COMPETITION POLICY AND LAW IN CHINA, HONG KONG AND TAIWAN

This book is the only comprehensive guide to the competition regimes of China, Hong Kong and Taiwan. Chinese developments are placed in the context of the adoption of competition regimes by developing and transitional states worldwide. The book also considers the pressure of transnational organisations on transitional states to adopt market-based economic strategies. The book adopts an inter-disciplinary approach considering the political, economic and legal issues relevent to competition policy adoption. The paradoxical phenomenon of Communist Mainland China seeking to adopt a pro-competition law whilst capitalist Hong Kong refuses to do so is explained and contrasted with the successful Taiwanese adoption of a competition regime over a decade ago. The underlying economic and political forces that have shaped this unusual matrix are discussed and analysed with a theoretical explanation offered for the existing state of affairs.

MARK WILLIAMS is an Associate Professor of Law at Hong Kong Polytechnic University, where he teaches Hong Kong company and commercial law and Chinese commercial law. He has a special research interest in competition policy and law generally, and more specifically with regard to East Asia. He holds an LL B from the University of Bristol and an LL M and PhD from the University of London, King's College. He is admitted as a solicitor in England and Wales and in Hong Kong. He has been European Union visiting lecturer in EC Law at Fudan University, Shanghai, as well as a visiting lecturer at East China University of Politics and Law, Shanghai; Peking University; Nanjing University, China and at Cardiff University Law School, UK. He has published widely on the subjects of Chinese commercial law and competition policy in Hong Kong.

COMPETITION POLICY AND LAW IN CHINA, HONG KONG AND TAIWAN

MARK WILLIAMS

CAMBRIDGE
UNIVERSITY PRESS

CAMBRIDGE UNIVERSITY PRESS
Cambridge, New York, Melbourne, Madrid, Cape Town, Singapore, São Paulo

Cambridge University Press
The Edinburgh Building, Cambridge CB2 2RU, UK

Published in the United States of America by Cambridge University Press, New York

www.cambridge.org
Information on this title: www.cambridge.org/9780521836319

First published 2005

Printed in the United Kingdom at the University Press, Cambridge

A catalogue record for this book is available from the British Library

ISBN-13   978-0-521-83631-9 hardback
ISBN-10   0-521-83631-X hardback

CONTENTS

PREFACE

The primary purpose of this book is to describe and analyse the competition law systems in place in Greater China. In order to do that, I decided that it was necessary, and appropriate, to place the extant systems in the context of the relevant economic theory that underpins competition regulation globally. The experience of developing and transitional states which have sought to adopt competition policy and law was also very illuminating in exposing common problems in the adoption process and so selected national cases have also been examined. The wider context of international developments in the competition law field have also played a part in the development of this branch of the law in Greater China and so they, too, are considered.

In order to accomplish my principal task, I also considered that, before undertaking a lawyer's analysis of the legal norms found in China, Hong Kong and Taiwan, it was essential to appreciate the historical, political and economic conditions of all three jurisdictions, for without that background knowledge the present state of competition regulation would be opaque and incapable of satisfactory explanation.

I have also attempted to create an explanatory theory from the facts I have found by use of a sociological methodology known as grounded theory, which allows for the construction of a theoretical explanation of the sometimes puzzling circumstances that pertain in competition policy and law in Greater China. The resultant hypothesis suggests that without a functioning democracy, which is explained in detail in the text, successful and effective adoption of a competition regime is impossible.

My excursus into the adjacent disciplines of history, economics and politics has not been undertaken without significant trepidation on my part, given that the whole of my higher education has been that of a traditional common lawyer, more at home with statutes and cases than with the nostrums of the social sciences. Nevertheless, I hope that my interdisciplinary approach to the subject of competition regulation in Greater China will be of some interest to the reader and, even though a theoretical explanation is offered to explain the present position, I have not altogether neglected the instincts of the practising lawyer, as will also be seen from the text.

I believe that political developments in both Mainland China and Hong Kong are central to understanding competition policy and this theme is explored fully in the text.

Currently, in Beijing, the various organs of the central government responsible for competition policy formation – the Ministry of Commerce, the State Administration of Industry and Commerce and the State Development and Reform Commission – are involved in a protracted power struggle to determine which body will win the considerable political and bureaucratic prize of controlling the new and powerful proposed competition authority. The original plan for an independent body appears to have been jettisoned in favour of an agency directly controlled by an existing bureaucracy. This volte face will have important implications both for the integrity of the system and the professionalism of the enforcement process. This in-fighting may also extend the decade-long delay in enacting a comprehensive statute; these matters are dealt with more fully in the text.

In Hong Kong, the post-colonial proconsul Tung Chee-wah, who has been Chief Executive since 1997, recently made an astonishingly frank admission of a fundamental weakness in his administration. On 13 January 2005, he stated in his annual Policy Address that 'these shortcomings and inadequacies have undermined the credibility of our policy-making capability and our ability to govern'. This *cri de coeur* proved to be Tung's political obituary and his resignation followed on 10 March 2005. His successor, Sir Donald Tsang Yam-kuen, a government servant of almost forty years' standing is unlikely to make any significant change to Hong Kong's sector-specific competition policy and so the existing bankrupt competition policy of the Hong Kong authorities is likely to remain unchanged. However, unexpectedly, a committee to review competition policy was announced in mid-March 2005 by the Financial Secretary, Henry Tang; the committee will report in 2006, so change could be in the wind.

This paradox of Communist Mainland China seeking to legislate a competition statute, whilst capitalist Hong Kong resolutely refuses to do so, will be fully explored, and, hopefully, satisfactorily explained in the text which follows. The anomalous position of Taiwan in competition matters, as regards Mainland China and Hong Kong, will be contrasted with the experience of those jurisdictions to illuminate what I consider are the necessary prerequisites for the adoption of an effective competition regime.

Clearly, political considerations are fundamental to understanding both the *status quo ante* and the future direction of competition policy in Greater China and this justifies my attempt at an interdisciplinary approach to this intriguing subject.

I have endeavoured to state the law, as I understand it, as at 1 December 2004.

MARK WILLIAMS
School of Accounting and Finance
Li Ka-shing Tower
Hong Kong Polytechnic University

30 April 2005

ACKNOWLEDGEMENTS

This book is the product of a number of years' study and appreciation of Greater China. I first came to live in the Far East in 1995 during the dying days of British imperial possession of Hong Kong. Since that time, I have tried to understand something of the history, politics, economics and the legal systems of the Chinese peoples and such small appreciation as I have of these large subjects would not have been possible without the assistance of many people.

In Hong Kong, my initial introduction to staff at Peking University and Nanjing University was made possible by Mr Khaw, the Academic Registrar of Hong Kong Shue Yan College. The College President, Dr Henry Hu and the Principal, Dr Chung, were also instrumental in encouraging my study of the laws of China. Paul Stables of Shue Yan College was also most helpful in debating many issues with me.

I must thank my late colleague Dr C. A. Ong of the Hong Kong Polytechnic University for his encouragement and helpful suggestions on parts of the text. My students Brian Tso and Vincent Tang were also indispensable in assisting me in locating additional references as was Gwendoline Wong, of the HKPU library. I must also thank my various friends in Hong Kong who encouraged and cajoled me into completing the text. I am also grateful to various officials at the Hong Kong Consumer Council, the Office of the Telecommunication Authority and the Information and Broadcasting Bureau who provided me with valuable information. I must thank Sin Chung-kai, one of the Democratic Party legislators, for the assistance he gave me in understanding his Party's attempt to introduce limited competition legislation in Hong Kong.

In China, I must thank academic colleagues at Peking University, Professor Wu Zhipan; at Fudan University, Shanghai, Professors Zhang Naigen, Lu Zi'an and his wife Sophie; at East China University of Politics and Law Professors Si Pingping, Feng Jun and Chen Zidong; at DongHua University Shanghai, Ms ShenYan, and at the Chinese Academy of Social Sciences, Professor Wang Xiaoye. I also owe a great debt to my former

Fudan students Ji Wenhua (now at the Ministry of Commerce, Beijing), Xie Junhui (now studying in Berlin), Lin Lixin (now studying in the United States) and Zhang Jinsong (now a postgraduate student in the United States). My thanks are also due to many officials of the Chinese government who assisted my understanding of government policies and procedures.

In Taiwan, I greatly appreciated the assistance given to me by officials at the Fair Trade Commission, Taipei.

In Switzerland, I must thank Robert Anderson at WTO for information concerning the Jenny Working Group and Phillippe Brussick of UNCTAD for allowing me to attend their seminar in Hong Kong.

In London, I own a sincere debt of gratitude to Professor Richard Whish of King's College for his guidance and encouragement. I also wish to acknowledge the great help given to me by Dr Megan Walters, who not only introduced me to the world of grounded theory methodology but also suggested that it had a useful application in explaining the complex relationships between politics, economics and competition law.

In Cardiff, I wish to thank Professor Duncan Bloy for reading extracts of the text and making several very helpful suggestions. Lesley Green is also to be commended for her sterling efforts to read my dreadfully written manuscript amendments and for committing them to type so efficiently.

Finally, I would like to thank all the editorial staff at Cambridge University Press and in particular Kim Hughes, Jane O'Regan, Jean Field and Anna-Marie Lovett, who have shown great patience in the face of various delays in completing the manuscript, some of which were due to rapid developments in the law and other to the exigencies of life but none of which we were able to control.

ABBREVIATIONS

ACT	Asia Container Terminals Limited
AM	Administrative Monopoly
APEC	Asia-Pacific Economic Co-operation
ASEAN	Association of South-East Asian Nations
ATV	Asia Television Limited
BA	Broadcasting Authority
BL	Basic Law
BO	Broadcasting Ordinance
Cap.	chapter
CBRC	China Banking Regulatory Commission
CCNM	Centre for Co-operation with Non-Members
CCP	Communist Party of China
CD-R	CD recordable
CECIA	Hong Kong Chief Executive's Council of International Advisers
CEO	Chief Executive Officer
CFA	Court of Final Appeal
CLP	China Light and Power Company Limited
Cmd	Command Paper
CNAC	China National Aviation Corporation
CNPC	China National Petroleum Corporation
COMPAG	Competition Policy Advisory Group
CPC	China Petroleum Corporation
CPRC	Constitution of the People's Republic of China
CROC	Constitution of the Republic of China
CT	City Telecom
CTI	Committee on Trade and Investment of APEC
CTV	cable television market
CWHK	Cable and Wireless Hong Kong
DPP	Democratic Progress Party
DSB	Dispute Settlement Body

EC	European Community
ECC	Electricity Consumers Concern
ECJ	The Court of Justice of the European Communities
ECR	European Court Reports
EIU	Economic Intelligence Unit
EPS	Easy Pay System
ETS	external telecommunications services
EU	European Union
FTC	Fair Trade Commission
FTL	Fair Trade Law
GATS	General Agreement on Trade in Services
GATT	General Agreement on Tariffs and Trade
GDP	gross domestic product
GITIC	Guangdong International Trust and Investment Corporation
GLC	government-linked companies
HKE	Hong Kong Electric Company Limited
HHI	Herfindahl-Hirschman Index
HIT	Hong Kong International Terminal
HKBN	Hong Kong Broad Band
HKCC	Hong Kong Consumer Council
HKCTV	Hong Kong Cable Television Limited
HKSAR	Hong Kong as a Special Administrative Region
HKSARG	Government of Hong Kong as a Special Administrative Region
HKT	Hong Kong Telecommunications Limited
HKTel	Hong Kong Telephone
ICN	International Competition Network
ICPAC	International Competition Policy Advisory Committee
IMF	International Monetary Fund
KCRC	Kowloon-Canton Railway Corporation
KMT	Kuo Ming Tang
LEGCO	Legislative Council
LPG	liquefied petroleum gas
MAP	Federal Ministry for Anti-Monopoly Policy and Support of Entrepreneurship
MIT	Massachusetts Institute of Technology

MOEA	Ministry of Economic Affairs (Republic of China, Taiwan)
MOFCOM	Ministry of Commerce (People's Republic of China)
MOFTEC	Ministry of Foreign Trade and Economic Co-operation (People's Republic of China)
MSAR	Macau Special Administrative Region
MTL	Modern Terminals Limited
MTRC	Mass Transport Rail Corporation
NAFTA	North American Free Trade Agreement
NATO	North Atlantic Treaty Organisation
NGO	non-governmental organisation
NPC	National People's Congress
NPCSC	National People's Congress Standing Committee
NPL	non-performing loans
NRDC	National Development and Reconstruction Commission
NT	New Taiwan dollar
OAA	Osaka Action Agenda
OECD	Organisation for Economic Co-operation and Development
OFTA	Office of the Telecommunications Authority
OFTEL	Office of Telecommunications (UK)
OOCL	Orient Overseas Container Line
PBOC	Chinese Central Bank
PCCW	Pacific Century Cyber Works Limited
PRC	People's Republic of China
PRI	Pardido Revolucinario Institucional
RDEL	Residential Direct Exchange Lines
RMB	currency of the PRC known as the Yuan or RMB (People's money)
RoA	return on assets
ROC	Republic of China on Taiwan
RoE	return on equity
RPM	resale price maintenance
RTHK	Radio Television Hong Kong
s., ss.	section, sections
SAIC	State Administration for Industry and Commerce
SAR	Special Administrative Region

SDERC	State Development and Economic Reform Commission
SDRC	State Development and Reform Commission
SETC	State Economic and Trade Commission
SLC	substantially lessen competition
SME	medium-sized enterprises
SOASAC	State-owned Assets Supervision and Administration Commission
SOE	State-owned Enterprise
SPDC	State Planning and Development Commission
SSNIP	significant and non-transitory increase in price
STDM	Macau Society for Tourism and Entertainment
TA	Telecommunications Authority
THC	terminal handling charge
TNC	transnational corporation
TO	Telecommunications Ordinance
TPM	Trigger Point Mechanism
TRIPS	Agreement on Trade-Related Intellectual Property Rights
TVB	Television Broadcasts Limited
UK	United Kingdom of Great Britain and Northern Ireland
UNCTAD	United Nations Conference on Trade and Development
UN set	United Nations Conference on Trade and Development, *The set of multilaterally agreed equitable principles and rules for the control of restrictive business practices* (1980)
US, USA	United States of America
USC	United States Congress
VAC	Veterans Affairs Commission
VOC	Dutch East India Company
WTO	World Trade Organisation
Yuan	Currency of the PRC, known as RMB (People's money) or the Yuan

Journal abbreviations

| *AM Ec Rev.* | *American Economic Review* |
| Chi-Kent L. Rev. | Chicago-Kent Law Review |

Cmd	Command
CML Rev.	Common Market Law Review
ECLR	European Community Law Review
Geo. Wash. Int'l L. Rev.	George Washington International Law Review
HKCFAR	Hong Kong Court of Final Appeal Reports
HKLRD	Hong Kong Law Reports and Digest
HKLJ	Hong Kong Law Journal
J Law and Econ.	Journal of Law and Economics
J World Comp.	*Journal of World Competition*
JBL	Journal of Business Law
J. Pol. Econ.	*Journal of Politics and Economics*
JCL	Journal of Contract Law
LFCE	Ley Federal de Competencia Economica
NCILCR	North Carolina International Law Review
NY J. Int'l Law and Pol.	New York International Law and Policy Review
OJ	*Official Journal*
s., ss.	section, sections
Stan. L. Rev.	Stanford Law Review
SWJLTA	South-West Journal of Law
UCLA Pacific Basin Law Journal	University of California, Los Angeles Pacific Basin Law Journal

1

Introduction and methodology

1.1 Scope of the book and a definition of China

> If monopoly persists, monopoly will always sit at the helm of government... If there are men in this country big enough to own the government..., they are going to own it.
>
> Woodrow Wilson, *The New Freedom* (1913)

So said the late President Wilson about the linkage of concentrated economic and political power some ninety years ago, in the context of the United States of America. These were the same concerns that had prompted the passage of the Sherman Act 1890 to control the giant industrial trusts that developed in late nineteenth-century America and appeared to many to threaten democratic institutions.[1]

This text will seek to demonstrate that Wilson's observation is still relevant today in considering law and policy development concerning economic competition in China, Hong Kong and Taiwan. Each jurisdiction exhibits facets of the posited relationship between economic and political power in those jurisdictions' differing approaches to competition policy making and the adoption of a comprehensive law to enforce the political choice of a pro-competition policy. In China, the political monopoly of the Chinese Communist Party previously led to a complete state monopoly of economic power. This economic policy was effectively abandoned in 1978 and the following discussion of competition policy and law in China results directly from that seismic shift. China now appears to have decided that a set of rules is needed to regulate the socialist market economy.

In Hong Kong, the existence of concentrations of economic and political power in the same hands also dictates policy towards the regulation of

---

[1] Ernest Gellhorn and William E. Kovacic, *Anti-trust law and economics*, 4th edn, New York: West Publishing (1994). Disappointment with the effectiveness of the Sherman Act led to the adoption of the Clayton and Federal Trade Commission Acts in 1914 to strengthen anti-trust regulation.

competition and has led directly to the government's open hostility to the introduction of comprehensive legislation. But, interestingly, it is the private ownership of economic assets that causes competition problems in Hong Kong, not a dominant publicly owned sector, which is, in contrast, the root of Mainland competition problems.

In Taiwan, the politics and economics of authoritarianism gradually gave way, during the 1980s and 1990s, to a more pluralist form of politics and with that political reformation a fair competition law was enacted to police the newly liberalised economy. However, before examination of competition policy can begin, it is necessary to define China.

The expression 'Greater China' is often used as a useful phrase to avoid the political pitfalls of comparing the *de jure* separate jurisdictions known as Mainland China, Hong Kong and Macau and the *de facto* separate jurisdiction of Taiwan. For convenience, in this thesis the words 'China' and 'the Mainland' are used interchangeably and since Mainland China forms the largest constituent part of the People's Republic of China, the abbreviation PRC is also sometimes used in the restricted sense of applying only to Mainland China.

Hong Kong, as a Special Administrative Region (HKSAR) of the People's Republic of China, has its own political, economic and legal system distinct from the Mainland. This is guaranteed in international law by the Sino-British Joint Declaration 1984, a treaty within the meaning of the Vienna Convention on the Law of Treaties 1969,[2] and deposited at the United Nations. Domestically, Article 31 of the PRC Constitution (CPRC)[3] provides that 'The state may establish Special Administrative Regions when necessary.' The Basic Law (BL) of the HKSAR was adopted by the National People's Congress and Promulgated by the President of the PRC on 4 April 1990.[4] This is the governing constitutional document establishing the HKSAR as from 1 July 1997. Article 1 provides that Hong Kong 'shall exercise a high degree of autonomy and enjoy executive, legislative and independent judicial power'. This 'one country, two systems' approach is confirmed to continue for fifty years from 1997 and, further, that the socialist system and policies 'shall not be practised in Hong Kong

---

[2] United Kingdom Treaty Series 58 (1980), Cmd. 7964; 1155 United Nations Treaty Series 331. See Article 80: only treaties registered with the United Nations may be invoked before the International Court of Justice but nonetheless remain valid as between the parties.

[3] For an English translation of the Constitution of the People's Republic of China, see China Laws for Foreign Business, vol. 4–500, CCH Asia, loose leaf (1999).

[4] The Basic Law of Hong Kong Special Administrative Region of the People's Republic of China www.info.gov.hk/basic_law/flash.html.

during that period'.[5] However, the recent (April 2004) 'interpretation' of the Basic Law by the Standing Committee of the National Peoples Congress,[6] which effectively vetoed the adoption of universal suffrage for the election of the Hong Kong Chief Executive in 2007 and the Legislative Council in 2008, has caused acute political controversy in Hong Kong and calls into question the real ambit of the 'one country, two systems' formulation of the former supreme PRC leader Deng Xiaoping.

Macau SAR has similar autonomy to Hong Kong based on its own Basic Law which came into effect on 20 December 1999 and is, in essence, similar to the Hong Kong version. Macau does not have a competition regime, has a very small economy and is, therefore, not considered in this book.[7]

The position of Taiwan is controversial. The PRC and most of its population regard Taiwan as an integral part of China: 'Taiwan is part of the sacred territory of the PRC. It is the lofty duty of the entire Chinese people, including our compatriots in Taiwan, to accomplish the great task of reunifying the Motherland.' [8] Taiwan has *de facto* independence and is thus considered a renegade province by the PRC government. The population of Taiwan appears to be divided between those who consider the Republic of China on Taiwan (ROC) as the legitimate government of the whole of Chinese territory, those who consider Taiwan to be an independent state with no territorial claim on the Mainland and that there is no legitimate PRC claim to Taiwan and, thirdly, those content to allow the current ambiguous *modus vivendi* to continue for the sake of peace and economic prosperity. A recent Taiwan enactment to sanction direct plebiscites on

---

[5] Article 5 BL.

[6] Decision of the Standing Committee of the National People's Congress on issues relating to the methods of selecting the Chief Executive of HKSAR in 2007 and for forming the Legislative Council of HKSAR in 2008, 26 April 2004 http://www.info.gov.hk/cab/cab-review/eng/basic/pdf/es5200408081.pdf.

[7] A very large proportion of the Macau economy is based on the gambling industry that has historically been monopolised by Hong Kong based tycoon Stanley Ho. His company STDM (Macau Society for Tourism and Entertainment) provided 63 per cent of government revenue in 2002. STDM recently lost its gaming monopoly and two new entrants have pledged to invest some US$2.2bn in new casino facilities. Macau's gambling shake up 4 December 2003 http://news.bbc.co.uk/1/hi/world/asia-pacific/3287755.stm. The first rival 'Las Vegas-style' casino to the STDM monopoly, The Sands, opened in May 2004. Competition has now begun in earnest in the Macau gaming industry for the first time. See 'New casino mobbed', *The Standard* (Hong Kong), 20 May 2004.http://www.thestandard.com.hk/thestandard/news_detail_frame.cfm?articleid=47695#intcatid=1.

[8] See preamble to the CPRC, above.

constitutional matters[9] may result in further political tension among the people of Taiwan who may, at some time in the future, vote for *de jure* separate statehood from the PRC. The Mainland government has warned that any such unilateral declaration by Taiwan would result in military action being taken by the People's Liberation Army to prevent the division of national sovereignty.[10] The island of Taiwan is currently governed under the authority of the Constitution of the Republic of China (CROC)[11] adopted on 25 December 1946, which still claims the whole territory of China extant at that date.[12] In practice, the ROC only exercises authority over Taiwan and its dependent islands in the Taiwan straits.

Thus, what is sometimes referred to as Greater China can be divided into the following jurisdictions: a socialist Mainland, 'The People's Republic is a socialist state under the people's democratic dictatorship led by working class'[13] based on 'democratic centralism',[14] non-socialist Hong Kong and Macau SARs[15] and the ROC on Taiwan whose constitution states it to be 'a democracy of the people, to be governed by the people and for the people'.[16]

Economically, the PRC is constitutionally based on 'the socialist system . . . [of] public ownership of the means of production'[17] and the state-owned economy is said to be the leading force in the national economy.[18] Exploitation of man by man is stated to have been replaced by the principle of 'from each according to his ability, to each according to his work'.[19] However, Article 11 stipulates that 'the non public ownership sector comprising the individual economy and the private economy within the domain stipulated by law is an important component of the socialist market economy'.[20] Further, Article 15 CPRC elaborates that 'the state practises the socialist market-directed economy'.[21] The state also promises to 'permit the private economy to exist and to develop within the limits prescribed by law . . . [and] to protect the lawful rights and interests of the private economy'.[22] Under Article 18 CPRC, foreigners too are allowed to invest in China. Thus, the PRC's current official economic policy is

---

[9] http://www.gio.gov.tw/taiwan-website/4-oa/20040301/2004030101.html and http://www.gio.gov.tw/taiwan-website/4-oa/20040203/2004020301.html.
[10] For example see *China Daily*, 31 May 2004 http://www.chinadaily.com.cn/english/doc/2004-05/31/content_335212.htm and *China Daily*, 26 May 2004 http://www.chinadaily.com.cn/english/doc/2004-05/26/content_333820.htm.
[11] The Constitution of the Republic of China www.gio.gov.tw/taiwan-website/5-gp/yearbook/appendix3.htm.
[12] Art. 4 CROC.   [13] Art. 1 CPRC.   [14] Ibid. Art. 3.   [15] Confirmed by Art. 5 BL.
[16] Art. 1 CROC.   [17] Art. 6 CPRC.   [18] Ibid. Art. 7.   [19] Ibid. Art. 6.
[20] 1999 amendment CPRC.   [21] 1993 amendment CPRC.   [22] 1988 amendment CPRC.

ambiguous – a socialist state that tolerates private ownership of economic assets, which form an important component of a socialist market-directed economy. These inherent contradictions exist as a result of a political imperative to improve China's economic performance whilst maintaining the people's democratic dictatorship led by the Chinese Communist Party (CCP);[23] the relevance of these constitutional matters will be considered later in the text.

Hong Kong was always portrayed by its pre-1997 colonial government as a bastion of free enterprise and ferocious economic competition. The HKSAR Basic Law confirms that Hong Kong will not be required to practise socialism until at least 2047[24] and that private ownership of property shall be protected[25] by the common law system extant before 1997.[26] Thus, the *status quo ante* was preserved on the retrocession of sovereignty to the PRC.

Taiwan's constitution provides for a social-democratic dispensation of economic assets and 'seeks to effect equalisation of land ownership and restriction of private capital in order to attain well-balanced efficiency in national wealth and people's livelihood'.[27] Further, private wealth and privately operated enterprises might be restricted by law if deemed 'detrimental to a balanced development of national wealth and people's livelihood'. But private productive enterprise shall 'receive encouragement, guidance and protection' from the state.[28] It is also provided that 'public utilities and other enterprises of a monopolistic nature shall, in principle, be under public operation but may be permitted by law to be owned by private persons'.[29] Thus, Taiwan's constitutional position is of a classic social-democratic mien based on the Swedish model, exhibiting a statist bent apparently sceptical of the benefits of economic competition.

So much then, for the theoretical positions of these three jurisdictions in relation to their economic structures. This book will seek to demonstrate that these constitutional positions do not in fact, reflect the reality of the economic structures extant in any of the jurisdictions considered here. Discussion of the situation as regards China will be found in chapters 4 and 5. The Hong Kong position will be analysed in chapters 6, 7 and 8 and Taiwan's competition regime will be considered in chapter 9. The results of the analysis and a synthesis of the overall findings are offered in chapter 10. The conclusions drawn from the evidence might be surprising because, as is often the case, appearance and reality in China are often very different.

---

[23] Preamble to CPRC.   [24] Art. 5 BL.   [25] Ibid. Art. 6.   [26] Ibid. Art. 8.
[27] Art. 142 CROC.   [28] Ibid. Art. 145.   [29] Ibid. Art. 144.

Having described the constitutional arrangements of the three jurisdictions under study, the remainder of this chapter will seek to set the
rationale for this enquiry (1.2) and the objectives of this book (1.3), to
explain the methodology adopted (1.4) and provide an explanation of the
structure of the work (1.5).

1.2 Rationale and research questions

The rationale for undertaking the research necessary for this study of
China flowed from two factors – the size and potential importance of
the economic restructuring process under way in the formerly socialist
economy of China and the relatively growing global importance of the
Chinese economy, coupled with the existing significance of the Hong Kong
and Taiwanese economies. As regards China, a desire to understand what
new regulations the Chinese government proposed as a replacement for
the state planning process that had existed hitherto as the principal tool of
economic management also stimulated the author's curiosity. The nature
of the socialist market, the means of policy formation, the particular policy
pressures that affect the Chinese government, the process of legislation
and the effectiveness of law as a practical method of enforcing policy
choices, were all issues that needed to be understood. Also worthy of
consideration were developments in competition policy in former socialist
states and through the auspices of international organisations as China
emerged from a state of self-imposed autarky and was faced with new
policy choices. The accession of China to the World Trade Organisation
(WTO) would also have a considerable, though perhaps unpredictable,
effect on China's economy but clearly domestic producers would now face
more competition than in the past.

A quite different set of issues was evident in relation to Hong Kong. The
Territory's reputation as the paradigm example of a 'laissez-faire' economic model was often assumed without critical assessment, and so was
ripe for investigation. An interesting anomaly was that whilst Hong Kong
claimed to have a free, open and competitive market, the government, cu-
riously, was openly hostile to both a domestic competition statute to protect the competitive process and also to any move by the WTO even to discuss multilateral rules on competition policy. The unusual phenomenon
of a marked concentration of economic and political power in the same
hands suggested that the official explanation of Hong Kong's policy stance
might not be entirely accurate and so merited detailed examination and
analysis.

As regards Taiwan, its separate economic and political development from Mainland China seemed to have contributed to its decision to legislate a comprehensive competition law in 1992. Even though a law existed, one needed to investigate how well it was operating in practice. Against this background, it seemed possible that lessons could be learnt by Mainland China and Hong Kong from Taiwan's adoption process, given their cultural similarities, which might be useful in their consideration of policy choices.

Traditional comparative law methods could not be employed fully in this undertaking, as there was no developed competition jurisprudence in either China or Hong Kong, and so a broad-based process of investigation was needed to include the relevant historical, political and economic environment within which competition policy was developing in each jurisdiction. Traditional legal analysis would be employed, where appropriate, but this narrow approach would not be an adequate framework to analyse and explain the existing competition situation in China and Hong Kong and so an interdisciplinary approach was adopted.

Thus, the rationale for the study of competition policy development in China and Hong Kong was essentially that the subject was inherently interesting, little of relevance had been published on the topic by legal academics and the importance of China, Hong Kong and Taiwan to the world economy justified an enquiry into their domestic competition systems. This was especially so in view of the enhanced economic globalisation fostered *inter alia* by the establishment of the WTO in 1995 and the organisation's subsequent activism in studying the interrelationship between competition law and trade. Competition is one of the so-called 'Singapore Issues'[30] and might yet lead to the internationalisation of competition regimes through WTO mechanisms, though as a result of the collapse of the September 2003 WTO ministerial meeting in Cancun, Mexico, the fate of the Singapore Issues is now very uncertain, especially as it appears that the European Union may now be prepared to drop its advocacy of WTO competition negotiations for the time being as part of the process of re-starting a new round of trade talks.[31] This is exactly what transpired in July 2004 when the EU agreed to withdraw its insistence on

---

[30] The term 'Singapore Issues' relates to a set of discussion topics first identified at the 1996 WTO ministerial meeting held in Singapore. They are: trade and investment, trade facilitation, transparency in government procurement and trade and competition policy.
[31] *World trade talks near collapse*, BBC, 9 December 2003. http://news.bbc.co.uk/1/hi/business/3304663.stm and Singapore issues: clarification of the EU position, European

competition policy being included in the new round of trade liberalisation negotiations at the WTO.

1.3 Objectives

In light of the focus on China and Hong Kong, but bearing in mind the international situation and the position of Taiwan, this book seeks to:

- investigate the experience of selected developing countries and countries in transition in adopting competition law and apply those insights to the study of China, Hong Kong and Taiwan;
- appreciate international developments in competition law and policy and how they affect decision-making concerning competition policy in China and Hong Kong;
- examine and analyse the development of competition policy and law in China, Hong Kong and Taiwan;
- assess critically the existing and proposed legal rules governing competition in China, Hong Kong and Taiwan;
- rationalise and explain the situation observed by use of grounded theory methodology so as to create a testable hypothesis that has both internal and external validity and is generalisable;
- make a contribution to the stock of knowledge concerning competition law and policy in China, Hong Kong and Taiwan and produce a theoretical explanation of the circumstances necessary to ensure that competition law adoption is effective.

1.4 Methodology

A way of thinking about and studying social reality.[32]

Adopting a methodological approach in order to create new theory or a hypothesis in law is not very common. Given the subject matter of this enquiry – nascent competition law in China, Hong Kong and Taiwan – and the need to understand more fully the underlying and replicable aspects of the results discovered, explicit recourse to a systematic structure of investigation, analysis and synthesis that could lead to the

Commission Communication, 31 March 2004 http://trade-info.cec.eu.int/doclib/cfm/doclib_section.cfm?sec=182&lev=2&order=date.

[32] This definition is offered by Juliet Corbin and Anselm Strauss in *Basics of qualitative research: techniques and procedures for developing grounded theory,* London: Sage (1998), p. 3.

postulation of a testable explanatory hypothesis, seemed not only advisable but necessary.

This book is not a traditional exposition and analysis of a mature 'black-letter' common law subject. Rather, it is an investigation into a developing legal and policy field in distinct communities that do not share all or many institutions familiar to mature common law or civil law jurisdictions, although, of course, Hong Kong exhibits much greater similarity with other common law jurisdictions than does China, as a result of colonisation by the British between 1841 and 1997.

The use of analytical tools to make sense of the discovered information and then to use them to uncover hidden or obscure core issues in each jurisdiction required more than traditional deductive or analogical reasoning, so beloved of the common lawyer. This is the justification for this brief discussion of methodological issues and the adoption of a methodological approach in this book. This is the means by which a testable hypothesis will be created and this will form the benchmark against which the results discovered will be measured in the concluding chapter. Through the use of a methodological approach and the adaptation of a social science paradigm, a useful and testable hypothesis is generated which may be of wider application to the study of competition law, especially in developing countries likely to adopt a competition regime for the first time, than merely to the jurisdictions examined here.

This section will now examine a number of issues:

- the design of the research method actually undertaken;
- the nature and rationale for adopting a methodological approach in this book;
- the nature of research paradigms including the nature of the relationship between the enquirer and the enquired;
- the utility of traditional methods of legal research in relation to this project;
- grounded theory as a basis for conducting legal research;
- how data collection and analysis was undertaken;
- data sources; and
- the utility, contribution to knowledge and limitations of this book.

1.4.1 How is legal research typically carried out?

Legal research is, in some ways, a singular pursuit. It does not follow traditional scientific methods of developing theory and subsequently collecting data to test against the theoretical construct. Legal researchers tend not to develop theoretical paradigms and then conduct empirical research. The methods of social or political science research involving the subjective evaluation of opposing theories are not those of the law, except in jurisprudence. Management science and economics which look to the testing of theory by the use of models against quantitative data and statistical analysis are again largely alien to the lawyer, whether as a practitioner or as an academic. The exception is criminology. Data collection from populations of research subjects may be obtained to assess the accuracy or otherwise of preconceived conceptions of criminals' propensity to offend or how they might react to particular sanctions or what may cause offending behaviour. But lawyers tend to view this as social science – a branch of sociology or psychology, not 'hard law'.

Legal research has traditionally meant the ability to seek out information in the form of written law by way of case decisions or statutory material or the views of academics or practitioners from journals or textbooks. After obtaining the raw material, the lawyer then has to understand the legal issues and follow the reasoning of the legislature or the court in order to gain an insight into the law. The ability then to extrapolate principle from case decisions is a cardinal virtue, highly prized by other lawyers and clients alike. For, if the lawyer can predict the decision of a court in respect of a novel or even a clear case, then the costs and uncertainties of litigation can thereby be diminished.[33] The same skill of analysis and exposition is also prized in academic lawyers.

Competition law, however, is an exception to the non-theoretical approach. Explicit recourse to economic theory is essential to understand the basic precepts and policy goals of competition policy. Economics is the *raison d'être* of competition law; the law is the handmaiden of economic theory, its actualisation in the real world of business.

As Whish says: 'Competition law is about economics and economic behaviour, and it is essential for anyone involved in the subject . . . to have some knowledge of the economic concepts concerned.'[34] Posner agrees: 'One thing that has long been clear, however, is that anti-trust deals with what are at root economic phenomena.'[35]

---

[33] The value of prediction as a vital lawyer's skill was lauded by Oliver Wendel Holmes in his highly influential essay *The path of the law*, 10 Harvard Law Review 457 (1897).
[34] Richard Whish, *Competition law*, London: Butterworth, 5th edn (2003), p. 1.
[35] Richard A. Posner, *Anti-trust*, University of Chicago Press, 2nd edn (2001), p. 1.

1.4.2 The rationale for methodology

All research has methodology, either implicit or explicit. Common law research tends to follow implicit rules for the conduct of research, which are discussed below. These often unstated assumptions about how to conduct research do not accord with the approach of other disciplines where explicit use of methodology to provide the building blocks of theory is the norm.[36] However, one might pose the question, is this lack of explicit use of methodology and theory in law a strength or a weakness?

The author's interest in research methodology was kindled as a result of commenting on a draft PhD thesis written by Megan Walters[37] on the subject of decision-making in the management of the property estate of Hong Kong Telecom (now PCCW). Exposure to the approach adopted in her thesis aroused the author's interest as to whether the grounded theory she utilised could be adapted to analyse the author's research data concerning competition law and policy in greater China. Clearly, the nature of the subject matter was quite different. Her thesis was concerned with the collection, by interview, of data concerning the views and actions of property managers in response to a changing market/regulatory structure in the Hong Kong telecommunication market. This book is concerned with the description and analysis of the current state of competition regulation in greater China, suggestions for reform and prediction of future developments. At first blush, it appeared that there was little or no assistance that the methodology she had adopted could render in this endeavour.

However, upon reflection, issues concerning the nature of the known, the relationship between the researcher and the researched and the inherent limitations in any research activity caused by 'human frailty', convinced the author that explicit recourse to methodology and the creation of theory in a work of this type was appropriate. Two alternative models of methodology were considered, namely the verification approach and the grounded theory approach,[38] both of which are used in social

---

[36] See Corbin and Strauss, *Basics of qualitative research.*

[37] I am indebted to M. R. Walters not only for her enthusiasm for methodology but also for alerting me to the precepts of grounded theory that have been adopted here and for her assistance in adapting the Corbin/Strauss approach to fit legal research of the type undertaken here. Her thesis is entitled 'Institutional economics of corporate real estate management; a case study of Hong Kong Telecom', University of Hong Kong Library (2002).

[38] Barney G. Glasser and Anselm Strauss, *The discovery of grounded theory: strategies for qualitative research,* New York: Aldine Publ. Co. (1967), pp. 10–15.

science research. The verification approach involves two stages, namely the initial formulation of or the use of an existing hypothesis, followed by a test of the hypothesis in a defined social environment, usually involving some form of quantitative analysis.[39] This method was rejected as the author had no knowledge of or any particular preconceptions about an existing hypothesis. Further, quantitative verification of results would not be possible. Therefore, the grounded theory approach was chosen as it very well matched the process that had actually been undertaken in this research; grounded theory is explained in section 1.4.5. The author did not develop a theory in the ether and then seek to test it. Rather, curiosity as to the existence and nature of competition regulation in China was stimulated by an employment secondment to Hong Kong and the observation of the very striking difference in the role law played in China when compared with familiar common law jurisdictions. This ignited the spark of the author's curiosity to discover more. The resulting seven-year odyssey of data collection led the author to consider how a mass of information could be organised, analysed and comprehended. A conclusion was reached that exposition and analysis were not enough and that one further step should be attempted, the creation of a theory, the definition of which to Corbin and Strauss is: 'A set of well developed concepts related through statements of relationship, which together constitute an integrated framework that can be used to explain or predict phenomena.'[40] It appeared to the author that this is what legal research seeks to achieve but by implicit rather than explicit means. Consequently, the adoption of grounded theory as the framework for the creation of a hypothesis seemed a reasonable and appropriate way in which to proceed.

One was also driven to consider what, if any, linkages could be made between observed phenomena in greater China and other places that had adopted or were considering the adoption of competition policy. The notion occurred to the author that the results of this investigation should not be treated in isolation and that an attempt should be made to link core issues common to other jurisdictions.

The use of a methodological approach allowed the author to consider these issues systematically and create an overarching hypothesis in an attempt to explain them.

---

[39] Barney G. Glasser, *Basics of grounded theory analysis,* Mill Valley, Calif.: Sociology Press (1992), p. 16.
[40] Corbin and Strauss, *Qualitative research,* p. 15.

1.4.3 The nature of research paradigms

As Dr Walters says: 'Research involves an enquiry into a phenomenon to enable knowledge and understanding to be enhanced. In order to do this, questions concerning the phenomenon to be studied and the type of knowledge sought must be considered to identify an appropriate strategy to conduct the enquiry.'[41] The core object of enquiry in this work is the current state of competition policy in greater China and the probable future direction of competition policy in each jurisdiction. Competition policy, for present purposes, includes the political decisions and directions given by government to economic actors, actual legislation currently in force concerning competition and the rules governing sectors of the economy regulated by mandatory regimes.

Actual regulations and laws can relatively easily be obtained and analysed. The effectiveness of their enforcement can be discerned objectively, though with some severe limitations in relation to Mainland China. However, given that this enquiry is not only historical but also prospective, in that it seeks to discern the future direction of competition policy, a substantial element of subjective assessment and extrapolation of the available evidence on the part of the researcher is inevitable. Thus, it appeared appropriate to consider different paradigms for undertaking the research in hand. Paradigms are a basic set of beliefs that guide action taken in connection with disciplined enquiry.[42] In Dr Walters' opinion, 'the researcher's view of knowledge and the nature of reality will determine the enquirer's choice of methodology for conducting the research, as much as the characteristics of the phenomenon under investigation'.

Paradigms for research have been hotly debated for many years. As Dr Walters explains, Kuhn reviewed the impact of paradigms on the development of new ideas and theories.[43] The categorisation of paradigms is dependent upon the researcher's response to ontological, epistemological and methodological questions, which normally follow the paradigm adopted within the researcher's own academic discipline. Guba provides the following definitions:[44]

Ontological   What is the nature of the 'knowable'? Or, what is the nature of reality?

---

[41] The structure of the following discussion is substantially adopted from chapter 3 of M. R. Walters' PhD thesis, Institutional economics of corporate real estate management.
[42] Egon G. Guba, The paradigm dialogue, London: Sage Publications (1990).
[43] Thomas S. Kuhn, The structure of scientific revolutions, University of Chicago Press (1962).
[44] Guba, The paradigm dialogue, p. 18.

Epistemological	What is the nature of the relationship between the enquirer and the enquired?
Methodological	How should the enquirer go about discovering knowledge?

Guba suggests four categories of research paradigm – positive, post-positive, critical theory and constructivism. A précis of Guba's and Dr Walters' description of these categories follows. Positivism posits that reality can be firmly known. This is the scientific approach to the natural sciences adopted in the seventeenth century by European scientists. Physical phenomena can be observed; ontologically reality exists and is observable. The observer is detached from, and objective about, the phenomenon observed. Methodologically, positivism relies upon hypotheses or questions stated in advance, which are then subject to empirical tests such as experimentation. Collected data can be tested for reliability through statistical and other techniques.

Post-positivism accepts the positive approach but is sceptical of the actual ability of the observer to remain in Olympian detachment from the subject of the enquiry; it posits that one can never be completely sure that the truth has actually been uncovered. But it still maintains that ontologically the truth is ultimately discoverable. If then humans are frail and inherently liable to subjective contamination, can remedial steps be taken to rectify the perceived deficiencies? Adaptation of the methodology used may provide an answer. If human intellectual and sensory capabilities are deficient as a means of establishing objective truth, then results based on many sources of data will provide a better check that the truth will be found and will limit the distortions of the individual perception and interpretation of the researcher.

Critical theory suggests that paradigms reflect the choices of researchers undertaking the enquiry. The way researchers see the world and the values they hold must influence the epistemological question of 'what is the nature of the relationship between the enquirer and the enquired?' Critical theorists, the feminist critique and Neo-Marxism hold that nature cannot be seen as really there, except through the lens of the value system of the researcher. Thus, values enter into every field of enquiry that inevitably raises the question of whose values should prevail. Ontologically the critical theorists have much in common with the post-positivists, seeing the world as critical realists. Reality exists but cannot ever be fully understood. Epistemologically they vary from the post-positivists as to the degree to which the researchers' own values affect the outcome of the enquiry. Post-positivists adopt an objective approach modified by human frailty, whereas critical theorists require that a subjective assessment must be taken so that who the enquirer is and exactly what values one holds are crucial in evaluating the outcomes of the research. Methodologically they wish to eliminate false consciousness and rally observers around a common (true?) point of view.

Constructivism rejects the previous three paradigms at the ontological level. It postulates that reality cannot be said to be 'out there' but exists in multiple forms in the mental constructs of the researcher. Everyone has their own version of reality, socially and experientially based, local and specific, and dependent for form and content on the person who holds it. Ontologically, if there are many different interpretations of the research (as many as there are people producing the results or reading them) then realities are multiple and the search is for more sophisticated constructions, not 'reality'. Epistemologically, researchers take a subjective view and the identity and values of the observer are clearly important, as that is the only way to establish reality in the mind of the enquired. Thus, ontology and epistemology are combined, the nature of reality and the nature of the relationship between the enquirer and the enquired are inseparable. Methodologically, the enquiry is qualitative and includes two aspects – hermeneutic (or interpretative) and dialectic. The hermeneutic aspect seeks to depict individual constructs as accurately as possible whilst the dialectic compares and contrasts the individual constructs with existing constructs. This paradigm does not seek to achieve a common view, as would critical theory, but rather to reconstruct the world at the point at which it exists.

The key question is – are these paradigms important? Kuhn suggests they are, for two reasons.[45] Firstly, to determine how the particular piece of research should be done and secondly, to determine how acceptable the results would be to one's academic peers in the same discipline.

In Dr Walters' view, 'addressing the questions of the ontological, epistemological and methodological characteristics of any particular researcher in relation to a given piece of research output may assist other researchers from other academic disciplines that adopt different paradigms to comprehend the basis upon which the work was done'. Lawyers and social scientists may work in different ways. However, in the final analysis Tesch's[46] view on research validity must be correct: 'Basically, there is only one

[45] Kuhn, *Scientific revolutions.*
[46] Renata Tesch, *Qualitative research: analysis types and software tools,* London: Falmer (1990).

requirement for research: that you can persuade others that you have indeed made a creditable discovery worth paying attention to.' In legal research, this clearly involves the persuasion of one's qualified peers that a piece of work is respectable by publication in a reputable journal or through a respectable publisher. Peer review is the essential quality-control regulator but lawyers tend to be professionally rather homogeneous as regards their approach to research and theory. Thus, perhaps, explicit use of theory and an overt reliance on social science methods might be judged heterodox, even to the point of heresy or, worse, irrelevance. In this book, the use of a methodological approach and the attempt at greater generalisation of the results discovered into theory is justified by the nature of the subject matter. Orthodox common law research methods may be different and rely on traditional assumptions, as examined below, which, it is suggested, are not entirely relevant to the subject matter of this study.

1.4.4 The nature of legal research

Traditional legal study seems to be singularly distant from the issues discussed above. The approach of lawyers to research does not easily fit into any of the paradigms outlined. The common lawyer tries to uncover the abstract principle underlying a decision of the court or the statute under consideration and then to fit the case or statute into the existing schema, making allowance for distinguishing decisions that do not follow orthodox lines. Most lawyers would consider themselves positivist in the sense that they believe that legal rules are 'out there' and can be discovered. They would justify this on the basis that breach of the rule has actual real consequences and *in extremis* the court can sanction those who do not obey the command of the law.[47]

However, it is submitted that traditional methods of common law research are not of much assistance to this project, due to the nature of the enquiry and the subject matter involved. But one commonly practised technique familiar to common and civilian lawyers will be employed here, namely the comparative approach. China is essentially a codal country, though at present much of the legal code remains unfinished. The nature of China's legal system and its impact on competition law matters will be discussed later. However, the current statutory provisions concerning unfair competition and the proposed comprehensive anti-monopoly law

---

[47] This suggests a very Austinian view of the law.

do have analogues in common and civilian law. The draft anti-monopoly law draws heavily on European Community (EC) competition law and practice and thus it will be both necessary and desirable to employ comparative techniques when analysing the proposed new law. The current competition provisions in Hong Kong are, by contrast, the familiar common law provisions concerning torts, breaches of contract or infringement of intellectual property rights but with no specific statutory provisions, save in respect of telecommunication and broadcasting, where EC-type provisions have been adopted.

This book will, in addition to considering the comparative legal paradigm, also refer to economic, political and social phenomena. However, it is not concerned with the quantitative economic methods of modelling nor with a detailed consideration of political or social theory, but, given the nature of the enquiry, reference will be made, in outline at least, to these issues where relevant in the text. The purpose of considering the various research paradigms mentioned above is to demonstrate that whilst law has its own idiosyncratic research culture, the fundamental issues addressed in this chapter are of relevance and importance to provide an intellectual underpinning for this work. The research undertaken to produce this book was not a traditional 'black-letter' law enterprise and thus it is justifiable to consider the approach of the social sciences to academic research. However, that is not to say that more traditional legal research techniques should be abandoned but rather that they should be used to illuminate aspects of this work, where relevant to the subject matter under discussion.

1.4.5 Grounded theory

Grounded theory was originally developed by two sociologists, Glasser and Strauss.[48] They proposed making comparisons between data to identify, develop and relate concepts. Grounded theory means that theory is derived from data, systematically gathered and analysed through the research process.[49] It is submitted that grounded theory is of utility to this study, due to the particular circumstances of the jurisdictions examined. In grounded theory, the researcher does not begin the project with a preconceived idea in mind but allows theory to emerge from the data. The researcher must, of course, delimit the subject of the investigation,

[48] Glasser and Strauss, *Grounded theory.*
[49] Corbin and Strauss, *Qualitative research,* London: Sage (1998).

otherwise data collection is impossible and useful research questions cannot be asked. Grounded theory relies on the creativity of the researcher as well as critical analysis of collected data. It requires rigour in data collection but creativity in the researcher's ability to identify variables, ask pertinent questions, make comparisons and create an ordered schema from the mass of data collected.[50]

In this study, data collection involved asking appropriate questions of interviewees, collecting written materials from multifarious sources and then attempting systematic analysis. At times this process was daunting, particularly in China, a distinctly foreign country with very considerable dissimilarities of academic and governmental culture, language and a relative paucity of published data. These difficulties were exacerbated because the subject matter of the investigation was in a process of constant change and evolution, thus creating considerable uncertainty for the researcher. Consequently, the results at the end of the process cannot constitute the 'right' answer; simply they provide the basis for a little less uncertainty about competition policy developments.

Grounded theory requires that once the researcher has completed analysis of the available data, ideas generated by the processing of the data begin to coalesce into theory. But this raises the question of the validity of the ideas that emerge and their reliability to act as the constructs of a hypothesis. Yin suggests that, to be confident of the validity of generated theory, the researcher should use multiple sources of evidence, establish the veracity of the information and review the data with knowledgeable interlocutors.[51] Once the validity of the constructs has been ascertained, the links between the constructs that go to form the hypothesis and the evidence gathered must be tested. This provides the internal validity of the developed hypothesis.

The development of the hypothesis by this means clearly relies to a greater extent upon the 'judgement' and background of the researcher, as will the way in which the data has been collected. Part of the researcher's background will include his knowledge of the relevant literature. This knowledge of the external context of the study will help to reconfirm the external validity of the research. Similarities and differences with similar research situations observed and reported by other workers in the field, will help to confirm the external validity of the project. This also aids external validity by making explicit the relationship between the existing

---

[50] Guba, *The paradigm dialogue*, p. 13.
[51] Robert K. Yin, *Applications of case study research*, London: Sage (1993).

body of knowledge and the new findings. The developed hypothesis will also provide new insights and hopefully create new knowledge about the topic, thus making a novel contribution to the field.

The findings might well accord with existing knowledge or they may be in conflict; this may be because the findings are incorrect, resulting from an internal design fault of the project or it may be that special circumstances cause the data to be idiosyncratic due to external factors unique to the subject matter. Whether the results 'fit in' with previous patterns or not, new insights should be achieved and knowledge increased.

1.4.6 Data collection, limitations, interpretation and evaluation

In addition to traditional library resources, it was necessary to undertake a number of field trips to Mainland China and Taiwan and to seek primary data from relevant individuals in all three jurisdictions through correspondence or interview. Much of the data pertinent to Mainland China was not publicly available or was classified as *neibu* (internal or confidential) to the government. Some of this data was provided to the author on the basis of confidentiality and so the identity of some informants has been protected, for fear of allegations of divulging 'state secrets'.

Significant amounts of data, especially regarding Mainland China, were written in the Chinese language and so translated versions had to be procured, which might compromise analysis and evaluation. However, all reasonable care was taken to ensure the veracity of the information obtained. In addition to these matters, the personal characteristics of the author needed to be considered as a local Chinese writer might legitimately have quite different impressions of Chinese efforts in the competition law field.

In order to interpret the data collected as accurately and as objectively as possible, so assisting in construct formation and theory generation in accordance with grounded theory, Yin's suggestion of using multiple sources of data, establishing the veracity of the information and reviewing the data with competent interlocutors was undertaken.[52] As explained above, multiple data sources were accessed and cross-checking with officials and academics was conducted to establish the veracity of any findings. Presentation of findings at international conferences and publication in journals of preliminary findings is evidence that substantial peer

---

[52] Ibid.

review has been undertaken.[53] However, it should be remembered that this verification was of preliminary findings and due to the longitudinal nature of this project not all material included here has been subject to detailed peer scrutiny. It is submitted that both the internal and external validity of the data has been secured, so far as is possible, in accordance with grounded theory requirements.

The enquiry undertaken revealed a paradox to the author, which the analysis undertaken below seeks to explain. The issue was this. China is the last remaining major communist power. Its official ideology rejects the market and with it economic competition. But not only is China moving rapidly towards an economy primarily based on capitalist means of production but it also ostensibly wishes to protect the competitive process by the use of competition law. On the other hand, Hong Kong, a *sine qua non* for 'red in tooth and claw' capitalism, denies the utility of government intervention to protect competition. This situation called for an investigation to discover what factors lead to these diametrically opposed policy decisions. A legitimate question arose as to whether they can be explained as rational policy choices or whether there are ulterior political or economic motives that drive policy formation. In any event, one needs to question prospectively whether a pro-competition policy or law would actually be effective in either China or Hong Kong. As regards Taiwan, the question is to what extent the adoption of competition law has been successful.

These are the issues that this book seeks to answer. This is done through the analysis of data; the use of analogous country case studies where relevant; comparative analysis of the existing and proposed legal provisions and the exploration of the socio-economic and political milieu, both domestically and internationally, in which policy has been formed

---

[53] China and the WTO Accession Conference, Zhuhai, December 1998; China and the EU Conference, Wuhan University, China, January 1999; Asia Pacific Law and Economics Conference, Bangkok, July 2000; China and the WTO Conference, Australian National University, Canberra, March 2001; Mark Williams, 'Economic Regulation: A Competition Law for the PRC', China and Zhuhai in the Globalisation of the World Economy, Conference Proceedings, 6–7 December 1998; Mark Williams, *Implications of the EU Competition Law for China's competition legislation*, 97(6) Wuhan University Law Review (1999), pp. 1–7; Mark Williams, *Analysis and suggestions on the outline Anti-Monopoly Law of the PRC*, Contemporary Legal Studies, Fudan University Press, Shanghai (2001), Part 1; Mark Williams, *Competition law developments in China*, JBL (May 2001), 273–98; Mark Williams, 'Consumer law in China', 18(2) UCLA Pacific Basin Law Journal (Spring 2001), 252–72; Mark Williams, *Introduction to general principles of PRC contract law*, 17 JCL (2001), pp. 13–36.

in each jurisdiction. As will be seen in the penultimate chapter, this book postulates the following hypothesis:

Competition law can only be effective in a functioning democracy

The basis of this formulation is the data presented in the later chapters, adopting a grounded theory approach to allow the creation of this explanatory hypothesis.

1.5 Structure of the book and summary of chapters

In light of the objectives explained in section 1.3 above, this work has been structured to reflect, hopefully, a logical and rational examination of the subject. This section seeks to mention briefly the underlying issues that will be examined in detail later.

Chapter 2 seeks to provide a succinct review of the relevant economic, political economy and legal literature relevant to the concept of economic competition and the political structures that underpin market-based economies. The experience of emerging economies and transitional states which have attempted to adopt competition policy and its enforcement through new legal regimes is analysed, as it is particularly relevant to China's situation. A number of countries' experiences are examined and the lessons learnt considered. The comments of academic observers are noted for later reference to China and Hong Kong.

Chapter 3 seeks to examine the internationalisation of competition law through various international organisations, principally the United Nations Conference on Trade and Development (UNCTAD), the Organisation for Economic Co-operation and Development (OECD) and the WTO, though the impact of initiatives of the regional organisation Asia–Pacific Economic Co-operation (APEC) and the newly established International Competition Network (ICN) will also be mentioned. This involvement of international organisations in competition policy formation has had an impact on both China and Hong Kong and has been welcomed as positive and supportive by China, where the government is surprisingly receptive to the protection of competition, but the opposite is true of Hong Kong. The HKSAR government is hostile to international rule adoption that would lead to a requirement for Hong Kong to legislate domestically and was one of the leaders of opposition to international rule-setting or even discussion of the topic by the WTO. This interesting paradox, given the different official political economy of China and Hong Kong, forms a central and continuing theme throughout the analytical chapters devoted to these jurisdictions.

Chapter 4 provides a detailed examination of the environmental factors germane to competition policy evolution in China – historical, economic and political factors are described and subjected to analysis. Chapter 5 considers the academic debate in China concerning competition policy and law, how the government has been investigating and debating competition law options and how the international community has contributed to this process. Existing competition rules are analysed and compared with relevant analogue legislation elsewhere. Existing drafts of an anti-monopoly law are scrutinised and some observations offered as to the practicality of legislating and implementing a comprehensive competition law in China.

Chapter 6 considers the historical, economic and political context of Hong Kong, illuminating in particular the political structure that exists following the resumption of Chinese sovereignty in 1997, and the nature and structure of the domestic economy in contrast to the externally traded sector.

Chapter 7 investigates the competition policy formation process in Hong Kong and examines the role of the Hong Kong Consumer Council (HKCC), the involvement of academics and other relevant actors. The HKSAR government's 1997 Response to HKCC proposals for a new comprehensive competition law and the establishment of the Competition Policy Advisory Group (COMPAG) are examined. Competition failures in the Hong Kong domestic economy are identified and analysed and an explanation of government hostility towards the enactment of a comprehensive competition statute is attempted.

Chapter 8 concentrates on three regulatory regimes that the HKSAR government insists exemplify its measured, sector-specific approach. The extant regulation of the electricity industry through a non-statutory scheme of control, and competition law rules in the broadcasting and telecommunication sectors, contained in the Broadcasting Ordinance (Cap. 562) and the Telecommunications Ordinance (Cap. 106) are analysed.

Chapter 9 attempts to investigate the history of competition policy adoption in Taiwan, the economic and political setting within which the crucial decision to adopt competition policy was taken and then to manifest that political decision through the enactment of the Fair Trade Act 1992. An analysis of the principal features of the law and an assessment of the success of the first decade of adoption is attempted.

Chapter 10 synthesises the results of the analytical chapters 4 to 9 and then subjects them to further scrutiny in the light of the grounded theory methodology approach explored in chapter 1. The insights provided, especially by Kovacic as explained in chapter 2, concerning the essential features of any successful adoption of a new competition regime will be considered in light of the analytical results obtained as regards China and Hong Kong. The constructs of the hypothesis are then identified from the analysed data and the hypothesis is proposed. Again, in accordance with grounded theory, the hypothesis is tested for both internal and external validity, with the Taiwan experience offered as an analogue. Finally, some suggestions to palliate the competition situation in Hong Kong and China are offered.

1.6 Conclusion

This chapter has sought to explain the geographical extent of this enquiry and to set out the constitutionally mandated economic and political environments that pertain in greater China. The methodology adopted in this book has been explained in the context of common lawyers' general antipathy to overt theorising in the majority of academic legal research. The wisdom of this isolationist tendency has been questioned, especially in respect of methodologies developed in the social sciences that might have relevance to some legal research subjects, particularly, it is submitted, the object of enquiry in this book. However, it is recognised that competition law is a notable exception to the common law's generally antithetical stance on explicit reference to theory. Consideration has been given to several competing ways of developing theory in academic research and it has been proposed that grounded theory is a suitable intellectual framework to be utilised in this work, given its non common law subject matter. The design, data collection and analytical methods used have been explained and the limitations of the work discussed. The hypothesis to be created has been set out, so that it can be borne in mind whilst the substantive analysis undertaken later is considered by the reader.

2

Competition theory and the experience of states adopting competition law

2.1 Introduction

The focus of this chapter is to analyse the current literature relevant to the theory of competition and then to review the arguments – economic, political and legal – as to the desirability of developing countries, countries in transition and small economies adopting competition law. Opinion is sharply divided as to whether or not, as a matter of economic theory, such a policy decision is justified, never mind the political and practical issues that an aspiring adopter would need to address.

There is a considerable literature concerning the economics of competition and the adoption of a competition law regime. Those who have been intimately involved in the drafting and implementation of new competition systems hold a plethora of divergent views. In many cases, comprehensive competition law systems have been adopted by states without the appropriate infrastructure to support effective implementation. This often creates the worst possible scenario of a superficially sound system that is in reality nothing but a hollow shell. This bleak picture is often the result of a well-intentioned but fickle commitment by international aid organisations. Often they propose (or require) the adoption of competition law but do not then provide resources for the efficacious rollout of the new pro-competition measures, so that the institutional structure is fatally weakened before the system has even been put into operation. Political and governmental weaknesses then compound this flawed approach. Further, a one-size-fits-all mentality is often apparent, that demonstrates either a bias towards the foreign consultants' own familiar but complex system and/or a lack of knowledge of the realities of government and law enforcement in the recipient country. Another reason for inappropriate wholesale adoption might be the desire by the adopting country to emulate the perceived prestige or success of the foreign system, without appreciating the vital importance of adopting a system to fit local objectives and taking into account local capacity to operate a competition system. China is a developing country[1] with a transitional economy and has a number of ideological, institutional and human-capacity problems that seriously call into question the wisdom of adoption at this time and the ability to enforce a new pro-competition legal regime. Hong Kong is small economy (by some measures) and there are legitimate issues to consider as to the need for and operation of a competition system in such economic conditions. Taiwan has transformed from a state-guided protectionist entity into a more open economy that now enjoys WTO membership and has adopted a competition regime as part of the process of economic and political liberalisation since the mid-1980s. Thus, the issues discussed here are directly relevant to the three jurisdictions.

The picture that emerges from the literature is mixed. The arguments for and against adoption of a competition regime have had a part to play in the policy discussions and decisions of both China and Hong Kong. The hostile attitude of the Hong Kong government to competition law, avowedly the paradigm of the free market, is paradoxical. This is especially so as the policy stance of the socialist PRC government has been much more benign towards the creation of a competition regime in the Mainland. This clear dichotomy of views is all the more remarkable given that, logically, one might have imagined that the respective governments would take the opposite stance to that which they actually do. This curious state of affairs will be explained and relevant competition policy issues will be analysed in the later chapters devoted to China and Hong Kong respectively. Taiwan, in contrast, made the policy choice for adopting a competition law system almost two decades ago and now has a functioning system in place.

2.2 Competition terminology and the nature of economic competition

Various technical terms are used in this book and so it is advisable that, for the sake of clarity, they are defined at the outset. Competition in its ordinary usage means a contest in which people try to do better than their rivals.[2] In relation to commerce, the UK Competition Commission has considered competition to be 'a process of rivalry between

---

[1] China was admitted as a member of WTO on this basis.
[2] *Oxford paperback dictionary*, 4th edn, Oxford University Press (1994).

firms . . . seeking to win customers' business over time'.[3] Rival firms operate in a given product market, which has geographical and temporal components; these considerations are central to the concept of any given market. The mechanism of economic rivalry, as opposed to a politically driven economic system, is the process of competition.

To decide if competition provides beneficial economic outcomes, one must consider the economic theory of perfect competition and contrast the results of such a system with that of a market without competition of any kind, that is, a monopoly.

Classical economics predicts that the most beneficial structure for any market is that of perfect competition, where both individual consumer welfare and social welfare are maximised. The expected benefits of competition include greater consumer choice in terms of quality coupled with the lowest possible price; monopoly would provide exactly the reverse of these benefits – high prices with little or no choice. Thus, competition results in a felicitous combination of maximised economic efficiencies – productive, allocative and dynamic – so reducing wastage of social assets to a minimum combined with maximisation of individual consumer welfare or satisfaction.

Monopoly, conversely, will result in rent-seeking behaviour by the incumbent who will be able to reduce supply of the relevant good, increase price and fail to improve the product. Lethargy and waste of resources is the prerogative of the monopolist. Thus, the classical school would suggest that the operation of Adam Smith's invisible hand provides an unmitigated good.

This theoretical paradigm of perfect competition is, however, most unlikely to occur in reality as it presupposes a very large number of buyers and sellers of similar or near-identical products, all of whom have perfect market information. No barriers to entry or exit of the relevant market exist, whether they be financial, geographical, physical or legal. These assumptions make even the theoretical existence of perfect competition seem improbable, let alone a reality of commercial life in our very imperfect world.

Whilst perfect competition is a chimera, absolute monopoly is almost as unreal. Only where legal privilege grants absolute territorial exclusivity to a sole supplier of a non-substitutable product, for example water or electricity, can a true monopoly exist. But even in such 'natural' monopoly

---

[3] See *Merger references: Competition Commission Guidelines*, London (June 2003), para. 1. 20.

industries attempts have been made worldwide to introduce competitive pressure to reduce costs and improve quality and choice, though not all attempts have been unqualified successes.[4] Thus, competition authorities are usually concerned with a range of market conditions from near monopoly or markets with dominant incumbent suppliers, who can exert market power and act quasi-independently of competitors or customers, to situations where some level of competition does exist, but firms seek to merge or collaborate actually or potentially to weaken competitive rivalry between them.

Moreover, perfect competition also presupposes that both consumers and business operators always act in a strictly rational and logical way, the sort of ideal utilitarian personified by the fictional Victorian industrialist, Thomas Gradgrind, in Charles Dickens' novel *Hard Times*.[5]

But business people and consumers rarely act as rational calculating machines and motives as diverse as greed, megalomania, indolence and personal loyalty may all sway the weak human actor away from the true path of *homo economicus*. Further, classical theory exists in a static environment where technological change is disregarded and dominant players never become dinosaurs. Reality is very different from these artificial and restrictive assumptions.

Thus, if perfect competition is so far removed from the daily economic market place, perhaps policy makers may simply reject the notion of seeking to achieve an unobtainable objective in favour of a more realistic policy goal.

The perspective of history now seems to indicate clearly that, however far market-orientated economies are from the attainment of perfect competition, they do, in most instances, produce better economic outcomes than those achieved by central planning. Most of the world's population now live in states committed, to some extent or other, to market-based

---

[4] Electricity deregulation in California and the privatisation of railways in the UK have been poor advertisements for the benefits of competition (though they are probably better categorised on failure of regulatory structures, rather than competition per se). Gas and electricity in the UK and telecommunications in UK and Hong Kong are industries that have shown substantial benefits to consumers since the introduction of competition.

[5] 'A man of realities. A man of facts and calculations. A man who proceeds upon the principle that two and two are four, and nothing over ... with a rule and a pair of scales and the multiplication tables always in his pocket, sir, ready to weigh and measure any parcel of human nature, and tell you exactly what it comes to. It is a mere question of figures, a simple case of arithmetic.' Charles Dickens, *Hard Times*, London: The Folio Society (1983), p. 2.

economies and so it is necessary to fashion theoretical models to adapt to this reality of imperfect competition. If imperfect competition is the best we can hope to achieve, have economic theorists provided a convincing analytical framework to explain the extant reality and to serve as a good policy objective for policy makers to seek to achieve?

As long ago as the 1940s, economists had developed a theory of 'workable competition'.[6] This is an acceptance of the implausibility and impracticality of even seeking to attain a state of perfect competition; achieving the most competitive market possible in the relevant circumstances is the limit of the theory's ambition and satisfactorily defining the theoretical parameters of even this limited goal is problematic.

More recently, a new model has been suggested of 'contestable markets'.[7] This theory emphasises the need for free entry to and exit from any given market by firms, so that, should incumbents engage in rent-seeking behaviour, a new producer will enter the market, compete away the supra-competitive profit and then exit the market without impediment. This theory may be applicable in apparently oligopolistic markets. A good example may be the Hong Kong external telecommunication market where previously dominant players now constantly complain that as soon as they seek to raise prices, a new participant will enter, offer services, and then disappear as prices fall back to their original level. Entry to and exit from this market is both easy and relatively cheap. Licences to operate are readily available and the purchase of wholesale circuit capacity from infrastructure owners with excess capacity ensures that the large operators are constantly harassed by the gnat bites of small, transient, competitors.

Yet another formula is that of 'effective competition'. This is a policy goal adopted in relation to competition analysis, especially in relation to mergers, not only in the UK[8] but also in the EC Merger Regulation.[9] Effective competition embodies the notion that the objectives of competition policy and the enforcement authorities is to ensure that market players are subject to a reasonable degree of competitive pressure either from other market players or consumers or both.

---

[6] John Clark, *Toward a concept of workable competition* 30 AM Ec Rev 241–56 (1940).
[7] David Bailey, *Contestability and the design of regulatory and anti-trust policy* 71 AM Ec Rev 178–83 (1981).
[8] See Utilities Act 2000, ss. 9 and 13; OFTEL, *Achieving the best deal for telecoms consumers* (January 2000).
[9] Regulation 4064|89, OJ[1989] L395/1 as amended by Regulation 1310|97, OJ [1997] L 180/1.

As will be seen later, this book will suggest that attempting to operate a pro-competition policy regime successfully through a competition law is fraught with difficulties. The possibility of abusive enforcement, and even outright failure when the policy is executed in a state that does not enjoy a 'functional democracy', is high; this concept will form the basis of an explanation of why effective adoption and enforcement of competition policies and laws are so problematic in most transitional economies. A full explanation of this notion will be provided later in the text.

In addition to these 'human frailties', which might undermine rational decision-making by market players, other matters are just as troublesome to the classical conception of economics. Politicians and their electorates may pay lip-service to competition in theory but when competition, especially from foreign operators or large corporations, causes perceived harm to local interests, the practical commitment to a free and competitive economic system can waver or collapse. The political costs associated with greater competition may be a decisive influence on economic policy, whereby laissez-faire may give way to crude mercantilism. Concerns about industrial policy (national champions), strategic national interests (such as defence) or access to vital commodities or employment opportunities (especially in politically sensitive constituencies) or regional development or political hostility to foreign ownership of domestic assets may hold a greater sway over policy decisions than adherence to the goal of more competitive markets.

None of this is new. In *Wealth of Nations*, Adam Smith railed against what he saw as the distorting and malign policies of mercantilism operated by eighteenth-century British governments that sought to promote the interest of the merchant princes by various legislative measures, including the grant of geographical monopolies in relation to foreign trade, by restricting the colonial carrying trade, imposing high import duties and export subsidies. He famously considered that the removal of these governmental restrictions on foreign trade would promote the economic health of the nation and thereby increase its total wealth. As a result of the mechanisation of production in Britain in the late eighteenth and early nineteenth centuries, giving British manufacturers a huge cost and so competitive advantage over their rivals, the merchant princes became zealous converts to the twin concepts of free trade and laissez-faire. Thus, it is no surprise that where a nation has superior technology or skill it will espouse economic liberalism, but where it does not or suffers from a high cost base of production, siren domestic voices will complain of 'unfair' or 'malignant' competition. Thus, it can be expected that all nations who have expressed fealty to the principle of competition will make exceptions to equal treatment as and when political imperatives trump rational economic analysis. This truism of political life can be observed in all countries. For example, the USA imposing illegal safeguard duties on steel imports in 2002,[10] the European Union (EU)'s overtly protectionist policies in relation to agricultural products and China's imposition of a discriminatory set of measures to restrict foreign-related merger and acquisition activity in 2003.[11] Policy themes such as these will be discussed, as appropriate, in the text that follows.

In addition to questioning the wisdom of unrestrained competition, there may also be other obstacles. Clearly, the issue of the minimum scale of production of an industry is important, as some markets may be only able to support one or a very small number of competitors. Small economies are particularly vulnerable to high concentration ratios, and so, it is suggested, they need appropriate pro-competition policies even more than larger economies to restrain rent seeking and to enhance economic welfare by preventing the inherent disadvantages that afflict small economies from being accentuated.[12] The Hong Kong government refuses to accept this analysis and insists that a combination of free trade policies and minimal government interference in business is sufficient and so a comprehensive competition law is not needed; the truth of this assertion will be analysed later.

In developing countries, the market demand for a product may be very small, at least initially and so competition may be inimical to other politically set goals, especially in newly established or developing states. Nation building, national champions and chauvinism may all trump the economic case for competition at least in the initial stages of industrial development. In South Korea, Japan and Taiwan the promotion of rapid industrialisation and strategic concerns relegated questions of social, and especially consumer, welfare to a distant secondary importance to that of industrial policy. However, as their economies matured, especially during the 1980s and 1990s, these jurisdictions too became more conscious of the need to promote economic efficiency in their domestic economies, and new pro-competition legislative instruments, together with a more

---

[10] WTO Appellate Body United States – Definitive safeguard measures on imports of certain steel products WT/DS248/20, 16 December 2003.

[11] These regulations will be analysed later in section 5.7 below.

[12] For a detailed discussion of special difficulties faced by small economies in deciding on an appropriate competition strategy. See Mical S. Gal, *Competition policy for small market economies*, Cambridge, Mass.: Harvard University Press (2003).

aggressive enforcement policy, have been in evidence during the last several years; the case of Taiwan will be considered in detail later.

Consequently, it can be seen that the argument in favour of a pro-competition policy are not always overwhelming but, nevertheless, it is now true to say that the argument that more competitive markets do produce better economic results, is accepted by more countries then ever before with over eighty states[13] now having partial or comprehensive competition laws, many of which have only been adopted within the last fifteen years. The factors that determine whether they are effective in achieving their objective will be considered later in this chapter.

2.3 The objectives of competition policy

Whilst the theoretical underpinnings of competition law are somewhat opaque and to some extent contradictory, so too are the objectives of national competition legislation. For example, the EU has had a fixation on the creation of a single EU-wide market; the USA has at various times sought to protect small and medium-sized enterprises (SME) or, as political and economic fashions change, to pursue an unalloyed goal of economic efficiency. Whilst economics forms the theoretical justification for governmental involvement in business decision-making, political choices produce the legislative instrument and inform the enforcement emphasis of any given jurisdiction. As politics change, so does the rationale for, and the implementation of, competition policy.

Various goals (some of them inconsistent) can be identified as the aims of competition policies internationally. The most obvious and politically popular objective, especially in democratic states, is consumer protection, not merely by ensuring contestable markets or effective competition but by imposing penalties or prohibitions in particular cases or by requiring structural adjustments in a delinquent industry. Imposing direct controls over a malefactor, for example setting maximum prices, might be politically popular but cannot be justified in any but the most exceptional case, as, logically, if the operator is subject to competitive restraint, the invisible hand of the market mechanism should self-correct to produce the optimal outcome. Further, excessive consumer protection can so damage an industry that it may choose not to reinvest in new capital goods but to seek a better return elsewhere. In Hong Kong, the complaint of

---

[13] UNCTAD, *Directory of competition law authorities*, 13 March 2002, TD/B/COM.2/CLP/18. http://www.unctad.org/en/docs//c2clp18.en.pdf.

market players is that regulatory policy and 'over competition' has so reduced profitability in the telecommunication industry that infrastructure
is not now receiving adequate investment to ensure continued technical
superiority when compared to regional competitors, such as Singapore.
Short-term populism, the operators state, will cause long-term damage
to an essential industry. This argument will be considered later in the
analysis of the Hong Kong telecommunications sector.

Another populist cause is that of equity and the notion that the over-
concentration of economic power in a few hands is inherently dangerous.
The argument runs that this may imperil the functioning of democratic
institutions. This indeed has been a major concern in the USA and formed
the *raison d'être* of the Sherman and Clayton Acts.[14] The reverse is also
true. In Hong Kong, those who currently hold the levers of economic
power also, directly or indirectly, control the policy-formation process
and so, unsurprisingly, the Hong Kong government has been a vociferous
opponent of domestic or international legislation on competition; a full
analysis of this phenomenon will be offered later.

Equality arguments, in the sense of promoting the interests of the
SMEs, usually locally or family-owned concerns, from the ravages of effective competition from more efficient, large rivals is often an explicit
competition-policy goal. Diversity of ownership and fairness to the 'little
guy' are good political slogans but bad economics, especially in the eyes
of the Chicago School. Bork considers such arguments antithetical to the
sole legitimate goal of competition policy – economic efficacy – and as
little more than rank sentimentality.[15] European views about the unde-
sirability of over-concentration of economic power and the political need
for a plurality of ownership, especially by small business, were championed by the Freiburg School, also known as the Ordoliberal movement.
Their views were formed in the context of German industrial policy of the
Wilhelmine and later Nazi Reichs and are considered in more detail below.
They undoubtedly had an effect on EC competition law.

Other diverse goals have also influenced competition policy – the need
to promote regional development, to maintain high employment levels,
to protect home industry from foreign ownership or domination so allowing the growth of national champions and to protect industries vital to

---

[14] See Hans Theorelli, *The federal anti-trust policy – organisation of an American tradition*,
  Baltimore: The Johns Hopkins Press (1955), pp. 226–7 and 564–8; also, Rudolph Peritz,
  Competition policy in America 1888–1992, Oxford University Press (1996).
[15] Robert H. Bork, *The anti-trust paradox: a policy at war with itself*, New York: Basic Books,
  Inc. (1978).

national military defence are all matters that inform, or impede, rational and consistent policy choices in this field.

A former EC competition commissioner exemplified the vital issue of placing competition policy goals in the context of the society within which they operate. Karel Van Miert said:

> The aims of the European Community's competition policy are economic, political and social. The policy is concerned not only with promoting ef-ficient production but also achieving the aims of the European treaties: establishing a common market, approximating economic policies, promot-ing harmonious growth, raising living standards, bringing Member States closer together, etc. To this must be added the need to safeguard a pluralistic democracy, which could not survive a strong concentration of economic power.
>
> If competition policy is to reach these various goals, decisions must be made in a pragmatic fashion bearing in mind the context in which they are to be made: the realization of the internal market, the globalization of markets, economic crisis, technological development, the ratification of Maastricht Treaty.[16]

This statement was made some ten years ago and demonstrates a re-markably wide set of objectives for competition policy to achieve. These stated objectives clearly demonstrate the particular concerns of the de-veloping EU entity, whose structural features are markedly different from the unified single market of the United States. Whether this still repre-sents the true agenda of EC competition policy may be open to question. In America, there is no doubt that the influence of the Chicago School on policy objectives is still ascendant and that the primary emphasis of policy enforcement is on economic efficiency and consumer and social welfare.

Thus, whilst the two most mature and influential competition law systems have fundamental differences in terms of objectives, the same will inevitably be true of other states. They may be less economically developed, have markedly different economic structures or systems of law or political problems such as authoritarian governments or a high level of corruption or a feeble system of justice or public administration. Social norms such as deference to authority or wide socio-economic differences or lack of a developed consumerist culture or a participatory political culture, may all call into question the appropriate and achievable goals of a competition policy and the legal regime used to enforce the adopted policy

[16] Speech by Commissioner Karel Van Miert, 'Frontier-free Europe', 5 May 1993.

choice. These issues will be considered below in relation to developing and transitional states, so as better to inform the later analysis of the extant competition systems in China, Hong Kong and Taiwan.

2.4 Economic analysis of law

The notion that law could and should be analysed by the use of economic concepts, is relatively recent, though Holmes suggested it over a hundred years ago.[17] An economic approach to law was pioneered by economists who had been primarily concerned with competition issues but the expansion into other legal areas began in the early 1960s with Calabresi in relation to torts[18] and Coase[19] on social costs. More than thirty years ago, Posner published one of the most celebrated works in this field, *Economic Analysis of Law*.[20] This book has been extremely influential, especially in the United States, in promoting the use of economic analysis of law in all fields of legal endeavour, even those such as racial discrimination, drug addiction, theft of works of art, sexual activity, religious observance or flag burning, none of which are usually associated with obvious economic concerns. Clearly, the legal rules relating to the ownership and disposition of property, corporations and the maintenance of competition in a market have a more obvious connection with economic analysis. In competition law, the explicit reference to economic theory is obvious and the use of economic analytical tools in reaching administrative or judicial decisions is absolutely embedded in the practices of competition authorities and courts worldwide. Thus, economic analysis of law is an obvious prerequisite to work in this field of legal endeavour.

2.5 Current economic theory and the justification for adoption of competition law

There are several core economic issues that affect policy analysis of competition theory and it is apparent that there has been a move away from the neo-classical microeconomic view of rational human behaviour, information flows and the potential of attaining a state of more perfect

[17] Holmes, *The path of the law,* 10 Harvard Law Review 457, 474 (1897).

[18] Guido Calabresi, *Some thoughts on risk distribution and the Law of Torts,* 70 Yale LJ 499 (1961).

[19] Ronald Coase, *The problem of social cost,* 3 J Law and Econ. 1 (1960).

[20] Richard Posner, *Economic analysis of law,* New York: Little, Brown & Co. (1973), 5th edn, New York: Aspen Law and Business (1998).

competition. Instead, alternative methods of economic analysis attempt to explain the actual functioning of markets in terms of chaos theory, game theory, uncertainty and mutual expectations as more reliable guides to market phenomena.

Contemporary economics considers that markets in states of more or less equilibrium where concentration determines competitiveness do not exist but rather that they are institutions in a constant state of evolution, where information is in a state of flux and competition is determined by the ability of actors to innovate their own processes and to integrate their production with rivals to produce enhanced returns. Another key element in competition theory, the definition of relevant market is also being critically reassessed. Substitutability in a given place at a given time is not taken to be the only determinant of the relevant market. Foreseeable future innovation, it is suggested, must also be taken into account as consumers in economic exchange may also consider the possibility of an innovatory product being available soon and so discount price accordingly.

An even more fundamental attack on classical theory is the notion that Pareto optimality is flawed and that more emphasis should be placed on productive, rather than allocative efficiency.[21] Loasby takes the view that the emphasis on perfect competition as the normative policy standard is inappropriate and the achievement of increasing productive returns may run counter to conventional wisdom:

> The commitment to Pareto optimality as a basis – apparently the only basis – for scientific welfare economics leads rather naturally to Samuelson's well-known assessment: 'Increasing returns is the enemy of perfect competition. And therefore, it is the enemy of optimality conditions that perfect competition can ensure.' The assessment is correct; but why not reverse the order? The optimality conditions, and the perfect competition which can deliver them, are the enemy of increasing returns and, therefore, of economic progress as understood by Smith and Marshall. The fascination with Pareto optimality and perfect competition is a major obstacle to understanding economic development.[22]

The vital issue of institutions and their effect on market expectations is also now considered to be of great importance. It has long been accepted that in an uncertain world firms will commit to new investment

[21] Thomas Jorde and David Teece, eds., *Anti-trust, innovation and competitiveness*, Oxford University Press (1992).

[22] Brian Loasby, *Equilibrium and evolution: an exploration of connecting principles in economics*, Manchester University Press (1991), p. 25.

only so long as they have a reasonable expectation of obtaining a return on their investment.[23] One vital factor in this decision-making process is inevitably subjective, that is the institutional setting in which the decision is made. The importance of a reliable judicial system, effective protection of property rights and contractual freedom cannot be overstated.[24] Another branch of economic research – New Institutional Economics – fostered by Douglass C. North, has emphasised the importance of the type and quality of social institutions that support markets in determining economic performance. Institutions, whether formalised as laws or merely social conventions, can provide part of the explanation of the observed differentials in economic development around the world[25] North has recently extended his analysis by providing an explanation of the way in which societies create their institutional infrastructure is also a determinant of their economic performance.[26] He suggests that a society's adaptive efficiency is crucial, which he defines as how effective a society is in developing stable, fair, productive and accepted institutions which are flexible enough to change in the face of altered political or economic circumstances. Some authors suggest that only democracies can provide the environment for sustained institution building combined with the innate flexibilities that allows for successful adaptation and change.[27]

Thus, the new paradigm has shifted from the idealistic and formal neo-classical vision of competition to a more fluid, evolving and realistic picture of the business world.

In the context of developing economies Frischtak suggests:

> A competitive environment is a necessary condition for countries to follow an efficient development path but it is not sufficient. At the very least it is essential to have a class of traders willing to shift to industrial activities. The

---

[23] G. B. Richardson, *Information and investment*, Oxford University Press (1960).

[24] The vital importance of property rights and their promotion and protection in creating wealth has been popularised by a highly influential book, *The mystery of capital*, which seeks to explain why poor countries remained mired in poverty whilst a few Western nations (and some of their former colonial possessions) were able to create conditions in which capitalism was able to flourish and produce unprecedented wealth. Hernando de Soto, *The mystery of capital: why capitalism triumphs in the West and fails everywhere else*; New York: Basic Books (2000).

[25] Douglass C. North, *Institutions, institutional change, and economic performance*, Cambridge University Press (1990).

[26] Douglass C. North, *Understanding the process of economic change*, Princeton University Press (2005).

[27] Morton H. Halperin, Joseph T. Siegle and Michael M. Weinstein, *The democracy advantage: how democracies promote prosperity and peace*, New York: Routledge (2005).

least developed countries need to build up their industrial endowments, markets, and institutions before they can use competition to the fullest advantage as a tool of industrial policy.[28]

Thus, if this is the case, the soundness of the theoretical basis upon which the edifice of competition regulation currently rests may be open to question.

As far as legal commentators are concerned, the pre-eminent voice on the proper object of a competition regime is that of Posner. In his seminal book *Anti-Trust Law: An Economic Approach* he championed the Chicago School view that the only proper object of competition law was the promotion of economic welfare.[29] This was not universally accepted at that time but in his second edition he opined:

> Almost everyone professionally involved in anti-trust today whether as litigator, prosecutor, judge, academic or informed observer – not only agrees that the only goal of anti-trust laws should be to promote economic welfare but also agrees on the essential tenets of economic theory that should be used to determine the consistency of specific business practices with that goal.[30]

Others however consider that competition law and its enforcement do more economic harm than good and that bureaucratic second-guessing of the market should not be tolerated. They argue that competition laws should be cut back to an absolute minimum – say, limited to prohibitions of cartels only as suggested by Bork[31] or even completely repealed as advocated by Armentano.[32] Others worry about the transfer of economic decision-making away from individual firms to government. As Amato puts it:

> It is a fact that within liberal society itself one of the key divisions of political identity (and hence identification) is between these two sides: the side that fears private power more, and in order to fight it is ready to give more room to the power of government; and the side that fears expansion

---

[28] C. Frischtak, B. Hadjimichael and J. Zachau, *Competition policies for industrialising countries*, Policy and Research Series no. 7, World Bank, Washington, D.C. (1989).

[29] Richard A. Posner, *Anti-trust law: an economic approach*, University of Chicago Press (1976).

[30] Posner, *Anti-trust*, p. ix.   [31] Bork, *The anti-trust paradox*.

[32] Dominick T. Armentano, *Anti-trust policy: the case for repeal*, Washington, D.C.: Cato Institute (1986).

of government more, and is therefore more prepared to tolerate private power.[33]

However, despite these doctrinal concerns most commentators would concur with Professor Whish:

> despite the range of different theories and difficulties associated with them, competition does seem to possess sufficient properties to lead to policy choice in its favour. Competitive markets seem, on the whole, to deliver better outcomes than monopolistic ones. This is why competition policy has been so widely embraced in recent years; there is probably a greater global consensus on the desirability of competition and free markets today than at any time in the history of human economic behaviour.[34]

This author agrees and this book will seek to demonstrate how the governments of China, Hong Kong and Taiwan seek to deal with (or tolerate) competition problems within their jurisdictions.

2.6 The political dimension – political economy and business regulation theory

2.6.1 Political theory and market competition

In addition to the academic debate on the economics of competition policy, clearly the political setting of a particular jurisdiction will be of crucial importance to the choice of whether or not to embrace a competitive market mechanism and then how best to optimise economic outcomes and protect the market thus created.

The German Ordoliberal and Social Market theories that came to prominence in the 1940s and 1950s best exemplify the modern adaptation of the classical political economy of Adam Smith and David Riccardo to contemporary market regulation in liberal democracies. The progenitor of Ordoliberalism was Walter Eucken. His approach was to attempt to chart a middle course between pure laissez-faire and state-dominated politico-economic structures. The basic idea was that politico-legal and politico-economic decisions form part of an economic constitution, which is created by a general political decision to determine how the economic life of

---

[33] G. Amato, *Anti-trust and the bounds of power – the dilemma of liberal democracy in the history of the market,* Oxford: Hart Publishing (1997), p. 4.
[34] Whish, *Competition law,* p. 15.

the nation is to be structured.[35] This concept of an economic constitution was further developed in his book *Grundlagen der Nationalökonomie* (The Foundations of Economics). This work contains an elaborate scheme of classification of economic orders, with two central models, the centrally planned economy and the market economy, which is divided into twenty-five sub-forms of supply–demand relationship, ranging from monopoly to perfect competition. In a later work *Grundsätze der Wirtschaftpolitik* (Principles of Economic Policy) Eucken develops his theory of the intimate interdependency of policy, the economic orders and society. He then uses this synthesis to analyse the laissez-faire period of German economic development, which he suggests lasted until the end of the 1870s. Later economic development in Germany is characterised by him as the 'experimental period' where government intervention expanded, providing protectionist measures that fostered further monopolisation and cartel formation. He criticised the emergence of monopolies and oligopolies as subverting the legitimate interests of other social actors and of undermining *Rechtsstaat* (Rule of Law). Eucken's analysis is criticised by Sally on the basis that it underestimates the role of public policy considerations stipulated by classical economists and that it also downplayed the role of the state in promoting industrial combinations.[36] Eucken also analyses the effect of centrally planned economies and strongly argues that this system destroys economic freedom to dispose of property and so subverts the rule of law by replacing it with the naked exercise of political power.

So, in Eucken's view, unrestrained private economic power creates monopolies, which development is enhanced by government protectionist measures, which ultimately lead to complete state domination of the economic order through central planning. Thus, power, whether private economic power or monopolised state power, is the force that needs to be controlled because it can distort or destroy the price mechanism as the primary allocator of resources and also has the effect of destroying individual freedom. This analysis seems nation-specific to Germany but there may be a kernel of logic applicable universally. His solution to these perceived evils is to protect the competitive mechanism. To do this it is necessary to establish *Ordnungspolitik* (policy of order – an economic constitution).

---

[35] Walter Eucken, Franz Bohm and Hans Grossmann-Doerth, 'The Ordo Manifesto of 1936', in Alan Peacock and Hans Willgerodt, *German neo-liberals and the social market economy: origins and evolution,* New York: St Martin's Press (1989), pp. 23–4.

[36] Razeen Sally, *Classical liberalism and international economic order*, London: Routledge (1998), pp. 109–10.

As Sally puts it '[this structure] behoves the state to set up and maintain the institutional framework of the free economic order, but it should not intervene in the price-signalling and resource allocation mechanism of the competitive economic process'.[37]

The 'policy of order' is an elaborate construct involving a number of constitutive and regulatory principles. The constitutive components include: a functioning price system, stable monetary values, open markets including the prohibition of closing markets by private entities even through the use of intellectual property monopoly rights, sanctity of private property, freedom of contract, full liability for entrepreneurs in the sense of no limited liability corporations so as to tie risk taking to responsibility for the consequences of that risk-taking behaviour, stable policy choices and an equality principle, such that all the enumerated elements are given equal weight due to their interdependency. The main principle of regulation he suggests, to allow the economic order created by the principles to function, is that of a vigorous, intrusive competition policy backed by stern legal sanctions given to an independent competition authority with the objective of establishing the classical vision of perfect competition.

Eucken's model can be criticised as overly rational and rigid in structure dependent on a belief that human beings can 'create' a perfect order, for the centrality of an unrealistic goal – classical perfect competition – as the rationale for the whole edifice and also, for the politically naïve belief that a powerful economic policeman, in the form of a competition authority, can always be entrusted to exercise Olympian detachment in making essential policy choices in economic management. Further, as F. A. Hayek suggests, Eucken's liberalism, in the classical sense, was distinctly 'restrained'.[38]

However, despite these weaknesses, one should not underestimate the importance of his ideas – protection of property rights and legalism, the sound money policy of the Bundesbank and the power of the *Bundeskartellamt* in economic management, as well as the centrality of individual liberty in the constitutionalism of West Germany, all suggest that Eucken's thought did have an important influence on Germany's post-war institutional reconstruction.

Another influential German thinker in this field was Franz Bohm. His thought was more in line with classical liberalism and he emphasised his

---

[37] Ibid. p. 111.
[38] F. A. Hayek, *The rediscovery of freedom: personal recollections*, University of Chicago Press (1992), p. 190.

theory of the *Privatrechtsgesellschaft* (private law society). The centrality of the law in protecting individuals from state or group interference or unwarranted coercion by other individuals and by the protection afforded to free bargaining – contracts – as the basis of the free market economy. Free contracting explicitly requires limitations of state power and the power of interference by others on an individual's liberty. Law should merely state negatively what is not permitted, rather than be used to construct an economic system. Bohm has faith in the random operation of the invisible hand of the market, restrained from excess purely by negative legal injunctions. However, limitations on the power of the state would include the prevention of the protection of monopoly or cartel power by protectionist measures and the condemnation of anti-competitive behaviour by market-distorting actors on the basis that this constituted an unwarranted interference with the liberty of other individual market players. The basis of Bohm's fixation with legalism was, apparently, his experience as a German government servant in the 1920s, where he witnessed, first hand, direct manipulation of government policy by powerful commercial combines, that typified the nexus of industrial and political power in both Wilhelmine and Weimar Germany, unrestrained by legal prohibitions.

Another strand in the post-war neo-liberal German school of thought was the concept of the *Soziale Marktwirschaft* (social market economy). Alfred Muller-Armack was the originator of this conception of a moderated but market-orientated economy, an implicit balance between free markets and social protection. Whilst this bringing together of two potentially antithetical concepts – markets and social protection – might appear improbable, Muller-Armack appropriated the concept of subsidiarity, drawn from the Roman Catholic dogma, to construct his vision of a socially moderated market. Subsidiarity emphasised self-reliance or reliance upon others in small communities where power should be concentrated. Only if the individual or small unit could not provide the necessary function identified as necessary by the lower organisational tier should an upper level of government became involved. Muller-Armack also advocated economic rights for members of society including state subsidies to small businesses, workers rights to involvement in business decision-making and Keynesian policies of public spending in recessions. This interventionist model is clearly at odds with classical or even the Ordoliberal concept of economic organisation. Nevertheless, the close association of both the Ordoliberals and Muller-Armack with leading figures in German politics and positions in the higher civil service and

Federal Parliament in the 1950s, ensured that the neo-liberal agenda was crucial in German economic recovery, the *Wirtshaftswunder*, which restored German industrial might in the thirty years following 1945.

The German neo-liberal model discussed here is interesting for three reasons. First, it posits a close relationship between concentrated economic power and political influence (as was suggested by Woodrow Wilson, see section 1.1). Secondly, the emphasis on preserving competition by law, impartially enforced, so as to ensure economic liberty and, thirdly, the social-politico-economic 'good' of competition as part of the liberal-democratic dispensation of a state.

Essentially, these theorists saw, from the German perspective, that private power can distort economic markets and can mobilise governmental power actually to close markets completely. Even democracies were not immune from capture by powerful vested-interest groups, either by commercial oligarchies or over-mighty trades unions. As Sally says: 'Collective action by organised interests, as well as government intervention, culminates in the corporatist conflation and collusion of public and private power.'[39] These conclusions should be borne in mind when the actual politico-economic matrix in both China and Hong Kong are analysed later and when the postulated hypothesis of this thesis is examined in chapter 11.

2.6.2 Regulation of international business

An important facet of domestic economic regulatory regimes is the impact of the process of international rule setting especially in the face of increased globalisation, particularly with the establishment of the World Trade Organisation (WTO). The ways in which a particular subject matter is captured by an international forum and then internationalised are analysed by Brathwaite and Drahos.[40] They suggest that the process of capture and rule setting is driven by a contest between two divergent political forces, namely harmonisation (pro-international rules) and national sovereignty (anti-international rules). The process that determines which force succeeds is governed by the complex interplay of two phenomena, which they label 'principles' and 'mechanisms'. The parties that utilise the process include both state and non-state actors – transnational

---

[39] Sally, *Classical liberalism*, p. 125.
[40] John Brathwaite and Peter Drahos, *Global business regulation*, Cambridge University Press (2000).

corporations (TNCs), professional bodies, non-governmental organisations (NGOs) and, in rare cases, individual politicians or academics. Whether the prospective subject to be regulated internationally is successfully absorbed into the process or not, and whether harmonisation or national sovereignty wins out, is a highly intricate contest between the various stakeholders utilising the weapons of the principles and the mechanisms alluded to above. Often it is impossible to predict with certainty whether a particular subject matter will be internationally regulated or not, and this is certainly true of the internationalisation of competition law, as will be seen in the next chapter.

The principles used to play the international regulatory game identified by Brathwaite and Drahos include transparency (pro-internationalisation), national sovereignty (which may be watered down to a principle of mutual recognition of rules), national treatment vs. reciprocity and an emerging neo-mercantilism labelled 'strategic trade'; deregulation in the form of freedom from restrictions, lower costs of production vs. global best practice, free flow of information (not including the abandonment of intellectual property rights), and finally the rule of law in preference to arbitrary, naked, political judgements.[41] The mechanisms by which the principles are used include military coercion, economic coercion, economic 'rewards', modelling (voluntary or enforced transplantation of an existing model or system including legal systems), reciprocal adjustment (states shift the regulatory policy in response to a shift by another) and capacity building (technical assistance by advanced states so as to enhance the ability of other states either to adopt or comply with internationalised norms).[42]

The process described and analysed by Brathwaite and Drahos is of great complexity and considerable antiquity, though the spread of international norm setting has gathered pace in the last fifty years, particularly where American TNCs have perceived the process to be advantageous to them.[43]

As regards competition law adoption in Hong Kong or China, the process of internationalising the subject of competition law has been viewed with keen interest. Hong Kong has been a member of the WTO since its inception and has been a leading opponent even of the inclusion of discussions on whether to commence negotiations on the topic. This matter

---

[41] Ibid. chapter 21.   [42] Ibid. chapter 22.

[43] For a full discussion of the regulation of transnational corporations see P. T. Muchlinski, *Multi-national enterprises and the law*, Oxford: Blackwell (1999).

is considered later. China has not, thus far, entered the dialogue at the WTO on the subject, but since having acceded to membership the voice of the Mainland government on the possible internationalisation of competition law may well be heard more clearly in future.

2.7 Development economics and competition law adoption

A number of important issues need to be considered which, whilst separate, are inextricably interconnected. First, a doctrinal issue occurs as to whether developing countries and transitional states should, as a matter of principle, adopt and enforce a competition law regime. Secondly, if a competition system is to be adopted, what are the necessary conditions for successful adoption? Thirdly, once a decision to adopt has been made, what type of legal framework is appropriate and fourthly what institutional structures should be established to administer and enforce competition rules? Once these matters have been discussed, the actual experience of states that have adopted will be considered.

2.7.1 Theoretical disputes

Commentators are divided about the wisdom of developing and transitional states adopting a pro-competition system. Some suggest that the first step in economic liberalisation of an economy, reducing external barriers to import penetration to allow foreign goods access to domestic markets and so providing competition,[44] is sufficient of itself and that a competition law is largely irrelevant. Others suggest that this policy does not produce the extent of change that might be anticipated.[45] This might be due to collusion between domestic producers and the home government, which a domestic competition law will not solve as it will either not be enforced at all or only cosmetically. Further, due to weak government processes and capacity, identification of 'public interest' as a synonym for 'producer interest' is assured, so that competition law will be

---

[44] Robert D. Cooter, 'The theory of market modernization of law: economic development through decentralised law', in *Economic dimensions in international law: comparative and empirical perspectives*, ed. J. S. Bhandari and A. O. Sykes. London: Sage (1998), p. 275.

[45] Moses Naim, 'The launching of radical policy changes, the Venezuelan experience: 1989–1991, in *Venezuela: democracy and political and economic change*, ed. J. S. Tulchin (1992), p. 56.

ineffective and may even lead to public disillusionment with markets.[46] Others consider that this analysis is too pessimistic and that cartelisation and non-tariff barriers are complementary and the establishment of a competition authority can promote competition advocacy and counter producer bias by government.[47] The advocacy of a competition authority, both within government and to the public at large, may be a counterweight to recalcitrant anti-market forces that benefit from the *status quo* and so may be another argument in favour of adoption. The entrenchment of the economic gains from a programme of privatisation may, it is argued,[48] require the operation of a functioning competition law, though presumably the format, timing and regulatory structure of the industry needs also to be considered in the calculus of the necessity of a competition law at any given stage in the liberalisation process. Another viewpoint is that time and effort is better spent facilitating domestic trade by the removal of legislative and administrative barriers within the national borders[49] and promoting greater investment in transport facilities to enable easier internal trade.[50]

The view is also propounded that developing countries need a competition regime, not principally to enforce destructive domestic competition but rather as a weapon against foreign domination of the local market by TNCs, through their organic growth or via merger activity.[51] Competition law might also counter the pernicious activities of internationally organised cartels which disproportionately injure developing countries.[52] In many cases, a development-orientated policy has been suggested to be more beneficial to the national economy than the premature adoption of a system based on efficiency, one that would promote productivity through greater levels of investment funded by high and sustainable profits. In this

---

[46] A. E. Rodriguez and M. D. Williams, *The effectiveness of proposed anti-trust programmes for developing countries*, 19 North Carolina Journal International Law and Commercial Regulation 209 (1994).

[47] C. Conrath and B. Freeman, *A response to The effectiveness of proposed anti-trust programmes for developing countries*, 19 North Carolina Journal International Law and Commercial Regulation 233 (1994).

[48] Jean-Jacques Laffont, 'Competition information and development', in Annual World Bank Conference on Development Economics (1998), p. 253.

[49] Annette W. Brown, B. Ickes and B. Ryterman, 'The myth of monopoly: a view of industrial structure in Russia', pp. 38–9, World Bank, Policy Research Paper No. 1331 (1993).

[50] Laffont, *Competition information and development*, p. 245.

[51] A. Singh and R. Dhumale, 'Competition policy, development and developing countries', Working Paper No. 7, November 1999, South Centre, Geneva, http://www.southcentre.org/publications/competition/toc.htm.

[52] *Seamless Steel Tubes Cartel*, Case T-78/00 *Sumitomo v Commission*.

context, the examples of Japan and South Korea are used to support the notion of priority being given in developing countries to industrial, as opposed to, competition policy.

In contradistinction, other more orthodox views suggest that an active competition policy can, in fact, strengthen markets and so enhance the attractiveness of a country to foreign investors; such a policy, it is argued, promotes the strengthening, not the enfeeblement, of domestic producers, so that in the long run they will become fit enough to compete with foreign market players, as well as ensuring faster and more healthy economic growth.[53]

Another argument in favour of adoption is that private restraints of trade in the domestic markets of transitional economies also require the discipline of a competition regime. Kovacic suggests four scenarios to justify adoption, all of which deal with horizontal restraints.[54] First, a prohibition on cartels would send a clear signal, especially to service providers which were previously encouraged to fix prices or output levels by the state through trade associations, that such conduct was now unacceptable. Second, a properly enforced competition law would prevent collaboration or co-operation between firms which was required by the preceding central planning system. Thirdly, anti-cartel measures would protect the public procurement process from exploitation, especially as the public sector often makes up a substantial portion of many transitional economies. Lastly, anti-cartel measures would also allow the protection of the transitional economy from paying artificially high prices as a result of international cartels in basic commodities that often impinge disproportionately on developing and transitional economies. All of these arguments are sound but they do presuppose a level of capacity to enforce measures appropriately, which many transitional economies do not possess. However, by emphasising the concentration of effort on horizontal restraints, which are often thought to be the most pernicious anti-trust offence, the benefit to be obtained is enhanced to the adopting state.

The methods of economic reform and the sequencing of the process is also hotly disputed. At one end of the spectrum the minimalists would argue that merely opening borders to external trade, facilitating internal economic exchange through a secure property rights system with good

---

[53] Sam Laird, *Transition economics, business and the WTO*, 22 (1) Journal of World Competition Law 171, 184–5 (1999).

[54] William Kovacic, *Institutional foundations for economic legal reform in transition economies: the case of competition policy and anti-trust enforcement*, 77 Chi-Kent L. Rev 265 (2001), 293–7.

adjudication and 'clean' government is sufficient to ensure the success of markets that will spontaneously develop and force the sell-off of inefficient state enterprises who will have to compete with foreign entrants and domestic competitors, so bringing the benefits of the market to consumers. The maximalists, on the other hand suggest that nothing less than a comprehensive competition law, rigorously enforced, will ensure the success of an economic liberalisation programme. Kovacic suggests a middle course of fitting the comprehensiveness of competition law coverage and the manner and form of its implementation to local economic circumstances and local capacity to implement the appropriate policy choice.[55] This approach accepts the desirability of a competition law system, in most jurisdictions, but tailors the regime to the specific circumstances extant in the country concerned. Concerns of this nature are clearly at issue when consideration is given later to the Chinese environment for adoption of a competition law.

The cultural and the politico-legal context within which a competition regime operates should also not be forgotten. Many developing countries have chronic institutional and systemic problems that create enormous uncertainty, which is inimical to a good investment environment. One view suggests that domestic producers crave a tolerable measure of certainty in order to make future investment decisions. This can only be achieved by horizontal or vertical collusion to provide a reasonably certain framework within which to operate, given that the macro-environment is hostile. Such conduct should not, therefore, be condemned out-of-hand. This view suggests that competition law may worsen the situation by allowing greater official intrusion into business decision-making with potentially baleful effects.[56] The power of control and direction that a competition law may give to incompetent or corrupt officials over a fledgling private sector to seek corrupt payments in return for favourable competition law treatment or to direct economic activity in a direction that suits political imperatives, not economic logic, is a considerable one in states with frail governmental institutions. These matters are of particular relevance to Mainland China, as will be explained later.

Additionally, in states that are liberalising the whole economy, an issue of real concern is the priority to attach to competition policy and the sequencing of adoption, when there are so many other imperatives that

[55] Ibid. pp. 299–301.
[56] Ignacio De Leon, *An alternative approach to policies for the promotion of competition in developing countries*, 6 SWJLTA 85 (1999).

will also require attention, such as the drafting of substantive laws to create property rights, or statutes to establish banking, insurance and capital market regimes. The skilled professionals who drive the whole reform process are a scarce commodity and so it is argued that competition law should only be attempted when a functioning market economy has been established and market-related problems have become apparent; rushed adoption in inauspicious circumstances not only misallocates resources but may also divert attention from more important and pressing needs.[57]

The issue of whether and when China should adopt a competition regime is of considerable significance not only to the progress of the domestic reform process but also to the fate of the huge quantities of foreign direct investment that has been poured into China by foreign businesses that seek to participate in the domestic market. A botched attempt at adoption or partial, incompetent or discriminatory enforcement could have damaging consequences for the development of the private domestic sector, if government uses the new 'competition' powers to shelter incumbent and inefficient state firms on the basis that they are adversely affected by 'unfair' competition. Increased foreign participation in the domestic market, so recently conceded by China as part of the WTO accession agreement, might be weakened or subverted by the use of a competition statute to prevent the acquisition of 'monopoly' positions by foreigners through mergers or organic growth in the domestic market. The possible outcome of adoption in China is assessed later with these concerns in mind utilising the available evidence as to government involvement in the socialist market.

In Hong Kong, many of these arguments are irrelevant as the HKSAR has a mature economy, with abundant financial and human resources sufficient to operate a competition system, should the government make the political choice to proceed with legislation. The reason why the government has chosen to adopt a 'sector-specific' approach, with full competition regimes only in the telecommunications and broadcasting industries, will be considered later.

Taiwan has already adopted a comprehensive competition regime in 1992 and so the later discussion will concentrate on a retrospective consideration of the adoption process and the effectiveness of the systems implementation to date.

---

[57] Paul E. Godek, *A Chicago-School approach to anti-trust for developing nations*, 43 Anti-Trust Bulletin 261 (1998); *One U.S. export Eastern Europe does not need*, 15 Regulation 20 (1992).

A conclusion as to the wisdom or folly of adoption of any kind of competition regime or when adoption should take place cannot be ascertained with certainty. Real economies in real countries exhibit too many variables of economic structures and political/social institutions to allow for a scientific comparison of adopter and non-adopter states; empirical evidence is hard to come by and may not be of use in making an objective assessment of the merits of adoption. However, whatever the theoretic arguments, the reality is that, for better or worse, large numbers of developing and transitional states have adopted, or are soon to adopt, new competition law systems. In the next section the experience of adoption by various countries will be assessed as this will be a useful context within which to consider the position of China, Hong Kong and Taiwan.

2.8 The experience of transitional and developing economies that have adopted competition regimes

In this section, the experiences of several world regions that have recently adopted competition regulation will be examined. Both Eastern Europe and the countries of the former Soviet Union and much of Latin America have embraced more open international trading regimes as well as implementing active competition policies since the early 1990s. There is a significant literature on both regions and it will not be possible to analyse the experience of each country individually in detail. Thus, the particular economic, structural and institutional characteristics of each region will be identified and common lessons and problems will be identified. The case of Egypt and Thailand will also be mentioned. Clearly, there are many differences between the examined regions and China and Hong Kong but it is likely that some, if not many, of the issues that perplex the competition authorities of these countries will also be of interest should China eventually adopt a competition regime, as the problems encountered in these regions have certain common features with the Chinese situation, though they are different to those which concern Hong Kong.

2.8.1 The case of Latin America

First, let us examine the experience of the Latin American countries. In 1992, Mexico[58] enacted a comprehensive competition law.[59] Mexico is of

---

[58] For a full account of the Mexican situation to 1995 see Sergio Garcia-Rodriguez, *Mexico's new institutional framework for anti-trust enforcement*, 44 De Paul Law Review 1149 (1995).
[59] Ley Federal de Competencia Economica (LFCE), 24 December, 1995.

particular interest as a potential analogue for China in respect of competition law adoption. This is because both countries have a long history of single party authoritarian government – in Mexico, the Partido Revolucionario Institucional (PRI) since the 1920s and in China, the Communist Party of China (CCP) since 1949. Further, both countries strictly concentrated economic power in the hands of the government and both closed their economies to foreign participation as a result of preceding bloody civil warfare and foreign economic domination. They both pursued statist economic policies based on import substitution and an absence of competition in most sectors of the economy. In both countries these policies turned formerly almost entirely agrarian countries into industrial powers of some consequence, but both paid the same economic price in terms of wildly inefficient domestic production which could not compete in world markets. Subsidies from the state treasuries to inefficient producers meant that other essential public spending was displaced and thus scarce resources were wasted.

In the 1970s, Mexico strengthened protectionism by further restricting foreign investment and barring it altogether from industries deemed 'strategic'. Foreign technology transferred to Mexican firms was restricted so that the foreign originator could not control its use and the registration of foreign intellectual property was made difficult to accomplish. Essentially Mexico's policy was one of minimal foreign participation in its economy.

However, in 1982 the price of oil collapsed and brought about a financial crisis as a result of earlier massive foreign borrowing based on oil receipts. The collapse precipitated a deep recession, inflation and capital flight. The government was forced to change course and over the decade to 1992 a mass privatisation campaign was undertaken with over 900 state businesses being privatised, foreign trade liberalised, and the former restrictive regulatory regime repealed. Foreign participation in the economy was allowed, respect for intellectual property rights enhanced and ultimately Mexico agreed to join the North American Free Trade Agreement (NAFTA). This was as much a political decision as an economic one in that the PRI hoped to ensure its hold on political power by creating the conditions for increased prosperity and to prevent a slide back to protectionist policies by a subsequent leader. Again, parallels with China are interesting to note. China opened its door to foreign participation as a result of thirty years of economic mismanagement and many believe that the leadership's obsession with joining the WTO is a political as much as an economic decision, to link

China irrevocably to the world economy and prevent a lurch back to isolationism.

Mexico thus needed to ensure that its economy became more competitive and a new competition law regime was seen as a vital complement to NAFTA. In fact Mexico had long had an anti-monopoly law but it had simply not been enforced due to the lack of a dedicated enforcement body and the political/economic aims of state policy. The lack of enforcement taught domestic industries that the most important goal for them was to manipulate the massive web of state regulations that shut out competitors, rather than improving products, responding to the market and cutting costs of production. The financial sector was seen by Garcia-Rodriguez as a paradigm example of the lethargy and inefficiencies of the system, which often spawned corrupt practices to maintain economic rents; this real example provides some evidence of the theoretical positions outlined above.

Concentrations of economic power were also very marked – a single firm had 60 per cent of the national cement market, five firms controlled 70 per cent of the construction industry, the telecom provider had a 90 per cent market share. All of these firms had been under state control but by the early 1990s they had been privatised. Clearly, active competition enforcement would be needed to ensure that the market was not foreclosed by abuse of dominant positions.

Given this state of affairs the Mexican government enacted the Federal Law of Economic Competition in December 1992. For the first time the law was to be given a clear objective of: 'protecting the process of competition and free market access through the prevention and elimination of monopolies, monopolistic practices and other restrictions that deter the operation of the market for goods and services'.[60]

The law contains all the usual prohibitions against abuse of dominant position, and restrictive agreements; qualifying mergers are also subject to control. Space does not allow for a detailed treatment of the provisions. A new competition enforcement commission with wide powers was established with the specific remit of enforcing the new law through primarily administrative investigations and sanctions.

In respect of enforcement Garcia-Rodriguez identifies five main problem areas.[61] Firstly, the novelty of the law creates a problem for business and lawyers to understand the concepts and provisions of the new law. Secondly, when the Competition Commission declines to act in a particular case affected firms or consumers may not bring

[60] Art. 2 LFCE. [61] Garcia-Rodriguez, *Mexico's new institutional framework.*

private actions for damages. Thirdly, as a civilian country the Commission cannot use decided cases as precedents, so increasing the burden upon it to prove each new case individually. Fourthly, the political connections of dominant market players ensure that some sectors are still able to seek shelter from investigations into their market conduct. The example of the broadcasting monopolist *Telvisia* that controlled 90 per cent of the broadcast market and was a major generator of revenue to the government was cited. Despite repeated concerns about anti-competitive behaviour, no investigation into its activities had been launched by 1995. Fifthly, there was a lack of co-ordination between the Competition Commission and the regulators of controlled industries, which continued to erect barriers to entry and to protect incumbent monopolists.

A most interesting issue in Mexico's case is also the regional convergence and mutual enforcement issues brought into focus as a result of NAFTA. Co-ordination between the US, Canadian and Mexican authorities will undoubtedly become increasingly important, especially in relation to the application of extraterritorial enforcement based on the effects doctrine. Thus, it can be observed that many of the theoretical matters discussed above have indeed been encountered in the case of Mexico.

Turning now to other Latin American states, De Leon's analysis accords primarily with that of Garcia-Rodriguez.[62] However, he emphasises the institutional and cultural aversion to competition amongst many of the business elite in the region, where a small politico-economic class dominates economic decision-making. He claims that entrenched cultural values and sociological factors create major obstacles to achieving more competitive markets. He cautions that a thorough understanding of the historical factors that shaped the development of institutions and the society in which they operate is essential to ensuring the success of the market-liberalisation policies that have been pursued for the last twenty years. He contrasts the Spanish and Portuguese colonisation processes with economic and social developments in Europe and North America. The new colonies were Crown possessions and the assets in terms of land and other resources belonged exclusively to the Monarch. Robust private business never developed as licences and permissions were granted by the Crown or its imperial delegates, giving monopoly privileges to the selected

---

[62] Ignacio De Leon, *The role of competition policy in the promotion of competitiveness and development in Latin America,* 23 (4) Journal of World Competition Law 115 (2000).

few and discouraging private capitalist enterprise. Little changed in the nineteenth and twentieth centuries as republican governments obtained independence from the colonial power, the state merely being a substitute for the Crown.

The result of this statist approach was clearly observable up to the economic restructuring that began in the 1980s and still has a powerful underlying influence on the region's economies. The *rentier* culture was buttressed by myriad governmental schemes of control and regulation, which also promoted private restrictive practices. The whole paradigm of economic management was one of top-down *dirigiste* command and control; enterprise, risk taking and entrepreneurship were not worthy of economic or social value. Concentrations of industries in the region were very high, reflecting the nature of economic management. De Leon argues that this concentration of industrial power led to a significant misconception after the regional economies were liberalised, namely that these concentrations were the result of private collusion. He believes that in reality these phenomena were actually the result of the inherited historical structures and the pervasive and dominant anti-competition cultures that prevailed in these countries. The wholesale adoption of competition regimes based on the US or EU model would not be sufficient to overcome these deep-seated structural impediments to competitive markets. He makes the point that the origin and economic and social background of both the US and the EU were very different to the Latin region and thus, he believes, imported competition law regimes are fundamentally unsuited to regional conditions. Policy instruments, other than those actually adopted, might have been more appropriate to existing conditions. However, he agrees that the political imperative of signalling a dramatic shift of paradigm away from the state development model and towards reliance on markets is of great significance.

He considers that the greatest enforcement challenge is to shift the cultural perceptions and practices of the business community and of the government officials that still wield economic regulatory powers away from the knee-jerk statist response and towards an acceptance of competition as the normative position. Thus he believes that the competition advocacy role of the enforcement authority is a vital element in the successful application of the new competition regimes.

He considers three conditions to be essential for the successful implementation of competition regimes in the region – suitable definition of the policy agenda, the establishment of a usable institutional infrastructure and a vigorous campaign to win the hearts and minds of the public and other specifically interested groups. Clearly, the achievement of these tasks is not easy. As regards policy objectives he suggests a broader interpretation of competition policy aims to encompass not just efficiency but also a fuller appreciation of the vital impact of regulated industries, given the structural history of the region and, in his view, the lesser importance of private restraints. He suggests:

- stricter alignment of regulatory rules with pro-competition goals;
- flexibility in the face of market change, and a speedy and transparent dispute-settlement mechanism;
- reduction of the opportunity for bureaucratic interference;
- enhancement of public consultation and participation prior to finalisation of new regulatory rules;
- special sectoral regulation should be strictly justified and always aligned with the competition law unless there is an overwhelming reason not to do so;
- in networked industries emphasis should be given to access to the essential facilities of the incumbent;
- attempts should be made by government to establish voluntary industry standards and codes of conduct.

As regards institutional issues, he considers the prevention of institutional capture by interest groups as being of prime importance. To this end he suggests:

- an independent enforcement agency insulated from overt or covert political manipulation with a collegiate decision-making process, rather than granting decisional powers to a single person;
- the body should be accountable to the public via a parliamentary scrutiny committee and the publication of annual reports;
- separation of the investigation, prosecution and adjudication functions;
- transparency of procedures and rules; and
- suitable funding for staff and administrative costs.

He suggests a vigorous competition advocacy role for the enforcement body: the nurturing of pro-competition consumer groups and business organisations so as to foster a competition culture will allow the enforcer greater leverage to influence government rule making and to garner public opinion when difficult decisions against powerful incumbents have to be taken.

Thus, he concluded that because the underlying socio-cultural background, in the form of an overwhelming preponderance of state power, is very different from the US or the EU, competition policy must be adapted to suit the society in which it operates. The decade-old reforms are now under stress from three groups – the elite that has lost some of its economic power, middle-class managers in formerly state firms who face more uncertainty and greater demands to be productive and workers who also face similar pressures to be more productive for no extra remuneration. His final view is that whilst opposition to a more competitive economic culture is growing there is a real chance that the change to a more market-oriented economic policy will survive, but he warns against simple transplantation of developed world competition models to developing countries, as they will surely founder in such an uncongenial environment.

There are some similarities in respect of the power structures described in Latin America and those of China but there are also considerable differences, especially in relation to industrial concentrations. China's modern economic development was based on Maoist precepts of a decentralised cellular economic structure for several diverse reasons – economic (self-sufficiency), political (fear of invasion) and practical (difficult terrain and very weak transport infrastructure). These issues and the competition implications will be considered later.

It is both interesting and constructive to compare the similarities and differences of the Latin American experience of adoption with that of Eastern Europe and the former Soviet Union countries. Clearly, the organisation of economic structures was much more ideologically driven in these nations before 1989 than was the case of Latin America. It would be trite to observe that Marxist-Leninism considered competition to be the antithesis of rational, scientific and productive state planning and that public ownership of the means of production, distribution and exchange was the only correct way in which to organise economic activity. The cause of economic reorganisation in the former communist countries was a much more overt rejection of socialist politics than the reason for reform in Latin America, which was primarily driven by a foreign-educated elite who wished to improve economic performance, rather than achieve the overthrow of a complete system of government.

2.8.2 The case of Russia and the former Soviet satellites

Economic change in Eastern Europe and the Soviet Republics was sudden and extensive, often involving the imperfect privatisation of swathes of the economy, sometimes by highly dubious means that often had the effect, especially in Russia, of creating vast new private monopolies controlled by a clique of oligarchs. The concurrent failure to provide adequate and effective definition of property rights, a transparent and functioning stock market and the lack of an effective competition regime, have resulted in a very spotty record of creating contestable, never mind competitive, markets. The incestuous links between the oligarchs and politicians has assisted them in maintaining their control of large sectors of the domestic economies, allowing monopoly rents to be obtained and has done little to improve economic performance. The picture throughout the whole former Eastern Bloc region is very mixed, however, with the front-running EU candidate states being beacons of relative success, whilst the further east one looks the more dispiriting the picture becomes.

There is an extensive literature on Russia, its former satellites and countries in transition but only a selected sample of views is examined here. Russia adopted a law 'On Competition and the Limitation of Monopolistic Activities on the Goods Market' with OECD technical assistance in 1991. The law has been amended several times, most recently in 2002, and a complete overhaul of the competition regulation system is currently under way to rationalise administration and enforcement, and clarify coverage, especially merger thresholds and agreements that restrict competition. Improvements to the legal powers of investigation and enforcement are also envisaged.[63] The enforcement agency is not independent of government but is rather the Federal Ministry for Anti-Monopoly Policy and Support of Entrepreneurship (MAP).

Russia, in many respects, appears to have a number of similar problems to Mainland China in promoting a market-orientated economy. They include a culture of extensive government control of economic decision-making, numerous state-owned monopolies protected by sponsoring ministries, complex and overlapping bureaucracies responsible for economic matters, abuses of government power by state officials to protect local interests or favoured sectors from competition (often accompanied by widespread bribery), weak and ineffective enforcement of pro-competition rules resulting from a lack of appropriately qualified officials and a fragile legal system with a questionable grasp of the rule of law. The issue of abuse of administrative powers by local governments to protect locally affiliated producers and so partition the national

---

[63] Speech by Ilya Yuzhanov, Russian Minister of Anti-Monopoly Policy and Support of Entrepreneurship at the OECD Global Competition Forum, 12 and 13 February 2004.

market is very similar to the phenomenon called Administrative Monopoly (AM) in China; this matter will be considered in detail later. The problems listed here are unsurprising given Russia's Soviet legacy, where the Central Plan, not the markets, determined economic activity for over seventy years. Severely concentrated markets were a notable legacy of the Soviet system, though the government reports that some market concentrations are reducing.[64] However, the Russian government still directly controls prices in many markets, especially in transport and energy and the actual effectiveness of MAP in many areas of economic activity is suspect. The Russian government has officially acknowledged a number of weaknesses in the current system,[65] which include limited anti-cartel enforcement particularly in the oil and gas industries[66] and inadequate investigatory and penalty powers. Western opinion is sharply divided over the success or otherwise of the economic changes in Russia over the last fifteen years, with some seeing the whole enterprise as being fundamentally flawed whilst others take a much more optimistic view.[67]

Recently, the OECD published a voluntary peer review of the Russian competition system.[68] The conclusions of the review were that whilst there had been a complete transformation of many economic and legal structures and the creation of a competition-based market economy was stated to be a central goal of the state as stated in legal instruments including the Constitution, the articulation of this goal in practice was relatively weak. This was because of shifting policy priorities, crash privatisation programmes and economic crises during the last fifteen years. However, whilst a basic set of pro-competition legislation did now exist it

---

[64] See Contribution from the Russian Federation, OECD Global Forum on Competition, 30 January 2002. CCNM/GF/COMP/WD (2002) 2.

[65] See Challenges/Obstacles faced by Competition Authorities in Achieving Greater Economic Development Through the Promotion of Competition, Contribution by Russian Federation, OECD Global Competition Forum 2004, CCNM/GF/COMP/WD (2004) 2.

[66] Ben Slay and Vladimir Capelik, 'Natural monopoly regulation and competition policy in Russia', *The Anti-Trust Bulletin* (Spring 1998), pp. 229–60.

[67] Those with a relatively pessimistic attitude towards Russia's reforms include Richard Pipes, 'Flight from freedom: what Russians think and want', *Foreign Affairs*, May/June 2004; D. Triesman, 'Russia renewed?' *Foreign Affairs* (November/December 2002); Jerry Hough, *The logic of economic reform in Russia*, Washington, D.C.: Brookings Institution Press (2001); Bernard Black, Reiner Kraakman and Anna Tarassova, *Russian privatisation and corporate governance: what went wrong?*, 52 Stan. L. Rev. 1731 (2000); whilst others are not so pessimistic: A. Shleifer and D. Triesman, 'A normal country', *Foreign Affairs*, March/April 2004.

[68] Competition law and policy in Russia – An OECD peer review (2004). http://www.oecd.org/dataoecd/10/60/32005515.pdf.

required extensive overhaul as did the structure and focus of the competition authority. Specific recommendations included a substantial narrowing of the authority's responsibilities so as to allow for concentration on competition-enhancement measures. The substantive competition rules needed to be redrawn with greater clarity to assist in the creation of a more certain legal environment. The onerous and unnecessary notification of restrictive agreements and merger agreements of no competition importance should be abandoned. A new, credible penalty regime was needed as were new and effective powers of investigation. Human capital quality needed improvement so as to enhance economic analysis. Transparency in decision-making with clear explanation of decisions with reasons was an urgent requirement as was the need to explain and publicise decisions via the media to businesses and the public. Shortly after the completion of the Report, the newly re-elected President Putin restructured the Russian government with the abolition of MAP and the creation of a new Federal Anti-Monopoly Authority. This new body will apparently be more competition focused, having shed several of its regulatory and consumer affairs responsibilities. However, the detail and implementation of these changes will have to await new legislation and so any improvement on the previous state of affairs will have to be tested by experience.

Turning to individual former Soviet satellite jurisdictions, all the EU candidate states of east-central Europe have been obliged to model their newly minted competition laws on that of the EU as a result of the requirement of the *aquis comunataire*.[69] At least formally, they all have in place recognisable competition regimes with the usual enforcement structures but the effectiveness of the new laws varies substantially, due to some or all of the factors mentioned above. In the case of Bulgaria, Hoekman and Djankov conclude that enforcement has not been particularly effective with the vast majority of actions taken relating to 'unfair competition' issues rather than market failure problems.[70] The true province of competition enforcement – anti-cartel activities, abuse by dominant market players – was not really addressed for a variety of reasons. In fact, the law also had some provisions that worsened the competitive situation by

---

[69] It is a fundamental requirement of membership of the European Union that all member states' domestic laws must comply with the existing corpus of EC legislation. Once a new member joins, all future EC legislation domestically will apply as stipulated by the Treaty of Rome. See Josephine Steiner and Lorna Woods, *Textbook on EC Law*, 8th edn, Oxford University Press (2003).

[70] See Bernard Hoekman and Simeon Djankov, 'Competition law in post-central-planning Bulgaria', *The Anti-Trust Bulletin* (Spring 2000), p. 227.

preventing managers from leaving their posts to take employment with rivals for fear of divulging trade secrets or confidential customer-related information. Those hard-core anti-monopoly cases that were brought before the Bulgarian courts for prosecution were either dismissed or inadequate remedies were awarded, which did not rectify the structural problems identified.

In Poland, the Czech Republic, Slovakia, Hungary,[71] the Baltic States and Slovenia implementation appears to have been much more effective and national laws have been recently revised, due to their accession to the EU on 1 May 2004. The performance of these states appears to be an excellent advertisement for the successful adoption of competition regimes in transitional economies but it should be noted that all these countries underwent political as well as economic transformation over the last fifteen years. The relationship between their relatively successful adoption of competition law and the stability of their democratic political institutions should be stressed; politically inspired or corruptly organised capture of state institutions appears not to have occurred to any great extent. This presumably is a result of their relatively stable political institutional arrangements and a national commitment to market-orientated economic solutions. Further, this conclusion is fortified by the fact that the new members have had to satisfy the Copenhagen Criteria,[72] adopted at the EU Summit in 1993. Accession countries are required to have:

- stable institutions guaranteeing democracy, the rule of law, human rights and respect for and protection of minorities;
- an existing functioning market economy and the capacity to withstand competitive pressure and market forces within the Union; and
- the ability to take on the obligations of membership, including adherence to the aims of political, economic and monetary union.

It is tentatively suggested that for the successful adoption of a competition regime, the enumerated political factors are the real determinant of success. If this is so, can China hope to emulate these countries or will the potential adoption fail? These issues will be fully considered in the relevant chapters devoted to the PRC. In Hong Kong, different considerations

---

[71] For assessment of the early stage of competition law implementation see Carolyn Brzezinski, *Competition and anti-trust law in Central Europe: Poland, the Czech Republic, Slovakia and Hungary*, 15 Michigan Journal of International Law, 1129 (1994).

[72] European enlargement – an historic opportunity, EU Commission. http://europa.eu.int/comm/enlargement/intro/criteria.htm.

apply as will be seen later, but the decisive influence of political arrangements on the successful competition law adoption is also a compelling
explanation of the existing situation in the HKSAR.

2.8.3 Egypt and Thailand

Other developing countries have had a difficult time enacting and enforcing competition law as part of economic reform packages. Egypt embarked
on an economic reform programme in 1991, which included privatisation and structural adjustments to various economic sectors. Egypt did
not have a comprehensive competition law but as part of the package
of reform measures one was anticipated from the early 1990s. However,
there were repeated delays in promulgation and none had been enacted by
2000. The reasons for the delay were attributed to several causes including fear of the reimposition of heavy-handed government regulation of
commerce, excessive use of unfair trading allegations by rivals, lack of coverage of extra-legal businesses so unfairly burdening legitimate business,
lack of skilful public officials to implement the law and fear that corrupt
practices would lead to differential and partial enforcement. The principal opponents of a competition law were a small circle of well-connected
business leaders, who had extensive influence over policy makers, and
whether the fears concerning implementation mentioned above were justified or not these siren voices were successful in impeding enactment.
Further, the delays can also be attributed to other considerations namely
the incapacity of officials to comprehend and accept the new economic
paradigm, lack of international pressure to complete the reform process,
the relatively low priority of the legislation, and the lack of co-ordination
between ministries and the weak administrative and technical capacity of
relevant civil servants.[73]

In the case of Thailand, a new competition law was introduced as part
of the economic reform process set in train by the Asian Economic Crisis
of 1997–8, which originated as a run on the Thai currency in July 1997.
This exposed serious structural flaws in the Thai banking sector and in the
legal system. The new Competition Act 1999 adopted a legal framework
largely based on EC law with an additional catch-all 'unfair competition'

---

[73] Bahaa H. Dessouki, 'Privatisation in emerging economies: some aspects of the creation
of a new legal infrastructure – a case study of Egypt', PhD thesis, Senate House Library,
University of London (2000), chapter 5.

provision purportedly borrowed from the Taiwan Fair Trade Act 1992.[74] A competition commission was established to enforce the law. Five years after the law's adoption it is generally considered to have failed substantially. This is due to several reasons including the design of the enforcement body, which is headed by the Minister of Commerce, and so has no structural, legal or financial independence from government. The commission consists of sixteen members, none of which are full time or necessarily expert in competition law and practice. The commission is dominated by representatives of big business. The government, since 2001, has been in the hands of a pro-business party, Thai Rak Thai, headed by the country's richest man, whose family control the quasi-monopoly mobile telephone business, Shin Corp. The law has been rendered completely ineffective, as the operative provisions on abuse of a dominant position and merger control have been inoperable due to the Cabinet's refusal to pass the necessary implementing secondary legislation. Only four investigations have been undertaken, two of which aborted due to the lack of implementing secondary legislation. The other two cases involved allegations of 'unfair trading' by foreign-owned operators in the Thai retail and motorcycle supply markets. The retail case was dropped due to political pressure from foreign chambers of trade and the motorcycle case has been handed to the public prosecutor for the institution of criminal proceedings as the law only contains criminal sanctions. Both the latter cases were riddled with procedural failures and not a single investigation has been launched since 2001 in respect of any domestic business sector. Domestic business interests have been hostile to the implementation of the law for a variety of reasons including a genuine concern about the government's ability to administer the law fairly and more self-serving concerns about the intrusion of foreign businesses into the previously well-protected Thai domestic market and the need to create national champions capable of taking on TNCs. In 2003, the WTO Secretariat concluded in its Trade Policy Review that enforcement had been 'weak'.[75]

The dismal enforcement history of the Competition Act 1999 stems from several factors:

- structural flaws in the design of the law;
- the nature and composition of the enforcement body;

---

[74] See Sakda Thanitcul, 'Competition law in Thailand: a preliminary analysis', *Washington University Global Studies Review*, vol. 1, no. 1 and 2 (Winter/Summer 2002), pp. 171–84.

[75] http://www.wto.org/english/tratop_e/tpr_e/tp_rep_e.htm#thailand2003.

- the lack of capacity and resources of the officials entrusted with enforcement;
- the inherent conflicts of interest of ministers who on the one hand benefit from monopolies and cartels via their private business interests, whilst on the other have a duty to protect the public interest in competitive markets; and
- a lack of credible competition advocacy by the government or the commission who have not philosophically or politically accepted the case in favour of markets.[76]

The influence of powerful business interests to delay competition legislation enactment in Egypt and the neutering of the new competition system in Thailand by entrenched vested interests provide interesting lessons for the adoption process in both China and Hong Kong, though the nature of these influences is different. In Hong Kong, the political influence of business has allowed the creation of an effective road block to enactment; in China state enterprises may well subvert the implementation of a new competition law, just as they have prevented enforcement of much of the existing pro-market legislation. The case of Thailand also foreshadows considerable misgivings about the capacity of the Chinese authorities to implement fairly and impartially any comprehensive competition law that may be enacted, as will also be explained below.

2.9 The importance of competition advocacy

An issue that has received increasing attention in relation to successful adoption is that of competition advocacy, particularly in developing and transitional economies. Initially, the formulators of policy change – ministers, legislators, and officials – must be convinced of the superiority of markets as a means of economic organisation, in most parts of the economy, as a first step in successful adoption. Once the policy makers are convinced of the need for markets, then other key stakeholders, who include academics, the media, business and consumers, must also be brought onside. If any of these groups is not philosophically committed to the pro-market ideology, successful implementation is doubtful. Advocacy promotes and reinforces the creation of a 'competition culture' which is often at odds with the *status quo ante* in many, if not most, developing and transitional states. Specific country examples of the need

---

[76] Williams, 'Competition law in Thailand: seeds of success or fated to fail?' *J World Comp.*, 27(3) (2004), pp. 459–94.

for an economic cultural shift have been given above and need for this change in mindset is certainly true of Mainland China, as will be considered later. Whether government or business in China has really accepted this conceptual change remains an open question.

In addition to competition policy and law advocacy and adoption, other key elements are also essential prerequisites to competition policy success, namely the definition and protection of property rights, a bankruptcy law, establishment of a working capital market, a structurally sound banking system and a robust administrative and legal system. Should any of these infrastructural supports to competition be absent or seriously impaired, the success of competition policy is also less likely.

Further, the identity of who should take on responsibility for the vital advocacy function, not only before enactment but also once a competition statute is in place, is important. The pre-enactment propaganda function must be undertaken by politicians but once the initial hurdle of enacting legislation is overcome, then the identification and empowerment of an official responsible for advocating competition policy, both within government and to the public, is essential.

Conrath and Freeman hold a positive view of the effectiveness of competition authorities in advocating the benefits of competition and their ability to actually influence and overcome other parts of the government apparatus that attempt to legislate anti-competitive regulations that favour the producer interest.[77] They give an example from Poland concerning the attempt by the Agriculture Ministry to enact 'equalising tariffs' to protect farmers; a vigorous publicity campaign by the competition authority, mobilised public opinion and the ministry was obliged substantially to cut back the protective measures originally proposed.

Similar situations can also be enumerated in Hong Kong, whereby the Consumer Council, a statutory non-civil service body is charged with investigating anti-competitive behaviour and publicising its results, though it has no enforcement powers. This advocacy role causes industry and the Hong Kong government considerable embarrassment and sometimes leads to a pro-competitive result. Its advocacy of a pro-competition stance has encouraged debate on the issue in Hong Kong and may have led to new policies being adopted, especially in the telecommunication sector. The role of the Hong Kong Consumer Council will be discussed later.

---

[77] Conrath and Freeman, *A response to 'The effectiveness of proposed anti-trust programmes for developing countries'*.

In relation to competition advocacy in China, there are various bodies that might undertake this function but a fundamental impediment is likely to be the level and depth of ideological commitment to the concept of markets and competition as the primary regulatory mechanism. Another problem is that consumer advocacy in China is undertaken by a government body, part of the government hierarchy, and as such has no legal or financial independence; straying too far from perceived official and Party orthodoxy or challenging stated government policy would be impossible.

Taiwan's Fair Trade Commission, which administers the competition regime, takes competition advocacy seriously with a specific statutory mandate to publicise the case for a pro-competition policy, ensure that wide media exposure is given to both investigations and imposed penalties, to hold formal educative symposia for businesses, trade associations and officials and to make the case for pro-competitive policies direct to other government entities.[78]

The special importance of competition advocacy in developing and transitional states has been a topic of increased prominence in many international fora in recent years. The OECD,[79] UNCTAD, [80] APEC and Association of South-East Asian Nations (ASEAN)[81] and in particular ICN[82] have all discussed and embraced the notion that advocacy is a vital role for any competition authority in newly adopting states.

2.10 The design of competition regimes and institutional infrastructure

The design of a competition regime and the institutional architecture to implement policy and to enforce the law in newly adopting states is a matter of critical importance as to whether adoption is carried out successfully.

---

[78] Hwang Tzong-Leh, Chairman of the Taiwan Fair Trade Commission, 'Building a Competition Culture', Contribution from Chinese Taipei, OECD Global Forum on Competition, 17 and 18 October 2001. CCNM/GF/COMP/WD (2001) 17.

[79] OECD Report to Fourth Meeting Global Forum on Competition, 12 February 2004. www.oecd.org/dataoecd/13/42/2789 2500.pdf.

[80] UNCTAD Secretariat Report on Review of technical assistance, advisory and training programmes on competition law and policy, 23 April 2002. http://www.unctad.org/en/docs/c2clp29.en.pdf.

[81] See East Asian Competition Forum web site at http://www2.jftc.go.jp/eacpf/01_01.html.

[82] ICN, *Report of advocacy working group* (2002) and associated documents. http://www.internationalcompetitionnetwork.org/advocacydocuments.html.

Kovacic has provided an insight into the process of designing competition policy reforms in a number of countries in transition.[83] He has also provided suggestions for the establishment of the appropriate institutions that support effective implementation. He considers that there are three main benefits that flow from the adoption of pro-competition policy regimes:

- the provision of an institutional voice within government to promote markets and oppose excessive state intervention in the economy;
- the ability to deal with market failure in the private sectors of the economy and any attempt to create private restraints on competition that were formally matters of state policy; and
- the establishment of competition advocacy and enforcement institutions that encourage acceptance of market reforms and act as light-touch 'economic policemen' to reassure the population that they are not subject to exploitation in the new economic paradigm.

Kovacic supports the analysis that the particular social, cultural, legal and political environment in which competition law is to be implemented is crucial in deciding whether pro-competition policies will be successful; in this he concurs with De Leon and Garcia-Rodriguez.

He identifies several common characteristics of transitional economies – the pervasive role of the state, a residual influence of state planning, and the effect of the previous phenomenon of the 'informal economy' (that is, the black market, that flourished as a result of state planning failures). He suggests that former blackmarketeers can form the nucleus of new entrants to the new market economy. He stresses the vital importance of institutional structures to the success of the market reform process. The lack of qualified civil servants, lawyers, accountants and economists, the culture of wide and opaque discretionary powers, the lack of effective review by qualified courts and the desperate lack of resources for even the most basic of administrative functions can cause the failure of a new competition regime. He also mentions that a multiplicity of simultaneous reform measures can confuse priorities, encourage a culture of non-enforcement of the nominal legal provisions and militate

---

[83] William Kovacic, *Designing and implementing competition and consumer protection reforms in transitional economies: perspectives from Mongolia, Nepal, Ukraine and Zimbabwe*, 44 De Paul Law Review 1197 (1995); *Getting started: creating new competition policy institutions in transitional economies*, 23 Brooklyn Journal of International Law 403 (1997); *Institutional foundations for economic legal reform in transition economies: the case of competition policy and anti-trust enforcement*, 77 Chi-Kent. L. Rev. 265 (2001).

against effective enforcement, causing enduring suspicion of capitalism by government and the public alike which may also provide a very significant hurdle, so hindering acceptance of the reform process.

Kovacic also suggests that there are additional unfavourable conditions that can inhibit the successful adoption of a competition policy. These include: the lack of a supportive academic infrastructure to undertake research and to educate lawyers and officials; weak professional associations and consumer groups to reinforce a pro-competitive policy stance; unrealistic public and governmental expectations about the speed and effect of competition policy implementation. The novelty of truly independent quasi-governmental enforcement bodies can provoke bureaucratic resistance or a fear that such an authority could be captured by business or corrupt elements and that the newly established more representative and accountable political structures might be thus undermined. Weaknesses in official statistical information and business record-keeping can also be a major problem in the necessary analysis of the definition of overall market size and the share enjoyed by any individual operator. Lack of continuing and appropriate practical support from aid organisations who can often lose enthusiasm after the initial legislative act has been achieved can cause the new system to become moribund as a result of domestic institutional frailty and the plethora of factors mentioned above.

Thus, he considers it vital that a thorough understanding of the societal context of the country in question is essential before drafting a tailored law that fits well the priority needs of the economy in question. Simplicity is his watchword, given the severe resource constraints and the multiple problems of institution building, advocacy and structural factors. He believes that the advocacy role of the new institutions is a vital component of the work of new competition bodies as is a careful and phased implementation of the newly enacted law. He also recommends regular evaluation of the effectiveness of the new law, to see whether it should be modified in the light of experience and whether enforcement has been successfully implemented.

He also suggests that transitional states face problems not encountered by developed-country anti-trust agencies.[84] These include overhangs from the state planning system such as significant government-mandated barriers to entry to imports and foreign direct investment; domestic business registration processes that inhibit or prevent the

---

[84] Kovacic, *Institutional foundations for economic legal reform in transition economies*, pp. 301–10.

establishment of new firms that would compete with existing state enterprises; complex and arbitrary taxation regimes; direct control over the prices of some commodities and restrictive employment laws. He also highlights a number of other matters that have particular significance to China – fragile political acceptance of competition; weak domestic competition policy and enforcement expertise in either economics or law; dysfunctional courts; poor government transparency; existence of pervasive corruption; shortages of resources and poor statistical data. All of these issues will be encountered when China's position is analysed.

Recently, the OECD[85] endorsed this view by emphasising the importance of effective competition policy which is an 'essential prerequisite for economic development, growth and rising levels of economic welfare'.[86] Further, the essential factors for successful adoption of competition policy were identified as being:

- Building a competition culture by ensuring that key stakeholders – politicians, public servants, the business and legal community, sectoral regulators, academics and the press, as well as the general public – are convinced of the need for and benefits of competition.
- Ensuring that institutional distortions in the form of laws, regulatory structures, licensing regimes, procurement policies, investment restrictions and product standards, do not hinder, so far as is possible, the promotion of a competitive environment.
- Mandating the head of the competition authority with the task of public advocacy of competition policies both within government and to industrial sectors and to the public generally.
- If a competition law exists, whether it has effective substantive provisions; whether the stated objectives of the law operate to promote non-competition objectives and whether other instruments might be more efficacious to achieve these non-competition goals; whether the skill level of the personnel involved in the system – officials, lawyers and judges – is appropriate; the quality of political support; the funding, competence, transparency and independence of the competition agency; and finally, active co-operation with other government bodies.

The OECD has also published a very interesting survey of the actual institutional design of the thirty-seven participating nations who attended

---

[85] Capacity building for effective competition policy in developing and transitional economies, 16 April 2003, OECD Joint Global Forum on Trade and Competition CCNM/GF/COMP/TR (2003)13.
[86] Ibid. p. 3.

the 2003 OECD Global Forum on Competition. The most striking feature of the survey results was the wide variety of models adopted worldwide, ranging from a specific ministry or division of a ministry integral to the central government structure to constitutionally independent agencies entirely divorced from government influence. There was also great variation in methods of appointment of officials, budgetary matters, mandated tasks including the prominence and nature of advocacy, competences in terms of investigation, adjudication and appeals. The OECD survey concluded that:

> Several aspects of the design of a competition authority are linked to the traditions and institutional structure of the country and could not – or only with difficulty – be set up in a different way than is customary for comparable public administrative bodies in the jurisdiction ... evidently there is no one optimal design given the objectives that have been adopted for the competition agency or the functions that have been allocated to it ... it is difficult to ascertain whether these alternative approaches are optimal without also looking at the country specific factors such as its legal and administrative traditions, stage of development, political realities etc.[87]

Assessing the effectiveness of competition institutions once they are established is another matter of qualitative evaluation. Trebilcock and Iacobucci suggest several normative factors to be taken into account when making an assessment.[88] They include independence, which they consider a complex matter inextricably entwined with accountability, at least in a representative democracy. Expertise and detachment from conflicts of interest are also needed. Transparency in investigation, adjudication and enforcement are required but a balance must be struck with the need for commercially sensitive information to be kept confidential. The need for and desirability of administrative efficiency must be weighed against procedural fairness and other due process considerations. The virtue of consistency and thus, predictability, must sometimes yield to the need for flexibility, especially as competition analysis can often turn on specific factual issues such as delimiting the relevant geographical or product market or assessing dominance. Thus, creating a calculus of the effectiveness of a competition agency is not a simple task.

---

[87] *The objectives of competition law and policy and the optimal design of a competition agency*, 5 (1) OECD Journal of Competition Law and Policy, 36–7 (2003).
[88] Michael Trebilcock and Edward Iacobucci, 'Designing competition institution', *World Competition*, 25(3) (2002), pp. 361–94.

Dabbah suggests that measurement of the success of a competition system involves both the extent to which competition advocacy is embedded in the competition system and the degree of openness a domestic system has to international developments in sister jurisdictions of a similar level of economic development and sophistication.[89] These suggestions are no doubt sound but they do presuppose most of the normative factors identified by Trebilcock and Iacobucci above.

Thus, the decision to adopt, the objectives of a competition policy, the substantive provisions of the law to enforce the policy and the institutional structures created to administer the law, all need very careful consideration bearing in mind the specific idiosyncratic factors of the jurisdiction concerned. A one-size-fits-all approach is doomed to failure and the initial decision on whether to adopt at all must be considered in light of the political and economic circumstances that pertain in the particular jurisdiction at the specific time that policy decisions are to be made. Competition law, of itself, will not create a market economy and a competition law should only be adopted if the political decision has been taken to embrace markets with competition as the principal regulator. Competition law's basic function is to allow markets to operate. Thus, with regard to China, very considerable questions remain as to whether the government is ideologically committed to markets, rather than to state management of markets. Also, the notion that competition law decisions should be made by a pro-competition independent adjudicatory body that is also blind to the nationality of market players is questionable in China. These issues will be considered later in the text. In relation to Hong Kong, a model for a comprehensive competition law already exists in the telecommunications and broadcasting sectors along with suitable institutional arrangements, as will be explained later. For Taiwan, the decision to legislate and the design of its enforcement system was taken many years ago; the issue to be considered is how effectively they operate in practice.

2.11 The balance of convenience – for or against adoption?

The preceding discussion has, to some extent, pre-empted the question of whether to adopt at all. The balance of economic argument seems to favour adoption but not everyone concurs with this analysis. The main criticisms of introducing a competition law in developing countries are:

---

[89] Maher M. Dabbah, *Measuring the success of a system of competition law: a preliminary view*, 21(8) ECLR 369–76 (2000).

- competition laws are prone to be misapplied in an arbitrary and corrupt fashion that can discourage growth and investment;[90]
- competition can be best encouraged by free trade policies allowing the import of goods, and then ensuring good infrastructure (including customs procedures as well as physical infrastructure – sea and air ports, roads and railways) to improve the flow of goods across borders and also within the state;[91]
- competition law diverts political and legislative resources away from more fundamental issues such as the development of legal protection of property rights, the introduction of a workable contract law and the establishment of an effective court system and legal profession to protect the rights newly created;[92]
- poorly constructed competition regimes that do not take into account the conditions on the ground and are sensitive to local needs and capabilities will not only fail but will lower respect for the institution of law and the market mechanism;
- international aid donors quickly lose interest and commitment to competition law issues in transitional states, fail to provide continuing support and thus, there is a significant risk of creating a worse situation than that which pertained pre-reform;
- prohibition of developing countries' participation in export cartels (oil producers: OPEC, Malaysia: the Tin Cartel, Jamaica: the Bauxite Cartel, Brazil: the Coffee Cartel) could harm their primary source of export earnings;[93]
- domestic competition laws can be used as a Trojan Horse to allow multinational companies to gain a foothold and overwhelm local producers;
- small, free and open economies have no need for a competition law as imports will discipline monopoly rent seeking (this is an especially important argument as regards Hong Kong and will be addressed later in the text);
- a number of economies lauded as 'economically free' by the Fraser Institute and the Heritage Foundation do not have domestic competition

---

[90] See V. E. Capelik, 'Should monopoly be regulated in Russia?' 6 *Communist Countries and Economic Transformation* 19 (1994), pp. 22–4.
[91] See Cooter, 'Market modernization of the law'; Brown *et al.*, The myth of monopoly.
[92] Paul Godek, 'One U.S. export Eastern Europe does not need', *Regulation*, 20 (Winter 1992), p. 21.
[93] F. M. Scherer, 'International competition policy and economic development', Discussion Paper No. 96-26, Zentrum fur Europaische Wirtschaftsforschung GMBH (1996).

laws[94] (though Singapore has recently decided to adopt, leaving Hong Kong's government somewhat exposed in its resolute refusal to legislate); and [95]

- competition law can be used inappropriately to address non-competition issues, for example, administrative monopoly in China. This is really a political control, or rule-of-law, issue, not a competition concern. However, it is a major or even a primary reason for adopting a competition law.

Thus, for developing countries or transitional economies with a relatively weak commitment to markets and which have other grave institutional and governance problems, such as China, competition law will not be the panacea to create a well-functioning market economy that delivers economic growth and prosperity. In fact, as will be suggested later, adoption in such circumstances might actually harm, not promote, market economy development.

2.12 Conclusion

It must be admitted that all the issues mentioned above, both in favour of and against adoption have to be taken into account if a pro-competitive economic reform package is to be successful. But it is submitted that the criticisms listed in paragraph 2.11 above are not really arguments to deny the efficacy of competition regimes in any given economy, merely conditions to ensure that the reform is a success and not a failure. These are not reasons for non-adoption of competition law, just for the implementation of an appropriate law for the nation concerned, with exemptions and transitional provisions to be enacted as needed but subject to the caveat of the necessary political commitment and suitable institutional structures.[96] The trend towards competition law adoption to implement

---

[94] See www.heritage.org and www.fraserinstitute.org, and also generally a discussion of the arguments for and against developing countries, adoption of competition policies in Fredrique Jenny, 'The interface between competition policy and trade, investment and economic development', WTO Symposium held in Geneva on 27 October 1997.

[95] Singapore's Ministry of Trade and Industry began consultations on a draft Competition Bill in April 2004. http://www.mti.gov.sg/public/CMN/frm_OTH_default.asp?cid=2035.

[96] In his doctoral thesis, 'Privatisation in emerging economies', Dessouki considers the issues and problems identified in this chapter and arrives at similar conclusions to those found here. He opines that infrastructural problems have held up competition law adoption in Egypt and that any attempt to create an ambitious law would probably lead to failure.

a pro-competitive economic policy certainly seems to be one that is increasingly popular as a component of economic management in many countries worldwide.[97] Whether this is as a result of a Damascene conversion to the wisdom of market economic solutions as the policy option most likely to provide the best economic outcome or merely a transient, superficial fashion amongst the community of nations remains to be seen.

As far as the governments of China and Hong Kong are concerned, economic management is as important to them as to any other government. The process of policy formation and implementation in these two jurisdictions will form a core component of the analytical chapters to follow. Further, the issues of an assessment of whether a 'free and open economy' is always a competitive one, especially for non-traded services, will be discussed later in connection with the analysis of the Hong Kong situation. The specific relevant literature on China and Hong Kong will be extensively analysed in the appropriate chapters below.

A third issue of importance which will be addressed in the next chapter is the growth of opinion supporting the introduction of mandatory multilateral provisions to set global standards for competition regime adoption by all states. The history of this movement originates in the failed draft Havana Charter of 1948,[98] when, paradoxically, the United States was the foremost proponent of international standard setting in this field; the leading proponent of multilateral competition law is now the EU, with America decidedly reticent about whether or not the issue should be part of the next round of trade liberalisation negotiations at the WTO.

This chapter has sought to examine the theoretical controversies relevant to the economics of competition and the adoption of pro-competition legal regimes that support market-orientated economic reform programmes in developing and transitional economies and to extract useful common issues that will later be used to analyse the competition situation that pertains in China and Hong Kong.

---

[97] See Whish, *Competition law*, p. 1.
[98] Havana Charter for an International Trade Organisation, UN Doc. E/Conf. 2/78 (1948).

3

The international perspective

3.1 Introduction

This chapter will seek to trace, in outline, the influence of the international organisations on promoting interest in, and adherence to, comprehensive competition policy and the adoption of competition law in countries worldwide. In addition to mere promotion, some states, via international organisations, advocate that standardised competition provisions ought to be incorporated into public international law, so that signatory states to an international treaty would be obliged to enact compatible and effective laws domestically. Some have even advocated that such an international commitment should be enforceable via the Dispute Mechanism of the WTO. Indeed, the greatest progress in this regard has been made since the 1995 establishment of the WTO. However, there is no consensus, as yet, that those formal negotiations will in fact actually take place. Indeed, the likelihood of a consensus on the start of formal discussions on the issue now seems remote following the collapse of the ministerial meeting of the WTO in Cancun in September 2003 and the subsequent decision of the principal proponent of negotiations, the EU, to de-link this subject from other trade issues to be discussed as part of the proposed new round of multilateral trade negotiations.[1]

Despite the lack of internationally agreed standards, much progress has been made worldwide in enacting competition statutes. International organisations have been very active in promoting competition policy and law, as well as providing technical assistance to facilitate adoption. On occasion the implementation of modern competition policy and law has

---

[1] See European Commission, Singapore issues: clarification of the EU position, 31 March 2004. http://trade-info.cec.eu.int/doclib/cfm/doclib_section.cfm?sec=182&lev=2&order=date

been a condition of assistance to sovereign states that have found themselves in financial crisis.[2]

The twin trends of individual country adoption and the parallel resurgence in interest in legislating binding international law norms have not gone unnoticed in China. As part of China's opening to external influences and its policy of seeking to adopt international legal practice into its domestic system, it will be suggested below that the spread of competition law and the international interest in multilateral rules has galvanised, to some extent at least, influential policy makers in China not only to observe developments but to seek to imitate the international trend towards acceptance of the notion that competition rules are a prerequisite of an efficiently functioning market economy as much as an effective property or contract law. However, the actual motivation behind China's apparent enthusiasm for competition law adoption remains unclear. The possibility exists that the decision to legislate may not have been entirely motivated by a desire to adopt purely free market solutions to economic problems and to use competition law to protect the competitive process. A latent desire to re-assert some state control over the growing private sector of the economy composed of both domestic entrepreneurs and foreign investors may also have been a motivating factor, especially as the state sector faced contraction as a result of greater competition unleashed by WTO accession; this theme will be considered later.

China has not been required to adopt competition law as a result of outside pressure, nor was this a requirement of WTO accession. China has, nevertheless, been active in engaging with international organisations in its efforts to learn about international trends in competition law and policy as well as seeking specific technical assistance in drafting a competition law from organisations such as UNCTAD and OECD. China has also sought bilateral assistance and information from a number of individual countries. Thus, it will be argued that, far from ignoring international developments in this area, China has taken an active and indeed proactive interest in competition law issues. Having joined the WTO in December 2001 evidence suggests that China would have been broadly supportive of efforts to begin negotiations towards the creation of a mandatory, enforceable, international set of rules in the competition law area within the

---

[2] For example, Indonesia was required, as a condition of the IMF rescue package signed in January 1998, to enact a competition statute. See Law no. 5/1999 Concerning the Prohibition of Monopolistic Practices and Unfair Business Practice.

over arching WTO framework,[3] though this may be of academic interest only given the current state of play at the WTO in relation to the Doha Development Round.

However, even more interesting in this regard is the attitude of Hong Kong. The HKSAR government has persistently and consistently opposed the notion that open economies need a competition law to ensure a competitive trading environment. As a founder member of the WTO, Hong Kong China has been in the vanguard of members who oppose even the discussion of the adoption of mandatory multilateral rules within the WTO framework. This visceral opposition will be examined and explained in the subsequent analytical chapters concerning Hong Kong.

Clearly, it is not unusual to see two members of the WTO take opposite positions on any given policy matter. But for two members within the same nation state to do so would be unprecedented. However, one might argue that this is merely an example of the effective operation of the 'one country, two systems' formula propounded by the former paramount leader Deng Xiaoping and thus shows that the implementation of his innovative political formula for the resumption of sovereignty after 1997, is robust; recent political developments, whereby Beijing has vetoed the early adoption of universal suffrage in Hong Kong, seem to suggest the opposite.[4]

A final, if not even more perplexing fact concerning WTO discussions on competition policy is the position of the other 'China' – officially Chinese Taipei (in official WTO parlance) or the Republic of China, Taiwan. This third Chinese entity to hold separate membership of the WTO, was only allowed to join after the PRC had completed its own accession process to the organisation.[5] This Chinese member government is the only one of the three which has a functioning competition law that is effectively implemented; a detailed analysis of the Taiwan position will be undertaken later. Taiwan will probably be in favour of WTO

---

[3] In April 2002 at the UNCTAD Regional Seminar in Hong Kong the Chinese delegate was very positive in respect of opening negotiations at the WTO on competition law inclusion within the WTO framework.

[4] Decision of the Standing Committee of the National People's Congress on issues relating to the methods of selecting the Chief Executive of HKSAR in 2007 and for forming the Legislative Council of HKSAR in 2008. 26 April 2004 http://www.info.gov.hk/cab/cab-review/eng/basic/pdf/es5200408081.pdf.

[5] As mentioned in the first chapter, Macau SAR has also been a member of the WTO since 1 January 1995, thus there are four 'Chinese' members of the WTO. MSAR's competition policy is outside the scope of this book.

negotiations on competition policy inclusion at the WTO,[6] though the prospect of those negotiations now seems to be receding.

What a singular conundrum this situation presents. The PRC may adopt a domestic law and be neutral or in favour of WTO adoption. Hong Kong refuses to introduce any comprehensive domestic legislation and is against even holding discussions within the WTO, for fear that multilateral rules might oblige the HKSAR government to legislate. Taiwan would probably support international rules on the basis of its successful adoption of competition law. This matrix of opinion will be fully considered later.

3.2 The role of international organisations

The gathering pace of globalisation over the last fifteen years has caused a fundamental reorientation in transitional and many developing economies. One of the responses to these economic changes has been the increasing acceptance of the need for domestic competition law regimes worldwide. This policy choice did not occur in a vacuum. Many multilateral and international bodies have taken a keen interest in the issue of internationalising competition law rules. One option is to promote domestic adoption in developing and transitional states. The World Bank, the International Monetary Fund (IMF) and the OECD have been the main catalysts in promoting, encouraging or even in some cases requiring, adoption. UNCTAD has limited its role to information sharing and providing assistance to member states that have made the choice to adopt but does not, as an organisation, proselytise adoption. Regional organisations, such as APEC and ASEAN, have also played an educational and informational role in promoting discussion of the advisability of adoption in developing Asian states and small economies. The establishment of ICN as a forum for competition authorities to develop possible alignment of procedures, sharing best practice and offer capacity-building assistance on an agency-to-agency basis is a relatively new development. Allied to these educational endeavours is the issue of informal or formal co-operation on case handling where there are cross-jurisdictional issues to be resolved, whether in terms of evidence gathering or in terms of cross-border mergers. Beyond these measures there has also been a considerable debate, both at an academic and a diplomatic level, about the legitimacy of creating some form of international set of rules through a

---

[6] This proposition was confirmed by an official of the Taiwan Fair Trade Commission during a research visit to Taipei in September 2002.

multilateral treaty. This might take the form of basic competition regulations that would be advisable for sovereign states to adopt on a voluntary basis. This is the minimalist approach as exemplified by the UN Set drawn up by UNCTAD.[7] An intermediate option would be to require WTO members to enact basic competition legislation domestically but not to include review of the operation of the local competition system within the purview of the Dispute Settlement process. This would minimise interference with individual state sovereignty, save perhaps for a requirement of non-discriminatory treatment under basic WTO national treatment rule. The alternative maximalist approach is for the negotiation of a common set of harmonised, binding rules in the form of a competition code (that would trump conflicting national rules) in an appropriate forum, probably the WTO. This issue of international common minimalist or maximalist rules is highly controversial, especially since the WTO set up the Jenny Working Group in 1996. The remit of Jenny was to examine and study the issue, with the prospect of beginning actual negotiations in the next trade round, the commencement of which was delayed by the debacle at Seattle in 1999. As a result of the Doha Declaration and the failure to reach agreement at Cancun, the issue of incorporating discussions of competition policy at the WTO seems to be off the diplomatic agenda for the time being.

This chapter will briefly review the role of each of the organisations mentioned and will also mention in outline the ongoing academic debate on the issue of the merits of internationalising competition rules and if that were to be done, the format that would be most appropriate. Thus, this chapter will attempt to give an overview of developments emanating from these organisations and will attempt to assess the impact of their deliberations on the attitude and position of the Chinese and Hong Kong authorities in respect of their adoption of a competition regime.

3.3 The United Nations Conference on Trade and Development (UNCTAD)

The UN became involved in developing international anti-trust rules immediately after the conclusion of the Second World War but the failure of the United States to ratify the Havana Charter meant that it was never incorporated into the General Agreement on Tariffs and Trade (GATT)

---

[7] *The set of multilaterally agreed equitable principles and rules for the control of restrictive business practices*, GA Res. 35/63, adopted in 1980.

in 1948. However, the UN has been involved in the competition policy arena for several decades. In 1980, the General Assembly of the UN unanimously adopted the UN Set.[8] This resolution recommends all member states, both developing and developed, to adopt competition legislation and effective implementation mechanisms. It also calls for international action to control restrictive business practices. The Set is not binding but has been influential in encouraging adoption of competition regimes, especially in developing countries.

In 1998, UNCTAD produced a study report that reviewed the empirical economic literature and concluded that competition enhances economic growth and development.[9] It found that domestic firms faced with competition at home were better able to compete abroad than national monopolies. Further, the study found that there was compelling evidence that effective implementation of competition policy enhanced consumer welfare and economic efficiency. UNCTAD provides a great deal of technical assistance to countries who wish to adopt competition law in all regions of the world, for example Vietnam is in the final stage of drafting a national competition law which was promulgated in 2003 largely as a result of the technical assistance proffered by UNCTAD.[10] UNCTAD also has an educational role and holds regional seminars giving advice and providing information on competition law and policy. One was held in Guangzhou, China in December 2001 and another in Hong Kong in April 2002.

UNCTAD has produced a model law as a non-prescriptive pattern that covers all aspects of competition regulation with detailed explanatory notes to the main text.[11] Countries are urged to utilise the model law but in a flexible way that suits their own particular needs and is appropriate to their economies, socio-cultural norms and the available infrastructure to operate the chosen legislation. It should be noted that UNCTAD does not specifically endorse a comprehensive internationally enforceable code; it currently advocates domestic adoption but it does not rule out comprehensive or limited international rules. In a paper to the WTO competition study group in 1998,[12] UNCTAD took the view that developing countries had to weigh carefully whether a multilaterally agreed code with WTO enforcement provisions would be in their national interest. On the positive side, this might help developing countries that are the prey of

[8] Ibid.   [9] TD/B/COM.2/EM/10/Rev.1.
[10] See www.unctad.org/en/subsites/cpolicy/index.htm.   [11] Ibid.
[12] Phillippe Brusick, 'Trade and competition policy: a developing country perspective', Symposium on Competition and the Multilateral Trading System, 16 July 1998, WTO, Geneva.

international export cartels. The victimised country might be able to request the home authorities of the firms concerned to take appropriate action or seek information and co-operation or act themselves either alone or in concert with others. However, the rigour of immediate and complete adoption and effective enforcement might severely damage weak home industries unless there was a flexible application or a substantial 'grace' period. It also considered that extensive competition advocacy would be needed domestically to educate the home producers and consumers.

Another aspect of UNCTAD's work is the provision of assistance to developing countries on the issue of whether they should support the commencement of negotiations at the WTO on incorporating some type of competition law framework into the WTO regime. This was catalysed by a declaration at the Doha ministerial meeting of the WTO in November 2001.[13]

As a result of this decision UNCTAD undertook four regional information seminars, one of which was held in Hong Kong in April 2002. Delegates from twenty Asian countries attended including representatives of China and Macau. Noticeably, the HKSAR government was not represented officially but the semi-independent Hong Kong Consumer Council sponsored the meeting. The ambivalence of the HKSAR government to competition issues was well illustrated by its absence from the meeting.

The meeting amply demonstrated the variety of opinions concerning domestic competition law adoption in the Asian region, the lack of knowledge and limited capacity of several countries to enact and thereafter to enforce a comprehensive competition regime. Interestingly, the Chinese delegation broadly supported the notion of negotiations and subsequent adoption of competition rules into the WTO framework. The purpose of these seminars was to inform developing countries about the issues that they should consider when deciding upon their national stance on whether the WTO should commence negotiations on a binding multilateral competition framework. In addition to the capacity issues raised by many nations present, the development perspective and effect of competition policy and law enforcement was also keenly expressed. Many delegations fretted about whether a competition regime would be at odds with their national industrial and development strategy. Time and again the examples of Japan and Korea were used to illustrate the point that these

---

[13] The Doha Ministerial Declaration www.wto.org/english/trtop_e/dda_/dda_e.htm#doha declaration.

countries had achieved rapid development by government-facilitated and directed investment strategies. The encouragement of close industrial alliances and the provision of significant protection from outside competitors via external government barriers to market entry and the open or tacit acceptance of anti-competitive agreements, mergers and monopolies, were seen by some as a successful model for economic development. However, it was pointed out that the current world trade regime had now changed fundamentally with the establishment of the WTO and also that such strategies had been found to have serious flaws in the 1991 Japanese crash and the 1997 Asian Economic Crisis.

UNCTAD thus provides a valuable forum for discussion and information exchange amongst the sovereign member states of the UN, in an informal and non-negotiating setting. The experiences of developing countries that already have competition laws can be shared with states that do not have a competition regime. Thus, whilst UNCTAD pursues a positive pro-competition stance with valuable research output and provides a forum for expert and diplomatic discussions, as well as advocacy and practical technical assistance, it does not specifically endorse a binding multilateral framework. China's participation within UNCTAD provides support for the assertion that the central government has been watching the international situation carefully and remains positively disposed towards acceptance of binding international rules on competition, whilst the ambivalent stance of the HKSAR government is noticeable. Taiwan, as the Republic of China, was a founding member of the United Nations in 1945 but in 1971 the General Assembly voted to recognise the PRC government as the legitimate representative of China.[14] Thus, Taiwan does not take part in UNCTAD functions as it is not a member of the United Nations.

3.4 Organisation for Economic Cooperation and Development (OECD)

This body has a much smaller membership than the UN with thirty member states[15] which have, as common characteristics, commitments to democratic government and market-based economies. The organisation is a research and discussion forum with no plenary legal powers, though

---

[14] See United Nations General Assembly Resolution No. 2758, 25 October 1971. http://sources.wikipedia.org/wiki/UN_General_Assembly_Resolution_2758.
[15] OECD Membership http://www.oecd.org/document/58/0,2340,en_2649_201185_1889402_1_1_1_1,00.html.

it can and often does make non-binding recommendations on various social, governmental and economic matters some of which are very influential. The OECD has established a competition committee, which has prepared a number of influential reports and recommendations, especially on targeting hard-core cartels.[16] The OECD also has active relationships with a further seventy countries and has become increasingly concerned with competition promotion issues in recent years. The Centre for Co-operation with Non-Members (CCNM) undertakes responsibility for the OECD's dialogue with transition and emerging market economies to share institutional and policy options. Through the OECD Global Forums, managed by the CCNM, members and non-members address a number of issues that are transnational in nature including competition. The OECD Global Forums on Competition have been held annually since 2001; four such events have been held so far in October 2001, February 2002, 2003 and 2004.

The OECD has become active in the competition law field in recent years and provides considerable technical support in the competition law and policy area for non-member countries that request such assistance. The OECD has paid particular attention to the effects of hard-core cartels[17] and has made a formal recommendation to members to tighten enforcement of competition rules and to increase penalties. A recent report indicated that between 1996 and 2000 119 hard-core cartel cases were investigated by member countries' competition authorities and the sixteen largest cartels affected trade valued at US$55 billion and in some cases caused a 50 per cent mark-up on the market value of the goods concerned. It was suggested that for every cartel identified, six or seven were not detected.[18] Clearly, the economic effects of these cartels was not confined to the domestic economies in which they operated but would also, to some extent at least, have affected nations that did not have effective sanctions or the capacity to enforce such regulations as they did possess.

In addition to providing technical assistance to member and non-member countries in drafting and implementing competition laws, the OECD also actively advocates the domestic adoption of competition rules and their effective enforcement. This advocacy campaign is implemented

---

[16] OECD Competition Committee reports on cartels and other competition issues http://www.oecd.org/document/39/0,2340,en_2649_37463_2474407_1_1_1_37463,00.html.

[17] OECD Council Recommendation to Members 1998, http://www.oecd.org/pdf/M00018000/M00018135.pdf.

[18] OECD Report on the nature and impact of hard core cartels, 8 April 2002, http://www.oecd.org/pdf/M00028000/M00028445.pdf.

by providing detailed empirical economic analysis of the harm caused by anti-competitive activities and by hosting workshops and seminars that provide an opportunity to inform delegations from developing countries about the issues.

The Global Forums, mentioned above, have addressed a number of important topics.[19] Participants include developed and transitional and developing states. The OECD has attempted to convince developing states that competition law does not necessarily mean accepting complete laissez-faire policies or abandoning industrial policy or that it would inhibit foreign investment. The content of the substantive provisions, the nature and emphasis of enforcement and the format of the competition authority, should reflect the economic, political and resource realities of the nation concerned. The goals of a competition policy are suggested to be promoting and protecting the competitive process and promoting economic efficiency, with other non-competition goals being reserved to other policy instruments. The OECD has championed the case for adopting a competition regime by reason of increased innovation and growth, reduction of economic waste and increased consumer welfare, especially for developing countries by tackling the pernicious effects of international and domestic cartels. The abuse of dominance especially by regulated monopolists has been discussed and, in the cases of Russia and China, the abuse of governmental powers to restrict competition. The case for promoting co-operation between competition authorities especially in merger notification and cartel cases has been made as well as the need to ensure that sanctions are painful enough to deter would-be transgressors. The methodologies of investigation, tools such as leniency programmes for whistle-blowers, the benefits of competition advocacy, especially in transitional and developing states, have been stressed. The nature, architecture and optimal features of a competition authority have been discussed but were not suggested to be key to optimal performance; though independence from political influence is important, funding and sufficient qualified personnel are suggested to be vital. There was also a consensus that competition policy was possibly more important in small economies than in large ones but the approach to be adopted in small economies should be tailored to the specific idiosyncrasies of that economy and should not necessarily

---

[19] A full summary of all the matters discussed thus far is included in a recently compiled document to accompany the 2004 Global Forum on Competition. See www.oecd. org/dataoecd/13/42/27892500.pdf.

follow the system employed by large economies. The OECD has also
prepared a number of interesting publications on the topics discussed
including Capacity building for effective competition policy in developing and transitional economies[20] and The Objectives of competition
law and policy and the optimal design of a competition agency.[21] The
OECD has also instituted a system of voluntary institutional and competition system peer audits, South Africa was audited in 2003 and Russia
in 2004.[22] The report on Russia makes very interesting comments on the
unwieldy nature of the Russian enforcement authority, the inadequacy of
substantive law, the complexity and opaqueness of enforcement and sanctioning powers and the over-broad responsibilities of the then responsible
body. Following President Putin's re-election in March 2004, the restructuring of the Russian government subsequently announced may have
advantageous consequences for competition policy effectiveness. Reference has been made to some of the Report's findings in the previous
chapter.

Thus, OECD takes a more focused and purposive stance than
UNCTAD. This is not surprising as it is an organisation of developed
countries which might be expected to promote objectives that are common to the membership of the organisation, namely the enhancement of a
competitive domestic market that is open to imported goods and services
provided by those member countries. This advocacy and educational role
may of course be simply a matter of disinterested philanthropy to promote
the economic welfare of non-member states but this may be unlikely in the
realpolitik world of international economic diplomacy, where national interest is the abiding policy objective and philanthropy is rarely seen. China
has been a keen recipient of OECD technical assistance and several seminars have been held in China to discuss competition-related issues and
to assist with and comment on draft Chinese competition statutes.[23] The
role of the OECD with regard to the assistance proffered to China will be
mentioned again in chapter 5.

Hong Kong is not a member of OECD and has not requested any
technical assistance; this is unsurprising given the government's hostility
to legislating in this field.

[20] 4 (4) OECD Journal of Competition Law and Policy (2003).
[21] 5 (1) OECD Journal of Competition Law and Policy (2003).
[22] OECD Competition law and policy in Russia, OECD peer review (2004) http://www.oecd.
org/dataoecd/10/60/32005515.pdf.
[23] Seminars were held in Beijing in December 1997, November 1998, October 1999 and in
Shanghai in December 1999.

Both China and Taiwan have attended several of the global forums and their contributions relating their opinions concerning and experiences of competition law adoption and enforcement will be discussed, where relevant, in the text to follow. Hong Kong has been a notable absentee from the forums, presumably because the HKSARG does not accept the philosophical case for a competition law.

3.5 The World Bank and the International Monetary Fund (IMF)

These organisations have differing objectives. The World Bank is primarily a non-commercial lender to governments to provide funds for the development of public-sector-type projects, which are not economic or commercial propositions, to commercial banks or where the credit of the recipient country is poor and commercial entities will not lend. The IMF is the international lender of last resort when a country faces a financial crisis and needs immediate or medium-term financial assistance to overcome an extant crisis. Both organisations impose terms prior to granting loans and the 1997 financial crisis in Asia exposed some of the conditions upon which assistance was forthcoming, including, in the case of Indonesia, a requirement to improve and effectively implement comprehensive competition laws.

Thus, their advocacy of pro-competition policies may be coercive rather than merely persuasive. In the case of Indonesia, the nature of the law promulgated and more importantly the willingness or ability of the domestic government to enforce it effectively is clearly open to severe doubt.[24] Lack of follow up and long-term assistance can render adoption ineffective. In the case of Thailand,[25] the World Bank sponsored drafting of the law was not followed up with any effective education or training or long-term secondment of foreign officials to assist in implementation. Consequently, the Thai authorities have sought assistance from the OECD to implement the law more effectively but the problem of resources as well as political will in Thailand make effective enforcement elusive. This situation exactly correlates to the risks identified by Kovacic previously in chapter 2

---

[24] Ningrum Natasya Sirait, 'Indonesia's experience with its competition law and challenges ahead', paper presented at the Asian Law Institute Inaugural Conference, 27–28 May 2004 at the National University of Singapore.

[25] Details of the Thai experience, thus far, with competition law have been related in the previous chapter.

of this book and may cause disillusionment with competition law by other potential adopter developing countries. Neither China nor Hong Kong has been subject to any pressure from either organisation to adopt competition legislation as neither has sought the type of financial assistance that involves the acceptance of loan conditions requiring the promulgation of competition regimes.

3.6 World Trade Organisation (WTO)

The General Agreement on Tariffs and Trade (GATT), the predecessor to WTO, did not address competition law issues once goods had passed the national border. The Havana Charter (1948) did seek to include anti-trust rules as part of the international trade regime but was stillborn as a result of the failure of the United States Senate to ratify the treaty. Consequently, on its formation in 1995 the WTO, which now administers the GATT and other multilateral trade agreements, did not have an explicit mandate to police potentially restrictive business practices that could impede the flow of goods and services internationally. There are a few limited but nevertheless important competition provisions contained in various WTO agreements.

Article VII of the General Agreement on Trade in Services (GATS) provides that each member state will ensure that any monopoly supplier of a service in its territory will not, in supplying the monopoly service in the relevant market, act in a way that is inconsistent with that member's obligations relating to most-favoured-nation treatment under Article II and any other specific liberalisation commitments made by that member. Further, where the monopoly supplier competes directly or indirectly through an affiliated company, that member will ensure that the supplier in question does not abuse its monopoly position in one market to dominate another adjacent market in a manner inconsistent with its treaty obligations. These provisions also apply in the case of exclusive service suppliers, where a country, formally or in effect, authorises or establishes a small number of service suppliers and substantially prevents competition among these suppliers on its territory. GATS Article VIII (3) authorises the Council for the Trade in Services to act in connection with a complaint by a member against a monopoly supplier of a service of any other member, by requesting information from the member state concerned. Article VIII (4) provides a notification mechanism of any grant of monopoly service supply rights.

Article 8 of the Agreement on Trade-Related Intellectual Property Rights (TRIPS) recognises that appropriate measures may be needed to prevent (a) the abuse of intellectual property rights by the holder and (b) recourse by rights holders to practices that unreasonably restrain trade or adversely affect the international transfer of technology. Article 40 (8) provides that some licensing practices or conditions pertaining to intellectual property rights which restrain competition may have adverse effects on trade and impede the transfer and dissemination of technology, and allows members to control such abuses in their national laws.

In relation to telecommunications, specific mention is made of the prevention of anti-competitive practices by suppliers of telecommunication services either alone or in concert. The use of cross-subsidisation, collusive use of information provided by competitors that harms competition and unreasonable delay or the refusal to provide technical or other relevant commercial information about essential facilities are all outlawed.[26]

This piecemeal approach is selective and unsatisfactory and provides weak enforcement mechanisms, though any breach of a treaty obligation may result in a reference to the Dispute Settlement Body (DSB) by a member state and ultimately to the imposition of trade sanctions if the complaint is upheld. As yet, the only competition-related dispute has been between the United States and Mexico.[27] This concerned the international interconnection charges levied by the dominant Mexican telecommunications supplier, Telmex. The complaint alleged that the Mexican government had given an exclusive mandate to Telmex to set interconnection rates with US telecommunication operators and that these rates were excessive and not cost based and so in breach of GATS commitments. Apparently 80 per cent of Mexico/United States telephone traffic originates in the US and as a result of the high interconnection fees, US consumers had allegedly been overcharged by upwards of US$1 billion since 2000. On 2 April 2004, a Dispute Settlement Panel found Mexico in breach of its GATS commitments.[28] They found that Telmex did

---

[26] The texts of the various WTO agreements can be found at http://www.wto.org/english/docs_e/legal_e/legal_e.htm.

[27] For general information concerning the background to the dispute, see the US State Department Press Release dated 12 March 2004 http://usinfo.state.gov/ei/Archive/2004/Mar/15-584765.html.

[28] Mexico – Measures affecting telecommunications services – Report of the Panel WT/DS204/R.

not adopt a cost-based methodology to set interconnection rates and that Telmex had engaged in anti-competitive practices which were unrestrained by Mexican law and granted Telmex exclusive authority to set rates. Further, Mexico had failed to ensure that US carriers operating within Mexico were able to lease lines to provide resale services, though there was no breach in the refusal to allow US carriers using leased lines to complete calls originating in the US. Mexico did not accept the panel's adverse finding and the US did not accept the ruling on the use of lease lines by US carriers to complete calls in Mexico that originated in the US. Despite this, the matter is not to be appealed as the Dispute Settlement Body adopting the Panel Report on 2 June 2004 settled the dispute.[29] The settlement agreement provides for a new market-based mechanism for setting international connection rates and also allows for the liberalisation of the leasing of domestic capacity. This outcome appears to be a practical settlement of the particular dispute but provides little clarity or certainty as to the extent of WTO competition competence, since both parties were dissatisfied with aspects of the Panel's analysis and conclusions.

The inclusion of general competition provisions into the WTO system has received a great deal of attention since the decision in 1996 at the Singapore ministerial meeting of the WTO, when it was agreed: 'to establish a working group to examine the relationship between trade competition policy'. The Jenny Working Group began work in 1997 and facilitated a number of symposia, inviting many leading experts to express their views on the subject, to expose the main areas of disagreement and to analyse the complex interactions arising from trade and competition policy. Suffice to say that a large volume of literature has been generated in the form of annual Working Group reports,[30] that summarise the discussions of the Group and collections of papers examining all relevant issues.[31]

Opinion has been sharply divided on many basic issues and in particular whether the WTO was the appropriate forum to even hold discussions on the subject, let alone to proceed to actual negotiations on the issue.

---

[29] Mexico – Measures affecting telecommunications services – Notification of Agreement WT/DS204/7.

[30] Reports of the Working Group on the Interaction between Trade and Competition Policy to the General Council (1997–2003) WT/WGTCP/1–7.

[31] See generally the WTO web site pages devoted to competition policy at http://www.wto.org/english/tratop_e/comp_e/comp_e.htm#top. For the minutes of meetings, see WT/WGTCP/M/1–22. For other documents, see WT/WGTCP/W 1–246.

The EU has been the prime supporter of actual negotiations and the US a leading sceptic. However as part of the inevitable diplomatic compromise to agree the final political declaration at the Doha ministerial meeting in November 2001, a decision was taken to keep the issue on the agenda. The disarray at the Cancun ministerial meeting in September 2003 and the subsequent capitulation of the EU[32] probably means that an overarching agreement on WTO competition rules has been indefinitely postponed if not abandoned.

The Doha Declaration did explicitly recognise that the developing world is not yet in a position even to fully comprehend many of the complex issues that need to be addressed, so that they can decide whether to consent to opening negotiations or not. This seems somewhat odd given that the Jenny Working Group has been discussing exactly these matters since 1997; if developing countries have not grasped the issues after seven years of debate, then it seems unlikely that the necessary consensus needed at the WTO is likely to come about in the foreseeable future. In all probability the decision on whether to negotiate will form part of the diplomatic horse-trading that will take place once the current trade round has been completed, though that may be several years away. Full understanding of the issues is unlikely to be imparted easily or quickly, notwithstanding the efforts of the Jenny Working Group, UNCTAD and OECD. The mandate of the Jenny Working group was extended after Doha with a directive to focus on developing country issues: core principles of competition law to include transparency, non-discrimination and procedural fairness but its future existence is now clearly in doubt. From the developing countries' point of view adoption of competition rules, voluntarily or through an agreed multilateral mechanism, is a vexed issue and has been discussed previously.

Hong Kong was a member of the WTO throughout the period of the Jenny Working Group's deliberations and strongly opposed the notion of multilateral talks, as this would have run counter to the domestic position of the Hong Kong government, which will be fully explained later. China was not a member at the relevant time but the Chinese position will now be of considerable interest, as China became a member in December 2001; any new talks about talks or actual negotiations will include China. The same applies to Taiwan.

---

[32] *Singapore issues: clarification of the EU position*, EU Commission, 31 March 2004.

3.7 Asia Pacific Economic Co-operation (APEC)

This body was established in 1989 as a regional forum on trade and investment matters and acts as a channel of communication between Asia-Pacific nations. Currently, APEC has twenty-one members including the PRC, Hong Kong and Taiwan. APEC was not established by treaty and has no rule-making powers. Decisions are reached by consensus and in any event are non-binding.

In 1994, the Bogor Declaration was adopted which stated that one of the goals of APEC was to:

> complete the achievement of our goal of free and open trade and investment in the Asia-Pacific no later than the year 2020. The pace of implementation will take into account differing levels of economic development among APEC economies, with the industrialized economies achieving the goal of free and open trade and investment no later than the year 2010 and developing economies no later than the year 2020.[33]

In November 1994, as one of the measures to facilitate this long-term goal, APEC Ministers agreed that the Committee on Trade and Investment (CTI) would develop an understanding of competition issues, in particular competition laws and policies of economies in the region and how they affect flows of trade and investment in the APEC region. They would also identify potential areas of technical co-operation among member economies. In 1996, the Osaka Action Agenda (OAA) work programmes for competition policy and deregulation were combined.

As a result of the 1997–8 Asian financial crisis APEC Ministers endorsed the APEC Principles to Enhance Competition and Regulatory Reform and approved a plan of subsequent work to strengthen the markets in the region in 1999 at the Auckland ministerial meeting.

In 2001, leaders agreed that the OAA should be extended to 'reflect fundamental changes in the global economy' since the Osaka agreement. This would include additional study on measures to strengthen the functioning of markets. The implementation of competition policy and deregulation provides markets with a framework that encourages market discipline, eliminates distortions and promotes economic efficiency. Therefore,

---

[33] *APEC leaders' declaration Bogor* (1994). http://www.apecsec.org.sg/apec/leaders__declarations/1994.html.

competition policy and deregulation is one of the key elements contributing to both future progress and the extension of the OAA. Thus, one of the topics APEC has studied and made proposals on is competition law and policy, especially since the 1996 WTO decision to establish the Jenny Working Group. APEC has adopted a pro-competition policy approach, encouraging information sharing between member states, holding annual competition policy meetings, and establishing a competition law and policy database.[34]

Additionally, APEC has been active in education and capacity-building initiatives and over the last few years has held training programmes to promote economic competition both on general competition issues as well as on specific sectors regulation such as electricity, transport, telecommunications and financial services. APEC has also begun holding joint training sessions/seminars with the OECD on competition matters.[35] For example, in 2002/3 meetings were held to consider competition advocacy, capacity building, recent developments in competition law and policy especially relating to cartels, abuse of dominance and mergers.[36]

Thus, APEC is actively engaged in pro-competition advocacy in order to facilitate the long-term objective of more free and open markets in the region. As regards competition law, most of the APEC members have some form of regulation, though some, such as Hong Kong, do not. The diversity of substantive rules, administrative structures and capacity to enforce the law amongst the members is very great and the feasibility of attaining the Bogor objective must be dubious given the range of political, economic and social differences within this most heterogeneous region.

3.8 International Competition Network (ICN)

ICN is an organisation without a secretariat or a physical home. The genesis of ICN was the recommendation of the final report of the International Competition Policy Advisory Committee (ICPAC).[37] This committee was

---

[34] See http://www.apeccp.org.tw/.

[35] *APEC Convener's summary report on competition and deregulation* (2003). http://www. apecsec.org.sg/apec/apec_groups/committees/committee_on_trade/competition_policy. downloadlinks.0004.LinkURL.Download. version 5.1.9.

[36] APEC *Training programme on competition policy*, 2003/SOMII/cpdg/006, 24 May 2003.

[37] For details concerning ICPAC see, http://www.usdoj.gov/atr/icpac/icpac.htm.

established by the then US Attorney General Janet Reno and her Assistant Attorney General for Anti-Trust Joel Klein in 1997 with a mandate to consider international competition policy and law developments in the light of globalisation, and in particular to consider issues such as transnational merger control, the relationship between trade and competition and methods to improve co-operation between competition authorities. ICPAC's Final Report was delivered on 28 February 2000[38] and one of its recommendations was as follows:

> The Advisory Committee recommends that the United States explore the scope for collaborations among interested governments and international organizations to create a new venue where government officials, as well as private firms, non-governmental organizations (NGOs), and others can consult on matters of competition law and policy. The Advisory Committee calls this the 'Global Competition Initiative' and that this should be focused on 'greater convergence of competition law and analysis, common understanding and common culture'.[39]

At a conference in Brussels in September 2000, both Assistant Attorney General Klein and EU Competition Commissioner Mario Monti endorsed the establishment of such a forum as did the next US Assistant Attorney General for Anti-Trust, Douglas Melamed. The international Bar Association subsequently organised a conference in England in February 2001 which also endorsed the foundation of the new organisation. In October 2001 a meeting of the senior competition officials of fourteen jurisdictions launched the ICN, with its first annual conference being held in Naples in September 2002.

The ICN is an organisation devoted solely to competition law enforcement and is, thus, unique. Its membership, as at June 2004, comprises some sixty-five national and regional competition authorities from all parts of the globe and is voluntary and open to any national or regional competition authority. ICN has no rule-making functions and its focus is to specific projects. If consensus is reached, ICN may issue statements of 'best practice' and implementation is entirely a matter for individual members. Developed, transitional and developing economies are represented.

---

[38] ICPAC Final Report http://www.usdoj.gov/atr/icpac/finalreport.htm.
[39] See ICPAC Final Report, chapter 6, p. 1.

So far ICN has established working groups on the following substantive issues:

- Mergers.[40]
- Capacity building and policy implementation[41] including special emphasis on the case for competition policy adoption in developing and transitional states, advocacy,[42] institutional design, and capacity assistance programmes.

Additionally, ICN holds annual conferences at which many topics of substantial interest have been discussed.[43]

ICN is clearly a very focused body which has none of the disadvantages of offending political sensibilities on sovereignty issues that would inevitably arise in the more formal setting of the WTO. The adoption of 'best practice' statements, is at most 'soft law' but the peer pressure to conform might be more beneficial in reality than the distant threat of possible trade sanctions as a result of a WTO-like dispute settlement process. The ability to have a focused and directed approach to the actual issues of investigation, analysis and enforcement of competition law may well prove very valuable to authorities from developing and transitional states that have severe resource and personnel constraints. The 'hands on' approach of officials and practitioners with practical experience of case handling may yet prove more beneficial than wrangling over the precise justification of competition law adoption or the exact wording of potential competition law statutes. ICN is able to concentrate on states that have already made the choice to adopt competition law and thus the improvement of implementation in recent adopter jurisdictions is the real benefit that might flow from its operations.[44]

---

[40] Several interesting documents have been produced which can be assessed at http://www.internationalcompetitionnetwork.org/mergersdocuments.html.

[41] ICN Capacity and technical assistance report (2003) http://www.internationalcompetitionnetwork.org/Final%20Report_16June2003.pdf.

[42] ICN advocacy report (2002) http://www.internationalcompetitionnetwork.org/advocacyfinal.pdf.

[43] For full details of matters discussed at the three annual ICN conferences held to date see
http://www.internationalcompetitionnetwork.org/annualconference2002.html
http://www.internationalcompetitionnetwork.org/annualconference2003.html
http://www.internationalcompetitionnetwork.org/annualconference2004.html.

[44] For an assessment of the ICN and its prospects see Mario Todino, 'International competition network: the state of play after Naples', *World Competition*, 26(2) (2002), pp. 283–302.

At present, Taiwan is a member of ICN as it has a dedicated competition statute, the Fair Trade Law 1992 and a competition agency, the Fair Trade Commission, but neither China nor Hong Kong are members. This is unsurprising since neither jurisdiction has a specific comprehensive competition law or enforcement agency. China's does have the Anti-Unfair Competition Law 1993, which contains some competition related provisions, and the State Administration for Industry and Commerce (SAIC) is the competent authority for enforcement. Presumably since China has participated in OECD Global Competition Forums and intends to move to comprehensive legislation, it will also join the ICN in due course. Hong Kong, at present, only has competition provisions in two sectors, telecommunications and broadcasting, with two separate organisations responsible for enforcement. Given the HKSAR government's antipathy towards comprehensive competition legislation, early membership for Hong Kong is unlikely.

3.9 Conclusion

The international perspective on competition rules is very complex, with multiple organisations all having different policy motivations and objectives. China, Hong Kong and Taiwan are intimately concerned with these developments and play an active part in shaping international policy. But, particularly in the case of China, the recent upsurge in international activity in this field has, it is suggested, had a direct effect on the domestic policy making process which will be discussed later. The interesting position may arise whereby China could be broadly in favour of international competition rules, should WTO discussions ever eventuate; but Hong Kong will oppose them, even though they are part of the same state. Taiwan is also now a member of the WTO and has a fully functioning competition regime. So, it appears that China may be one country but with three views and experiences of competition regulation.

It is clear that the international developments in this subject over the last decade have been influential in opening Chinese official thinking to the possibility of legislating in this field. Hong Kong, on the other hand, has been an active sceptic in the WTO discussions, presumably hoping to prevent negotiations taking place at all. Hong Kong has also boycotted the OECD and UNCTAD and is not in a position to join ICN. It will be suggested later that this is primarily because Hong Kong is keen not to be placed under a binding international obligation to legislate a domestic competition statute or even to explore adoption as a policy option, as this is diametrically opposed to stated HKSAR government policy. Thus, it can be seen that international developments have had a direct impact on policy decisions in both China and Hong Kong but, perversely, in the opposite direction to that which one might reasonably expect those jurisdictions to take.

Finally, there is a large literature on current and future trends in the internationalisation of competition policy and law, which has not been considered in the text. Readers interested in the debate are directed to the appropriate sources, some of which are identified below.[45]

---

[45] A selected sample of the literature additional to that available on the WTO web site includes: Richard Feinburg, 'Anti-trust policy and international trade liberalisation', 14(4) *J World Comp.* 13 (1991); Manuel Agosin and Dainna Tussie, 'Globalisation, regionalisation and new dilemmas in trade policy and development', *J World Comp.* 15(4) (1992), p. 92; Elenor Fox and Janusz Ordover, A. 'The harmonisation of competition and trade law: the case for modest linkages of law and limits to parochial state action', *J World Comp.* 19 (2) (1995), p. 5; Charles Stark, *Anti-trust in the international business environment* 27(3) NYJ Int'l Law and Pol. (1995); Ignacis de Leon, *The dilemma of regulation. International competition under the WTO system*, 18 (3) ECLR 163 (1997); Ignacio de Leon, 'Should we promote anti-trust in international trade?' *J World Comp.* 28 (1997), p. 35; M. C. Malaguti, 'Restrictive business practices in international trade and the role of the WTO', *J World Trade* 32 (1998), p. 117; Edward M. Iacobucci, 'The interdependence of trade and competition policies, *J World Comp.* 22 (1998), p. 5; Roger Zach, ed., *Toward WTO competition rules*, The Hague: Kluwer Law International (1999); Bernard Hoekman, 'Competition policy, developing countries and the WTO', Policy Research Paper No. 2211, World Bank, Washington (1999); Samuel Laird, 'Transition Economies, Business and the WTO', *J World Comp.* 22 (1)(1999), p. 171 (1999); Olivier Cadot, Jean-Marie Grether and Jaime de Melo, 'Trade and competition: where do we stand?', *J World Trade* 34 (3) (2000), p. 1; Jung Yongjin, 'Modelling a WTO dispute mechanism in international anti-trust agreement: an impossible dream?' *J World Trade* 34 (2000), p. 89; C. A. Jones, 'Towards global competition policy? The expanding dialogue on multilateralism', *J World Comp.* 23 (2000), p. 95; K. C. Kennedy, *Foreign direct investment and competition policy at the WTO*, 33 Geo. Wash. Int'l L. Rev. 585 (2001); Alexandre Grewlich, 'Globalisation and conflict in competition law', *J World Comp.* 24 (3), (2001) 367; Giuliano Amato, 'International anti-trust: what future?', *J World Comp.* 24 (4) (2001) 451; Edward Swaine, *The local law of global anti-trust*, 43 William and Mary Law Review 627 (2001); Christian A. Conrad, 'Strategies to reform the regulations on international competition', 26 (1) *J World Comp.* 101 (2003); K. C. Kennedy, *Competition law and the WTO: the limits of multilateralism*, London: Sweet and Maxwell (2001).

4

China and economic regulation – history, politics and economics

4.1 Introduction

Competition law in China[1] is a developing subject. As part of the government's policy of restructuring the planned economy of the past into a 'socialist market' economy,[2] a mechanism to ensure an efficient allocation of economic goods is a key policy goal. At present there is a patchwork of miscellaneous laws and regulations[3] that seek to prevent the most damaging anti-competitive activities found in the transitional Chinese economy but a strong theoretical foundation to support the competitive mechanism is currently lacking, as is a comprehensive legal code to set the market rules. However, since at least 1994 the central government has

---

[1] China refers to the People's Republic of China and not to the Hong Kong or Macau Special Administrative Regions or to the Republic of China on Taiwan. Different legal systems and policy considerations apply to each of these other areas, none of which has ever adopted the socialist economic system or rule by the Chinese Communist Party.

[2] This term is used in Article 15 of the Constitution of the People's Republic of China adopted on 29 March 1993 but is not defined or explained. There are clearly inherent contradictions within the phrase 'socialist market' but nevertheless the policy of restructuring the Chinese economy has progressed without significant interruption since the inception of the Open Door policy at the Third Plenum of the 11th Communist Party Congress in 1978.

[3] They include, *inter alia*, State Council regulations prohibiting the implementation of regional barriers in the course of market economy activities (2001); The interim provisions on carrying out and protecting socialist competition, State Council (1980); The Anti-Unfair Competition Law (1993); The Prices Law (1997); The Law on Bidding and Inviting Tenders (1999); The Interim Measures for the Merger of Enterprises (1989); The Provisions on the Prohibition of the Restriction on Competition by Public Utility Enterprises (1993); The Law on Electric Power, The Decision of the Party Central Committee and the State Council Prohibiting Government or Party Organisations Engaging in Business Enterprises (1984); The Circular on Breaking Regional Market Blockades and Further Promoting the Circulation of Commodities (1990) and The Opinions Concerning the Establishment and Development of Enterprise Groups (1992). There are numerous other local laws and regulations.

been considering its options.[4] State organs have been studying competition regimes around the world, seeking to gain insight into how different governments police free-market systems. The help of international organisations, particularly the OECD, has been sought, to enhance capacity building. Detailed consideration of the work of the Drafting Committee and the influence of these international consultations will be given in the next chapter.

The purpose of this chapter is to introduce the background historical, political and economic developments in China since the foundation of the People's Republic in 1949, to consider the political infrastructure within which competition law and policy are developed and to explain some of the idiosyncrasies of the Chinese system that have a direct bearing on competition policy formation and implementation including opacity and local protectionism.

The key elements of the infrastructure to support an effective competition system as identified by Kovacic[5] – the academic community, government structures and the legal system including the competencies of lawyers – will be examined.

This chapter will assist in better understanding the complexities of modern China and the various cross-currents that continually buffet the Chinese people and their government. One small facet in a very complex picture is the impact of policies that will increase economic competition in a domestic economy that has traditionally been highly uncompetitive and shielded from foreign participation. To perceive better the plethora of forces at work today in China, an understanding of the context is vital. Having examined the background issues and infrastructural matters, the next chapter will concentrate on analysing current laws and the drafts of the PRC proposed anti-monopoly law.

4.2 Modern history of China and major political events

> China, though it may perhaps stand still, does not seem to go backwards.
>
> Adam Smith, *The Wealth of Nations* (1776)

---

[4] The Anti-Monopoly Law Drafting Committee was jointly established in May 1994 by the State Administration of Industry and Commerce and the State Economic and Trade Commission.

[5] Kovacic, *Designing and implementing competition and consumer protection reforms in transitional economies*.

4.2.1 National identity

The history of modern China, for present purposes, began on 1 October 1949, the date of the proclamation of the foundation of the People's Republic by Mao Zedong, Chairman of the Communist Party of China. He famously remarked that: 'The Chinese people have . . . now stood up. The Chinese have always been a great, courageous and industrious nation; it is only in modern times that they have fallen behind . . . [today] we have closed ranks and defeated both domestic and foreign aggressors . . . Ours will no longer be a nation subject to insult and humiliation.'[6] This peroration referred to the fact that for the preceding century intrusive foreign powers had forced open, by military means, the economy of the Chinese Empire to foreign trade and then made increasing political demands for the cession of territory or other politico-economic concessions. These foreign predations have had a long-lasting effect on the Chinese psyche, which was in any case always tinged with an innate sense of superiority and insularity. The English name 'China' is a foreign invention; the Chinese name for the country is Jung Guo (literally Central Country or Middle Kingdom, that is, the centre of the world). As Spence says: 'Chinese pretension to universal Asian overlordship [was based on] the assumption that China was the "Central" Kingdom and other countries were, by definition peripheral, removed from the cultural centre of the universe.'[7]

China's traditional disdain for foreigners and foreign entanglements is well illustrated by the reaction of the Emperor Qianlong in 1792 to the visit of the British envoy Lord McCarthy, who was famously sent away with a flea in his ear, with no trade treaty or diplomatic presence conceded by China. The Emperor wrote to King George III: 'As your Ambassador has seen for himself, we possess all things. I set no value in the objects strange and ingenious and have no use for your manufactures.'[8] Many in China still bridle with a deep sense of injustice as a result of the nineteenth-century foreign incursions into China. A rabid nationalism can be whipped up at any time the government chooses. Recent examples include the mass hysteria in 1996 supporting military sabre-rattling and missile 'practice' to intimidate the Taiwan electors who were choosing their first freely elected president Lee Teng-hui. The author personally witnessed university students in Nanjing cheering every time the television showed a missile being fired. This typical reaction evidenced a passionate

---

[6] Philip Short, *Mao: a life*, London: Hodder and Stoughton (1999), p. 419.
[7] Jonathan Spence, *The search for modern China*, 2nd edn, New York: Norton (1999), p. 182.
[8] Jasper Becker, *The Chinese*, London: John Murray (2000), p. 113.

and reckless desire for unification of the motherland at any price. Again, in 1999 the masses were on the streets to excoriate the Americans over the deaths of the three Chinese 'journalists' at the Chinese embassy in Belgrade as a result of the NATO smart-missile 'mistake'. In April 2001, the American spy-plane that was forced to land at a Chinese military air base on Hainan Island after a mid-air collision incident between American and Chinese military aircraft created similar scenes.

The sense of difference between the Chinese and all others is very striking; nationalism and ethnic identity are synonyms, in fact, if not in law.[9] Separate treatment of 'foreigners' is deeply ingrained in the Chinese government machine, formally in terms of separate legal rules for nationals and foreigners and informally in terms of treatment by organs of the state. In the nineteenth century, Britain insisted that the Chinese term *yi* (barbarian) should not be used in Chinese documents describing the British.[10] Historically, until the forcible opening of China to foreign trade in the middle of the nineteenth century, foreigners were constrained by Imperial edict to deal only with the cohong merchants at Guangzhou for a few months of the year.[11] A modern example is the recent and ongoing campaign against Falun Gong, branded by the Chinese government as an 'evil cult' or even a 'terrorist organisation' after the events of 11 September 2001. In order to extirpate it from the body politic, Chinese adherents are arrested and detained for indefinite periods for punishment and 're-education through labour'. However, foreign practitioners who make public demonstration of their affiliation to the movement are merely arrested and deported. Oddly, the Chinese state in practice often deals more favourably with individual foreigners than with its own people. A further illustration of this separate treatment was that, until the adoption of the new contract law,[12] China had two quite separate contract laws, one for foreigners and one for the Chinese. The Foreign Economic Contract Law was considerably more favourable than the domestic version. This differential and more favourable legal treatment may have originated in the extraterritorial application of foreign law to non-Chinese nationals resident in the Treaty Ports.[13] The notion of 'equal

[9] The Nationality Law of the PRC (1980).
[10] An article in the Treaty of Tianjin (1861) quoted in Spence, *The search for modern China*, p. 182.
[11] The cohony was a group of Chinese merchants selected by the Imperial authorities who were given exclusive rights to deal with foreign traders. Each merchant was allowed to deal only with foreign traders of a particular nationality. For an explanation of the Chinese Imperial trading system see Spence, ibid. pp. 117–23.
[12] Williams, *An introduction to general principles and formation of contracts.*
[13] See Spence, *The search for modern China*, pp. 123–8.

treatment under the law' is a very recent idea in China and the National Treatment[14] standard under WTO rules will be a difficult concept for Chinese officials to accept as they have habitually segregated their treatment of persons and products according to nationality.[15] The government 'also discriminates against its own people with rural residents being unable, until very recently, to change their legal residence status to move to an urban settlement, for fear of mass migration to the cities, so causing chaos; in practice millions exist in a legal twilight zone as rural migrant workers enjoying few legal rights in the cities where they temporarily live and work.

4.2.2 Foreign incursions and the end of the Chinese Empire

Protect the country – kill the foreigner.[16]

The first political/economic demands in the nineteenth century were made by the British following the First Opium War. This resulted in the cession of Hong Kong Island and opened five other ports, the Treaty Ports,[17] to British commerce and the protection of resident consular officials, including the extraterritorial application of English law to non-Chinese nationals.[18]

Up to that time foreign trade was extremely restricted. The system devised by the Chinese from 1757 to 1842 was that twelve merchant houses, the Hongs, were nominated to deal with the trade representatives of twelve non-Chinese countries. This monopoly system of nominated traders was conducted in one of twelve 'factories' on an island in the middle of the Pearl River at Canton, now Guangzhou, for a very limited time each year. Foreigners were forbidden to live in China at all, except for the tiny enclave of Macau, which was administered from the early sixteenth century to

---

[14] The notion that foreign goods should be accorded the same treatment by the authorities of a state as home-produced products is a fundamental rule of the GATT/WTO system. See John H. Jackson, *The world trading system: law and policy of international economic relations*, 2nd edn, Massachusetts: MIT Press (1997).

[15] This has been confirmed yet again by a new set of interim merger regulations that apply only to foreign firms who acquire Chinese enterprises, see the next chapter. As regards official PRC policies on how foreigners should be handled, see Ann-Marie Brady, ' "Treat insiders and outsiders differently": the use and control of foreigners in the PRC', *The China Quarterly*, 164 (2000), pp. 943–64.

[16] Slogan of the anti-foreigner movement I Ho Chuen (The Boxers), China 1900.

[17] They were the cities of Guangzhou, Fuzhou, Xiamen, Ningbo and Shanghai.

[18] See Treaty of Nanjing 1842. From the Chinese viewpoint, this was the first of the 'unequal treaties' to which China was subjected by the foreign powers in the nineteenth century. The Chinese government, both nationalist before 1949 and communist after 1949, never accepted the validity of the cession of Hong Kong to Britain.

1999 by the Portuguese. China refused to buy any foreign goods but was prepared to sell tea, silk and porcelain to the foreigners in exchange for silver. This constant drain of silver out of the coffers of the British East India Company, which held the British monopoly of trade with the east until 1834, caused not only resentment but also smuggling of the one commodity Chinese people did appear to want – opium produced by the Company in Bengal. The dispatch of a new Governor General, Li Zexu, to Canton by the Emperor to prohibit the illicit opium trade and the outflow of silver from the Empire, resulted in the gunboat diplomacy so favoured by Lord Palmerston, the British Foreign Secretary at the time. The price of Chinese military defeat was a British territorial presence in China until 1997.[19]

Other nations quickly advanced their claims for, first, trading rights and then political concessions, including the fabulously successful foreign settlements at a small village called Shanghai. By the end of the nineteenth century, the Qing dynasty, weakened by inflexible political structures, a civil service steeped in Confucian literature but not the diplomatic and technological arts of the modern age, civil war and constant political demands by foreign powers and its own xenophobic population, collapsed in 1909. The boy Emperor Pu Yi was deposed in favour of a republican president, who later tried to found a new imperial house.

The weak republic struggled on in to the 1920s when the newly aggressive and imperialist Japanese first occupied the whole of industrial Manchuria in northeast China and in 1936 commenced open hostilities to conquer the whole country. In the meantime, the Chinese Nationalist Party had split into the mutually loathing CCP and the Kuo Ming Tang (KMT), led respectively by Mao Zedong and Chang Kai-shek. China from the 1920s to 1949 was in a constant state of chaos caused by both civil war and Japanese invasion.

4.2.3 The victory of communism

Long live the great, glorious and always correct Chinese Communist Party.[20]

The final victory of the CCP was not a foregone conclusion by any means, but to the winner the spoils. Mao had never been a great enthusiast for

---

[19] For a full treatment of the trading situation, the course of the First Opium War and its consequences, see Spence, *The search for modern China*, chapters 6 and 7; also F. Welsh, *A history of Hong Kong*, London: Harper Collins (1997), chapters 2, 3 and 4.

[20] Sign welcoming delegates, CCP Congress, Guangzhou, August 1977.

Stalinist Russia and was wary of escaping the embrace of the imperialist capitalists only to fall into the clutches of the Russian Bear, who had always been a predatory northern neighbour.[21] The short-lived Sino-Russian friendship lasted barely eleven years before an ideological split severed political and economic ties, leaving China almost entirely isolated. The United States continued to recognise the remnant state of the ROC, now confined to the island of Taiwan, as the legitimate government of the whole of China, until the adroit diplomacy of Kissinger sponsored an American volte face in 1971, whereby the PRC was recognised as the legitimate government of China and the ROC on Taiwan was sidelined.

Domestically, Mao inspired a cult of personality to rival any of his imperial predecessors and plunged the country into ever more convoluted devotions to his leadership. The Anti-Rightist Movement in 1957 sought out anyone of privileged background, education or any foreign connection, to be denounced as a traitor and punished accordingly. The Great Leap Forward, begun in 1959, was a disastrous utopian fantasy that resulted in the greatest man-made famine in history with upwards of 30 million Chinese starving to death before the enforced communisation of agriculture was partially abrogated in 1962.[22] With old age leading to ever greater paranoia Mao unleashed yet another calamitous political campaign, the Great Proletarian Cultural Revolution 1966–76. This orgy of destruction, mob violence and massacre almost spiralled into civil war. Almost all of Mao's veteran colleagues of the Long March era were internally exiled or executed or otherwise met an early death.[23] By 1976, on Mao's death, China was still in a state of lawless chaos and desperately poor.

The assumption of supreme state power by Deng Xiaoping in 1978 and his subsequent decision to abandon China's isolation and take steps to open the country to limited foreign intervention in economic matters has transformed China's economic and political importance. Despite the Tiananmen 'Incident' in 1989 and the politico-economic blip that

---

[21] Port Arthur (now Dalian) was occupied by the Russian Empire in 1898 as the terminus of the great trans-Siberian railway giving access to an ice-free Pacific port, as were large tracts of territory.

[22] Jasper Becker, *Hungry ghosts*, New York: Owl Books (1996).

[23] Deng Xiaoping was purged in 1966 and again in 1976, President Liu Shaoqi died as a result of deliberate medical neglect and Lin Biao apparently tried to organise a *coup d'état*, lost his nerve and his plane was shot down over Mongolia as he tried to escape to Russia. For full details see Short, *Mao: a life*, above.

occurred afterwards, China's gross domestic product has soared,[24] mainly as a result of private enterprises, both foreign and domestic, that have transformed China into the twenty-first century's 'workshop of the world'[25] and into a member of the capitalist trade club, the World Trade Organisation, in December 2001.[26] In 2003, over half of the top 200 exporters were firms from Taiwan, Hong Kong or other foreign nations; the top exporter was a Taiwan-owned computer component manufacturer. These 200 firms exported goods worth over US$96 billion, almost half of all China's exports in 2002.[27]

The entry of China into the WTO has extensive political as well as economic significance. Reformists in the CCP see membership and the treaty obligations entered into as a guarantee of continued expansion, economic openness and transparency which might hold out the prospect of political reformation too. The hardliners fret about this and criticise that China gave away far too much to gain membership of the WTO and that China is now on the road back to the pre-1949 era with foreign capitalists poised to capture and dominate the Chinese domestic market. This political reaction was clearly evident in 1999 after the Americans publicised the concessions that Premier Zhu Rongi had made to win American approval of China's membership. Further, it was noticeable that, even two months after China's accession to the WTO, no Chinese-language version of the accession agreements was available in China, presumably because of political concerns.[28] It is clear that the Chinese public and many in government had very little understanding of the nature and the consequences of WTO membership for China, especially the far greater access to China's markets now guaranteed to foreign enterprises. The economic consequences of membership are considered below.

[24] China's GPD per capita at current prices was US$342 in 1990 and US$777 in 1998, *Statistical year book*, 45th issue, United Nations, New York (2001), chapter 18, p. 133.
[25] Exports of clothing, footwear, electronic goods, bicycles, fancy goods etc. In 1990 China's exports amounted to US$62 billion; in 1999 they were US$195 billion. Ibid.
[26] The PRC formally became a member on 9 December 2001 and Chinese Taipei (Taiwan) a day later. China now has four seats at the WTO table including Hong Kong and Macau as separate customs territories.
[27] 'Foreign firms shine among China's top 200 exporters', *South China Morning Post*, 19 June 2003; see also Nicholas Lardy, 'The role of foreign trade and investment in China's economic transformation', *The China Quarterly* 144 (1995), pp. 1065–82.
[28] 'China guards details of its WTO Agreement', *Asian Wall Street Journal*, 3 December 2001.

4.2.4 Contemporary political issues in China

There are many other political issues of major importance when considering competition policy in China. The first of these is that the most effective competition regimes operate in democratic societies. China is not a democracy. There has been no accompanying political reform to mirror the great economic changes that have occurred in China since 1978. The political structure is one of orthodox Leninist party domination of all aspects of political life in China. Other token political parties do formally exist and NGOs appear to flourish. However, appearance and reality in China are very different. All the non-communist political parties, NGOs, charities and religious organisations are subject to strict registration procedures and supervision by the state. The state and the party are formally separate but the Chinese constitution presumes and guarantees the leading role of the CCP.[29] The new leadership of state and party that took office in March 2003 seems to appreciate that the present political structure is untenable and on National Day, 1 October 2003, State President and Party General Secretary Hu Jin-tao made a speech endorsing 'socialist-democracy'; precisely what this might mean in practice remains to be seen.[30] Thus, in theory and practice, no activity considered 'political' in China escapes the control of the party. In such conditions, where both large sections of the economy and all political life continue to be monolithically controlled, the key research question that this book attempts to answer is whether an effective competition policy can be fashioned or enforced in China. The existing Chinese political structure faces a central dilemma, namely the inherent contradiction of encouraging economic freedom and protecting the competitive process, whilst maintaining strict authoritarian control of all other aspects of civil society.[31] This issue will be considered in the analytical chapter 5 to follow and in the concluding chapter.

Another major political concern, caused by monolithic political control is the soaring growth of corruption. The complex bureaucratic procedures governing all aspects of economic life in China and the decentralisation of economic/political decision-making in commercial matters, coupled with extensive discretion, very low official salaries and the lack of effective supervision, conspire to ensure that corruption is both widespread and

---

[29] Preamble to the Constitution of the PRC as amended 15 March 1999.
[30] 'Hu's worthy goals still far from realisation', *South China Morning Post*, 2 October 2003.
[31] Hao Yufon, 'From rule of man to rule of law: an unintended consequence of corruption in China in the 1990s', *Journal of Contemporary China* (1999), pp. 405–23.

endemic. Corruption in China is systemic. The frequency and widespread nature of periodic anti-corruption campaigns by the CCP and the state, reinforce the common perception that corruption is simply out of control. Over the five years from 1997 to 2002, the CCP inspection department investigated 790,000 party corruption cases, resulting in 780,000 cadres being either jailed, executed or subjected to internal party discipline.[32] The CCP considered this campaign a great success but these shocking figures only confirm the impression that corruption is rampant. The respected international survey organisation, Transparency International, in its 2001 Global Corruption Report, said:

> China faces the region's greatest challenge in reining back corruption … the cost of corruption is estimated at 2–3% of GDP by Morgan Stanley Dean Wittier but an internal assessment by Professor Hu Angang of Tsinghua University, Beijing put the figure as high as 15–16% of GDP and that 15–20% of all public project funds leak into private hands. The officially investigated cases reached 45,000 in 1999, a 15% increase over 1998.[33]

Even senior party figures acknowledge the seriousness of the situation: 'Historical experience has shown that the exercise of power without restraint and supervision inevitably leads to corruption. We face the destruction of our party and of our nation if we fail to fight corruption and promote clean government.'[34]

The prevalence and corrosive effect of corruption causes deep resentment amongst ordinary Chinese people and the economic inefficiencies that result thereby clearly affect competitiveness. The actual amounts involved are staggering. Two recent examples illustrate the seriousness of the problem. In December 2001, Wang Xue-bing, the former Chairman of the Bank of China, one of the four state-owned banks, was arrested on corruption charges. The amount allegedly embezzled was in excess of US$500 million.[35] This was a minor matter when compared with the Xiamen case. Lai Changxing was the head of an import/export business, the Yuan Hua Group, in the Special Economic Zone of Xiamen. He allegedly corrupted hundreds of the city government officials including

---

[32] 'Crackdown on corrupt cadres hailed as big success', *South China Morning Post*, 15 October 2002.
[33] Transparency International web site at http://www.globalcorruptionreport.org/gcr2001. html at p. 11.
[34] Li Peng, Chairman of the Standing Committee of the National People's Congress, 9 March 2001 quoted in the *2001 Global corruption report.*
[35] 'Former Bank of China President facing prosecution', *Financial Times*, 9 July 2002.

the mayor, the chiefs of police and customs and various provincial and military officials, one of whom is now a minister in Beijing. The scam involved the smuggling of commodities into Xiamen during the mid-1990s worth some US$5 billion, causing a loss to the Chinese exchequer of some US$3 billion. He is currently fighting extradition from Canada whence he fled to escape arrest.[36] The increasing frequency of major corruption cases continues unabated. On just one day two former heads of major state-owned enterprises (SOEs) were condemned for corruption – Gao Yan, chairman of the State Power Corporation and Zhu Xiaohua, chairman of the State Council's own commercial finance arm, China Everbright Group.[37] In a 2003 report, the People's Procurate (State Prosecution Service) analysed trends in corruption in China. In the 1980s, corruption was relatively low level and low value but by the late 1990s it had become institutionalised, with entire departments or even whole regional governments being implicated and involving huge sums. This systemic cancer may not be susceptible to cure.[38] In 2003, Guangdong Province, adjacent to Hong Kong, reported investigating 1,239 cases of 'high level' corruption; 200 cases involved sums of at least US$125,000 and 30 cases involved over US$1 million. Additionally, the CCP reported that this province had the highest number of fugitive Party members; over 2,000 were missing, the majority having absconded overseas to escape criminal prosecution for corruption.[39] One analyst has suggested that corruption in China has had three distinct phases, all linked with economic distortions in the market.[40] The first type of corruption was in the 1980s and involved the manipulation of state-mandated commodity prices and market prices. The second, in the 1990s, involved smuggling, due to very high import tariffs and restrictive quota regimes. The third in the new decade concerns real estate. The key here is that the wholesale price and supply of land is low, even zero and is controlled by state officials, whilst the market price of new residential or commercial property is high. In such an environment, especially as there has been a run-away real-estate boom in much of China, corrupt land deals seem to dominate the high-profile reported cases, such as that of Zhou Zhengyi, the Shanghai

---

[36] 'If he goes back, he will be toast', *South China Morning Post*, 3 July 2002.
[37] 'Power producers' shares reel from tariffs cuts and former Everbright chief given 15 years for graft', *South China Morning Post*, 11 October 2002.
[38] 'The swelling cancer of corruption', *South China Morning Post*, 1 September 2003.
[39] 'Two Guangdong officials accused of taking bribes', *South China Morning Post*, 21 February 2004.
[40] 'The ultimate source of corruption', *South China Morning Post*, 3 November 2003.

property tycoon who reportedly corrupted very high level Bank of China officers in Hong Kong in return for credit lines in excess of US$225 million.[41] Corrupt land dealings may even reach to ministerial level, with the removal from office of Tian Fengshan, Minister of Land Resources in October 2003.

The political cost of the corrosive effect of corruption and the unofficial abandonment of Marxist ideology, together with the collapse of cradle-to-grave social provision, will further destabilise the political situation. A remarkably frank assessment of the seriousness of the problem is given by Huang Weiding,[42] but his prescription to cure the malady is merely heightened propaganda campaigns, more 'socialist democratic politics' and greater supervision; these measures are unlikely to be any more successful in the future than they were in the past. Apparently in desperation, the central government may rely on methods adopted under the Empire; special anti-corruption officers recruited and paid centrally will descend on regional officials to conduct spot checks and take remedial action. Again, the likelihood of this measure being successful is very small.[43]

The increasing economic pressures over the next five years as a result of WTO entry may well cause the alienated and destitute masses to turn to political turmoil as the only method of effective protest in the authoritarian Chinese state. The prevalence of disaffection as a result of economic hardship has already become widespread. One worrying issue for the government is massive unemployment in the agricultural sector which currently sustains over 500 million of China's vast population, as a result of cheaper agricultural imports following WTO accession, which reduces tariffs, abolishes quotas and grants much greater access to foreign agricultural products.[44] It is expected that a minimum of 9.6 million farmers will have to leave agriculture. The same phenomenon will also occur in many manufacturing and service industries, particularly the SOE sectors. For example, vehicle manufacture import tariffs will fall from 80–100 per cent to 25 per cent in 2007; it is expected that of the present 120 manufacturers only perhaps 30 will survive the market opening, with 3 or 4 dominating the market, all linked to a foreign giant.[45] Millions of

---

[41] 'Shanghai property mogul stands trial', *Shenzhen Daily*, 21 May 2004.
[42] Huang Weiding, 'Fighting corruption amidst economic reform: the awakening of the next economic power house', in *China's century*, ed. Lawrence J. Brahm, New York: Wiley (2002) above.
[43] 'Imperial tactics enlisted in anti-graft fight', *South China Morning Post*, 27 August 2003.
[44] Saywell and Wilhelm, 'Seeds of change', *Far Eastern Economic Review*, 29 June 2000, p. 44.
[45] O'Neill, 'WTO delivers mixed blessings', *South China Morning Post*, 1 October 2001.

workers will be redundant. In the oil industry, redundancies of up to 30 per cent have occurred since 2000. In Daquing, a city in Chinese Siberia completely dominated by the state oil firm, 80,000 out of 300,000 workers have been declared surplus to requirements. The problems of unemployment will worsen as the region's oil reserves deplete very rapidly in the next few years.[46] The growing inequalities in income and wealth risk incurring the wrath of the dispossessed and creating social instability.[47]

Demonstrations are increasing in size and frequency in all parts of China. In April 2002 alone, huge demonstrations occurred in the old heavy-industrial heartland in Manchuria (Shenyang), thousands of workers demonstrated after being laid off at their former work places and at the CCP headquarters.[48] The potentially destabilising effect of these public demonstrations is the greatest political threat to the stability of the current Chinese government. The domestic and international consequences of such instability are impossible to overstate, given that the PRC is the world's most populous country, with approximately 1.3 billion people.[49]

These political rigidities are a consequence of the fact that there has been very little political reform since the death of Mao, whilst the economic landscape has been transformed. It is interesting to speculate how long this situation will endure but the likelihood of a peaceful political transformation is improbable. In more than 4,000 years of recorded Chinese history the demise of a dynasty (and for these purposes the CCP is a dynasty) has never been accomplished without violence.[50] A country with no democratic traditions of any kind and great deference to history is unlikely to undergo such a transformation without recourse to traditional methods of effecting political change. This, undoubtedly, is a Cassandra scenario; but many knowledgeable observers are of the same opinion.[51]

Even the central government now seems to be taking doomsday scenarios seriously. The State Development and Economic Reform Commission

---

[46] O'Neill, 'Nearly one third of city's oil workers out in the cold', *South China Morning Post*, 10 April 2002.

[47] 'Wealth gap looms as nation's greatest threat', *South China Morning Post*, 3 October 2002.

[48] Jasper Becker, 'Workers in a state of disunion', *South China Morning Post*, 23 March 2002.

[49] *China statistical year book*, Beijing, 2000.

[50] The only two examples of peaceful political transformation in China were the retrocession of Hong Kong and Macau to China in 1997 and 1999 respectively and the transfer of power in Taiwan to Chen Shibien in March 2001; this will be discussed later.

[51] The most trenchant of these is Gordon Chang, *The coming collapse of China*, Random House, New York (2000).

(SDERC) presented a report to the leadership listing various potentially fatal problems for China's continued economic development; they
included *inter alia* globalisation, foreign trade, agricultural dislocation,
income disparities, unemployment and social disorder. The report warns
that mass migration from the poor hinterland to the more prosperous
cities, increased unemployment and social disorder caused by rapid economic change could spell disaster.[52]

The political outlook for China in the next ten years is one of increasing
instability caused by the economic dislocation that will result from the
more competitive environment ushered in by greater foreign access to
the domestic market and the restructuring or collapse of the SOE. It
remains to be seen whether the economic growth created by a more open
economy can provide sufficient wealth that can be equitably distributed
to the masses who will bear the brunt of the economic hardship of this
new paradigm. If the economic gains are not distributed sufficiently to
the dispossessed, then the political future of China is grim indeed.[53] The
omens are not good, given the current huge inequalities in China, which
have been magnified enormously by the endemic corruption of the CCP
and the government, which increasingly treats state assets as a private
resource for individual enrichment.[54]

These fears have played a vital part in forming the policy choices currently being made by the government in relation to competition policy.
The political issue is whether China can afford not to become more competitive. China's political leaders appear to be still undecided as to whether
the balance of advantage lies in adopting a comprehensive competition
law or not. The policy debate continues in Beijing, whilst technical prepa-
rations have been made for the introduction of a comprehensive competition law. The detail and current state of these technical and doctrinal
debates will be considered in the next chapter.

---

[52] 'A wake up call for China's new leaders', *South China Morning Post*, 30 August 2003.
[53] Commentators have varying views about China's political future. For a selection of these
see Michael Oksenberg, 'China's political system: challenges for the twenty-first-century',
The China Journal (45) (2001), pp. 21–35; Pan Wei, 'Towards a consultative rule of law
regime in China' *Journal of Contemporary China* 12 (34) (2003), pp. 3–43; Zhao Sui-sheng,
'Political Liberation without Democratisation: Pan Wei's proposal for political reform',
Journal of Contemporary China, 12 (35) (2003), pp. 333–55; Larry Diamond, 'The rule of
law as transition to democracy in China', *Journal of Contemporary China* 12 (35) (2003),
pp. 319–31.
[54] See Chang, *The Coming Collapse of China*, pp. 246–9; 'Troubles ahead for the new leaders',
The Economist, 16 November 2002; X. L. Ding, 'The illicit asset stripping of Chinese state
firms', *The China Journal* (2000)(43), pp. 1–28.

4.3 Economic policy 1949–2004

4.3.1 Economic socialism Chinese style

We don't talk politics anymore. Why should we? Who is our leader now?

Money is our leader.[55]

The communist experiment began in 1949 and was implicitly abandoned in 1978. The economic history of China is far too large a subject to receive detailed treatment here. The immediate victory of the CCP in 1949 caused panic amongst the established Chinese business community in the major cities. Many fled to Taiwan and others to Hong Kong; most of the major tycoons in Hong Kong either themselves fled the communist takeover or are children of parents who did the same.[56]

China then embarked on a policy of creeping nationalisation until by 1954 almost all economic activity was 'owned' or controlled by the state. China sought to ape the economic development processes of Stalinist Russia by a concentration on heavy industry as the major driving economic force. Steel, chemicals, coal, heavy engineering were all emphasised in accordance with the state plan, which distributed the factors of production. Market mechanisms were taboo. Line ministries were established to administer whole industrial sectors but China did not follow the Stalinist model precisely by establishing vast single enterprises in one particular location that would produce all the nation's supply of a particular commodity. Rather, a cellular structure was established. This was for two principal reasons – firstly, China's transport infrastructure is very poor except between the major cities (this was even more pronounced fifty years ago) and the transport of a commodity from a distant plant would have been impossible. Secondly, Mao had a military/ideological belief in the necessity for each region to be as self sufficient as possible, primarily as a result of China's experience of invasion by the Japanese. Dispersal of key industries would ensure the ability to continue resistance to an aggressor, even if large parts of the country were occupied. This was the so-called Third Line strategy. Whatever the political and practical imperatives that

---

[55] Mr Zhang, a Beijing Merchant, in P. E. Tyler, 'Riches tasted, China hungers for freedom', *New York Times*, 30 May 1997.

[56] For example Tung Chee-wah, the Beijing-appointed post-colonial Chief Executive of Hong Kong, is the son of the founder of the largest Chinese shipping empire. Mr Tung senior simply sailed his ships away to Hong Kong from Shanghai in 1949. Most of the leading textile manufacturers dismantled their equipment and established new enterprises in Hong Kong.

drove this policy of duplication of capacity, it has had an increasingly baleful economic impact since the move towards more market-orientated mechanisms of economic management, as huge over-capacity now exists in most industries. Thus, it has been impossible to develop economic nodes for particular industries (for example, like Detroit in the USA for vehicle manufacture) and as a result of the absence of economies of scale the products made are wildly uncompetitive.[57] For example, although China has more than 120 vehicle manufacturing plants, only two have the capacity to product 500,000 units, eight can produce 100,000 and ninety-five less than 10,000 units. Apparently this extremely fragmented structure will be rationalised not by market forces but by administrative fiat via the National Development and Reconstruction Commission (NRDC).[58] This example can be duplicated in most industrial sectors in China.[59]

Another consequence of this policy was the dispersal not only of industry but also the duplication of political authority over a particular industry. As a result of China's size and population, regional governments often have far more practical power than do the distant mandarins of Beijing. Consequently, the intriguingly named 'mother-in-law' problem arises. A given plant is often said to have 'too many mothers-in-law' who issue contradictory instructions to state enterprises that can cause managerial paralysis, at worst, or at best profound confusion as to the role of the management or the strategic direction the enterprise is to follow. Examples are legion and this phenomenon partly explains the appalling condition of the state industrial sector in China.

A further consequence of the hydra-headed legacy of Maoist economics is the rampant abuse of local administrative powers by provincial and local governments to protect local producers and so their tax bases and local jobs, by impeding internal trade. This is discussed in section 4.7 but it is clear that China still lacks a single internal market for goods and services. In this respect it has the problem identified in the EU fifty years ago but in China's case within a single, unitary, nation state. It will be seen in the next chapter how EC competition law has been chosen as the Chinese model and 'Administrative Monopoly' – the Chinese name

---

[57] *China: Internal Market Development and Regulation*, World Bank, Washington (1994); *China's Emerging Private Enterprises: Prospects for the new Century*, International Finance Corporation, Washington (2000).

[58] Chinese Government to Rationalise Auto Sector, Ministry of Commerce, 19 August 2003, http://english.mofcom.gov.cn/article/200308/20030800118569_1.xml.

[59] 'TV makers feel the pinch', *South China Morning Post*, 4 November 2002 (40–50 current producers, expected to fall to less than ten over five years).

for this abuse of governmental power and the consequent local protectionism – has a whole section of the draft anti-monopoly law devoted to it.

The bankrupt state of most of China's SOEs is a major concern especially as increased foreign competition with them in China's domestic market in the future will further weaken their already dismal finances. Mass restructuring and huge job losses may be the inevitable result of WTO membership.[60] Local protection may well not be able to shield the SOEs for much longer from a more competitive environment.

4.3.2 Economic restructuring

In 1978, at the Plenum of the CCP, a critical decision was endorsed to embark on a policy of 'opening' to foreign influences. This was to be strictly confined and limited to economic interaction. Initially, several Special Economic Zones[61] were established on the periphery of the Chinese land mass as almost separate territories where 'socialist' economics was not practised, and normal government regulation of customs duties, together with rules on exporting by non-state trading companies, taxation and employment simply did not apply. The most successful of these zones has been Shenzhen, geographically larger than its immediate southern neighbour, Hong Kong. As a result of high land and wage costs, Hong Kong manufacturers flooded across the border to establish manufacturing plants of all types, especially clothing, footwear and electrical/electronic goods.

The state has, until recently, adopted a decidedly ambiguous attitude towards the existence, nature and scope of private enterprise in the domestic economy. After the initial decision to open the economy partially to foreign capitalism to conduct export-oriented manufacture, the vast bulk of the domestic economy remained in state hands. However, over the last twenty-five years, the government has gradually relaxed the restrictions on domestic private business and indeed has now formally recognised that

[60] Edward Steinfield, *Forging reform in China: the fate of state-owned industry*, Cambridge University Press (1998); 'Dream car hit the skids as China joins WTO', *The Times*, 10 March 2002; 'Liberalisation to put squeeze on China's insurers', *South China Morning Post*, 20 April 2002; 'Lines drawn over retail invasion', *South China Morning Post*, 9 April 2003. For an assessment of the social changes that WTO membership may bring see Kye Woo-lee, 'China's accession to the WTO: effects and social challenges', *China Perspectives* 33 (2001), pp. 13–24.

[61] These were Shenzhen, Zhuhai, Xiamen and Shantou; many other 'special' zones and areas were created later.

private ownership of capital is 'an important component of the socialist market economy'.[62] This constitutional acceptance of capitalism is a major landmark. But the legal protections in place to define and enforce property rights are limited and largely ineffective. This issue will be considered further in the next section. The phrase 'socialist market economy' as used in the constitution to identify correct economic orthodoxy, is not defined in the constitution or anywhere else. However, it seems to suggest some form of mixed economy with a significant state sector. There has been no 'big bang' privatisation as occurred in the former Soviet Bloc countries following the political changes of the early 1990s. However, China has been very active in altering the relationship of the state to the SOEs and collectively owned enterprises.[63]

In the first place, China has developed two stock markets, one in Shenzhen and another in Shanghai. Listing on the market has been governed, as least until very recently, by exclusively political, rather than economic or regulatory considerations. Access to the market to raise capital from the Chinese public was seen as a political privilege to be awarded to favour large SOEs which needed a capital injection that neither the state nor the state banks were willing or able to provide. Well over 90 per cent of the listed companies on the Chinese stock markets are state-owned enterprises in which less than 25 per cent of the voting shares have been sold to the public. The process of listing has been governed by the ability of influential SOE managers to lobby national politicians; domestic private businesses have been almost totally excluded from raising capital in this way. The result has been a large number of flotations where many of the companies, even after ten years on the market, have never made a profit or returned a dividend to their shareholders. Further, corporate governance standards in China are weak and rarely if ever enforced;[64] private share-holders have no power to determine corporate appointments and the Party Secretary in each company remains the ultimate arbiter of business decisions. Inevitably the management of these companies rarely

---

[62] Art. 11, PRC Constitution states: 'The non-public ownership sector comprising the individual economy and the private economy within the domain stipulated by law is an important component of the country's socialist market economy. The state protects the lawful rights and interests of the individual economy and the private economy', as amended 15 March 1999.

[63] For a history of state-owned enterprise reform from 1978 to 1999, see Lawrence J. Brahm and Steven X. M. Lu, *State Owned Enterprise Reform in China*, 25 Asia Business Law Review, pp. 18–23.

[64] See the section *Strengthening enterprise governance* in *China in the world economy: the domestic challenges*, Paris: OECD (2002), pp. 44–6.

acts in the interests of the shareholders. Reform of this situation is one of the key recommendations of a recent OECD report.[65] The government reorganisation carried out in March 2003, after the assumption of power by the new leadership, established several new state economic bodies responsible to various aspects of restructuring the economy in readiness for the increased competition fostered by WTO accession. The new State-Owned Assets Supervision and Administration Commission, has been tasked with consolidation, restructuring or disposing of most of the remaining 159,000 SOEs. This body wants the retained SOEs to be run as businesses, not state agencies. Whether this will be achieved is an open question.[66] A recent APEC report[67] praised progress so far but domestic commentators were sceptical. Chinese economist and director of the World and China Institute, Li Fan, characterised China's record on transparency as 'appalling' and the state still 'monopolised significant portions of the economy... financial reforms remain slow, state banks won't commercialise any time soon and SOE control markets like they own them'.[68]

4.3.3 The problem of the SOEs and the banks

Most large-scale listed enterprises in China still do not behave as profit-maximising entities. The listed or unlisted SOE is still regarded as a pillar of the socialist economy and continues to provide employment for hundreds of millions of urban workers as well as cradle-to-grave social benefits such as housing, health care, education, social welfare and pensions. These provisions benefit not only existing workers but also pensioners and employees' dependants. The inefficiency of the system has been thoroughly explored in several books,[69] which conclude that the parlous state of the SOEs could yet create a banking crisis that could then lead to a great economic political and economic upheaval.

The alarming state of SOE/bank affairs has been alluded to by the OECD:

---

[65] Ibid.

[66] 'Market-driven directors sought for state firms; Welcome steps in state sector shake-up', *South China Morning Post*, 8 October 2003.

[67] IAP Study Report China 2003, APEC, 2 June 2004. http://www.apec.org/apec/news_media/media_releases/020604_reportchinaprogress.html.

[68] 'APEC report is accused of glossing over faults', *South China Morning Post*, 4 June 2004.

[69] Nicholas Lardy, *China's unfinished economic revolution*, Washington, D.C.: Brookings Institution Press (1998). Steinfeld, *Forging reform in China*.

A severe vicious circle has developed. Poor enterprise performance con-
tributes to bank non-performing loans and lowers bank profits by eliminating much of their core market. By themselves, financial institutions
cannot hope to restore their financial solvency unless and until enterprise
[SOE] performance improves substantially. But high non-performing loans
make it difficult for the banks to provide for enterprise restructuring needed
to improve their performance. This vicious circle is aggravated in China
by the behaviour derived from traditional relations amongst financial institutions, SOE and the government that reforms have not yet decisively
transformed.[70]

In 1998, the weaknesses of the SOE system were acknowledged by the new
Premier, Zhu Rongi. He enunciated a policy of 'letting go the small/weak
and strengthening the big/strong'. This policy encouraged the implicit
privatisation of a very large number of the small SOEs and co-operative
enterprises, but there were no proper systems in place to ensure a rational
disposal of state assets. Even valuing state assets is a next-to-impossible
task, as, in the absence of a market for the property concerned, any administrative assessment of true value is at best guesswork and at worse a corrupt tool to ensure the speedy disposal of public assets at giveaway prices
to favoured recipients.[71] This process led to many allegations of peculation
and corruption. Further, even though the policy of 'letting go the small'
has removed many of them from effective state control, the large SOEs still
dominate heavy manufacturing, engineering, petro-chemicals, oil and the
utility sector as well as aviation, banks, insurance, financial services, railways and telecommunications. None of these sectors has been strengthened by the marketisation promoted by the Premier. The financial results
of the remaining SOEs continue to worsen and many commentators consider that the impact of the WTO accession will trigger implosion.[72] Yet
another round of privatisation of up to 150,000 smaller SOEs and the
administrative consolidation of the remaining larger enterprises into 196
holding groups was mooted by the government in late 2003;[73] at this stage,
it is impossible to say if this policy will be implemented or what effect it will
have.

[70] OECD, *China in the world economy* pp. 22–3.
[71] 'The real worth of state-owned assets', *South China Morning Post*, 15 September 2003, and
'Unreal valuations revisited', *South China Morning Post*, 22 September 2003.
[72] Chang, *The coming collapse of China*, chapter 3.
[73] 'Market-driven directors sought for state firms', *South China Morning Post*, 8 October
2003.

The dangerously insolvent SOE sector has been funded by policy loans from China's state banks, which in their turn are also insolvent by internationally accepted criteria.[74] The state banks have 99 per cent of the domestic savings market, with the four largest controlling 75 per cent of the sector.[75] Chinese people have few choices when it comes to investment. They can deposit their savings with one of the four state banks, buy speculative investments in one of the stock exchanges[76] or they can keep the cash under the bed. China has one of the highest saving rates in the world, averaging 40 per cent of disposable income, equivalent to US$720.9 billion.[77] This great ocean of liquidity is then lent out by the state banks. However, the great majority of the bank loans are to the SOE sector; the private sector of the economy is effectively excluded from borrowing from the state banks. In 1999, the Chinese Central Bank (PBOC) admitted that 25 per cent of the loans were 'non-performing'. A year later, the PBOC explained that the bank had transferred US$157 billion of these non-performing loans to asset management companies. But even after this re-capitalisation programme the PBOC in 2000 announced that non-performing loans still comprised 25 per cent of the bank's assets. Thus, the re-capitalisation has achieved nothing and the problem continues to worsen.

However, the statistics provided by the PBOC are not accepted as an accurate reflection of the true insolvency of the state banks. In 1999, Standard and Poors opined that the true level of bad debts was 70 per cent. Deutsche Bank concluded that 50 per cent of the loans were bad debts. Accordingly, the true financial status of the state banks is that they are horribly insolvent. The picture becomes more alarming when it is appreciated that loans to the SOEs are not only rolled over indefinitely but that the total owed is actually continuing to increase, even excluding the unpaid compounded interest on existing loans, in order to make up the shortfall in the revenues of the SOEs. Thus, no matter what re-capitalisation of the banks takes place, the bad debts will continue to increase inexorably unless most of the SOEs are liquidated, the debts are converted to equity and the state completely re-capitalises the banks and partially recoups its outlay by effective privatisation. But these options are probably politically impossible.

---

[74] OECD, *China in the world economy.*   [75] Ibid. table 4 at p. 20.
[76] China's stock markets have a poor reputation, with frequent allegations of fraud practised by industry insiders to inflate share prices artificially. 'Landmark stock fraud trial ends', *South China Morning Post*, 2 April 2003.
[77] Ibid at p. 123.

By the end of 2003, yet another re-capitalisation of the state banks was being floated by the government, the third in four years. The new plan appears to be to reduce non-performing loans to 15 per cent and improve capital adequacy ratios from 5 per cent to 8 per cent. This might be financed by the government selling bonds to produce the cash to infuse the moribund banking sector. This attempt to correct the structural failures in the system is likely to fail, just like the previous attempts, because the haemorrhage of funds to insolvent SOEs cannot be reduced for fear of triggering their outright collapse.[78]

The true financial position of China's state banks is incomparably more serious than the position of the banks in Thailand, Indonesia and South Korea prior to the Asian financial crisis of 1997. By 2003, Standard and Poors considered that China's banks were the worst in Asia, with an estimated 50 per cent bad debts and a recovery rate of less than 20 per cent. Comparable figures for Australia were 3 per cent bad debts and a 70 per cent recovery rate. Many commentators, including the Director General of the WTO, are very concerned that China's state banks are vulnerable to a financial crisis caused by their policy of lending to SOEs and the unprecedented effect of domestic competition from foreign banks that will develop subsequent to WTO accession.[79] Since 2003, foreign banks have been able to conduct local currency business with Chinese companies; by 2007 they will be able to transact business with Chinese retail customers.[80] This will allow, for the first time, Chinese individual and private businesses to withdraw their vast deposits from state banks and place them with foreign institutions. This could lead to a liquidity crisis, with the state banks being unable to fund cash withdrawals or additional lending to the SOEs. If this were to occur, there would be a full-scale financial crisis, the dire effects of which cannot be overstated. Chang believes that such a crisis could lead to the collapse of the Chinese state.[81]

In order better to address the deep-seated and dangerous condition of the state banks, the government in April 2003 removed banking supervision from the purview of the People's Bank of China and established

[78] 'Massive bailout proposed for banks', *South China Morning Post*, 26 August 2003; 'Bank bailout will fail without deeper reform', *South China Morning Post*, 26 August 2003.

[79] Panitchpakoli Supachai and Mark Clifford, *China and the WTO: changing China, changing world trade*, Singapore: Wiley (2002), chapter 12 and epilogue.

[80] This was a key financial services market opening commitment made by China as part of its bilateral agreements with the US and EU that broke the log-jam in WTO Accession talks.

[81] Chang, *The coming collapse of China*.

the China Banking Regulatory Commission (CBRC), which is authorised to supervise and regulate banks, asset management companies, trust and investment companies and other deposit-taking institutions. The CBRC appears to be taking the inherited situation seriously and has said:

> The targeted banking institutions include: the top five banking organizations with highest Non Performing Loans (NPL) ratios; the banking organizations with a rising stock or ratio of the NPL; the top five banking organizations with highest expected loss ratio of non-credit assets; and the banking organizations that are noted for poor management of off-balance-sheet activities or involved in illegal or rule-breaking activities. The targeted bank customers refer to the customers whose outstanding balance of the NPLs exceeds one hundred million yuan, and who have five or more affiliated enterprises with the aggregate outstanding balance of loans exceeding one hundred million yuan.[82]

The CBRC's first annual report makes for sober reading as the list of problems revealed is both very frank and equally disturbing but at least the magnitude of the task ahead appears to be understood, especially as the government has a settled intention to list two of the state banks overseas to obtain new capital and to attempt to commercialise their operations, so as to compete with the foreign banks who will have full access to the Mainland market in 2007.[83]

However, administrative attempts to reduce the ratio of NPL to total assets may be creating a very undesirable consequence. Since the NPL cannot be reduced or disposed of, bank managers need to make new loans to increase total loan assets, so reducing the percentage of the NPL to that now larger total.[84] This has been achieved by reckless lending to the newly liberated real-estate market, especially for new apartments and offices. This appears to be creating a real-estate bubble of huge proportions financed by bank lending. Approximately US$100 billion in loans was poured into property development projects in China between January and August 2003, almost 50 per cent up on the same period in 2002. This sum is equivalent to the total investment in real property in Indonesia, Thailand and Malaysia combined in the decade prior to their financial collapse in 1997. The spending is nationwide, not simply limited to the most advanced eastern cities. Many suspect that the bubble

[82] CBRC Press release, 25 March 2003.
[83] See Setting a new stage in China's banking regulation and supervision, CBRC, 11 March 2004. http://www.cbrc.gov.cn/english/.
[84] 'Mody's report: Nation to continue banking reform', *China Daily*, 9 June 2004.

is fuelled by corrupt land transactions between officials, developers and bank employees. In October 2003, the crisis deepened with the removal and probable arrest of the Minister of Land Resources on suspicion of corruption.[85] Should the property bubble burst, the already dreadful bad debt totals on state banks' books would spiral. If that were to happen, the consequences might be extremely serious.[86]

In response to the deteriorating inflation position and reports of wide and indiscriminate lending by the banks to finance real-estate projects, aluminium and cement plants (generally owned by local governments), the central authorities took heavy-handed action early in May 2004. The State Development and Reform Commission (SDRC) of the central government announced that local price-control agencies were empowered to control, by administrative means, 'excessive' price increases of over 4 per cent per annum and that new capital investment projects that might increase inflation were to be halted for three months.[87] In Guangdong, the Governor has announced that the construction of golf courses should be suspended, all development of new cement-manufacturing plants, government buildings, golf courses, exhibition centres, logistics parks and shopping malls would be reviewed and land-use policy and bank lending tightened.[88] In fact, the effect of this administrative 'signal' from government resulted in a complete suspension of all new bank lending nationwide for a limited time. This credit crunch might result in an economic soft-landing, but this is by no means certain. This Draconian use of blunt administrative fiat is hardly the act of a government committed to market solutions to economic problems. Pragmatically the central government may have had no choice but to act as it did. However, this throws into sharp relief the fact that China does not have a functioning market system; when the chips are down the government controls the economy by administrative order. Thus, it is legitimate to consider to what extent the government is really committed to allow the market, via competition, to act as the primary economic regulator, reserving to itself only macro-economic levers to adjust market conditions.

The economic challenges, particularly the condition of the SOEs and the dangerously exposed banking sector, have considerable implications for competition policy. These major components of the economy are presently in a weakened condition. The effect of increased competition

[85] 'Land minister is suspended for alleged graft', *South China Morning Post*, 22 October 2004.
[86] '$729bn flows into property projects', *South China Morning Post*, 25 September 2003.
[87] 'Mainland acts to keep price increases in check', *South China Morning Post*, 10 May 2004.
[88] 'Guangdong to restrict investment', *South China Morning Post*, 12 May 2004.

from external actors could trigger a disastrous economic crisis. The paradox is that without a more competitive environment, neither the banks nor the SOEs will have any incentive to effect substantive reform. The vital political and economic question is how competition can be introduced without causing the death of the patient. It will be argued that a comprehensive competition law cannot, of itself, solve these deep-rooted economic problems, but that without a workable and effective competition law and policy, the economic situation of the whole economy will worsen and a primary incentive to become more competitive will be lost. However, should a competition law be enacted, grave doubt exists as to whether it can be implemented.

Competition law is clearly no panacea for China's economic problems but it might form a valuable component in the ongoing reformation of the Chinese economic system, if implemented fairly and competently. This prescription is endorsed by the recent OECD Synthesis Report on China's accession to the WTO.[89] In addition to advising the adoption and effective implementation of a competition law, the Report also makes the following comments and policy recommendations to stabilise the structure of the economy and provide a sound basis for economic change:

- Credit allocation is inefficient and financial discipline weak. The solvency of financial institutions should be restored and the diversity of financial institutions should be encouraged to develop capital markets. The capital adequacy of institutions should be restored and regulatory barriers removed, allowing the development of domestic joint stock banks and greater foreign participation in the banking sector.
- Regional fragmentation is a serious problem. A development strategy with uniform national conditions and allowing internal capital mobility should be developed. Regional protectionist barriers should be removed and the central/local fiscal relations need to be reformed.
- Corporate governance reforms have had limited success. Remaining weaknesses in governance structures, whilst clarifying property rights and strengthening market incentives, need to be addressed. In the near term, improve independence and accountability of managers and boards of directors and remove restrictions on trading of SOE shares as soon as possible and take other steps over the longer term to improve financial market discipline.

---

[89] OECD, *China in the world economy.*

- Ambiguous property rights hamper corporate governance and mechanisms for business sector restructuring. Bankruptcy and other insolvency mechanisms are too weak to allow resources to be re-deployed from firms that are not competitively viable. Development of a coherent framework and supporting laws ensuring that property rights are well defined and apply equally to all economic segments. Establishment of a more uniform framework for insolvency and strengthen the autonomy and enforcement powers of bankruptcy courts. In the near term, clarify and strengthen the SOE rights to property and other assets; clarify rules governing use of and acquisition of state assets by non-state entities. Enact a comprehensive bankruptcy law with uniform rules and clear rights of debtors, creditors, and shareholders; clarify responsibility for the debt of failing enterprises to banks and social benefit funds so that they do not block exit.[90]
- Competition is uneven across sectors; anti-competitive practices and in some cases legal/regulatory frameworks impede entry or limit competition among incumbents. Development of a comprehensive framework for fostering competition nationwide with clear definition of the responsibilities of government agencies. In the near term, enact a comprehensive competition law; and establish a clear code of conduct sanctioning anti-competitive practices by government entities. Except for natural monopolies, open sectors now reserved for the SOEs to other enterprises.
- Weak financial discipline encourages misallocation of resources, weakens incentives of enterprises to operate efficiently and poses risks to financial stability. Strengthen the independence and capabilities of financial regulators/supervisors; improve the ability and incentives of financial institutions and markets to provide discipline. In the near term, restore solvency to financial institutions while continuing to improve their accountability for maintaining sound prudential standards. Move rapidly to strengthen enforcement powers of financial supervisors. Improve transparency and remove restrictions on financial markets that inhibit discipline.
- Laws and regulations are poorly and unevenly enforced. Strengthen the independence of the judiciary and clarify its jurisdiction. Reduce the judiciary's financial dependence on government and political

---

[90] See also Louis Putter Man, 'The role of ownership and property rights in China's economic transition', *China Quarterly*, 144 (1995), pp. 1047–64; Peter Ho, 'Who owns China's land? Policies, property rights and deliberate institutional ambiguity', *The China Quarterly*, 66 (2001), pp. 394–421.

authorities and strengthen the jurisdiction of courts over government agencies.[91]

Some of these issues have already been addressed above; others will be analysed below. All of these matters explain the particular economic circumstances of China and assist in understanding the complex and, in some respects, unique problems that confront Chinese policy makers when making decisions concerning economic regulation.

4.4 Government structures and personnel

4.4.1 Decentralisation

The constitution of the PRC stipulates that China is a unitary state and guarantees the primary role of the Communist Party in guiding the state. State power is organised on a central and local level. However, China is not a federation and theoretically all political power derives from the centre. Thus, political authority cascades from the centre to the periphery. The constitution insists, of course, that all state power is in the hands of the people.[92]

The People's government is organised in various levels. The Central People's government in Beijing has responsibility for all aspects of national policy. The provincial governments, municipal and county authorities theoretically implement national decisions at the local level whilst also amplifying the often-vague national policies and laws. The inherent conflict of the division of political power is one that has bedevilled decision-making and law enforcement in China; particularly since the reform process began in 1978.

The policy of decentralisation of political power after the disastrous experience of the later Mao years led to many provincial and local authorities ignoring or subverting the centre's political and economic commands. The policy of economic experimentation in the special economic zones and later the eastern coastal provinces led to undoubted economic gains but at the price of weakened political control and great confusion as to the pace of economic reform and the rule-making powers of local government. The interpretation of conflicting national and local regulations has been and remains a major practical problem for business. This has caused great uncertainty amongst the business community, as well as for

---

[91] Adapted from conclusions in Boxes 1 and 2, OECD, *China in the world economy*, p. 43.
[92] Art. 2, Constitution of the PRC as amended 15 March 1999.

lawyers, who often find it difficult, if not impossible, to give authoritative legal advice. This chaotic situation has to some extent been addressed by a new statute defining the distribution of law-making powers.[93] However, the situation remains highly confused.

The classic example of this political and economic waywardness was the provincial administration in Guangdong. This is the economic powerhouse of the Pearl River Delta region, adjacent to Hong Kong. By the mid-1990s, it had become almost *de facto* economically independent of the central government. This situation came about as a result of a political agreement between Deng Xiaoping and the provincial leaders, whereby they were allowed extensive economic autonomy in return for political loyalty, particularly after the Tiananmen Square events of 1989. Deng's Southern Tour of September 1992 praising capitalist production methods in Shenzhen and Guangdong reconfirmed economic reform and cemented the political accommodation allowing Guangdong extensive economic autonomy. However, this political consensus broke down in the mid-1990s as a result of the physical incapacity of Deng and the reassertion of effective political control by the centre consequent upon economic mismanagement, widespread corruption, excessive inflation and the insolvency of the Guangdong government borrowing and investment company, the Guangdong International Trust and Investment Corporation (GITIC). This entity had borrowed large sums from foreign banks in hard currency and in 1998 was peremptorily closed down by the central authorities, leaving foreign bankers exposed. The bankers maintained that lending to GITIC was equivalent to sovereign debt. The central government denied this and a confused liquidation process once again underscored the lack of clear political and legal regulation.[94]

The confusion of roles and imprecision between the legitimate authority of the various levels of government is compounded by the revenue question. Most tax and other sources of revenue in China, including the grant of valuable concessions or land use rights with the exception of customs duties, flows into the coffers of local or regional government. Central government revenue sources are very fragile and often dependent on revenue transfers from the richer provinces to the central treasury. This ill-defined process considerably weakens the central government's room

---

[93] Legislation Law enacted 15 March 2000.

[94] O'Neill, 'Crackdown on investment firms with bad loans cuts contagion effects; GITIC closure heralds Beijing resolve', *South China Morning Post*, 8 October 1998.

for manoeuvre and also is at the root of several other painful dilemmas in Chinese public administration.

Firstly, most public services are funded locally, including the local branches of national ministries as well as the system of People's Courts. This leads to the weakness or even the inability of the central government to enforce its economic policies at the local level. As most funding and personnel issues are in the gift of local politicians and not the national authorities, loyalties are often divided sharply. Secondly, local protectionism and AM, twin vices that are particularly pernicious in China and for which no effective remedy has yet been found by the national authorities, are also partly caused by the need of local government to ensure maximum revenues, which largely derive from the profits of the locally owned SOEs and taxes on local businesses. Weakening the local tax base by allowing freer internal trade is, therefore, fiercely opposed by local administrators as they fear a net loss of revenue. This situation explains the need for an overhaul of the public finance mechanism, so as to neutralise one of the reasons for local government opposition to a unified internal market. Mere legislative commands from far-away Beijing are unlikely to be an effective remedy for this aspect of the problem, given that China does not have the rule of law and in any case the local authorities control the People's Courts. Many previous regulations have been made to deal with this issue, all of which have been ineffective. Yet another legislative attempt will be made if the new anti-monopoly law is enacted. A whole section of the current draft anti-monopoly law is devoted to this subject but whether mere legal formulations will be effective to meet this challenge is open to serious doubt because the root of the problem is a complex matrix of political vested interest, revenue concerns and little regard for the rule of law. The issue is examined more closely below.

4.4.2 Dual control

In addition to the confused relationship between the central and local authorities, there is also the perplexing phenomenon of dual state and party control at every level of government and in every state-owned enterprise.

The structures of state power are exactly mirrored by the organisation of the Communist Party. This duplication of role and function ensures that the party's political role is enforced surreptitiously throughout all state institutions as well as through all other economic units owned by the state or held collectively. In practice, the role of the official state functionary and that of the party secretary are sometimes combined in one person but often are held by more than one individual; this can lead to serious conflicts within organisations between the official post holder and the party secretary. This phenomenon is carefully examined in relation to the steel industry in Steinfeld's study of the contemporary Chinese steel sector.[95]

This confusion as to lines of authority in government is deep rooted in post-1949 China. The confusion caused by contradictory laws and regulations, the arbitrary exercise of state power, the conflict inherent in the dual control of government and the SOEs, all contribute to the singular nature of the Chinese government machine. The structural weaknesses identified in this section have a direct bearing on the adoption and subsequent enforcement of any new anti-monopoly law in China. These peculiar institutional structures of China will make effective implementation of a competition law very problematic.

4.4.3 Personnel

A rather more prosaic issue is that of personnel and resources within the government machine, specifically whether China's civil servants would be capable of comprehending a competition law system and subsequently enforcing it. This is a critical matter in deciding whether, even if China does legislate in this area, such a law can be administered effectively and impartially. Leaving aside issues of corruption, it is competence and experience that will determine whether China is able successfully to legislate and implement a fully functioning competition system.

The drafting and legislative process is discussed in the next chapter. Problems are all too readily apparent there. But consideration also needs to be given to the capacity of human resources. Many of China's civil servants are relics of the state-planning era and have little or no formal education in market economics. Even fewer have a legal education that would equip them with the necessary intellectual tools to manipulate the complex factual, economic or legal issues concerned in competition analysis.

Most graduating Chinese students want to find employment in the private or foreign-owned sector; government service even in the main cities is, at best, seen as a way to make good contacts within the government machine before leaving to seek one's fortune in business. Salaries are very low, structures rigid and highly orientated to deferential obedience and

---

[95] Steinfeld, *Forging reform in China.*

promotion is based on seniority and loyalty, rather than merit. Thus, the government does not necessarily attract the highest-calibre students, though, of course, some very able recruits do enter government service with a genuine public service ethic. Notwithstanding poor initial pay and conditions, such individuals hope that they might rise quickly in the bureaucracy, which desperately needs to improve its level of competence in a fast-changing, internationalising and ever more complex administrative environment. Older cadres who dominate the higher reaches of the civil service, however, are often in post for historical political loyalty and not because of ability; the concept of accelerated promotion is not much in evidence in China. For example, none of the ministers in the State Council is under fifty years of age[96] and most of them are sixty. Further, it should be remembered that, in China, there is no separation between overtly political posts and administrative civil-service-type positions; there is a seamless promotion and transition process between party, bureaucracy (which includes the judiciary) and ministerial office, for which seniority and (sometimes) merit are the determining factors.

On a philosophical level, most civil servants are officially aligned to the CCP doctrine of the 'socialist market'; intellectual gymnastics of a sophisticated kind are needed to reconcile socialism with market competition. A lack of real philosophical commitment to a market-based, as opposed to a heavy-handed governmental regulatory role, is probably as serious and pernicious a problem as lack of formal education. Without a real belief in markets, any competition regime runs the risk of overt manipulation to achieve government-mandated, as opposed to market, solutions to economic problems.

It should be borne in mind that China's civil service is of considerable antiquity and the current organisation clearly still identifies with the Imperial civil service of the past. The mindset of government in China is that of an obligation to active government, in the sense that government in China equals not only the ability but the right to command and control all aspects of public life: what is not specifically allowed by government, is prohibited. By way of example, until recently Chinese citizens had no freedom to choose their employment, contract a marriage or place of residence without permission. Ownership of any significant private property or engaging in business was prohibited. Economic activity was the prerogative of the state plan, not of individual initiative. China's neo-Confucian

---

[96] For details of senior PRC government personnel see http://english.peopledaily.com.cn/ data/organs/statecouncil.shtml.

mindset of enforced social harmony and the paternalistic role of the state as guardian and guide of the 'broad masses' is deeply embedded in the government psyche. Clearly, this world-view is fundamentally at odds with the ideology of economic liberalism that accepts the chaotic but creative process of competition as the principal economic regulator.

A cynic, or perhaps a realist, might suggest that China's apparent acceptance of markets is superficial and they have been allowed as a necessary evil to assist China to accumulate the necessary wealth and power to regain the motherland's rightful place in the galaxy of nations, namely as the central kingdom. Private domestic business and foreign direct investment and their participation in the domestic market are tolerated by government in order to attain that goal. However, the lack of control over domestic private markets is deeply unsettling and problematic to China's bureaucracy. Competition law may well provide just the tool required to reassert official control over the private economy, whilst loudly proclaiming adherence to the notion of markets and competitive processes. Competition law may also be used to ensure a level of protection to the SOE and assist in the creation of national champions to fulfil a national industrial policy. Competition law, of the EC model, provides broad open-textured language capable of wide legitimate interpretation, substantial powers to proscribe conduct and the right to impose penalties. This instrument may be the means to reassert official control lost during the years of economic experimentation since 1978; in other words, this may be the means by which the Empire strikes back.

Thus, at one level, the traditionally minded civil servant might welcome a competition law that allows the true rulers of China to regain their diminished economic authority that has been attenuated by economic change;[97] other officials may actually be convinced of the need for markets and the adoption of a competition law to police them in a fair, transparent and unobtrusive manner. However, one will only be able to come to a conclusive conclusion after the adoption and implementation of any new legislation. Thus, even if China does not harbour these Machiavellian[98] ulterior motives for competition law adoption, it must remain a very open question as to whether China's governmental institutions or its civil servants do, at present or probably for the foreseeable

---

[97] 'Triumph of a 1,000-year-old bureaucracy', *South China Morning Post*, 7 June 2004.
[98] Niccolo Machiavelli, *The Prince*, ed. Quentin Skinner and Russell Price, Cambridge University Press (1988).

future, have sufficient commitment or capacity successfully to operate a comprehensive competition regime in good faith.

4.5 Law making

The origin of the PRC's current legal system can be traced back to the adoption of the first constitution in 1954. Currently, primary legislative power is exercised by the National People's Congress (NPC) and its Standing Committee. Theoretically all power belongs to the people.[99] However, China does not adopt the Western doctrine of separation of powers and the constitution does not recognise the need for a system of checks and balances between the legislative, executive and judicial branches of government. The constitution provides that the NPC and local people's congresses should be the dominant power centre. Nationally the NPC is the ultimate organ of the state's power and the Standing Committee is its permanent manifestation. In reality, the NPC has over 3,000 deputies and meets for only two weeks in March every year. Most legislative activity is undertaken by the Standing Committee or via delegated legislation by the State Council, the executive arm of the central government.

Law-making powers in China are distributed on the basis of a hierarchy. At the apex is the NPC and its Standing Committee, next comes the executive central government known as the State Council and the base of the pyramid is formed by local people's congresses and their standing committees. This hierarchy was confirmed by the new Legislation Law enacted in 2000.[100] Constitutionally, the NPC is the only organ allowed to enact basic laws (which are not defined) and to amend the constitution. It has a supervisory role and it can also delegate authority to the Standing Committee and State Council to promulgate secondary legislation.[101] The Standing Committee has approximately 150 members and it is elected by, and responsible to, the NPC.[102] Only NPC deputies can serve on this Standing Committee, and this is a full-time appointment.

---

[99] Art. 2 Constitution of the PRC. Recent political demonstrations in Hong Kong since the publication of the central government's refusal to allow universal suffrage in both coming elections has prompted the use of the slogan 'Return Power to the People'. Apparently this phrase in Chinese is deeply offensive to the CCP, who had adopted this epithet as a revolutionary slogan decades ago. Democrats in Hong Kong may agree to drop its use to placate Beijing if a rapprochement between the government and the democrats occurs. *South China Morning Post*, 11 June 2004.

[100] Enacted on 15 March 2000 and effective 1 July 2000. It is too soon to say whether this attempt to bring order to the chaotic law-making system will function effectively.

[101] Art. 62, Constitution of the PRC.   [102] Ibid. Arts. 65, 66 and 68.

Regular meetings are held for approximately ten days every two months. A small subcommittee handles day-to-day matters. The Standing Committee also has administrative support from a secretariat and a Legal Affairs Commission that prepares briefing documents and drafts some statutory provisions. Unfortunately, many regulatory matters are drafted by individual ministries and thus the quality of legislative drafting varies considerably. There is no core Parliamentary Counsel-type office to ensure consistency and uniformity of usage or language. Thus, many laws are vague and inconsistent either by design or by default.

The precise division of competence between the NPC and its Standing Committee remains unclear. Recently, China adopted a Legislation Law, as mentioned above, but it is too soon to tell whether this new dispensation will prove effective. The law provides that legal superiority should descend in accordance with the level of the legislative enactment. Thus, constitutional rules will trump all other legislative enactments, law enacted by the NPC will override rules or regulations made by the State Council or local people's congresses and local regulations will be subordinate to all legislation enacted by higher state organs. Whilst this structure is theoretically sound, it is impossible to say whether it will prove effective in practice. Previous experience militates against a satisfactory outcome, especially as local courts will have the job of resolving legislative conflicts and, as will be seen, they are incapable of acting independently of their local-authority sponsors. Thus, where conflicts arise, it is highly likely that local legislation will still be regarded as the determining legal provision. In a recent well-publicised case,[103] a local judge, Li Huijuan, in Henan province in central China applied the provisions of the national legislation law to a dispute between two local seed companies. She preferred the relevant national law to a conflicting provincial law. The Provincial People's Congress reacted furiously, denouncing her verdict as 'illegal . . . and an encroachment on the function of the legislative body'. She was subsequently removed from her post by the Provincial High Court. In a comment on the case, a Beijing university law professor opined that whilst the judge's verdict was a correct statement of the law, she had no constitutional power to declare the local regulation invalid due to its contradiction of the national law. She should have referred the issue to the NPCSC, who alone had power to rule on the validity of legislation. This episode neatly exemplifies the limit of judicial power in China and the complete control by political organs of the judicial branch of government. The case also highlights the fact

---

[103] 'Judge sows seeds of lawmaking dispute', *China Daily*, 24 November 2003.

that there is neither separation of powers nor judicial security of tenure in China. Further, it illustrates the point that conflicts between local and national laws are still extensive.

However, the existing legislative arrangements in China have undoubtedly improved substantially since the commencement of the reform process in 1978. Law making is now considerably more professional; the number and quality of draftsmen available and the educational attainment of Chinese legislators has markedly improved. The importance of a more transparent, logical and professional approach to the construction of a comprehensive legal system has been appreciated by the government as a necessary precondition for an effective market-based economy. The construction of a comprehensive and rational legal corpus is proceeding but will take many years to complete. Politically, the NPC has a reputation of being little more than a rubber stamp; its credentials as an effective legislative and supervisory organ have still to be proved.

4.6 The legal system, the courts and lawyers

China's legal system will be a vital component in ensuring that any future competition law can be effectively enforced. Without a suitably advanced legal culture, a mature and sophisticated judicial system with well-educated and honest judges and a highly educated, skilled and professional cadre of lawyers, no competition law system can hope to succeed. The question to be addressed in this section is whether China possesses such a system and the personnel to staff it.

4.6.1 Concepts underlying the legal system in China

In Imperial China, law was principally concerned with punishments for the infraction of the criminal code. Law in China has a very long pedigree. Legalism as a philosophical model for the organisation of the state began over 2,500 years ago. Guan Zong (645 BC) stated that: 'The ruler is the creator of the law. The ministers are the keepers of the law and the people are the object of the law.' The Legalist system was concerned with coercive measures to compel compliance with the law; subjects were expected to obey because of fear of punishment, not out of loyalty to the ruler or respect for the laws of god. Officials were also expected to obey without question. As Shang Yan (338 BC) noted: 'Officials are responsible for maintaining the law and performing duties but those who act in violation of the law of the king should be executed without the possibility of pardon:

that punishment should also be extended to members of their families to the third degree.' To emphasise the autocratic nature of all Imperial instructions to civil servants, orders to them always ended with the advice 'Tremble and obey!'

It is interesting to ponder how different the Chinese state is today from the Imperial autocracy of two millennia ago. The government has continued to emphasise that it wishes to perfect a rule-by-law system (*yifa zhiguo*) as opposed to a rule-by-man system (*renzhi*). However, this emphasis is a reaction to the disastrous personality-dominated arbitrary rule of Mao and the Gang of Four in the 1960s and 1970s. In 1998, at the annual meeting of the NPC, President Jiang Zeming confirmed that the objective of the Central Government was to build a complete legal system for the PRC by 2010. This does not imply acceptance of a rule-of-law system on Western lines with separation of government powers, independent courts and actual respect for individual rights when they conflict with government interest. In the 1999 revision of the Constitution, the phrase *yifa zhiguo* was used for the first time and gives the impression of ruling through law or by law. However, it also implies continued subordination of law to the exercise of state power.[104]

It is extraordinary that over these millennia the mindset of China's leaders seems to have maintained a remarkably consistent notion of the proper ambit of law – namely a coercive instrument of state power. If this is so, there can be little confidence that an anti-monopoly law will not be administered in this way should a competition regime be enacted. There is little evidence of any substantial change in traditional attitudes, in fact quite the opposite, and those who hold the levers of power now and for the foreseeable future will be quite unwilling or unable to shrug off the weight of historical precedent. This conception of law and the ambit of state power are antithetical to Western notions of the proper interface between exercise of power and the role of law and its disinterested administration.

Formally China's legal system adopts the civilian model. This follows from the transplantation of amended European civilian codes by the Republican government in the 1920s and 1930s. This system was abrogated in 1949 with the establishment of the PRC. However, China still considers itself part of the civilian family of law; it is clearly not a common law

---

[104] See Pitman Potter, B. 'The Chinese legal system: continuing commitment to the primacy of state power', *China Quarterly*, 159 (1999) p. 674; Leila Choukroune, 'Rule of law through internationalisation: the objective of the reforms', *China Perspectives*, 40 (2002), pp. 7–21; Chen Jian-fu, 'Implementation of law as a politico-legal battle in China', *China Perspectives*, 43 (2002), pp. 26–39. See also the Henan seed case mentioned above.

system. The role of the court has long been seen as that of the application of the law in individual cases; judges have no special authority as regards interpretation of the written law. In fact, the PRC constitution specifically states that interpretation of the constitution or of any statute is a matter for the Standing Committee of the NPC.[105] This subordination of the court to the political sovereign is also of very long pedigree. The Legalist School took the view that there was little difference between laws, regulations and administrative orders. Imperial officials doubled-up as judicial officers; there was no separate cadre of judges. The fixed schedule of punishments was not designed to limit arbitrary power but rather to implement the imperial will. Thus, officials had as little discretion in legal matters as possible. Adjudication of cases was simply another aspect of government activity; deciding what the law meant was the prerogative of the sovereign, not subordinate officials. There was no special training in law and the judicial function deserved no special respect or elevated status.

Unlike common law courts, Chinese courts have no power to interpret law; that role is reserved to the NPC.[106] The role of the NPC in determining what the law means in China was dramatically demonstrated in the cause célèbre of the Hong Kong Immigrant Children Case.[107] Hong Kong was established as a Special Administrative Region (SAR) of the PRC on 1 July 1997 following the 1984 Joint Declaration between the United Kingdom and the PRC. The Declaration was implemented by the enactment of a mini-constitution for HKSAR by the central government: the Basic Law (BL) of HKSAR. It recognised *inter alia* the right of independent adjudication of all legal cases that arose in Hong Kong. Under the BL, certain persons were recognised as permanent residents of Hong Kong, including children of such residents. Many thousands of these children who were resident in other parts of China prior to 1997 claimed that the BL now entitled them to emigrate to the HKSAR, which they had not been entitled to do under the previous colonial dispensation. The HKSAR government imposed emergency influx control by ordinance that limited their right of entry and settlement. The affected persons applied to the court for a declaration that the immigration scheme was contrary to their rights as permanent residents within the meaning of the Basic Law. The case continued to the Hong Kong Court of Final Appeal (CFA),

---

[105] See Art. 67 of the Constitution and Art. 42 of the Legislation Law.
[106] Ibid.
[107] *Na Ka Ling & Others v Director of Immigration* (1999) 2 HKCFAR 4; *Ng Siu Tung & Others v Director of Immigration* [2002] 1 HKLRD 561.

the successor body to the Privy Council. The CFA ruled in favour of the children and struck down the immigration ordinance as contrary to the BL, declaring that the wording of the BL was clear and unambiguous. The HKSAR government disagreed with the court's interpretation of the BL and under Article 159 of the BL referred the matter to the NPCSC in Beijing for 'Interpretation'. The NPCSC, using highly dubious means, ruled that the clear words of the BL did not mean what they said and had to be read in the context of a political declaration of a non-competent body made five years after the enactment of the BL. This saga clearly showed that judicial independence in the interpretation of law is not accepted by the central government; indeed the NPCSC opined that the HKSAR courts should have referred the interpretative decision to them by way of a preliminary reference before seeking to apply the law to the instant case. Thus, it is clear that when legal rights clash with government interest in China, the official interest will always trump an individual right because a political body, controlled by the CCP, is the ultimate arbiter of legal meaning in China. This case demonstrates that even when the political settlement of the HKSAR and its insulation from the Chinese legal system is at stake, along with investor confidence, government interest will always have a higher priority. No clearer demonstration of the role of law in contemporary China can be given.

Remarkably, the historical view of the role of law and of judicial officers remains readily apparent in the contemporary Chinese system. Consequently, it is clearly open to doubt as to whether such a system can deliver sound and reliable adjudication on the complex issues involved in competition law disputes which will inevitably also include politically sensitive issues such as rights of monopoly SOEs and the rights of private and foreign enterprise to compete in the Chinese market. It must be acknowledged that the systematic subordination of law to state interest is so deep seated in the Chinese psyche that impartial adjudication seems very unlikely to be achieved in the foreseeable future.

4.6.2 Lawyers

Law itself and the nascent legal profession was effectively subverted in 1959. The Anti-Rightist political movement was designed to secure Mao's hold on all levers of power and law was seen as unnecessary to achieve his political objectives. University law departments were closed down, courts became simply the forum for political deviants to admit their guilt publicly and receive the imposition of punishment. Judges were appointed for their class credentials; a university education in any subject was sufficient to disqualify one from appointment as it indicated a bourgeois background and political unreliability. This attitude to law was quite disastrous.

By 1978 according to official figures,[108] China had only 212 qualified lawyers in the whole country, all of whom were geriatric survivors of the previous years of political disfavour and had received their legal training prior to 1949. All the others had been 'liquidated' as class enemies or re-educated. Legal study was only revived in 1978, thus even the most prestigious law school in China has little more than twenty-five years of contemporary history. The loss of two generations of legal personnel is the fundamental reason for the lack of qualified senior personnel in contemporary China. It also partly explains the weaknesses in the Chinese legal system as a whole.

Legal education in China is now conducted at most national and provincial-level universities. An undergraduate degree takes four years of full-time study, a master's degree a further three years. Selection to China's university is via a national university entrance examination; only about 2 per cent of school leavers can expect to enter a university.[109] The system is highly selective and rote learning is a major component of all education in China. Application of law by problem solving is relatively rare. Qualification as a lawyer is based on success in the nationally administered Lawyers' Examination, for which no university degree is required nor is any undergraduate or post-graduate study of law. The examination is essentially a memory test of multiple-choice questions. Thus, to become a lawyer merely requires an excellent memory and a good knowledge of orthodox political thought, which is also an integral part of the examination. There is no training in lawyers' skills or any system of practical training. Passing the examination grants immediate access to legal practice. In 1999, China had 110,000 qualified lawyers, only 50 per cent of whom had a bachelor's degree in law and only about 4,000 of whom were officially qualified to deal with foreign-related work.[110] Needless to say, the quality of lawyers in China varies dramatically.

The 1996 Lawyers Law attempted to clarify the status of lawyers, who until that time were officially described as 'state legal workers'. They worked directly in government departments or the SOE or legal collective

---

[108] Speech by Jia Wugong of the PRC Ministry of Justice, June 2000.
[109] *China Statistical Year Book*, Beijing (2000).
[110] See speech by Jia Wugong above.

units; private practice for profit was illegal. Subsequent to the new law, lawyers could form partnership businesses, but this has only been so for the last eight years. Firms are on average very small by Western commercial standards, the largest employing about twenty lawyers. Legal experience is limited by the nature of the education system and the lack of comprehensive training. In time, the situation will improve as many major foreign commercial firms have recruited PRC-qualified lawyers to prepare for an expansion of China-related business, and the pursuit of a foreign legal qualification is a prize eagerly sought by most talented Chinese law students.

Collectively, lawyers do have a representative body, the All China Lawyers Association; it formally represents lawyers' interests but is not a functioning professional body as it has no control over entry to the profession or any disciplinary functions. These matters are entirely in the hands of the Ministry of Justice, which sets admission standards, the national qualification examination and administers a disciplinary system. Thus, the profession is not independent of the government in any meaningful way but at least lawyers as a whole are no longer seen as civil servants. However, the depth and range of experience, the professional independence and sophistication of lawyers make it difficult to believe that the very complex issues of competition law could be competently advised upon by the vast majority of Chinese lawyers. Recently, the poor conduct of lawyers and quality of much legal advice in China was highlighted by the Beijing Justice Bureau. Poor or non-existent service provision, even after payment of fees in advance, was a serious problem as, indeed, was corruption. Lawyers who bribed judges for favourable verdicts were not uncommon. Zhao Dacheng, the responsible official at the Ministry of Justice, opined that much of the profession suffers from 'inept management and lacks credibility'. [111] Therefore, whether in government service or acting for enterprises the range, quantity and quality of legal advice must be highly suspect. Only four or five thousand lawyers in the whole country are competent to deal with 'foreign' law, which is shorthand for commercial literacy; the number who have even heard of competition law would probably number less than several hundred.

Thus, again the capacity of the Chinese system to administer a comprehensive competition regime adequately must be open to very serious doubt. There are grave deficiencies that cannot be adequately remedied without considerable allocation of very scarce resources of qualified

---

[111] 'Beijing to tighten rein over lawyers', *China Daily*, 12 April 2004.

teachers and practitioners to training a cadre of lawyers to administer any new competition law system.

4.6.3 The court system and judges

The formal structure of People's Courts resembles a Western hierarchical model – Basic, Intermediate, Higher and the Supreme Court[112] and so appears to mirror Western models. But appearances are very deceptive in China. The national Ministry of Justice formally controls the court system but in reality it is administered on a local level by the ministry branches at provincial, prefectural and county level. All funding and personnel matters are decided and funded locally. The judiciary is not independent of government either theoretically, formally, administratively or managerially; the courts are simply another part of the People's Government. As a result of local funding, decisions are habitually subject to overt and covert interference by local political interests and individual decisions considered 'sensitive' are never made by the judges who hear the case but by the adjudication committee, chaired by the Party Secretary of the judicial administration who may or may not be officially a judge.

In addition to this institutional structure, which inhibits impartiality, lack of competence and corruption are endemic within the system. Most judges have no legal education or training whatsoever. A recent example was the appointment in 1998 of a new presiding judge in the Higher People's Court of a major city in east China, a very high-profile position with many vitally important commercial disputes to adjudicate in one of China's largest and most cosmopolitan cities. The appointee was a trade union official who deserved promotion. Unfortunately, no position of suitable seniority in the bureaucratic hierarchy was vacant, except for the chief judge's post. Thus, he was appointed but unfortunately had no legal knowledge at all; he promptly enrolled at a local university for a course of evening classes.[113]

Lack of any knowledge of law may also be compounded by corruption. Numerous cases have come to light of corrupt appointment of highly unsuitable persons. The impact of overt corruption is clearly a problem as the Judges Law forbids *inter alia* lawyers meeting judges about forthcoming cases, treating judges to dinners and the giving of presents. Cases of corrupt practices are legion and appear frequently in national

---

[112] Organic Law of the People's Court adopted in 1954, amended 1979 and 1983.
[113] This information was imparted to the author by academic sources in China.

newspapers. For example, in 2002 the former President of Liaoning Higher People's Court was dismissed from the CCP for corrupt practices for accepting bribes worth the equivalent of millions of US$ and taking advantage of his position to allow his son to earn illegal profits.[114] Another recent case involved the former president of the Guangdong Higher People's Court who was arrested for accepting bribes worth in excess of US$ 1 million.[115] Domestic critics are fierce in the denunciation of the quality of Mainland justice: 'China's courts remain as corrupt as ever. It is well known that lawyers act as the white glove of the judges and collect lots of money under the table and sell their decisions to whomever pays the highest price.'[116] Many judicial posts are filled by retired army officers whose primary function is to punish criminals. Such appointees' ability to handle complex commercial matters such as competition law is clearly dubious in the extreme. Further, the abysmally low official salaries are sure to promote corrupt practices to facilitate even a modest lifestyle. Salaries may be only US$200 to 300 per month. This level of pay is completely inadequate to attract high-calibre candidates, who can earn ten or twenty times as much in private legal practice. Thus, again, the capacity of most Chinese judges to adjudicate competition cases would be weak or non-existent.

The inherent weaknesses in court structure and personnel have not gone unrecognised by the central government. An unprecedented rise in complaints from the public about judicial corruption in the late 1990s led to a year-long nationwide 'rectification campaign' in 1998.[117] In that year, 2,512 judges were disciplined for malpractice; the figure had dropped to 1,080 in 2001.[118] In June 2003, the Supreme Court issued a

---

[114] 'Top official thrown out of party for corruption', *South China Morning Post*, 17 September 2002.

[115] 'Guangdong court chief faces graft claims', *South China Morning Post*, 24 October 2002.

[116] Li Baiguang, Director of the Beijing Residents' Research Centre, quoted in 'APEC report accused of glossing over faults', *South China Morning Post*, 4 June 2004.

[117] The plethora of 'inspections' by the Supreme Court Disciplinary Department and the Ministry of Justice, not to mention those conducted by the CCP Discipline and Inspection Office, are all rather reminiscent of the plot of Nikoli Vasilievich Gogol's masterpiece *The Government Inspector* (1836). The play satirises the consternation caused to the corrupt local officials of a nameless Russian town by the rumour of the imminent arrival of an incognito Imperial inspector. The venal functionaries flatter and bribe the person they believe to be their nemesis for a favourable report to higher authority but the joke is that he is not the real inspector at all but rather a penniless traveller. The *bona fide* inspector arrives just as the impostor departs. For a new English translation see http://www.methuen.co.uk/governmentinspectormse.html.

[118] 'Supervision mechanism set up to supervise judges', *China Daily*, 9 October 2002.

thirteen-article judicial conduct code,[119] which yet again exhorted judges not to:

- Torture prisoners to extract confessions.
- Manufacture evidence.
- Abuse their powers to violate the rights of litigants.
- Accept bribes.
- Accept free meals.
- Engage in profit-seeking business ventures.
- Secretly meet with litigant's lawyers.

However, these exhortations appear to have had little effect. In January 2004, Wuhan Central China, the city's Intermediate Court President, apologised for thirteen of his judicial colleagues who had been condemned for corruption; two of the most senior were later imprisoned for periods of thirteen years and six and a half years respectively. In April 2004, the head of the 'inspection group' of the Supreme Court exhorted judges not only to abide by the new code of conduct but also not to allow 'their spouses, children and immediate staff' to interfere with the administration of justice and to avoid nepotism.[120] By June 2004, the Minister of Justice and the Chief Justice of the Supreme Court were, yet again, proposing a crackdown on corrupt judges. The persistence of the problem was attributed to low official salaries and the large differential between judges' pay and the profits of private practice.[121] In order to try to improve judicial quality and to recruit more suitably qualified judges, the Chief Justice has mooted the appointment of rich, older lawyers, rather than ex-army officers or callow fresh graduate students as career judges; he referred to this practice as traditional in common law jurisdictions.[122] He also suggested substantially increasing official salaries to attract and retain talented personnel; however, he did not specify where the resources to finance these reforms would be found.[123]

Another basic flaw in the Chinese court system is the very great difficulty or impossibility of enforcing a judgement against a resisting

[119] 'Code issued for preventing corruption among judges', *China Daily*, 20 June 2003.
[120] 'Judges slated for stricter scrutiny', *China Daily*, 8 April 2004.
[121] 'Judge: "bad apples" don't spoil court', *China Daily*, 12 January 2004.
[122] Perhaps the Chinese Chief Justice should consult the British Lord Chancellor who has some little experience in these matters. For details of the English process of judicial appointments see http://www.dca.gov.uk/judicial/appointments/jappinfr.htm.
[123] 'Lawyer–judge relation needs to be regulated', *China Daily*, 5 June 2004.

defendant.[124] Enforcement has to take place in the place of domicile of the debtor. Local courts often simply refuse to recognise a 'foreign' judgement; that is, one made by a court outside the judicial district. If the judgement is recognised, local institutions and court officers will often refuse to co-operate in the seizure of assets. This can often be as a result of overt political protection of an important local business interest or a well-connected individual. This phenomenon is well documented and a fundamental impediment to a functioning judicial system. A respected Chinese legal scholar Cao Si-yuan has argued that businesses, whether foreign or Chinese, have a less than 1 per cent chance of enforcing a judgement against a defeated opponent in its home judicial district. He attributed this to local protectionism – judges support local firms because they are employed and paid by local government.[125] Doubtless the enforcement of competition rulings would suffer the same fate. Improvement in this aspect of the Chinese system is a vital component in building an effective judicial machine.

It is abundantly clear that if a satisfactory adjudicatory system for competition law cases were to be established, selection and training of a cadre of competent lawyers and judges would be a condition precedent to the effective operation of the system. This will be a complex, slow and expensive operation but it must be carried out before any effective system could be introduced. Thus, it remains to be seen if China has the understanding of the complex nature of the systemic, legislative, administrative and personnel matters needed to administer competition law adequately. Further, China also requires the political will and the resources to fund a large-scale undertaking, never mind access to sufficient expertise, either foreign or domestic, to operationalise a competition law. Whether China can fulfil these pre-conditions is very much an open question.[126]

4.7 Administrative Monopoly and local protectionism

This governmental system also generates another Chinese phenomenon – Administrative Monopoly. This can be defined as the misuse by government, at all levels, of administrative powers, both legal and extralegal, to promote, manipulate, impede or prevent economic activities.

---

[124] Donald Clarke, 'The execution of civil judgements in China', *The China Quarterly* (141) (1995), pp. 65–79.

[125] 'Foreign companies "Can't win in courts"', *South China Morning Post*, 20 January 2003.

[126] All of the matters mentioned in this section are amplified by Donald J. Lewis in 'Governance in China: the present and the future tense', in Brahm, *China's century*.

Administrative Monopoly is very widespread and is regarded as pernicious by most Chinese writers[127] as it inhibits the rational distribution and use of economic resources and causes enormous waste and duplication. Examples of AM include differential taxation applied to goods from outside the 'home' territory, outright boycotts of 'foreign' goods, physical blockades at provincial or municipal boundaries, the use of administrative permits in a discriminatory fashion, orders to all state business answerable to the local government only to purchase supplies from local manufacturers. Forced tie-in sales of unrelated goods to benefit favoured producers and discriminatory administrative directions to local state banks to support local state enterprises with credits are also common. Further, abuses include the creation of profit-seeking enterprises within the local government structure which also act as the local administrative organs responsible for regulating a particular trade; needless to say such an inherent conflict of interest would clearly damage competition.[128]

Actual examples of AM are easy to find throughout China. In Shanghai, to the author's personal knowledge, every taxi that plies for trade is of the same model, the Santana – an outdated Volkswagen sedan that was unsuccessful in Europe in the 1980s. Shanghai's municipal government controls the Shanghai Automotive Industrial Corporation, a state-owned vehicle manufacturer. Several years ago the German automotive giant Volkswagen set up a joint-venture operation in Shanghai with the local firm to produce the Santana. To ensure that sales from the favoured producer would be satisfactory, the local government in Shanghai, a city/region of in excess of 13 million people, produced two regulations. The first decreed that only Santana cars would be licensed for use as taxis in the region and the second that all 'foreign' automobiles – that is, cars manufactured outside the Shanghai municipal area, but sold in Shanghai – would be subject to higher car-licensing fees and an additional sales tax. These measures added about 10 per cent to the purchase price. Both measures were at odds with national 'free trade' policies, they reduce choice

[127] Zhang Shufang, *Analysis of administrative monopoly and legal measures that can be taken to counter it*, 4 CASS Journal of Law (1999); Shi JiChun, *Definition and regulation of administrative monopoly in China*, 3 Frontiers of Jurisprudence (1999), Law Publishing House, Beijing; Wang Xiaoye, *Studies in competition law*, Beijing: China Legal System Press (1999).

[128] Judge Chen Hu of the Higher People's Court, Beijing, in a speech given to a conference jointly hosted by the Court and the Institute of European Affairs, Chinese Academy of Social Science held at Beijing on 19 June 2004.

and increased cost for consumers and are a blatant example of local protectionism.[129]

Other abuses of administrative power can also be found in the service sector. China Telecom, the national telephony provider, had a policy of requiring new telephone service subscribers to purchase the handset from it before Telecom would agree to install a telephone line. The local gas monopoly also had a similar policy with regard to the supply of gas to consumers who were required to buy a cooker before gas could be laid on. These tie-in sales were outside their legally granted monopoly; in law consumers were entitled to purchase equipment from whomever they chose. Interestingly in this case, also in Shanghai, the municipal government intervened on behalf of the consumer and sought to enforce the current Anti-Unfair Competition Law. The consumers, backed by local officials, here succeeded in forcing the monopolists to back down. The consumers won because these two monopolists are nationally accountable and so the municipal government had no vested interest to protect. It may be that the political kudos of protecting local consumers and the possible promotion of local equipment suppliers trumped the political influence of the national monopolists.

These examples are merely emblematic of a chronic problem that is found throughout China. Local protectionism has very serious implications. Firstly, it props up local uneconomic industries that generally produce lower quality and higher priced goods. Secondly, it prevents the efficiencies of economies of scale, as larger and more productive units cannot easily gain access to markets outside their local area and certainly not to the regional or national market. Thirdly, it prevents the establishment of nationally recognised branded goods or chain stores to the detriment of efficient companies seeking to develop national market penetration. Fourthly, the over-capacity inherent in such a structure prevents the rationalisation of the SOE as local governments may superficially comply with central government orders to close a local production unit but as soon as the government inspectors leave the locality, production is recommenced. Clearly, such sabotage of national policies by local politicians inhibits restructuring. It also leads to the continued haemorrhage of state bank funds to loss-making, inefficient, publicly owned businesses, which in turn leads to a shortage of funds for productive enterprises and an intensification of the insolvency problems of the banks themselves.

---

[129] Further examples of local protectionism can be found in Trish Saywell, 'China's city limits', *Far Eastern Economic Review*, 14 October 1999.

The duplication of industrial capacity, mentioned above, is a direct consequence of the Maoist policy of regional domestic self-sufficiency. The needs of strategic defence also played a part in the dispersal of industry – the so-called Third Front policy, whereby military defence in depth could be ensured by the ability of each region to supply itself with the war materiel needed for a defensive war. With the end of the isolationist Cold War mentality, China is still burdened with massive over supply of industrial capacity in many sectors. This hangover from the policies of the state plan and self-sufficiency is the root cause of local protectionism.[130]

The protectionist 'beggar-thy-neighbour' attitude prevalent in China is reminiscent of the protectionist policies of nation states in the 1930s during the Great Depression or the activities of individual states of the United States which led to the passage of the Federal Interstate Commerce Act to prevent internal protectionism. Another comparator is the European Union. It too had an overriding economic objective in the founding European Community (EC) Treaty,[131] to create a single, common market for goods, services, capital and labour.[132] However, myriad national rules and government policies inhibited the creation of a single market. After many years of near paralysis, the Court of Justice of the European Communities in the Casis de Dijon[133] decision quickened the pace of intra-European free trade. The Single Market Project in the 1980s that was prefigured by the adoption of the Single European Act 1986 also had internal trade liberalisation as its objective. The reduction of governmental restrictions of intra-European trade was reinforced by the active enforcement of the EC Treaty's competition provisions[134] as well as promotion of competition regimes at the national/member state level. The net effect of the removal of official barriers to trade, vigorous implementation of competition law and more active enforcement of the rules on

---

[130] In 1987, 80 factories in 21 provinces produced refrigerators, over 100 factories in 26 provinces produced televisions, and 300 factories in 28 provinces produced washing machines. This atomisation of production facilities shows how difficult it is to achieve economies of scale or national market penetration. This sectoral fragmentation may well have been reduced since 1987 but the underlying problem remains. *China: internal market development and regulation*, Washington, D.C.: World Bank (1984).

[131] Art. 2 EC Treaty as amended OJ C340, 10 November 1997.

[132] Ibid. Art. 3.

[133] *Rewe-Zentral AG v Bundesmonopolverwaltung fur Branntwein* (Case120/78) [1979] ECR 649.

[134] Arts. 81 and 82 EC as amended.

public procurement[135] and state aids[136] has been substantially to complete the creation of a single EU market. The result of the completion of the single market has been assessed by the EU Commission as increased employment, increased economic growth and reduced inflation;[137] these are benefits that China now seeks to emulate.

Thus, what the Chinese categorise as administrative monopoly is not the action of business enterprises but rather use of local government power to prevent the creation of a unified, single, internal market in China. It is, therefore, strictly a single market issue, not a competition matter. The relevance of the European experience has not been lost on the Chinese government. As will be seen later, the jurisprudence and policies of EU market integration have had a major influence on Chinese policy making.[138]

But can the beneficial outcome of trade liberalisation and increased economic welfare as seen in the EU be replicated in China?

Superficially, the attempt to remove government-created barriers to internal trade through the agency of the proposed anti-monopoly law would be an appealing one if it were able to create an integrated internal market in China. But the achievement of this felicitous outcome may be problematic, for several reasons. First, Europe is not China, not only in a geographic sense but also in terms of political, administrative and economic structures. Seeking to achieve the benefits of a single market strategy based on competition law alone is to betray a basic misconception as to the role of a competition statute. The true purpose of a competition law is to ensure that privately created barriers to competition are efficaciously dismantled. Government barriers to trade within a single unitary state require political reformation, especially in China, where numerous previous attempts to deal with the problem by central regulation have failed. Political, not legal, action is what is needed to remedy the problem. This brings into play the second major difference between the EU and China – the rule of law. China does not now and is unlikely to

---

[135] For example, the Directives on Public Works (71/305) and (93/36), Public Supplies (77/62) and (93/37), Public Services Procurement (92/50) and Public Utilities (93/98).

[136] Art. 87 EC as amended.

[137] Commission Report, *Impact and effectiveness of the single market* at http://europa.eu.int/comm/dg15/en/update/impact/smsumen.htm.

[138] This was confirmed by Zhang Chen Yang, Deputy Director of the Department of Treaty and Law, Ministry of Commerce, who is one of the leading members of the anti-monopoly law drafting committee in a speech give at a conference jointly hosted by the Court and the Institute of European Affairs, Chinese Academy of Social Science held at Beijing on 19 June 2004.

enjoy for the foreseeable future a competent and uncorrupted system for the administration of justice with concomitant respect for judicial independence and for judicial pronouncements that will be obeyed by erring local administrations. If the attempt to rein in unruly local authorities has failed for the last twenty years, it is unlikely that a new law will make a great deal of difference.

This view is confirmed by a senior government official responsible for enforcement of the existing regulations that in theory outlaw administrative monopoly. In respect of the prospects of a new competition law succeeding where the existing rules have failed, he said: 'Therefore, considering the failure of the [1993] Law, it is reasonable for us to expect that the actions of eliminating competition carried out by local government would still be a big challenge to enforce anti-trust law in the future. A competition authority would be hard to correct or punish the actions of local government [sic].'[139] Consequently, it can be seen that China's problems with market integration are, whilst not unique, more intractable due to the nature of political structures and weak adherence to the notion of the rule of law, as opposed to the rule of man. The Chinese judicial system can offer little assistance in overcoming the barriers erected by administrative monopoly, whereas in the EU the Court of Justice has taken a leading role in creating the single market.[140]

Whether a competition law in China can overcome the administrative monopoly problem is dubious, given the institutional, environmental and capacity problems illuminated above. Further, the administrative monopoly phenomenon demonstrates that China should not be viewed as a monolithic whole but rather as a loose confederation of economically separate fiefdoms, with an outwardly strong central apparatus but whose actual central government's power is severely limited. An analogy may be made with China's imperial past and the old Chinese proverb that illustrates a ruler's limitations 'The mountains are high and the Emperor is far away.'[141] China, as a result of its geographical size and huge population, has historically been governed by imperially sanctioned administrators who were often able to achieve a considerable degree of autonomy, whilst maintaining outward loyalty to the centre of power upon which their own legitimacy ultimately depended.

[139] Xue Zheng Wang, 'Challenges/obstacles faced by competition authorities in achieving greater economic development through the promotion of competition', Contribution from China, OECD Global Competition Forum, 13 February 2004 CCNM/GF/COMP/WD(2004)16.
[140] *Rewe-Zentral* case above.   [141] Traditional Chinese proverb.

The example of Guangdong during the Deng Xiaoping era was cited above.

4.8   A change to market solutions? The rationale for adoption

The historical Chinese political-economy model, whether Imperial or communist, has always been based on interventionist state-mediated outcomes. This system may be in the process of breaking down. The case for this proposition is as follows. Firstly, the impact of the growth of the private sector business, where the state has inevitably fewer opportunities to intermeddle, is a significant new factor in the equation. This internal force may lead to the adoption of a more rational distribution of economic resources by the intervention of the invisible hand of the market, to paraphrase Adam Smith.[142]

Secondly, the central government has realised that stern measures need to be taken to curb local protectionism, as the overall economic welfare of the nation is severely impaired. A World Bank report[143] in 1994 found that between 1985 and 1992 retail goods 'exports' from one province to another declined from 36.6 per cent to 27.6 per cent. This shrinkage of internal trade is a very worrying trend for the central government and seems to confirm the existence of severe impediments, which conspire to pauperise many regions of China. There is no evidence to suggest that this trend has been significantly reversed in the last ten years. The realisation of the worsening situation caused the government to undertake an extended study of foreign competition law and policy. This may have produced a consensus in government circles that a comprehensive competition law with credible enforcement powers is an urgent economic necessity to try to achieve a more efficient and less wasteful use of scarce economic resources.

Thirdly, the government is anxious to encourage enterprise mergers to produce 'national champions' and, as administratively sponsored amalgamations have proved either difficult to achieve or of dubious economic value, competition and market forces may be allowed to do what the state has found difficult or impossible to achieve.[144]

Fourthly, China's entry into the WTO will lead to market opening in many closed sectors of the domestic economy. Competitive pressure on

---

[142] Adam Smith, *The Wealth of Nations* (1776).
[143] *China: internal market development and regulation*, World Bank (1994).
[144] See Wang Xiaoye, *Necessity of and conditions for an Anti-Monopoly Law in China*, Institute of European Studies, Chinese Academy of Social Sciences, Beijing (2001).

domestic firms will increase and the government is worried that many domestic businesses will be too weak to compete effectively with foreign transnational corporations with billion-dollar promotional budgets, streamlined production and distribution channels, goods of international quality and deep enough pockets to sustain loss-leaders. The government fears that such business methods may enable foreign firms to capture market share and destroy indigenous producers. The nightmare scenario for Beijing is that companies such as Ford, Unilever and Sony will dominate the Chinese market and destroy China's ability to create world-beating companies. Therefore, the country needs to employ effective measures to tackle abusive anti-competitive behaviour, cartelisation and mega-mergers, which it does not perceive to be in its national interest. In fact, new merger rules concerning foreign takeovers of Chinese firms were enacted in April 2003. They will be analysed in the next chapter.

Consequently, China's government may have come to a consensus that competition policy is a legislative priority. However, whilst it appears that China will now proceed to legislation, maybe as soon as 2005, it is also apposite to ask whether the proffered rationale for adoption represents the real reasons for this policy choice.

In a submission to the 2003 OECD Global Forum on Competition, the Mainland government suggested that the objectives of the proposed new anti-monopoly law were: 'the prohibition of monopoly, safeguarding fair competition, protecting the rights and interests of businesses and consumers and the public interest and guaranteeing the wholesome development of the socialist market economy'.[145] The same submission also suggested that the phrase 'public interest' may include the protection of employment and the preservation of the general 'economic situation'. As the objectives were not ranked in order of priority, 'the ambiguity might lead to the overstress on [sic] public interests, thus impairing the competition objective'.[146]

This concern is clearly justified given the poor pro-competition achievements of the current legislative provisions and the weak enforcement of them by the existing administrative machine, in both market-competition matters and administrative monopoly. Further, as was suggested above, the underlying motivation for the enactment of the new monopoly law may not be the promotion competition in the market but

---

[145] Contribution of China, OECD Global Competition Forum, 10–11 February 2003, CCNM/GF/COMP/WD(2003)1, p. 3.
[146] Ibid. p. 4.

rather the reassertion of control by the bureaucracy over the wayward private sector. After all, China is still a socialist state and practises a socialist market economy, not a market economy. China also has the largest and oldest government administrative machine ever known and so the suspicion must be that the state will continue to play a dominant role, for the foreseeable future, in China's economic development, especially given the monopoly role in political leadership arrogated to itself by the CCP.

Government in China is, and always has been, about control. The majority of the Mainland economy is still controlled directly or indirectly by the state and this situation is unlikely to change in the near term. The much-heralded privatisation of smaller SOEs by the former Premier Zhu Rongi that began in 1998 has sold off some 50,000 small enterprises but there remain some 159,000 enterprises in state ownership as of 2004. The ones sold so far are mostly very small scale. A further round of disposals is in the offing but even after that has been completed, the total sell-off will still only represent a maximum of 20 per cent of the total state sector value-added services reckoned by reference to their value in 1997; thus, even after all envisaged privatisations are completed the state will still control 80 per cent of what it owned in 1997 and the government has no intention of disposing of these, the crown jewels of the socialist market economy.[147] Therefore, it is legitimate to question the government's commitment to private ownership of business and the primacy of markets, with competition as the principal regulator of economic activity.

However, this does not necessarily mean that government is hostile to a restricted Chinese-owned private sector. The private part of the economy is now not only tolerated but protected as a partner in economic development of China. Patriotic capitalists, previously denounced as class enemies, are now welcomed into the ranks of party membership.[148] By allowing entrepreneurs to become members of the CCP, the state is

---

[147] Carsten Holtz quoted in 'The mission creep at the great sell-off', *South China Morning Post*, 14 June 2004.

[148] The Chinese Communist Party amended its constitution at the 16th National Congress of the CCP on 14 November 2002 so as to allow capitalists to apply for membership, though the amendment is not quite so blunt. Article 1 in chapter I of the CCP Constitution has been revised as follows: any Chinese worker, farmer, member of the armed forces, intellectual or any advanced element of other social strata who has reached the age of eighteen and who accepts the Party's Program and Constitution and is willing to join and work actively in one of the Party organisations, carry out the Party's decisions and pay membership dues regularly may apply for membership in the Communist Party of China. For details see http://www.chinadaily.com.cn/en/doc/2002-11/08/content_143105.htm. http://www.china.org.cn/english/features/49184.htm.

subtly reasserting some control over private-sector operators who will be ensnared and enmeshed into the fabric of the *ancien régime*.

China has had the most sophisticated and long-lived bureaucracy in the world; the term 'Mandarin' was appropriated by the British in the nineteenth century to describe the omniscient cadre of post-Northcote–Trevelyan[149] officials which inhabited the upper reaches of the British civil service. The Chinese imperial civil service was a genuine meritocracy and this tradition still, to some extent, holds good today. The mentality of this elite group in China is of not only a right to govern but also a duty, which ineluctably leads to an assumption that power equals control. It is hard to believe that the combination of the Chinese civic-service tradition, coupled with a one-party state, and an ideological base of Leninism, unchecked by countervailing centres of political authority, will produce the essential concept of limited government that is necessary to operate a pro-market competition law system. Thus, the very notion of the proper ambit of government functions in China in not propitious to the successful operation of a competition law system.

Further, the adoption of competition law based on the EC system has sufficiently broad and open-textured language to allow wide discretionary enforcement and creative, but possibly prejudicial, interpretation. In fact, an EC-based system in China could be precisely the tool to reassert control over the developing domestic private sector that does not accept the blandishments of CCP membership. An additional benefit would be to curb the undesired encroachment of foreign enterprises in the Chinese domestic market. These nefarious objectives could be achieved whilst at the same time ostensibly accepting the advice of OECD, the World Bank, the IMF and jurisdictions such as the United States and the European Union[150] to adopt and implement a competition law.

---

[149] The Northcote–Trevelyan Report (1854) identified ministerial patronage as one of the main reasons for the British civil service's reputation, at the time, of endemic inefficiency and public disrepute. The establishment of a meritocracy based on public examination and selection by a Civil Service Commission greatly improved the calibre of public officials. http://www.civilservicecommissioners.gov.uk/history.htm.

[150] For example, the OECD promotion of competition law adoption by capacity building and propaganda measures can be seen on their website at http://www.oecd.org/topic/0,2686,en_2649_37463_1_1_1_1_37463,00.html. As regards the EU, Competition Commissioner Monti has keenly promoted Chinese competition law adoption and visited Beijing in November 2003 to press his case, see 'Europe sees need for monopolies regulator', *South China Morning Post*, 25 November 2003. In May 2004, a formal bilateral competition dialogue between the EU and China was established, *EU–China agree terms for bilateral competition dialogue*, European Union Press Releases – European Commission IP/04/597, 6 May 2004.

These views have been recently publicly corroborated by Chinese official Xue Zheng Wang of the State Administration of Industry and Commerce which enforces the existing pro-market rules. He is quoted fully below:

> Anti-trust law is supposed to be against private anticompetitive conduct and is not supposed to be applied to the markets that are controlled or regulated by the government . . . competition authority that is responsible to enforce anti-trust law, as a part of the government, would barely be able to deny other government agencies' actions . . . China economy is regulated or controlled by government in many aspects although it has made a big jump towards free market economy in the past twenty years. By now, China economy is still called a government-guided-type one. That is to say, government remains powerful and active in various markets that should be free from intervening. Sometimes the government even gives direct orders to state-owned enterprises. For instance, the State Council restructured the petrol industry by combining state-owned oil enterprises into two groups of corporate in 1998. After the reshuffling, China National Petroleum Corporation (CNPC) monopolised the production of petrol in 12 provinces in northern China, as well as the downstream business like refining and retailing, while China Petroleum & Chemical Corporation (CPCC) 19 provinces in southern China. Lots of small-and-middle-sized private oil companies went out of the business because of the monopolisation of the two groups. In the same year, so called 'self disciplined price' took place in industries like steel, chemical, farmer using truck and building material. The price was actually done through the combining effort of large state-owned enterprises and trade unions and two government organisations, which are identified as regulators of the industries above. The government organisations believed that destructive competition is carrying on in these industries and thus the government must step in . . . Certainly the situation of market in China will be improved for the government is making great effort to keep itself from intervening on the market too much. However, it will have a long way to go. It would be naive to expect that the government would withdraw completely and quickly from the areas that it used to occupy. Therefore, it would still be a big challenge for successful enforcement of the future's anti-trust law in China.[151]

This frank admission by a senior government official of the real part played by the Mainland government in economic affairs is reinforced by the language of the most recent amendment of the PRC Constitution.

---

[151] Contribution of China, OECD Global Competition Forum, 12–13 February 2004. CCNM/GF/WD(2004)16.

In March 2004, Article 11 was amended from: 'The State protects the lawful rights and interests of the individual and private sectors of the economy, and exercises guidance, supervision and control over the individual and the private sectors of the economy.' To read:

> 'The State protects the lawful rights and interests of the non-public sectors of the economy such as the individual and private sectors of the economy. The State *encourages, supports and guides the development of the non-public sectors of the economy* and, in accordance with *law*, exercises supervision and control over the non-public sectors of the economy.' (My italics)

This amendment appears to emphasise the role of the state in *guiding the development* of the private sector through the use of *law*. This seems to confirm the notion that law, competition or anti-monopoly law, will be the government's instrument of choice to guide and control the private economy.

4.9 The academic community

> What should our policy be towards non-Marxist ideas? As far as unmistakable counter-revolutionaries and saboteurs of the socialist cause are concerned, the matter is easy: we simply deprive them of their freedom of speech.[152]

One of Kovacic's[153] prerequisites for developing countries adopting competition law is the soft infrastructure of a supportive academic community that can provide philosophical underpinning, expertise and support of the market system by way of publications of all types, the education and training of lawyers, economists and skilled administrators who will operate the system and assist in advocacy programmes to enlighten and encourage community support of a pro-competition law and adjacent policy through the mass media.

In China, the academic community is large and generally supportive of the economic reform programme pursued by the government for the last twenty-five years. As will be seen in the literature review of Chinese writings in the next chapter, most authors support a pro-competition policy. However, China's universities are not mirrors of Western institutions. They are subject to intense political scrutiny and direction by the

---

[152] Mao Zedong speech, 'On the correct handing of contradictions among the people', 27 February 1957.

[153] Kovacic, *Designing and implementing competition and consumer protection reforms* and *Getting started.*

parallel control structures of the CCP. Freedom of speech is not an acceptable political notion in China. Publications are subject to censorship and must conform to the party line; failure to do so will result at least in non-publication and possibly more serious consequences.[154]

Thus it is often the case that lawyers and economists who have been domestically trained over the last twenty-five years have more knowledge of Marxist philosophy, Deng Xiaoping and Jiang Zheming thought than substantive law and a full grasp of the practical application of market economics. The curriculum of university study is rigidly controlled by the Ministry of Education. No variation is permitted from the national curriculum, and the orthodoxy of political education (compulsory Marxism) is carefully policed by the CCP that maintains a system of control in every university department. The true centre of decision-making on all matters, including staff appointments, is often in the hands of the party secretary and not in those of academic post holders.

What can be taught or published is subject to political fashion but it is undoubtedly the case that there is much more room for academic debate and publication than was the case twenty years ago. Advocating the use of markets as an economic regulator twenty-five years ago would have resulted in compulsory re-education in a *laogai* (a reform through labour camp). That is not the case now. Calling for market solutions within the limits of the 'socialist' market is the current orthodoxy. But political fashions can and do change in China with sudden and unpredictable consequences. Should the competition ushered in by greater domestic market opening to foreign goods and services cause too serious economic and social dislocation, one can imagine that the academic advocates of such pro-opening policies could become political scapegoats; this has happened on countless occasions in the past in both imperial and communist China.[155]

Thus, this leads to the interesting questions of how secure is academic support for a pro-competition policy and will it evaporate should political

---

[154] The author has gained these insights into the Chinese university system following extensive teaching experience and research visits to several universities in Beijing, Shanghai and Nanjing between 1996 and 2003. Indeed, a Chinese-language version of this book was refused publication in Mainland China because of conclusions reached by this author. However, it is likely that another publisher will be found in Hong Kong.

[155] The best example of this intellectual criticism of the CCP was the Hundred Flowers Campaign (1957). This movement encouraged public criticism of the CCP for five weeks. When the volume of protest became too great, the CCP clamped down with the Anti-Rightist Campaign branding 300,000 academics as 'rightists'. This designation effectively ended their university careers. See Spence, *The search for modern China*, pp. 541–3.

fashion change? Given the authoritarian nature of Chinese government, such a risk must be substantial but given that a major shift in policy seems unlikely at present, academic support on a political level appears secure, for the moment at least.

Another major issue is whether the academic community can provide the education and training of the professionals that a competition system will undoubtedly need to staff a competition authority and provide a cadre of competent lawyers to advise enterprises. At present, competition law is touched on in a few leading university law schools as a part of courses such as International Economic Law and Domestic Economic Law. But such courses are relatively scarce and are often taught at a very theoretical level, given that staff have no experience of competition law in practice or an effective domestic court system. Thus, foreign expertise might be needed to train the trainers but can sufficient qualified personnel be found and remunerated and if so, where would the resources be found? Academic salaries are extremely low in China, approximately US$100 to 300 per month. Qualified foreigners might command that sum per hour. Clearly, the domestic system would find it impossible to justify such a huge budget for this purpose. Thus, if domestic resources cannot be found, would international organisations provide capacity-building funds to kick-start the education process? The scale of such aid to make an appreciable impact makes this unlikely and experience in other developing countries does not offer much optimism in this regard.[156]

4.10 Competition advocacy

In the opinion of Kovacic and other commentators and organisations, competition advocacy is a vital component of successful competition law adoption. Kovacic considered that a consistent and effective pro-competition message has to be given to consumers, producers, workers and government and that without this educative process no competition regime in a transitional economy would work well. In the Chinese context, forceful advocacy of market solutions to economic problems is particularly problematic for several reasons. The constitution provides that the People's Republic of China is a socialist state, albeit with the acceptance

---

[156] Similar problems have been identified by Maher M. Dabbah, 'Building global anti-trust policy: law and politics', PhD thesis, University of London (2001) and also by Bahaa H. Dessouki in relation to Egypt in 'Privatisation in emerging economies: some aspects of the creation of a new legal infra-structure – a case study of Egypt', PhD thesis, University of London (2000).

that the private sector is an important part of the socialist-market economy. Thus, at a philosophical level, there is no whole-hearted commitment to markets as the sole or even main regulator of the economy. Secondly, given the absence of free speech and the strict control of all media outlets by the organs of the state and the CCP (including the internet), the ability to propagandise in favour of market solutions may well be limited or restricted by the official ambivalence to market economics. Any prospective competition authority might be hamstrung by this inherent contradiction and officials in charge of competition policy might be reluctant to test the bounds of current political orthodoxy for fear of making a political 'mistake' and suffering criticism or sanctions as a result. Thus, it is submitted, that any advocacy on behalf of competition would inevitably be limited and half-hearted. This would especially be so if the immediate effects of greater market openness were to be higher unemployment and social unrest. Consequently, one of Kovacic's primary requirements for successful adoption may well be missing entirely or fatally weak.

4.11 Conclusion

This chapter has attempted to outline the historical, political and economic background against which any comprehensive competition law would operate. It is the assertion of this book that competition policy and law, especially in respect of the anticipated outcomes that may flow from adoption of a comprehensive law, cannot be attempted without a sound understanding of the context within which the law will operate in a particular jurisdiction. This is especially apposite in relation to a country that operates on fundamentally different principles to liberal democracies. China is different not only from Western democracies but also from the other formerly communist countries of the Soviet bloc, in terms not only of economic and political organisation but also as regards history and culture. Basic implicit assumptions about the operation of the economic and legal systems that hold true in the West simply do not apply in China. Thus, any attempt to analyse competition law in China must take these differences fully into account or else be fundamentally flawed.

5

Existing and proposed Chinese competition provisions

5.1 Introduction

The historical, political and economic conditions of China explored in the last chapter have set the scene for a discussion of the current position of competition policy and law in China. The purpose of this chapter is to analyse the present state of the debate on competition policy in academic and government circles, consider the existing legal provisions dealing with competition issues, examine the policy formation process and to comment upon the current drafts of a comprehensive competition statute under consideration by the PRC authorities. The chapter will conclude with consideration of whether the proposed provisions are necessary, sufficient or appropriate to deal with the perceived defects in the regulation of China's 'socialist market'.

5.2 Chinese domestic literature on competition policy and law

The debate as to the nature, form and extent of the economic reform process in China is and has been a very contentious subject. These issues concerning the marketisation of the Chinese economy are hugely important not only to the 1.2 billion Chinese but also to the rest of the world economy. A fully marketised and efficient China would dwarf the world's largest economy, the United States, by a large margin.[1] The economic, political and military implications are not hard to discern. Some have suggested that the twenty-first century will be China's century.[2] Internally, the difficulties of attaining that grand vision are all too clear to see and were illustrated in the previous chapter. However, there are many in

---

[1] Typical of this optimistic literature is W. Overholt, *China: the next economic superpower*, London: Weidenfeld and Nicolson (1993), p. 21, where the suggestion was made that China's economy would be larger than that of the USA by 2004 based on calculation by Lawrence Summers, then Chief Economist of the World Bank; needless to say this has proved somewhat over optimistic.

[2] Brahm, *China's century*.

China who do not accept that China's economic future necessarily lies in reliance on market mechanisms to regulate economic activity. Some do not accept capitalist ideology and emphasise the socialist part of the official politico-economic orthodoxy, as was discussed in the previous chapter.

Politics is the fundamental determinant of the nature of the economic system that a country chooses to adopt. China from 1949 to 1978 practised a variant of Soviet state socialism, with Maoist refinements, especially in respect of the isolationist and self-reliant policy foisted on China and symbolised by the country turning its collective back on the rest of the world for thirty years. China was to survive and prosper without foreign participation in her affairs; autarky was the order of the day. The result was little improvement in the general poverty of the population but at least there was the goal of one day attaining the promised land of communism and everyone was, at least, equally poor (except perhaps for the Party hierarchy). This inherent egalitarianism certainly did have some attractions to the communally minded and propagandised Chinese population.

The primacy of ideological purity was vitally important in the socialist phase of China's history; accusations of heterodoxy could have, literally, fatal consequences. The intellectual underpinning of the socialist paradigm was provided by an amalgam of Marxist–Leninist dogma overlaid with 'The Thoughts of Chairman Mao'. The advent of Deng Xiaoping and his pragmatic reform agenda caused Party ideologues a dilemma. It is beyond the scope of this book to examine in detail the intellectual contortions required to square the socialist-market circle. But a sketch of the academic and officially sanctioned competition policy literature will be attempted below.

It should be kept in mind that even academic literature is subject to censorship to ensure that the bounds of politically acceptable debate are observed.[3] Control of the media is a dominating concern of the Party apparatus as it seeks to control all information flows, including the material available on the Internet.[4] Given the political sensitivity of the inherent contradiction between a market-oriented mechanism and the official orthodoxy, competition and particularly the issues of the proper ambit of state regulation, control and direction, are highly sensitive. The consequences of a more competitive environment, less state control and

---

[3] For a discussion of current censorship practice in China, see chapter 11, 'The Stinking Ninth', in Becker, *The Chinese*.

[4] In September 2002, for example, all Chinese access to the Google search engine was suspended for upwards of ten days and traffic diverted to government-controlled portals, *South China Morning Post*, 21 September 2002.

potentially greater unemployment, especially in the short term, reach into the core of political sensitivity in China.

Given the nature of the issues inherent to the doctrinal debate on competition, academics and relevant government officials are given relatively more freedom to express their opinions in the specialised academic media. This is because such publications are not normally circulated to the general population. Further, foreign-language publications and sources are also subject to less rigorous censorship, again because the 'spiritual pollution'[5] inherent in such publications will not infect the masses.

The summary that follows is based on articles originally written in the Chinese language. Thus, the author is reliant on translated material and so there must be a risk that the material upon which the discussion is based may not be a fully accurate representation of the original author's views. However, a competent English/Chinese reader has verified the accuracy of the translations and checked all the materials and the English versions; if the material was originally written in English that is stated.[6]

The academic debate in China on competition policy and law issues is necessarily subject to the political limitations already mentioned but also to significant intellectual limitations caused by the relative lack of academic learning concerning the theoretical and particularly the practical implications of free-market operations. An acute shortage of academic exchanges to enhance the capacity of the academic community to engage fully in the highest quality of debate, practical resource limitations such as very poorly funded and stocked libraries, very low academic salaries that necessitate the taking of second jobs for economic reasons and the relative isolation of the academic community caused by lack of funds for travel all create significant hurdles. Problems of language comprehension, given that most international academic intercourse is conducted in English, also causes difficulties. Consequently, some of the published literature in China is of limited quality and there are occasionally fundamental misconceptions about the nature and function of markets. The 'light-touch' philosophy of competition law, as opposed to intrusive regulatory regimes, is also sometimes misunderstood. Finally, there is often terminological confusion displayed in the written sources. Unfair competition (in the sense of misleading or untrue advertisements, trade-mark misuse, passing-off and counterfeiting) and true competition policies (measures

---

[5] The phrase originated in 1983 to counteract the influences of Western political ideas.
[6] Some of the materials are officially published and translated, others are not. Many internal documents have been made available to the author by Chinese academics and officials.

to maintain contestable markets) are often used interchangeably. Accurate definitions and the difficulty of translating Western technical terms into Chinese cause much confusion. This is the environment within which the academic debate in China is conducted.

The leading competition law academic in China is Professor Wang Xiaoye of the Chinese Academy of Social Sciences, the premier social science research organisation which is very influential in the policy making process of the Chinese state, as it is responsible directly to the State Council. She is one of the few Chinese academics who have a thorough understanding of Western competition law systems as she read for a PhD in competition law at the Max Planck Institute of the University of Hamburg. The policy-making organs of the State Council on competition law issues often consult her. She has written extensively on the subject of Chinese competition law and is a firm proponent of the immediate adoption by the PRC of a comprehensive competition statute.

She has written extensively in Chinese[7] and displays a comprehensive knowledge of the entire compass of competition policy and law issues. She has considered that the size, complexity and level of development of the Chinese economy necessitates the enactment and active enforcement of a comprehensive competition law. She considers that the tasks an anti-monopoly law should perform are to break up administrative monopolies (previously defined) and facilitate an economically efficient market structure by promoting competition, not the protection of competitors. This should be achieved by ensuring that damaging collusive agreements are banned, the creation of too dominant firms via mergers is regulated, and the abuse of dominant market power should be prohibited. She views the present legal regime (examined below) as incapable of meeting these goals to enable the creation of an efficient market. She considers the law to be fragmented and incoherent, the penalties for breach to be far too low and

---

[7] Wang Xiaoye, 'Anti-monopoly law under the conditions of the socialist market economy', *Journal of Chinese Social Sciences*, Beijing, 1 (1996), *Regulation of Administrative Monopoly*, Beijing: Intertrade, Vol. 4 (1998), *Investigation on legislation to control mergers in China*, Beijing: People's Publishing House (1997), *Anti-Monopoly Law should regulate the activities of public companies in the market*, 5 Chinese Academy of Social Science Journal of Law (1997), *Studies in competition law*, Beijing: China Legal System Press (1999) (a collection of papers and articles), Necessity of and conditions for an anti-monopoly law in China (working paper in English), Institute of European Studies, Chinese Academy of Social Sciences, Beijing (2001); 'Expert urges swift drafting of anti-monopoly law', *People's Daily*, 1 July 2002; *The prospect of anti-monopoly legislation in China*, Washington Global Studies Law Review, 201–31 (2002) (in English); quoted in 'Pressure for anti-monopoly law grows', *Financial Times*, 25 May 2004.

the enforcement body (SAIC) too weak. This body lacks the necessary political leverage to confront powerful local and national vested interests, both political and economic. She has exposed the fallacy that an anti-monopoly law would inhibit industrial reorganisation or mergers to enhance the efficiency of the economy or would prevent the establishment of the larger-scale enterprises needed to compete on the world stage. She does not consider that a new law would be used discriminatorily against foreign firms and is convinced that the introduction of a comprehensive law is long overdue; she attributes the continuing delay to departmental infighting as to who should have the sought-after role of enforcement agency.[8]

Many authors offer descriptions of foreign competition law systems and consider whether they are relevant to China's specific situation. Xu Shiqing has described American anti-trust history;[9] Liu Dashing has considered the experiences of foreign countries that have competition law and concluded that they should be examined but not slavishly followed in China because of that country's special economic and political conditions.[10] It is noticeable that the literature concentrates on developed-country economies and 'advanced' systems of competition regulation; developing countries' experiences and those of the formerly socialist nations who have adopted market-oriented economic reforms are not really the subject of much Chinese academic interest, though a convincing case can be made out that these very countries have far more in common with China than Germany or the United States. This lack of interest may be due to the aspirational desire of Chinese commentators for China to borrow only 'best practice' so as to emulate developed economies or, perhaps, more likely, the experience of developing and formerly socialist countries is more difficult to find in the available academic literature, especially that available to the Chinese academic community. However, one author, Wang Baoshu,[11] explicitly recommends that China should seriously consider the experiences of developing nations who have adopted competition law and transitional economies.

Qi Duojun has provided a comprehensive and incisive *tour d'horizon* exposing the fallacy that competition law prevents amalgamations which

---

[8] As quoted in 'Pressure for anti-monopoly law grows'.

[9] Xu Shiqing, *Talks on American anti-monopoly law*, 1 Political Science and Law, Shanghai Academy of Social Sciences (1994).

[10] Liu Dashing, *The new field of anti-monopoly legislation in our country*, 82 Chinese Legal Science (1997).

[11] Wang Baoshu, *Comments upon anti-trust law application to administrative monopoly*, Journal of the Graduate School of the Chinese Academy of Social Sciences, 5 (1998).

foster economies of scale, the AM problem, definitions and categorisations of types of monopoly, monopoly considerations and the position of the SOEs, consideration of the deficiencies of the current legislative framework, the need for and shape of a competition statute and its attendant enforcement machinery as well as extra-territorial enforcement and the effects principle.[12]

One very prominent area of debate is the phenomenon of AM. The concept springs from the decentralised power structures found in the Chinese government and the lack of effective legal supervision of administrative acts, all of which were examined and analysed in the previous chapter. The definition of AM and how it is to be differentiated from economic monopoly is one that has taxed many Chinese writers. Hu Ruying considers that AM is a monopoly maintained through administrative instruments by administrative organs within a strict political hierarchy.[13] Hu Weiwei agrees but uses the words administrative powers, rather than instruments.[14] Zhang Deling, however, offers another view: that AM is formed by a combination of administrative powers and market strength.[15] Wang Xiaoye and Zhang Shufang[16] consider these definitions lack concentration on the central element of the abusive and illegal nature of the defined conduct, which is formally prohibited under China's current legislation. This definitional controversy is important as the other types of monopoly – state-mandated monopolies and pure economic monopolies – need to be differentiated, so that they can be accorded differential treatment under any new comprehensive statute. All the writers agree that AM is a very serious threat to the establishment of a national market in China and that local protectionism inhibits internal trade and economic restructuring.

However, some commentators, such as Shi Jishun[17] and Xie Junhui,[18] consider that AM is not part of the ambit of anti-monopoly law at all. They

---

[12] Qi Duojun, *Research problems in Chinese anti-monopoly legislation*, Wuhan University Law Review (1998).

[13] Hu Ruying, *Competition and monopoly: micro-economic analysis of socialism*, Shanghai: Shanghai Shanlian Publishing House (1998).

[14] Hu Weiwei, *Anti-monopoly law is a necessity in China*, 3 Jurisprudence (1995).

[15] Zhang Deling, *Monopoly and anti-monopoly legislation in China's contemporary situation*, Economic Studies, 6 (1996).

[16] Wang Xiaoye, *Causes and analysis of Administrative Monopoly and legal measures against it*, 4 Journal of Law, Chinese Academy of Social Sciences, 4 (1999).

[17] Shi Jishun, 'Anti-monopoly law analysis', *Intertrade*, 4 (1998) and *Definition and regulation of Administrative Monopoly in China*, 3 Frontiers of Jurisprudence (1999).

[18] Xie Junhui, Briefing note on Administrative Monopoly (1999), prepared specially for the author's research.

think that the abuse of governmental power should be subject to proceedings under the administrative Procedure Law and is properly the subject of judicial review and a remedy for the problem should not be added to a competition statute that should deal with economic actors, not political/administrative law issues. The addition of measures to deal with AM would compromise the central function of a comprehensive competition law statute. The correct way to remedy AM is through political measures and the strengthening of the rule of law to control administrative abuses that are already illegal under various existing laws. The task is to strengthen current legal procedures, the courts and respect for and enforceability of the law generally. Setting up another new administrative body to enforce a competition law would inhibit a more vital issue, that of increasing general respect for and compliance with the legal system. Including AM provisions in a competition law statute would be wrong in principle. One might add that whilst this point of view is correct doctrinally, the current debilitated state and the fundamental problems of the courts mean that such a course of action, namely, excluding AM from an actively enforced competition law, would inevitably mean that the AM problem would not be effectively tackled at all for the foreseeable future and the size and importance of the problem demands a practical remedy, even if that does not fit neatly into an academically pure schema. Nevertheless, the vital issue of whether or not AM can be effectively remedied is a moot point. Without a new political settlement that includes a much strengthened concept of the rule of law, any method chosen to deal with AM is unlikely to succeed.

Wu Hongwei gives an interesting explanation for the development and tenacious persistence of AM.[19] He considers that one of the reasons for the continued vigour of AM is the result of budgetary changes introduced in 1994. These had the effect of shrinking departmental budgets nationwide and, to make up the deficits and maintain spending and personnel levels, local government embarked on an extra-legal revenue raising round of imposing administrative penalties and charges. Further, promoting local industry and thus increasing local taxation revenues via the turnover tax also enhanced the local officials' career prospects, providing another motive for AM. On the issue of how to tackle AM, Wu Hongwei agrees with Shi and Xie that AM should not be remedied via a competition statute. He considers that the defect is due to political and administrative reasons and so should be dealt with by clarifying overlapping responsibilities

---

[19] Wu Hongwei, *A discussion on China's Administrative Monopoly and avoidance*, 6 Jurists' Journal (2001).

and imposing clear lines of accountability, improving internal administrative supervision via a central inspectorate and reorganising public finances to remove the main need to raise extra-legal revenues. He also notes that corrupt practices are not surprising when officials' salaries are so inadequate and suggests that higher salaries, coupled with intensive supervision, would also help to address the issue.

Huang Xin and Zhou Jun consider AM to be the primary obstacle to establishing a working national market and that the primary task of an anti-monopoly law would be to tackle this phenomenon.[20] They consider the Chinese market to be not unduly concentrated as enterprises are relatively small scale. This is true in national terms but they fall into error by not fully appreciating that the relevant market is not the national one (due to the absence of a national market in most goods and services) but the local or provincial geographic-product market; difficulties in the distribution system and poor transport facilities exacerbate the problem. Thus, their assertion that anti-competitive practices are not a serious problem is based on a fallacy. Zhang Ru-ping[21] also made the same error. Other than this error, Huang and Zhou's views on the pernicious nature of AM and the ineffectiveness of the numerous legislative prohibitions and exhortatory provisions were put down to traditional causes – overlapping and contradictory regulations, weak enforcement, split administrative responsibility, insufficient penalty provisions and powerful vested political and economic interests that frustrate enforcement. Lu Jong-xing, Chang Li-ying and Chang Ni conclude that the range of fines, vague definitions in respect of infractions of the current law, practical problems in investigation of complaints, gathering evidence, problems of deciding upon the correct type and level of punishment, difficulties of enforcing decisions, often come down to the old hydra of local protectionism, inadequate respect for legal rulings and the incompetence of local officials.[22]

Evidence of anti-competitive practices is given in several articles including one by Wang Cunxue.[23] He mentions incidents all over China of collusive price setting in the colour-film processing market in December

---

[20] Huang Xin and Zhou Jun, *An approach to the legislative control of Administrative Monopoly and monopoly practices*, 3 China Jurists' Journal, National University of Politics and Law, Beijing (2001).

[21] Zhang Ru-ping, *Analysis of abuse of market power*, 3 Jurists' Review (1998).

[22] Lu Jong-xing, Chang Li-ying and Chang Ni, 'Analysis of twenty years of China's anti-unfair competition laws' in *Collected Works of the 9th Chinese Economic Law Theoretical Meeting* (2001).

[23] Wang Cunxue, *Price cartels and their regulation in China's market economy*, 2 Modern Law Science Review (1998).

1998, five department stores in one city fixing prices of washing machines, fifty-one petrol-station operators in a given city setting minimum prices and dominant white goods manufacturing adopting resale price maintenance (RPM) with threats of refusals to supply if RPM was not maintained. He concludes that such practices are common in China and injure consumer interests.

Merger control is considered by Wang Chundi[24] who discusses the possibility of a merger-control regime in China. He suggests the turnover threshold trigger points for merger investigation, raises market definition issues, public interest issues, crisis situations, economic efficiency matters and industrial reorganisation criteria. He also summarises international regimes and ponders on their relevance to the Chinese situation.

Regarding the administration and enforcement of a comprehensive competition law regime, all the authors are united – current administrative arrangements under existing legislation are ineffective in policing the pro-market rules and a new structure will need to be established that has strong powers and sufficient resources adequately to enforce any new law. Wang Xianlin[25] considers the pros and cons of establishing a two-tier administrative system with judicial review of decisions or a specialist competition tribunal, whether such an authority would concentrate purely on competition issues or whether consumer protection would also be under its aegis, as in Australia, or continue to be policed by a separate body. He made the point forcefully that China should consider the options carefully and not blindly copy a developed country's systems without considering China's own particular circumstances. He advocates a centrally funded authority with regional offices, and that the authority be responsible only to the State Council, with no reporting to or influence by provincial or local governments, to prevent institutional capture. The authority should have a small number of high-quality members who should be professionally qualified economists, accountants and lawyers. They should be full time and not affiliated to any other government or business grouping to ensure independence. It should have the full panoply of investigatory, penalty and enforcement powers as well as power to promulgate detailed subordinate legislation and rule-making powers. The authority should be able to deal with AM issues and would also be the merger-control authority.

[24] Wang Chundi, *Monopoly through merger*, 3 Jurists' Review (1998).
[25] Wang Xianlin, *An approach to the establishment of an anti-monopoly law enforcement authority and its functions*, China Administrative Supervision Journal (August edition, 2000).

Another interesting adjunct to the debate was the establishment on a
Peking University sponsored web site of a discussion forum in English
on competition law issues.[26] This site in 2000 published a lively and interesting spectrum of views, some emanating from a Seminar on the
Frontiers of Economic Laws held by the Law School of Peking University
in July 2000. Wang Zixuan and Wang Qiangxiang, two of the contributors, opined that the forthcoming entry of China into the WTO hastened
the need for China to adopt a comprehensive competition law because
'a great number of multinational corporations will enter the Chinese
Market which will possibly do harm to Chinese consumers' interests and
the development of Chinese enterprises. In this sense, anti-monopoly law
is significant in maintaining the stability of Chinese society and promoting
the development of China's national economy.'[27]

Some, however, do not accept the need for a competition law. Tan
Yong-mei and Chen Xiao-chun[28] consider that the challenges faced by
Chinese industry after WTO accession require a stronger industrial policy
of government-sponsored mergers and a state-directed industrial investment to encourage the development of national champions. They think
that monopoly laws are riddled with uncertainties and anomalies, so that
they are unworkable. Questions such as what share of a market creates
dominance, how should relevant markets be defined, whether to apply a
per se rule or a rule-of-reason approach are all too vague and uncertain.
Further, regulating competition would take up too much court time and
government resources, which justifies a 'do-nothing' policy.

Other government voices agree. Li Chang-quing and Ma Hong-mei,[29]
senior officials at the State Administration of Industry and Commerce,
consider that the time is not right for promulgation of a comprehensive
competition law. They argue that a competition law is only necessary
when the market economy system has been perfected and as this has
still to be achieved competition law at this stage is premature. They state
that Chinese industry is not concentrated by international standards (the
non-concentration fallacy mentioned above). They opine that the current Prices Law can control excessive price demands by dominant firms.
They again deploy arguments about lack of consensus as to monopoly
thresholds and abusive conduct to justify rejection of legislation on the

[26] http://www.chnlaw.com/LegalForum/hottopics/index.asp.
[27] See Wang Zixuan, Peking University, ibid. contribution to the web site mentioned.
[28] Contribution posted at www.chnlaw.com above.
[29] Li Chang-quing and Ma Hong-mei, 'China should postpone drawing up an anti-monopoly
law', Draft Article for publication in *Economic Daily*, Beijing, February 2002.

subject. Further, as a proposed competition law would overlap with existing legislation, it should not be enacted as this would cause confusion. Finally, there is no consensus as to the shape of an enforcement body. They are however, worried about AM and the possible domination of Chinese markets by foreign firms.

The anti-legislation arguments outlined above are not convincing. The technical definitional issues are not unique to China and do pose real difficulties but other jurisdictions have exactly the same problems; they choose to overcome them, not to abandon competition regimes on the basis that it's too difficult to make choices. The non-concentration fallacy has been exploded above and the arguments that existing legislation would be sufficient misses the whole point of having a comprehensive law so that overlap can be swiftly dealt with by the selective repeal of contradictory provisions. One might wonder whether the real reasons for official opposition might be more to do with a bureaucratic 'turf' war than principled, rational opposition to a competition regime in China. In any event, if the suggestion made in the last chapter that competition law enactment may be a method of re-asserting control over the private economy and foreign interlopers is correct, official objections will surely fade away.

Other more thoughtful officials support a pro-competition policy and a complete legal regime. Wu Wenlong, a senior official at the State Economic and Trade Commission, the department charged with restructuring the planned economy and the overall direction of policy towards the SOEs, is a firm proponent of a comprehensive competition regime. In 1998, he opined that the need for rapid legislative action on the issue was clear.[30] He noted that a competition statue was included in the eighth five-year legislation plan for the NPC, a draft law had been under preparation for some years and that there was growing appreciation in academic circles that legislative action was necessary to assist in the restructuring of the economy and to increase economic efficiency to prepare Chinese industry for the more competitive post-WTO entry domestic economic conditions. He considered that legislation was an essential component of 'perfecting the socialist market economy'. He recited all the classical arguments in favour of an active competition policy. He also added that such legislation would complement the ongoing transformation of the planned Chinese

---

[30] Wu Wenlong, 'An economic constitution; a discussion of some ideas and problems in legislating a Chinese anti-monopoly law', *Intertrade*, 4 (1998), writing under the pseudonym Zhen Fa.

economy to a more market-orientated one. He also hoped that such legislation would assist in dealing with AM, the transformation of government functions and provide a means to curb *fanpai* and *la lang pei* corporations.[31] He also noted that most developed countries with a market economy have a competition law to provide light-touch regulation
of the market. He dismissed fears over legislative overlap and the non-
concentration fallacy. He suggested that a competition law would also
provide redress for small and medium-sized firms and, in particular, allow
privately owned firms to enter and compete in currently closed markets.
It would also provide the tools to discipline, on a non-discriminatory basis, multi-national corporations that might abuse a dominant position in
the capital-intensive, technological or service sectors that will be opened
to foreign direct investment after WTO entry. This approach to the issue
of adoption is clear, rational and logical but whilst he argues cogently
for competition law, the forces of inaction are considerable, consisting
as they do of powerful political and economic vested interests which can
only suffer a loss of political and economic power should competition
law be enacted and vigorously enforced. One weakness of Wu's position
is that it is a somewhat idealised one and the important issue of adequate
administrative capacity and the ability to enforce adjudicated penalties
is not addressed squarely. The implicit assumption is that a comprehensive competition law can be impartially administered and enforced; this
assumption is one that may well not be justified.

In respect of the dangers to Chinese domestic industries posed by
stronger foreign competitors, senior political figures are alert to the issue
but their concern is balanced by a realisation that without the spur of
increased foreign and domestic competition China's domestic industries
will find it difficult or impossible to improve their lamentable efficiency
record. Chen Qing-tai, a very senior figure in the central government,
frankly suggested that the government needed to change its policies fundamentally:

> The government should no longer meddle in the allocation of resources,
> instead it should strive to ensure that the market functions well in resource

---

[31] *fanpai* (literally turned-over or transformed corporations). They are government regulatory units that transform themselves into quasi-commercial enterprises but retain a
privileged position in the market, often the grant of a monopoly or a concession, through
often corrupt connections (*guanxi*) with their former sibling government departments. *La
lang pei* (literally pulled-together couple or marriage) is the phenomenon of administratively arranged commercial amalgamations, which may have no economic logic but which
might serve the political or social requirements of a particular government department.

allocation. Joining the WTO is a strategic approach taken by China to promote the establishment of market economy. The Chinese government aims
to solve the deep-rooted systematic and structural problems hindering economic development through wider market opening and deepening reform.
The formation and growth of enterprises should be as a result of market
competition, not government intervention ... [which] should endeavour
to create an environment of fair competition for enterprises ... and provide equal market access for private enterprises so that they can take part
in market competition.[32]

This acceptance of a market-orientated solution as the correct path for
China is welcome, as is the candour displayed in the realisation of the
nature and magnitude of the macro-political and economic challenges
that China faces. However, whether the central government can effectively implement a market-orientated solution is very uncertain, given
the background issues of rampant corruption, the huge vested interests
of the SOEs and local governments' preference for maintaining of the
status quo, never mind the ever-present danger of a SOE-induced banking failure resulting in massive social unrest. Administrative, personnel
and legal-system weaknesses only compound the problem of implementation of a comprehensive competition law.

Thus, it can be seen that academic debate along with contributions
from informed government officials has been tolerably open and frank,
especially given the great sensitivity over open debate in China. The balance of informed opinion is in favour of competition law in principle
but the devil is in the detail. The next section will examine and analyse
the current competition law provisions, consider their effectiveness in
Chinese market conditions and reach some tentative conclusions about
reform.

5.3 Current competition law provisions

The regulation of the competitive process is not entirely neglected in
Chinese law. Substantive rules go back as far as 1980 when the State
Council issued regulations[33] that *inter alia* no products should become
subject to monopolised control unless authorised by law and that efforts were to be made to break down regional blockades. Needless to say

---

[32] 'Government's changing role', *China Daily*, 25 April 2002.
[33] *Interim provisions on carrying out and protecting socialist competition*, State Council, Beijing
October 1980.

twenty-five years later these concerns still remain an issue in Chinese economic life. Neither those regulations, nor any of the rules that followed them, have proved to be effective.

5.3.1 The Anti-Unfair Competition Law 1993 and its enforcement

The principal statute is the 1993 Anti-Unfair Competition Law,[34] which was enacted by the Standing Committee of the National People's Congress. This statute is primarily a consumer protection law. It is not a complete competition code. It addresses a miscellany of issues including passing-off (Article 5), business bribery (Article 8), false and disparaging advertising (Article 9), protection of confidential business information and trade secrets (Article 10) and false prize sales (Article 13). However, it does have something to say about pure competition issues. Monopolists are forbidden to use predatory pricing policies to destroy embryonic competitors (Article 6), other businesses are also forbidden to engage in similar tactics (Article 11) and forced tie-in sales of unrelated goods are prohibited (Article 12). Bid-rigging is outlawed (Article 5). Finally, AM conduct is expressly prohibited (Article 7). Government organs are enjoined against restricting freedom of choice of suppliers of products, restricting arbitrarily the business freedom of operators and abusing administrative powers to prevent or restrict the marketing of non-local products within their administrative area. Consequently, it can be seen that one of the most pressing issues for China, the AM problem, was already identified as a significant problem ten years ago; it will be recalled that the 1980 State Council Regulations addressed the same matter. However, in China there is a world of difference between the expression of legislative will and execution in practice. The recurrent and intractable nature of AM was emphasised yet again by the promulgation on 21 April 2001 of another administrative circular outlawing AM practices;[35] presumably this Regulation was issued because the previous measures were ineffective. The new Regulations largely set out which organ can overrule the decisions of other manifestations of the state but do little to provide a remedy to those who suffer from administrative abuse as a result of the illegal conduct. If the provisions of Article 7 of the 1993 law had been effectively enforced, the issues alluded to in the 2001 Regulations would not be of importance

---

[34] An English translation can be found in *China Law and Practice*, 18 November 1993, pp. 31–9.
[35] *Regulations of the State Council prohibiting the implementation of regional barriers in the course of market economy activities*, Beijing, 21 April 2001.

today. However, they remain a nested problem of major significance because, whilst the national legislative will is apparent, the mechanisms of enforcement provided by the statute are weak and are incapable of overcoming the realities of local political power.

Enforcement of the 1993 Law is provided for in Articles 16 to 19. Powers of investigation, the requirement of the subjects of the investigation to co-operate and provide information and records as required by the inspectors, are included. Penalties are set out in Articles 20 to 29 and include both financial penalties and injunctive powers to prevent the recurrence of prohibited conduct. Article 30 provides for higher levels of government to supervise lower levels, for example, for provincial governments to supervise municipal authorities.

The enforcement authority is the SAIC, a national organisation answerable vertically to the State Council, the permanent executive arm of the Chinese government. However, this body was until 1999 functionally organised at each lower level of government and was funded and partially responsible to that corresponding level, down to the county level of government. Therefore, if the municipal government of city X was imposing a blockade or a discriminatory licensing or taxation regime against 'foreign', that is non-local Chinese goods, it was the municipal branch of the SAIC that was responsible, in the first instance, to investigate its sponsoring local authority. Needless to say, few investigations were pursued with vigour, when the subjects of their potential investigations controlled the pay, promotion and privileges of the local SAIC staff.[36]

The seriousness of these problems for the credible enforcement of the 1993 Law was recognised by the central government in 1999, when the SAIC was reorganised to make all SAIC branches responsible to the Provincial level of government, so by-passing the county and prefectural government administrations, who were thought to be the principal sponsors of AM blockages. It has been suggested by SAIC officials that this restructuring exercise has improved the enforcement record of the competition provisions over the last five years in respect of trading entities but no empirical data to prove this was produced.[37]

In 2001, the State Council renamed the SAIC and changed its bureaucratic status to a full ministerial body, upgrading it from a vice-ministerial organ, so as to give it enhanced administrative authority within the

---

[36] Information provided to the author by officials at the SAIC headquarters in Beijing, May 2000.
[37] Contribution of China, OECD Global Forum on Competition, 10–11 February 2003, p. 3. CCNM/GF/COMP/WD (2003)1.

government structure. This was the prelude to a political sponsored enforcement campaign under the slogan 'strengthening and standardizing the order of the market economy'. Yet again, the main focus was to attempt to create a national market within China and to break down monopolistic structures and regional blockades. This effort followed a similar political campaign in 2000 entitled 'countering administrative barriers and acts of restricting competition by public utility enterprises'. In that year, the SAIC dealt with 56 cases of administrative monopoly, and 785 cases of public-utility-related competition cases; this was claimed to be a 'remarkable success'. No details of the nature or seriousness of these cases are available, nor the penalty or enforcement action taken, nor an assessment of whether the remedies applied actually rectified the existing problems or prevented new abuses occurring. In reality, the number of cases is very small, given the size of China's population, economy and vast government-operated business sector and hydra-like bureaucracy. Further, if these campaigns and bureaucratic changes were effective, why does a new anti-monopoly law have to be established with a completely new bureaucracy to administer and enforce the new prohibitions? The truth appears to be that current arrangements are not working; this is tacitly admitted by the SAIC itself.

In the Chinese submission to the 2001 OECD Global Forum on Competition,[38] Wang Xuezheng of the SAIC admitted there were major problems in enforcement especially in case related to SOE's or government. They included:

- The lack of a legal definition of monopoly, renders enforcing the 'prohibition of monopoly' as mandated in various regulations impossible.
- Lack of clarity in the definition of cartel practices means that open cartels are common.
- Weak control of administrative monopoly as a result of 'a lack of strict regulatory mechanism and effective legal restriction'.
- The strength and power of sectoral monopolies, in SOE utilities such as gas, telecommunications, taxi services, and health care. [Note that these cases are in the publicly owned sector. These abuses of dominance are not carried out by the private sector or foreign-owned businesses.]
- Penalties are very light (maximum administrative fine of RMB200,000) [approx. US$25,000] and so there is no deterrent effect on national enterprises. Some acts such as tie-in sales and predatory pricing do not

---

[38] Contribution of China, OECD Global Forum on Competition, 17–18 October 2001, pp. 4–5. CCNM/GF/COMP/WD (2001)10.

attract penalty sanctions at all. Other penalty provisions are based on the confiscation of 'illegal gains' but these are difficult or impossible to calculate.

- China's enforcement agency has superficially all necessary enforcement powers without the need to prove a case in court. However, as at the end of 2000 China had some 5.35 million domestic enterprises [one or other form of SOE], 200,000 foreign owned business entities, 1.76 million larger private enterprises and 25.71 million small or family businesses. Given this number of entities, the SAIC found difficulty in administering the law, notwithstanding having some 68,000 employees [not a small government department by most standards!]. Quality of personnel was a serious problem, with SAIC rarely employing economists or qualified lawyers.[39] Internal capacity problems were exacerbated by the fact that many Chinese enterprises had 'low legal accomplishments and some do not cooperate with law enforcement and ... [given] that courts cannot enforce their own cases [sic], it is difficult for them to assist administrative authorities'.
- Overlapping and duplication of functions between enforcement bodies caused confusion as to who has authority to enforce the various pro-competitive provisions in a number of conflicting laws and regulations.

Thus, the true picture of law enforcement is not optimal. As regards anti-competitive acts by business, enforcement is also thought to be weak for similar reasons to those already enumerated: the protection afforded by local political interests normally trumps the ability of the SAIC to act. It can also be seen that the 1993 statute is incapable of dealing with many commonly found competition-related problems – abusive conduct by monopolists, cartel operations, oligopoly situations, vertical restraints or mergers, as these phenomena are not regulated by the provisions of the 1993 Law.

As regards direct government-sponsored abuses, the Administrative Monopoly problem, there has been no improvement since the 1999 restructuring of the SAIC. This has been officially admitted by the SAIC itself:

> the unfair competition practices done by government or government agencies are still under the supervision and check of their sponsoring authorities. In practice, we have found that the government or government agencies

[39] See Contribution of China, OECD Global Conference on Competition, 12–13 February 2004, p. 3. CCNM/GF/COMP/WD(2004) 16.

are seldom punished for their unfair practices, as the objectives such as regional development, the increase of the revenue of local government and employment generally prevail over the objective of competition protection in dealing with such cases. Therefore, it is evident that the unfair competition of government and government agencies is still rampant.[40]

This was again amplified and explained, in specifically political terms, by SAIC official, Wang Xuezheng:

> The [1993] Law has not, however been effectively enforced yet. The higher authority of the incumbent usually does not pay seriously [*sic*] attention to the violating actions, partly because that they [*sic*] have the same interest in it. It is hard to find a successful case that a higher authority performed actively to correct a violating action of a local government, say nothing of punishing responsible officials [*sic*].[41]

In respect of the prospects of success of the proposed new anti-monopoly law in tackling AM issues he went on to say: 'Therefore, considering the failure of the [1993] Law, it is reasonable for us to expect that the actions of eliminating competition carried out by local government would still be a big challenge to enforce anti-trust law in the future. A competition authority would be hard to correct or punish the actions of local government [*sic*].'[42]

5.3.2 Miscellaneous legislation with pro-competition provisions

Thus, it seems that enforcement of the existing competition statute has been weak and generally ineffective; the prospects for the success of any new anti-monopoly law may also be poor. The 1993 Law is not the only statute to regulate anti-competitive practices; other statutes also have pro-competition provisions. The Prices Law 1997 has some provisions aimed at competition issues.[43] For example, Article 14 provides:

> Operators may not carry out any of the following unfair pricing acts:
>
> (1) collude with others in manipulating market prices, thereby harming the lawful rights and interests of other operators or consumers;
> (2) dump merchandise below cost in order to force out competitors or to monopolise the market, thereby disturbing the normal order of production and business and harming the interests of the state or the

---

[40] Ibid.   [41] Ibid.   [42] Ibid.
[43] Adopted at the 29th meeting of the NPCSC, December 1997.

lawful rights of other operators except for the disposal of fresh produce, seasonal or over-stocked merchandise.

The terms manipulation, the test of harm, below cost, intent, monopolise, and normal order of production are not defined. No suggestion of dominance as a requirement in Article 14(2) is made. The provisions are clearly unworkable and do not appear to comprehend basic microeconomic concepts. Penalties are provided in Article 40 and Article 41 provides a right of action to consumers who have suffered loss as a result of price-fixing conduct. On 30 August 1999, the Tender Invitation and Bid Law was enacted by the NPC Standing Committee, which *inter alia* prohibits collusive tendering in Article 32; this merely reiterates Article 15 of the 1993 Law. On 8 November 2002, the *Interim Regulations for Restructuring of State Owned Enterprises Utilising Foreign Investment* were published by the State Economic and Trade Commission (SETC) and the SAIC. Article 9.1 of the Regulations specifies that in the case of restructurings that result in monopolies or otherwise hinder fair competition, government shall examine and call evidence before approving such a transaction.

On 7 March 2003, the *Interim Provisions for Merger and Acquisition of Domestic Enterprises by Foreign Investors* were jointly promulgated by various government bodies. The Provisions require transactions by foreigners to acquire domestic businesses, that meet certain thresholds, to be reported and investigated by the authorities so that potential competition concerns can be adjudicated upon. A detailed discussion of the Provisions follows later, especially in light of their overtly discriminatory nature – they only seek to control foreign acquisitions in the domestic market.

On 18 June 2003, SDRC issued the *Interim Regulations on Prohibition of Monopolistic Pricing Acts*, which are effective from 1 November 2003. They have been stated by the SDRC to be a 'preliminary exploration of antitrust legislation'. Under Article 2, a new concept in Chinese law namely, monopolistic pricing is introduced. This is defined as: 'acts of business operators, in collusion with other operators, or by abusing their dominant position in the market, to manipulate market prices and disrupt the normal order of production and operations, thereby harming the lawful interests of other operators, consumers or the public interest'. Article 3 provides a definition of a market dominant position as: 'being determined according to the market share of the subject operator, the degree of interchangeability of the subject products and the difficulty of market entry for new competitors'. Another interesting addition to the Chinese patchwork of regulations is for the first time an explicit ban on RPM. Article 5 provides: 'Business operators shall not exploit their dominant positions to set the resale price of the goods when sold to distributors.'

This appears to link the concept of a market-dominant position, as defined in Article 3, to RPM. Thus, apparently only an operator with market dominance is prohibited from enforcing RPM; other operators may do so.

Various other prohibitions are also enumerated in the *Interim Regulations* including price manipulation and cartels, exorbitant prices, dumping and predatory prices, and discriminatory pricing; this is merely a reiteration of prohibitions already found in other laws and regulations. Enforcement is by administrative action via the SDRC with powers to order the suspension of infringing conduct and financial penalties. Article 13 also provides for the reward of informers and protection of their identity.

Once again the diffuse and overlapping nature of these latest regulations, the weak and duplicitous enforcement mechanisms and the lack of a coherent strategic vision on competition matters, is all too evident; they seem to be yet another stopgap measure until a final decision on a complete competition code, and who should enforce it, emerges from the government machine.

Thus, the Chinese central government seems to have realised the limitations of its current policy armoury. New issues continue to crowd in on the economy caused by increased problems of the solvency of the state-owned business sector, the expansion of the private economic sector, the threats to domestic producers represented by WTO entry and intensified foreign competition, not to mention the aggravation caused by administrative barriers to internal trade. From this position, as long ago as 1994, the government resolved to undertake a full-scale review of competition policy; the saga of competition policy formation in China will now be related.

5.4 Competition policy making 1994 to 2000

> All state affairs which have not yet been decided upon, or which have been
> decided upon but not yet been made public [are secret].[44]

In early 1994, the Chinese central government took a decision to set up a working group[45] to study the need for China to adopt a comprehensive

---

[44] Chinese Law, Regulations on guarding state secrets (1951).
[45] My information concerning the detailed discussions of the Working Group comes from personal interviews with several members of the committee, and access to the original

competition policy as part of its ongoing economic reform programme. The stated aims of the interdepartmental working group were to consider the necessity for a competition law and then, if appropriate, to proceed with drafting a statute. The group was led jointly by two departments of the State Council namely, SETC and the SAIC. The SETC had several roles including managing the amalgamation of state-owned industries into viable and more commercially run organisations, economic policy advice to central government and promoting competition policy as part of wholesale restructuring of the economy into a 'socialist-market economy'. The SAIC is the body charged with granting business licences to enterprises and enforcement of business-related laws including the 1993 Anti-Unfair Competition Law, as we have seen above. Additional members were co-opted as necessary from various industrial ministries such as telecommunications, posts, railways and aviation who have control of important state monopolies. Further, members from the NPC legislative affairs committee also formed part of the working group.

The first meeting was held on 12 May 1994. It decided that a comprehensive competition law was a necessity in order to:

- facilitate the establishment of the socialist-market economy and promote modernisation;
- assist in the development of a legal system to enforce rules that promoted the socialist-market economy;
- deepen enterprise reform;
- promote the transformation of governmental functions in the economic sphere;
- align China with international practice in matters of economic regulation.

The group decided that any law they recommended should be compatible with China's socialist-market system, an attempt to create a unified, open and orderly national market by breaking down regional economic boundaries and creating a fair trading environment. This was to be achieved by using legal rules equitably and ensuring impartial enforcement. In order to attain a system that was feasible to operate, slavish copying of any particular foreign system was to be avoided but the variety of foreign control systems would be carefully studied and evaluated, before arriving at a solution that would be practical in the Chinese context.

minutes and briefing papers prepared for working group meetings. As these were internal official meetings, information was divulged to me for the purpose of my research on the basis of strict anonymity. Thus, no further attribution is provided.

The group set a preliminary target date for completion of a draft competition law at the end of 1995; this proved wildly optimistic. The first
outline draft actually appeared only in 1999, and final legislation is still
awaited in 2005, a full decade after the process began.

During 1994 work proceeded to collect the views and inputs of state organisations responsible for various industrial sectors – tobacco, construction, pharmaceuticals, metallurgy, telecommunications, posts, electricity
generation and distribution, chemicals and civil aviation. Many of the industrial ministries made a case for special treatment or exemption from
competition rules to be introduced citing the national interest, the need
to take advantage of economies of scale, or the disastrous consequences of
cut-throat price competition. Industry lobbies were also consulted. They
were worried about regional blockades, the demarcation line between
permissible and impermissible competition, and the need to have a clear
distinction between acceptable economies of scale and monopolisation;
they fretted that the mere size of an undertaking might make it impermissible, rather than its behaviour in the marketplace. Expert views were also
sought from academics. They generally worried that making a distinction between economic monopoly and abuse of administrative powers of
governmental organs would not be an easy task, given China's singular
governmental structures and practices. Further, information was sought
on a number of countries' monopoly control regimes. Work was done on
the systems operating in Japan, South Korea, Germany, the United States,
the United Kingdom, Australia, New Zealand, the Philippines, Hungary,
Canada, the European Union, Mexico, Poland, Jamaica, Venezuela and
Taiwan.

During 1995 and 1996, work continued on studying international systems of control with translations of laws being carried out and summaries
of individual regimes being undertaken. Also, an economic analysis of
various important Chinese industries was carried out which showed, interestingly, that most of them were not unduly concentrated, save for
explicit utility monopolists such as telecommunications, railways, power
generation and petro-chemicals. However, the actual scale of some of the
business units was enormous in absolute terms due to China's size and
population. Whilst on a national scale concentration was not theoretically alarmingly high, the reality was that each producer tended to operate regionally and so may well have had absolute dominance in a whole
province or region of China that might easily contain between 50 million
and 100 million consumers. By any measure, such large-scale operations
with regional dominance were not subject to effective competition, given

the regional protectionism previously mentioned. Further, the difficulties of transport and distribution over such large geographical distances, as are encountered in China, all conspire to provide considerable barriers to entry to regional markets. It may be that the Working Group in using a national perspective and with an eye to industrial consolidation, economies of scale and the industrial policy of promoting national champions, may have lost sight of the need to promote economic efficiency by competitive means at the consumer level. In effect, the definition of relevant markets was deficient.

The fulfilment of the legislative timetable had slipped significantly and in early 1997 some members of the Working Group moved for more rapid progress towards legislating a competition law. However, by the end of 1997 little headway had been made. A conference was held in Beijing in December 1997, supported by the OECD, at which international experts were present. The conference chairman expressed a desire to proceed swiftly with legislation, but to date (mid 2005) nothing has happened. In November 1998, a seminar was held jointly by the central government and the OECD to discuss a draft competition law. Another meeting was held at the Paris headquarters of OECD in October 1999 in preparation for a seminar held in Shanghai in December 1999 to discuss legislating China's competition law. The outcome of that meeting was broadly positive towards the draft law but several important issues remain unclear and they may not be remedied until after finalisation of a legislative draft is presented to the NPC or the NPCSC: there is no timetable for this as yet. Significant battles have to be fought over the scope and coverage of the legislation, its definitions and thresholds for triggering action, the powers, organisation, control and penalty provisions that will be granted to the enforcement agency. The role of the State Council and whether it will be competent to grant appeals from decisions of the enforcement body or provide exemptions to industries or businesses that breach the law's provisions are also major issues that are, as yet, unresolved.

The original timetable for legislation was thrown severely off course for several reasons. Firstly, it is clear that there is a division in government circles between those who believe that competition and free markets will more quickly and efficiently modernise and galvanise Chinese industry and those who have looked with admiration at Korea and Japan and seek to emulate their economic success by adopting a dirigiste state-sponsored industrial policy. They prefer an active, interventionist policy with government playing a major role in directing investment flows to protect and promote industrial national champions. Unfortunately for proponents of this view the Asian Economic Crisis of 1997 exposed how precarious the economies of Japan and South Korea really were in the more globalised world of today compared with the relatively protectionist, halcyon days of the 1950s and 1960s. Further, Japan and South Korea were the Cold War allies of the United States which was prepared to accept import flows from these countries without reciprocation from them in opening their markets fully to American products, so long as they remained unwavering opponents of world communism, as represented by the Soviet Union and the People's Republic of China. The Americans and Europeans are today unlikely to accept such a benign stance towards China as fellow members of the WTO. Within five years of accession, China is committed to make wholesale revisions to its market-access arrangements and to reduce substantially the tariff walls, that protect so many of China's creaking smoke-stack industries.[46] Realistically, the protectionist, state-sponsored route is not a viable alternative for China to pursue in current global economic conditions. But arguments about industrial policy have hindered progress towards a consensus on the adoption of a competition law.

Secondly, the technical issues of competition law are highly complex and international opinion on best practice is divided. In this climate, the Chinese have adopted a sensible approach to studying as many alternative systems as possible before seeking to fashion their own model to fit with their particular political, economic and social norms. The process of evaluation has taken longer than expected and the learning curve has perhaps been steeper than anticipated at the beginning of the exercise.

Thirdly, the power centres of all levels of government have been anxious to protect their power, influence and budgets. Substantive adoption of a workable competition policy will inevitably reduce the role and power of all levels of government. This has been a very serious impediment to rapid progress. Real or fictitious issues of principle, drafting, thresholds, enforcement and exemptions have, no doubt, extended debates about the precise form and content of a competition law significantly. Delay clearly serves the interests of industrial ministries and powerful local interests, who see their empires of patronage and control dissolving, in the face of, ironically, a more centralised economic regulatory mechanism.

Fourthly, for several years the prospect of WTO entry seemed a distant prospect as talks with the US and the EU ran into the sand. However,

---

[46] China–USA Trade Agreement, 15 November 1999 and China–EU Trade Agreement, 19 May 2000.

with the US deal agreed in November 1999 and the EU in May 2000, the prospect of wide-scale multinational access to China's domestic markets was now a tangible reality, rather than a theoretical possibility. China became a member of the WTO on 9 December 2001 and by 2006 will be facing intense foreign encroachment on its previously protected home ground. This may well be the crucial factor that speeds up the progress of legislation. Concern about foreign domination of Chinese markets is a real spur to competition legislation. Indeed, the new foreign-related merger control regulations issued in April 2003 address precisely this issue; they are analysed in section 5.7 below.

Fifthly, as always, finding legislative time in the calendar is problematic, especially when the principal legislative organ meets only once per year for a single two-week meeting. A law of this significance would probably require the endorsement of the full NPC, rather than the politically less significant imprimatur of the NPC Standing Committee. There has been continued indecision in finalising the draft and a further version appeared in October 2001. The next section will analyse the 1999 draft and then a commentary will follow on the changes made in the 2001 and 2004 versions.

5.5 The Draft Anti-Monopoly Law 1999

5.5.1 Objectives and definitions

The 1999 draft basically chooses the EU approach to competition law.[47] Articles 81 and 82 of the EC Treaty are adopted almost verbatim and merger control by reference to turnover thresholds is established. However, an additional element in the draft is the prohibition of administrative monopoly practices. An independent regulator is envisaged with effective enforcement powers including investigatory procedures and administrative powers to prohibit condemned conduct and impose financial penalties. Again, as with the substantive law, this is a strikingly similar regime to that of the EU. In view of the increasing likelihood of legislative action based on the 1999 draft, it is desirable to analyse these proposals.

Article 1 states that the law's purpose is to prevent monopoly behaviour, defend the competitive process, protect the legitimate interests of consumers and operators and promote the healthy development of the socialist market economy. It might be thought that some of these objectives

---

[47] An English version of this draft was prepared for an OECD-sponsored seminar held in Shanghai late in 1999.

are in conflict or even mutually exclusive particularly the protection of competitors as opposed to the protection of the process. But the interests of protected competitors must be 'legitimate' and so one might argue that they have a legitimate interest in the preservation of the competitive process, which is all they can demand, rather than intervention to protect market players no matter what effect this might have in relation to overall economic efficiency.

Broad aims for competition policy that are not always compatible are nothing unusual.[48] If the provisions, when enacted, are used solely to promote economic efficiency, then another of the perceived goals of the Chinese government, that of integrating the national market, may suffer. However, the imperative of market integration may not be as powerful a political objective as it was in the case of the EU, where rigid market segmentation along member state boundaries was the cardinal sin to be extirpated at all costs. Even in Europe this approach may well now have been softened as a result of the single market policies of the last two decades, which have resulted in substantial improvements in market integration.

In China, the competing needs for market integration and increased economic efficiency may, in fact, be complementary, given the urgent need to remove administrative barriers to intra-regional trade. This may, other things being equal, also promote consolidation within industries that are more exposed to competition and less able to seek the protection of the local government authorities. Thus, market integration and economic efficiency may be complementary objectives in China's case. But, if consolidation were to go too far, problems of dominance would clearly be a major concern. Attaining a balance between consolidation and competition should be the ultimate goal of Chinese policy makers. But that will be very difficult to achieve and, in the final analysis, it depends on political factors, which are not the primary concern of competition policy makers and enforcers. However, given China's political environment and governmental structures ignoring the political dimension of competition policy would be naïve in the extreme.

Article 2 contains definitions. The law regulates 'operators' who are legal persons, other economic organisations and individuals who are engaged in commodity operations (presumably production, distribution or sale of manufactured goods, raw materials or agricultural products at a

---

[48] In the EU competition policy may have conflicting goals. See Steiner and Woods, *Textbook on EC Law* (2000), pp. 189–95.

profit). The provision of services at a profit is included in the definition of commodity. Presumably, non profit-making governmental functions such as provision of education services or health services would not be included but private enterprises in these sectors would be. Difficulties of definition and coverage are potentially serious and the distinction between what is a government body providing not-for-profit services and commercial enterprises is particularly perplexing in an economy where the army runs hotels, telecommunication businesses, farms and universities and central government departments raise revenue by operating restaurants and night clubs. Monopoly behaviour is also defined in terms of 'abuse of market domination status' alone or in collusion whereby competition in a given market is excluded or restricted. This definition is very much in line with EU law in Article 82. The term 'given market' is also defined both by reference to geographical area and in relation to a particular commodity. It would appear that the notions of substitutability and cross-elasticities of demand must be taken into account in deciding what amounts to a market share of a particular commodity. This problem is very familiar in EU law and has spawned many leading cases[49] and substantial official guidance as to how the EU Commission arrives at a definition of the relevant market in specific cases.[50] It is submitted that if the draft Chinese law were enacted, reference to the principles of EU law in this regard would prove to be both appropriate and instructive. Article 4 expressly enjoins government departments at all levels to promote competition and desist from abuse of their administrative powers to restrict competition.

5.5.2 Abuse of dominance

Part Two of the draft then turns to the substantive prohibitions. Article 7 prohibits abuse of 'market dominance', which is defined in Article 8 as a sole operator in a given commodity market, or where an operator has an 'overwhelming position' in a given market 'which is difficult to enter' (presumably where there are significant barriers to entry). Article 8 (4) states that market domination status can be assumed when the market share of a single operator reaches 50 per cent or where two operators together have 66 per cent or three operators together have 75 per cent of a

---

[49] *United Brands v Commission* (Case 27/76) [1978] ECR 207.
[50] Commission Notice on the *Definition of the relevant market for the purposes of community competition law* (1997) OJ C372.

given market. Under Article 9 operators with dominance shall not unjustifiably set, adjust or maintain prices or supplies of commodities, impede access to the market of competitors, prevent or obstruct the entrance of new operators to the market or harm consumers. Other activities are also outlawed, price discrimination or the imposition of differential terms of supply (Article 10), incitement of intimidatory conduct by other operators against competitors (Article 11), forced tie-in sales (Article 12), predatory pricing (Article 13) and monopolisation of distribution channels (Article 14).

5.5.3 Restrictive agreements

Part Three of the draft deals with restrictive agreements of either a horizontal or a vertical nature. Under Article 15 agreements, of whatever nature, between competitors that restrict competition are prohibited. Examples are provided of prohibited conduct which include price-fixing or price maintenance, bid-rigging, restrictions on quantities or the quality of goods supplied, exclusive territoriality, exclusive dealing with suppliers or customers, restrictions on utilisation of new techniques or equipment and collusion to exclude or remove competitors. Article 16 specifically bans resale price maintenance. However, just as in Article 81(3) in EU law, the draft in Article 17 then provides for exemptions from the prohibitions on condition that they are conducive to overall economic development and the public interest, that competition is not thereby eliminated and that the regulatory authority grants a waiver. Examples are then provided of the types of agreement that might be favourably received by the regulator. They include agreements to adopt new technology, improve product quality, raise economic efficiency, reduce costs and standardise specifications and to undertake research and development. Small and medium-sized businesses that co-operate to improve efficiency are granted favourable consideration (presumably a *de minimis* exemption). Crisis cartels are also potentially permissible.

Article 18 provides for offending agreements to be notified to the regulator, who may grant exemption. However, agreements that create or reinforce market dominance or relate to price-fixing or price maintenance cannot be exempted. Notification must take place within fifteen days of inception of the restrictive agreement Article 19 and within one month a decision must be made by the regulator who may condemn the agreement, ratify it or make it subject to conditions. It is generally accepted that horizontal agreements of the most blatant type – production limitations and price fixing – are very common in Chinese industry[51] and vertical restraints are equally prevalent.[52] Consequently, it is submitted that the real level of restrictive agreements must, in reality, be very great and unless there is a system of block exemption or even the non-application of the provision to most vertical agreements, the administrative system to adjudicate individual exemptions will break down. The draft law provides power for the regulatory body to make delegated legislation, in similar fashion to the EU Commission's powers. Presumably, these matters could be dealt with in such subordinate legislation.

5.5.4 Merger control

Part Four then turns to merger control. Article 20 defines a merger situation as occurring in one of five circumstances:

- the outright combination of two or more operators;
- the acquisition by one operator of more than one third of the issued capital of another;
- the purchase or lease of all or most of the assets of another operator;
- entering into an arrangement whereby there is effective management of one operator's business by another;
- direct or indirect control of another operator's business or personnel appointments or removals.

Article 21 envisages control of the mergers whereby application for ratification of a merger proposal must be submitted to the regulator. The thresholds for notification are:

- the merged enterprise has more than a 50 per cent market share of a given commodity market; or
- one of the potential merger partners has a 25 per cent market share of a given commodity market prior to the merger; or

[51] For example, on 20 January 2000 the Chinese Automobile Industry Association announced a decision by the ten domestic automobile manufacturers that they would not compete with each other on price and would agree a tariff of automobile prices, *China Daily*, 3 March 2000. In June 2000, nine television manufacturers formed a price alliance to co-ordinate the retail prices of televisions, *China Daily*, 31 July 2000.
[52] For example, refusals to supply to support resale price maintenance agreements are commonplace. In July 2000 a television manufacturer, Changhong, announced that it had suspended supplies of its television sets to Guomei, a large Beijing retailer, as a result of the store reducing the retail price of its products without the manufacturer's agreement, *China Daily*, ibid.

• one of the potential merger partners has a turnover volume in excess of an administratively defined amount, which is not mentioned in the draft.

Under Article 22 the application for ratification must contain relevant information on the enterprise's business, assets, employees, sales volume, profit margins and taxes paid. Company annual reports and financial statements, production and operational costs, prices, an assessment of the effects of the merger relative to the overall economic social and public interest and the rationale for the merger must be provided by the applicant. The time for notification is not made clear. It appears to be an *ex post facto* notification system rather than a preliminary approval procedure. However, logically, where enterprises realise that they are about to sign a merger agreement they could make the validity of the contract conditional on approval from the regulator.[53] The regulator then has two months under Article 23 to make a decision on the application, but this can be extended. There is a presumption against any merger that creates or strengthens market dominance or even one that merely restricts competition. Mergers must improve market competition before they will be ratified under Article 24 but there is an overriding power under Article 25 for the State Council to approve a merger that promotes the national economic, social or public interest.

Clearly, there is an inherent tension between Articles 24 and 25. Article 24 seems unrealistically pro-competition. Mergers between substantial competitors must reduce competition to some extent; they can hardly promote competition by reducing it! But if the merger promotes other sorts of economic or technical progress or creates new products and competition is not eliminated, mergers can be beneficial. Article 24 needs to reflect a more realistic approach to merger control. Despite this pro-competitive stance, Article 25 proceeds to drive a coach and horses through this policy. This is, unashamedly, a tool to promote a national champion policy. There are no countervailing requirements of technical improvements or even that any competition remains at all within a given market. Article 25 could allow the creation of new-scale monopolists. Consequently, if enacted in this form the integrity of the merger control regime could very easily be undermined, especially given the traditional interventionist policy of industrial ministries. If ratification is refused or not sought the

[53] Contract Law 1999 (PRC) Article 45 states: 'The parties may agree to attach conditions to the effectiveness of the contract.'

regulator may, under Article 26, prohibit the merger or require divestiture or reinstatement of the status quo ante or impose a financial penalty.

5.5.5 Administrative Monopoly

Part Five deals with the Chinese peculiarity of Administrative Monopoly. The oddity of a monolithic, single party, non-democratic government having to issue a legal prohibition to prevent other parts of the same government from breaking or abusing its own administrative powers is an unusual phenomenon. But as mentioned above the Balkanisation of political power in China concomitant with an ineffective rule of law makes these explicit provisions necessary, although in many respects they simply reiterate the matters alluded to in other regulations (see section 5.3).

Article 28 prohibits government organs from obtaining supplies of commodities from a single supplier or from using administrative measures to restrict or exclude legitimate competition. Article 29 deals with regional protectionism and forbids the use of administrative powers to restrict the inflow or outflow of commodities to or from a particular locality. Article 30 prohibits a range of governmental conduct, namely: forced mergers and forced association agreements between operators; compulsory alignment of prices; forced purchase or sale of commodities by operators; and administrative orders requiring operators to desist from competing or to set output limits or to limit product ranges. Some of these prohibitions are perfectly logical but the prohibition of forced mergers could be more perplexing. Clearly, mergers in the state-owned enterprise sector is a pressing issue. Consolidation in certain industries such as automotive and steel is an absolute national priority if industries such as these are to have any chance of competing in the more open trading environment that should eventuate after the transitional phase of WTO membership has passed. Administratively sponsored mergers are a political necessity and so, perhaps, this provision is aimed at purely localised forced mergers to form uneconomic conglomerate enterprises that have no commercial logic behind them at all and are merely necessitated by local political factors, rather than economic ones. Presumably, central-government-sponsored mergers of state-owned industries would not be affected or would be exempted by the State Council under Article 25.

At present administratively sponsored prohibitions against competition are very common in many industries. A recent example has been price discounting in the airline industry. In recent years the monolithic

China National Aviation Corporation (CNAC) that controlled all aspects of civil aviation in China was broken up to form a civil aviation regulator who controlled all civil airports, air traffic control and regulatory matters and separate operational airline businesses. Some of the operators have even been listed on the Hong Kong stock market, such as China Eastern Airline, though the state retains majority control. Surprisingly, once freed from the shackles of the CNAC, the operating companies began to compete on previously monopolised routes and began offering discounted fares. In 1998, some of the airlines began to suffer losses but instead of withdrawing from the market they complained to CNAC who immediately ordered a cessation of 'malignant competition'[54] and imposed regulations in 1999 to establish a uniform national tariff. However, the travelling public was irate[55] with CNAC's imposition of higher fares and passenger traffic fell precipitately by some 3 million in 1999.[56] In July 2000, the CNAC announced that the operating airlines would be reorganised into three major groups and the new entities would once again be allowed to compete on price. It is suggested that such conduct is widespread and that the draft provisions are aimed at curbing such behaviour. By 2002, after eighteen months of tense negotiations, three holding companies, Air China, China Southern and China Eastern Airlines had been established by the administrative fiat of CNAC. The 'directed reform', whereby these three entities now control the nine largest operational airlines in China, which have an estimated 80 per cent market share,[57] was not inspiring confidence. The government-controlled *China Daily*, opined that the forced mergers, whereby economically stronger entities were required to take over all the assets as well as the large liabilities of weaker operators, had not strengthened, the industry overall and had not made the airline sector more able to meet foreign competition. The weak operators had been 'incompetent in cutting costs . . . had hundreds of thousands of redundant employees and failed to demonstrate good management skills'.[58] Such shotgun marriages of SOEs may not be successful in a competitive market.

---

[54] See *China Eastern Airlines Today Magazine*, July 2000, p. 18, per Li Zhongming, President of China Eastern Airlines.
[55] See a series of articles in *China Daily*, 17 November 1999, 27 April 2000, 24 May 2000.
[56] See *China Daily*, 30 July 2000.
[57] Jia Fuwen, President of Shandong Aviation, 'Soaring in the sky with the wings of Qi Lu', *Air Travel*, CNAC, May 2004.
[58] 'China admits aviation reform plan falls short', *South China Morning Post*, 5 November 2002.

5.5.6 Administration and enforcement

Part Six of the draft establishes a new regulatory body to administer the competition law. Its remit is to formulate competition policy and subordinate regulations, investigating and enforcing the competition law, conducting non-adversarial market structure investigations and preparing and publicising a list of operators who dominate a given market (Article 31).

The regulatory body is to be established under the auspices of the State Council and will not be answerable to functional ministries or local governments; its tasks are to be undertaken independently and without interference from individuals or bodies (Article 32). The independence and status of the regulator is crucial to the successful implementation of competition law in China. Institutional capture by vested interests and discriminatory application of the rules would utterly undermine the objectives of the draft law. Central government officials involved in this policy area are fully aware of the vital importance of this issue and needless to say there are voices within the apparatus of government that seek to subvert the independence of any regulator in this field. However, the recent reorganisation of China's central bank, the People's Bank of China, into a strong headquarters with regional outposts, has militated against institutional capture by individual provincial governments, as was the case before reorganisation. Article 39 of the draft law also allows the regulatory body to follow the model provided by the central bank. To reinforce the prestige and seniority of the regulatory body, Articles 33 to 35 provide that the chairman of the regulatory body will hold the rank of minister with two deputies with the rank of vice-minister. The chairman will be appointed by the NPC and the State Council will appoint the six other members of the body (who should be legal or economic experts). Strict duties of confidentiality are imposed on members in respect of all commercially sensitive information that comes to their knowledge as a result of the regulatory functions (Article 37). Members will have a term of office of five years and can only be removed in specified circumstances – ill health, criminal conviction or breaches of statutory duty (Article 38). Decisions of the regulatory body will be made by voting and a two-thirds majority is needed (five out of seven members) to adopt decisions. Investigatory powers are granted to the regulatory body for cases involving breach of the draft law in Articles 41 and 42. However, there is a crucial weakness in that the regulator can only investigate breaches of the Administrative Monopoly provisions and therefore report to the offender's higher authority. The regulator cannot take punitive or injunctive measures against the offending department. This is a major flaw. Given the nature of government, this provision may render the draft law a paper tiger, as Administrative Monopoly is one of the most serious components of the uncompetitive economic situation found in contemporary China. It appears that the industrial and administrative organs of the state are not prepared to countenance the interference of a new body in what they regard as their 'back yard'.

The result of this enforcement lacuna may well undermine the whole coherence of the structure of the draft law let alone the impartial and vigorous enforcement of its principle objectives. A new round of discussion and negotiation must be undertaken so that this weakness can be eliminated; if this is not done, the draft law may well be rendered largely ineffective, as sponsoring departments are very unlikely to take vigorous action to correct the anti-competitive activities of their subordinate organs. Sufficient powers to enforce the competition law against other government organs must be given to the regulator, so that the law can be enforced impartially against both enterprises in the state and private sectors and against government organs. Without this, the law may well not only be a failure but may also undermine confidence that the central government is serious about promoting competition law in China. This would be a most unfortunate consequence and might throw into doubt China's real commitment to the market-opening commitments made to the United States and the European Union in the WTO accession agreements. It could also result after the transition period in bilateral trade disputes. For all these reasons this provision must be amended.

The general investigatory powers awarded to the regulator include questioning witnesses, requiring the production of records of all sorts and entry upon premises including residential premises to conduct searches (Article 42). All decisions of the regulator must be made public but any confidential information discovered in the course of an investigation must be kept secret (Article 43).

5.5.7 Penalties and sanctions

Part Seven of the draft deals with penalties and related matters. Under Article 44 abuse of a dominant position, cartel operations and resale price maintenance are all grouped together. The punishments that may be awarded include a cease-and-desist order, confiscation of 'illegal income' and a fine of up to three times the 'illegal income'. In the most egregious cases the business licence of the offender may be cancelled. As in EC law, it is the regulator that acts as investigator, prosecutor, jury and judge. This agglomeration of roles has been criticised in the past[59] but in the case of the EU there has always been recourse to originally the Court of Justice, or now to the Court of First Instance when an investigated party was dissatisfied with either a procedural error or the quantum of the penalty imposed.[60] The courts have power to vary penalties up or down or dismiss any case where the Commission had committed a procedural error, not proved its case or had erred in law or made a wrong determination of fact.[61]

In the draft law Article 51 provides a right to seek reconsideration of a decision by the regulator, which must be launched within fifteen days of receipt of the decision or appeal, may be made directly to the People's Court. A question must be raised, however, as to whether many judges in the Chinese court system will have the dual competence required to comprehend fully the complexities of the economic and legal issues that may well arise in cases of this type. It is suggested that it will be necessary to make administrative rules to assign these cases directly either to the Higher People's Court or to the Supreme People's Court in Beijing due to the danger of local or regional partiality of provincial tribunals favouring the investigated enterprise or a lack of competence of judges to deal with cases of this nature. Reference to the Supreme People's Court would also have the advantage of adding weight to any legal opinions to be made on competition cases and this body would be less influenced by local or departmental protectionism.

Another problem with Article 44 is the issue of 'illegal income'. No definition of the phrase is given in the draft law and no method of calculation of this sum is prescribed. Consequently, given the vagueness of the phrase adopted, the calculation of 'illegal income' will be extremely problematic, if not impossible. If no calculation can be made, no confiscation can occur and no penalty can be imposed. This is a major flaw. A definition of the phrase must be made to ensure that calculation can take place. Alternatively, the EC law method of penalty calculation[62] whereby reference is

---

[59] Tom Lenaerts and Walter Vandamme, *Procedural rights of private parties in community administrative proceedings* (1997), 34 CML Rev. 531.

[60] See Regulation 17/62 (1959–62) OJ (special edition), p. 87, especially Article 17.

[61] See *National Panasonic v Commission* (Case 136/79); *Music Diffusion Française v Commission* (Case 100-103/80); *Transocean Marine Paint v Commission* (Case 17/74); *Hoechst v Commission* (Case 46/87).

[62] Regulation 17/62 ibid. Article 15(2) Euro 1,000 to 1,000,000 or up to 10 per cent of turnover in the preceding year.

made to a percentage of turnover could be adopted as the penalty provision that would prove more usable and certain. It will also be necessary to set guidelines for the imposition of the level of any penalty imposed; this could be achieved through delegated legislation.[63] Currently, the provision, as drafted, is unworkable. Further, even if 'illegal income' is defined, the penal provision of three times 'illegal income' is unlikely to prove a deterrent. The level of the penalty provision is much too low to deter or punish serious breaches of competition rules. A large monopolist is unlikely to worry about such low penalties and will simply pay the fine and carry on abusing the other market players or the consumer. The law will not achieve its objectives without much more stringent penalty provisions. Also, there is no provision for repeat offenders or for offenders who ignore or evade stop-and-desist orders made by the regulator to receive exemplary punishment. The draft law should make clear that repeat offences would be punished more severely and that ignoring the orders of the regulator would have serious consequences.

Other lesser offences under Articles 10, 11, 12, 13 and 14 are dealt with even more leniently with stop-and-desist orders, confiscation of 'illegal income' and a small fine of a maximum of RMB200,000. These penalties suffer from the same defects as those alluded to above. This provision must be amended to reflect the fact that even these breaches of the law can have serious economic consequences and are taken very seriously by the authorities. Penalties at this level will not have a salutary effect.

Article 46 deals with qualifying mergers that have not sought ratification by the regulator. The penalty is set at a fine between RMB100,000 and RMB1,000,000. Unscrambling of the unauthorised merger is also possible under Article 26. Again the financial penalties are really very low and should be substantially increased by a factor of 10 to make the penalty more realistic, especially when one may be dealing with enterprises that have a net worth of billions of RMB.

Articles 47 and 48 give a statutory right to a victim of anti-competitive behaviour to bring an action in the People's Court to recover losses arising from the unlawful behaviour. The level of compensation is by reference to actual loss or the offender's illicit profits plus the investigation expenses. This formula is open to the same criticism as made earlier in respect to the regulator's enforcement penalties. Further, private persons apparently cannot request injunctive relief, though, clearly, they should be able to do

---

[63] The EU Commission has published its guidelines on the imposition of fines in competition cases (1998) OJ C9/3.

so. The addition of a specific statutory right to private recompense also accords with the directly applicable nature of Articles 81 and 83 of the EC Treaty, whereby individuals injured by unlawful conduct can claim injunctive relief as well as damages from the courts of their member state.[64] In the United States, plaintiffs can claim treble damages and injunctive relief against defendants who breach the anti-trust rules.[65] Given the limited experience in assessment of damages and the potentially powerful effect of private enforcement actions, damages calculations should be made punitive to encourage injured plaintiffs to take action, especially where they cannot persuade the regulator to act. Such action could also be a deterrent to potential and actual offenders. Private enforcement can be a powerful tool to force compliance with the law. China should consider adopting a treble-damage rule for these reasons. China already has an analogous provision in consumer law whereby a consumer who is the victim of a fraud in the provision of goods or services can claim double the consideration paid for the product.[66]

Another power that the draft law lacks is that of divestment in monopoly or oligopoly situations. As mentioned above, divestment orders are possible in objectionable merger cases but the limitation to financial penalties only in monopoly and oligopoly cases in the draft law are possibly a mistake. In British competition law, divestment orders have been used under the provisions now contained in the Enterprise Act 2002, previously under the Fair Trading Act 1973.[67] The relevant minister can exercise this power after an adverse finding in a Competition Commission Report on structural problems found in a given industry. A classic example was the action taken by the Conservative government in the late 1980s to require divestment by dominant brewery companies of part of their tied estate of public houses and a requirement that the remaining tied outlets would have to offer for sale at the affected outlets at least one beer produced by a rival brewer.[68] The object of these requirements was to weaken the regional dominance of several of the brewers and to allow customers more choice of product. The effectiveness of the orders in achieving their aim is debatable but they did inject a significant change into the brewing

---

[64] *Garden Cottage Foods v Milk Marketing Board* [1984] AC 130 and *Cutsforth v Mansfield Inns* [1986] 1 CMLR 1. Also see Notice on co-operation between national courts and the Commission (93/C 39/05).

[65] Clayton Act ss. 4 and 16 38 Stat. 730 (1914).

[66] Article 49, Protection of Consumers' Rights and Interests Law (1993).

[67] See ss. 131–6, Enterprise Act 2002 (UK).

[68] UK Monopolies and Mergers Commission report, *The Supply of Beer*, Cmd 651 (1989).

industry in Britain. Despite the recent overhaul of British competition law to align it more closely with the EC model,[69] the investigation and divestment powers under the old Fair Trading Act 1973 Provisions were retained by the new legislation, as they may be a more appropriate remedy than a financial penalty in a situation of chronic market failure.[70]

The US system also has provision for divestment powers[71] to be exercised in suitable monopolistic and oligopolistic situations. The courts have used the power sparingly even where the US government has demanded such orders[72] but in some major cases such as *United States v AT & T*[73] and currently *United States v Microsoft Corp.*[74] the courts have required the restructuring of major industries. In the Chinese context, it is submitted that such investigation and divestment powers would be very useful in many potentially serious market-failure situations of oligopolistic competition or in pure abusive monopoly cases. Consequently, it might well be advisable to add such a power to the armoury arrayed in Part Seven of the draft law. This would add significantly to the powers available to the Chinese regulatory authority.

5.5.8 Exemptions

Part Eight of the draft law contains miscellaneous provisions. It provides for the enactment of detailed implementation and enforcement rules: the complete exclusion of the exercise of intellectual property rights and various utility services – post office, railways, the electricity, gas and water industries or from the purview of the law. The exclusion for the utility sectors is only for five years from the implementation date. It is arguable that the exclusion of such a significant block of industries from the application of the competition law is damaging to the integrity of the whole system envisaged by the draft law but at least the exclusion is limited to a fixed period of five years. In the UK most utilities are now subject to sectoral regulatory regimes that have competition as one of their objectives. The

---

[69] Competition Act 1998 (UK).

[70] See D. Parker, *The Competition Act 1998: change and continuity in U.K. competition policy*, Journal of Business Law (July Issue) 283 (2000).

[71] 26 Stat. 209 (1890) Sherman Act ss. 4 Federal Courts have power to 'prevent and restrain violations of the Act'.

[72] See Ernest Gellhorn and William E. Kovacic, *Anti-trust law and economics*, 4th edn, New York: West Publishing (1994), pp. 134–6.

[73] 552 F. Supp. 131 (D.C. 1982).

[74] US District Court, Washington D.C., C.A.98–1232 http://usvms.gpo.gov/ save that the Federal Appeal Court substantially overturned the divestiture orders of the lower court.

sector regulators have concurrent powers[75] with the general enforcement authorities (the Office of Fair Trading and the Competition Commission) as regards investigation and penalties. A member of the UK Competition Commission has suggested[76] that 'some of the most interesting challenges under the new Act will arise [from regulating the utility sector]'. Therefore, it is submitted that the mere exclusion of these industries from the ambit of the draft law is not enough, the law should take account of them and their activities should be subject to scrutiny.

An interesting point to note is that telecommunications is not in the excluded category. This sector is dominated in China by China Telecom, which holds well over 90 per cent of the whole vast Chinese telecommunications market. China Telecom's charges verge on confiscation, rather than a fee for service, and the cost of long-distance and particularly international calls is prohibitive.[77] It appears that this state leviathan was not sufficiently politically favoured to be included in the list of utilities that can escape the strictures of the draft competition law. The government seems to consider, therefore, that the telecom sector should be subject to the rigours of market competition, presumably to force the pace of the modernisation of China's telecommunications infrastructure. China Unicom, the only licensed competitor at the moment, has faced massive interconnection problems and other impediments to it carrying on its business from an incumbent reluctant to share its market.[78] The whole sector would undoubtedly benefit from foreign investment, which would increase consumer welfare by providing choice and also at the same time lower prices. Under China's WTO accession agreements, foreign interests will be able to own up to half of Chinese telecommunication businesses and liberalisation of the industry is now gathering pace.[79]

5.6 The 2001 Draft modifications

In October 2001, a conference was organised by the central government, sponsored by the joint drafting committee, to consider further

---

[75] UK Competition Act 1998 s.54 and Schedule 10.
[76] Parker, *The Competition Act 1998*, pp. 297–300.
[77] In 1998, 20,000 complaints were made to the Chinese Consumer Association concerning low quality and high prices in the telecommunications sector, *China Daily*, 15 March 1999.
[78] *China Daily*, 15 January 1999.
[79] Announcement of new regulations on foreign involvement in the telecommunications industry by the Chinese Telecommunications Minister, Wu Jichuan, *China Daily*, 26 September 2000.

amendments to the 1999 draft[80] in light of comments made and issues raised by concerned parties.[81] It became apparent that official bodies other than the SETC and the SAIC had a number of objections to the proposed legislation. There was clearly a turf war in progress as the SETC had crucially made amendments to the effect that the proposed competition authority would come under its aegis; other government departments feared losing some of their regulatory powers and were also unhappy that their officials had not been part of the drafting group.

The arguments raised by the State Planning and Development Commission (SPDC) were essentially self-serving as it feared losing some of its price-control functions in the domestic market if a competition authority under SETC was established. It objected to the proposed legislation on principle and maintained that since the domestic market was not well developed, Administrative Monopoly should be controlled by reform of government structures and existing agencies' powers of enforcement should be enhanced, so that there was no need for the creation of a new body. Both the Ministries of Railways and Aviation proposed that as railways and airports were natural monopolies they should be exempted from the scope of the proposed law. The Ministry of Finance, which had no vested interest, supported the legislation and a single competition authority. The Ministry of Communications wanted to retain control of competition within its industry. All of these objections were entirely predictable and probably mean that consensus is far from being achieved. The matter will languish in legislative limbo unless it receives strong political backing that will break the bureaucratic log-jam.

In order better to appreciate the evolutionary process between the 1999 draft and the 2001 draft, the substantive changes found in the 2001 document will now be examined. The first major alteration is an explicit declaration of the extent of the application of the law. The new provisions provide that the law will apply to:

- conduct that affects the market for goods or services within the territory of the PRC;

---

[80] The 2001 modifications have not been officially published in Chinese or in English; this is an internal working document but clearly shows important policy shifts since the 1999 draft.

[81] The author has been especially fortunate in receiving information on the nature and content of the discussions at this meeting from a participant, who cannot be identified for reasons of confidentiality.

- the conduct of government agencies who abuse their powers to restrict competition; and
- conduct that takes place outside the territory of the PRC but which affects Chinese markets.[82]

The definition of markets is widened to include reference to close substitutes,[83] in addition to products of the same type.

The scope of forbidden behaviours that operators with market power cannot lawfully engage in is also widened to include 'interference with other operators' business activities' and 'conduct that obviously harms consumers'.[84] No definitions are given of these terms and they clearly widen the types of censured conduct. It may be that they extend the scope of egregious conduct beyond that which is properly within the purview of a competition statute. Also, these extensions, in the Chinese context, give too enhanced discretionary powers to the competition authority, so giving rise to a fear that they might be used in a partial or heavy-handed way.

The competition authority is given new powers to define market-domination status[85] and dominant players are prohibited from charging higher prices than would be usual under competitive conditions.[86] The rule-making powers are unobjectionable but the prohibition of high prices on pain of penalty is a power too far. In the absence of abusive behaviour or artificially erected barriers to entry, the market should encourage competitors into the arena to compete away the monopoly profit; civil servants should not be involved in determining 'fair' prices. This may give a hint that the bureaucrats still have not ideologically bought into the idea of the invisible hand of the market operating to set prices and hanker after the old pricing mechanism provided under the state plan.

A new ban on refusals to deal without objective reasons is also included in the prohibited abuses of a firm with market power.[87] With respect to collusive agreements, none with clauses that sanction market domination or reinforce such a position or fix prices shall be considered for exemption by the competition authority.[88] The competition authority will now have an extended period of two months to consider exemption for qualifying agreements, rather than the one month in the previous draft,[89] and further supplementary rule-making powers concerning procedure and the criteria to be used in assessing the agreement are added.[90] Another new clause

---

[82] New draft (2001) Article 2.   [83] Ibid. new Article 3.   [84] Ibid. new Article 8.
[85] Ibid. new Article 9.   [86] Ibid. new Article 10.   [87] Ibid. new Article 13.
[88] Ibid. new Article 19.   [89] Ibid. new Article 21.   [90] Ibid. new Article 22.

allows the authority power to approve, cancel, amend the agreement or order a cease-and-desist order.[91]

The merger provisions in Part IV are recast. The English version (provided to the author by official sources) uses the terminology 'convergence of economic power', which is now defined as the acquisition of control of other operators. 'Control'[92] is not defined, a serious error; the 1999 draft did have a clear threshold test. However, the market-share threshold of the converged business which triggers a requirement to receive administrative permission to merge is reduced from 50 per cent to 33 per cent[93] but there is no minimum turnover requirement; this may be a simple drafting oversight as it appears to mean that any merger, irrespective of its economic consequence that creates a firm with 33 per cent of any market is notifiable. This would not appear to be a sensible threshold for a national notification procedure or to have any economic justification.

The period within which the authority must adjudicate on a merger is extended from two to three months. Further, the balancing provisions in the 1999 draft of a requirement to show an improved post-merger competitive environment and advantages that outweigh the disadvantages, is removed. This appears reasonable, as the former provision seemed to provide an almost impossible test to ensure approval.

Turning to AM, a very extended definition of prohibited activity is added.[94] The prohibitions now include:

• requirements that local materials or services be used in commercial operations;
• physical blockades at local boundaries or at points of entry;
• discriminative charges or administrative burdens;
• use of different technical standards or duplicating testing or other procedures to exclude non-local goods;
• creation of local commercial or maintenance of local monopolies;
• exclusion of non-local bidders from tendering processes; and
• prohibiting the establishment of non-locally owned businesses and their investment in categories of commerce.

As regards enforcement, one idea appears to have been dropped, namely the function of maintaining an official list of entities that satisfy the definition of market dominance.[95] Additionally, some bureaucratic 'face' has been saved by adding a function of advising state organs on any of their

[91] Ibid. new Article 23.   [92] Ibid. new Article 24.   [93] Ibid. new Article 25.
[94] Ibid. new Article 33.   [95] Ibid. new Article 38.

rules or regulations that have an anti-competitive effect; but this is an advisory role only, there is no power to dictate or strike down incompatible rules.

A worrying change is that in the 1999 draft the proposed competition authority had a high-powered board of seven with a chairman of ministerial rank and two vice-chairmen of vice-ministerial rank. This would place it at the top of the bureaucratic pyramid – a vital issue if it is to carry out its functions effectively. In China, the rank of the head of the organisation will determine not only its budget but also its precedence and, thus, authority. This is all-important in the culture of the Chinese state. The new draft omits the composition and ranking of the senior personnel. Also, the original proposal was that the NPC would select the three top post-holders; this too is now absent.

Further, the duty of confidentiality of authority members is omitted but retained for more junior staff,[96] as are provisions on fixed terms of five years and entrenchment of members' tenure, unlike the 1999 draft. The rules governing the conduct of investigation, official meetings and voting on authority decisions are dropped. It appears that the original effort to ensure independence and incorruptibility have been significantly watered down. This might signal that the original intention of a powerful central body with 'clout' is now being undermined by the bureaucratic opponents of effective competition enforcement. The new body may be emasculated by lowering its status. Another manifestation of the strength of the vested interests in the bureaucratic state is the new provision that suggests that the competition authority may seek a compromise with an investigated malefactor,[97] whereby a 'recommendation' may be made which if accepted will result in the investigation being terminated without penalty. This appears to be a very Chinese method of 'saving face' and is probably designed to allow government departments to promise to desist from illegal acts without the imposition of a public penalty.

The penalty provisions of the new draft are also amended. In respect of abuse of dominance the 1999 proposals were, at least partly, unworkable in that in addition to injunctive prohibition orders and criminal sanctions, the financial penalty was limited to three times any 'illegal income'. This would be difficult to calculate and might have resulted in a very small penalty with regard to potentially serious abuses or ones that originated from a very large enterprise, so any retributive or deterrent effect might be nugatory. The new provisions retain the injunctive and criminal

---

[96] Ibid. new Article 45.   [97] Ibid. new Article 43.

powers but amend the financial penalty provisions to allow for a maximum RMB 1 million or 15 per cent of annual turnover as the sanction.[98] This is a much more sensible method of calculation and an appropriate level of sanction, in line with international norms. Further, this applies to all abusive conduct of whatever type, whereas the 1999 draft differentiated, to some extent illogically, between types of abuse as regards level of penalty with some offences having a maximum penalty of only RMB 20,000 under the 1999 provisions, which was laughably low. In respect of collusive agreements, the 1999 draft stipulated similar penalties to those for abusive conduct. The new draft provides for stiffer penalties, though, interestingly, less punitive than that for abusive conduct, which seems odd given the universal condemnation of hard-core cartels internationally and the increasing international trend towards criminalisation of cartel operations.[99] The new penalty provides for a maximum fine of either RMB 50,000 or up to 10 per cent of turnover, but with no criminal sanction.[100]

One is driven to consider why these proposals now differentiate between the abuse of dominance and collusive conduct and why collusive agreements are seen as deserving a lesser maximum penalty than monopoly practices. One reason might be that collusive or co-operative behaviour is not seen in China as being as reprehensible as monopolistic behaviour given the high premium given to group activities by Chinese society. Another reason might be the perception that collaboration might be necessary in some markets and the group exploitation of consumers is not as reprehensible as single-firm monopoly gouging that might be considered as a wholly inappropriate and selfish activity.

As regards failure to apply for permission to merge in appropriate cases the old provision stipulated a punishment of RMB100,000 to RMB 1 million; these were low but in addition divestment powers were also available. The new provisions provide for fines of RMB100,000 to RMB 5 million,[101] in addition to divestment. These are obviously significantly more punitive. Further, the lack of any enforcement penalties as regards AM was a serious flaw in the 1999 draft but the new draft rectifies the lacuna by providing for administrative but not judicial sanctions. Responsible officials at local government levels who impose regional blockades in contravention of Article 34 may be subject to demotion or dismissal

---

[98] Ibid. new Article 46.

[99] For example, in the United Kingdom, s.188 Enterprise Act 2002 creates a new 'cartel offence' with maximum penalties stipulated in s.190 of up to five years' imprisonment and /or an unlimited fine.

[100] New Article 47 (2001) draft.   [101] Ibid. new Article 48.

or even criminal sanctions.[102] In relation to other manifestations of AM, the new draft provides that the competition authority may investigate and 'demand' cessation. Demotion, dismissal or criminal action may be taken against culpable individuals.[103] These new provisions are an improvement on the 1999 proposals but they still appear to be very weak. Admonition from higher authority has been tried for over twenty years and has been completely ineffective. Therefore, one must be very sceptical as to whether, given the apparent demotion of the stature of the competition authority related above, these provisions will effectively tackle the problem. The criminal sanctions will be equally toothless as identifying exactly who, in a very collective style of decision-making especially in government, was responsible for making and/or implementing the impugned act. Thus, the likelihood of these measures being successful is slight.

As regards compensation to wronged individuals a right to compensation is maintained, again with the Beijing Intermediate People's Court having exclusive jurisdiction,[104] presumably for the same reasons as mentioned above. In relation to financial penalties imposed by the competition authority should the malefactor not pay the penalty, the authority can instruct the debtor's bank to deduct and pay over the fine levied.[105] Finally, a vital issue is left until last – exemption. The 1999 draft exempted from implementation for five years all public utilities – posts, electricity, gas and water – with the exception of telecommunications. In the 2001 draft these exemptions are omitted. This is a very important development given the well-catalogued abuses of the public sector utilities. Thus, it appears that all sectors are now to be within the ambit of the new draft with no sectoral exemptions at all. This would be very surprising. It is assumed that this is an accidental omission and any law finally adopted will include a list of exempted industries.

5.7 Control of enterprise mergers – only foreigners need comply

In late 2002, the central government published a set of draft regulations to control foreign related mergers. These draft rules were announced by the Ministry of Foreign Trade and Economic Co-operation (MOFTEC) though actually promulgated by several government organs. This was done without any prior warning or consultation. Presumably the

---

[102] Ibid. new Article 49.   [103] Ibid. new Article 50.
[104] Ibid. new Article 51.   [105] Ibid. new Article 54.

gathering pace of foreign-related acquisitions or the perceived foreign
threat to WTO liberalised sectors, panicked the government into the creation of this new regulatory scheme in the absence of a general competition
law to control undesirable mergers that threaten to concentrate unduly
ownership of sectors of the Chinese market in foreign hands, that were
not already directly controlled by the state. It should be noted that these
provisions are *ad hoc*, are stated to be 'interim provisions' and apply only
to foreign acquirers of a Chinese target entity. Presumably these 'interim'
provisions will be repealed when a finalised general competition statute
eventually emerges. The original draft was completed and promulgated
on 7 March 2003, entering into force on 12 April 2003.[106]

Article 1 states that the objectives of the Provisions are to 'promote
and standardise foreign investment, implement national allocation of resources, ensure employment, safeguard competition and the safety of the
national economy'. Clearly, the hand of bureaucratic control hovers over
market mechanisms to direct national resource allocation, to protect inefficient but substantial providers of jobs and ensure 'safety', which is
probably a euphemism for protecting the nascent national champions
that China is seeking to create and promote by administrative means.
Examples have already been given of this administrative sponsorship of
'bigness' in relation to the automotive, the airline and the steel industries
in earlier sections of this book. Another purpose of these rules appears to
be to prevent foreign domination of sectors of the domestic market. Market information already shows that, as of 2002, foreign firms dominated or
had substantial shares of various markets, even before the WTO liberalisations took effect. Kodak had almost 50 per cent of the photographic film
market, Nestle about 40 per cent of the instant coffee market, Proctor and
Gamble had 30 per cent of the hair-care product market, Hewlett-Packard
had 25 per cent of the commercial internet-server market and Epson
30 per cent of the computer-printer market.[107] This phenomenon alarmed
the Chinese authorities into creating these interim regulations in an attempt to slow down or prevent further encroachment by foreign firms on
other domestic markets by the acquisition of domestic enterprises. This

---

[106] The official title of the regulations is the *Interim provisions on mergers and acquisition
of domestic enterprises by foreign investors*, order of the Ministry of Foreign Trade and
Economic Co-operation, the State Administration of Taxation, the State Administration
for Industry and Commerce and the State Administration of Foreign Exchange, order
No. 3 of 2003.

[107] 'Beijing's anti-trust package may trip up multinationals', *South China Morning Post*,
24 October 2002. The quoted statistics were produced by Market Research Data.

is paradoxical, as many of the foreign entities with large market shares have obtained this market position as a result of the purchase of SOE assets from the government. Central government policy may, therefore, be thought to be somewhat schizophrenic; on the one hand government wants more foreign investment and technology transfers and to be rid of the loss-making SOEs, but on the other frets about the very organisations that it has brought to birth by selling public assets to foreign acquirers. Part of the explanation may be different priorities between government organs and also a possible lack of co-ordination between central and local government, given the extremely confused and opaque enterprise ownership structures in the PRC.

Organic growth is not restricted by these rules but presumably the speediest way for foreign multi-nationals to gain market presence and market share is via the acquisition route, which could also provide vital local market knowledge in China's fragmented domestic market as well as access to local distribution channels.

Article 2 defines that the Provisions apply when foreign investors purchase the shareholding interest in a domestic enterprise, subscribe for any increase in share capital of a domestic company or when a foreign entity purchases the assets of a domestic enterprise. The term 'company' in the first two classes presumably means entities established under the provisions of the PRC Companies Law 1994 but the terms 'enterprises' in the third phase is wider and would include the SOEs and collectively owned enterprises. The purchase of assets of these entities would be the only method of acquisition, as they do not have a share capital capable of being purchased.

Article 3 requires the foreign acquirer to comply with all relevant laws, to be 'fair, reasonable, and honest', to act in 'good faith' and to 'compensate with equal value' the seller of shares or assets. Further, they are enjoined not to 'cause excessive concentration, eliminate or restrict competition, disrupt the social or economic order or damage the interests of society or the public'. Needless to say none of these requirements or prohibitions is defined and so whether they are so much verbiage or may have a significant chilling effect in practice on foreign-related merger and acquisition activity is yet to be seen. The crucial issue of 'equal value' has been recently highlighted as a significant practical problem in China-based merger and acquisition activity. Elaine Lo, a solicitor with Hong Kong based Johnson, Stokes and Master who have acted in a number of China-related merger and acquisition cases opined that the need for official endorsement of the sale price by the State Owned Asset Supervision and Administration

Commission may 'break a transaction'; state perceptions of SOE asset values are often unrealistically high.[108]

Article 4 re-emphasises that certain industrial sectors are still closed to foreign participation whether through merger and acquisition activity or otherwise.

Article 6 provides that approval of qualifying transactions shall be undertaken by MOFTEC (now Ministry of Commerce (MOFCOM)), and the re-registration of the merged or acquired entity will be completed through SAIC.

Article 7 provides that in an equity purchase transaction the successor entity (usually a Foreign Invested Enterprise under Chinese law) will also be responsible for any of the old domestic company's obligations. The creditors' rights against the old entity survive the acquisition and are transferred to the new owner. Provision is also made for other arrangements to protect creditors.

Article 8 further interferes with freedom of control by mandating the use of a Chinese valuer to confirm the price to be paid for either shares or assets. Any transfer at an undervalue is 'prohibited' but it is not clear what constitutes an 'obvious low price', which is not defined. It is not clear whether such an undervalue sale renders the contract of sale void or whether some other consequence follows. Article 9 provides complex rules concerning the time for payment by the acquirer of the Chinese shares or assets. Article 10 provides detailed rules regarding the conversion status of the Chinese domestic entity into a foreign-owned investment vehicle.

Articles 11 to 16 provide for Chinese law to apply to transactions; choice of a foreign law to govern the agreement is prohibited. This is quite contrary to the freedom to choose the governing law of a contract as stipulated in Article 126 PRC Contract Law 1999; this is a retrograde step. Additionally mandated is the disclosure of identity of the acquirer and various other information. Further detailed requirements are made for documents to be submitted for regulatory inspection and approval. Article 17 provides a thirty day time limit for approval or rejection, though, if competition issues arises, the limit may be extended.

Article 19 provides the triggers that cause a requirement for examination and so objection to the merger or acquisition on the basis of excessive concentration. Should any of the following criteria be met, special notification must be given to MOFCOM and SAIC, that is to say:

---

[108] 'Merger and acquisition on the rise as China eases restrictions', *South China Morning Post*, 31 May 2004.

- any party to the transaction has a turnover in excess of RMB 1.5 billion;
- the aggregate number of Chinese enterprises merged or acquired exceeds ten in a related industry (Note: There is no turnover threshold or market share requirement);
- market share in China of any party is 20 per cent or more;
- market share of the new entity post merger or acquisition will be 25 per cent or more.

The terms 'related industry' or 'market share' are not defined.

Further, should any government department, trade association or competitor consider that any merger or acquisition involves a 'considerable market share or if other important factors exist which seriously impact market competition, the national economy, people's livelihood or state economic security', then they can require the foreign investor to refer the matter to MOFCOM. Again, none of the operative terms are defined.

Article 20 allows MOFCOM/SAIC to convene a 'hearing within ninety days of the date of receipt of all necessary documents' [presumably from the proposed foreign investor as detailed in Articles 11–16]. At an unspecified time after the conclusion of the hearing, MOFCOM will render a decision (presumably for approval, rejection or conditional approval; however, MOFCOM's powers are not explained anywhere in the provisions).

Article 21 attempts to deal with merger and acquisition activity outside China where the parties own assets or have enterprises within China. These provisions apply where any party to an 'offshore transaction' [not defined] owns assets in China worth RMB 3 billion or more, where the turnover of any party in China exceeds RMB 1.5 billion, the market share in the Chinese market of any party exceeds 20 per cent, the market share in China as a result of the transaction exceeds 25 per cent and when the number of foreign invested enterprises in China owned by any party to the transaction exceeds fifteen [no market share or turnover threshold required].

MOFCOM may grant approval for the transaction based on whether the result would be an excessive concentration in the domestic market, harm domestic competition or damage consumers' interests. The consequences of a MOFCOM refusal to grant approval are unclear as no powers or penalties are provided and the extraterritorial implications of such a purported refusal to approve an essentially foreign–foreign merger are difficult to define, given the vague and ill-thought-out nature of these Provisions.

Article 22 provides that if the parties can show that the result would improve competition conditions in the market, restructure a failing enterprise and safeguard employment, introduce new technology, managerial skills and improve the enterprises' international competitiveness or improve the environment, approval will be granted notwithstanding the concentrative effect.

These regulations are the first attempt by China to regulate concentrations. They seem to borrow concepts and procedures from Western merger control regimes but they exhibit many serious and obvious defects:

- There was little or no initial consultation with stakeholders before the emergence of the initial draft in October 2002.
- They were promulgated by ministerial regulation, not primary legislation and exhibit all the hallmarks of being prepared to address sectoral hobbyhorses, rather than a rational economy-wide regime to prevent harmful concentrations of economic power.
- The Provisions only apply to foreign acquisitions, despite the fact that the major concentration problems in China are with domestic SOE dominance in so many sectors, not with foreign monopolists. The Provisions unfortunately exhibit an underlying discrimination based on national origin, which clearly breaches the spirit, if not the letter, of basic non-discrimination philosophy of the WTO agreements.

There are numerous and fundamental drafting defects, for example 'related industries', as regards mergers, are not defined, neither is 'market share' or 'off-shore transaction'. What precisely constitutes 'Obviously lower consideration' paid for assets or shares, which allows a transaction to be vetoed, is clearly problematic. Other issues of concern include:

- The derogation from freedom of contract, the re-imposition of an intrusive examination and approval process of contractual documents by government and the meddling in the details of the transaction itself, also involves a retrograde return to state interference in micro-management of individual economic transactions.
- The specified thresholds for merger scrutiny are illogical and arbitrary.
- There are no confidentiality rules, so that commercially sensitive information contained in documents submitted to MOFCOM/SAIC could be divulged to commercial rivals.
- There is no explanation of the powers or penalties MOFCOM could utilise.

- No explanation of the adjudication process is given, neither are there any guarantees of independence or the qualifications of the adjudicator. Thus, clearly serious doubts arise as to whether the process will be transparent or fair. No right of appeal by way of administrative review or to the court is provided, though as an administrative decision, presumably, a disgruntled applicant could apply to the People's Courts for relief under the Administrative Procedure Law.
- No guidance on substantive or procedural matters, such as precisely to whom and how application should be made under the Provisions, is given.
- Lawyers in international practice confirm that this is a matter of considerable concern. Jonas Koponen of Linklaters has succinctly summed up the current position – 'there exists an obligation to file, but no directives on how to make the filing . . . also, officials tend not to be particularly open to discussing these issues either, so, for the moment the procedure resembles something of a black box'.[109]

These Interim Provisions constitute a profound disappointment given their numerous and obvious defects. They represent a throwback to deep intervention by government in the nascent market economy in China. This appears to be based on political considerations, not on a commitment to a more transparent, non-discriminatory rules-based system. All the good work done previously to produce a comprehensive, well drafted, transparent competition law has been significantly undermined by this development. What is even more concerning is that it emanated from MOFTEC (now MOFCOM), one of the lead agencies involved in the preparation of the general competition law. Hopefully these merger rules will quickly become a dead-letter when China's anti-monopoly law supersedes it, but as to when this will happen, no definite indication, at present, has been given.

A further discouraging straw in the wind indicating that a general law may not be imminent was the promulgation of yet another set of administrative orders to prohibit cartel pricing and excessive monopoly profits.[110] Recent history seems to show that whilst the Chinese authorities are aware of competition issues, there is a clear lack of policy or coherence over what to do; the most likely cause is the philosophical divide between the progressives who favour more market-orientated solutions and the

---

[109] E-mail correspondence with the author, 23 June 2004. Quoted with the permission of Mr Koponen.
[110] See the State Development and Reform Commission (SDRC) *Interim regulations on prohibition of monopolistic pricing acts June 2003*, discussed above.

conservatives who remain attached to traditional methods of command and control. Further, the previously discussed bureaucratic turf war as to the shape, content and implementation of a new general anti-monopoly law continues to rage. Yet another draft version of the Anti-Monopoly Law appeared in March 2004.

5.8 The 2004 Draft Anti-Monopoly Law

Between the preparation of the 2001 draft and the completion of the 2004 draft law, several relevant and important events occurred in relation to competition policy. First, China joined the WTO and, subject to the phase-in period of up to five years, faced, for effectively the first time, the real prospect of foreign penetration, and thus competition for market share with the SOE, in many key domestic markets. Second, there was a wholesale change in the leadership of both the CCP and the State in March 2003. Third, as a result of the sweeping personnel changes at the top, the central government machine was also overhauled at the same time, with the abolition of some economic departments of state and the creation of new entities with correspondingly new responsibilities. Unfortunately the boundary of authority between these new organs is no better defined than the demarcation between their predecessors; there is considerable confusion of roles and responsibilities, and this continues to plague the finalisation of a comprehensive competition policy, the establishment of an executive agency and the enactment of a comprehensive statute.

As regards changes in government agencies, the old MOFTEC and SETC were abolished and merged into a new Ministry of Commerce (MOFCOM). A new planning agency, the State Development and Reform Commission (SDRC), was created as was the State Owned Assets Supervision and Administration Commission (SOASAC), an organ purportedly to hold government ownership of the SOE and to accelerate the reinvigorated privatisation policy. The role and functions of the SAIC were unchanged. It appears that MOFCOM was given the lead role in further refining the draft anti-monopoly law. Lu Fuyuan was appointed the new Minister of Commerce in March 2003 and stated, soon after his appointment, that unification of the domestic market and the introduction of a comprehensive competition law was a priority.[111] Unfortunately, it

---

[111] 'Commerce Ministry defines its policy goals', Ministry of Commerce Press Release, 25 March 2003. http://english.mofcom.gov.cn/article/200303/20030300077225_1.xml. Lehman Bros. Newsletter, March 2003. http://www.lehmanbrown.com/insights_

soon became clear that the new minister was seriously ill and was replaced by Bo Xilai, the former governor of one of the old industrial provinces in northeast China, in February 2004. In March 2004, the new draft of the anti-monopoly law emerged. The new 2004 draft has been sent to the State Council for further consideration, as it proved impossible to settle a crucial issue, namely which department of state was to be responsible for administration and implementation of the anti-monopoly law. It is understood that both SAIC and MOFCOM considered that they could undertake the job of economic policeman but given the track record of SAIC over the last decade in enforcing the 1993 Law and MOFTEC in drafting the 2003 Interim Provisions on Mergers and Acquisition of Domestic Enterprises by Foreign Investors, there appears to be no reason to believe that either body is capable of competently administering a new and potentially more intrusive regime. Consequently, in view of this disagreement, the State Council has been called upon to adjudicate and, thereafter, pass the draft on to either the NPC or its Standing Committee for legislative enactment. The author has been informed by senior officials involved with this process that major substantive changes to the 2004 draft by the State Council are unlikely and that enactment will probably take place in 2005. Thus, it is appropriate to analyse the terms of the latest draft and to consider how this version differs from its predecessors; only the major differences and changes will be highlighted.

The basic structure of the 2004 draft remains based on the EC model. A strong administrative authority is envisaged to enforce a broadly worded economic-based competition system. Chapter one provides definitions. Article 1 outlines objectives similar to the earlier drafts, whilst Article 2 defines jurisdictional coverage in a similar way to the 2001 draft. Jurisdiction is extended to monopolistic behaviour in relation to economic activities in China and coverage also extends to activities that occur outside China that have an economic effect within the PRC. Thus, China appears to follow the stance adopted by the USA, as regards extraterritoriality, rather than the more limited doctrine of effective implementation utilised by the EU.[112] Article 3 defines monopoly activities, against which the law

---

newsletter_ March2_2003.htm#1. Fiducia Management Consultants http://www.fiducia-china.com/News/2002/1306-1455.html.

[112] The seminal cases in the US are *United States v Aluminium Co of America* 148 F2d 416 (2nd Cir.1945) where Judge Learned Hand espoused the American rule in respect of the effects doctrine; this was subsequently confirmed in the US Supreme Court in *Hartford Fire Insurance Co. v California* 509 US 764 (1993). In the EU, a more limited doctrine which relied on implementation, as opposed to the mere economic effects of a restrictive

is said to be directed. There are four manifestations of monopoly enumerated, namely: monopoly agreements; abuse of market domination, excessive concentrations of market power and administrative monopoly. Article 4 defines market operators as legal persons, other economic organisations and individuals engaged in the production, purchase or sale of commodities, which includes services. Unlike the 2001 draft, close substitutes are not mentioned explicitly. Markets are defined in terms of a geographic area, a specific commodity combined with a temporal component. The law is also extended, by Article 55, to encompass the decisions of trade associations and similar institutions that adversely affect competition.

Under Article 5, all government departments and agencies are required to take action to create and maintain a fair and open trading environment, whilst Article 6 empowers the competition authority to enforce this law to prevent and punish monopoly behaviour and to encourage and protect fair competition. This is as close as the draft gets to explicitly authorising competition advocacy by the authority. By virtue of Article 7, the government encourages, supports and protects all enterprises and individuals who should exercise 'social supervision' of monopoly activities; this appears to be a provision designed to protect whistle-blowers and to encourage the provision of incriminating information to the competition authority. The article also exhorts government organs not to support monopoly activities nor shelter offenders.

Chapter two is concerned with the prohibition of monopoly agreements. By Article 8 operators are forbidden, by contract or other means, to engage in the following activities which restrict competition – price fixing, bid-rigging, restricting the production or sale of commodities, allocating markets, restricting the purchase or sale of new technology or equipment, co-ordinating boycotts or engaging in other conduct that restricts competition. It appears that the 'restriction' of competition need not be serious and there is no *de minimis*. However, the authority will have power to make delegated legislation by way of implementation rules and, presumably, this issue will be dealt with by guidelines or implementing rules. There is substantial alignment here with the 2001 draft. Exemption from the prohibition can be obtained from the competition authority if the agreement is conducive to overall economic development, is in the public interest and does not substantially damage competition. The agreement

---

agreement, was explained by the ECJ in *Wood Pulp* Case 114/85. For a full discussion of the effects doctrine and extraterritoriality, see Whish, *Competition Law*, chapter 12.

must be filed with the competition authority and must cite one of the following justifications:

- The agreement upgrades technology, improves product quality, enhances operational efficiency or promotes research and development.
- Such agreements are common amongst small and medium-sized enterprises and improve management efficiency and competitiveness.
- The agreement amounts to a crisis cartel due to serious declines in sales volume or over-production or market changes in the relevant industry.
- The course of conduct undertaken may be restrictive of competition but is conducive to economic development and is beneficial to the public interest.
- The agreement must be refused exemption within sixty days of filing or else it is deemed to be approved under Article 11.

Chapter three prohibits abuse of market-domination status. Article 14 prohibits the abuse of a 'market-domination status' that interferes with the operational activities of other market operators and excludes or restricts competition. Article 15 defines 'market-domination status' in exactly the same way as was originally conceived in the 1999 draft. Once market domination status is determined the substantive prohibitions become relevant. The following are prohibited:

- Sale of commodities at 'higher than normal' prices – Article 17.
- Sale of commodities at 'lower than normal' prices in order to exclude or harm competitors; sales of commodities below cost of production are also prohibited – Article 18.
- The use of unjustified price discrimination – Article 19.
- Refusals to supply – Article 20.
- Forced transactions by use of threats or other unjustified means with the aim of eliminating fair competition from other operators – Article 21.
- Forced tie-in sales or unreasonable trading conditions – Article 22.
- Forced exclusive dealing by distributors or terms of supply that prohibit distributors from dealing with competitors' products – Article 23.
- Resale price maintenance – Article 24.

Chapter four seeks to control enterprise mergers. Article 25 states that a 'convergence of economic power' means:

- where one enterprise takes over another or two or more enterprises combine together, whether or not this results in the formation of a new enterprise;

- where one enterprise acquires control of another through the acquisition of shares or assets [Note: 'control' is not defined];
- where two or more enterprises form a relationship by which one has power to appoint the management or exercise control over the other directly or indirectly or through a joint venture structure.

This definition appears to be narrower that the one attempted in the 1999 draft.

Under Article 26 the potential convergence of economic power triggers a requirement to pre-notify the competition authority if market share of the applicant enterprises exceeds limits to be defined by State Council. The 2004 draft does not set the trigger thresholds, as did the 2001. The procedural and approval criteria provisions are similar to those under the 2001 draft. The authority has ninety days from notification to reach a decision on approval, conditional approval or rejection under Articles 28 and 29. A merger can be prohibited on grounds that it would restrict or prevent competition, hinder healthy development of the national economy or damage the social or public interest. However, the authority would have discretion to allow a merger that did restrict competition but had countervailing benefits to the national economy or that were in the public interest.

Chapter five prohibits AM. The provisions in the 2004 draft are essentially the same as in the 2001 version.

Chapter six deals with establishment and powers of the competition authority; the provisions of the 2004 draft are similar to the earlier version, save that the investigatory powers are enhanced; the identity, and composition and bureaucratic rank of the authority is not identified in the draft. This central bone of contention must be decided by the State Council.

Chapter seven provides penalties for breach of the statute. In respect of monopoly agreements, the draft provides for a maximum financial penalty of RMB 5 million; the previous draft stipulated a fine of RMB 50,000 or up to 10 per cent of the previous year's turnover. For abuses of dominance, the new draft proposes a penalty of up to RMB 10 million plus a private right of damages as well as possible criminal liability in certain situations; the 2001 draft proposed a maximum penalty of RMB 1 million or up to 15 per cent of the previous year's turnover. With respect to qualifying but unauthorised mergers, the proposed penalty is now a maximum fine of RMB 10 million or an obligation to unscramble the merger; the previous draft suggested prohibition, or required the unlawful combination to be de-merged as well as attracting a fine of RMB 100,000. The punishments for breach of the Administrative Monopoly provisions are recast. Under the old draft, cessation of the conduct could be demanded by higher authority and responsible officials sanctioned by the disciplinary process, with theoretical criminal liability too. The new draft provisions under Article 47 provide that where unlawful administrative rules or regulations have been adopted in breach of Article 35, so infringing on the prohibition of abuse of administrative power, the offending department's supervising authority shall have power to revoke or amend the offending regulations and to administratively punish the responsible official who may also be criminally liable. Under Article 48, where departments carry out activities that restrict competition in breach of Articles 31 to 34, the power to require cessation is granted to the new competition authority, not to the supervisory authority of the delinquent state organ. Additionally, the competition authority can impose administrative sanctions on the offending official. Further, if a market operator has gained a benefit as a result of the illegal acts of the offending department, the competition authority is empowered to confiscate the illicit profit and to fine the operator up to RMB 1 million. Article 49 provides a private right of action for victims of competition offences. Under Article 52, penalties can be enforced through the People's Court. Under Article 53, a request for re-consideration against liability and/or size of penalty can be lodged with the competition authority within sixty days; if after the announcement of the re-consideration the party remains dissatisfied, he can appeal to the People's Court or they can exercise the right of appeal directly to the Court, without prior application to the authority for reconsideration.

The current draft is, in many ways, a curate's egg – good in parts. Most of the structure and content is similar to the 1999 and 2001 versions, and so evidencing a coalescence of official thinking as to the substantive and procedural aspects of the system. Whilst this stabilisation is welcome, the defects in some of the substantive provisions remain. Details of process will have to await implementing regulations, other matters of concern relate to omissions.

The competition authority is given no clear mandate to advocate pro-competition policies either within government or to business operators or to the wider public. After over a decade of discussion and debate, the structure, administrative position and independence of the competition regulator is still undecided. This betrays deep divisions within the bureaucracy and that an ongoing power struggle continues to be fought within government over which department should control the new organisation. The intensity of this division shows the importance of the new authority, as it will wield very significant powers over the state-owned, the domestic private and foreign-owned sectors of the economy as well as over central and local governments' economic prerogatives.

The State Council may have to fudge the issue of a strong, powerful and dedicated agency in favour of maintaining bureaucratic harmony. The decision to award the new regulatory body to one of the contending bureaucracies will surely influence how the new law is implemented and the direction of anti-trust policy in China. At the time of writing (March 2005), MOFCOM's Vice-Commerce Minister, Yu Guangzhou, announced that the anti-monopoly law would be promulgated by the end of 2005.[113] As regards administration of the new competition regime, MOFCOM had suggested that a political compromise was being considered, namely, that mergers and AM would be supervised by MOFCOM, the SAIC would police abuse of dominance and cartels whilst the National Development and Reform Commission would enforce the provisions on bid-rigging and price fixing.[114] Clearly, if this arbitrary and illogical division of administrative responsibilities were to occur, any chance of a coherent development of competition policy would be lost. The outcome of the political horse-trading within Beijing's corridors of power is, at present, unknown; however, it appears that the final decision will be taken during 2005.

This compromise mentality is also evidenced by the new penalty provisions. On the one hand, the maximum nominal penalty is substantially raised but the real sting, the percentage of turnover maxima, is dropped, so reducing the overall deterrent effect. This is especially in relation to nationally organised monopolies; the new maximum penalty will be effectively insignificant, even if it were to be imposed.

On the other hand, penalties for Administrative Monopoly abuses are strengthened, to some extent, by the granting to the proposed competition authority sole jurisdiction to sanction erring state bodies when they operate the various forms of administrative blockage or protection. This ousting of the authority of the delinquent's superior bureaucratic manager is an improvement on the previous sanctioning regime. But the retention of the superior's jurisdiction when the lower-level body creates new illicit regulations is unfortunate as this method of enforcement is unlikely to be more successful in the future than it was in the past under

---

[113] 'Foreign firms curb Mainland pursuits', *South China Morning Post*, 6 December 2003.
[114] China to issue anti-trust law in 2005, CRIENGLISH.com, 4 March 2005. http:// yuanguangzhou2. mofocm.gov.cn.

the 1993 law. This example neatly illustrates the political-bureaucratic compromises that have been negotiated between the interested official stakeholders to get the draft anti-monopoly law to the current stage of development.

On a more positive note, there are two matters worthy of attention as a result of their omission from the draft. First, no sectoral exemptions are mentioned, even for limited duration, as were included in the 1999 draft. This is clearly positive for the potential development of a comprehensive pro-competition system. Second, the draft does not overtly discriminate on grounds of the nationality of the business operator in any 'monopoly' situation identified in the draft law. This development is also to be welcomed as it retreats from the protectionism and overt discrimination evidenced in the Interim Merger Provisions of 2003. However, the lack of discriminatory treatment on the face of the draft, does not necessarily mean that differential treatment will not occur in practice; only experience of the administration and enforcement of the law will determine whether fair and equal treatment will be afforded to all market operators.

If the new law substantially follows the 2004 draft and provides for a strong, central administrative unit with suitable resources, the pro-competition forces within government will have won a significant battle. But it is far too soon to say whether they will win the war to entrench a pro-competitive, market-based economic system in China.

5.9 Current competition concerns in China – merger mania

The previous sections have attempted to explain and analyse the existing substantive rules on competition and their enforcement in China as well as the proposals for a new comprehensive anti-monopoly law.

The long-running adoption saga may now be drawing to a close and this section seeks to identify competition concerns that are in the fore-front of policy makers minds, as of mid-2004, and which will inevitably colour the final form of the statute that emerges from the legislative process, probably in 2005. At present, there are several issues that are of immediate importance, namely, the continuation of Administrative Monopoly problems, and a huge wave of merger and acquisition activity in many sectors especially in the beer and automotive industries. Further, there is an increasing worry in the mind of the Chinese government about the actual or potential dangers of increased foreign participation, or even dominance, in various domestic markets. Of particular concern are the photographic film, coffee, computer software, soft drinks, packaging and vehicle tyre markets.

During 2003, a merger wave accelerated through Chinese industry. Interestingly, statistics appear to show that the majority of acquirers were Chinese entities, rather than foreign multi-nationals. Apparently, for the first nine months of 2003, 30.8 per cent of acquisitions were by Chinese buyers whilst only 15.8 per cent were by foreign acquirers; the other 50.4 per cent were acquired by connected parties, the majority of whom were probably also domestic.[115] Many of the mergers notified were government inspired and administratively sponsored, rather than purely market-driven decisions; the wisdom of these arranged marriages will only be ascertained in due course as China's market becomes more open to foreign-owned competitors. During 2004, the pace of foreign acquisitions appeared to be speeding up[116] especially in the beer industry[117] and there was also massive new foreign investment in the automotive industry.[118]

At the same time, the existing rules on foreign-related mergers appear not to have been rigorously enforced, leaving a regulatory and compliance black-hole, presumably for fear that enforcing the regime is both impractical and may have the effect of scaring off much-needed foreign direct investment.

The Chinese government is also acutely aware of the dilemma it faces from a potential public opinion backlash against the perceived or real increase in foreign participation in the domestic market. Several industries have complained about alleged 'unfair business practices' by foreign participants. For example, in February 2004, representatives of China's retail sector were incensed by the increasing presence in China of foreign-owned hypermarkets, which have fundamentally shaken up the sector. There are apparently now over 300 large-format stores in China with many more developments in the pipeline; foreign retailers now apparently have a market share of approximately 8 per cent from a zero base a decade ago. Domestic retailers demanded government action to curb

---

[115] Draft anti-monopoly law completed, Xinhua, 29 October 2004.
[116] 'Merger & Acquisitions on the rise as China eases restrictions', *South China Morning Post*, 31 May 2004.
[117] 'Full-scale takeover war waged for brewery', *South China Morning Post*, 2 June 2004.
[118] 'Car industry driving towards gridlock', *South China Morning Post*, 23 May 2004. The wisdom of foreign automobile manufacturers' headlong dash to increase capacity in China is likely to cause disastrous over-capacity in the industry resulting in a radical consolidation and bankruptcy for many players. See 'A leap over the cliff', *Financial Times*, 25 August 2003.

potential foreign dominance.[119] However, the plea for overt protection will not, apparently, be heeded,[120] though one can easily imagine that a partial enforcement of a competition law might well provide just the relief hard-pressed local firms request.

In light of these concerns, and the stated policy of MOFCOM to swiftly proceed with enactment of a comprehensive anti-monopoly law, the agitation in favour of legislation intensified in 2004.[121]

In January, reports in the press announced that legislation was imminent and would be submitted to the March 2004 session of the National People's Congress;[122] this announcement proved to be erroneous. Reports of the bureaucratic 'turf war', mentioned above, also surfaced in the press as did concerns that, in light of the discriminatory nature of the 2003 Interim Provisions on mergers, foreign investors would receive either discriminatory treatment *de jure* and/or *de facto*.[123] Others were concerned that any new competition agency would be subject to irresistible political pressures by domestic interests to favour Chinese operators at the expense of foreign competitors.[124]

In May 2004, the SAIC published a report entitled 'The Competition-restricting Behavior of Multinational Companies in China and Counter Measures'.[125] The report took over a year to prepare and alleged that 'foreign business giants were building monopolies in China'. To support this allegation the report stated that Microsoft's operating system and Tetra-pac's packaging products respectively enjoyed 95 per cent market shares in China and that Eastman Kodak had a 70 per cent share of the photographic film market.[126] The report also alleged that some (unnamed) transnational companies had used their dominant positions in technology, brand recognition, capital resources, and management skill 'to suppress competitors and maximise profits'. This view alone seems to confirm

---

[119] 'China's open and shut case for WTO', *South China Morning Post*, 11 February 2004.
[120] 'Lines drawn over retail invasion', *South China Morning Post*, 9 April 2003.
[121] China making important progress on competition laws, Xinhuanet, 25 November 2003.
[122] 'China to complete anti-trust law', *China Daily*, 12 January 2004.
[123] *Will protectionists hijack China's competition law?*, International Financial Law Review, 1 January 2004.
[124] 'Anti-trust raises abuse fears', *South China Morning Post*, 13 January 2003.
[125] *Journal of the State Administration of Industry and Commerce*, vol. 5 (2004), May 2004.
[126] Kodak has been very aggressive in acquiring market share via the acquisition route in China. In a series of deals, Kodak has acquired from the Chinese government various former SOE film manufacturers, the last of which was the acquisition of 20 per cent of China Lucky Film in October 2003. 'Kodak pays US$100m for Mainland stake', *South China Morning Post*, 24 October 2004.

that the SAIC does not really understand the nature of market competition; surely the alleged behaviour is precisely what a competitor should do – maximise the firm's comparative advantages so as to destroy competitors and increase market share and profits. In the absence of abuse of a dominant position, the criticised conduct seems to be entirely unobjectionable; the SAIC does not appear to agree.

Allegations were also made of predatory pricing, exclusionary conduct by the purchase of exclusive advertising rights and discriminatory price gouging in the Chinese market. Refusals to deal and runaway acquisitions of Chinese rivals were also cited as manifestations of an insidious attempt to build monopoly positions and corner markets, especially in the software, photographic film, mobile phone, camera, vehicle tyre and the soft packaging materials markets. The report seems erroneously to conflate two issues – the building of market share and the actual or potential abuse of market power. Needless to say, the cited foreign market participants strongly refuted any misconduct or of seeking to monopolise Chinese markets. The report concluded that the State Council should proceed without further delay to approve the enactment of the new anti-monopoly law.[127] The report is interesting for several reasons. First, it concentrated on alleged monopoly positions and abuses by foreign-owned businesses in China; no mention was made of the dominance and abuses by the much larger number of SOE monopolies in China. Secondly, the weakness in comprehension of competition principles exhibited in the report appears to indicate a lack of capacity to undertake the necessary analysis of complex competition law issues and consequently, this deficiency does not augur well for appropriate implementation of any comprehensive anti-monopoly statute; the report was clearly a political document as much as a technical market analysis.

Given the increased interest in competition issues in 2004, the pressure on the government to legislate soon appears to be growing. Senior officials involved in the adoption process have indicated that the new law will be enacted in 2005, that it will be non-discriminatory in substance and application and that it will be enforced fairly and transparently. However, given China's track record on competition matters and the manifest capacity issues raised in these two chapters, a final verdict on the success of adoption and implementation must be withheld until the legislation is

---

[127] 'Pressure for anti-monopoly law grows', *Financial Times*, 25 May 2004. 'Anti-monopoly law "to benefit all businesses"', *China Daily*, 2 June 2004. China wary of monopoly of transnational companies, Xinhua, 25 May 2004.

promulgated, the detailed implementing regulations and guidelines have been issued, an enforcement body established and actual decisions have been made.

5.10 Implementation

A comprehensive competition law has been on the Chinese government agenda for over ten years. Significant progress has been made in educating government officials, politicians, and business people in the economic arguments of the benefits of competition over state planning in the allocation of economic resources. But government has, nevertheless, tried a number of more interventionist policies such as officially sponsored industry associations to ensure orderly markets, forced mergers and price-fixing cartels in industries facing over-supply or suffering from 'malignant' competition. However, these have failed to solve the chronic problems of over-supply of many commodities. Cartel action to set minimum prices or restrict supply, has ended in failure. Chronic over-supply and deflation have continued to afflict the Chinese economy, until very recently. Further, the insolvent SOEs do not go out of business, as state banks are required to continue to support local politically sponsored producers. Industrial ministries still try to force administrative mergers of enterprises to create 'national champions' which are unlikely to be economically successful unless state banks continue their uncommercial lending policies, as their equivalents once did in Thailand, Indonesia, Korea and Japan. Monopolies continue to thrive as a result of government fiat and the abuse of administrative power by exclusive purchasing, differential taxes and blockade are still clearly in evidence. These phenomena continue to plague and artificially compartmentalise the national market, so impeding the growth of internal trade and the process of specialisation that is so badly needed in the Chinese economy. Adding to the pressure on Chinese policy makers is the entry of China into the WTO, with the expected onslaught of foreign corporations on a much greater segment of the domestic Chinese market.

Thus, the major competition problems that the Chinese economy actually suffers from are not a result of the actions of profit-orientated, privately owned firms in a laissez-faire market, rather they are the result of too much *government* intervention in all aspects of the economy, whether by reason of state firms abusing their dominant positions, the SOEs engaging in officially sponsored cartels or new monopolies being created by government-inspired mergers. The administrative monopoly problem is clearly *not* a free market competition issue. In contrast, true competition problems that arise from the actions of domestic private business or from foreign participation in the Chinese domestic market are so insignificant in their economic impact, at least for the present, and for the near future, that they cannot constitute a sound justification for the enactment of a comprehensive competition law system. Thus, the question that must be addressed is, if the true 'competition' problems in the Chinese market are really matters of state policy and control of the economy, can a competition law system *simpliciter* be justified or should some other policy choice be made that would be more appropriate and likely to succeed in providing an efficacious remedy to the identified deficiencies?

It appears, from the evidence identified above, that China may not need a competition law at present for several reasons. First, the extant problems are not, in reality, the subject matter of classical competition law concerns. Second, competition law, if enacted, is unlikely to remedy the malady because the problem has been misdiagnosed and so the wrong treatment has been prescribed for the patient. Third, the medicine suggested will not be effective for this particular patient because of the individual characteristics of the patient whose constitution and other capacity weaknesses will inhibit the proper functioning of the cure and, indeed, the cure may make the patient's condition worse, by erecting new barriers to effective market functioning as a result of granting government new interventionist powers that it does not presently possess over the domestic and foreign-owned private sectors. Thus, competition law may be the wrong policy choice for China in current circumstances.

What, then, is needed to cure the identified symptoms? Perhaps, given the experience of other developing and transitional economies, nothing short of a philosophical sea-change, as regards the proper ambit of state intervention in economic matters is needed, as well as full-scale divestment of state ownership of business, together with a root-and-branch restructure of the organs of political control including the courts, along with their respective personnel; this, clearly, is a very tall order. But evidence from other jurisdictions suggests that this is precisely what is needed to ensure a functioning and effective competition law system. These issues will be considered further in chapter 10.

Despite these concerns, it seems that the Chinese government has concluded that, as central planning did not provide the socialist utopia promised by Marx and Mao and that the confused concept of a socialist market has also led to considerable imperfections in the economy, the only credible alternative is to foster a more competitive environment, so as to unlock China's true economic potential. However, whilst China may want the fruits of capitalism, the government seems intent on not relinquishing too much control over the 'commanding heights' of the economy to domestic private interests or to foreigners; core industries will remain SOEs and competition law may be used to discipline unruly market participants. Conservative forces have managed to restrain a full-blooded commitment to competition by waving the shrouds of economic, social and political instability as reasons to delay the implementation of full marketisation. This equivocation has not reduced the pressures of the failure of the current policies to make the SOEs more efficient and the pro-competitive effects of WTO entry are now likely to force the government to legislate a competition statute to rationalise the confused web of existing regulation, which is both incoherent and inconsistent. This tool may also provide government with greater power over the sector of the economy that it does not already directly control.

Several matters need to be considered as to whether the proposals, as now contained in the 2004 draft law, are a serious attempt to make the Chinese economy more efficient.

Firstly, huge doubt must remain as to whether the government is, from top to bottom, ideologically committed to allowing the invisible hand of the market to regulate the economy, rather than the hand of the bureaucracy. All indicators show that whatever the small band of central government pro-marketeers hope, the bulk of the government machine is addicted to control and that the proposed competition law fatally injures this their fundamental *raison d'être*; evidence of this is provided by the new merger rules, explained above. Thus, this first ideological hurdle may prove determinative of the success or failure of pro-competition policy. The basic instinct of micromanagement by the Chinese state is nothing new and breaking the instinct of millennia would involve a real cultural revolution requiring basic political change in the shape of democracy, which would implicitly include a constitutionally limited role for the state and an effective rule of law. Thus, it is argued that, without such a root-and-branch change, competition policy will not be a success. Indeed, whilst a competition law may well be enacted soon, the likelihood of a good faith and competent enforcement of such a law is low. Evidence of the existing weaknesses of technical capacity and the immense domestic political hurdles to successful implementation, have been outlined above.

An object lesson in what is needed to succeed with a competition policy, by way of contrast, is to consider the situation that now prevails on Taiwan. For thirty years after 1949, Taiwan was subject to direct military and then autocratic control with just as much bureaucratic interference in all aspects of life as in the Mainland. But a decision in 1984 to alter radically the economic structure of the island led to representative government becoming a reality, which led to the first direct presidential election in 1992. Competition law was part of the politico-economic reform package. Taiwan promulgated its Fair Trade Act in 1992 and it has been a notable success.[128] It is submitted that it is no coincidence that the two developments occurred in tandem. It is proposed that a functioning democratic political structure is a concomitant to the enactment and effective administration and implementation of a competition statute. A definition of the terms 'functioning democracy' and the characteristics of 'effectiveness' will be explained in chapter 10.

Secondly, it is submitted that the 2004 draft law may be overly ambitious. The proposed statute laudably seeks to deal with all the issues that a comprehensive competition policy should seek to address – monopoly power, restrictive agreements, oligopoly, mergers and an internal free market. But it is suggested that it is not realistic for China to attempt to take on all these complex and contentious issues at once. An incremental approach might be a better strategy. China's administrative capacity and the skill base of its public servants may be insufficient to handle the very complex technical issues arising out of the adoption of a comprehensive competition policy. Consequently, if the draft law is enacted in substantially the same form as it now appears, thought might be given to selective implementation of its provisions in a phased programme. The prohibition of cartels might be the easiest aspect of the draft law to implement first. This would allow the regulators to gain experience of implementation and to overcome problems on a relatively small scale before being faced with the great complexities of detailed fact finding and economic analysis required in many other anti-competitive situations.

A further difficulty is that a national body capable of enforcing a comprehensive competition law in a country the size of China will need a small army of highly qualified accountants, economists and lawyers who are ideologically committed to competition policy in order for it to function effectively. A major issue is whether China has the financial resources and a talent pool of such personnel available and if so, would they be interested in civil service employment at salaries of US$200–400 a month?

---

[128] Information concerning the Taiwan Fair Trade Law can be found at www.ftc.gov.tw_. The competition policy and law system of Taiwan will be examined and evaluated in chapter 10.

Such a salary is low for professional middle-class urban dwellers, especially for those working in the private sector. Additionally, the prestige, job security and fringe benefits of government service are diminishing in value, whilst the demand for skilled commercial lawyers in China is exploding as WTO entry has caused an exponential growth in demand for competent legal advice from well-qualified personnel in respect of all aspects of trade-related liberalisation. Given the current shortages of lawyers – there are only 110,000 qualified attorneys in China – to serve a population of 1.25 billion and that many do not even hold a law degree,[129] it is improbable that sufficient high-quality personnel can be found to staff the competition regulatory body.

The vital matter of the status of the competition authority also needs to be thoroughly considered by the State Council. Given the operating environment extant in China a high status and high-powered body is vital for success; the 2004 draft law leaves the decision as to the identity and status of the enforcement body undecided.

Finally, if this analysis is correct, the weaknesses of the draft law, as identified above, need to be considered and rectified to have a properly functioning, rational structure. It is suggested that the implementation of a comprehensive law may well prove impossible to achieve, even with the full political backing of the central government.

5.11 China's position measured against success criteria

In chapter 2 it will be recalled that Kovacic,[130] elucidated a number of criteria that he thought were necessary to ensure the successful adoption and implementation of a pro-competition policy, supported by law. He considered that strong institutional structures were essential to ensure the success of new competition regimes in developing economies. He stressed the need for qualified personnel, a reduction of discretion and opacity in decision-making, a robust independent legal system, and adequate financial and physical resources to enable a system to function effectively. Above all, the government and people of a territory that proposed to adopt competition policy must be convinced of its purpose and desirability as well

---

[129] In a recent speech, Jia Wuguong of the PRC Ministry of Justice stated that in 1979 China had 212 qualified lawyers and in 1999 had 110,000, only 50 per cent of whom had a Bachelor's degree in law and only 4,000 were qualified to deal with foreign-related work. Most law firms had fewer than twenty employees.

[130] Kovacic, *Designing and implementing competition and consumer protection reforms in transitional economies* and *Getting started*.

as any potential costs, such as short-term higher unemployment when inefficient protected industries contract as a result of a more competitive environment. He also saw competition advocacy as a vital function of any competition authority in explaining and convincing the population and industry of the merits of a pro-competition policy. Other support-ive infrastructure in terms of academic institutions to train personnel and to reflect on competition problems, strong civil society institutions – professional associations and consumer organisations to help reinforce a pro-competition political agenda – are all needed to ensure the successful introduction of competition policy. Finally, government objectives for the initial introduction of a new competition regime should not be too ex-pansive; limited milestones of success should be erected to judge whether the new policy has been effective; over-ambitious goals would usually not be met. These observations appear to be very relevant to the situation in China as identified here. China is weak in many of the areas men-tioned for historical and political reasons, which have been discussed in some detail above and in the previous chapter. If one carefully scrutinises China's record against the Kovacic criteria, one might fairly conclude that any competition regime adopted in China will face formidable obstacles to becoming effective, notwithstanding doubts as to the sincerity of the government's commitment to market competition as the prime economic regulator and whether ulterior motives, as discussed earlier, are the real motivation for adoption.

5.12 Conclusions

China has made remarkable progress in economic restructuring in the last twenty-five years. However, a great deal remains to be done. Compe-tition law is clearly one of the major policy tasks that is necessary if China is to complete its transformation from a centrally planned economy to a market-focused one. This chapter has sought to demonstrate that the adoption and proper implementation of a comprehensive competition law will be a key test of the level of political support for the marketisa-tion of the Chinese economy. It will also evidence the commitment of the government to advance the cause of the rule of law and to honour the spirit and the letter of its market-opening commitments made in the WTO accession agreement. This chapter has sought to identify some of the major problems that are apparent in the draft competition law and to suggest remedies for those defects. Unless the wider political and eco-nomic issues are resolved, a workable set of competition rules adopted and a genuine internal market developed, the goals of greater economic efficiency and the ability of domestic industry to survive market opening, will not be achieved. Additionally, China faces great difficulties in the implementation and enforcement of any comprehensive competition law due to weak infrastructure and human-resource deficiencies. The eventual success or failure of a pro-competition regime in China cannot, at present, be predicted with certainty, but the issues exposed and analysed in these last two chapters will be used to construct a testable hypothesis in chapter 11.

6

Competitive Hong Kong? Myths, perceptions and reality

Monopoly is a terrible thing, till you have it.[1]

6.1 Introduction

This chapter will seek to explain the unique historical, political, social and economic features of Hong Kong as a precursor to a detailed examination of the state of competition within the domestic economy of Hong Kong and the HKSAR government's policies regarding the regulation of competition.

Hong Kong has been perceived very differently depending on the identity of the observer. To imperialist apologists it was the exemplar of enlightened colonial government whereby the mixture of small, competent, uncorrupted, paternalistic government coupled with a dynamic work-orientated population produced nothing less than an economic and social miracle. The dismay of Lord Palmerston, on being informed that Hong Kong Island had been annexed to the British Empire by Captain Elliot, the local British plenipotentiary in 1841, expressed in the oft-quoted retort 'a barren rock with scarcely a house upon it',[2] has proved to be a significant underestimation of the Territory's economic potential. In 1997, at the time of the retrocession of the colony to China, Hong Kong's GDP per capita was higher than that of its colonial possessor.[3]

However, to the Chinese patriot Hong Kong represented an open sore that had oozed shame for 150 years as a humiliating reminder of national

---

[1] Rupert Murdoch, *The New Yorker* (1979). Mr Murdoch is a member of the Hong Kong Chief Executive's Council of International Advisers (CECIA) established in 1998 to offer economic advice to the HKSAR government. He is the Chairman and Chief Executive of News Corporation, one of the world's largest vertically integrated media companies and he is also CEO of Fox Entertainment Group.

[2] As quoted by Spence, *The search for modern China*, p. 158.

[3] GDP per capita in Hong Kong in 1997 was US$26,287 and in the United Kingdom US$22,488, *Statistical Year Book*, 45th Issue United Nations, New York (2001), chapter 18, p. 133.

weakness and successful foreign aggression and encroachment upon the territory of China. The resumption of sovereignty in 1997 represented a triumph of national reunification, as did the return of Macau in 1999, after almost 450 years of Portuguese 'administration'.[4] The only outstanding territorial impediment to complete national reunification was the stubborn refusal of the Taiwanese people to countenance 'rejoining' the Motherland.

Thus, perceptions of Hong Kong's political status have always been polarised and very much influenced by the identity of the observer. The same is true of its economic status. Hong Kong has been lauded as the world's freest economy with little government interference in business decisions, a paradigm example of a market, as opposed to government-regulated, economic system. The 'red in tooth and claw' capitalist work ethic of the territory's people has been admired and often the nature of its economic structures have been uncritically assumed to be competitive, often buttressed by right-wing North American economic think-tanks that produced ranked lists of economic freedom.[5] These international plaudits have been gleefully seized upon by HKSAR government officials as proof of the apparent competitive nature of Hong Kong's economy. But it is the contention of this book that the assumption of the inherently competitive nature of Hong Kong's economy is fundamentally flawed. A crucial distinction must be made between the internationally traded part of economic activity, where Hong Kong's record is indeed an exemplary one and the non-traded domestic economy, which, it is submitted, is very far from being open and competitive. Structural imperfections abound, as do examples of collusive business practices.[6] Monopoly abuses that benefit the operators of some businesses, producing considerable but unquantifiable, supra-competitive profits which are detrimental to the efficient operation of the domestic economy, are common. However, it must be admitted at the outset that hard data to prove this contention

---

[4] Officially Macau was not a colony of Portugal but merely a Chinese territory administered by Lisbon; this was a diplomatic face-saving fiction. Originally the Portuguese were allowed to occupy Macau for trading purposes in 1555 as a reward for destroying a troublesome band of local pirates which the Chinese authorities had been unable to eradicate. No treaty of cession of territory was ever formally signed. See S. Shipp, *Macau, China: a political history*, Jefferson, N.C.: McFarland & Co., Inc. (1997), chapter 2.

[5] The Fraser Institute in Canada produces an annual report, Economic Freedom of the World, see http://www.fraserinstitute.org/economicfreedom/index.asp and the US-based Heritage Foundation produces its annual Index of Economic Freedom, see http://www. heritage.org/research/features/index/.

[6] See detailed discussion of these issues later in this chapter and in chapter 7.

conclusively is very difficult to provide. The HKSAR government has no legal powers of economic investigation and most business operators refuse to answer government or academic enquiries on the grounds of commercial confidentiality and, in any event, they would have everything to lose and nothing to gain from the public exposure of collusive or monopolistic practices.

The HKSAR government stoutly refuses to accept that there are any market imperfections in the Hong Kong domestic economy because they allege that there is no compelling evidence of them.[7] But this lack of evidence results from wilful blindness on the part of officials objectively to evaluate the evidence that is available and further results directly from the lack of any legal powers to investigate competition complaints that are made. The evidence of market failures, which will be marshalled below, is dismissed by the government as not being indicative of a widespread problem. In any event, the government's official philosophy is hostile to economic interventionism and constantly repeats its mantra of adopting market-based solutions to economic problems, not bureaucratic ones. However, the truth of this assertion is questionable and whether the government operates as a benign umpire in the economy and does not stoop to dirty its hands in direct economic management is doubtful. For example, several sectors are heavily regulated – transport and electricity, or dominated by the public sector – housing, education and medical services. Sometimes active intervention in markets is clear and obvious – direct purchase of Hong Kong equities in 1998 and manipulation of the property market in 1999 and 2002 or the developing of essential facilities such as trunk roads, container terminals at the port, or the new airport at Chep Lap Kok. These issues are discussed below. It will be argued that the portrayal of Hong Kong as the world's freest economy is a myth supported by a carefully rehearsed propaganda campaign and does not reflect the reality of much of Hong Kong's domestic economy.

The government's position on competition regulation is that a general competition law cannot be justified and a strong case must be made even for sector-specific regulation. This is so, even though, as will be shown, Hong Kong operates a confusing and contradictory web of industry regulation in energy supply (electricity and gas), transport (rail, ferries, buses and the port) but full pro-competition regulation in telecommunications and broadcasting. Thus, Hong Kong's refusal to legislate a general

---

[7] See HKSAR Government, *Response to the Consumer Council Report on Competition* (1997).

competition law is very perplexing and the government's case will be carefully examined in an attempt to rationalise its policy stance.

If logic is not the basis of the government's stance, then can the rationale for the government's hostility to competition regulation be explained? It will be suggested that the position of the HKSAR government as regards the domestic economy is intellectually dishonest. To assert that there is no competition problem to address because there is no evidence is disingenuous. The lack of evidence results from the absence of compulsory disclosure powers. The argument is circular and unpersuasive. To adopt a position of philosophical scepticism towards competition regulation is a respectable one, though very hard to maintain in respect of hard-core cartels, as even the most libertarian Chicago School anti-trust adherent does not support toleration of this collusive activity. The government's position that some sectors need full-blown pro-competition provisions (broadcasting and telecommunication) but the rest of the economy does not need any competition regulation at all is unusual to say the least. There has been no justification of this illogical and baffling stance, other than a constant repetition of the government's propaganda mantra that Hong Kong has the freest economy in the world.[8] It will be submitted that the underlying reason for the policy stance adopted is not a lack of evidence or an inability to legislate or enforce competition policy but rather the lack of a functioning democratic government. The concentration of economic and effective political power in the hands of a small economic, oligarchic elite that benefits from collusive economic practices and would suffer from a competitive market, is the real reason for the government's overt and illogical hostility to regulation, in the public interest, in this field. The analysis that follows will support this assertion and will also provide evidence for the more general hypothesis postulated in the final chapter.

Thus, the central theme of the three chapters analysing the Hong Kong situation is to explain how capitalist Hong Kong, which one would assume would wish to protect the competitive process by which it apparently prospered, on the one hand is resolutely against the introduction of a general competition law, but on the other supports sector-specific regulation of various industries, where it perceives without much or even any empirical evidence that there has been market failure. This is a most

---

[8] For example, Daniel Cheng of the Trade and Industry Bureau asserted as much in *Hong Kong Service Economy*, vol. 7, February 1999. He is just one amongst many loyal civil servants who endlessly repeat the government line, with various degrees of credulity. Also, see the HKSAR government web site http://www.isd.gov.hk/eng/index.htm (Information Services Department of HKSAR Government).

singular state of affairs and the explanation of this conundrum can only be found by understanding the social and political structures in Hong Kong. It is submitted that powerful forces continue to propagate the myth of an open domestic economy with no market imperfections, in order to ensure that their own economic welfare is safeguarded. This feat can be achieved because of the nature of the political structures in Hong Kong, which are directly or indirectly controlled by those same oligarchic forces. It is submitted that the concentration of effective political power in the hands of a small group of entrenched oligarchs is the core reason for the government's intransigent and illogical policy.

The government's hostility to competition regulation has also extended into the international arena where it opposes even the discussion of competition issues as part of the next round of trade liberalisation talks at the WTO.[9] The interesting spectacle of the HKSAR government arguing against competition rules at WTO level, and the Central Chinese government being agnostic or even in favour, could raise the prospect of this divergence of views being aired in public. This again would be a most singular event; two administrations from the same country taking opposing stances on the same issue – but even more bizarrely, it would be competitive, capitalist Hong Kong that is against incorporation of competition rules and communist China that would be in favour. Ironies of that magnitude are not common even in the realpolitik world of international diplomacy.

The key questions to be addressed in this and the next chapter are:

• Is Hong Kong's domestic economy open to competitors?
• Are there indications of failures of the competition mechanism?
• If there are failures, what are the most appropriate remedies to take in the public interest?
• Does the government's prescription of a sectoral approach work in theory or in practice?

In order to understand the extant state of affairs in Hong Kong this chapter will:

• consider the relevant historical events of Hong Kong's colonial foundations and development;

[9] See the annual reports, working documents and minutes of the Jenny Working Party, http://www.wto.org/english/tratop_e/comp_e.htm. The position of HKSAR government on multilateral competition provisions is clearly set out at various places by the Hong Kong Representative.

- examine the political institutions of government both pre-1997 and the political settlement under the post-1997 Basic Law;
- describe and analyse the social and cultural make-up of Hong Kong society as relevant to economic matters;
- explain the nature of economic change and development in Hong Kong including the pressures that the territory now faces as a result of China's accession to the WTO and the vital issue of economic integration of Hong Kong into the economy of the Pearl River Delta Region of Guangdong province as relevant to competition issues in Hong Kong;
- examine and analyse the competition policy debate in Hong Kong from 1992 to 2003, and
- seek to explain the reasons for the government's stance on general competition regulation.

The next chapter will concentrate on an analysis of current sectoral competition regulation in Hong Kong and consider what future developments in the competition regime are likely in light of domestic and international pressures for change and reform of Hong Kong's economic structures.

6.2 History

Hong Kong island was acquired by Britain as a result of the peace treaty formally ending the First Opium War in 1842; the island was ceded in perpetuity. The Kowloon peninsula was added as a result of the treaty concluding the Second Opium War in 1858, again in perpetuity. The larger section of the colony, the New Territories, were ceded by lease for ninety-nine years from 1898.[10] The attraction of Hong Kong island was that it provided one of the only sheltered, deep-water, harbours along the whole of the extensive south-east China seaboard and was in close proximity to the Pearl River delta and the extensive navigable waterways of southern China. As mentioned above, the British home authorities were not best pleased with this new addition to the Empire and would have preferred a more geographically hospitable site, as Hong Kong island has virtually no natural flat land at all and had no established trading tradition; at the time of cession Hong Kong island was a remote settlement of local fisher-folk with no significant agriculture or any industry.

[10] See Spence, *The search for modern China*; and Welsh, *A history of Hong Kong*, chapters 1 to 5 and 11.

But, as with Singapore, location was the decisively important factor in Hong Kong's success, along with the magnificent harbour that could accommodate ocean-going schooners and steam ships, which had a much larger draft than Chinese ships of the period. Waves of emigration from the troubled Mainland provided a hard-working and business-orientated population and trading became the colony's economic focus. Thus, as was often the case in British imperial expansion, the flag followed trade.

Hong Kong rapidly became a centre for the entrepôt trade in East Asia. The population grew to 283,905 by 1900[11] and continued to increase substantially to 1.6 million up to the outbreak of the Second World War, due to chronic political instability, civil war and the Japanese invasion of China. The population fell precipitately during the Japanese occupation to 600,000 and then grew dramatically to 1.8 million in 1947 and to over 3.1 million in 1960 as a result of the re-ignited civil war and the subsequent communist victory.[12] The basis of Hong Kong's economy was transformed in the 1950s by the flight to the Territory of wealthy Mainland industrialists, mainly from Shanghai, who brought with them industrial hardware, know-how and capital. Hong Kong became a textile, light-industrial and shipping centre of the first rank but by the 1970s land and labour costs were making it uncompetitive.

Fortuitously, the Mainland changed political and economic direction and began a process of welcoming inward investment from Hong Kong compatriots who within ten years had removed almost all of Hong Kong's manufacturing base to Guangdong, especially to the special economic zone of Shenzhen, where socialist economic rules did not apply. This became the trigger for huge economic development in the Chinese Guangdong region to the north of the Territory which became the premier export-processing region of China, though headquarters and back-office functions remained in Hong Kong, so that they could benefit from the huge service industry supporting the export trade – banking, insurance, shipping, air transport, accountancy and legal services. The environmental conditions in terms of a free and open governmental system, respect for human rights and the rule of law coupled with very low corruption rates, when compared with other jurisdictions in the region, meant that Hong Kong became the nerve centre for the huge surge in Chinese exports of manufactured products over the twenty-year period from 1980 to 2001.[13]

[11] Hong Kong Colonial Census 1901, Registrar General, Hong Kong Government.
[12] Hong Kong Departments of Commerce and Industry and Census and Statistics (1969).
[13] China's exports were as follows (US$ billion): 1990 US$62, 1992 US$84.9, 1994 US$121, 1996 US$151, 1999 US$195.

The major political event affecting this economic boom was the signing, in 1984, of the Joint Declaration by Britain and China, which settled the fate of Hong Kong – the Territory would return to Chinese sovereignty, with very significant regional autonomy, in 1997. Despite the political reassurances there was a serious drain of talent of educated middle-class people during the 1980s, which accelerated dramatically following the Tiananmen Square events in 1989.[14] The arrival of Chris Patten as the last Colonial Governor in 1992 signalled a heightened political commitment to maintaining and buttressing civil and political rights and an attempt to entrench them in the post-1997 settlement. Political relations between Britain and China in the period between 1992 and 1997 were at times strained, which added to the political uncertainty of the population. The reform of the Legislative Council (LEGCO) franchise, instituted by Patten, was scrapped upon the resumption of Chinese control, so maintaining the essential features of the pre-reform Council that was and now continues to be effectively dominated by business interests, with only one-third of seats subject to direct universal suffrage.[15] This percentage changed to 50 per cent in 2004 but due to the need for agreement by simple majority of both the directly and functionally elected portions of the legislature, business interests will retain an effective veto even after the 2004 election. The executive arm of government is largely unchanged in structure from the pre-1997 model, save that now the Chief Executive has promoted a political appointment system to replace a civil-service-led government.[16] Efforts to create a legislature and Chief Executive chosen by universal suffrage are on hold; it was constitutionally possible to introduce full democracy for the 2007 election of the Chief Executive and the 2008 Legislative Council election but a decision by the National People's Congress Standing Committee, in April 2004,[17] has effectively prevented that option. Expansion of the electorates of the functional constitutes may be considered to widen representation to some extent as a palliative measure.

---

[14] Net emigration in the early 1990s was running at about 60,000 per annum, Chief Secretary's Speech in London May 2002.

[15] See HSKAR Government Legislative Council http://www.legco.gov.hk/english/index.htm.

[16] The new system was instituted on 1 July 2002. Of the new 'political appointments' seven were former senior civil servants, four were businessmen and three were academics. None were elected. As for the Executive Council, in addition to the fourteen already mentioned a further five persons were appointed of which two were elected members of the LEGCO.

[17] Decision of the standing committee of the National People's Congress on issues relating to the methods for selecting the Chief Executive of the Hong Kong Special Administrative Region in the year 2007 and for forming the Legislative Council of the Hong Kong Special Administrative Region in the year 2008, 26 April 2004.

Local opinion was largely hostile to the central government decision to veto universal suffrage for the foreseeable future.[18] The liberalisation of the franchise has, however, come into even sharper focus as a result of the huge public demonstration in Hong Kong on 1 July 2003. Over 500,000 residents, well over 10 per cent of the whole adult population, took to the streets ostensibly to protest at the government's introduction of new legislation, mandated by Hong Kong's mini-constitution – the Basic Law – to tighten and extend the law on treason, sedition and subversion, commonly labelled Article 23. But most demonstrators also wished to register deep dissatisfaction with the leadership of Tung Chee-wah, the appointed post-1997 Chief Executive and to demand movement towards full political rights. This event was by far the largest expression of public dissatisfaction since 1997 and the repercussions are difficult to predict. In the immediate aftermath two government ministers resigned, the government withdrew the proposed subversion legislation and Beijing commenced a crash programme of economic measures to assist Hong Kong's ailing economy. After the decision of the NPC in April 2004, another huge demonstration was held on 1 July 2004, which protested about the lack of progress towards full democratisation.[19]

6.3 Political institutions

The nature of political institutions in any jurisdiction is a key factor in whether competition policy can be effective in promoting a competitive business environment and maximising consumer welfare. Hong Kong's present political institutions are substantially a legacy of the standard British colonial model, which has both strengths and weaknesses, which are readily apparent in the government machine that currently administers Hong Kong. This section will seek to describe the pre-1997 institutions and compare them with the present matrix as established by the Basic Law of the HKSAR. It will also comment on the nature of the structures found, the effective nucleus of political power and the impact of these arrangements on the attitude of the government towards competition policy formation and the ongoing debate on Hong Kong's future stance towards competition policy and law.

Under the Letters Patent and Royal Instructions, which formed Hong Kong's constitutional basis during the colonial era, governmental power

---

[18] 'On hold – Democracy in Hong Kong', *The Economist*, 1 May 2004.
[19] 'Champions of democracy', *South China Morning Post*, 2 July 2004.

was exercised essentially through the Royal Prerogative by a powerful Executive Governor who was appointed by the Crown on the advice of the British Prime Minister. The Governor stood in right of the sovereign as head of the civil and military government but subject to direction from Whitehall. The UK Parliament had no direct power over colonial administration but the Colonial and later Foreign Secretary was accountable to the UK Parliament for colonial affairs. Parliament retained ultimate authority to legislate for Hong Kong and any inconsistent local laws were superseded by imperial legislation. Following retrocession of sovereignty, the legal constitutional text of Hong Kong became the Basic Law.[20] This document emanated from the Central People's Government and is the foundation of the guarantee of the 'one country, two systems' formulation provided for in the Joint Declaration. The political structures of the Special Administrative Region are set out in chapter IV of the Basic Law. The Governor's post was re-titled Chief Executive,[21] to be appointed by an election committee effectively chosen by the central government. Tung Chee-wah was chosen in 1996 to be the first Chief Executive. In 2002, he was re-elected unopposed for a second term by an election committee of 800 Hong Kong residents. There is consistent pressure from democratic groups for the election of the Chief Executive to be undertaken by universal suffrage but no official proposals exist, at present, for change. The lack of any choice in the 2002 election was a blow to a more democratic method of selection. Political reform has now become an even more prominent issue following the 1 July 2003 demonstration, and the NPCSC decision of April 2004. A possible way forward is to expand significantly the size of the selection committee and to make it much more representative of the general population.

In colonial Hong Kong, the institutional organs included an Executive Council, which acted as a privy council to advise the Governor on administration of the colony and to promulgate policy decisions. The membership of the council was entirely a matter for the incumbent Governor and included, by tradition, the chief civil servants – the Chief Secretary, the Financial Secretary and the Attorney General as well as the General Officer Commanding HM Forces. Other civil servants were also often councillors but so were important figures from the commercial life of the colony. Government departments were headed by policy secretaries, career civil servants, who were effectively ministers appointed by and answerable to

---

[20] The Basic Law http://www.info.gov.hk/basic_law.
[21] Art. 43 BL.

the Governor and who held appointment on civil service terms, not on the basis of a popular mandate or by control of LEGCO. The Basic Law retained this system.[22] These arrangements were modified by the introduction of a system of political 'ministers' appointed by and answerable to the Chief Executive, but not removable by LEGCO, as of 1 July 2002.[23]

The government also consisted of a legislative arm and a Supreme Court. The LEGCO was originally an entirely appointed body; the Governor chose the legislators. Over time the body did become more representative of the population but progress was very slow and cautious, especially after the 1984 Joint Declaration, for fear of offending China. Patten introduced the widest franchise yet seen in Hong Kong during 1994 and elections based on this much-expanded functional constituency franchise were held in September 1995. China was incandescent with rage at what it perceived to be an attempt to create political instability in the pre-handover period. The changes were vetoed and the previous settlement reverted to after the resumption of Chinese sovereignty in July 1997, when an appointed provisional LEGCO took office for one year until an election took place in September 1998. Further elections occurred in September 2000 and September 2004.

The legislature elected in 2000[24] comprised thirty members representing functional constituencies (the total electorate of which is 175,606 electors),[25] twenty-four members from geographical constituencies (3.6 million electors) and six members via the election committee (800 electors), which is the same body that elects the Chief Executive. In the 2004 election the six election committee seats were abolished and the LEGCO became 50 per cent directly elected. From 2008, the method of electing LEGCO under the Basic Law could have been by full democratic franchise but after the April 2004 NPCSC decision vetoing such a change, there are, at present, no official proposals for conducting the election process in 2008. LEGCO must pass all primary legislation in Hong Kong and

---

[22] Ibid. Art. 48 (5).
[23] Speech of the Chief Secretary for Administration HKSAR, Donald Tsang, 17 May 2002 http://www.info.gov.hk/gia/general/200205/17/0517199.htm.
[24] Art. 66 BL.
[25] The 30 functional constituencies include accountancy, engineering, industrial (2), real estate, agriculture, finance, social welfare, architectural, financial services, info-tech, textiles, health, insurance, transport, commercial (2), Heung Yee Kuk, labour (3), wholesale/retail, import/export, legal, medical, district councils, education, sports and culture, tourism; 18 seats can reasonably be classified as 'business seats'. The number of electors per seat varies from 148 to 71,390. Hong Kong Electoral Affairs Commission Report on the 2000 LEGCO election at www.info.gov.hk/eac/index_en.htm.

has power to refuse supply and to question officials but limited power to introduce private members bills, which in any event are subject to veto by the Chief Executive. LEGCO has power to pass censure motions but no power to dismiss officials or the Chief Executive. Few officials have ever resigned as a result of political censure in Hong Kong but in July 2003 the Financial Secretary was forced out due to an ongoing criminal investigation, as was the Secretary for Security due to her inept and arrogant handling of the proposed Article 23 subversion legislation.

LEGCO has an unusual voting system.[26] Members are divided into two groups – functional constituency members (Group I) and geographical and election-committee-elected members (Group II). For a motion to pass, a majority is required in each group, thus creating an effective veto of the popular will as expressed by the geographical and election committee representatives.[27] This clearly entrenches the political power of the business group, given the composition of functional constituencies.

Thus, real political power is firmly in the hands of the executive arm of government in Hong Kong, that is the Chief Executive, the Executive Council and the civil service. It is interesting to note that commercial interests have paramount importance in the structures just described. The Chief Executive was a tycoon and owner of Hong Kong's largest shipping line;[28] the new ministerial system also has substantial representation for business people; the functional constituencies in LEGCO have a majority of business representatives and are there precisely to enhance the political power of business interests. It is interesting to note that in the 2000 election nine of the functional seats were elected unopposed and that the number of actual votes cast per functional constituency seat varied from 139 to approximately 13,000. By way of contrast, geographical members needed to receive a minimum of 300,000 votes to be in the running for a seat.[29]

Therefore, commercial interests clearly have predominant representation in Hong Kong's government and thus have a substantial say in policy and law making. It will be suggested that Hong Kong's inability to form a consensus to legislate a general competition law results directly from

[26] LEGCO Rules of Procedure, Part J, Voting, Rule 46 and 47, at www.legco.gov.hk/general/english/procedure/contant/partj.htm.

[27] Election Committee Representatives will disappear as from September 2004; these six places will become part of the expanded and directly elected geographical constituency.

[28] Tung's family business is Orient Overseas Container Line, Hong Kong's largest shipping business.

[29] See Report of 2000 Legislative Council Elections, HK Electoral Commission, http://www.info.gov.hk/eac/en/legco/2000_report.htm.

the interplay of these oligarchic commercial interests and their effective control of extant political power structures. Thus, it is suggested that the formation of policy is not undertaken in the interests of the population of Hong Kong as a whole but rather in the interests of the existing holders of concentrated economic power. Evidence to support this contention will be analysed below and will tend to support the hypothesis formed in the concluding chapter as a result of this analysis.

6.4 The civil service

Hong Kong's civil service has the reputation for being one of the most competent in Asia and the continuity of good government following the retrocession of sovereignty was seen as a key component in maintaining stability during the transition of power. Fears of interference and manipulation from the central government in Beijing have proved to be unfounded and good, competent, uncorrupted government in Hong Kong is corroborated by the assessments of various foreign governments, as well as the economic freedom think-thanks already mentioned. In marked contrast to China, number 57 on the Transparency International Corruption Perceptions Index,[30] Hong Kong is a model of rectitude holding position number 14, just below the UK and ahead of Austria.

Hong Kong's civil servants are career officials. They are trained to administer but not to innovate. Maintenance of a dogged loyalty to the orthodox government line is a prerequisite for advancement. The Chief Executive and his council decide on policy; they administer and defend it. As regards the ability of the civil service to administer a general competition law, the introduction of a competition regime in the broadcasting and telecommunications sector provides evidence that the Hong Kong government is quite capable of administering any future general competition system that might be enacted. A more detailed examination of the telecommunication and broadcasting competition regimes will be attempted in chapter 8, which will show that there is now growing institutional capacity to operate a comprehensive competition system. Thus, the ability of the government effectively to administer any general competition law that might be adopted is, therefore, assumed.

---

[30] See http://www.globalcorruptionreport.org/gcr2001.shtml Global Corruption Report 2001.

6.5 Legal institutions

Hong Kong's legal system is a variant of the traditional English common law system. A Supreme Court was established in early colonial times and subordinate courts have been created subsequently by Ordinance. The Basic Law essentially retained these familiar structures. Judicial power over Hong Kong cases is constitutionally given to the Hong Kong courts[31] with the apex being the Final Court of Appeal, which has a bench on which overseas common law judges are invited to sit with the permanent Hong Kong based justices.[32] Only one case concerning the right of Hong Kong abode for children of Hong Kong permanent residents, who had not been born in the territory, has caused grave concern about the autonomous nature of the judicial system since 1997. This cause célèbre was lost by the HKSAR government who referred the judgement of the Court of Final Appeal to the National People's Congress Standing Committee in Beijing who effectively reversed the court's ruling.[33] Despite this considerable setback the Hong Kong courts retain a robust common law independence of the government and there is no hint of criticism of the continued impartial administration of justice. The enforcement of judgements and orders of the court in Hong Kong is no different from those encountered in any developed economy; the rule of law is accepted and obeyed, by the general population as well as government bodies. There is no impediment here to the effective implementation of any future competition law.

The legal profession is divided as in England and Hong Kong is the base for numerous international law firms, which tend to locate their East Asia operations in Hong Kong. Professional standards are good but there has been recent criticism of falling standards of professional competence amongst new entrants to the profession.[34] Standards of competence, independence and expertise are generally high and the depth and international cross-fertilisation of the profession means that Hong Kong's legal professionals are entirely able to take on the task of offering world-class advice in

---

[31] Arts. 80, 81 BL.   [32] Art. 82 BL.

[33] *Ng Ka Ling v Director of Immigration* (1999) 2 HKCFAR 4. The decision in this case was reversed by the NPCSC as explained by Justice Bokhary in *Ng Siu Tung & Others v Director of Immigration* (2002) 1 HKLRD 561, at 652. As a result of this case, wags suggested that the court be renamed the Court of Semi-Final Appeal.

[34] Review of Legal Education and Training, Law Society of Hong Kong, August 2001 http://www.hklawsoc.org.hk/pub/news/societyupdates/20010813a.asp and speech of the Chief Justice of Hong Kong 14 January 2002 http://www.info.gov.hk/jud/whatsnew/html/speech/legal_yr_cj02.htm.

relation to competition law issues. Adjudication on competition matters could be undertaken by the courts or by a specialised tribunal, once suitable training had been given. Thus, it can be asserted with confidence that the judicial branch and the legal profession could play a full and efficient part in any future competition system devised by the government.

6.6 The academic community

Hong Kong has eight publicly funded tertiary institutions. They are essentially modelled on UK institutions. The BL guarantees freedom of academic research[35] and freedom of speech.[36] There has been one controversial event, the Robert Chung Affair, involving the apparent interference, by a senior aide to the Chief Executive, with the opinion-research polling activities of a political science researcher at the University of Hong Kong. Pressure was apparently brought to bear on senior academics to curtail Chung's research activities as they showed that the Chief Executive's popularity rating was very low. As a result of an internal enquiry, the Vice-Chancellor of the university resigned. Generally, however, the ability of academics to conduct research has not been impaired following the retrocession of sovereignty. The ability of the academic community in Hong Kong to contribute to the debate on competition policy is not in question. Several local academics have taken an interest in the subject but lawyers have not been in the forefront of the debate. The nature and extent of the academic involvement with competition issues will be discussed below. Should the government decide to legislate on this issue, the academic community should be able to provide intellectual back-up as well as specific, suitable training for the lawyers, economists and civil servants who would run the system.

6.7 Economic policy and structure

The government maintains that a general competition law is unnecessary as Hong Kong has a free-trade policy, with minimal interference with the import of goods from overseas and duty is payable only on petroleum

---

[35] Art. 34 BL.

[36] Ibid. Art. 27. There has been recent concern that anti-Beijing press commentators may be subject to pressure to tone down or end anti-Hong Kong or central government rhetoric, following the resignation of three popular local talk-show hosts who provide a popular outlet for anti-government sentiment. See 'Freedom of speech must be defended', *South China Morning Post*, 28 May 2004.

products, cars, cosmetics, alcohol and tobacco.[37] This free access of goods to the Hong Kong domestic market allows competition in some sectors to flourish. This analysis is generally supported by at least one of the authors of the Economic Freedom of the World Report.[38] The structure and nature of the Hong Kong economy according to the Economist Intelligence Unit[39] is that Hong Kong is primarily a trading economy. The total value of the foreign trade in goods was equivalent to 271 per cent of current-price GDP in the year 2000, compared with 16.9 per cent in Japan and 20.1 per cent in the USA. Hong Kong is a service centre for companies doing business with China and the structure of the economy has changed dramatically over the last twenty years. In 1984, manufacturing accounted for 24.3 per cent of GDP but in 1999 for only 5.7 per cent. Trade, banking, tourism and other service industries accounted for 85.4 per cent of GDP and a similar percentage of employment.

However, these statistics do not tell us much about the structure of the domestic economy. A striking feature of Hong Kong's economy is the nature and level of control vested in the hands of a small number of very large conglomerate groups, which may have real estate, telecommunications, food, energy, automotive, commodity, transport and retailing subsidiaries. The common corporate structure consists of interconnected subsidiaries and extensive cross-ownership. Most Hong Kong listed companies are controlled by family interests with interlocking share-holding structures that make corporate raids all but impossible and allow substantial minority family shareholders to retain effective control of most public companies. The nature of these interlinked corporations is a characteristic feature of the domestic economy and it is precisely those who control such companies that have both a vested interest in repelling competition as well as the political power, exercised directly or indirectly, to persuade government that competition regulation should not be introduced into the Hong Kong domestic market. This concentration of interlinked economic power in the hands of a few oligarchic families has not gone unremarked. In a report to the European Parliament in October 2000,[40] the rapporteur John Cushnahan opined as follows at page 16:

---

[37] Dutiable Commodities Ordinance Cap. 109.
[38] Fraser Institute, http://www.fraserinstitute.ca. Professor Robert Lawson expressed this view to the author in an e-mail.
[39] Country Profile, July 2001, at http://store.eiu.com/.
[40] A5-0284/2000, http://www2.europarl.eu.int/omk/sipade2?L=EN&OBJID=2663&LEVEL=3&MODE=SIP&NAV=X&LSTDOC=N.

Need for fair competition laws

The influence of the Li Ka-shing family on Hong Kong business life has been the subject of criticism from a number of sources within Hong Kong itself.

It has been alleged that this family's business operations account for somewhere between one quarter to one third of stock market capitalisation and include such sectors as telephones, mobile telephones, electricity, supermarkets and property.

Earlier this year local newspapers voiced concern at the increasing dominance of the Li family after Mr Li's son Richard Li Tzar-kai assumed control of Cable and Wireless HKT, the largest telecom operator in the area.

This followed in the wake of two other incidents. The awarding of the Cyberport project to Richard Li without the matter being subjected to a public tendering process attracted considerable controversy as did the fact that many exemptions were granted when Mr Li senior's Tom.com was being floated in the Growth Enterprise Market.

If there is any substance to these allegations they have significant implications for EU businesses that either trade with or locate their Asian headquarters in Hong Kong.

As the existence of fair competition laws and practices ensures a level playing pitch for Hong Kong firms when they compete in the EU marketplace, European Union businesses are entitled to reciprocation when they operate in Hong Kong.

The European Commission in their Third Annual Report on Hong Kong also noted the controversy surrounding competition policy.[41]

Mr Li Ka-shing is only the most prominent of the local oligarchs; there are many other wealthy and well-connected mercantile families in Hong Kong who have the preponderance of economic and thus political power, given the institutional structures that exist in Hong Kong.

The Hong Kong colonial and post 1997 governments have characterised their economic policy as one of 'positive non-intervention', in marked contrast to other regional neighbours (Japan and South Korea being the most obvious examples) who pursued a dirigiste industrial policy in the past. However, the official characterisation of Hong Kong's policy is open to question.

As Dr Lam Pun-lee says:

Apart from direct involvement in housing [some 50 per cent of the population live in government-owned flats], education [over 90 per cent of

[41] COM(2001) 431 Final 25 July 2001.

children attend government schools and all universities are subvented by the public exchequer] and medical services, the government controls major industries too.

All railway systems in Hong Kong are owned and run by the government.[42] Franchises have been granted to bus companies that enjoy monopoly rights in the provision of bus services. Taxis and mini-buses are both subject to entry control and with the exception of mini-buses are under fare regulation. Except for piped gas supply utility companies are under some form of direct government control. Water is supplied solely by the government, while electricity is supplied by two territorial monopolists . . . subject to a scheme of control.[43]

6.8 Land – a government monopoly

A vital, especially in the context of Hong Kong, and often overlooked issue of fundamental importance in relation to the structure of the domestic economy is the fact that the government is the sole owner of all land in the SAR.[44] All occupied land in Hong Kong is leasehold. This has been of tremendous significance in Hong Kong's history. Topographically the SAR is very mountainous, with a chronic shortage of flat building land; creating new building land from marine reclamation projects has been practised by the Hong Kong government for more than 100 years and increasing encroachment on Victoria Harbour is very politically controversial.

Hong Kong's economic success has acted as a magnet for immigration from Mainland China and the population of almost 7 million is accommodated in an urban area of approximately one-third of the size of Greater London.[45] The government is the monopoly supplier of land and has followed a policy of drip-feeding the market to ensure the maintenance of high land prices, so benefiting the public exchequer. The government

---

[42] This was true in 1997 but the government has disposed of 50 per cent of its ownership in the Mass Transit Rail Corporation since that time.

[43] Lam Pun Lee, *Competition in energy*, The Hong Kong Economic Policy Series, City University of Hong Kong Press (1997), p. 1.

[44] One exception is St John's Anglican Cathedral in the Central District of Hong Kong, which was granted a freehold site in 1841; since then no other freehold land grants have ever been made. All land in Hong Kong ultimately belongs to the government.

[45] Hong Kong has an approximate area of 1,091 sq. km, population in 1999 6.8 million; Greater London has 1,508 sq. km, population in 1998 7.1 million. In Hong Kong approximately 40 per cent of its area is country park and mountains so leaving a usable area of approximately 600 sq. km. Thus, Hong Kong has roughly the same population as London accommodated in one-third of the habitable land. *The Statesman year book*, 138th edition. New York: Palgrave (2002).

derives approximately 30 per cent[46] of its income from the sale of land or land premium fees or property-based taxes, fees or charges. Additionally, the government also imposes very restrictive conditions on land use of demised property, demanding a very high premium whenever a tenant requests a change of a restrictive use. At the end of the contractual term of the lease, the government then resells a new lease. The Basic Law extended the duration of all pre-1997 leases but lessees had to pay an additional government rent as consideration, as well as residential rates. Thus, the government captures land values four times over. Between 1984 and 1995 land prices rose by 700 per cent according to Jones Lane Wotton, international real-estate agents, with prices of residential land reaching an average of over US$3,145 per sq. foot in 1997. However, since that time prices have declined by more than 65 per cent from their peak.[47]

Hong and Lam have examined this dear-land policy in depth.[48] In their view: 'High property prices come as an unexpected, indirect consequence of the government land supply policy. Undeniably, leasing land gradually by the government has created an institutional environment that allows big developers to dominate the land and housing markets. This development encourages property speculation and in turn, leads to high property prices.'[49] The government's land-sale policy has encouraged the development of an oligopolistic market in development land, as such real estate is auctioned in large lots which cost hundreds of millions of Hong Kong dollars in up-front land premium fees, so purchasers must either have access to substantial bank credit lines or huge cash reserves. Small developers do not have these financial resources and so between 1991 and 1994, for example, seven developers provided 70 per cent of all new housing units; 55 per cent came from just four suppliers and one of them supplied 25 per cent of the total number.[50]

This land policy has had other very unhealthy economic effects: for example, in 1994, 45 per cent of the capitalisation of the Hong Kong stock market was made up of companies in the property and real-estate market, compared with 10 per cent in the UK. As regards investment expenditure,

---

[46] Hong Kong Consumer Council Report, *How competitive is the private residential property market?* (July 1996).

[47] 'We'll force up flat prices: Leung', *South China Morning Post*, 26 September 2002.

[48] Hong Yu-hung and Alven Lam, Opportunities and risks of capturing land values under Hong Kong's leasehold system, Lincoln Institute Land Policy Working Paper, Cambridge, Mass. (1998) WP98YH1.

[49] Ibid. at p. 18.

[50] Hong Kong Polytechnic University Study for the Hong Kong Consumer Council (1996).

60 per cent was property related and over 30 per cent of bank lending was to property and construction firms.[51] This does not include the value of residential mortgages to homebuyers. These proportions are unlikely to have changed substantially in recent years, even though the market has slumped since 1997. In response to the dramatic decline in values the government in 1998 halted all land sales in the hope of supporting the market, the clearest possible evidence of government intervention in a supposedly free market, by a 'non-interventionist' government. The government also quietly abandoned plans, announced in the first policy address after the handover in 1997, to provide 85,000 new flats per annum, 50,000 of which would be produced by government and aimed at low-income families for rent or sale. This was, and remains, socially necessary to alleviate excessive residential overcrowding. The balance of 35,000 units per annum would be provided by the private sector. As a result of the post-1997 slump in prices, the policy was abandoned secretly by the government.[52] Further, in September 2002 the government suggested additional direct intervention in the market 'to force up flat prices'.[53] This incident gives a glimpse of the true policy-formation process in Hong Kong.

This excessive concentration of investment in the real-estate sector in Hong Kong, caused directly by government policy, leads to two related evils. Firstly, government land policy has enabled the dominant property firms to accumulate huge cash reserves that facilitated the creation of an interlocking web of conglomerate companies that, through network effects, have had a substantial foreclosing effect on competitors who attempt to enter many market sectors. The dominant property firms have garnered vast profits over the last three decades in Hong Kong as a result of government policy. The entrepreneurs, or the family interests which control them, have acted rationally by diversifying into other commercial sectors by setting up conglomerate corporate structures that can be subsidised, directly or indirectly, or granted special business access by the parent or associated corporations. The network effect of these conglomerate structures can and does act to stifle competition from non-connected firms by the erection of high barriers to entry to the same or a connected market. For example, in the domestic fuel market, the choice of which energy infrastructure to install in a forty-storey block of residential flats begins at the planning stage. The consumer market is the

[51] Samuel Staley, Planning rules and urban economic performance: the case of Hong Kong, The Hong Kong Centre for Economic Research, University of Hong Kong (1994).
[52] 'Tung accused of housing cover up', South China Morning Post, 1 July 2000.
[53] 'We'll force up flat prices: Leung', South China Morning Post, 26 September 2002.

largest purchaser of fuel for hot water and cooking purposes. Gas and electricity utilities often offer deals to developers to allow the sole installation of piped gas or electricity for these purposes, with large subsidies being offered for use of relevant gas or electric appliances. As Dr Lam says:

> If developers took the interests of consumers into consideration they would choose the fuel supply system with the lowest costs. But structural impediments may prevent fair competition from taking place. Since the majority shareholders of the energy companies in Hong Kong are also majority shareholders in property development firms, a fuel supply system may be chosen on the basis of serving the interests of those shareholders, rather than those of the flat purchasers. Hong Kong Electric is controlled by Cheung Kong (Holdings) [Li Ka-shing's flagship property enterprise]; they may choose electric water heating systems over gas, despite the fact that gas may be cheaper. Similarly, Hong Kong and China Gas Company is controlled by Henderson Land Development, which may promote gas over electricity. This close association of energy companies with property developers has been enabling energy companies to increase sales by the prevention of fair competition.[54]

In 2003, political concern was expressed in LEGCO about the foreclosing of various markets in relation to newly completed residential estates. Telecommunications, retail outlets and property management services of specific housing developments were generally undertaken by subsidiaries of the real-estate developers and suspicions existed that only connected service providers were selected to supply services to completed estates and that competitors were not even invited to tender.

The suspicions of the foreclosure of markets and the obviously anti-competitive effect of such practices caused the government via the Competition Advisory Group (COMPAG) to seek research consultancy tenders from academic bodies and consultancy organisations, to discover the extent of the problem.[55] However, even if the investigation takes place, there are no legal powers to require developers to disclose tendering or selection procedures or documents. It is most likely that developers will claim that confidentiality concerns justify limited co-operation or they may refuse to disclose any information, justly pointing out that these are private contractual matters and of no concern to government. In short, their

---

[54] Lam, *Competition in energy*, p. 83.
[55] See COMPAG Assignment No. 1/2004, Consultancy study on competition aspects of cross-sector business operations of large real estate developers, 2 March 2004.

arguments would be: it is a private matter, you have no right to information and we have broken no law.

The assertion that the real-estate market has competition problems will be tested further in detail below when Consumer Council reports into the workings of some sectors of the domestic economy are discussed. Secondly, the combination of government land policy and the oligopolistic real-estate market has maintained artificially high real-estate prices that benefit the oligopoly members but impose higher than free-market costs directly through real estate prices or indirectly through higher than free-market rents to business. This has the effect of making Hong Kong a more expensive place to do business than other regional centres and in the long run may have a significant effect on the SAR's international competitiveness.[56] If these assertions are correct, Hong Kong's domestic economy is not the free and openly competitive environment alluded to by the government. This assertion must be tested against the factual situation pertaining in the Hong Kong domestic market; evidence to support this assertion is not easy to obtain. The absence of investigatory powers and the lack of publicly available information on many of these issues exacerbate the difficulties of proof but nevertheless evidence does exist to support this contention and it is presented below.

6.9 The competition debate 1992–2003 and sectoral investigations

The current competition policy debate has come about as a result of Governor Chris Patten's first policy speech to LEGCO in 1992. He said:

> Hong Kong is proud of its free and competitive markets. But a more sophisticated and prosperous community has become increasingly unwilling to accept unfair and discriminatory business practices. The public has already begun to voice alarm at the use of market power by suppliers in areas of special importance to the ordinary family's wellbeing . . . I shall ask my Business Council to put at the top of its agenda the development of a comprehensive competition policy for Hong Kong.[57]

---

[56] Whilst market rents have fallen very significantly in the last five years, they are still 50 per cent higher than rents for comparable property in Singapore, Hong Kong's major regional competitor and substantially higher than in Shenzhen just over the border in China.

[57] Hong Kong Legislative Council Official Record of Proceedings, 7 October 1992, p. 16.

As a result of this policy initiative the government commissioned the Hong Kong Consumer Council to undertake sectoral investigations including banking, supermarkets, gas supply, broadcasting, telecommunications and private residential property between 1993 and 1996. These reports were conducted without any legal power to demand evidence from persons concerned or to require the production of documents but most business operators did co-operate with the enquiries, to some extent at least.

6.9.1 Bank deposits

Under s.12(1)(a) of the Hong Kong Association of Banks Ordinance the Association was empowered to make rules regarding the maximum rates of interest payable on HK$ deposits of less than $500,000 or maturing in less than fifteen months.[58] S.21 (1) empowered the Association to discipline or expel any member acting in breach of any rules made by the Association. The Banking Ordinance effectively prevented restricted licensed banks or deposit-taking companies, who were not 'banks' as defined, from accepting deposits of less than HK$500,000 and HK$100,000 respectively or of repaying deposits on less than three months' notice. Therefore, these organisations were excluded from competing with banks for small deposits.

The effect of these legislative rules was to create an interest-rate cap for smaller deposits. The report found that the spread between deposit rates offered and lending rates was considerably higher than in other jurisdictions. The difference was 1.65 per cent higher for fixed deposits and 1.79 per cent higher for prime savings, so demonstrating that the legally sanctioned cartel was extracting a monopsonistic rent from depositors, allowing Hong Kong banks to become some of the most profitable in the world. The report opined that this cartel was extracting large supra-normal profits from small depositors and that the cartel arrangement should be dismantled in stages between 1995 and 1997. The government eventually accepted the recommendations but was very slow to implement its decision, partly as a result of the Asian financial crisis in 1997/8 and the political uncertainty created by the retrocession of sovereignty. Interest rates payable to depositors were finally liberalised in 2001.

---

[58] Are Hong Kong depositors fairly treated?, Hong Kong Consumer Council, 28 February 1994.

6.9.2 Domestic water heating and cooking fuel market

It should be pointed out that the vast majority of Hong Kong people live in multi-storey blocks of flats, usually some thirty to forty storeys high. Installation of network systems of wires, pipes and cables to provide water, gas, electricity and telecommunications, can practically only be done at the development stage of the building estate. There are, therefore, special characteristics to be considered when assessing the market for domestic fuels and telecommunications.[59] Further, most Hong Kong homes do not have space-heating systems due to the semi-tropical climate but do have need of air-conditioning units.

Domestic water heating and domestic cooking in Hong Kong are dominated by the use of gas as the primary fuel. This is for cultural and technical reasons. Chinese people prefer to cook with 'fire' as the use of the wok in cooking is essential and requires instant, very high temperatures; electricity does not suit this purpose. Ovens are rarely, if ever used, in domestic Chinese kitchens. As regards water heating, many Hong Kong flats do not have suitable electrical circuits to support instantaneous electric water heaters and gas is, again, the usual energy source. Gas can be supplied in three ways; firstly piped coal gas (known as Towngas) through the public piped network owned and exclusively operated by Hong Kong and China Gas Co. Ltd., secondly by a private piped network supplying liquefied petroleum gas and thirdly by portable individual LPG cylinders. Portable cylinders are inconvenient and LPG private networks in individual buildings are very rare for legal and technical reasons; no developer will plan for the installation of a Towngas pipe system and also a private LPG system due to the huge costs involved. Also, the Gas Safety (Supply) Regulations forbid the installation of LPG mains pipes along or across any public road and provide for stringent safety features for the bulk storage of LPG. Consequently, Towngas has a dominant position in the defined market of between 80 and 90 per cent.

Thus, Towngas is a private monopolist. It is subject to no scheme of control or regulatory regime as regards price. Over the ten-year period 1985 to 1994 the Report found that the rate of increase of Towngas prices had been consistently higher than operating costs. Needless to say Towngas was highly profitable; over the ten-year period from 1984 to 1994 the return on sales grew from 18.6 per cent to 36.8 per cent; operating margins grew from 27.8 per cent to 69.2 per cent; the return on capital was approximately

---

[59] Assessing competition in the water heating and cooking fuel market, Hong Kong Consumer Council, 1995.

16 per cent per annum. In comparison with US energy giants, Towngas was the most profitable utility provider in the world. In addition to the costs of gas supplied, the related markets of supply and maintenance of gas appliances were also dominated by Towngas, which supplied in excess of 90 per cent of gas appliances.

Towngas had been accused of abusing its dominant position by attempting to persuade developers to ensure that the gas supply was designed into residential buildings for cooking and water heating to the exclusion of suitable electrical circuits. If it were not so planned, a much higher connection charge would be levied at a later date. The electricity utilities suggested that this was an abuse of dominance in an attempt to exclude electricity from new flats as a method of water heating. The Report recommended the break-up of Towngas, the adoption of a common carrier system to allow other suppliers to use the Towngas pipe network and a switch over to natural gas from coal gas to increase sources of supply. In the meantime, Towngas should be subject to some form of regulatory control to increase efficiency and reduce costs. New flat developers should be required to install suitable electricity circuits as well as gas connections to allow consumers choice of water-heating fuel. An energy regulator to encompass both gas and electricity supply should be established to set standards and encourage effective competition in the domestic energy market.

Since the Report was published the government has not changed the regulatory environment to increase effective competition in the defined domestic energy market.

6.9.3 Supermarkets

Supermarket stores in Hong Kong are generally very small in size when compared to Europe, North America and Australasia.[60] This is primarily due to small site sizes and site scarcity. However, cultural preferences also play a part in this market structure. Chinese people tend to prefer to purchase fruit, vegetables, meat and fish fresh from traditional covered markets, locally known as 'wet markets', on a daily basis. Two factors also influence grocery shopping in Hong Kong. Firstly, most of the population does not own a car as most people live in flats with no or very limited car parking facilities. Secondly, very limited storage space exists in kitchens,

---

[60] Report on the supermarket industry in Hong Kong, Hong Kong Consumer Council, November 1994.

due to their tiny dimensions when compared to those typically found in other places. These two factors mean that a weekly shopping expedition to the supermarket to buy groceries, transport them by car and then store them in bulk is impossible. Thus, generally, 'supermarkets' in Hong Kong cannot be closely compared with those in other jurisdictions.

Notwithstanding these local peculiarities, the Consumer Council report adopted a government definition of supermarkets as 'establishments that engage in retail sales of general provisions including foodstuffs as one of the major items that use the self-service method'. Convenience stores and traditional wet-markets were excluded on the basis that they were not close enough substitute suppliers. It is a moot point as to whether this definition had a distorting effect on the report's findings to the extent of invalidating them. There were and remain no legal rules regulating entry into the supermarket sector.

Given this somewhat narrow definition two operators dominated the market. Wellcome and Park'N Shop chains had, at that time, some 70 per cent of the market. But if a wider definition was adopted, the government believed that the whole supermarket sector accounts for only 35 per cent of foodstuff sales. The two market leaders also grew significantly during the study period 1985 to 1993, squeezing the market share of other operators. Access to prime store sites, most of which were situated within the development envelope of new residential housing estates, so giving an almost captive customer base of residents, was seen as a key advantage. Park'N Shop is part of the Hutchinson Whampoa/Cheung Kong conglomerate controlled by the Li Ka-shing family and Wellcome is part of the Dairy Farm International Holdings, part of the Jardine Matheson group of companies, controlled by the British-based Keswick family. The report found that all new residential housing developments, owned by the respective parent companies, included a supermarket site operated by their respective grocery subsidiary. The Consumer Council saw this close relationship as a significant barrier to entry.

The dominant position of the two incumbents also gave them significant bargaining power over suppliers, including demands for exclusivity agreements. Choice of products within stores was relatively restricted, thus preventing inter-brand competition; prices of many similar/identical items were similar if not identical in the stores of either firm in close geographical proximity to each other but varied noticeably across the Territory. Price competition was minimal during the period of study, whether this was due to intense competition, covert collusion or an oligopolistic market could not be determined due to lack of information; the Consumer

Council had no power to require disclosure from investigatees. The 1994 report recommended monitoring of the supermarket sector, adoption of effective powers giving the ability to investigate anti-competitive complaints against incumbents and open tendering by developers for new supermarket sites to prevent 'tying'.

Since the report was published, the industry has become even more concentrated. In September 2000, the French Carrefour hypermarket retailer which had previously operated four large supermarkets in Hong Kong closed down, citing an inability to access large enough sites to accommodate its 'hypermarket' style of operation. In June 1999, a new entrant to the food retail market, adMart, which operated on a no-store, free home delivery basis, began operations. The two dominant firms responded offering competing free delivery services and by reducing prices on selected goods. The new entrant failed within eighteen months. The two incumbents then reduced the scale of the home delivery service and subsequently started to charge for the service. Allegations of abuse of dominance and predatory practices were made at the time but no hard evidence emerged and, in any event, even if they could be substantiated, they would not have been unlawful. In June 2001, the 34-branch GD Supermarket chain collapsed, probably as a result of management incompetence and employee fraud. As a result of these structural changes the combined market shares of the two principal incumbents has increased to 80 per cent of supermarket sales from 70 per cent a decade earlier.[61] In 2003, the Economic Intelligence Unit (EIU) conducted a survey[62] of the supermarket sector to investigate claims that the market was an effective duopoly and that the incumbents were attempting to increase their dominance by abusing their position by below-cost selling and intimidatory tactics to pressurise suppliers not to deal with competitors, such as the now-defunct adMart. The EIU concluded that whether or not the allegations were true was a matter for a competent competition authority to judge and that Hong Kong lacked the means to assess competition problems optimally.

In August 2003, the Consumer Council published another report[63] into the supermarket sector, as claims were made that despite over five years of deflation in the consumer price index the standard sample of foodstuffs from supermarkets had increased substantially in price during the

---

[61] 'Supermarket giants "will continue unchallenged"', *South China Morning Post*, 21 June 2001.

[62] *Closed shop?* Business Asia, Economist Intelligence Unit, 19 May 2003 vol. XXXV, no. 10.

[63] Report on competition in the foodstuffs and household necessities retail sector, Hong Kong Consumer Council, 11 August 2003.

same period. The two chains attempted to discredit the survey, saying its methodology was flawed. Hong Kong consumers were unimpressed by the stores' protestations but the operators claimed foul play and maintained that there was vigorous competition in the sector between the two of them and with other foodstuff suppliers. They denied that their profit margins were excessive but declined to produce any evidence to support this contention; there is no publicly available data to ascertain profit margins as neither Wellcome nor Park'N Shop are listed entities and their financial results are consolidated with other subsidiaries into the published results of their respective parents. Thus their true profitability is opaque and there exists no legal means to compel disclosure. Needless to say, the government has taken no steps to implement any of the 1994 Consumer Council recommendations concerning this sector or any action whatsoever to ascertain the true facts concerning the business practices or profitability of these two chains.

6.9.4 Broadcasting and telecommunications

Both these technology-based sectors were subject to government franchise and statutory regulatory regimes at the time the reports were undertaken.[64, 65] It will be convenient to consider them later in a separate section devoted to them in a subsequent chapter. They will be considered separately because they are the only two industries that are now subject to comprehensive, competition-orientated regimes, with full legal powers over both traditional sectoral regulatory matters as well as general competition provisions. The history of the industries, in terms of structure and regulatory environment, will be considered in detail, as will the Consumer Council reports, which may have helped convince the government to legislate in this field. The minutiae of the statutory schemes and the powers and effectiveness of the regulators will be critically examined in due course. But at this juncture a single question should be raised, namely, could competition problems be found in these two sectors, necessitating full regulatory intervention, but not in any other sector of economic activity in Hong Kong? The paradox inherent in the government's position is obvious. As will be seen later, the government

---

[64] Ensuring competition in the dynamic television broadcasting market, Hong Kong Consumer Council, January 1996.
[65] Achieving competition in the liberalised telecommunications market, Hong Kong Consumer Council, March 1996.

continues to maintain that there are no significant competition problems extant in most economic sectors; but following the government's own logic, the telecommunication and broadcasting sectors must have had competition problems to justify full competition regulation. The interesting question is, what was unique about these two industries that necessitated competition rules and was there clear evidence of competition failures in advance of legislation? These issues will be examined in a later chapter.

6.9.5 Residential property

The land policy of the Hong Kong government has been discussed in section 6.8. The importance of real estate to the overall Hong Kong economy and to individual citizens cannot be over-stated.[66] The scarcity of affordable property, endemic residential overcrowding, the very high percentage of income expended on mortgage repayments (58 per cent of disposable income from 1985 to 1994 and 73 per cent in 1995; in comparison the average in North America and Europe is 35 per cent),[67] all contribute to the mania for property ownership for residential and speculative purposes. Over 30 per cent of bank lending is for residential mortgages and over 45 per cent of the capitalisation of the Hong Kong stock market is based on property companies. However, between 1997 and mid-2004 the market has crashed from its peak in October 1997 by approximately 65 per cent.[68] This has proved a salutary lesson to many buyers who bought at the peak of the bubble and now have significant negative equity problems. Government policy in the housing market has been marked by great confusion and overt manipulation in an attempt to prop up and reverse the disastrous slide in prices. The official laissez-faire policy of the government has been exposed as a sham by this naked interventionism but even worse it has been ineffective in achieving its objective of stabilising prices, as a result of two recessions and rising unemployment, at its highest-ever level of 7.1 per cent (2002); in 1997 it was 2.2 per cent.[69]

---

[66] How competitive is the private residential property market? Hong Kong Consumer Council, July 1996.
[67] Ibid. pp. 1 and 2.
[68] 'We'll force up flat prices: Leung', *South China Morning Post*, 26 September 2002. This remained the position in October 2003.
[69] Statistics on Labour Force, Unemployment and Underemployment, Census & Statistics Department http://www.info.gov.hk/censtatd/eng/hkstat/fas/labour/ghs/labour1_index. html; unemployment remained at a similar level in October 2003.

The 1996 report was written against a background of unsustainable property price increases and rampant speculation. The special characteristics of the Hong Kong residential property market require explanation. Almost all the population is accommodated in apartments; houses are the preserve of the super-rich or rural agricultural workers or fisher-folk, groups which do not form a significant percentage of the total population. The report concentrated on only one sector of the total housing market – new private residential flats. This definition of the area of study can be criticised as ignoring the fact that over 50 per cent of housing units in Hong Kong are actually government-provided public housing and it also ignores the second-hand private flat market. The rationale was that these segments were not close enough substitutes and so formed distinct markets. In the case of public housing, stringent eligibility requirements and long waiting lists meant that it was not a substitute for new private housing. This may be tenable but in relation to private second-hand flats it appears less so. However, there is a marked cultural preference in Hong Kong towards the purchase of 'new' flats as opposed to second-hand ones.

Another justification for this view of the separateness of the new-flat sector is that banks operate quite different mortgage lending schemes depending on whether the property is new or second hand. New flats can be mortgaged for up to 80 per cent or more of value, repayable over twenty-five or more years. Additional top-up loans to purchasers may also be provided by developers. But for second-hand flats, banks will typically lend for a maximum period of forty years less the actual age of the building, generally for a period of only 10 to 15 years and at only 70 per cent of valuation. Thus, new flats' price per sq. foot is up to one-third higher than older property but perversely new flats are easier to buy, due to the mortgage lending policy of the banks.[70] Thus, this lending policy may also serve substantially to differentiate the new-flat market from the second-hand market. These factors may well justify the Consumer Council's market definition.

The report did expose a number of factors highlighting the extensive and intrusive role of the government in this market as the sole owner, and thus seller, of developable land, being the largest direct landlord in Hong Kong housing some 50 per cent of the population, the sole arbiter of land usage and change and being reliant on land-based revenues (including sale income, premium income for change of use, stamp duty, rents and rates) for up to 30 per cent of annual income. It is obvious that the government

[70] 'Old before their time', *South China Morning Post*, 28 June 2004.

has a number of clear conflicts of interest. Maintaining land scarcity drives up prices and direct revenues but increased sales of land depresses prices and so revenues. However, greater availability of affordable housing increases consumer welfare and enhances the economy's efficiency, by lowering a key cost of producing goods and services. This dilemma has still not been resolved. But it is submitted that the government, at the time of the report and currently, still plays a decisive role in the Hong Kong property market. Government protestations of minimal intervention in economic matters sound particularly hollow in respect of the real-estate market.

The main conclusion of the 1996 report was that the supply of new flats was highly concentrated; the figures have been quoted above. The report recommended that the government reduce perceived barriers to entry to the residential development market by reducing lot sizes to encourage new entrants into the market, improve its zoning and building regulation approvals procedures, improve residential land supply, rezone old industrial land as residential, improve forecasting techniques, outlaw anti-competitive practices and increase the transparency of government disposals of land.

The report's conclusions caused significant debate at the time of its release as the housing-market bubble peaked. Subsequent falls in prices have significantly improved the affordability ratio, at least for those in employment. However, as of 2004 prices remain high by international standards, even after the disastrous falls since 1997.

Professors Cheng and Wu[71] criticised the report's methodology, especially the narrow market definition and the conclusions that flowed from that definitional premise. They included second-hand flats in their market definition and found no anti-competitive problems. However, given the characteristics of the Hong Kong residential housing market, perhaps their criticism is not entirely justified. But they did agree with the report's conclusion that government land-disposal policies were at the root of the problem of the scarcity of development land.

Unfortunately, as a result of the property slump in the last seven years, the government has not increased land supply and has attempted to boost the market by reducing or ceasing the sale of development lots and completed government-subsidised flats. Land sales did resume on a very limited trial basis in spring 2004. Once the economy eventually rallies, the

---

[71] Leonard K. Cheng and Wu Chang qi, *Competition policy and the regulation of business*, City University of Hong Kong Press (1998).

property market may return to the bubble state of the mid-1990s, as Hong Kong's net population continues to rise by a minimum of 50,400 immigrants from the Chinese Mainland per annum, notwithstanding a natural increase of roughly the same number. Thus, with a net population increase of almost 100,000 per annum[72] demand for residential accommodation is bound to cause a rise in property prices, if the government maintains its current restrictive land sales policy. Improving competition in the provision of new residential units does not appear to be the government's first priority; supporting residential property prices does.

In June 2002, the government announced a wholesale re-organisation of its housing provision policy. Official targets for home ownership, set by the Chief Executive in 1997 at 70 per cent have now, apparently, been abandoned. The bureaucracy will be stream-lined in respect of government rental flats and the government will no longer build new flats for sale to the lower middle class, the so-called 'sandwich class'. People with moderate means will now get a direct financial subsidy by way of top-up mortgage loans.[73] Property developers have achieved a major goal: to get the government out of the market for private flat sales. The new financial packages will now be used solely for purchasers of private-sector-built flats.

What conclusions can be drawn from the various Consumer Council reports? First, they were the first systematic attempt to investigate and analyse the structures of various non-traded domestic economy sectors. Subject to the issues of market definition and the controversies that arose therefrom, the reports do provide evidence of structural impediments to competition in the markets studied. Second, the government's response was slow, hesitant and unconvincing. This antipathy was the result of several factors, namely, of the government's philosophical commitment to non-interventionism, the strongly held conviction that there are few, if any, competition problems in the domestic market and the political factors alluded to above. However, the assertion that political and economic power are so closely aligned as to be the major determinant of the government policy position is not accepted by the government.[74] Thirdly,

---

[72] Hong Kong's population was 5.674 million in 1991, 6.412 million in 1996 and 6.708 million in 2001. This shows a 1.034 million net increase over ten years, approximately 100,000 per annum www.info.gov.hk/censtatd/eng/hkstat. This rate of increase is projected to continue.

[73] 'Opportunity and challenge for new housing chief', *South China Morning Post*, 26 June 2002.

[74] At a meeting on 29 August 2002, the author confirmed this was the case with three senior civil servants of the Economic Development and Labour Bureau and the Commerce, Industry and Technology Bureau of HKSAR Government.

any assault on profitable business practices would be seen as unacceptable, especially by the oligarchic interests that directly benefit from them
and which also operate the levers of political control; this may well explain the government reaction to the Consumer Council Reports of the
mid-1990s.

6.10 The academic debate

During the 1990s, and at the same time as competition policy was highlighted by the Governor and the Consumer Council, an academic debate
also took place within Hong Kong as to the merits or otherwise of adopting a general competition law. Most of the contributors were economist
lawyers playing a decidedly reserved role. Professor Albert Chen, a leading
academic lawyer, noted the absence of competition law, and the lack of
a focused grass-roots movement supporting competition law. He opined
that a policy decision on adoption should depend on an economic cost-
benefit analysis. He thought that there would be additional compliance
costs for business if a competition law was introduced and that such a
new regime would foster 'uncertainty. . . as to whether particular business practices are lawful. Uncertainty is the antithesis of predictability
and calculability, which is normally associated with the rule of law. So
legal uncertainty is also a cost or loss from a welfare point of view.'[75]

With respect, this view somewhat oversimplifies the issue. Any new legal rule involves compliance costs; the key question is whether those costs
are balanced or exceeded by overall efficiency gains and a concomitant
increase in consumer welfare or not. If this argument was taken to its
logical conclusion, no new law would ever be enacted for fear of compliance costs. As for increased uncertainty that, with respect, depends on the
model adopted, the skill of the legislative draftsman, the clarity of subordinate legislation and guidelines issued by the enforcement authority and
the transparency and rationality of the application of the law to individual
cases. This is so with any law, not just competition statutes. It seems that
unfamiliarity with the concepts and precepts of competition law may be
the root of Professor Chen's anxiety, rather than the inherent complexity
or perversity of the law itself.

At about the same time, the Hong Kong Centre for Economic Research published a number of contributions in a single edition exclusively

---

[75] Albert Chen, *Competition Law and Hong Kong* 23(3) HKLJ 413.

devoted to the subject of competition law adoption.[76] Professor Richard Wong took the view that the only significant impediment to competition in Hong Kong was extant government regulation and the monopolisation of sectors of the economy.[77] He took a very sceptical view of the inherent value of anti-trust intervention, as exemplified by his understanding of the American experience. However, he did qualify this view as regards Hong Kong due to the lack of empirical evidence. He stated that competition was not an issue in manufacturing as Hong Kong producers were overwhelmingly export-orientated and were exposed to international competition. He did consider that the service sector might have anti-competitive inefficiencies but in the supermarket sector he thought the duopoly observed was merely a question of economies of scale.

He also considered that there were four areas of concern. They were:

- government monopolies in postal services, water supply, railway systems (then wholly government owned), health services (90 per cent of hospital beds), public housing (50 per cent of households) and education (between 75 and 84 per cent of school places and 100 per cent of university places);
- the government-sanctioned bank-interest cartel (since dismantled, see section 6.9.1 above);
- licensing in the professions, especially in medicine and law;
- franchising in road transport – buses, taxis and mini-buses, telecommunications, aircraft maintenance, air cargo terminals, container freight, electricity supply.

He concluded by opining that government actions were the most dangerous aspect of any anti-competitive problems that existed. His neoliberalism deserves acknowledgement and one suspects that if evidence were obtained to support the contention that widespread cartels and other barriers to competition existed, he would not be entirely against appropriate legislative measures.

Professor Leonard Cheng[78] opined that Hong Kong's free trade policy was a necessary but not sufficient spur to competition in the Territory because many goods and services are not traded. He listed real estate, retailing, transportation and utilities as major problem areas and thought

---

[76] Understanding competition in Hong Kong, HKCER Letters (1993) vol. 20 http://www.hku.hk/hkcer/articles/v20/rwong.htm.

[77] Ibid.

[78] 'A consensus for Hong Kong's competition policy?' *South China Morning Post*, 2 April 1999.

that to dismiss competition policy was an error. He went on to cite examples of banks, insurers, newspapers and the professions as open cartelists. Obvious oligopolists such as domestic housing suppliers were in danger of co-ordinated action but he found no hard evidence to support such a finding so he suggested that legal investigatory powers were needed to discover the facts. He noted the high level of cross-ownership and cross-shareholdings prevalent throughout the Hong Kong economy and fretted about the possible anti-competitive effects that this might imply. However, he worried more that a comprehensive law implied a big new bureaucracy which would be too intrusive and would encourage American-style litigation. He seemed to ignore the potential reduction in regulatory and scheme-of-control functions and that civil servants thus engaged could be redeployed or replaced by a competition authority. An overall increase in civil servant numbers would not be a certainty. As for intrusiveness, that would depend on the form and scope of the statute and the powers vested in an authority, as is certainly the case in respect of potentially increased litigation rates. The Hong Kong and US civil litigation systems have fundamental differences in terms of process, civil jury trials, discovery procedures, requirements of proof, levels of judge-awarded damages and contingency fees. Concerns about the flood-gates of litigation are misplaced; this is understandable as the author is an economist, not a lawyer, and these technical matters of procedure, whilst vital, may be overlooked by non-practitioners.

However, he concluded that it was vital to have full legal investigatory powers to uncover the facts, given that business would not voluntarily or fully disclose internal information or co-operate with fact-finding investigations. This observation was very perceptive, as may be seen from the difficulties encountered by the Consumer Council and COMPAG sectoral competition investigations. He appreciated that without hard information making decisions about competition policy and law would be a hostage to fashion and prejudice, not the result of a rational and critical assessment of the facts. Unfortunately, this is exactly the way in which the government did come to form policy in 1997 and subsequently; the obvious defects in that process and the outcomes achieved, will be explored later.

As can be seen, the debate on the general issue of competition regulation in Hong Kong was limited but essentially exposed the fundamental policy issues for debate and consideration by the authorities. As has been noted above, the sectoral competition investigations carried out by the Consumer Council were not universally welcomed either for their methodology or conclusions. Nevertheless, the Council completed a final report on the general competition situation for consideration by the public and the government. The following sections will analyse the Council's recommendations and the government's response.

6.11 The Consumer Council final report

In November 1996, the Consumer Council published a major report, *Competition Policy: The Key to Hong Kong's Future Economic Success*. The conclusions were that the sectoral reports had uncovered significant market imperfections and that there were other economic sectors that also suffered from similar problems but that, due to an absence of investigatory powers, the Council was powerless to conduct effective enquiries.

The report argued that by not having a competition law Hong Kong was lacking the necessary weapons to ensure that the domestic economy remained competitive, which in the long run would affect the Territory's ability to remain internationally economically competitive. The illustration of the then recent partial liberalisation of the telecom market was used to show how competition had substantially reduced prices and increased consumer welfare. Examples of neighbouring jurisdictions, Taiwan and South Korea, were also given of newly industrialised economies that had recently introduced competition laws. The advantages to business of fairness, consistency and the reduction of the overall regulatory burden on the economy as a whole were also stressed. Consumers would also benefit from lower prices, improved services and more choice. Thus, the Council strongly recommended the adoption of an effective competition policy in tandem with the enactment of a general competition statute to provide a transparent and effective method to deal with restrictive conduct. The competition policy suggested included a strong element of education and advocacy to promote its aims and objectives within government, the business community and amongst the general public. The government should adopt internal policies to ensure that its procurement and licensing systems adhered to pro-competition objectives; any new regulatory schemes should be subject to a competition analysis and the existing regulatory regimes should be examined with a view to abolition, with pro-competition provisions replacing them wherever possible.

As part of its twin-track approach, the report argued that a comprehensive competition statute should be enacted, based on the EC model, with four principal elements: prohibition of agreements between firms that prevent, restrict or distort competition, prohibition of abuse of a dominant position that prevents, restricts or distorts competition, prevention of abuse of collective dominance and a merger-control provision. The collective dominance and merger-regulation provisions would only be introduced as experience was gained from operating the two basic prohibitions. The usual range of financial penalties would be available and private entities injured by the unlawful conduct would be eligible for compensation from the Competition Authority. A small competition authority and an appeal body would be established to administer the law, based again on the EC model. The ordinary common law courts would not have jurisdiction in competition cases.

The report appeared eight months before the hand-over of Hong Kong to China. The government sought public consultation from December 1996 to March 1997 and received eighty-eight responses from commercial and academic respondents. An interdepartmental working party was set up and a formal response was published in November 1997 – *Competition Policy for Hong Kong*.

6.12 The government's Response

The Response began with an exposition of the government objective for competition policy – the promotion of economic efficiency. The government confirmed that it wished to promote free trade and competition, to be brought about with minimal government intervention in the economy and utilising a test of market accessibility and contestability.

The government claimed that:

- There were virtually no barriers to market access for local or international traders and manufacturers.[79] (This may be true of most of the economy which is not regulated or subject to government-mandated monopoly control but privately erected barriers do clearly exist.)
- Government policy discouraged unfair business practices.[80] (This contention related to consumer-protection measures, and was irrelevant to discussion of competition matters per se.)
- Funds had been allocated to the Consumer Council to investigate anti-competitive practices. (That may have been so but the Council had no legal powers to carry out fully effective investigations and the government had no legal powers to punish anti-competitive conduct.)

[79] *Competition policy for Hong Kong*, Trade and Industry Bureau, Hong Kong, November 1997, p. 5.
[80] Ibid.

- Regulation in some sectors was necessary but government ensured that any oligopoly or monopoly that existed would not unduly compromise service quality or price. (How does this assertion mesh with a government that philosophically denies the value of regulation and is ostensibly wedded to market forces? Government judgement will, apparently, thus prevail over market forces in some sectors, so apparently contradicting the government's fundamental policy stance.)
- Individual sectors of the economy vary and need different types of control mechanism. (This argument appears again to be at odds with the government's stated goal of minimum intervention, guided by the notion that competition generally provides the best solution to economic problems. Particularist regulations inevitably create anomalies unless guided by a coherent principle, which should be competition.)
- The Heritage Foundation and the Fraser Institute had ranked Hong Kong as having the highest degree of economic freedom in the world and so a non-intervention policy was justified. (The use of these indices as a justification for not enacting a competition law is erroneous as they only measure government restrictions on trade and government intervention in the economy; they have nothing to say about private restrictions or the structure of the private sector of the economy or the contestability of markets. Thus, using them to support the government's case is a gross fallacy.[81])

In respect of the Consumer Council findings the government commented that:

- The service sector was not insulated from international competition. New players were free to enter the market in line with WTO principles. (This may be so for some sectors such as banking and finance but not so

---

[81] The author contacted Professors Lawson and Gwartney at the Fraser Institute by e-mail in June 2002. They both took a sceptical attitude towards the efficacy of anti-trust legislation. Their prime concern, and the model of economic freedom they adopt, is that of freedom from government interference. The surveys do not consider private actions as inhibitors of economic freedom as they think that there is a qualitative difference between private and public restraints on trade. Thus, the index does not seek to measure private restraints at all. The Heritage Foundation Index of Economic Freedom adopts a different set of measures including prevalence of corruption, government non-tariff barriers, tax burden, rule of law, regulatory burdens, restrictions on banks, labour market regulation and black-market activity. Again, it does not seek to measure private anti-competitive practices specifically at all.

in the case of regulated professions, some of which appeared to tighten their entry barriers after 1997.[82])

- Hong Kong's lack of a competition law would not compromise the SAR's ability to participate in international fora. (This may be true but in the 2002 WTO Trade Policy Review members did question whether the absence of a competition law compromised the government's ability to promote competition.[83])

Notwithstanding the view that there were no serious problems, the government then decided to enhance its extant 'competition' policy on the basis that there was 'possible room for improvement'. It accepted that its policy needed to be more 'proactive, transparent and comprehensive'. In order to achieve these objectives it would:

- Issue a policy statement setting out objectives and principles to promote competition and require all government departments to adhere to them and encourage publicly funded organisations to do the same.
- Give emphasis to competition issues when submitting proposals to the Executive Council and review existing regulatory schemes to minimise entry barriers so as not to contribute to anti-competitive conditions in the economy.
- Establish a COMPAG to discuss competition policy development.

The effectiveness of these measures was open to question. It seemed that the government grudgingly accepted that some anti-competitive problems did exist but that leading by example and exhortation would provide a solution. Since the government plays a relatively minor role in economic affairs, on its own submission, it appears that pro-competitive policies affecting the public sector cannot have any effect on the problems identified by the Consumer Council, which all applied to the private sector.

As regards COMPAG, it is difficult to see what such a body could achieve. The Group was to have no legal powers to investigate, prohibit or punish anti-competitive conduct. Therefore, it is difficult to appreciate how a toothless talking-shop could adequately address the issues of concern that had been identified. The government assertion of COMPAG's potential effectiveness will be assessed in the later discussion of the competition situation in Hong Kong since its establishment.

The Response then proceeded to address the fundamentally important issue of whether Hong Kong should enact a general competition law to

---

[82] Lawyers, doctors, accountants, dentists and architects.
[83] Document no. WT/TPR/M/52 http://www.wto.org.

provide an enforcement mechanism, to include coverage of the private sector. In chapter 5 of the Response the government makes out its case. First, the government acknowledged the advantages of general legislation:

- demonstration of commitment to competition across all sectors, not only limited to public bodies;
- rendering unlawful 'unfair' business practices would promote healthy competition and protect consumer interests and complement existing consumer protection laws;
- abuses could be investigated and subject to sanctions, if substantiated; and
- Hong Kong's legal framework would be congruent with those of most of its developed trading partners.

However, the government did not concede that a comprehensive law would enhance economic efficiency, presumably because it contended that the sectoral regulation and free-trade policies achieved this central objective based on existing policies.

The government's argument to discount the advantages of a general competition law was then made out. The Response maintained that there were examples of policy objectives being achieved without the need for law. For example, free international trade and open-market policies were not regulated by legislation. An assertion was made that 'a competition law is not essential to a successful competition policy'. The analogy used to support the government's contention is erroneous. The absence of government trade-restraint regulation is not a comparator for the absence of law forbidding private restraints of competition. The absence of governmental barriers to trade is quite different in nature and effect to private agreements or behaviours to restrain competition. It is difficult to see how one can make a logical causative jump to say that the absence of law in one area of public policy justifies the absence of law in another; this is simply illogical. Further, the government did not quote a single example of a state that adopts this asymmetric approach to competition policy or one that has proved to be effective; the simple reason why the government did not point to extant examples is that none exists. An exhortatory policy without the force of law cannot, it is submitted, by definition, be effective in checking abuses which the government tacitly acknowledges exist.

The next proffered argument was equally weak. The government asserted that there is divergence between the substantive rules of states with competition regimes and thus there is no universal agreement as to the definition of prohibited acts. Consequently, a possible Hong Kong statute would inevitably be out of line with at least some other jurisdictions' law and thus any legislation would be subjective and open to 'legal challenge and litigation'. This point is so weak as to be embarrassing. It is trite to observe that the laws of different nations vary. The precise definitions adopted depend ultimately on judicial and political judgement. The government appears to suggest that it was incapable of making a political choice on a form of words. As to the legal challenge and litigation point, all statues in Hong Kong are subject to examination by the courts and may be measured against the Basic Law and Hong Kong's international treaty obligations. A competition law would be exactly the same. If one accepts the government's argument and takes it to its logical conclusion, no new law would ever be passed for fear that it would be subject to challenge. This argument is patently absurd.

The penultimate argument is even more perverse than the last. The government maintained that a general law is not as flexible as administrative guidance or sector-specific codes of conduct. The Response opined that a guide or code of conduct 'can still be binding on members. We can still find ways to exert "teeth" short of draconian legislative measures.' This statement is open to a number of fundamental criticisms. First, the assertion that administrative guidance or codes of conduct are more flexible may be true, but it has not been proved by the government with evidence. Secondly, it appears to support less transparency, rather than more. Thirdly, it deviates from the basic conception of the rule of law being superior to the rule of man. Finally, it does not explain how codes of practice are enforceable or what alternative 'teeth' the government had in mind (false ones, presumably!). The sheer illogicality of these assertions is deeply troubling; it seems to suggest that the government was trying desperately to think of any form of words, however implausible, to justify its policy stance.

The government dismissed the argument that WTO or APEC had formed a consensus in favour of competition law. It asserted that Hong Kong has always had a free and open market and so the structural impediments to competition that existed in other jurisdictions, necessitating a competition law to enforce a new economic order, are not an appropriate comparator to Hong Kong conditions. This argument has some merit but it presupposes that there are no competition problems or abuses and that the domestic economy is a free and open one with few barriers to entry. From the evidence presented above, such a sanguine view of competition conditions in Hong Kong is unjustified.

The government then attempted to build its case with additional objections. Firstly, legislation would be an 'apparent overkill'. The government's argument was that it is difficult to determine what effect any particular business practice would have on competition. It accepted (albeit with some reluctance) that 'certain forms of horizontal restraint like price-fixing and bid-rigging may not be fair to consumers or market partici-pants. But the effect on efficiency or market contestability is less clear.' Thus, it appears that the government only reluctantly accepts that naked cartel practices may have a deleterious effect. Even hardened Chicago School economists agree that such hard-core cartels have no utility to the economy but only to the participants, who through their conduct negate competition entirely. This ambiguity as to the damaging nature of cartels is a reason for doubting the sincerity of the government in promoting competition; it seems that even the most blatant abuse of markets is not perceived as a serious matter. The OECD and most major trading na-tions think exactly the opposite.[84] An explanation of this view might be because such abuses are thought to be a 'normal' part of business life in Hong Kong. Thus, defining them as unlawful is simply too unpalatable a step for the government to countenance, especially when the business interests in Hong Kong also comprise the pre-eminent political force in the Territory (as has been demonstrated above). It might be that alienat-ing such a constituency is simply politically impossible. The government then sought to justify collusive activities on the basis of enhancement of economies of scale or strengthening the quality of service, which 'should not be deterred by the application of a narrow form of competition policy'. Again the government apologia for blatantly anti-competitive practice is simply breathtaking and secret conspiracies are apparently better than open competition; this appears to be the government's *credo*.

Secondly, the Response suggested that any new general competition law would create uncertainty and so would be an additional and unacceptable burden on business. This excuse is quite lame. All laws have some element of ambiguity; competition law is no different. An enacted statute would no doubt provide for subordinate legislative rules to explain clearly what the law was aimed at and provide regulatory comfort to business people, as has been done in telecommunications and broadcasting ordinances. This argument may well be one deployed by business interests in any situation but a responsible government must weigh up the costs of a new regime

---

[84] See Recommendations of the Council concerning effective action against hard core cartels, OECD, c(98)35/Final, 14 May 1998 at http://www.oecd.org/dataoecd/39/4/2350130.pdf; and Report on the nature and impact of hard core cartels and sanctions against car-tels under national competition laws, OECD, DAFFE/COMP (2002)7, 9 April 2002 at http://www.oecd.org/dataoecd/16/20/2081831.pdf.

against the overall gain in economic efficiency and consumer welfare. The government appears to be listening only to one side of the debate and not taking into account the benefits that a competition law could provide. In any event, open markets and competition do create uncertainty; this is the spur to encourage firms to keep ahead of the competitors, rather than for them collusively to agree to continue to enjoy the quiet life of cartel.

Thirdly, the government opined that implementation would require expertise and a large bureaucracy. The identification of the need for expertise is correct, but for a government with the human and financial resources of Hong Kong this is not a real obstacle. As regards an increase in the number of civil servants, if the specific regulators were harmonised into a competition authority, the overall increase in staff need not be great. For example, the Irish Competition Office has twenty-five full-time staff.[85] Even if Hong Kong required double or treble that number, it would be a tiny percentage compared to the full-time establishment of over 170,000 civil servants. Again, the benefits that could accrue to the economy must be balanced against any net increase in costs.

Lastly, the government opined that a competition law would restrict business practices across the board and so compromise free and open trade policies, so ultimately undermining competitiveness. The response identified Hong Kong and Singapore, both often quoted as the most competitive economies in the world and neither have a competition law. This statement appears quite illogical. Firstly, competition law does not 'restrict business activities across the board'. This displays a fundamental misconception of the role and function of competition law. No business activities are restricted, save those that harm competition. Secondly, Hong Kong and Singapore may well be very competitive in relation to the external aspects of their economies. However, Hong Kong may well not have a competitive domestic economy, based on the evidence presented here and Singapore also does not have one as the government directly or indirectly controls, through government assets companies and state pension funds, a large percentage of the economy.[86] In any event, Singapore has now taken the policy decision to enact a general competition statute partly out of concerns about its competitiveness and partly as a result of various free-trade pacts recently made, especially with the USA. The HKSAR government

---

[85] Information given by the Head of the Irish Competition Authority at a conference on International Competition Law at Senate House, University of London, 17 May 2002.

[86] Some estimates put that percentage at close to 60 per cent, but this is hotly disputed by the Singapore government who suggest that it is as low as 13 per cent. 'Singapore Inc. II', *Business Times*, Singapore, 3 September 2002.

case is thus weakened by the defection of Singapore to the pro-competition law camp.

Thus the government concluded that the uncertainties created by enacting a competition law, 'especially amongst the business sector', outweigh the case in favour of adoption. Further, the government 'did not believe that the extent of horizontal and vertical restraints or abuse of market dominance is so pervasive as to merit general outlawing'.

Again the logic was flawed. All the available evidence from the Consumer Council's studies, limited as they were by a lack of investigatory powers, showed that there were serious problems in the sectors studied and that there were various other sectors that might have similarly serious defects in their markets, but the council was hamstrung in any attempt to investigate. The government's decision flies in the face of the evidence. The conclusion even contradicts itself by accepting that market defects were present but attempts to minimise their importance. A further contradiction is also apparent, namely that if the 'free market' policies were so successful, why was it necessary to introduce specific sectoral competition regimes for telecommunications and broadcasting, at the approximately same time as denying that problems exist elsewhere in the economy? The government cannot have it both ways: if non-intervention is justified generally, how can it be necessary in only two specific sectors? It is unclear what specific peculiarities make telecommunications and broadcasting unique.

A final argument deployed by the government is that Hong Kong is a small, open economy with low entry barriers and few regulatory prohibitions, so open trade can provide the necessary spur to competition by domestic incumbents. The second assertion has already been dealt with above, but as regards 'smallness' as a rationale for not adopting a competition law, some might concede that higher industry concentration ratios might be inevitable, given problems of accommodating numerous players in the market as a result of the constraints of economies of scale. These arguments alone, the government argues, justify a lack of a comprehensive competition law. Unfortunately for the Hong Kong authorities, Professor Mical Gal does not agree. In a recent book,[87] she demonstrates that it is precisely small economies that are prone to higher concentration ratios which need specifically tailored and enforced competition laws. She states that:

---

[87] Mical S. Gal, *Competition policy for small market economies*, Cambridge, Mass.: Harvard University Press (2003).

when trade barriers are reduced, competition policy plays an important rule in facilitating trade by reducing private barriers to the entry of foreign importers . . . the freer the trade, the stronger the incentives of firms to re-erect barriers and keep their historical advantage. Competition policy should [allow] foreign producers . . . to compete with domestic producers on fair and equal terms . . . [which] involves the formal right to compete . . . [as well as] the creation and enforcement of rules of conduct prohibiting anti-competitive behaviour . . . even in a small market with a liberal trade policy, competition policy has a critical role for increasing efficiency in the market by reducing or eliminating abuses of dominant position and the incentives of firms to collude.[88]

Professor Gal also suggests that 'market forces alone cannot achieve efficiency in small markets . . . that are characterised by high concentration levels and high barriers to entry . . . competition policy in a small economy is thus a crucial instrument with respect to determining domestic market structure and conduct and the intensity of competition'.[89] Thus, the Hong Kong government's arguments against the enactment of a general competition law, as set out in its 1997 Response, are exposed as unconvincing by the application of close analysis and critical assessment.

The government's decision in 1997 effectively to 'do nothing' did not end the debate on policy in Hong Kong. A number of anti-competitive incidents have continued to surface over the last seven years: COMPAG has been constituted, the Democratic Party has attempted to introduce a limited competition bill into LEGCO, the extant monopolies, duopolies and oligopolies have continued to be criticised at various times, as has the government's inept attempt to manipulate the housing market and to operate the electricity Scheme of Control. But on the positive side, full-blooded competition law has been introduced to the broadcasting and telecommunication sectors. All of these matters will be discussed below.

6.13 Conclusion

The government's visceral hostility to a general competition law is clear but the rationale and logic of the government's arguments are not; they are fundamentally flawed in many and obvious ways. The institutional schizophrenia exhibited by the government's muddled thinking on this issue has been amply exposed above and this is worrying because it calls into question, at a fundamental level, the good faith of the government

---

[88] Ibid. pp. 41–2.   [89] Ibid. p. 45.

policy making process. The rationale adopted by the government raises the question of whether the long-term public interest is the core reason for the policy stance or whether the policy merely shelters the economic interests of the merchant oligarchy.

In a recent article in the *South China Morning Post* Simon Pritchard said:

> Like its colonial predecessor, this government has a visceral dislike of anti-trust actions as a tool of economic policy.
>
> In reality this has meant a policy of supporting a relatively small group of firms earning high and predictable returns. Hong Kong has not been immune to competition in its domestic industries – witness telecommunications and, to a lesser extent, banks – but these are exceptions rather than the rule.
>
> To understand why, look no further than the family-run firm of the Chief Executive, Tung Chee-wah. As one of the major players in the highly cartelised global shipping industry, Orient Overseas Container Line (OOCL) has much to gain from backroom deals that carve up the global container trade.
>
> In the early 1990s OOCL and four other firms were found to have rigged the market in overland transport of containers on transatlantic routes and were fined US$18.3 million by the EC Commission.
>
> Tung Chee-wah was Chairman of OOCL at the time and while simply operating according to common practice, the case is a reminder of his perspective on the right relationship between firms and consumers.[90]

Thus, the former Hong Kong Chief Executive himself was previously at the helm of a cartel participant, which may help to explain the government's attitude towards competition policy. The closeness of the administration to leading business interests is exemplified by another little known fact, which only emerged as a result of new Hong Kong Stock Exchange disclosure requirements in April 2003. The former Chief Executive's family company OOIL and Cheung Kong/Hutchinson Whampoa Limited, Mr Li Ka-shing's flagship conglomerate, were financially connected. Cheung Kong/Hutchinson owned 9.08 per cent of OOIL.[91]

Cheung Kong/Hutchinson is one of Hong Kong's largest corporate groups. They control one of the electricity monopolists – Hong Kong

[90] 'Competition would make waves in the shipping trade', *South China Morning Post*, 4 July 2002.
[91] 'Tung firm buys back 9pc Li stake', *The Standard*, 9 August 2003. After the disclosure of this financial linkage in April 2003, OOIL bought back the 9.08 per cent interest in August 2003.

Electric; one of the supermarket duopolists – Park'N Shop; two other leading retail chains – Watson and Fortress; two of the leading property development companies – Cheung Kong and Hutchinson Whampoa, as well as one of the leading telecommunication companies – Hutchinson Telecom. For good measure, Hong Kong's dominant fixed-line telecommunications operator, PCCW, is also controlled by the Li family.

Thus, the closeness of big business to politics in Hong Kong is not only institutional but also through direct ownership linkages. Given these institutional and financial connections, the possibility of a change in government competition policy appears to be remote.

That the government leaves itself open to accusations of pandering to entrenched economic interests is concerning enough; but if the undoubted good government practices, for which Hong Kong is so renowned throughout Asia, are questioned in the future, it is possible that international capital's confidence in Hong Kong's level playing field will be undermined, so reducing Hong Kong's attractiveness as a place to do business.

Exactly these issues, competence in policy making and the nature of the relationship between government and business interests, were put into sharp focus by the former Chief Executive himself in his 2005 Policy Address to the Legislative Council,[92] when he made the following admission in relation to the performance of his administration: 'We also lacked a sense of crisis, political sensitivity as well as the necessary experience and capability to cope with political and economic changes. We were indecisive when dealing with emergencies. These shortcomings and inadequacies have undermined the credibility of our policy-making capacity and our ability to govern.' Despite this astonishingly frank admission, the Chief Executive then went on to reiterate his faith in Hong Kong's existing competition policy but at the same time also had to deny publicly charges of complicity between government and big business. He said 'While ensuring the efficiency of our free market and its capacity to create wealth, we also seek to properly balance the interests of different social strata and sectors. We are resolutely against "collusion between business and Government" and will strictly enforce our monitoring systems to eliminate any "transfer of benefits".'

Having delivered his own political obituary, Tung Chee-wah did the honourable thing and fell upon his sword some ten weeks later by

---

[92] The 2005 Policy Address, Working Together for Economic Development and Social Harmony, http://www.policyaddress.gov.hk/2005/eng/pdf/speech.pdf.

tendering his resignation as Chief Executive on 10 March 2005. He was succeeded by the Chief Secretary, in effect the second in command, Sir Donald Tsang Yam-kuen. Tsang will take control for an interim period of up to six months. After an 'election' for the top post, the new Chief Executive will serve out the remainder of Tung's second term. This became a matter of acute political and legal debate in Hong Kong as Article 46 of the Basic Law stipulates that the term of office of the Chief Executive shall be five years but Mainland officials have suggested that, despite the express wording of the Basic Law, the new leader will only serve until 2007. This matter has now been settled by an Interpretation of the Basic Law by the NPCSC on 27 April 2005. This has further damaged the credibility and integrity of the one country two systems formula. Tsang will now most likely win the forthcoming election on 10 July 2005.

As regards competition policy, this change in the leadership is unlikely to mean any substantial change of direction. Sir Donald Tsang, whilst undoubtedly a more accomplished political actor than his predecessor, is a scion of the civil service *ancien régime*. A colonial career civil servant of almost forty years' standing, he was the first local appointee to become Financial Secretary in 1995. A loyal Mandarin he has faithfully implemented policy for the whole of his career including the Cyberport project and, more recently, the West Kowloon Cultural Development; both of these imbroglios have attracted fierce criticism of the government for favouring property development interests over and above considerations of encouraging competition. He was, as Financial Secretary until 2001, directly responsible for COMPAG and so for the implementation of the government's sector-specific policy agenda. Attachment to the traditional economic policy and an uncritical acceptance that what is good for business is also good for Hong Kong will probably mean that complacency in respect of competition policy is guaranteed, especially as the domestic economy has strongly rebounded in 2005.

A critical but constructive engagement with structural economic imperfections such as the over reliance of government revenues on property income and the uncompetitive nature of much of the domestic economy, is unlikely. A light touch on the tiller of government and a course of steady-as-she-goes is probable. After seven years of tycoon-led government, the levers of power are now back where they belong, firmly in the hands of the rightful governors of Hong Kong, the permanent civil service. Just as under the British colonial system, government is now in a safe pair of hands, trusted by all those that matter – Mainland leaders in Beijing and the merchant oligarchs and administrative-grade civil servants in Hong Kong.

Executive-led government will be, in fact, executive-dominated government with economic policy being directed to be as business friendly as possible. Sir Donald can be trusted to lead Hong Kong back to the future.

Lamentably, it is likely that the same discredited competition policy will continue to be pursued by Tsang's administration, though there may be a change of direction following the announcement of the formation of a committee to review the workings of COMPAG in the March 2005 Budget speech. The explanation for this state of affairs is the overly close relationship between government and business interests and the existing political veto exercised by entrenched business interests who would be threatened by any move to open up Hong Kong's domestic economy to greater competition.

Implementation of competition policy in Hong Kong 1997–2004: economising with the truth

7.1 Introduction

Since the Hong Kong government's Response in 1997, the issue of competition policy has not faded into the background. Academic debate and investigation has continued, the Consumer Council has continued to lobby for a change of policy by government, some political parties have attempted to raise the matter in LEGCO, and civic organisations and the media have become more interested in the issue as Hong Kong's post-1997 performance deteriorated; concurrently the government has been faced with a continuing string of competition-related problems. COMPAG has been activated to handle competition issues and there have been major legislative developments in the telecommunications and broadcasting sectors. This chapter will seek to analyse the ongoing competition debate in Hong Kong.

7.2 Government competition policy in action: the Policy Statement

If the government's approach outlined in the 1997 Response were correct, one would have expected few, if any, competition-related problems since that time. However, this has not been the case. Particular issues will be identified and examined below as will the practical implementation of the Competition Policy Statement and the work of COMPAG.

In the next chapter, the interesting paradox of the government's stated position on competition regulation will be contrasted with the introduction of full sectoral competition regulation in two industries – telecommunications and broadcasting. This is the perfect example of the government's schizophrenic approach to this subject. Presumably only these two industries suffered from or were in danger of suffering anti-competitive activities so justifying the imposition of comprehensive regulation, whilst the rest of the economy did not suffer in this way, so justifying the lack of legislative intervention. The illogicality of this approach, as well as the flaws in this sector-specific approach, will be examined later.

In May 1998, the government published its Statement on Competition Policy.[1] This document stated that the government was committed to 'enhancing economic efficiency and a free flow of trade, thereby benefiting consumer welfare'. The government exhorted both private and public bodies to adhere to pro-competition principles. It stated that some business practices 'may warrant thorough examination' – price-fixing, bid-rigging, market allocation, sales and production quotas, co-ordinated boycotts and discriminatory standards. But even then the government did not condemn them outright. It went on to suggest that some behavioural conduct by operators with market power may need examination but not condemnation – predatory pricing, retail price maintenance, restrictive supply conditions. Again the well-worn mantra of Hong Kong as a small, externally orientated economy 'which is already highly competitive' was invoked to justify non-interventionist policies.[2] The statement then went on to outline proposed action, namely to raise public awareness of the ability of competition to enhance economic efficiency, identify government-imposed sectoral restraints, initiate pro-competition policies in government and public-sector bodies, encourage the private sector to be competitive, support the drawing up of voluntary codes of practice, be ready to accept competition complaints and provide a forum for discussion. The job of implementation was given to COMPAG but with no legal powers of any sort to do so.

7.3 The work of COMPAG

The 1998–9 COMPAG report identified a number of areas, which should be studied, and action taken thereafter, if necessary. They were: the establishment of a system to admit non-UK/Irish lawyers as barristers, opening up the system of selling government housing schemes, examining the introduction of competition in electricity supply, adopting of a common-carrier natural gas system for the piped-gas market, considering competition issues in the oil supply market, and amending various restrictive technical standards that may be anti-competitive. In telecommunication and broadcasting, note was taken of administrative steps to liberalise the markets. In financial services, various restrictive legal rules would be considered for relaxation including the minimum

[1] For the text of the Competition Policy Statement see http://www.info.gov.hk/tib/roles/psoc.htm.
[2] For criticisms of this assumption, see the quotations highlighted from Mical Gal's book, *Competition policy for small market economies*.

brokerage fee rules at the Hong Kong Stock Exchange, requiring all brokers to charge a minimum fee of 0.25 per cent (a sanctioned cartel) as well as implementing the Consumer Council recommendation to abolish the bank interest rate cap. Government tendering for supplies would be examined for anti-competitive effects. The cargo-handling industry would be investigated to assess the level of competition within the industry. The regulated rice importation scheme would be considered for abolition.

All of these initiatives would, if implemented, have beneficial effects on the competitiveness of the various markets affected, but the authorities would still not have any legal powers to investigate competition failures nor sanctions to penalise malefactors. Further, no overarching pro-competition rules were to be established, maintaining the inherent problems of overlapping schemes, differential treatment and the danger of regulatory capture. The core strategic incoherence was untouched.

The 1999–2000 COMPAG report outlined further pro-competition moves in both telecommunications and broadcasting, the detail of which will be examined in the next chapter. The bank interest rate cartel was to be scrapped in phases up to mid-2001. The minimum brokerage commission cartel was to be abolished by April 2002. However, in January 2002, the removal of the minimum commission rules was suspended because of fears about unemployment, as smaller brokerages could not compete with the larger operators. The government was panicked by the apparent possibility of 7,500 job losses and postponed the liberalisation.[3] In the energy market, a Consumer Council report into oil supply was considered, as were remedial measures to enhance competition. The conveyancing market for public housing was opened to tender, though the Law Society appeared to encourage the charging of minimum fees by tendering solicitors' firms. The price-control scheme was to be fully liberalised by 2003. As regards the major energy utilities, a consultancy report had concluded that interconnection between the two regional electricity monopolists was technically feasible. But action was subject to voluntary acceptance by the two incumbents. As regards gas supply, the proposal to establish a natural gas terminal in Shenzhen (just across the border from Hong Kong) opened up the possibility of introducing a common-carrier natural gas system. Various other liberalisations were reported including an objective set of criteria to allow lawyers to be admitted as barristers, opening maintenance contracts for public housing to open tender, encouraging the establishment of more private-sector schools and allowing the establishment of a

---

[3] 'Minimum brokerage fee to stay', *South China Morning Post*, 25 January 2002; the liberalisation finally came into effect on 1 April 2003.

third driving school. Also reported was the notorious decision in January 2000 of all six mobile phone licensees to increase basic charges by HK$20 concurrently on the same date. Unsurprisingly the Telecommunications Authority found that there had been collusion and the operators agreed to rescind the increase – uniformly. However, even though this was a clear breach of their licence conditions, no penalty was imposed. Thus, the report did show some improvement in competitive conditions in a limited range of markets over which the government had direct control or decisive influence. However, the lack of legally enforceable sanctions or even, where they existed, the reticence to use them, as in the blatant cartel activities of the mobile phone operators, undermines the government's credibility; it appears to be long on rhetoric but short on effective action. The prevarication in the utility liberalisation programme illustrates this well. The Consumer Council report into the gas industry was already six years old by 2000 and no effective action had been taken to introduce competition. The same was true of electricity.

The third COMPAG report, of 2000–1, again reported progress on identified areas of concern. Further liberalisation in telecommunications and broadcasting was reported, as was the inclusion of full competition provisions in the revised Broadcasting Ordinance and Telecommunications Ordinance. These are now the only industries that have full competition regimes; they will be examined in the next chapter. New consideration was to be given to breaking the exclusive rights of audience of barristers in the higher courts and the operation of the integrated retail payments system in Hong Kong. Liberalisation of the gas and electricity industries was again delayed by the need for further consultation and examination of options. Various other small liberalisations were confirmed in the areas identified in the preceding annual reports. A complaint of abuse of dominance in relation to the retail payments system was substantiated but as no competition rules had been broken only an additional investigation by the banking regulator could be undertaken to seek to improve the situation. Further, in October 2000 twelve Chinese-language newspapers simultaneously increased their cover prices by HK$1; the newspapers also published a common statement regarding the increase, indicating that it was a common decision of the industry to increase prices uniformly. It appeared to be another example of open collusion. The Home Affairs Bureau decided that this was not an anti-competitive practice as there were forty-seven registered newspapers, which actively competed for readers and there remained existing price differentials, even though prices for some publications had been increased. In the shipping industry the Hong Kong Shippers Council confirmed that all its members had uniformly increased charges because of exchange-rate risk. The government decided to investigate as the method of calculation was 'not transparent' to non-members. Further allegations were made concerning a cartel in the ready-mixed concrete market (a basic and very important industry in Hong Kong) but as an investigation was ongoing as to allegations of price gouging of the government Housing Authority no further investigation was proposed. Again this report confirms serious allegations of cartels being very active in Hong Kong in many industries and a lack of will on the part of the government to take measures to tackle private-sector competition abuses.

The most recent COMPAG report, 2002–3 claimed that 'Hong Kong thrives on competition [which] is more than a buzzword for businesses in Hong Kong – it is a concept that is ingrained in the local culture': such an assertion cannot be taken at face value, given the nature of the domestic economy and the evidence marshalled in this book. It seems odd that, if this is really the state of competition in Hong Kong, the government has seen the need to produce a policy statement, create COMPAG, produce new guidelines outlining anti-competitive acts (these will be analysed later) and imposed full competition regulation in telecommunications and broadcasting. Again the creation of detailed competition guidelines to 'encourage various sectors proactively to implement Hong Kong's competition policy' seems entirely superfluous, given the government's claim about the nature of Hong Kong's domestic economy; yet again the government has demonstrated that a high degree of proficiency in double-think is necessary to understand Hong Kong's policy on competition.[4] Notwithstanding the obvious contradiction between government sophistry and reality, COMPAG went on to report the usual litany of generally minor issues that it had considered during the year.

The new initiatives enumerated included drafting the Competition Guidelines mentioned above, legislation on mergers in the telecommunication sector (see detailed analysis in the next chapter) and various minor regulatory and public-sector tendering matters. Progress on previous issues was explained – no progress on electricity liberalisation, admission of barristers to practice in Hong Kong was now on a non-discriminatory basis, completion of the liberalisation of rice importation, liberalisation proposals for the parallel import regime for computer software. New licences for satellite broadcasting had been issued, a review of

[4] 'Double-think': the faculty of simultaneously harbouring two conflicting beliefs – coined by George Orwell in his masterpiece *Nineteen Eighty-Four* (1949).

retail payments systems had been undertaken, more trading rights at the stock exchange had been granted.

An important development, the tendering exercise to introduce a paperless electronic data interchange to interface trade-related documents with government regulatory processes, was reported. In the event, the selected tender was submitted by a joint-venture vehicle in which the government itself had a 42 per cent stake; some disquiet was expressed about the tendering and selection process and the fact that the winner, Tradelink, would have a monopoly of the electronic submission of trade documentation.[5] The government had a clear conflict of interest in adjudicating on the grant of the contract to create and operate the system, since it was a part-owner of one of the tenderers. The award of the seventeen-year franchise would greatly increase the value of Tradelink, not only as a result of the revenue to be gained from operating the system, but also as the development of the technology would have great export potential for the company. Interestingly, Li Ka-shing family firms had interests in all three companies that tendered for the project. Most of the other shareholders in Tradelink were the Hong Kong corporate elite and had substantial transport and logistic-related interests; they included Citic Pacific, Warf Holdings, Swire Pacific, Jardine Pacific, Hutchison Whampoa, Cathay Pacific, China National Aviation Corporation, HSBC, Modern Terminals, PCCW and Standard Chartered Bank. The shareholders might be thought of as a cartel of those concerned with the logistics industry in a joint venture with a government that has secured an official monopoly. This incident exemplifies the way in which Hong Kong government prefers to 'manage' business in the Territory – collaboration, leading to a cartel of interests that grants itself a monopoly. This incident, yet again, calls into question the government's real commitment to competition policy in Hong Kong.

The COMPAG report went on to list fourteen competition-related complaints it had received, the most important of which was a dispute between the two dominant supermarket chains and other pork-meat retailers. The wet-market retailers complained that the supermarkets had jointly reduced retail prices, in a predatory fashion, so as to increase their share of the fresh pork-meat market. COMPAG concluded that it could find no evidence of predation by the supermarkets and, even if there was, the pig-meat market would self-correct, as barriers to entry were low. This conclusion is suspect as, of course, COMPAG had no legal means to

---

[5] 'Tradelink's win spells loss for competition goal', *South China Morning Post*, 26 September 2003.

conduct a thorough investigation and demand production of documents or to take evidence on oath, as under existing Hong Kong law abuse of a dominant position is not unlawful.

The COMPAG report also asserted that the WTO Trade Policy Review 2002 noted that 'Hong Kong has a very competitive market, that Hong Kong's competition policy is a text-book case of the market economy at work' and that 'an all-embracing competition law might not be required in certain circumstances'.

This summary of the Trade Policy Review findings is misleading. Firstly, COMPAG ignored the criticism made by the WTO Secretariat (see below) and also that made by the EU.[6] Secondly, in reality only two comments praising Hong Kong's competition policy were recorded in the minutes. They were made by the representative of Macau, Hong Kong's neighbour and fellow Special Administrative Region of China, and by Mr Jara, the discussant on the panel, who was acting in a personal capacity *not* as the representative of his nation, Chile, nor of WTO members generally. This is specifically noted in the chairman's opening remarks.[7] The statement that 'members noted' that Hong Kong's competition policy was a text-book case and that competition law was not required in certain circumstance is incorrect; both comments were made only by Mr Jara in his personal capacity and this was not the consensus view of the committee, as claimed by COMPAG.[8] Thus, COMPAG has exaggerated the praise for Hong Kong's competition policy, misrepresented the view of an international body and ignored cogent and coherent criticism. This liberality with the truth is worrying and again seems to demonstrate the government's defensiveness and inability to counter reasoned criticism of its entrenched policy rhetoric; this dissimilation is worthy of the best British civil service traditions, which the Hong Kong government seems to have inherited. The selective choice of facts by COMPAG is reminiscent of Sir Robert Armstrong's famous remark made during the Spycatcher trial in Australia in 1986 about the necessity of sometimes being 'economical with the truth'.[9]

[6] See para. 57, minutes of the Trade Policy Review, Hong Kong – China, see http://www. wto.org WT/TPR/M109 – 17 February 2003.
[7] See para. 1 ibid.   [8] See para. 117 ibid.
[9] The phrase means to convey an untrue version of events by leaving out important facts. Sir Robert Armstrong was the British Cabinet Secretary in 1986. He was sent to Australia to give evidence in a trial to attempt to suppress the publication of the memoirs of Peter Wright, a former British Security Service agent, who held a grudge against the UK government over his pension entitlement. Wright sought to cash in on his experiences at MI5 by writing a book. The government's case for injunctive relief failed in Australia and ultimately in the UK too but the British House of Lords did find that Wright had broken an implied duty of

The final COMPAG-related development worthy of note in the 2002/3 report was the publication, in September 2003, of the finalised *Guidelines to Maintain a Competitive Environment*.[10] It is interesting to note that the draft version appeared in December 2002, some weeks after the specific criticism of lack of clarity and definition in Hong Kong's policy by the WTO Secretariat in the Trade Policy Review, mentioned above. It seems too coincidental that these two events were unrelated; authoritative, rational, external criticism clearly stung the government into action at least to define what they consider to be anti-competitive practices – something singularly lacking in the 1998 Policy Statement. The final version of the Guidelines states that their function is to 'assist in the implementation of the policy statement by assessing the overall competitive environment, defining and tackling anti-competitive policies and to ensure consistent application of policy across sectors'. First the document enumerates the essential elements required to assess the overall competitiveness of the economic environment including stable government, rule of law, free and open macro-environment, available market opportunities, pro-business and foreign investment policies, no trade or exchange controls, a clear and simple taxation regime, access to capital, a differentiated labour market, transparent immigration policies, good infrastructure and open access to information. Clearly, Hong Kong scores highly on most of those measures. Second, the effect of restrictive practices on market conditions needs to be assessed and government might be expected to act if either conduct limits market accessibility or impairs economic efficiency and is detrimental to the 'overall interest of Hong Kong'. To determine if market accessibility or economic efficiency is impaired, COMPAG will consider a number of factors to decide if competition, in a given market, has been or is likely to be prevented or substantially lessened:[11]

- the extent that imported goods or new foreign players in a given market may or do provide competition;
- the availability of close substitutes;
- the existence of restrictive government systems, barriers to foreign trade or legal regulation of the relevant market;
- the height of barriers to entry including economic, structured or strategic;

confidence to the Crown and ordered that he account in equity for any UK-derived profits. See *Attn. Gen. v Guardian Newspapers* [1990] AC 109.

[10] http://www.compag.gov.hk/reference/guideline.pdf.

[11] The 'substantial lessening of competition' test is the one adopted in the Telecommunication Ordinance Competition Provisions and has recently been defined by the Telecommunication (Competition Provisions) Appeal Board; see an analysis in the next chapter.

- the actual or likely competition effect of the practice on the given market;
- whether the act has or is likely to remove a competitor from the relevant market;
- the dynamic efficiency of the relevant market.

If restrictive practices exist that do create anti-competitive conditions, then a public policy test to determine justification based on economies of scale, prudent supervision, protection of consumers or incentives for innovation would be applied. In balancing the judgement, the determining factor would be the overall interests of Hong Kong, which would require consideration of the need for prudential supervision, service reliability, social need, safety or 'other public interest considerations'.

This very interesting and elaborate set of tests is all very well and good, but COMPAG seems to forget that it has no legal justification for the tests, no legal powers to conduct economic investigations or to require or compel private sector co-operation or even to obtain evidence. Further, it has no legal mandate to make findings and no legal powers of implementation or sanction. Thus, the tests provided are nothing more than phantasms drawn in the vacuum created by the absence of a general competition law; they are in a very real sense empty of meaning.

The Guidelines conclude by defining anti-competitive practices, abuse of dominance and procedures. The condemned practices include price-fixing, restrictions on supply, market sharing, discriminatory standards to prevent entry to a market (as in uniform admission rules to a profession), organised boycotts, and bid-rigging, market allocation or sales or production quotas. Abuse of dominance includes predatory pricing retail price maintenance, unreasonable price discrimination and tying of goods and services or the imposition of harsh trading conditions.

Businesses are again exhorted not to engage in the defined conduct and government departments are required to abide by these policy precepts. If exhortation does not work, then government promises to take appropriate administrative or ultimately legislative measures to tackle problems ad hoc.

Exactly the same criticisms can be made of the condemned conduct or behaviour as has already been made in relation to the COMPAG restriction of competition tests:

- No legal basis to promulgate them
- No legal powers to investigate or gather evidence
- No legal powers to remedy or punish malefactors

Further, it would also strain credulity to request industries under suspicion to co-operate in the investigation of complaints of breaches of the

Guidelines, given that, if proved, government has indicated it would 'take administrative or legal steps as appropriate to remove the anti-competitive practice' identified. Why should a business that conducts its business lawfully, voluntarily provide evidence that might lead to its own condemnation? No legal advisor to a business would recommend compliance with the Guidelines; indeed it might be negligent to do so, in the absence of any legal basis for the investigation or any legislative requirement to comply. Therefore, the promulgation of these Guidelines is little more than a paper tiger designed to look impressive, and to deflect reasoned and rational criticism of the government's chosen policy position.

The root question is why does the government apparently ignore significant competition failures in the private sector, take some measures in relation to the public sector and opt for full competition enforcement in telecommunications and broadcasting? The evidence, from COMPAG reports, appears to allow an inference to be drawn that the government's preoccupation, as regards the private sector, is not to interfere with the usual business practices in Hong Kong. The logical rationale for this must be that a political decision has been taken to this effect as demonstrably the government does not appear to act in the public interest in effectively promoting consumer welfare and economic efficiency in the private sector. The evidence presented tends to support the principal hypothesis of this book, which will be amplified in the final chapter.

7.4 Debate and community criticism of Hong Kong's competition policy 1997–2004

The community reaction to the Consumer Council Final Report and the government's Response was mixed. Cheng and Wu[12] were sceptical of the government's Response considering it too conservative and toothless. They thought that the lack of compulsory investigative powers was a fatal weakness in the Response and advocated a comprehensive law as the only effective method to allow for objective enforcement of a pro-competition policy.[13] The US Consul General and the Chairman of the American Chamber of Commerce both opined that Hong Kong did indeed need a general competition law.[14]

[12] Leonard K. Cheng and Wu Changqi, 'Time to lay down the law', *South China Morning Post*, 17 March 1998.
[13] Cheng and Wu, *Competition policy and the regulation of business*, pp. 239–53.
[14] 'Anti-monopoly body still on drawing board', *South China Morning Post*, 18 November 1997.

A scandal concerning the Law Society's attempt to set a minimum price for conveyancing tenders in 1999 caused an editorial in the *South China Morning Post*,[15] the leading English-language newspaper, to opine that unless there was legislation to ban price-fixing it would be impossible to prevent future abuses and that if Hong Kong was serious about emerging from its economic malaise in a lean and efficient state 'the need to introduce a more effective competition policy without delay' was clear.

As regards the domestic and services economy David Dodwell, the head of a Hong Kong based research think-tank opined that: 'Hong Kong's domestic and services economy [have] a labyrinth of monopolies, cartels, restrictive professional practices and exclusive distributorships which has created a costly domestic economy for which Hong Kong residents have to pay a high price.'[16] He went on to argue that high service costs were helping to make the Hong Kong export industry uncompetitive and that the situation he described above meant that local service providers would be increasingly unable to compete with global service providers as the services market opened up internationally. He thought that Hong Kong was losing out in education and medical 'exports' as Hong Kong attracted very few international students or overseas patients due to the exorbitant cost of higher education and medical services. He considered that the real-estate market was at the root of Hong Kong's competitiveness problem causing a very high cost base from which all other costs flowed. He listed the usual problem sectors already alluded to but added that trade mark and copyright laws to outlaw parallel imports was driving up the costs of most branded goods – videos, CDs, books, cosmetics and cars.[17]

---

[15] 11 September 1999.

[16] *Competition policy and competitiveness*, The Hong Kong Service Economy, Vol. 7, February 1999.

[17] The rules relating to parallel imports have now been ameliorated. As regards trademarks, the Trade Mark Ordinance was amended in 2000, effective 2003. By virtue of s. 20, the parallel import trade in branded goods was liberalised by adoption of the 'exhaustion of rights' doctrine. The section also protected trademark owners' rights in respect of goods that had been impaired in such a way as to damage the reputation of the mark. In respect of copyright, the Copyright Amendment Bill 2003, abolishes civil liability for persons who import copyright products and use them personally or in their own business s. 30 (2); criminal liability is also abolished s. 118 (2). In addition, the use of parallel imported software is also decriminalised by s. 118 A (2). However, traders in such goods remain both criminally and civilly liable. The 2003 Bill had not completed the legislative process as at 1 July 2004. These liberalisation measures were both hotly contested by business interests which had been accustomed to very high retail prices for branded goods in Hong Kong; clearly, the measures do assist price competition in respect of such goods in the Hong Kong market.

His conclusion was unambiguous: 'Oligopolies and cartels are widespread. Only a Competition Authority with proper legal powers ... [can be effective in protecting] local consumers, manufactures and Hong Kong's export competitiveness.'

Internationally, concern has been expressed in the columns of *The Economist*[18] and by the European Parliament.[19] Further, the down-rating of Hong Kong's competitiveness by the World Economic Forum[20] in 2001 caused some defensiveness on the part of the government; Hong Kong's position fell from third in 1999 to thirteenth in 2001 and to sixteenth position in 2004 in respect of micro-economic competitiveness. In the opinion of Professor Jeffrey Sachs of Havard Business School: 'Being a finance and trading entrepôt is necessary but not sufficient to maintain competitiveness.'[21] The government sought to down play this adverse ranking on the basis that the survey over-emphasised technology and innovation, areas of admitted weakness in the Hong Kong economy. The debate about Hong Kong's economic future and the role of competitiveness has also exercised politicians. Christine Loh, an influential former legislator and now head of the think-tank Civic Exchange, urged the government to explode ingrained myths about Hong Kong, one of which was that it had the freest economy in the world.[22] She opined that cartels dominate the domestic economy and that electricity, freight and container terminal charges were too high as a result of monopolistic practices; she advocated increased, effective competitive mechanisms.

Similar thoughts were echoed by a visiting American academic. Professor Richard Schmalensee, Dean of the MIT Sloan Management School, expressed astonishment that Hong Kong had no anti-cartel legislation: 'The fact that Hong Kong doesn't have a law against price fixing and basic cartel behaviour is fairly amazing... I don't see any reason why any economy wouldn't benefit from a law against cartels and enlightened merger policy.'[23]

Further scepticism was also forthcoming from an unexpected source. The WTO undertakes regular trade policy reviews of member states' compliance with the WTO obligations of membership contained in the various

---

[18] 'In few hands', *The Economist*, 2 November 2000; also Business Asia, Economist Intelligence Unit, *Closed shop?* 19 May 2003, vol. XXXV, no. 10.

[19] See A5-0284/2000, www2.europarl.eu.int.

[20] http://www.wef.org.

[21] Quoted in the *South China Morning Post*, 10 October 2001.

[22] 'Time to discard myths and build for the future', *South China Morning Post*, 4 February 2002.

[23] 'SAR urged to draft anti-cartel laws to foster competition', *The Standard*, Hong Kong, 15 July 2002.

plurilateral trade agreements. In November 2003, the WTO Trade Policy Review Report prepared by the WTO Secretariat considered, in relation to the government's sector-specific regulatory approach that:

> The existence of different rules for different sectors could lead to distortion of resource allocation because firms would choose to enter sectors with clear competition rules, so that they could not be coerced by incumbents. Moreover, regulations (for instance telecommunications) have to perform a dual role of traditional regulator and of enforcer of competition policy, which could compromise their impartiality. Different regulators may interpret competition provisions differently and possibly inconsistently. An independent competition body ... might well better promote and enforce competition.[24]

The secretariat also criticised:

- the lack of definition of anti-competitive practices in the government's competition policy statement;
- the omission of any mention of mergers or changes in economic structures that could be detrimental to consumer welfare and competition itself;
- the absence of any legally binding definitions of competition abuses;
- the impossibility of making complaints about anti-competitive abuses in the absence of any legal definition;
- the inability of COMPAG to adjudicate on competition abuses in the absence of definitions and the impossibility of granting remedies without legal authority to do so.

The report went on to note at paragraph 97: 'It is unclear whether the existing enforcement measures available to the various agencies responsible for competition policy are sufficient to constitute an effective deterrent to anti-competitive practices.'

The government generally welcomed the outcome of the review but refused to respond directly to the Secretariat's criticisms, beyond the usual mantra of asserting Hong Kong's free and open trading environment, or to media questions concerning the criticism of Hong Kong's competition policy. However, it should be noted, that the final communiqué gave Hong Kong a very good report as regards external barriers and internal government regulation of trade. Further, the absence of overt criticism in the final WTO panel report can also be attributed to the fact that the WTO does not have a specific mandate to police member's internal competition

---

[24] WTO Trade Policy Review Secretariat's Report, November 2003 at para. 92. http://www.wto.org/english/tratop_e/tpr_e/tp_rep_e.htm #hong_kong2002.

rules and that, at present, there is no agreement on minimum global rules or any enforcement mechanism.

In recent years, the media has taken up the cudgels on behalf of consumers in a row over the supply of fresh pork-meat, energy supply, and a host of other issues; this has occurred both in the Chinese language media, read by 95 per cent of the population, as well as the English-language press and all television broadcasters. The government's response to these complaints has been to set up reviews and half-hearted investigations which lack mandatory disclosure powers or any right to adjudicate or sanction. As a result, they have been ineffectual.

Another important community development has been the involvement of Civic Exchange, a local public policy think-tank, in debating and reporting on competition issues in Hong Kong. Early in 2003, four workshops were held to consider competition issues generally and the implications of competition regulation in three key sectors – telecommunications, electricity and transport. Four reports were published as a result,[25] the tenor of which was to urge government to clarify and simplify Hong Kong's regulatory structures by enacting a general competition statute so as to set common standards across industries, improve transparency and thereby enhance consumer welfare. Although the government was invited to participate in all the workshops and to respond to the debate, the offer was rejected and a response to the criticism of present policy was not provided.

However, not all voices have been unanimous in condemning the government's policy. Needless to say civil servants continued to praise and defend the government line at every opportunity.[26] In the media, Chan Wai-kwan expressed the view of many in business that the government's approach of a voluntarist, market-driven, non-interventionist policy best suits Hong Kong.

7.5 Consumer Council activity since 1997

Following the final competition report in 1996, the Consumer Council continued to play a prominent role in competition matters.[27] In addition to advocacy of a comprehensive competition statute, the Council has

---

[25] *Is Hong Kong anti-competitive? Competition policy and regulation*, Civic Exchange and CSLA Research, March 2003; Is Hong Kong's energy framework fair?; competition policy in the telecommunications sector – What's the answer to competition? http://www.civic_exchange.org/n_pub_cont_03_competition.htm.

[26] For example, Daniel Cheng, HKSAR's competition policy, *Hong Kong Service Economy*, vol. 7, p. 5; all HKSAR government web sites, especially www.info.gov.hk/info/compet.htm.

[27] All the information concerning Consumer Council activity is derived from the council's annual reports and other material published on its web sites http://www.consumer.org.hk.

undertaken the receipt and investigation of competition-related complaints from members of the public, organisations and businesses. It has also been commissioned by the government to undertake investigations into various industries and practices that appeared to be anti-competitive. The following are some of the more prominent competition issues that have confronted the Consumer Council over the last seven years.

In 1998, the Council attempted to investigate allegations of price-fixing in the fresh-chicken market. Fresh chicken, as opposed to frozen, is a very popular food for Hong Kong residents and forms a distinct market. The investigation noted a sharp price rise but due to lack of investigative powers, nothing could be substantiated. During 1998/9, the Council investigated allegations of a price cartel amongst school-textbook publishers. School pupils must have a copy of the nominated edition of a subject textbook, which they must purchase privately. Publishers offered standard discount inducements to schools to select their products. In July 1999, the publishers' trade association announced in newspaper advertisements that, as a result of the bad publicity generated by the investigation and parental anger, all the members of the association would offer a uniform 10 per cent discount on retail prices. It was pointed out to them by the Council that this was another example of cartelised behaviour, and that it was expressly discouraged by the government's competition policy statement.

In September 1998, newspaper reports suggested that an information-sharing exchange existed between two property developers selling new flats situated in close physical proximity to each other, to notify each other of sales tactics or price reductions. The matter was reported to COMPAG who opined that this was not a price-fixing agreement, market prices were falling and competition had not been impaired.

General dissatisfaction with the energy sector led to the Council launching a major enquiry. A very full report was published in January 2000.[28] The principal focus of the report was the state of the oil-supply industry. The Council found that the petrol, diesel and LPG markets were a tight oligopoly, exhibiting high degrees of vertical integration – import, wholesale and retail functions integrated into each oil company with three oil companies having 70 per cent of the LPG market, 80 per cent of the diesel market and 90 per cent of the petrol market. Relatively small sales volumes, limited room for market growth and high barriers to entry were also exhibited. Hong Kong had one of the highest price structures in the world, excluding taxation. There was no price competition at all at the

---

[28] Energizing the energy market, Hong Kong Consumer Council, January 2000. http://www.consumer.org.hk/energy/000112/english/sum-e.htm.

retail point of sale and prices were not even advertised outside petrol stations, as the same product was uniformly priced by all market participants. Government land policy on providing sites for stations also contributed a substantial entry barrier. The Council made several recommendations to loosen the market but in the absence of legal powers, little effective action was possible. In July 2000, the oil companies were again exposed as exploiting their oligopoly.[29] The government sought to encourage the use of ultra-low-sulphur diesel fuel as a result of an increasingly serious air-pollution problem. The new fuel was more expensive on the international market than traditional diesel and so a tax concession of 89 cents per litre was given to the companies. It was subsequently discovered that the world market price was not as high as had been anticipated, the companies had benefited from the drop in prices and none of the incumbent firms passed on the reduction, which amounted to 50 per cent of the tax concession, to consumers. Again the government and the Consumer Council were powerless to act. In May 2002, in answer to a question about sharp practice in the oil supply industry in LEGCO,[30] the Secretary for Economic Services replied by repeating the standard government mantra that Hong Kong has a free economy and that the government continued to rely on market mechanisms to control prices. The Secretary confirmed that the government had loosened licensing requirements and had relaxed planning requirements for new petrol-station sites. The answer again rejected any introduction of competition law to regulate the sector.

In August 2000, the Council investigated another important monopoly. In Hong Kong the use of debit cards to settle consumer transactions is widespread. The Easy Pay System (EPS) is operated by EPSCO Ltd., a joint-venture company owned by Hong Kong's major banks. It is the only networked system that allows merchants to operate a sales-desk terminal to process payments via customer debit cards. A group of merchant users complained to the Consumer Council that EPSCO had altered its merchant user tariff by substituting a 0.75 per cent of value per transaction charge in place of a flat fee of HK$2.00 per transaction, thus increasing the cost of usage enormously. The alternative forms of customer payment, cash, cheques (Hong Kong has no cheque guarantee card system), stored value cards and credit cards, were not considered close enough substitutes to EPS for various reasons. These included security/risk of theft as regards cash, cheques are not generally acceptable because of the risk of fraud,

---

[29] 'Pressure on oil firms to justify prices', *South China Morning Post*, 26 October 2000.
[30] Legislative Council Question No. 3 (Oral Reply), 8 May 2002.

stored value cards are only usable for low value transactions and credit cards have high transactions costs of 2–4 per cent. EPS as an electronic debit system has none of these disadvantages. Consequently, it formed a separate market in which EPSCO was dominant. The issue of abuse by EPSCO was then analysed and it was concluded that the lack of an effective substitute payment system allowed EPSCO to act unilaterally to raise prices with virtual impunity. No new entrant to the market was likely, given that the ownership of EPSCO was in the hands of all the major banks. The Council complained that its study was not as rigorously analytical of the cost structure of the payment system as it might have been because it had been denied access to financial data by EPSCO on the basis of commercial confidentiality. It recommended that competition needed to be introduced into the payments system but this could not be required as there was no legislative framework of compulsion. EPSCO was acting entirely lawfully.

In August 2003, the Council published a report[31] into pricing policy in the supermarket sector which showed that despite five years of deflation in the Hong Kong Consumer Price Index, the standard grocery sample had increased in price, the number of smaller supermarket operators had declined by 41 per cent during the period 1996 to 2001, and there were allegations of abuse of market dominance which could not be substantiated as the Council lacked investigatory powers. The incumbent operators denied the allegations.

However, there was a clear increase in market share by both dominant suppliers and credible allegations of abusive conduct. However, no proper investigation could be undertaken properly to assess market conditions or the veracity of the allegedly abusive behaviour due to lack of legal powers. When challenged, the government simply reiterated that it considered the food-retailing sector to be competitive and there was no evidence to justify any form of intervention.

7.6 Further competition issues

In 2001, three more competition issues were ventilated in the press. Simon Pritchard[32] commenting on competition in Hong Kong said:

> On Monday, Real Estate Association president Stanley Ho Hung-sun argued that real estate developers should collude in a pre-arranged pact not

---

[31] Competition in Food Stuffs, Hong Kong Consumer Council, August 2003 http://www.consumer.org.hk/mainmenu/english/eindex.htm.
[32] 'Policy writers lose the plot', *South China Morning Post*, 21 November 2001.

to buy land from the government's reserve list, thereby reducing supply and provide a kick to prices. Elsewhere, such comments would warrant investigation on anti-competitive grounds. But such a bizarre proposal is simply the corporate flip side of government efforts to manage land supply and prop up prices.

The official stance on competition reveals a cognitive disconnection over the nature of wealth creation and distribution that runs deep. A fixed currency regime leaves two options for becoming more competitive – costs can be cut or productivity enhanced . . . Yesterday the Liberal Party [pro-business party] argued for civil service pay cuts and less red tape. What he failed to mention was the multiple restrictive practices across the domestic economy that keep prices high at the expense of consumer welfare and competitiveness.

In November 2001, it became known that the President of the Hong Kong Travel Industry Council, Joseph Tung Yao-chung, had advocated that association members collectively boycott North-West Airlines after the company offered lower-price tickets direct to consumers via its web site. The Consumer Council said it was aware of the issue but had no power to investigate or prohibit such actions, should they be taken by travel agents. A member of the public who had made the complaint suggested that travellers should buy their air tickets abroad.[33]

In December 2001, it became known that for the first time in a decade that the volume of goods moving through Hong Kong's port had declined.[34] This was attributed to shippers increasingly using new port facilities in the Pearl River Delta in China but it also emerged that another cause was the very high costs of using Hong Kong's port facilities.[35] A government report stated that the high costs were the fault of the private-sector port operators. It analysed the costs as being 99 per cent attributable to terminal-related charges and not to publicly funded costs of pilotage, harbour dues and towage. As previously mentioned, the port is operated by an unregulated oligopoly headed by Hong Kong International Terminal (HIT) which is controlled by Mr Li Ka-shing's Hutchinson Group and Modern Terminals Limited (MTL) which is owned by a consortium of property-based companies – Warf/Wheelock, China Merchants and Swire Pacific. The Hong Kong Shipper's Council had complained[36] about very high port costs in their response to the government's

---

[33] 'Lack of anti-cartel law makes it necessary to buy tickets abroad', *South China Morning Post*, 31 December 2001.
[34] 'Port feels slow down chill', *South China Morning Post*, 12 December 2001.
[35] 'Touchy issues "holding up" port cost report', *South China Morning Post*, 1 January 2001.
[36] Letter to the Secretary for Trade and Industry, 28 February 1997.

consultation on the Consumer Council final report of 1997. These charges had risen consistently above the general inflation rate for more than ten years. They opined that:

> 'The uncontrolled and rapidly increasing THC [port costs] represent a heavy and unjustified burden on Hong Kong shippers. It reduces our competitive edge... and that of Hong Kong's position as a hub port. On the other hand the implementation of a competition policy and a competition law in Hong Kong would provide a more level playing field between shippers, shipping lines and terminal operators.'

In addition to the disputes concerning the THC, the long-term future of the vitality of the port is now a very significant issue.

Hong Kong's port is still one of the world's busiest and handles more than 90 per cent of the Territory's trade. According to the Census and Statistics Department, trading and logistics services accounted for 26.5 per cent of Hong Kong's gross domestic product and employed 24.1 per cent of our labour force in 2002. The economic contribution of Hong Kong's port is significant.

In recent years, Hong Kong's port has been challenged by the emergence of other ports in the Pearl River Delta region. The growth of container throughput in Hong Kong's port has slowed down while that for other ports in Shenzhen has expanded rapidly. It is possible that the prime position of Hong Kong's port will soon be overtaken by other ports. As the production base of Hong Kong manufacturers is now in the Mainland, it is logical that they import materials and export their finished products directly through Mainland ports. The competitiveness of Hong Kong's port will further be eroded after the removal of the quota system for textiles and clothing products in 2005, so allowing more direct export shipment from China. Some pessimists argue that even if the THCs and trucking costs were lowered, it may not be possible to revive the port of Hong Kong.

The dominance acquired by Hong Kong terminal operators has long been a controversial issue because, whilst there is no legal barrier to entry, the Hong Kong government has a mechanism to ensure that the industry has enough handling capacity and container ship berths to meet projected demand growth.

After the full completion of Terminal 9 (T9) in 2005, services of container handling at Kwai Chung Container Terminals will be provided by five companies – HIT, MTL, COSCO-HIT, CSX Corp and Asia Container Terminals Limited (ACT). In fact, HIT and COSCO-HIT can be considered as a single operator because both of them are controlled by the same parent company, namely, Hutchison Whampoa Limited. In

February 2004, it was reported that CSX was considering disposing of its Hong Kong interests and that its port assets could be bought by one of the other incumbent operators, so further concentrating the industry; the Hong Kong government has no merger review or control powers to veto this development, should this create additional competition concerns.[37]

Before the completion of T9, the two major players, namely, Hutchison Whampoa and MTL, had more than 80 per cent share of the market. There is a 'non-poaching' cartel agreement between these two major players. The cartel agreement can be easily enforced in a market with so small a number of players. Supra-normal prices might well be expected and indeed Hong Kong terminal charges are the highest in the world. Thus, it is clear that Hong Kong container terminal industry is highly concentrated.

Another special feature of the industry is the existence of a huge excess capacity held by the terminal operators, which is about 30 per cent of the total container throughput in 2003. The policy used to control the supply of terminal capacity by the government is called the 'Trigger Point Mechanism' (TPM). According to the TPM, the government commits not to grant the right to build new container terminals unless and until the quantity demanded for container handling services exceeds existing capacity by a certain amount.

But the TPM, the total capacity of the industry, is not determined by the government. Instead, the terminal operators can influence the amount of new capacity triggered by TPM because they can lower or raise the realised demand by raising or lowering their terminal tariffs. But the TPM does not take the pricing policy of the existing players into account when determining the handling capacity. In the last decade, terminal operators from Hong Kong have co-operated with Mainland enterprises to develop ports in Shenzhen. It has been suggested that the terminal operators have artificially inflated the THC in Hong Kong. By charging high prices, they can continue to enjoy monopoly profits, but if this diverts cargo to their new ports in Shenzhen, the operators still profit, as they also own these 'competing' facilities. They have also tried to delay the construction of the new terminal T9 in Hong Kong for several years, in order to maintain their duopoly position and vigorously oppose the construction of any new container berths on Lantau Island, near Hong Kong airport.

This bizarre state of affairs appears to be ignored by the government. The results of its non-intervention policy can now be seen. Hong Kong may have begun to price itself out of the ocean-shipping market.

---

[37] 'HK port shake-up to follow CSX asset sale', *South China Morning Post*, 12 February 2004.

Another recent competition issue to surface was the effective merger, in 2003, of two of Hong Kong's three franchised bus operators. Citybus owners, the UK Stage Coach group, sold its interest to one of Hong Kong's rivals, New World First Bus, so creating an effective duopoly between the merged entity, which will have a 25 per cent market share, and the dominant Kowloon Motor Bus which has the other 75 per cent. The franchised bus industry is subjected to a detailed regulatory scheme by government that specifies routes, frequency of service and cost of fares. The government was unconcerned about any anti-competitive effects on the basis of the availability to the public of other forms of transport. This was not the result of a merger investigation, since Hong Kong has no merger control system, save in telecommunication and broadcasting, but rather a reply to news reporters' questions by the Transport Secretary.[38] Yet again, this merger reflects the government policy of effectively allowing the concentration of economic power to proceed without substantial analysis of the potential for anti-competitive effects or consideration of the wider public interest.

The cartel-like behaviour has become more brazen. Bid-rigging is a criminal offence but only in respect of public-sector procurement contracts; bid-rigging in relation to private sector contracts is quite legal.[39] The government has provided no explanation for this double standard. In a recent case, a cartel of building suppliers was cleared of criminal bid-rigging, in a public-sector supply case, on the basis that there was insufficient evidence. The alleged conspirators had set up a front company to co-ordinate the bids, paid a 'membership fee' of HK$500,000 each and shared some HK$55 million (US$7.05 million) in excess profits between them. The defendants even sought legal advice as to whether their conduct amounted to an offence prior to the implementation of the scheme. The relevant contracts were worth approximately HK$115 million (US$14.74 million).[40] In the view of a leading politician and barrister, bid-rigging is even more rampant in the private sector than in public supply contracts,

---

[38] 'City Bus to be sold to owner of main rival', *South China Morning Post*, 10 June 2003.

[39] Section 6 of the Prevention of Bribery Ordinance (Cap. 201) provides that anyone who 'offers any advantage to any other person as an inducement to or a reward for or otherwise on account of the withdrawal of a tender, or the refraining from the making of a tender, for any contract with a public body for the performance of any work, the providing of any service, the doing of any thing or the supplying of any article, material or substance, shall be guilty of an offence'. S.7 prohibits the similar acts in relation to public-sector auctions.

[40] 'Judge clears cartel of fixing bids to supply gates', *South China Morning Post*, 17 March 2005.

yet the government refuses to extend the criminal provisions to include private sector contracts.[41]

Unfettered open cartel activity in several domestic markets has now been observed. The Hong Kong Laundry Services Association announced in the Chinese language press a joint agreement to raise prices in concert, ostensibly due to increased energy costs.[42] The Hong Kong Kowloon Vermicelli and Noodle Manufacturing Industry Merchants' General Association also released a joint notice, along with twenty suppliers, to announce a uniform increase in both the wholesale and retail price of flour-based products.[43] In April 2005, an open cartel of eleven driving schools representing some 80 per cent of Hong Kong's 900 driving instructors, called a press conference to publicise a fixed schedule of rates for driving lessons pegged to 1997 prices. This was justified on the basis that the demand for driving lessons had declined for both economic and demographic reasons, so adversely affecting driving instructors' incomes.[44] These examples serve to demonstrate that chronic competition failures are widespread throughout the domestic economy.

7.7 Conclusions to be drawn from the competition debate

Thus, what conclusions can be drawn about the nature of the Hong Kong domestic economy as a result of analysis of the COMPAG and Consumer Council competition activities? It seems clear that where the government itself has been the direct cause of anti-competitive practices or structures, some remedial action has been taken. In only two markets – broadcasting and telecommunications – has, ironically, a fully competitive environment been created by a derogation from the government's stated non-interventionist policy. In many other sectors, all the evidence points to a deeply ambivalent attitude amongst the business community and the government towards active competition. The preponderance of evidence shows that in many instances, co-operation and collusion are the preferred methods of doing business, rather than full-blooded competition. It is also suggested that the evidence presented above does not reveal the true extent of anti-competitive practices in Hong Kong. This is because there are no legal powers to investigate allegations of anti-competitive

---

[41] Fair Competition is Essential to the Preservation of Free Enterprise, Ronny Tong Ka-wah, Legislative Councillor, Article 45 Concern Group, Policy Paper No. 1, 9 November 2004.
[42] *Ming Pao* (a Hong Kong Chinese-language newspaper), 5 November 2004.
[43] 6 April 2005.
[44] 'Driving school cartel "stifling competition"', *South China Morning Post,* 8 April 2005.

practices and the government is philosophically wedded to the idea that there are no serious anti-competitive problems in the domestic economy. The government merely repeats the mantra that non-intervention is working admirably, so creating the 'freest' economy in the world, as recognised by international authorities on the subject, aside perhaps from the Commission of the European Union and the Secretariat of the WTO.

Hong Kong's government likes to boast of its commitment to a competitive economy and the economic freedom that Hong Kong apparently enjoys. The government's publicity machine basks in the reflected glory of international league tables that claim that Hong Kong is the 'freest' and, by subtle implication, the most competitive, economy in the world. In January 2004, the conservative American Heritage Foundation, in its 2004 Index of Economic Freedom, ranked Hong Kong as the world's 'freest economy' for the tenth consecutive year. The Financial Secretary, Henry Tang, was quoted by the government information service as saying that: 'We see the role of the Government as that of a facilitator that provides a business-friendly environment where all firms can compete on a level playing-field ... The Government will also maintain an appropriate regulatory regime to ensure the integrity and smooth functioning of a free market. We will spare no effort in preserving our strengths and in further improving ourselves where we can.' However, leaving aside political rhetoric, the government's position is not upheld by the available evidence, outlined above, which supports precisely the opposite conclusion, namely that there are serious competition problems in the Hong Kong domestic economy.

One must consider what other factors might determine government policy. One might speculate that the very business culture of Hong Kong is pro-cooperation as a direct result of the unpleasant experience of having to be so highly competitive in the international export market. It may be possible that such experiences have imbued businesses in the domestic economy with the idea that as competition is so tough outside it would be much more sensible to enjoy the quiet life at home. To paraphrase the words of a discovered US cartel operator, the customer is my enemy and the competitor is my friend.

Another possible explanation of government's ambiguous attitude to competition abuses is that, given the lack of legal prohibition of collusive conduct, business naturally gravitates towards the easiest method of doing business lawfully, namely co-operation, active or tacit. After all, in the absence of prohibition, why should firms compete when everyone in a small, isolated market has a highly profitable share of that market, entry by newcomers is difficult and the government's attitude is one of benign neglect. The government even publishes its ambivalent attitudes as policy, though now tempered by the new Guidelines. In such an atmosphere, it is unsurprising that the observed behaviour of many domestic businesses is collaborative.

Critically, the outlook of civil servants must be crucial. In Hong Kong, they are not only the servants but also the masters as they form a permanent government immunised from the rigour of removal by an electorate. They indeed have a monopoly of power. The very nature of their security of tenure, the assurance that they rule by right and a dogged determination to stick with a proven formula for economic success, means that even in the face of evidence of chronic competition failures, they remain wedded to a philosophy of denying reality and continuing a policy of benign neglect.

The civil service favours stability and maintenance of the status quo, which was the sole objective of policy leading up to the handover of sovereignty. They are also addicted to maintaining political power as they have formed the governing class for over 150 years. The cosy relationship of mutual respect and admiration between government and business has led to a Faustian pact – business largely stays out of administrative government and government stays out of business. As former President Jiang Zimin has often said, Hong Kong is a commercial city, not a political one; though this may now be changing. One might controversially argue that the government does not run economic policy in Hong Kong in order to serve the public interest, but rather to serve the interests of a section of the public that has most overt and covert political power – the commercial oligarchs. It is suggested that the root of this mutual admiration is the structure of political institutions in Hong Kong, which are now enshrined in the Basic Law. The lack of full democratic accountability of the government in Hong Kong is the basic reason for government hostility to the enactment of a general competition law – too many political interests that matter look upon a competition statute in the same way as they view universal suffrage as the method of selecting a government, that is, with a mixture of fear and loathing. The massive public demonstration of anti-government protest on 1 July 2003 has spurred the Beijing and HKSAR governments to embark on a new policy of bread and circuses to try to placate Hong Kong's disaffected public; bread in the form of boosting Mainland trade and tourism to Hong Kong to increase local employment and circuses in the form of lavish public relations campaigns, including a bizarre government-sponsored appearance by the Real Madrid soccer team in July 2003 and the Rolling Stones in November 2003. However, it appears unlikely that these tactics will achieve the desired goal of silencing the discontent of the Hong Kong electorate, as was demonstrated by the second record anti-government march that took place on 1 July 2004 when over 300,000 people again filled the streets.

The incestuous nature of the ruling civil service/commercial oligarchy relationship was castigated by Philip Bowering, a well-respected writer. Rather than summarise his argument, a substantial portion of the article is reproduced:

> There are two main [elite] groups in Hong Kong: big business and the senior members of the bureaucracy-related government-dependent bodies such as the judiciary and universities. Both have close links to professional bodies, especially lawyers and accountants.
>
> At the top of the business tree nowadays are the figures who dominate not just the property market but other aspects of the economy – utilities, retailing, telecoms – to the same or even greater extent than the chaebol ever controlled the South Korean one.
>
> Mostly they profit indirectly from, rather than contribute to, the international and China-directed trade in goods and services. They act like the government-linked companies (GLCs) that play a similar role in Singapore.
>
> The difference is that Singapore's GLCs are subservient to the political and bureaucratic leadership, while in Hong Kong the bureaucracy tends to follow their interests.
>
> Business elites are, naturally, to some extent self-serving. They need to bend policies in their favour. But they serve a purpose if they provide stability and set an example of industry, dependability and security.
>
> Hong Kong's business elite has, by and large, done that over the years. But what are we to make of the example set by the various companies that led an unfortunate and gullible public into believing inflated claims of future profits while friends in high places helped the process by waiving listing rules? The public lost billions, while some board members benefited substantially.
>
> One expects some of this in all markets. But societies where elites display blatant and unprincipled greed associated with the likes of Imelda Marcos and Tommy Suharto seem unlikely to be headed for success . . .
>
> This columnist has remarked before on how the senior bureaucrats, not content with high salaries and very comfortable pensions, have created new troughs from which they can feed – jobs outside the civil service pay scale but within the gift of the bureaucracy at the KCRC, the MTRC, the Monetary Authority, the Stock Exchange, and many more at lower-profile positions.

The bureaucrats may like to think they are big business figures who deserve salaries similar to those paid to business people who have succeeded in highly competitive international businesses. Why then did they join the low-risk civil service but now expect high reward?

There is merit in keeping some distance between the business and bureau-cratic streams of the elite. They ought to balance each other, keep society on an even keel where drive, imagination and the profit motive of the busi-ness elite are balanced by order, rules, commitment to the social goals that lie within the responsibility of government – education, health etc. That means not just keeping civil servants away from the quasi-public troughs but providing much stricter rules on moving to the private sector.

How many former administrative-grade civil servants have made decisions involving huge amounts of money – for example, land use – on the tacit un-derstanding a lucrative but undemanding job with the beneficiary company will be theirs for the asking once they decide to retire?. . .

The linkages also encourage civil servants to tolerate, or even actively en-courage, the anti-competitive practices that are rife in Hong Kong and have seriously damaged its overall competitiveness by raising costs and thwarting the entry of new and more dynamic players . . .

The bureaucrat fat cats seem to think it is their job to be pro-business, which in effect means being for the established elite and their profitable cartels, which are a burden on the overall economy and on small and international business in particular.

The civil service seems not to realise that its macro-economic, as well as social, purpose ought to be to create an environment of open competition that will allow new players and encourage all business equally. Its job is to prevent the emergence of monopolies and, where they exist, to regulate in the public interest rather than – as at present – provide easy profits regardless of efficiency.

The civil service and business elite linkages need to be broken. Civil ser-vants should stay in the service – or go completely outside it. They should be barred from running government corporations. Likewise, the rules sur-rounding the movement of upper level civil servants to private sector jobs should be governed by much tighter rules and monitored closely, in par-ticular to see whether they have been in a position to deliver rewards to prospective private employers.[45]

This symbiotic relationship between senior officials and the commer-cial oligarchs poisons the well of public policy formation on competition

---

[45] *South China Morning Post*, 14 January 2002.

issues as the vested interests of the business sector are prioritised over the welfare of the general population.

Thus, it is submitted that without either wholesale political reform or some form of binding international agreement, perhaps at the WTO, Hong Kong is most unlikely to introduce a general competition law under current political arrangements.

7.8 The political response to the competition debate: the 2000 bill

Despite the government's resolute determination to reject general legislative intervention in the competition field, not all political actors take the same stance. Political concern about competition is not a new phenomenon. In 1996, before the Consumer Council final report was published, the Legislative Council debated the issue. The then Secretary for Trade and Industry, Denise Yue Chung-yee, said that the government had an open mind as to the need for such legislation.[46] But she stressed that Hong Kong was one of the three most competitive economies in the world without competition law. Several pro-Beijing and pro-business members doubted the need for competition laws.

In 1999, following the publication of the government's Response and the Competition Policy Statement, the Democratic Party representatives in the Legislative Council sought a formal debate on competition policy.[47] The Consumer Council provided a submission to assist the debate. The Council reiterated its arguments in favour of a competition law that had been made in its 1996 final report. The Council restated the need for a transparent and non-arbitrary set of rules for the economic game and that the implementation of an effective competition policy needed a statutory basis. The government's sector-specific approach was criticised in that it was piece-meal and too rigid to cope with fast-changing markets, particularly in technology-based industries. The difficulty of narrow market definitions and the involvement of different government departments almost inevitably led to either overlaps, or gaps in regulation, or differential standards across sectors, which was not conducive to transparency or equitable treatment. The use of a licensee-based system inevitably proscribed the persons who could be regulated and might not have any basis in the reality of the market concerned. Examples were given of such problems in

---

[46] 'Laws on free competition urged to break up cartels', *South China Morning Post*, 30 May 1996.

[47] The debate took place on 27 January 1999.

banking, broadcasting, and telecommunication sectors. The Council also pointed out that as it had no powers of investigation or sanction, competition complaints were correspondingly few as the Council's ability to respond effectively was severely limited.

The result of the Legislative Council debate was intriguing. The motion urging the government to enact a general competition statute was carried by 18 votes to 3 with 2 abstentions from members representing geographical and election committee constituencies. However, the functional constituency members, dominated by business interests, refused to accept the motion and it was thus lost.

The Democratic Legislators were, however, not deflected from seeking to introduce a limited competition statute in the next session. Sin Chung-kai, Democratic Party LEGCO member, sought to introduce a Fair Competition Bill. The major provisions of the bill were:

- To outlaw collusive agreements that had as their object or effect the unreasonable diminution, distortion or prevention of competition in respect of substitute products. Exemptions were granted to trade-union activities, professional licensing bodies, consumer boycotts, and public functions specifically authorised by law.
- To provide a civil remedy in damages for acts in contravention of the bill and specifically authorise the court to grant injunctive relief as well as actual damages and punitive or exemplary damages where appropriate.
- The government was given discretionary power to take action on behalf of any victim of an unlawful act under the bill and was entitled in addition to injunctive relief to recover damages.
- Any contract term promoting collusive agreements was to be void at law.
- The government was empowered, but not obliged, to establish a public body to investigate complaints of anti-competitive behaviour and to propose further legislation should it consider that to be necessary.

However, in order to be discussed in the Legislative Council, the President of LEGCO had to be satisfied that the bill had no government expenditure implications.[48] The government secretariat had to provide an opinion on this matter to the President.

---

[48] Art. 74 of the Basic Law states: 'Members of the Legislative Council of the Hong Kong Special Administrative Region may introduce bills in accordance with the provisions of this Law and legal procedures. Bills which do not relate to public expenditure or political structure or the operation of the government may be introduced individually or jointly by members of the Council. The written consent of the Chief Executive shall be required before bills relating to government polices are introduced.'

The government opinion stated that:

- The bill would cause a large increase in government civil litigation expenditure, comprising additional staff needed to prosecute businesses that contravened the prohibitions created and the creation of a new specialised tribunal to hear cases. These additional costs would amount to HK$3million per annum.
- Direct civil litigation costs would be increased by between HK$30 million to HK$200 million per annum.
- The creation of a new body to advise the government on competition would cost an estimated HK$20 million–82 million per annum.
- Consequently, the total estimated additional expenditure would be between HK$53 million and HK$280 million per annum.

Thus, as this was a private members bill, to which the government did not lend support, under the Basic Law provisions the bill should not be discussed. As a result of this advice the President of LEGCO vetoed discussion of the bill.

The grounds of the government's opinion categorising the bill as one that would affect public expenditure were dubious. The bill gave the government discretionary power to prosecute civil actions, not a duty to do so. Thus, any increase in public spending was not mandatory, even if one accepts the government's rather unpersuasive case for the nature and magnitude of the costs involved. There would be no necessity to establish a separate tribunal or a competition advisory body; this was a political matter for the government. However, by categorising the bill as having financial implications discussion was terminated before the merits of the bill could even be discussed. In the unlikely event that the bill was passed, the government retained a further veto power in that the Chief Executive could decline to sign a bill into law.[49] However, by utilising the device of

---

[49] BL Art. 49 states: 'If the Chief Executive of the Hong Kong Special Administrative Region considers that a bill passed by the Legislative Council is not compatible with the overall interests of the Region, he or she may return it to the Legislative Council within three months for reconsideration. If the Legislative Council passes the original bill again by not less than a two-thirds majority of all the members, the Chief Executive must sign and promulgate it within one month, or act in accordance with the provisions of Art. 50 of this Law.'

Art. 50 states: 'If the Chief Executive of the Hong Kong Special Administrative Region refuses to sign a bill passed the second time by the Legislative Council, or the Legislative Council refuses to pass a budget or any other important bill introduced by the government, and if consensus still cannot be reached after consultations, the Chief Executive may dissolve the Legislative Council. The Chief Executive must consult the Executive Council before dissolving the Legislative Council. The Chief Executive may dissolve the Legislative Council only once in each term of his or her office.'

categorising the bill as a money bill, this eventuality was negated. Need-less to say this tactic of vetoing any discussion was not welcomed by the Democratic Party, who sponsored the bill. They strongly criticised the government's reasoning and its stance on overall competition policy and em-phasised that one of the bill's objectives was to encourage the government to review its strategy, as present policies did not adequately address Hong Kong's economic structures.[50] The bill had little prospect of success even if debate had been allowed, given the in-built pro-government/pro-business composition of LEGCO, as then constituted, and the particular nature of the LEGCO voting system (see above). However, the actions of the government were very revealing. It appeared to be anxious to stifle effective public debate on this sensitive issue, presumably on the grounds that the attempt to provide a smoke screen for the ineffectiveness of its competition policy by the establishment of COMPAG and ad hoc investigations by the Consumer Council, would become just too obvious. Public exposure of this policy failure in the forum of LEGCO might have proved just too embarrassing for the government to countenance.

7.9 Conclusion

This chapter has sought to examine competition conditions in the domestic Hong Kong economy and to submit government policy on competition to close scrutiny. The facts presented suggest a close relationship between the commercial oligarchs and the centres of political power, which explains the fundamental reason for the government's antipathy towards effective competition policy, despite clear evidence that the Hong Kong domestic economy has endemic competition problems. Government policy, if unchanged, may undermine Hong Kong's ability to provide an effective service centre for the greater China region and if that occurs Hong Kong's economic future is bleak indeed. An even more concerning issue is that the government appears to be less than frank in its competition policy pronouncements than the Mainland competition officials quoted in the previous chapters on China. Hong Kong's civil servants now seem to be so desperate to prove that their competition policy is credible that they have taken to spin-doctoring and economising with the truth.

---

[50] Press release on the government's opinion on the Private Member's Fair Competition Bill, Democratic Party Legislative Council Secretariat, 23 November 2000.

Electricity, telecommunication and broadcasting: competition regulation Hong Kong style

8.1 Introduction

The HKSAR government's public policy approach to competition regulation is founded on scepticism as to the need for, or desirability of, competition legislation. If competition failures can be identified and 'proved' to the government's satisfaction, consideration may be given to rectifying such proven market failures. Stated government policy is to employ exhortation to amend business practices, followed by administrative action to encourage change, with legislative intervention as very much a last resort. Such statutory intervention will be sector specific and confined to addressing only the competitive failures identified in the narrow sector to be regulated.

At first blush, this approach appears to be at least consistent with the government's philosophy of 'small' government and creative non-intervention in economic decision-making and might be thought to be a limited and proportionate response to specifically identified problems. This profound scepticism about the value of competition law does have some support from the academic authors of the economic freedom indices mentioned in the last chapter.[1] But whether this analysis is correct is questionable.

Firstly, as has been demonstrated in chapter 7, the government's case that Hong Kong's domestic economy is a structurally free and open one is decidedly weak. Secondly, the assertion that competition problems are few and minor flies in the face of the available evidence. Thirdly, the government has no legal tools to undertake economic investigations to discover whether or not sectors of the domestic economy are competitive. Thus, policy making must be undertaken on a reactive basis when

[1] See http://www.fraserinstitute.ca and http://www.heritage.org.

restrictive business practices become too obvious to ignore and decisions are based, at best, on partial information and, at worst, on assumption or prejudice. As was demonstrated in the preceding chapters, the government's basic assertions about the nature of the Hong Kong domestic economy are based not on objective evidence but on surmise that neatly conforms to the government's philosophical stance.

Given that the government has no legal powers of investigation of economic structures or competition failures, how does the government identify, as a matter of policy, those economic sectors that need to be subjected to intervention and, if intervention is required, how are decisions made as to which legal tools should be used to deal with the perceived problem? In order to answer these questions and to assess whether the government's claims that the sector-specific approach is a viable competition policy tool, it is necessary to consider some of the industries that are subject to regulatory or competition regimes. It is not possible for reasons of space to analyse more than three sectors. Electricity, telecommunications and broadcasting have been selected for this purpose. The electricity industry in Hong Kong is unusual for a public utility. It is organised on the basis of two private sector territorial monopolies and subject to government-mandated 'Schemes of Control'. Government is thus involved in a very intimate way with this sector, hardly the actions of a paradigm free-market apologist. It is necessary to sketch the history of government involvement in the electricity industry, the nature and effect of the Schemes of Control and the possibility of structural change in the electricity supply market, in order to assess the effectiveness of government policy in this sector.

Telecommunication and broadcasting are the only two sectors of the economy that are subject to comprehensive statutory competition rules. They also exemplify the government's sector-specific approach and the inherent limitations and complexities of this unique approach to competition regulation. An interesting issue here is why these two sectors were chosen for the application of full competition regulation, when other industries were not; they remain entirely free to monopolise, cartelise or merge as they see fit. Presumably there were clear and compelling reasons to justify intervention that is at odds with the government's laissez-faire approach. The following sections will address these issues and also attempt to assess whether the legislation in place is effective from both a policy and a legal perspective.

8.2 Electricity

I'll have my bond, speak not against my bond.[2]

Electricity is produced and supplied in Hong Kong by two privately owned territorial monopolists. Hong Kong Electric Company Limited (HEC) supplies Hong Kong Island and China Light and Power Company Limited (CLP) supplies Kowloon and the New Territories.

The history of the government's involvement in regulating this industry began with consumer dissatisfaction with a large price increase in 1952. In 1959, an official enquiry recommended compulsory acquisition of the two providers by the government. In 1964, following lengthy negotiations, CLP proposed a non-statutory contractual Scheme of Control to last for fifteen years to 1978. The stated objectives were to limit disposable profits whilst giving a reasonable return on capital to investors and at the same time to promote efficiency and expansion of supply. This balance was to be achieved by agreeing a rate of return on capital employed, with any 'excess' profits being credited to a development fund to be used exclusively to acquire additional fixed assets. Any interest earned on the development fund would be applied to reduce tariffs. A contractual document incorporating such terms was agreed and entered into by CLP and the government. HEC was not a party to this agreement but aligned its policies voluntarily with it until 1978, when HEC too entered into a similar contract with the government. A continuation agreement was reached for a further fifteen years; these arrangements were renewed again from 1994 to 2008.

In April 1982, Hong Kong Land Company Limited acquired 34 per cent of the equity of HEC, which was subsequently sold to Hutchinson Whampoa Limited, one of Mr Li Ka-shing's flagship conglomerates. Thus, Mr Li effectively controls the supply of electricity to Hong Kong Island. CLP is controlled by the Kadoories,[3] another of Hong Kong's business dynasties. Thus, Hong Kong's electricity supply is effectively controlled by two of Hong Kong's wealthiest families. As there is only one interconnection cable of 720MV for emergency use between the two providers, accommodating less than 10 per cent of installed Hong Kong based generating capacity,[4] the two operators have absolute territorial monopolies.

---

[2] Shylock in *The Merchant of Venice*, Act III, Scene iii.
[3] According to the 2002 CLP Annual Report, Kadoorie family trusts controlled 34.84 per cent of CLP Holdings Limited. http://www.clpgroup.com.
[4] See http://www.edlb.gov.hk/edb/response/4.htm.

The need for a rapid expansion of the electricity supply industry to service the growing industrialisation of Hong Kong in the period 1950 to 1980 was a primary consideration for the genesis of the Schemes of Control but market conditions changed following the relocation of heavy industrial users to new cheaper manufacturing sites in China after 1978.

The Schemes of Control allow for intrusive government monitoring of the producers' finances, prior approval of investment plans based on five-year projections and for guaranteed rates of return of 15 per cent on equity capital and 13 per cent on debt capital (to include the development fund which is treated as a liability). Any major change in generation, transmission or distribution capacity must be submitted to the government for approval and assessment. This is normally done on a five-yearly basis and includes projected expansion plans and proposed tariffs. Additionally, an annual tariff and audit review is also undertaken by the government. The companies are free to increase their tariff charges by up to 7 per cent above the projected tariff figure previously approved by the Executive Council in the five-year review. The Schemes of Control effectively guarantee the rates of return agreed and the producers are allowed to increase tariffs as necessary to achieve that return; no account is taken of technological or structural market changes. The Schemes of Control are contained in a contract (presumably in the form of a deed) and enforcement of the provisions by either party would be by an ordinary civil action for breach of contract with the normal contractual remedies of damages and injunction being available to either side; there has never been a dispute between the parties that culminated in litigation.

Dr Lam Pun-lee[5] has considered the economic effects of the Schemes of Control. On tariffs he finds that the real (inflation disregarded) tariff did not change in the twenty years from 1973 but even so Hong Kong was paying more for electricity than most of its Asian competitors. As regards the rate of return on equity investment, the 15 per cent return was very beneficial to shareholders when compared to that achieved by other Asian utility providers. Further, as the permitted rate of return on company debt is 13.5 per cent but the commercial cost of long-term debt is only 8 per cent, the producers can pocket the difference. This has directly encouraged over-investment and the two companies now have reserve generating capacity of about 45 per cent (1995 figures) whilst the international figure is approximately 25 per cent.[6] Dr Lam concludes:

---

[5] Lam, *Competition in energy.*
[6] These figures have not changed materially since 1995.

> As the permitted returns of the two companies are based on fixed assets, customers have to pay higher prices for unwanted excess capacity. Under the Scheme of Control, the companies can expand their capacity once their financial plans have been approved by government, regardless of whether the capacity is later found to have been useful or not... Further more, financial institutions are prepared to lend to the electricity companies at attractive rates to fund expansion. Thus they are able to earn the difference between the permitted rate of return (13.5%) and the cost of the debt (around 8%). The Scheme of Control is therefore a licence to print money. They can rely completely on debt financing to fund capacity expansion [which is then guaranteed a return of 15%].

Decisions relating to capacity expansion have caused the government acute political embarrassment. For example, the decision by the government in 1993 to allow CLP to construct a new gas-fired power station at Black Point fuelled with natural gas piped from China's Hainan Island, proved to be a costly mistake. As the capacity expansion was undertaken under the aegis of the Scheme of Control, CLP was able to obtain the allowed rate of return on its investment, notwithstanding that by 1998, when the plant went on stream, it worked at only 75 per cent of its planned capacity as the electricity demand forecasts upon which the decision to proceed was based proved to be wildly optimistic and therefore wrong. Instead of the managers and shareholders bearing a loss or at least reduced profits, the company was simply allowed to increase tariffs and so pass on the cost of the poor decision-making to the consumer. Worse, from a political standpoint, the government got the political blame for allowing the project to proceed.[7]

By 2002, little had changed. The government was apparently considering options for change but the Enron collapse and California electricity crisis of 2001 has bolstered the position of CLP and HEC. They both now make much of the security-of-supply argument to slow down or halt any tentative steps towards injecting competition into the electricity supply market. Another side-effect of the effectively guaranteed nature of profitability in the industry is that the companies have been able to secure loan capital at preferential rates to fund diversification into other markets – property development within Hong Kong and a plethora of other ventures in foreign markets: electricity trading in Australia, internet bandwidth ventures and television. The excessive rates of return guaranteed to producers have also helped to fund major investments in Mainland

---

[7] 'A tight hold on power', *Sunday Morning Post*, 8 March 1998.

China. Without the stability and predictability of their Hong Kong profit base it is questionable whether such expansion and diversification would have been possible. Thus, Hong Kong electricity consumers are directly funding the supplier's expansion and diversification, which, of course, benefits the producers' shareholders but does nothing for Hong Kong consumers. The Schemes of Control do not restrict such diversification.[8]

In January 2002, HKE increased its tariffs by 5.3 per cent, despite deflation in the consumer price index in Hong Kong. A motion to reduce the electricity company's guaranteed rate of return was debated in LEGCO. In responding to the debate the Secretary for Economic Services argued that it was more difficult to open up the industry to competition than in other countries. She said that as there was a contract between the government and the suppliers it would be difficult to institute change and that sharing supply via interconnection was problematic because the two companies had different capital investment structures.[9] This response is indicative of the government's confusion of roles in attempting sector-specific regulation without adhering in fact to a pro-competition stance. The Secretary was using the government's own folly in agreeing the Scheme of Control structure to excuse excessive monopoly profits for the providers and her emphasis on the return to investors in the companies, rather than the public interest, again underscores the government's real policy agenda in all competition matters; when business and consumer interests conflict, the protection of business interests always trumps consumer welfare. This dictum was postulated in the previous chapter.

Between 2002 and 2003, there was growing disenchantment with electricity supply arrangements. A group of property developers calling itself Electricity Consumers Concern (ECC) which included Sun Hung Kai Properties, Swire Properties, Hysan Development, Great Eagle Properties, Hong Kong Land, Hang Lung Properties and Warf Holdings, who operate large office developments and shopping malls on Hong Kong Island, began a political campaign to force HKE to reduce its tariffs. This development pitted one group of property tycoons against Mr Li Ka-shing, the controller of HKE; unsurprisingly, Mr Li's property companies, Cheung Kong and Hutchison Whampoa, did not join ECC. ECC commissioned a comparative economic analysis of electricity supplies from Dr Stephen Luk,[10] which demonstrated that:

---

[8] 'Two-headed relic', *South China Morning Post*, 5 February 2002.
[9] 'Motion urges lower maximum profit levels for power companies', *South China Morning Post*, 24 January 2002.
[10] Research paper on Electricity prices, November 2002.

- The schemes of control had directly led to substantial over-investment leading to 40 per cent excess generating capacity, well above the 25 per cent international norm required for security of supply.
- Both generators consistently over-estimated future demand for electricity.
- The Hong Kong Audit commission found that this overcapacity directly resulted in excess costs amounting to HK$720 per consumer per year being passed on in the tariff charged by CLP between 1996 and 1998.
- If the excess capacity were eliminated consumers across Hong Kong would each receive a rebate of HK$663 per annum.

In response to the criticism, Mr Li said that that the allowed rates were contractually agreed with government and that contracts should be honoured: 'Hong Kong must observe the rules and respect contractual obligations.'[11] The deputy chairman of HKE thought that requests for tariff reductions were 'ridiculous and bizarre'.[12] In fact, the Schemes of Control do not guarantee the maximum tariffs, they merely set a ceiling; lower tariffs could, of course, be charged by CLP or HKE, should they choose to do so. A critique of the Scheme of Control by the leading brokerage, CLSA,[13] suggested that Hong Kong consumers were paying 20 per cent to 40 per cent more than those in Singapore and that both the return on equity (RoE) and return on assets (RoA) allowed in Hong Kong were the highest in the world by a significant margin. CLP's RoE was about 17 per cent and RoA was about 13 per cent, whilst HKE achieved 11 per cent and 21 per cent respectively. Needless to say, the electricity incumbents are in no hurry to change present arrangements. The government is consulting on whether structural change in the industry is technically and economically feasible and proposals are expected to be ready for discussion in 2005, but no structural change will occur until 2008, at the earliest,

[11] See 'Li Ka-shing joins power debate', *South China Morning Post*, 18 November 2003. Mr Li's insistence on strict contractual observance is strikingly similar to Shylock's plea in the Merchant of Venice, 'I'll have my bond; I will not hear thee speak; I'll have my bond, and therefore speak no more.' Act III, scene iii and 'If you deny me, fie upon your law; There is no force in the decrees of Venice. I stand for judgement. Answer me: Shall I have it?', Act IV, Scene i; one must hope that Mr Li does not suffer the same fate as Shylock. The end of this spat between the tycoons was that both CLP and HKE chose not to increase tariffs in 2003 but they did not reduce them either. 'Power firms snub calls for tariff reductions', *South China Morning Post*, 11 December 2002.

[12] Per Canning Fok, Deputy Chairman of HKE as quoted in 'Utility chief says appeal for price cuts is bizarre', *South China Morning Post*, 9 November 2002.

[13] Anthony Wilkinson, *Critique of the Hong Kong Schemes of Control*, CLSA Emerging Markets, 26 February 2003.

when the current Schemes of Control lapse. Interestingly, in September 2003, the author was informed that at least CLP was privately preparing for some injection of competition into the electricity market post-2008. The company had commissioned expensive new computer software that can handle complex tariff structures and differential billing, so paving the way for an ability to deal with pricing in a deregulated market. Publicly, of course, both CLP and HKE continue to argue loudly for no change in current arrangements, especially after the outages in New York, London and Italy in 2003. However, suggestions for change have been made by various industry experts including Dr Lam, who has suggested that the post-2008 settlement should include open access to the grid, encouragement of new suppliers and freedom for consumers to choose from whom to buy electricity.[14]

The government's boast of being a light-touch and economically non-interventionist regulator is exposed as a sham by its electricity supply policy. The Schemes of Control involve the government in routine management decisions concerning basic commercial matters of production, capacity, prices and methods of financing the businesses. This is hardly the action of a non-interventionist, free-market champion. But, even so, the intervention is presumably biased towards economic efficiency and competition, so as to conform to the government's Competition Policy Statement. However, the clear evidence is that the current arrangements have exactly the opposite effect. They encourage over-capacity, skew investment decisions leading to inefficiency and wasted resources; they produce prices higher than in comparable markets outside Hong Kong and they insulate the incumbents from any commercial or competitive pressure to reduce costs or to innovate. Current policy may even encourage reckless diversification and poor investment decisions, given that the effective rate-of-return guarantees insulate shareholder dividends. They also expose the government to opprobrium when sanctioned investments later turn out to be unnecessary. The government takes the blame for approving them but the system, perversely, rewards rather than punishes the companies who can simply pass on the costs of their mistakes to customers, citing the government's approval of the plan as a justification for the higher tariff rates.

The ultimate effect of the Schemes of Control appears to be to protect the companies from competition and to insulate them from the consequences of commercial decision-making, with all risk being transferred to the shoulders of the tied electricity consumer, who has no choice but to pay the tariff agreed upon by the government with the suppliers. Having concluded that the present arrangements substantially benefit the producer, one might consider that the government has failed to act in the public interest as regards electricity supply. A possible reason for this is provided in the previous chapter. The only benefit the government can cite from present arrangements is security of supply but the costs imposed on Hong Kong consumers clearly outweigh this benefit, which could be achieved at much lower cost by greater interconnection between the two providers, additional interconnection with the Guangdong electricity grid and the encouragement of new entrants into the market to supply an electricity pool via an open grid system. Thus, it can be confidently asserted that the current structure of the electricity supply industry in Hong Kong is very far from ideal. The government's preferred option of sectoral regulation, even in this industry, which has been subject to it for almost forty years, is clearly a failure by any objective assessment and even by the government's own policy goals.

8.3 Telecommunication

8.3.1 Industry structure

Prior to 1995, Hong Kong Telephone (HKTel) was the government-franchised domestic monopoly service provider. HKTel was incorporated in 1925 and granted a fifty-year exclusive licence to provide telephone services. The company was not in public ownership and paid an annual royalty fee to the government for its franchise. The monopoly was extended in 1975 for a further twenty years. Government reserved the right to agree tariff charges but, until 1975, there was no formal scheme of control as in the electricity industry. Rising costs and the expiry of the licence in 1975 led to a renegotiation of the terms of the franchise. From January 1976, a Scheme of Control was established that was to last for twenty years; it set a maximum rate of return on shareholder funds of 16 per cent after tax, any surplus was to be set aside as to 80 per cent as a development fund and 20 per cent as a shareholder fund to be distributed as bonus shares. The development fund was to be treated as a liability and accrued interest at 8 per cent, deductible from the permitted return.

International circuits to and from Hong Kong were provided by a different company, Cable and Wireless plc, which was until 1981 wholly owned by the UK government, after which it was privatised. The company had a franchised monopoly for all international calls. After the parent company's privatisation, the Hong Kong operation was hived-down into a subsidiary company, Cable and Wireless Hong Kong (CWHK). In the same year, the Hong Kong government granted CWHK an exclusive licence for all international circuits for twenty-five years until 2006. In consideration for the monopoly, CWHK paid an annual royalty to the Hong Kong government and transferred 20 per cent of its equity to the government, which the government later sold. During 1983 and 1984, CWHK acquired a majority of the shares of HKTel and then merged with it to form Hong Kong Telecommunications Limited (HKT). This company later took over the stock-market listing of HKTel. HKT thus became an exclusive monopolist in both the domestic and international markets. The domestic market remained subject to the Scheme of Control.

By 1991, concern was being expressed about the monopoly position of HKT. A study by Mueller[15] concluded that the net profit on international calls had increased from 40 per cent in 1983 to 60 per cent in 1988 but this was lower than the actual profit. This was because HKT used international profits to subsidise local calls and if the subsidy was stripped out, the real profit was closer to 75 per cent. He recommended an end to cross-subsidisation and the early termination of the exclusive international franchise. In fact, the government had previously commissioned an external consultancy report in 1987. In 1991, the Booz Alan and Hamilton report recommended liberalisation of the local telecommunications market and the government accepted this advice.

As a preliminary administrative matter an Office of the Telecommunications Authority (OFTA) was established in July 1993. OFTA's role was not only to regulate the new market but also to guide the development of the telecommunications industry. This twin role will be considered later. The government then decided to liberalise the domestic fixed telecommunications network.[16] This process had already begun by September 1992, when three new entrants into the fixed-line market were licensed. They had to build new trunk cable networks themselves as part of their licence obligations, though they would be allowed access to HKT telephone exchanges and, crucially, interconnection with HKT to the local loop. This was essential as otherwise there would be no practical way to access business or domestic consumers, almost all of whom were

---

[15] Milton Mueller, *International telecommunications in Hong Kong: a case for liberalisation*, Chinese University of Hong Kong (1991).

[16] Position Paper – Hong Kong's telecommunications policy, Hong Kong Government, Economic Services Branch, January 1994.

located in multi-storey buildings with no possibility of duplicate wiring for telephonic equipment.

One vital issue that has not been satisfactorily explained, either by the government or by commentators, is why the government took the decision to liberalise the telecommunications market. Initially liberalisation affected only fixed networks, mobile telephony and value-added services but not international calls. The rationale for the basic liberalisation decision and the introduction of competition rules in telecommunication licences is nowhere spelt out. Presumably the government was concerned that Hong Kong's regulatory regime for telecommunications was an outdated and inefficient relic of colonial administrative practice and thus needed the spur of competition to ensure that Hong Kong would continue to be, and thrive as, an international communications hub. But, as we have seen, this mode of thinking did not apply to the electricity industry. Presumably, this was because there was no international or regional threat to the electricity industry, as was evident in the globalising telecommunications market and the need to ensure that Hong Kong's telecommunications infrastructure was able to support the burgeoning financial services sector.

Further, given the weighty business and political influence of the owners of the electricity duopoly, the government might have been obliged to turn a blind eye to obvious defects in electricity supply arrangements but was forced by increasing external competitive pressure to restructure telecommunications. Other factors may also have played a part in this crucial policy shift in the regulation of this industry. Commitments under the WTO Basic Telecommunications Agreement, to which Hong Kong was a signatory, have also been suggested as a reason for the fundamental shift in policy direction by the government.[17] Another reason may have been the need to attract new entrants into the Hong Kong market to create critical mass as a premier telecommunication hub in Asia and that without some rules to level the playing field, given HKT's overwhelming market dominance, no new investment would have been forthcoming from foreign investors. The concern about regional competitors stealing a march on Hong Kong was echoed in the most recent liberalisation policy to be announced: full liberalisation of fixed networks as from 1 January 2003.[18] An internal discussion paper stated that full liberalisation was needed as

[17] This was suggested to the author by officials at the Hong Kong Consumer Council (HKCC) and by Democratic Party researcher Simon Lo in an e-mail to the author, 30 May 2002.
[18] Announcement in LEGCO by the Information Technology and Broadcasting Bureau, 11 January 2002.

not to do so 'would be seen as a backward step, making us trail behind Singapore, in particular, as they implemented full liberalisation in April 2000'.[19] Thus, again it appears that pro-competition policies were forced upon a reluctant government only because of a perceived threat from external competitive forces and that it was proving impossible to insulate the 'domestic' industry from these forces. Clearly, where the government perceives an industry to be purely 'domestic', competition rules need not apply, as effective pressure to force change does not exist, so trumping the vested interests of the commercial oligarchs that control so much of the domestic economy.

Returning to the history of liberalisation of the fixed telecommunications sector, the Consumer Council published an influential report in 1996 on the telecommunication,[20] and in parallel the broadcasting[21] markets in Hong Kong, which they considered to be inextricably linked, especially in view of the blurring of traditional technological demarcations. The report made many recommendations to government on future policy towards the then nascent competitive telecommunications market. The report noted that Hong Kong was unique in having a private sector monopolist in complete control of the telecommunications market,[22] the fact that the government had chosen to liberalise domestic fixed networks but not international circuits (this did occur later) and that the penetration of mobile telephony was amongst the highest in the world.[23]

The report also recommended:

- Separation of functions and financial accounts within HKT Group companies and proper disclosure of information, especially in relation to the cross-subsidisation of domestic calls from international call revenues.
- Public disclosure of technical network information to facilitate interconnection.

[19] HKSAR Government discussion paper quoted to the author by an OFTA official in correspondence with the author, 21 June 2002.
[20] Achieving competition in the liberalised telecommunications market, Hong Kong Consumer Council, March 1996.
[21] Ensuring competition in the dynamic television broadcasting market, Hong Kong Consumer Council, 20 January 1996.
[22] In 1995, HKT had 99 per cent of the market for basic fixed-telephone services and an 88 per cent market share of outgoing international calls.
[23] 76 per cent of Hong Kong's population owned a mobile telephone in November 2000, *The Statesman's Year Book*, New York: Palgrave (2002) p. 464. By August 2003, the percentage had risen to an astonishing 95 per cent, with over 6,480,175 mobile subscribers. Key Telecommunication Statistics, 14 August 2003 http://www.ofta.gov.hk/datastat/eng_key_stat.htm.

- Provision for the sharing of essential infrastructure facilities occupied by the incumbent.
- That HKT be allowed interconnection to the local loop at reasonable cost and without delay.
- Non-discriminatory access to customers at their place of business or residence.
- A legal right for OFTA to inspect any commercial agreement between licensees and building developers or managers to check for tie-in or exclusive dealing agreements.
- That OFTA publicise the public's right to change to another fixed-line provider to offset HKT's overwhelming dominance.
- A review of interconnection charges.
- Greater public disclosure of interconnection agreements between licensees.
- Clarification of the definition of the precise scope of the exclusive international operation right.

The government responded by accepting almost all of the Consumer Council's recommendations and a new omnibus Telecommunications Ordinance was promulgated. As from 1 January 2003, the local fixed-network system has been fully liberalised and the performance requirements relaxed to encourage more entrants into the market. The aim of the policy is to increase broadband internet capacity. Subscribers to existing providers have increased from 51,000 in February 2000 and 543,000 in October 2001 to 1.1 million in August 2003,[24] a 22-fold increase in 3.5 years and at a monthly connection fee in the region of HK$150 (approximately £12), one of the cheapest in the world. Thus, in a little over ten years Hong Kong's fixed network has been transformed from a complete monopoly to one of full competition.

Turning to mobile telephony, this distinct market has had quite a different structure to the fixed networks. All through the 1990s the market was considerably more competitive than fixed networks, primarily due to the fast-evolving technology that provided new systems throughout the decade. Paging services were initially most popular, peaking in 1994, but the rapid decrease in mobile phone handset prices and service packages has eclipsed the paging market. Six personal communication services licences, in addition to the existing mobile licensees, were awarded in 1996 and by the end of that year subscriber numbers had reached 1 million, but by 2003 there were 6.4 million subscribers, over 95 per cent of the total

[24] Ibid.   [25] Ibid.

population.[25] In 1997 and 1998, two of the eight players in the market were subject to successful takeover bids, so reducing the competitors to six. This remains the position in 2004. The market is generally considered to be highly competitive, save for a specific incident to be mentioned later. There were no merger approval provisions in the then existing Ordinance and the licence conditions did not stipulate any oversight by OFTA. Number portability for consumers was a key development that leads to more effective competition in the mobile market.

As regards the international market, in March 1998 the government reached agreement with HKT to give up its exclusive licence eight years early, as from 1 January 1999. The incumbent was offered a compensation package which included a payment of HK$6.7 billion (approximately £500 million). HKT was also allowed to increase its basic tariff charges for land lines as a result of the removal of the cross-subsidisation of domestic tariffs from international call revenues. The liberalisation caused a dramatic reduction in international call prices and competition in the market means that Hong Kong now enjoys some of the cheapest international call tariffs in the world.

In August 2000, HKT was subject to a successful takeover bid by PCCW, a small communications company controlled by Li Ka-shing's son, Richard Li. Thus, control of the incumbent dominant provider passed into the hands of the Li family, who already had a considerable presence in the telecommunications market through Hutchinson Whampoa, a company controlled by the Li family and of which Richard Li was a director until 16 August 2000.

Prior to an amendment to the Telecommunications Ordinance in 2000, competition provisions were contained in the licences granted by OFTA but they were not backed by statutory provisions. Merger control in the sector was not implemented until the Telecommunications (Amendment) Ordinance became law in June 2003. During the passage of the Bill the main telecommunications operators conducted a furious lobbying campaign against the adoption of any merger-control provisions,[26] or alternatively if control was to be imposed they argued for provisions that would have been excessively weak. Details of the provisions eventually adopted will be discussed later.

Thus, in summary, the Hong Kong telecommunications market has been transformed by a complete change in the market environment, as a result of a policy decision taken by the government to promote a

---

[26] 'Telecoms reject Ofta M&A limits proposals', *South China Morning Post*, 4 October 2002.

pro-competition policy in the industry. The benefits to consumers in terms of an expansion of choice of services and reduction in cost have been dramatic. In essence, this is a paradigm example of the benefits of the creation of a competitive market in what was previously considered to be a natural monopoly. This has been achieved by the creation of a pro-competition regulatory framework and a fair and measured introduction of change in a rational and transparent fashion. The impact of new technology has also been a major driver of change. Implementation of the new rules of the game has been achieved successfully by qualified and competent civil servants. The competition law regime in telecommunications may provide a model for the eventual introduction of a general competition law in Hong Kong and the structure of OFTA may also be a blueprint for an authority to administer a comprehensive competition system.

However, telecommunication operators may have a legitimate sense of grievance. They complain that the government has not adopted an even-handed approach to economic regulation. They raise the complaint that the telecommunications market has been subjected to the full rigour of a comprehensive competition law regime, but all other industries in Hong Kong are exempt, save for broadcasting. The Hong Kong telecommunications industry also complains that as a result of a liberal policy on issuing of operator licences, the Hong Kong market is saturated, profitability is very low or even non-existent and, with the introduction of full merger control in 2004, consolidation of the industry is now more difficult than ever to achieve. The industry is also critical of the ethos and policy approach of OFTA in implementing its regulatory and competition rules. All of these issues were aired at a seminar hosted by Civic Exchange – a non-profit Hong Kong think-tank and Morgan Stanley in February 2003.

A report[27] was produced that analysed these concerns and suggested that:

- Current policy might reduce or prevent new investment in the industry as returns were too low, especially in the mobile market, and a more sustainable model had to be devised.
- More access to the Mainland Chinese market was needed to allow growth of Hong Kong based operators.
- Better checks and oversight of the decisions made by the Telecommunications Authority, which is constituted of a single individual, the Director of OFTA, and a more effective judicial appeal route were needed.

---

[27] *Hong Kong Telecommunications: What's the answer to competition?* 31 March 2003, published jointly by Civic Exchange and Morgan Stanley Hong Kong.

- Competition policy in telecommunications needed to be aligned with a general competition law so as to take account of cross-subsidisation by the large conglomerate companies that dominate the Hong Kong domestic economy.
- OFTA and government should encourage more collaboration and set clear goals for telecommunication strategy with evolving e-commerce applications.

In addition to these general issues, Michael Reede has identified some specific competition law challenges faced by OFTA in the current state of the Hong Kong telecommunication market,[28] namely:

> - Consumer protection may suffer as the current ferocious competition may tempt suppliers into misleading conduct.
> - The acceptable level of consolidation or concentration, via merger and acquisition activity, is unclear especially in respect of compatibility with the maintenance of a competitive market.
> - The possibility of collusive action by suppliers faced with continuing financial losses.

Obviously, the industry could be accused of special pleading and the logical way out of continuing unprofitability would be simply to exit the market, either by sale of the business to a competitor or simple closure of the business unit and a fire-sale of such assets as remain. One issue that may not be immediately apparent is that many of the market players in Hong Kong find the proposition of selling telecom assets at a loss to be unacceptable, especially if that means selling to a rival tycoon, who could gloat at his rivals' failure and cheaply purchase his rivals' assets. Most incumbents would prefer to subsidise telecom losses from profits originating in another part of their conglomerate empire, rather than 'lose face' by exiting the market in this manner. Thus, rational market behaviour cannot, necessarily, be expected from Hong Kong tycoons, who might face public humiliation in being seen to have been forced out of a telecommunications market.

As a result of the introduction of competition, the Hong Kong telecommunications market has undergone a transformation over the last decade and now faces a radically altered operating environment to that which pertained prior to liberalisation and the collapse of the hi-tech/telecom bubble in 2000.

---

[28] Michael Reede, Hong Kong's regulatory dichotomy, ibid. pp. 27–36.

OFTA has a very difficult job to do in safeguarding the currently competitive market, especially in the face of rapid technological change, and in operating sector-specific competition provisions in the vacuum of an absence of a general competition statute in Hong Kong. OFTA is faced with only having regulatory powers over licensees and this causes acute problems of regulatory authority as well as over the precise scope of those powers as regards adjacent markets and associated non-licensees. This issue of interlocking conglomerate corporate structures is a specific and complicating factor in the regulatory environment of Hong Kong, exacerbated by the lack of a general competition law. This, yet again, brings us back to the issue as to whether the sector-specific approach adopted by the HKSAR government works optimally.

The next section will consider the relevant legal issues.

8.3.2 Telecommunications competition provisions: definitions, overlap and entities regulated

The sectoral competition provisions are contained in the Telecommunications Ordinance (Cap. 106). ss.7I–N and s.35A (Investigatory Powers and Prohibitions), ss.32N–R (Competition Appeals) and s.36C (Penalties). These provisions have been in force since June 2000. New provisions on mergers have now been inserted into the Telecommunications Ordinance by virtue of the Telecommunications (Amendment) Ordinance 2003, which became law on 9 July 2003. The merger regime came into force on 9 July 2004 as a result of the finalisation of the Statutory Merger Guidelines. A new s.7P is added to the Ordinance to give power to the Telecommunications Authority (TA) to regulate mergers and to amend ss.32L, 32N and 32O of the Ordinance to allow for an appeal channel. Hong Kong now has a comprehensive competition framework for the telecommunications sector.

The objective of the following section is to analyse the legislative provisions and to consider whether they are technically effective in promoting competition. The analysis that follows is to some extent speculative, as few decisions pertinent to the competition provisions have yet been published by OFTA or the Appeal Board. However, the relevant decisions made to date are analysed below.

The competition provisions are 'sector specific' and so the ambit of the coverage of them is very important. The Telecommunications Ordinance (TO) only applies to the telecommunications market and to licensed operators within it. Therefore, the question arises to whom the TO provisions apply and what conduct is unlawful.

S.2 of the TO defines 'telecommunications', 'telecommunications service', 'communications' and 'telecommunications market'. Telecommunications means: 'Any transmission, emission or reception of communication by means of guided or unguided electromagnetic energy or both, other than any transmission or emission intended to be received or perceived directly by the human eye.' Telecommunications service means: 'A service for the carrying of communication by means of guided or unguided electromagnetic energy or both.'

Communications includes: 'Any communication

(a) whether between persons and persons, things and things or persons and things; and
(b) whether in the form of speech, music, or other sounds; or text; or visual images whether or not animated; or signals in any other form or combination of forms.'

Telecommunications market means: 'Any market for the provision or acquisition of telecommunication networks, systems, installations or customer equipment or services.'

It would appear that the definition of 'telecommunications' is designed to exclude application to broadcast television and also may not apply to internet transmissions, both of which are designed to be perceived directly by the human eye. The Broadcasting Ordinance (BO) is concerned with regulating television output, where ss.12 and 13 regulate television programme services transmitted by telecommunications. This clearly deals with television programming, but internet transmissions are not television programmes. Thus, does the TO or the BO regulate internet transmissions? There appears to be a lacuna. However, it might be argued that the definition of a telecommunication service is wide enough to cover internet transmissions, as it does not contain the exclusion of transmissions intended to be perceived by the human eye. By adopting a distinction based on technology between telecommunications and broadcasting and subjecting them to separate regulatory regimes, a grey area as to what is regulated and by whom is created. This is an unfortunate consequence of sector-specific regulation, especially when there are no fallback provisions in a general competition law that could plug such a regulatory gap.

This question of jurisdiction and the overlapping nature of the two Ordinances are important due to the blurring of distinctions between the various communications media. For example, PCCW/HKT was given a licence under the TO to operate a video-on-demand service, supplied via its fixed telephone network. The customer has access via a telephone line to a library of video films at any time of their choice and not subject to a fixed broadcast schedule. Thus, television pictures are provided by use of telephone lines and so the relevant regulatory statute is the TO not the BO. As will be seen later, this distinction as to which Ordinance applies can be legally significant. Technology will undoubtedly continue to create new methods of communication, which might be outside the ambit of narrowly drawn, technologically based regulatory structures. Clearly, a holistic approach is needed, at minimum, by merging the regulatory structures created under the TO and the BO. This problem of gaps in regulatory structure is well illustrated by a recent takeover case. Tom.Com, an internet venture floated in 2000 and controlled by Li Ka-shing. In August 2002, Tom.Com agreed to purchase 32.75 per cent of Asia Television Limited, Hong Kong's second terrestrial television broadcasting company. There were, at that time, no provisions to regulate this takeover in either the TO or the BO. Neither would apply in any event, as the acquisition of a television company by an internet company would not necessarily concentrate the television market and there are no takeover provisions in the BO relevant to competition issues. However, approval was required under the cross-media ownership provisions, not the competition provisions, of the BO. This issue will be highlighted later.[29]

This problem also has ramifications as regards the crucial issue of market definition. Clearly, for example, whether mobile telephony is a homogenous market or can be sub-divided by reason of accessibility to network coverage, cost, the nature of the handset and other factors such as G3 technology – that allows for the transmission of video pictures – could create separate markets. This would be an important matter as the regulatory regime is technologically specific and rigidly mechanistic in its approach to market definition. Further, the TO provisions are prescribed by the nature of definitions found in s.2 of the TO. They adopt a narrow, specific, common law approach, which, it is submitted, is inappropriate when significant flexibility is needed to decide accurately the nature of the relevant product market resulting from judgement calls as to the substitutability of alternative products.

---

[29] In the event the transaction did not proceed, apparently for commercial reasons but there was speculation that political objections from the PRC authorities may also have contributed to the collapse of the deal, 'Tom.Com–ATV deal collapsed on price differences', *South China Morning Post*, 21 August 2002.

Thus, at the first hurdle, the scope of the regulatory regime, a host of difficulties are thrown up that are caused, not by the concept behind substantive provisions of the regulatory system in place, but rather by the need (not for economic or legal reasons but partly for political reasons) artificially to isolate the telecommunications market to form a specific regulatory regime in order to conform to the government's politically driven mantra that sector-specific regulation works. This is a most unfortunate consequence of the government's stubborn refusal to yield to the logic of an overarching competition regime. Law is being used to fit a political orthodoxy and as a result the structure is fatally undermined.

Moving on from market definitions to the subjects of the law. The relevant provisions of the TO apply prima facie to the activities of a licensee or between licensees; only they are subject to the investigatory and the prohibitory provisions. Non-licensees are not liable to submit to investigation but they may have to provide information to the TA or be liable to a penalty for non-disclosure,[30] whether they are situated in Hong Kong or not and whether or not their conduct affects a telecommunications market. This could plausibly mean that in a conspiracy between a licensee and a non-licensee, where the non-licensee held all the evidence of the conspiracy, the TA might have difficulty in investigating a possible breach of the Ordinance. However, non-licensees cannot be liable for a substantive breach of the competition provisions or be subject to forcible entry or seizure of evidence, as the TA has no power over non-licensees and even if non-licensees were in breach of the TO provisions, they could not be subject to penalty, whilst the licensee would be, even if its part in the breach was minor. This enforcement problem is manifest only because of the narrow definitions necessitated by the government's misconceived sector-specific approach. The Banyan Garden case, discussed below, perfectly illustrates the severe limitations on effective enforcement of pro-competition rules imposed by this sector-specific approach.

8.3.3 Substantive prohibitions – abuse of dominance and restrictive agreements

Section 5 of the Ordinance provides for the appointment of a single civil servant to be constituted as the TA. Thus, all the powers exercised under the Ordinance are, in fact, the decision of a single person, not a statutory board or committee. The wide range and decisive nature of the powers

---

[30] S.36D, TO provides TA with power to require non-licensees to disclose relevant information.

granted to the TA have caused disquiet within the industry and amongst commentators.[31]

Turning now to the substantive prohibitive provisions. S.7K provides that:

> (1) A licensee shall not engage in conduct which, in the opinion of the Authority, has the purpose or effect of preventing or substantially restricting competition in a telecommunications market.

Conduct with intent to prevent or substantially restrict competition is sufficient; the conduct need not necessarily prevent or restrict competition and a dominant position is not required; the wrongdoer's intent is enough. Abuse of dominance is dealt with in s.7L. Thus, s.7K does not require any agreement between licensees to breach the prohibition but s.7K(2) specifically then goes on to provide examples of infractions of the section which do, predominantly, involve collusion and subsection 7K(3) specifically states that the conduct referred to in s.7K(1) makes unlawful collusive agreements, arrangements or understandings, onerous terms of supply or sale to or from another licensee or gives or receives preferential treatment involving an associated person that would disadvantage a competitor. This last provision appears to be an attempt to deal with the problems of cross-subsidisation of a licensee by an associated company or person. This is particularly problematic in Hong Kong given the web of tightly controlled conglomerate entities referred to previously. All the problems of jurisdiction mentioned above apply; only licensees are caught by the provisions, other persons are not. Associated persons do not break the law by colluding with a licensee and only the licensee is liable to punishment. This could hamper or prevent effective investigation and enforcement. Collusive agreements between licensees to fix prices or share markets are specifically prohibited in s.7K(2) (a) and (c).

Whether an infraction has occurred is subject to the 'opinion of the Authority'. However, the TA has power to promulgate guidelines under s.6D of the TO and under s.6(3)(a) 'must form any opinion or make any determination, direction, decision . . . only . . . on reasonable grounds and having regard to relevant considerations'.

Thus, the TA must exercise his discretion reasonably, based on sound and objective reasons. Consequently, it is submitted that whether or not the provision has been breached would depend on what, if any, guidelines

---

[31] See the Morgan Stanley/Civic Exchange report Hong Kong Telecommunications, 31 March 2003, containing Michael Reede's paper, Hong Kong's regulatory dichotomy.

under the TO had been issued on the subject, which might include exemption provisions. None, as yet, have been promulgated.

S.7L (1) prohibits a licensee from abusing its dominant position. Dominance is defined in s.7L(2) as 'the ability to act without significant competitive restraint from its competitors and customers'. In making an assessment of whether a licensee is dominant OFTA has statutory guidelines contained in s.7L(3) to assist it in making its determination. The factors listed are not exhaustive but include market share, the ability to make pricing and other decisions [free from concerns of rivals' or customers' reactions], barriers to entry to the relevant market, product differentiation and promotion and any relevant guidelines made under s.6D of the TO; a set of draft guidelines was put out to public consultation on 28 February 2004.[32]

Abuse of dominance is defined in s.7L(4) as: '[when] the licensee has engaged in conduct which has the purpose or effect of preventing or substantially restricting competition in a telecommunications market'. Dominance itself is not objectionable but abuse of that dominance is. Again, however, it should be stressed that the jurisdictional restraints of the TO are very clear; the prohibition only relates to conduct engaged in by a licensee. Non-licensees, for example suppliers of telecommunications equipment or the owners of essential facilities such as satellites, that are not themselves licensees under the TO but their abusive conduct has economic effects or is operationalised within a Hong Kong telecommunications market, are not affected by the prohibition in s.7L. This is a potentially significant defect, which again results not from a drafting error but as a direct result of the government's policy to limit competition regulation to a specific sector that has been overly narrowly defined. The badges of abusive conduct are exemplified but not exhausted in s.7L(5). They include predatory pricing, unreasonable price discrimination, non-related or unreasonable contractual restraints and enforced tying of supply to other service or equipment provision and discriminatory supply of services to competitors.

An issue relevant to dominance is whether s.7L is capable of dealing with the concept of joint or collective dominance.[33] The TO provision appears to contemplate that dominance is the prerogative of a single licensee only, given the statutory language employed: 'A licensee in a dominant position'

---

[32] Draft Telecommunication Authority guidelines on Anti-Competitive Conduct in the Hong Kong Telecommunications Market, OFTA, 28 February 2004.
[33] Monti, *The scope of collective dominance under Article 82 EC,* 38 CMLR 131 (2001).

(s.7L(1)). It might be argued as a matter of statutory construction that the singular noun employed can also carry the imputation of a plural noun[34] but one would need to take a purposive construction to arrive at that conclusion and the dictum in *Pepper v Hart*[35] is only of persuasive authority in Hong Kong. In any event, the statutory words appear to be clear and precise. If that is the case and dominance is restricted to a single licensee, then collective conduct falling short of an agreement or arrangement that would be caught by s.7K, would not be prohibited by s.7L. The 2004 draft Guidelines, mentioned above, take the view that collective dominance is contemplated by the section and that it can apply to more than one licensee acting collectively.[36]

An interesting example of how such a problem might arise occurred on 2 January 2000. All six mobile telephone operators in Hong Kong independently announced a simultaneous price rise of HK$20 to take effect the same day. On 3 January, the TA launched an enquiry into the price rises.[37] As a result of a very prompt investigation the TA was satisfied that there was evidence to show that there had, as a minimum, been a tacit understanding concerning price increases. This came about as a result of information-sharing by senior executives concerning the state of the mobile telephone market. They all knew, in advance, that their competitors were going to raise prices and by how much. There was apparently no evidence of a collusive agreement but the inference of an understanding could be made from the blatantly suspicious conduct of the licensees on 2 January 2000. The TA presented the preliminary findings to the licensees who all agreed to rescind the increases or allow customers to vary their service contracts without charge. At the time, the TA had only the licence conditions to rely upon, which were in substantially similar terms to s.7K (the statutory powers only came into force in June 2000) and so only had contractual powers to issue directions but not to impose a financial penalty. The importance of this case is that there was clear and obvious evidence of tacit collusion. If the operators had been more sophisticated in their co-ordinated actions and covered their tracks more thoroughly, the evidence of collusion might have been much more difficult to marshal. In that case, resort to the collusive dominance doctrine and use of s.7L would possibly have been a more advantageous line of attack.

---

[34] S.7(2) Interpretation and General Clauses Ordinance – (Cap.1).
[35] [1993] A.C.593.
[36] See CFTA, 'Draft Telecommucation Authority guidelines', para. 6.41.
[37] Case reference L/M T2/00 at http://www.ofta.gov.hk/c_bd/completed-cases/t2-00.html.

COMPETITION POLICY AND LAW IN CHINA

In a recent EC competition case, *Compagnie Maritime Belge Transports v Commission,* the ECJ opined that: 'collective dominance implies that a dominant position may be held by two or more economic entities legally independent of each other provided that from an economic point of view they present themselves or act together on a particular market as a collective entity'.[38] This notion would be of utility under the TO regime if the statutory language could be interpreted as bearing a plural meaning. Given the expressed view of the TA in the 2004 draft Guidelines[39] this approach could well be adopted in the future should a similar situation occur.

However, a major problem with the abuse of dominance provisions is the lack of effective investigatory powers and effective sanctions to prevent the non-licensee parent of a telecommunications licensee from subsidising, directly or indirectly, or giving preference to its subsidiary. As s.7L only catches the conduct of licensees, a determined parent company might be prepared to adopt measures designed to remove a troublesome competitor of its telecom subsidiary. In such a situation, the TA may have difficulty in preventing or punishing such conduct. This, yet again, raises the question of the effectiveness of the government's sector-specific approach.

S.7M is a consumer-protection measure and prohibits misleading or deceptive conduct and actually adds little to the existing statutory protections provided by the Trade Descriptions Ordinance and common law contract and tort, save that it does allow the TA to discipline licensees who engage in such conduct. In fact, the OFTA web site contains numerous complaints of misleading advertising claims made by licensees;[40] unsurprisingly most of the complaints originate from other telecommunication operators.

S.7N is a provision to prohibit discrimination by a dominant licensee. This provision appears to be unnecessary as it overlaps with s.7L(5)(b).

8.3.4 Merger control

A major legislative lacuna in the original provisions was the absence of any form of merger control. This omission came to be embarrassing when, in 1998, HKT acquired Pacific Link Communications, which resulted in HKT's share of the mobile market increasing, at the time, to 40 per

---

[38] [2000] 4 CMLR1076, para. 36.
[39] CFTA, 'Draft Telecommunication Authority guidelines'.
[40] http://www.ofta.gov.hk.

cent. The TO licence under which Pacific Link operated specified that TA approval was required in certain circumstances. Thus, when substantial changes in the ownership of a licensee were made involving the transfer of the licence to an acquiring entity, approval was needed; in other cases, for example, a simple sale of assets, permission was not needed. The analysis undertaken by the TA in this case was ill conceived and was criticised as inadequate.[41] In a subsequent consultation paper[42] the TA argued that this form of regulation is unsatisfactory. Originally, the government proposed amending the Ordinance by secondary legislation, so avoiding close scrutiny by LEGCO. After extensive criticism, the government relented and decided to introduce primary legislation. In May 2002, the government published the Telecommunications (Amendment) Bill, which *inter alia* provided for a statutory form of merger control in the telecommunications sector.

In a brief on the bill to LEGCO,[43] the government reiterated that its policy goal in the telecommunications sector was to 'promote fair and effective competition [and] . . . to safeguard the level of competition in the market'. The then existing provisions were accepted to be inadequate and unclear, leading to a fear of regulatory risk that was of concern to the operators' professional advisors. The government had, therefore, decided to legislate in the hope of clarifying the thresholds that would trigger regulatory involvement in the acquisition process and to specify the tests and procedures that would be followed by OFTA is assessing relevant transactions.

The bill proposed an *ex post* system of control whereby, in the opinion of the TA, in any case where a change in ownership or control of a licensee would substantially lessen competition in a telecommunications market, directions might be given to remedy the mischief by requiring divestiture or modification of ownership or control; failure to comply would result in the imposition of administrative penalties under the TO, including the issue of directions, the imposition of a financial penalty or suspension or cancellation of a TO licence. A voluntary pre-merger notification procedure was also provided whereby the TA could give *ex ante* comfort to an acquirer, that the TA has no competition objections to a proposed merger. The TA was to be authorised to promulgate guidelines to explain the criteria it would adopt in deciding competition concerns and the

---

[41] Cheng and Wu, *Competition policy*, p. 176.
[42] OFTA, *Consultation paper on the regulation of mergers and acquisitions*, April 2001, at
   http://www.ofta.gov.hk/report-paper-guide/paper/consultation/cp20010417.pdf.
[43] See OFTA web site above, under reference ITBB CR 7/13/14(02) Pt. 3.

method of analysis to be used. The merger-control provisions would only apply to acquirers who are themselves licensees; non-licensees would not be affected. A right of appeal to an Appeal Board was provided against determinations or sanctions imposed by OFTA.

The bill did not provide statutory guidance on the market-share thresholds that would trigger TA scrutiny. The TA indicated, in its April 2001 consultation paper, that the TA had in mind that the trigger for a competition investigation would be any transaction or series of transactions that resulted in the change in ownership or control of at least 15 per cent of the voting shares or where a person acquired effective control over a licensee. Further, the TA also opined that it might wish to receive notification of any ownership changes that exceeded 10 per cent of the voting capital or of any change in actual control. These matters have now been largely resolved following passage of the bill.

The provisions that finally emerged were significantly different from those originally proposed by government, especially as regards the threshold triggers that would allow for regulatory oversight.[44] The Telecommunications (Amendment) Ordinance 2003 now provides that the merger control powers of the TA apply when 'changes in relation to a licensee' occur. Three such 'changes' are specified in the amended s.7P(16):

- Material influence over a licensee, which is defined as when a person or his associates becomes the beneficial owner of more than 15 per cent of the voting shares of the licensee;
- Effective control over a licensee occurs when a person or his associates becomes the beneficial owner or voting controller (a broad definition is provided in s.7P(18)) of 30 per cent of the voting shares of a licensee and
- Majority control over a licensee occurs when a person or his associates becomes the beneficial owner or voting controller of (i) more than 50 per cent of the voting shares of a licensee; or (ii) acquires the power by virtue of any provision in the memorandum or articles of association or any other instrument regulating a licensee or any other corporation, whereby the affairs of a licensee are conducted at the behest of any person.

Under s.7P(6) where any of the above events is contemplated, it is possible, on a voluntary basis, to seek the TA's consent to the transaction. The TA

---

[44] For an analysis of the finalised provisions see Michael Reede, *New merger approval process for Hong Kong's telecommunications sector*, Hong Kong Lawyer, September 2003.

has power under s.7P(7) to approve or reject the proposal, subject to conditions to ensure the maintenance of competition in the relevant telecommunications market. Such prior approval immunises the acquirer or the licensee from further pro-competitive action by the TA. Pre-approval is likely to be given only after the TA has allowed for a period of public consultation and the submission of objections by interested parties. Such pre-notification is not required under the provisions but it is likely that it will be sought in most cases, as not to do so would run the risk of a subsequent unfavourable assessment by the TA which might involve the forced unscrambling of the deal.

If one of the threshold tests is satisfied, the TA is able to investigate the transaction and to assess whether the effect of the change is likely to 'substantially lessen competition' (SLC), the test adopted under the Australian Trade Practices Act. In committee, an amendment was successfully introduced which inserted a public benefit counter-weight to a finding of a SLC, so that even where SLC occurs a merger may yet be approved because a 'substantial public benefit' resulting from the merger can be discerned. This concept is clearly problematic and will be discussed below in light of the statutory Merger Guidelines that amplify these provisions.

S.6D(ii)(aa) and Schedule 3 provide a list of factors TA must take into account when deciding whether there is likely to be an SLC. These include the height of barriers to entry; market concentration; the degree of market power, profitability of the merged entity; dynamic changes in the market; elimination of competitors; the extent of vertical integration, the impact on competition; the availability of substitutes and the extent of post-merger competition in the relevant market. The TA's analysis is not limited to these factors, other relevant matters may also be considered.

8.3.4.1 The merger guidelines

After successful passage of the bill, OFTA issued a set of draft merger guidelines in August 2003.[45] Two extensive rounds of public consultation then followed before a finalised version was published on 4 May 2004. The new merger provisions contained in the amendment Ordinance then were brought into effect on 9 July 2004.[46]

The first draft of the guidelines to the new merger-control powers were published in August 2003 and suggested that:

---

[45] Consultation paper issued by OFTA, draft merger guidelines, 4 August 2003.
[46] Telecommunication Authority guidelines: mergers and acquisitions in the Hong Kong Telecommunications Markets, 4 May 2004. http://www.ofta.gov.hk/frameset/industry_index_eng.html.

- If the relevant combined market share of the entities were less than 15 per cent, there would be no detailed investigation or intervention. If the combined market share is over 40 per cent, a full investigation is likely. Where market share was between 15 per cent and 40 per cent, a case by case approach would be followed.
- Acquisitions by financial institutions would be exempt, subject to conditions.
- The TA's powers under s.7P (mergers) would not be used concurrently with those under s.7K (conduct of a licensee) and s.7L (abuse of dominance) or relevant carrier licensee conditions.
- An economic assessment of the relevant market would be made to analyse potential anti-competitive effects of any merger.
- The factors that must be taken into account before reaching a decision in merger cases include those set out in Schedule 3 TO, as well as taking into account any countervailing public benefit should an SLC be likely to occur.
- As regards market definition, OFTA will adopt the 'hypothetical monopolist' test in defining the appropriate product and geographic market within which to apply the test to establish whether the merged entity would be able to impose a small but significant and non-transitory increase in price (SSNIP); this was suggested to be the principal analytical tool employed to determine whether an SLC may occur.
- The objective of the analysis was to protect the process of competition, not competitors.
- 'Substantiality' was admitted to be subjective[47] and not well suited to economic analysis, save that it eliminates *de minimis* cases, and so TA would adopt a test of creation or enhancement of market power to determine SLC.
- An elaborate set of factors would be taken into account in deciding whether market power was likely to be created or enhanced; these are too voluminous to be detailed here.
- Procedures to be followed included the provision of informal advice, in prior consent and *ex post* cases.
- The proposed timetable for decisions was:
  - Where prior consent is sought, a preliminary investigation would be conducted within one month and if no serious issues were uncovered, consent would also be given at that time. If a full investigation were

---

[47] For the view of the Competition Appeal Board on the definition of 'substantial', see Appeal No. 4 of 2002.

needed, it would be concluded within a further three months. Thus, four months would be the maximum time for approval or rejection in this instance.

  ○ *Ex post* investigation should normally be concluded with 3 months of the commencement of the case.

- Confidentiality was to be respected in all aspects of the merger investigation process.
- A prior-consent investigation was to incur a maximum fee of HK$200,000.

The draft guidelines were subject to public comment. The industry responded[48] to the draft guidelines by the end of September 2003. The views expressed may be summarised as follows:

- AT&T was worried that the *ex post* system might provide too weak a set of remedies, should a dominant operator merge with another provider, as 'unscrambling the egg' after the event might prove too difficult. They suggested that in the case of a dominant player *ex ante* permission was more appropriate.
- British Telecom suggested more forthright encouragement by OFTA to potential merger parties to seek guidance; that the competition analysis be split into a geographical and product component; that public benefit defence should be better defined, and questioned how behavioural remedies could be enforced.
- CM Tel considered that price reductions, as well as increases, should be included in the SSNIP test, that cluster markets should include consideration of purchasing behaviour and that information concerning any proposed merger should be kept private by OFTA unless it proceeded.
- Smartone criticised the draft guidelines as departing from HKSAR government's 'small government' philosophy and complained about the structure, intent and procedures under the draft guidelines. They also criticised what they perceived to be a lack of clarity as regards market definition, substantiality, barriers to entry and the public benefit defence. The burden of compliance was also seen as excessive.
- HKCTV was concerned that the guidelines did not comprehensively address the issue of technological convergence.
- Telstra requested a more detailed definition of the concept of market power, substantiality, market definition, barriers to entry, market concentration, and considered the benefit to the public defence too narrow.

---

[48] http://www.ofta.gov.hk/frameset/home_index_eng.html.

- New World Telecommunications sought a policy statement of OFTA's philosophical stance to merger review and the objectives sought to be achieved, as well as a clarification of the burden of proof, more detail on market definition, and more substance on pre-merger consultations.
- Hutchison Telecom thought the guidelines philosophically anti-merger, that Hong Kong's special characteristics should be considered and that higher concentration ratios might be permissible than in larger jurisdictions. Corporate restructuring should be exempt and the *de minimis* threshold test needed elaboration. The draft guidelines were not practical enough and needed to be tailored to the subjects of regulation – carrier licensees. The substantiality test and associated burden of proof needed more clarity as did market share thresholds. More latitude should be given where a 'failing firm' was to be acquired, and a generous interpretation should be given to the public benefit defence.
- PCCW suggested that some broader principles needed emphasis, namely that the telecommunication industry required continued and increased capital investment and that mergers can contribute to this process. A broad explanatory policy statement was required, especially as the TA is a single individual, similarly an enforcement policy needs to be framed. The draft guidelines consisted mainly of principles and frameworks; they need to be more fully fleshed-out with examples to illustrate how they would operate in practice. Recognition of the positive aspects of mergers should be made explicit, as should the high risk of regulatory failure, especially in a fast-evolving, technologically intensive industry like telecommunications. The burden of proof should be made explicit and the vexing issue of the overlapping provisions in carrier licensees and the Ordinance should be clarified. A more sophisticated set of tools should be used to define market share and concentrations by utilisation of the Herfindahl–Hirschman Index (HHI). Failing firm mergers should be treated leniently and the public benefit defence should be more explicitly and generously interpreted.

Thus, the overall reaction of the industry was that the draft guidelines were too theoretical, and should be more concrete and tailored towards small economies like Hong Kong with a general policy statement to provide substantially more detailed examples, so as to provide practical guidance to practitioners and concerned parties.

Again, it was noticeable that there was a clamour for a more generous view of mergers as a positive development and the absorption of failing firms so as to assist market consolidation. The industry view seemed to be that this would encourage greater investment and recognise the public benefit that mergers might promote. Clearly, there is some force in these observations but they can also be criticised as self-serving in an industry that wishes to consolidate and sees these new merger provisions as an unwanted and unnecessary hurdle which would to prevent restructuring.

Following the publication of a second set of draft guidelines and another round of consultation, the final version was promulgated in May 2004. The most important features of the final provisions that diverge from the original draft are:

- An apparent policy shift to an explicit statement of the beneficial aspects of mergers, emphasising the benefits of enhancing economic efficiency and stressing that mergers would only be prohibited or unwound, where other remedies cannot be devised.
- The burden of proof that a merger would substantially lessen competition was explicitly placed on the TA to the civil standard. As regards the public benefit defence to a finding that a merger would create an SLC, whilst this would be raised by the acquirer, this was a matter for the TA to decide upon, presumably acting judicially and adopting the civil standard.
- The adoption of 'safe harbour' provisions, namely the CR4 Ratio test, whereby if the post-merger combined market share in the relevant market of the four (or fewer) largest firms (CR4) is less than 75 per cent, and the largest merged firm has a market share of less than 40 per cent, the TA would be unlikely to undertake a detailed investigation. Where the CR4 is 75 per cent or more, the TA is unlikely to investigate if the combined market share of the merged entity is less than 15 per cent of the relevant market. The second 'safe harbour' provision is the adoption of the HHI. The TA is unlikely to investigate where the HHI of the post-merger market is less than 1,000 (an unconcentrated market). In post-merger markets with an HHI of 1,000 to 1,800 (moderately concentrated), mergers that increase the HHI by less than 100 would be unlikely to trigger investigation but those that increase the HHI by more than 100 would normally require investigation. In a post-merger market with an HHI of more than 1,800 (highly concentrated), mergers producing an increase in the HHI of more than fifty, would be investigated.
- More specificity in relation to market definition was provided.
- Elaboration of the considerations to be taken into account when the efficiency or 'failing firm' defence is raised.

- Elucidation of the principles to be applied in relation to the 'public benefit' defence.

The 'public benefit' defence requires some discussion. This was inserted as an amendment to the government bill and no definition of this term is provided by the Ordinance. The guidelines explain that if a merger or potential merger does create an SLC in the relevant market, the acquirer will need to raise the defence and provide explicit details of the purported benefit to the public that outweighs the SLC, including the magnitude and timing of the benefit and all appropriate supporting evidence. Any potential 'benefit' to the public might be considered, including consumer benefits such as innovation, wider choice, higher capacity, better quality services or continuity of service. Non-consumer benefits might include the enhancement of Hong Kong's international competitiveness.

In an opinion on the appropriateness, utility and compatibility with international best practice of the guidelines to achieve government competition policy objectives in relation to mergers in the telecommunications sector, Professor Richard Whish opined[49] that the public benefit defence 'seems to me to be specific to Hong Kong law'. After mentioning the position in various other jurisdictions as regards non-competition/public interest defences, he went on to say that 'wherever possible, merger control should be applied purely with competition policy and the maintenance of competitive market structures in mind and that a real danger exists of undermining the effectiveness of law if other considerations are allowed to influence decision-making'. However, he thought that the 'interpretation given to the "public benefit test" in the guidelines [was] a sensible approach'.

Overall then, the guidelines appear to demonstrate that OFTA has the ability to create a workable, suitable and potentially effective merger-control regime in Hong Kong. However, since no merger activity has occurred in the telecommunications sector as yet, the true efficacy of the substantive provisions and the decisional process has yet to be tested. Given the concerns often voiced in the Hong Kong telecommunications sector about low profitability and the need for consolidation, so as to justify new capital investment, a merger and acquisition wave might occur. But the reluctance of incumbent owners to sell to their rivals may yet prevent forced sales or 'marriages of convenience' that would tarnish the

---

[49] Opinion of Professor Richard Whish on the Telecommunications Authority guidelines: mergers and acquisitions in the Hong Kong telecommunications markets, 29 April 2004, http://www.ofta.gov.hk/frameset/industry_index_eng.html.

image of the selling tycoon. Only time will tell if pride will outweigh the rational economic considerations of the need to consolidate a possibly over-crowded market.

8.3.5 *Investigative powers, penalties and appeals*

As regards investigation of alleged infractions of ss.7L–N and the merger control provisions, the TO provides investigatory powers.

S.7I requires that anyone who provides a public telecommunications service shall supply the TA with any information in the manner and at the time specified relating to its business that may reasonably be requested in order for the TA to carry out its statutory functions. Business confidentiality is no defence, even if that is a contractual obligation but immunity from suit for breach of a contractual confidentiality clause is provided.

S.35A provides the TA with power at all reasonable times to enter the premises of a licensee, to require production, inspection and copying of documents (which includes information stored on any computer) or accounts, relating to a telecommunications business operated by the licensee. Contravention of this provision is a criminal offence with a maximum penalty of six months' imprisonment and/or a substantial fine.

S.36D provides that if the TA has reasonable grounds to believe that persons, other than licensees, have information relevant to any investigation, a notice may be served in writing upon that person to disclose the requested information or produce any relevant document within a reasonable, specified, time. If the person objects to production, he can state his reasons to the TA, who must consider them and may thereafter serve a further notice accepting his objection and withdrawing the request or informing him that the TA will seek an order from a magistrate compelling production. Failure to comply with any court order for production is an offence, as is the giving of false information or the destruction, deletion or alteration of any relevant document.

S.36C provides for the imposition of penalties on licensees by the TA or by the High Court for breach of any licence condition, any provision of the TO or regulations made thereunder or any direction issued by the TA. The administrative penalty that can be imposed is a maximum of HK$200,000 for the first breach by a licensee, HK$500,000 for the second and HK$1 million for the third. The TA may also require the offending licensee to publicise information relevant to the breach to the public or to any person nominated by the TA. The offender may also be required to publish at its own expense corrective advertisements in the media. If the penalties mentioned above are considered by the TA to be inadequate, application to the High Court can be made seeking the imposition of a financial penalty of 10 per cent of the offender's turnover in the relevant telecommunications market or HK$1 million, whichever is the higher. The TA is enjoined not to impose penalties that are disproportionate to the breach. S.36C(5) limits the TA's sanctioning powers considerably. An offender cannot be subject to administrative sanction, as opposed to the sanctions that might be imposed by the High Court, unless the TA has given him reasonable time to comply with the breached provision. Presumably, if the offender can cure its offence within a reasonable time, no penalty can be imposed.

As regards the merger control provisions, s.7P(10) provides that if the thresholds, mentioned above, have been satisfied and there has been an SLC, the TA has power to require the licensee to take any action considered necessary to eliminate the anti-competitive effect discerned, including divestiture. Failure to comply would allow the TA to issue further directions, impose a financial penalty or to suspend or cancel the carrier's licence.

Finally, s.32 N–R provide for the establishment of a Telecommunication (Competition Provisions) Appeal Board. This body consists of a legally qualified Chairman or Deputy Chairman and two other members. The Board has jurisdiction to hear appeals under the competition provisions of the TO. Powers to compel witness attendance with documents are provided. Questions of law may be referred to the Court of Appeal for determination by way of case stated, as a preliminary issue. The establishment of an independent appeal channel is a useful safeguard against errors of fact or law committed by the TA, given that power is in law reserved to the Telecommunications Authority, in reality a single individual.

8.3.6 Recent competition decisions

There have been several recent adjudications concerning abuse of dominance and bundling by the TA and the first final judgement by the Appeal Board was published in September 2003.

In case T210/02, Hong Kong Cable Television Limited (HKCTV) was accused of abuse of its dominant position in the supply of pay-TV services by attempting to increase its market share in the pay-TV market and domestic broadband internet market by bundling its pay-TV service with the broadband service offered by its affiliated company, i-cable. The bundled package was offered at a discounted price. The complainants alleged that this conduct amounted to an abuse of dominance that would ultimately prevent or restrict the establishment of new service providers in both the pay-TV and domestic broadband internet markets.

The bundled service was offered by HKCTV as a promotion to new customers only between 19 September and 31 December 2002. New customers could choose the bundled service or separate subscription. HKCTV maintained that its offer of a promotional package to new subscribers, for a limited time, was not an abuse of dominance, merely a marketing tool to attract new customers and was not intended to be predatory. In any event, the effect on the broadband market would have been *de minimis*.

The TA considered that the relevant product markets identified were:

(i) the pay-TV service market;
(ii) the supply of broadband network services;
(iii) the supply of broadband internet access services.

HKCTV participated in (i) and (ii) and i-cable in (iii).

The TA noted that only (ii) and (iii) were telecommunications markets, subject to regulation under the TO.

Given the nature of the complaints, only market (iii) was relevant and that was further limited to domestic, as opposed to business, consumers. The TA accepted HKCTV's submission that narrowband and broadband access were separate markets for the following reasons:

• High-speed access via broadband was required to access certain content, which could not be satisfactorily achieved using narrowband.
• Broadband offered an 'online' or 'always-on' feature, that narrowband could not.
• Narrowband utilised a telephone line exclusively and unless a second line was installed, use of voice telephony was impossible. Broadband could use the same line without interrupting voice telephony traffic.
• Broadband subscription was relatively more expensive compared to narrowband, which demonstrated that consumers were prepared to pay more for broadband, given its superior characteristics over narrowband access.

The geographical market was the whole of HKSAR. The TA's analysis then proceeded on the basis that the relevant market was that of the supply of broadband internet service access (iii) above, HKCTV was not dominant in that market, where there were fifteen active suppliers, but it was dominant in the pay-TV market (i) above. Further, i-cable is one of the fifteen players in the market (iii). This market is currently structured so that four players hold 90 per cent of the market, with i-cable not being the largest operator, holding less than 25 per cent. No player is dominant in the opinion of the TA and entry to the market is not obstructed, barriers to entry not being high. The complaint raised the issue of whether HKCTV was leveraging its position in market (i) to unfairly i-cable advantage in market (iii). OFTA proceeded to conclude that HKCTV had preferred i-cable when offering the bundled package but the issue of law was whether such conduct breached s.7K TO by placing a competitor at a significant disadvantage by restricting competition in market (iii) above. The bundled promotion offered significant incentives – twelve months' free broadband internet access and no installation fee, subject to also subscribing for the pay-TV service. Given the market structure, the take-up rate of pay-TV and broadband internet services and that most new pay-TV customers would not, at the same time, have the need for a new broadband connection, the competitors of i-cable in the broadband domestic-access market were not significantly disadvantaged and thus, the bundled service did not prevent or substantially restrict competition.

As regards possible predatory pricing, which the TA defined as pricing below cost with a predatory purpose to eliminate a competitor and an ability to recoup the losses resulting from the predation, in fact, the offer of free broadband internet access for twelve months related to new pay-TV customers only and lasted for fifteen weeks; there was no evidence of competitors exiting the broadband access market and barriers to entry were relatively low. Thus, the bundling was not predatory, given its short duration, lack of industry complaints and lack of evidence of predatory purpose. Consequently, there was no breach of the carrier licence or of s.7K and s.7L TO.

This is the first published abuse decision by OFTA which gives an insight into the modes of analysis adopted. It appears that the examination of the evidence was thorough and the conclusions reached were soundly based. However, it should be noted that the structural flaws in the legislative scheme exclude from review the pay-TV market which is regulated under the Broadcasting Ordinance. This consequence results directly from the HKSARG's sector-specific policy and this case shows that this artificial regulatory segmentation is highly unsatisfactory.

The second reasoned decision on predation and anti-competitive behaviour, case T55/03, concerned fixed-price fee plans for external telecommunications services (ETS) offered by PCCW, the previously monopoly operator in this market in Hong Kong.

The international call market was opened to competition from 1 January 1999. PCCW's market share of the overseas business telephony and valued-added services market has fallen. By common consent, these markets are the most profitable segments of all the overseas call markets.

PCCW offered business users a fixed price for a certain quantity of usage to either any destination or to a restricted number of eight countries – China, Australia, Canada, Japan, Singapore, Taiwan, the UK and the USA. Complaint was made that the price offered was below the cost of the relevant services plus the mandatory universal service contribution. Thus, the offers were either predatory and/or anti-competitive under s.7L and s.7K TO.

PCCW responded to the allegations as follows:

- PCCW was not dominant in the ETS market which was highly competitive with minimal barriers to entry and thus was restrained by competition from predatory pricing.
- The fixed-fee plans were limited in scope, and would only affect a small percentage of outgoing ETS traffic.
- Competitors of PCCW are also offering similar schemes, some with even lower prices than those offered by PCCW.

The TA concluded that:

- The relevant market was the entire market for ETS, regardless of destination, as one scheme applied to all destinations and the restricted scheme covered countries to which about 80 per cent of total ETS calls were made.
- There were low barriers to entry to the ETS market, there are over 200 market operators, the product is undifferentiated, ETS was highly price sensitive and users regularly switched providers with little, if any, customer loyalty. Providers regularly entered and exited the market.
- PCCW did not have a substantial share of the ETS market during the relevant period from January to June 2003 and thus PCCW is not able to act free from competitive restraint. Further, the TA had declared PCCW non-dominant in the ETS market in October 2002, so removing onerous regulatory pre-approval of tariff alterations by OFTA.
- New entrants to the market had precipitated a price war, leading to significantly lower price packages being offered to domestic and business consumers. Many providers had responded by offering ever more tailor-made tariff plans to customers; PCCW's fixed-fee plans were not exceptional.

TA concluded that in light of the above analysis, PCCW was not engaging in predatory pricing as barriers to entry were low with many suppliers and new entrants, so even if existing competitors were eliminated, new entrants would quickly enter the market. Additionally, PCCW was not dominant in the ETS market. As regards anti-competitive conduct below-cost pricing was not necessarily anti-competitive, especially when the supplier was not dominant or did not have significant market power. Other operators offered even lower prices than PCCW, thus there was no evidence that PCCW had engaged in anti-competitive conduct.

This second case also demonstrates a good, clear analysis of the relevant market conditions and the conclusions drawn are logical and soundly based on the facts. Thus, in the first two cases determined and published by OFTA, under s.7K and s.7L, the system of adjudicating competition complaints appears to be working well. The pity is that this type of rational, evidence-based, investigation is not available outside the narrow markets of telecommunications and broadcasting.

A third important case, T261/03, concerned bundling of telecommunication services as part of the management fee for a residential housing estate. Banyan Garden is a large residential housing estate developed by the Cheung Kong Group, who appointed their subsidiary company Citybase as property manager. In September 2003, Citybase contracted with Hutchinson Multimedia and PowerCom to supply broadband internet and with Hutchinson Global Communications to provide residential land-line telephone services to all the residential units in the development. All of these companies are effectively part of the Cheung Kong/Hutchinson conglomerate and are 'associated persons', as defined by s.2 TO. Unit owners were required to pay for these telecommunications services as part of the management fee they were charged by Citybase under the terms of their leases. Some residents complained that they had no choice as to whether they wanted these services or not and also that, whether they utilised them or not, they still had to pay the full management fee. Competing telecommunications providers also complained that they were effectively prevented from competing for customers, given that residents of Banyan Garden would have to pay for their services, in addition to that part of the management fee that related to telecommunications services provided by the incumbents.

OFTA proceeded to investigate a possible breach of s.7K(3)(c) whereby a licensee is prohibited from engaging in conduct, which has the purpose or effect of preventing or substantially restricting competition in a telecommunications market. The prescribed conduct includes the giving by a licensee to, or the receipt by the licensee from an associated person, of an unfair advantage, if a competitor could be placed at a significant disadvantage or whereby competition would be prevented or substantially restricted.

During the course of the investigation, OFTA became aware that this type of contractual arrangement, whereby the telecom associate of a conglomerate property firm was granted preferential access to new housing developments without any competitive tendering process, was widespread in Hong Kong.

The obvious problem in disposing of this case was the limited ambit of the competition provisions in the Telecommunications Ordinance which are sector-specific and only *prima facie* apply to telecommunications licensees and not to other economic actors. The TA explicitly acknowledged the problem: 'para.70 . . . In the absence of a general competition law in Hong Kong, the application of sector specific telecommunications laws outside their designated area would be a cause of concern. Accordingly, potential competition issues that may be identified outside the scope of the present regulations may suggest that a broader regulatory framework would be beneficial to the economy.'

After an analysis of the facts surrounding the granting of the supply contracts, the TA found that PowerCom had received an advantage over its competitors from an associated person, namely Citybase. However, there was no evidence that either PowerCom or Hutchinson Multimedia had known that they had received that advantage. Thus, the TA considered in light of this fact, the supplier of the advantage should be the target of regulatory action, not the recipient, but as Citybase was not a telecommunications licensee, the TA had no jurisdiction to act. The TA found that: 'para.87 . . . In the TA's view, if the conduct of the non-licensee does raise concerns about prejudicing fair competition in a telecommunications market, it is not a matter that can be dealt with under the sector specific regulation under the existing Telecommunications Ordinance.' The TA went on to opine that:

> para. 88 . . . for an advantage to be considered 'unfair' within the meaning of s.7K(3)(c), some sort of culpability must be attributed to the licensee in question. In other words, the licensee is entitled to be regarded as innocent in circumstances where it can be shown that it honestly held, upon reasonable grounds, a belief in the existence of facts that the advantage being bestowed upon it by its associated entity was not an 'unfair' advantage.

Therefore, neither licensee received an advantage within the meaning of s.7K (3) (c). Additionally, the TA found, though it was unnecessary given its decision on the meaning of 'unfair advantage', that the nature of the selection procedures did result in a disadvantage to competitors and that they could be significant but given its findings that there was no unfair advantage, no action could be taken.

This narrow interpretation of the section significantly restricts the ambit of an already limited jurisdiction. The fact that, in essence, the fiction of the corporate veil[50] was used to prevent an imputation of knowledge of the advantage to the licensees is unfortunate. Here we are confronted with a tightly held corporate structure and the normal practice in similar factual situations appears to have been that services for new building estates were essentially tied 'in-house'. It is clear that the licensees enjoyed an advantage over their competitors, who were at a double disadvantage. Non-group providers were effectively unable to compete at the 'wholesale' level as a result of Citybase's contractual procedures and were also unable to compete for the business of individual consumers at the retail level, as they would be unlikely to want to pay twice for the provision of telecommunication services. The decision of the TA seems to be an unduly lenient approach and weakens the effectiveness of the pro-competition provisions of the Ordinance. The TA was clearly mindful of the policy environment within which it has to operate and appears to have chosen a deliberately conservative interpretation of the law. Thus, it seems that the best advice to corporate conglomerates is to ensure that there is no evidentiary paper trail of accepted in-house contractual practices and the law will not interfere with those arrangements. However, the real root of failure to deal effectively with a clear and apparently widespread anti-competitive practice is the government's sector-specific policy. A further worrying matter, in the context of the specific circumstances of the Hong Kong telecommunications market, is the fact that this type of tying as between the estate management subsidiaries and the telecommunications subsidiaries of the dominant property developers is a widespread phenomenon. Whilst on a case-by-case basis this may not be significant, collectively the effect may well be substantial. As Hong Kong has no provision for statutory economic investigations of sectors that appear to have structural impediments to

---

[50] See the celebrated case of *Salomon v Salomon & Co Limited* [1897] A.C.22. As to when a common law court will disregard the corporate veil in cases involving group companies, see the judgement of English Court of Appeal in The Albazero [1977] A.C. 774 per Roskill LJ at p. 807; but for a very different view, see Lord Denning in the Court of Appeal judgement in *DHN Food Distributors Ltd. v Tower Hamlets London Borough Council* [1976] 1 WLR 852. The argument about the treatment of nature of the separate identity of group companies was continued latterly in *Woolfson v Strathclyde Regional Council* 1978 SC(HL) 90 and again in *Adams v Cape Industries plc* [1990] Ch. 443.

competition, the concern of the TA, as highlighted above, drives home the point that even an isolated sectoral regime, as in telecommunications, may be inhibited from successful operation by the artificial limitations placed on the scope of OFTA competition enquiries by the legislation.

This trilogy of cases appears to confirm the inherent limitations of a sector-specific regime and to emphasise that the absence of a general competition law inevitably causes significant problems of scope of application and jurisdiction. Notwithstanding the overly legalistic and conservative application of parts of the regime, where fine legal niceties, rather than the economic effects of the relevant conduct appear to have greater weight, the system of investigation and adjudication appears to display the core competences needed to examine competition issues and so could form the nucleus of a general competition authority, should a policy decision be made to establish one in Hong Kong. The policy environment, along with, perhaps, an overly common law approach to interpretation, rather than a more purposive methodology, would need to be addressed, should the OFTA competition branch become the vanguard of a proto-competition authority.

On 15 August 2003, the Appeal Board gave judgement in the first fully contested appeal under the competition provisions of the Ordinance.[51] The facts were that PCCW had applied to the TA for permission to offer a lower-than-published tariff price to the residents of fourteen newly completed residential multi-storey housing estates for Residential Direct Exchange Lines (RDEL). The promotion was to last for ten months and only related to the specified estates. PCCW was dominant in the RDEL market covering the whole of Hong Kong territory and its carrier licence required the consent of the TA before offering discounts to its published tariffs. For the purposes of the appeal, it was agreed that the relevant market was RDEL for the whole of Hong Kong and not limited geographically to the residents of the fourteen relevant estates. Both the licence and the TO contained pro-competition provisions upon which the TA relied to refuse permission to PCCW on the basis that the price reduction would have the 'purpose or effect of preventing or substantially restricting competition contrary to General Conditions 15 and 16 [of the licence]'. The TA also relied on s.7K, s.7L and s.7N of the Ordinance. The Appeal Board made a number of important preliminary decisions that will affect subsequent cases:

[51] PCCW–HKT Telephone Limited versus the Telecommunication Authority. Appeal No. 4 of 2002.

- Jurisdiction. The appeal was conducted as a re-hearing and the Board decided that it was entitled to consider any fresh or other evidence it thought appropriate and any legal submissions based upon them; it was the Board's opinion of all relevant matters that was decisive.
- Burden of proof. The Board decided that the burden of proving breaches of the Ordinance rests with the TA. The standard of proof to be adopted was held to be the civil standard, based upon the balance of probabilities. In this case, the TA did not seek to prove an intent to 'prevent' competition or that PCCW's subjective purpose was to restrict competition. The TA sought only to prove that the objective effect of the promotion would have been to 'substantially restrict competition' in the RDEL market under s.7K, s.7L, and s.7N.
- Substantial restriction of competition. The Appeal Board proceeded to define this crucial concept before considering whether, on the facts of this case, the forbidden effect was likely to have occurred if the promotion had proceeded. The Board noted that no definition was provided in the Ordinance and the phrase was used in all three of the relevant sections. The construction of the phrase was to be undertaken with the legislative intent in mind that lay behind all the sections taken together and construed in light of the examples provided in each section. Thus, the phrase had the same meaning in each section, but whether or not there was a substantial restriction of competition was a question of fact to be determined by reference to the evidence and in light of the particular conduct concerned. Further, not every restriction will be substantial. An effect will substantially restrict competition if it is large enough to be 'worthy of consideration for the purpose' of the relevant prohibition, so citing with approval the dictum of Lord Mustill in *R. v Monopolies Commission*[52] which emphasised that the contextual background must be given proper weight. The Board disapproved the TA's construction of substantiality and chose to emphasise context, stating that the effect had to be at least 'significant' but need not be big.

The Board eschewed reference to decisions of the Court of Justice of the European Communities on the basis that EC law was to be considered in light of the purposes of the Treaty of Rome and that the Hong Kong telecommunication legislation was enacted in quite different circumstances, both in terms of legal and regulatory frameworks.

---

[52] [1993] 1 WLR23, p. 28H.

Turning to the questions of fact in the present appeal, the Board found that price was a significant motive in the choice of provider of RDEL services. The discount offered by PCCW in this promotion was either 20 per cent or 40 per cent over the ten-month period, depending on whether the waiver of installation charges was taken into account. PCCW was likely to enjoy a 20 per cent increase in sales in the fourteen relevant housing estates, which translated into a loss to PCCW competitors of approximately 4,400 RDEL customers who represented approximately 1 per cent of all RDEL subscribers in the whole of Hong Kong (which had been agreed as the relevant market). The Board held that the proposed promotional offer was not below PCCW's long-run average incremental cost and so was not predatory. The Board observed that price competition from a dominant incumbent only becomes anti-competitive when it has the 'purpose or effect of preventing or substantially restricting competition'. Importantly the Board determined that the legislative intent of the Ordinance was: 'not to favour new entrants to the market, but rather to seek to ensure that competition itself is not harmed because new entrants suffer substantial and unfair competitive disadvantage by reason of anti-competition conduct by the dominant provider'. The Board accepted evidence from Professor Kay that in deciding whether there had been a substantial restriction of competition one had to ask:

- Would the extant promotion occur in a competitive market?
- Would efficient entrants or competitors be excluded, as opposed to merely losing market share?
- Does the promotion give the dominant firm an advantage it would not have had in a normally competitive market?

The Board decided that, on the evidence, the tests were not met, so no substantial reduction in competition was likely to occur. The Board refused to look at the effect simply in terms of the fourteen relevant estates but measured the competitive effect by reference to the whole RDEL market in Hong Kong. As a result of this crucial determination of market definition, the Board held that whilst competition might be restricted to some extent it was not 'substantial' within the meaning of the provisions of the Ordinance.

The Board went on to state *obiter dicta* that simply because the TA had failed in this specific case, it should not be seen as a green light for multiple selective offers which would each individually be *de minimis*, so avoiding the wider legislative intent of maintaining competition in the relevant telecommunication market, but collectively would substantially restrict competition. The TA was urged to investigate each case on its merits and the totality of the evidence. Presumably this would mean that if PCCW pursued a pattern of similar conduct, the cumulative effect could be taken into account in any future determination.

This decision of the Appeal Board is clearly important as it sets out the Board's approach to its own jurisdiction and procedure, the burdens of proof, the meaning of substantial restriction of competition, as used in the TO, and that the legislative purpose of the competition provisions is to protect competition, not competitors. Consequently, a number of very important matters have been clarified and presumably, unless overturned on further appeal to the Hong Kong Court of Appeal on a point of law, the TA will follow the definitions and determinations made by the Board in considering future cases.

8.3.7 Assessment of the telecommunications competition regime

Some comment can now be made about the general tenor of the telecommunications competition provisions. The scheme is stated to be sector specific and, thus, subject to criticisms of narrowness of definition as made above. The effect of the lack of an overarching competition regime is that consideration of the position of TO licensees in isolation is dangerous. This methodology does not reflect the complex technological and commercial realities of the actual market for telecommunication services in the economic sense. Attempting to ring-fence the telecommunication market by the use of narrow legalistic definitions is illogical in the face of rapid technological convergence, innovatory commercial entrepreneurship and the conglomerate structure of much of the domestic economy.

As we have seen, Hong Kong telecommunications law now has the full panoply of internationally recognised provisions necessary to deal with competition issues – horizontal agreements, abuse of dominance and mergers, although the power to deal with oligopolies is to some extent uncertain. However, the question arises as to whether the existing framework is as effective as it could be.

Clearly, there are a number of defects in the current arrangements, some are structural, and some are related to drafting. But, as was admitted above, a comprehensive assessment is difficult, as there have only been a few determinations by the TA and only one by the Appeal Board under the relevant statutory provisions.

This leads to an obvious question – disregarding structural or drafting defects – namely, what was the reason for the historically limited nature of OFTA competition activity? Two possible answers present themselves, namely, a dearth of competition problems or a lack of institutional will to tackle them.

If one considers the evidence displayed on the OFTA web site concerning competition complaints, it is clear that the incumbent licensees continually snipe at each other about alleged misleading advertisements, but specific competition complaints have been relatively few, though they have increased significantly. Does this mean that the rivals are all competing fiercely and the complaints about misleading conduct are a symptom of that keen competition or has this been merely a proxy for actual competitive activity? It would seem that the logical conclusion is that the market is competitive, but there have been some intimations that this might be the wrong inference to draw.

Firstly, the clearly collusive behaviour of the six mobile telephone operators in January 2000, related above, raises the suspicion that the informal exchange of information or the tacit agreement that resulted in all six market players acting in exactly the same way at exactly the same time is an indication of, at minimum, regular commercial contacts between the industry players, especially where all the incumbents have a common concern, namely falling profit margins across the industry. The consensus that was presumably reached was that prices were uniformly too low for all the suppliers. Obviously, by their blatant conduct, the licensees thought that either they were not doing anything wrong, in the sense that their conduct was not unusual in the commercial world in Hong Kong, or that they would not be caught and punished. It must be presumed that they did not seek any legal advice about the clear and obvious breach of their license conditions by acting in this collusive manner or that they made a commercial decision to ignore any advice that was given. Either way, it suggests that the mode of making business decisions in Hong Kong is more co-operative than competitive. However, one might argue that this was a single isolated occurrence.

Secondly, as regards abuse of dominance, there have been continual complaints about the conduct of PCCW/HKT as regards the sharing of essential facilities, interconnection and the ability of subscribers to change suppliers in accordance with OFTA guidelines. Such reluctance of the incumbent dominant operator to accept the unpalatable realities of a liberalised market is not unique to Hong Kong. In April 2001, New T&T, a rival entrant in the fixed telecommunications market, made public a number of serious complaints.[53] New T&T accused PCCW/HKT of delaying or refusing to allow subscribers to change providers and overcharging for interconnection to local loop circuits. This dispute was resolved by OFTA without a formal complaint being made.[54] PCCW is the obvious target of competition complaints, being the largest single operator, and has attracted increasing numbers of complaints during recent times.

Thus, the evidence that exists as regards actual decisions and extant complaints is to some extent inconclusive as to whether the Ordinance provisions have been fully effective or not but there is growing evidence that the competition provisions are now bearing fruit, producing an increasing number of decisions to protect competition in the telecommunications market.

Turning now to structural, as opposed to operational matters, there remains no official government explanation as to what precisely marks out the telecommunications market as unique and qualitatively distinctive from all other sectors of the economy, with the exception of broadcasting, that justified the adoption of sectoral comprehensive competition regulation. However, an insight into government thinking as to why the telecommunications market should be singled out for competition regulation can be gleaned from the following passage, taken from a Legislative Council briefing document:

> 11 . . . Our conclusion is that it is the government's policy not to have an over-arching competition law or competition authority in Hong Kong. Because of the structural features of the telecommunications industry including high concentration levels, high barriers to entry, through high sunk costs, scarcity of radio spectrum and high levels of vertical integration, a sector-specific merger and acquisition regime is necessary to prevent over-concentration of market power in a few operators and undesirable cross-ownership.[55]

Thus, the government's rationale for its asymmetric competition policy appears to be the purported unique structural features of the telecommunications market. But if high concentration ratios, high sunk costs leading to high entry barriers and high levels of vertical integration justify regulation in this industry, why does this logic not apply equally to the gas, electricity, oil, property and supermarket markets in Hong Kong which all exhibit some or all of the same structural features. If this were the

---

[53] 'Phone rival accused of stifling competition', *South China Morning Post*, 25 April 2001.
[54] This was confirmed to the author by OFTA in July 2002.
[55] Information Technology and Broadcasting Bureau Briefing Paper to LEGCO, 3 May 2002 Ref.: ITBB CR 7/13/14 (02) Pt. 3.

justification for regulating the telecommunications market, then logic
would dictate that competition law should apply equally to other sectors
that display similar characteristics. But is this stated rationale really the explanation for sector-specific regulation? It is suggested that the underlying
reason for government activity in this sector has more to do with the fact
that the government was concerned that a once cosy, domestic and international colonial era monopoly was simply unable to operate effectively
to supply consumer and, more crucially, business demand for ever more
sophisticated telecommunication services. The ability to communicate
and trade is Hong Kong's *raison d'être*. If business could not efficiently
and cheaply take advantage of falling international call rates and upgraded
communications infrastructure, which give a small, resource-deficient,
export-dependent, trading entity its international competitive edge, then
the business sector generally in Hong Kong would suffer. Regional competitors, especially Singapore, are the fundamental reason why the government has acted contrary to its stated competition philosophy. What
was once a domestic industry has become, ineluctably, an international
one subject to the rigour of foreign competition. Other less technological, home-market industries are not subject to the same pressures and
in these cases the producer interest in high profits at low risk continues
to trump the interests of consumers due to their preponderant political
power.

The future wellbeing of the telecommunication industry is a vital concern to the service-reliant Hong Kong domestic economy. Clearly, two
matters are crucially important for the sector's continuing health – how to
ensure continued capital investment so that Hong Kong's infrastructure
remains state-of-the-art so as to provide Hong Kong service industries
with a competitive advantage. Secondly, how to maintain a vigorous and
competitive market within Hong Kong's relatively small domestic economy. Clearly, merger policy implementation and the apparently prosaic
issue of continued hobbling of PCCW by forced access to its local loop and
restriction of bundling requirements resulting from its dominance in various telecommunications markets are very challenging. PCCW wants to
be declared non-dominant[56] and forced unbundling to be ended. PCCW
says that present arrangements are a disincentive for it to invest to up-
grade its copper wires with optical fibre. But rivals say that competition
will be imperilled if PCCW's shackles are removed. PCCW has now been

---

[56] PCCW–HKT has made several applications to OFTA for declarations of non-dominance
in various telecommunications markets including business direct exchange lines (8 August
2003). Favourable decisions on this and Type II interconnection would unfetter the
presently hobbled leviathon.

released from the ex ante restraints placed on its pricing and promotional policies, in various market segments, on the basis that a market has now been established in many of the sub-telecom markets it formally controlled. OFTA announced on 13 January 2005 that PCCW would surrender its existing licence and the replacement would be subject to an *ex post* regulatory regime, so that the company no longer had to seek prior approval for promotional and tariff alterations. A system of *ex post* regulation for PCCW now prevails.[57] OFTA has a very difficult path to tread between the Scylla and Charybdis of too much regulation of the newly competitive market and too little; any regulatory mistake could seriously weaken the newly competitive market.[58]

Finally, whilst the logic of legislating for competition in telecommunications is ostensibly a rational decision, is this also true in relation to broadcasting, which did not face the same globalising forces as telecommunications? There was no WTO agreement relevant to broadcasting and the politically sensitive nature of television meant that transnational ownership is rare and subject to many national-interest exceptions. Further, broadcast media are subject to particular cultural and language issues that do not necessarily apply in the telecommunications market. The obvious question that presents itself is why broadcasting in Hong Kong has been subjected to the rigours of competition regulation, as a second exception to the policy of non-intervention espoused in the 1997 Competition Policy Response. This conundrum is considered next.

8.4 Television broadcasting

The television broadcasting market in Hong Kong has also undergone substantial change in recent years. This section will concentrate on the domestic television service market and not the stated aim of the government to foster Hong Kong as the premier regional media hub. Thus, the use of Hong Kong as a base for broadcasting operations aimed at audiences outside Hong Kong will not be discussed, as it does not affect the competition situation within the domestic Hong Kong market.

Traditionally, Hong Kong has not had a public service television broadcasting station but has had a government-owned and run radio

---

[57] http://www.ofta.gov.hk/en/tas/ftn/tas20050113.pdf.
[58] OFTA is currently consulting on the new licensing scheme for mobile phones on the expiry of existing second-generation licences, the principles and costing of local loop access charges (continued OFTA mandated prices or through commercial negotiations between network owners and service suppliers), most importantly on type II interconnection (connection by rival suppliers to fixed networks local loop) and on guidelines to define abuse of dominance. See http://www.ofta.gov.hk/frameset/home_index_eng.html.

broadcaster – Radio Television Hong Kong (RTHK) – which provides and broadcasts several Cantonese and English-language radio channels. However, RTHK does produce public service and current affairs television programmes that must be broadcast by the two licensed commercial terrestrial broadcasters – Asia Television Limited (ATV) and Television Broadcasts Limited (TVB) – as stipulated in their license conditions. RTHK is a department of the government, staffed by civil servants being editorially independent from the government, though having no legal or financial independence. RTHK relies on a block grant from the Treasury and has no means of raising revenue by way of advertising or via a specially hypothecated tax.

The domestic commercial television service market has two terrestrial free-to-air licensees ATV and TVB. They each have an English-language and a Cantonese language channel. The audience for television services is overwhelmingly dominated by demand for Cantonese-language programming; Cantonese speakers make up over 95 per cent of the Hong Kong audience as well as a huge number of viewers who have access to Hong Kong television broadcasts in neighbouring Guangdong province in the Chinese Mainland. By common consent, ATV is a distant second in the competition for the Cantonese-speaking audience, with TVB dominating this market segment. It is estimated that TVB has 75 to 80 per cent of the audience and, consequently, a corresponding share of advertising revenues.

In July 2002, Tom.Com Limited, the internet/media company controlled by Li Ka-shing and backed by his flagship Cheung Kong Holdings and Hutchinson Whampoa Limited, sought to acquire 32.75 per cent of ATV.[59] This acquisition was subject to approval under the Broadcasting Ordinance. An assessment of this development will be made later.

In addition to the two terrestrial, free-to-air, broadcasters there are also a number of domestic pay-television operators:

- PCCW/HKT previously offered a video-on-demand service via its telephone network that allows subscribers to view films of their choice at any time by using a decoder attached to the telephone socket. This service operated from 1998 to 2002 when it ceased operations for financial reasons.
- HK Cable TV owns the only dedicated cable network and operates the largest subscription cable TV operation in Hong Kong with some 560,000 subscribers, over 90 per cent of the pay-TV market.

[59] 'Tom.Com buys a one third stake in ATV', *Financial Times*, 10 July 2002; 'Tom converges on grail', *South China Morning Post*, 12 July 2002.

- Galaxy Satellite Broadcasting is a wholly owned subsidiary of TVB, the dominant terrestrial incumbent.[60] It is subject to licence conditions: that it cannot begin broadcasting operations until it has diluted TVB ownership by at least 50 per cent. It recently had to apply for a licence variation to extend the period allowed for divestiture to 28 February 2003, due to its inability to find an equity investor as a result of the economic downturn in the worldwide broadcasting industry.[61] It will begin operations by the end of 2003, having found a foreign investor.
- Pacific Digital Media, a new market entrant.
- Yes Television Hong Kong, also a new market entrant.
- In late 2003, PCCW/HKT began to offer television programming via its broadband internet system. Now TV is a bundled broadband internet, domestic telephone and television service package.
- Yet another domestic telephone/broad-band/television content service is being rolled out by Hong Kong Broad Band (HKBN), a subsidiary of CTI, a major telecommunications player in the Hong Kong market.[62]

This diversity of suppliers has come about as a result of the Broadcasting Ordinance Cap. 562, promulgated in July 2000 and, perversely, the licensing of broadband suppliers under the Telecommunications Ordinance who can now offer television programme content due to technological innovation. The law was comprehensively revised as a result of several complementary forces. In January 1996, the Consumer Council completed and published a report on the future structure of the broadcasting market.[63] The report noted that the environment for broadcasting was changing rapidly especially as a result of new technologies of transmission – cable, satellite, digital and compression technologies allowing use of the telephone system to deliver pictures, sound and the internet. The report recommended a forward-looking, flexible and streamlined regulatory regime, especially in view of the likelihood of technological convergence between the different media. Thus, an inclusive regulatory regime that was technologically neutral was suggested. The purpose of the regime should be to support a level playing field for all market players

---

[60] Complaint of predatory pricing by Hong Kong Cable Television Limited, Broadcasting Authority Preliminary Investigation Report, June 2002, Complaint Number BA1/2002.
[61] http://www.info.gov.hk/itbb/english/legco Ref. ITTB (CR) 9/4/2/(01) Pt.9, 9 July 2002.
[62] 'Pay-TV players face price war', *South China Morning* Post, 25 September 2003.
[63] Hong Kong Consumer Council, Ensuring competition in the dynamic television broadcasting market (1996).

and to prevent market domination so that local and minority interests were adequately reflected in the output of broadcasters whilst maintaining minimum broadcasting quality standards.

In particular the Council recommended:

- That the regulatory framework should be based on a division of the carrying media and the content/programme providers.
- Providers should be encouraged by the system to provide new technologies as they developed and not be obstructed by the needs of the regulatory regime adopted.
- Licence conditions should be made public.
- The adoption of safeguards to prevent market dominance by multimedia companies.
- That foreign ownership restrictions be relaxed.
- That telecommunications operators be allowed to supply video-on-demand services on condition that other providers could also use the telephone network for the same function.
- That further television broadcasting licences be granted to increase the number of market participants.
- Legislation to adopt specific anti-competitive prohibitions with tougher penalties in a new Ordinance.
- The rationalisation of license fee/royalty payments.
- The adoption of new administrative arrangements to ensure that broadcasting, telecommunications and other communication technologies were all subject to overall oversight by one government policy bureau.

The new government policy on broadcasting was announced in the 1998 White Paper Review of Television Policy.[64] In December 1998, the Executive Council approved the policy recommendations contained in the Review, which sought *inter alia* to:

- Widen programme choice.
- Encourage investment, innovation and technology transfer in the broadcasting industry (not that use of broadband internet as a delivery mode was not contemplated as part of this liberalisation).
- Ensure fair and effective competition in the provision of services.
- Protect decency and taste.
- Promote Hong Kong as the premier regional broadcasting and communications hub.

---

[64] See http://www.info.gov.hk/itbb/english/paper/doc/tv-eng.exe.

One of the key recommendations to enhance competition was the decision to allow competitors to have access to the fibre-optic cable network
that HKCTV had built since receiving a monopoly cable licence in 1993.
This would provide access to the essential network facility of the cable
infrastructure already in place, that by 2000 was accessible to 91 per cent
of households in Hong Kong.[65] Due to lack of spectrum availability, the
launch of additional terrestrial stations was very problematic. However,
with the availability of a fibre-optic cable, real competition, in terms of
consumer choice, could be introduced by competing content providers,
even though pay-TV and free-to-air TV might not be direct competitors
in the same market.[66] Needless to say that even with provisions for fixing a
fair interconnection fee the incumbent was not pleased with this decision,
as was the case of HKT in the telephone market.[67]

Another competition issue was the clear dominance of TVB in the
domestic terrestrial market. TVB apparently maintains strict contractual
non-competition clauses with all its major star performers. By signing
up potentially talented artists at an early stage in their careers, it prevents them from performing on rival channels. Both ATV and HK Cable
TV wanted to introduce a legal mechanism to forbid such onerous employment stipulations in the interests of stars being able to perform for
other providers, should they wish to do so. This would allow them to
buy the services of Canto-pop stars and thus increase audience share. The
audience-attraction power of the major Cantonese artistes is very influential in maintaining high audience-rating figures in Hong Kong and may
be likened to the star system used by the Hollywood movie industry in the
1930s to retain the services of elite performers.[68] The competitors argued
that without the freedom to employ the leading Canto-pop stars they
would never be able to compete effectively, on a level playing field, for the
majority Cantonese-speaking audience. The Executive Council chose not
to intervene in this issue but, later, in the Broadcasting Bill government
briefing note to LEGCO,[69] the government appeared to change its mind,

[65] Annual Report 2000–2001, Broadcasting Authority, http://www.hkba.org.hk/hkba/
chinese/ba_annual_report/Hkba.pdf.
[66] Decision of the EC Commission in MSG Media Services, OJ L.364/1, 31 December 1994;
Review of BSkyB's position in the wholesale pay TV market, Office of Fair Trading, London,
December 1996.
[67] 'Exco approves wide changes to TV market', *South China Morning Post*, 11 December 1998.
[68] The long exclusivity clauses have some resemblance to the situation in the George Michael
case *Panayiotou v Sony Music Entertainment (UK)*, *The Times*, 30 June 1994.
[69] *Legislative Council Brief Broadcasting Bill*, 28 January 2000 at http://www.info.gov.hk/itbb/
english/legco/doc/LegBrief-BB(Eng).doc. File ref. ITBB(CR)9/19/1(00) Pt. 7.

allowing the Broadcasting Authority (BA) to promulgate statutory guide-lines under Clause 4 of the Bill, which could address such issues.

In the Guidelines subsequently issued by the BA in February 2001, after successful passage of the Bill, the issue of artistes' contractual restrictions was specifically mentioned:

> 14. Competition issues arising from artistes' contracts are not exempted from the provisions of the Ordinance and as such are subject to the same prohibitions as any other agreement [caught by s.13(1)BO]. However, it is unlikely that any individual artiste's contract in itself could have the purpose or effect of restricting competition. Nonetheless it must be said that even individual agreements may fall foul of the competition provisions in certain circumstances depending on a number of elements. These, for example, may include the immense popularity of the artiste; the restrictive terms in the agreement being repeated in a number of similar contracts affecting other artistes; and the licensee in question being dominant in the relevant market. However, issues arising from or concerning artistes' contracts will be dealt with by the BA in the same way as any other competition case.

Another very problematic issue created by the government's sector-specific approach is that the convergence of telecommunication technology, especially broadband internet delivered by dedicated cable, via the copper telephone cable or even wireless delivery systems, is not adequately and rationally regulated. Delivery of content by such innovatory methods other than 'broadcasting' to the airwaves or a traditional dedicated tele-vision cable system, clearly calls into question the current sector-specific regime.

In this technical environment and given the Hong Kong population's love affair with technology and the voracious appetite to adopt new methods and devices, the attempt artificially to partition the converging telecommunication and broadcasting markets in Hong Kong is illogical and ineffective. The new internet television content services are all licensed under the TO and not the BO, so making the distinction superfluous and meaningless. The government's obsession with its sector-specific regula-tory mantra looks even more nonsensical in this sector than in others. By June 2004, even the government had to admit that convergence was a force that could no longer be ignored and announced that amalgamation of the BA and OFTA was under consideration along with a reformulation of the regulatory regime.[70] However, the Secretary for Commerce, Indus-try and Technology also stated that substantive change would take 'a very

[70] 'Telecoms, broadcast watchdogs may merge', *South China Morning Post*, 29 June 2004.

long time to achieve . . . years'; thus, the current regime will persist for the foreseeable future.

A final matter to be mentioned in this section is why the government concluded that broadcasting should be opened up to competition, when the globalising forces at work in telecommunications were not as clearly relevant or obvious in this market. The best answer appears to be that the government wished to enhance Hong Kong's role as not only a communication hub (hardware) but also a content hub (software). Hong Kong has traditionally had a major Chinese-language film and television production industry, with content exports to Mainland China, Taiwan, other Asian countries and to the Chinese Diaspora worldwide. Conscious of the fact that technological convergence meant that hardware without software would not be an attractive investment proposition for new entrants and also that without a clear set of pro-competition rules to create a level playing field, foreign investors might not enter the market, the government had to act.

The new BO became law on 7 July 2000.

8.4.1 Competition provisions in the Broadcasting Ordinance

The competition provisions of the BO consist of provisions very similar to, but not identical with, those contained in the TO; there are substantial differences that will be highlighted later. The BO divides the broadcasting market dependent upon whether the licensee wishes to aim predominantly at the domestic Hong Kong market, either free-to-air or by subscription, or the non-domestic market, where licences are available to a wider class of applicants. Domestic licences can be granted only to companies that are 'ordinarily resident in Hong Kong'.[71] Elaborate definitions of the nature of 'ordinarily resident' are included in the BO.[72] Thus, competition issues might arise as to the number or identity of eligible participants able to invest and participate in the domestic market. There are also elaborate definitions of 'disqualified persons'[73] who are not permitted to 'exercise control'[74] over domestic broadcasters.

These provisions clearly limit the class of persons who may be licensees or interested in a licensee. But these ownership restrictions to prevent cross-media ownership in the public interest are common in many

[71] BO s.8(4).   [72] S.8(4)(a) and (b).
[73] Schedule 1, Part 2, defines an extensive list of such persons, who include holders of another television or sound broadcasting licence, an advertising agency, a proprietor of a local newspaper, their associates or voting controllers, as defined in Schedule 1, Part 1 BO.
[74] S.3(2) of Schedule 1 BO defines this as being *inter alia* a director, principal officer, beneficial owner or a voting controller of more than 15 per cent of the voting shares in the company.

jurisdictions. Of themselves, they do not give rise to specific competition complaint and in any event the BO does allow the Chief Executive in Council to exempt applicants.[75]

One such case was in relation to Richard Li, son of Mr Li Ka-shing. On 17 October 2000, the Chief Executive exempted Mr Li from the restrictions mentioned above, in relation to his ownership of 15 per cent of PCCW/HKVOD, a company controlled by PCCW as a result of its takeover of HKT. He was *prima facie* a disqualified person because he was an associate of his father who controlled Metro, a sound-broadcasting licensee and he was also a director of Hutchinson Whampoa, the parent of Metro. A competition impact assessment was made that purported to show that the application for exemption would not adversely affect competition in the relevant television broadcasting market and exemption was given, subject to conditions requiring Mr Li to resign as a director of Hutchinson and other safeguard measures.[76]

In 2002, Tom.Com, another Li family company, sought to acquire 32.75 per cent of ATV,[77] and regulatory approval needed to be sought to exempt Mr Li Ka-shing from the disqualified-person provisions of the BO. This application would not have been as straightforward as the exemption granted to his son. Mr Li presumably would not have been prepared to give up his directorships of his flagship companies. That could have posed a dilemma for the government, as to whether to drive a coach and horses through the cross-media ownership provisions of the BO. If they had granted the exemption, the cross-ownership provisions would be brought into disrepute. Political pressure from the Democratic Party was also brought to bear on the government not to allow an exception, so as to preserve plurality of ownership in the broadcast media.[78] In the event, the transaction did not proceed, for reasons that remain murky, and so the issue was not tested.[79] In November 2002, a substantial change of ownership did occur but it had no competition implications.[80]

The principal competition provisions in the BO are to be found in s.13–16, s.25, s.26 and s.28. S.13 is a mirror provision to s.7K TO but it is not identical. The statutory language used is not congruent. Both provisions

[75] Schedule 1, s.3(3) BO.
[76] See http://www.hkba.org.hk at File ref. ITTB (CR) 9/11/3 (00) Pt 6.
[77] 'Tom.Com buys one third stake in ATV', *Financial Times*, 10 July 2002.
[78] 'Tung urged to block Tom.Com bid', *South China Morning Post*, 20 July 2002.
[79] 'Tom.Com–ATV deal collapsed on price differences', *South China Morning Post*, 21 September 2002.
[80] 'ATV share sale', *South China Morning Post*, 11 November 2002.

forbid conduct of a licensee that has the purpose or effect of preventing or substantially restricting competition but the BO also forbids mere 'distortion' of competition too. Therefore the BO provision appears to be somewhat wider than the TO provision. If so, why is this the case? Both amended Ordinances were enacted within six months of each other but identical provisions were not employed. The conduct condemned is that of the licensee. The authority may not take into account[81] the conduct of other persons. When considering breach of the prohibition in the BO this extends to direct or indirect agreement to fix prices, which is wider than the words used in the TO. The BO also includes a longer list of matters to be considered as prohibited including agreements limiting or controlling production, markets, technical developments or investment. Such terms are contractually void under the BO[82] but not the TO.

From the published statutory Guidelines it appears that, as regards anti-competitive agreements, the Authority will generally consider that restrictive agreements between parties who have less than a 25 per cent share of the relevant market will not normally have appreciable market power and so the effect on the market will not be appreciable.[83] Further, restrictive agreements were exempted from the operation of the prohibitions for a period of two years from 28 January 2000.[84]

A major innovation in the BO is that the Authority has the ability to grant individual exemption to agreements that contravene s.13(1) but the TO contains no such exempting provision. Thus, the prohibition is absolute in the TO but not in the BO, even though the conduct may be exactly the same. Whether this is a policy decision or merely a drafting oversight is difficult to ascertain. On 29 August 2002, the author questioned senior officials of the Information, Technology, Telecommunication and Broadcasting Bureau but they were unable to explain the conundrum, save to say that different drafting teams were responsible for the two ordinances and that as they were concerned with different markets, it might be appropriate to have different provisions. When the logicality of this position was put to the officials they merely repeated their rationale.

The same observations about the limited range of the prohibitions – the conduct must 'affect' a television service market and only a licensee is liable

---

[81] S.13(2) BO.
[82] S.13(3) ibid.
[83] Para. 57(c) of the Guidelines for the application of the competition provisions of the Broadcasting Ordinance, 16 February 2001 at http://www.hkba.org.hk/hkba/english/guides/guideeng.doc.
[84] Ibid. Para. 13.

to penalty – apply to both Ordinances. However, the BO contains a very cryptic provision in s.15(1): 'the conduct of an associate of a licensee or the position of the associate in a television programme service market, may be considered for the purpose of section 13 or 14'. Presumably this is an evidentiary matter and does not affect the extent of coverage of the prohibition to an associate of the licensee. It would appear that an associate would also be under an obligation to supply relevant information to the Authority in a competition investigation of a licensee's activities under s.28(1).

S.14 prohibits abuse of a dominant position. The prohibition and the definition of dominance is the same as that found in the TO, as are the examples given of potentially abusive conduct, save that the formulation of the purpose or effects of the licensee's conduct is the same as in s.13 above, namely it too includes distortion of competition as also being prohibited.

S.15 has no equivalent in the TO. Firstly, it provides that the conduct of an associate of a licensee may be taken into account in assessing the activities of the licensee; this was referred to above. It is, however, s.15(2) that is really interesting in that it creates a new statutory tort providing a private right of action for a person who suffers loss as a result of the anti-competitive activities of a licensee or of any other breach of a licence condition:

> S.15(2) A person sustaining loss or damage from a breach of s.13(1) or s.14(1), or a breach of a licence condition, determination, or direction relating to that section, may bring an action for damages, an injunction or other appropriate remedy, order or relief against a licensee who is in breach.
>
> (3) No action may be brought under subsection (2) more than 3 years after
> (a) the commission of the breach; or
> (b) the imposition of a penalty in relation to the breach, whichever is the later.
>
> (4) For the avoidance of doubt, it is hereby declared that the breach ... occurs when the Broadcasting Authority forms the opinion referred to in s.13(1) or S.14(1) respectively.

There is no parallel provision in the TO.[85] It is interesting to see the express creation of a private right of action resulting from breach of a competition

[85] The author spoke to the draftsman of this provision on 21 October 2002. He confirmed that this provision was inserted as a government amendment to the bill but he had no recollection of the policy reason for the government decision.

provision. This type of right has only been developed by case law with regards to EC law[86] but has always been an integral part of US anti-trust jurisprudence.[87] Proving breach of statutory duty might be problematic on evidential grounds but if the Authority has previously found a breach utilising its statutory powers of investigation (see below), the issue may not be relevant. However, it may still be very difficult for a plaintiff to prove causation and quantum of damage or for a court accurately to assess the evidence, given that Hong Kong courts have little or no experience of taking the pure economic evidence that might be proffered in competition law cases. The remedies are much wider than simply damages as injunctive relief may also be sought. It is unfortunate that the injured party has to take all the time and expense of a civil action; granting the Broadcasting Authority power to award a remedy to an injured private party might have been a more convenient way of providing adequate recourse, though the technical issues alluded to above concerning causation and quantum would apply equally to an administrative adjudication. The Consumer Council recommended in its final 1997 Competition Report that a new Competition Authority should have power to award compensatory damage to an injured private party.[88] There have been no cases under this provision.

S.16 provides the Authority with power to issue a 'cease and desist' order to a licensee in breach of the competition provisions. There is no direct equivalent under the TO but the Telecommunications Authority does have power under s.36B(1)(a)(ii) to issue directions to a licensee to comply with the provisions of the TO.

As regards investigatory powers, s.25(1) provides power to the Authority to require a licensee or any other person 'employed or engaged in connection with the relevant business' or any 'associate' (as defined above) who has relevant information to produce any documents or records of any sort for inspection, removal or copying and provide any explanation of them as requested. These powers seem to extend to persons who are wholly unconnected to the licensee's business, arguably non-licensees who may be engaged in collusive activities in a market related to a broadcasting services market but which can affect a relevant market.

---

[86] *Garden Cottage Foods Ltd. v Milk Marketing Board* 1984 A.C. 130.

[87] Sherman Act 1890 – 15 U.S.C.

[88] Apparently this new statutory tort was not government policy when the Broadcasting Bill was drafted but was inserted during the committee stage in LEGCO. Information provided in answer from the ITT Bureau on 29 August 2002.

S.25(3) enables a magistrate to issue a search warrant but only if access to any premises has first been requested and denied or where denial of access is likely. Presumably this is not limited merely to premises owned or controlled by a licensee but to premises occupied by other relevant persons.

S.26 provides a wider power to obtain information from any person who may have information relevant to a breach of the BO. The Authority must serve notice in writing on that person specifying the nature of the information sought and giving a date for compliance. The person may make representations as to why the information should not be disclosed and this must be considered by the Authority. If the disclosure request is ignored, the Authority must serve a notice stating that it will seek a court order for production from a magistrate. Failure to provide the information ordered or providing false information or destruction or alteration of information is an offence subject to a criminal fine and/or up to two years' imprisonment. This is a mirror provision to s.36D TO.

S.28 provides for penalties that may be imposed for breach of the competition provisions. The administrative penalties are similar to those contained in s.36C TO, save that there is no provision for publication of information or corrective advertisements as provided for in s.36C (3A) TO. The ability to seek greater penalties from the High Court for serious breaches of up to a 10 per cent of relevant turnover or a HK$2 million fine, are also similar to the TO provisions.

Another anomaly is, however, that the relieving provision in s.36C(5) of the TO is not repeated in the BO; the Authority here does not have to give a licensee in breach a reasonable time to remedy his conduct before being able to apply a penalty. The Authority has also intimated[89] in its statutory investigation guidelines that it would be minded to impose either a statutory warning, or in more serious cases, a direction, or in very serious cases or where a warning or direction has been ignored, a financial penalty applied either through administrative action or by an application to the High Court. Revocation of a licence is also not ruled out. This reticent approach to enforcement may be counterproductive as it may send a weak signal to industry players. Perhaps a more vigorous stance on dominance and collusive practices would have been preferable.

---

[89] Para. 41 of the Competition investigation procedures, 16 February 2001 at http://www.hkba.org.hk/hkba/english/guides/procedeng.doc.

There are two further major areas of divergence between the provisions of the TO and the BO. First, the treatment of appeals from competition decisions of the Broadcasting Authority to those of the Telecommunications Authority. As we have seen above, in the TO a specialised independent competition Appeals Board has been established. There is no such provision in the BO. Appeal here is merely administrative to the Chief Executive in Council under s.34 BO. The elaborate safeguards of an independent, authoritative body built into the TO provisions are missing from the BO, as is the ability to apply to the Court of Appeal for determination of a point of law. This is a significant weakness in the structure as regards procedural and substantive fairness in the adjudicative process. An independent counterweight and oversight of the executive's administrative powers is always desirable. In the BO, the appellate procedure is entirely 'in house', with no independent appeal route, save for an action for judicial review, with all the limitations inherent in such actions. It is difficult to understand why the TO competition Appeals Board was simply not empowered to hear competition appeals under the BO too. This would have made eminent sense. Again there is either some important policy reason for this omission or it may simply be a drafting error. Policy reason might include the maintenance of the fiction that sector-specific regulation is workable, even in sectors as closely aligned as telecommunications and broadcasting. In fact the author raised this issue with the HKSAR government officials responsible for broadcasting at a meeting on 29 August 2002. They confirmed that in the government's view broadcasting and telecommunication were distinct sectors and there was no necessity to have congruent appeal procedures; sector-specific regulation was the policy instrument adopted by the government and they refused to accept that this was an illogical or irrational position to adopt.

The second major area of difference is that of the lack of a specific merger control provision in the BO. The BO provisions are similar to the provisions found previously in the TO but they have now been amended by the 2002 Telecommunications (Amendment) Ordinance. The previous TO provisions had been found to be unworkable. Exactly the same argument can be made for the current BO licence provisions but the government has not sought simultaneously to amend the BO provisions utilising the 2002 Telecommunication Bill to do so. This appears to be yet another casualty of the misguided sectoral approach to competition regulation. Again, the responsible officials at the Policy Bureau confirmed that this indeed was the government position; they again refused to accept that any illogicality was involved.

8.4.2 Competition cases under the new Broadcasting
Ordinance provisions

Since the amendments to the Ordinance came into effect in 2000 there
has only been one relevant competition case. In March 2002, three new
entrants to the pay-TV service market, Yes Television, Galaxy Satellite
and Pacific Digital Media, lodged a complaint with the Broadcasting Authority. They alleged that HKCTV, the dominant incumbent with over
90 per cent of the pay-TV market in Hong Kong, had abused its dominant position by engaging in predatory pricing designed to weaken the
new players and/or eliminate them from the market. In June 2002, the
Authority issued a Preliminary Enquiry Report.[90] Under the procedures
set out in the statutory Guidelines issues in February 2001,[91] the Authority will undertake a preliminary investigation to determine whether there
is a case to answer and whether to proceed to a full investigation. From
para. 23 of the Guidelines, this is anticipated to be a non-threatening investigation that envisages: 'an exchange of correspondence or meetings
with the complainant and/or the subject of the complaint and/or other
interested parties or potentially interested parties as well as reference to
precedents in previous investigations'. This approach seems to confuse
the role of an honest broker or mediator with that of an investigatory
body that needs to establish facts, and to collect and preserve evidence of
wrong doing as its primary objective. This is because the person under
investigation has every reason to dispose of evidence and frustrate the
enquiry, given that its actions may not only be a statutory tort giving
rise to a claim for compensation but could also, theoretically, result in a
huge fine and/or the revocation of the broadcasting licence. The 'cards on
the table' approach, in which everyone co-operates in a friendly fashion
to dispose of the difficulty, seems somewhat inappropriate.

In this case, the complainants were about to launch their competing
services following the liberalisation of the broadcasting regime. Yes TV
and Pacific Digital commenced operations on 22 February 2002. On 21
January, HKCTV announced a promotional package whereby it reduced
its monthly subscription from HK$298 to HK$198 for new customers who
subscribed before 14 March 2002, effective until 31 December 2002. This
was a 34 per cent discount on the normal service fee. On 8 March 2002,

<hr/>

[90] Complaint of Predatory Pricing by Hong Kong Cable Television Limited. Complaint Number BA1/2002 at http://www.hkba.org.hk/hkba/english/whats_new/PER.doc.
[91] Guidelines for the application of the competition provision of the Broadcasting Ordinance,
16 February, 2001 http://www.hkba.org.hk/hkba/english/guides/guideeng.doc.

another promotional offer was announced, effective for new customers who subscribed before 30 June 2002, whereby their monthly service fee would be reduced to HK\$166.80 per month for one year. The complainants accused HKCTV of predatory conduct. After seeking information on a voluntary basis, the Authority issued its Preliminary Report and found that HKCTV had not breached the statutory prohibitions.

The analysis carried out considered that the relevant market was the pay-TV market, irrespective of method of delivery excluding the free-to-air television sector. This finding concurred with numerous similar determinations in other jurisdictions. Unsurprisingly, HKCTV attempted to argue that the market was the total TV market but this contention was rejected. Given that HKCTV had 560,000 out of 600,000 subscribers to pay-TV services, HKCTV was found to be dominant. The Authority considered that in order to succeed a complainant had to show that the conduct complained of was the direct cause of competitive injury. The complainants were unwilling or unable to supply such evidence that they had been weakened or potentially eliminated from the market and thus, decided the Authority, without further evidence of the intent or purpose to prevent, distort or substantially restrict competition, HKCTV was not in breach of the statutory provisions. The Authority was fortified in that conclusion by the fact that HKCTV had in previous years launched even deeper price-cut promotions at a time when it was a single monopoly provider.

Whilst the reasoning of the Authority appears to be superficially acceptable, it does seem to exhibit one substantial weakness. This is because the decision was predicated by caveats that the conclusion was justified given that there was no evidence provided by the complainants and 'on the information available' of a malign purpose on the part of HKCTV. It must be obvious that any evidence of such an unlawful purpose would not have been available to the complainants. Such information, if it existed, would be contained in internal memoranda or e-mails or in conversations between the senior management of the incumbent monopolist, who had every incentive to seek to strangle the newcomers to its formerly exclusive market at birth. It seems that the investigation undertaken was flawed. To have been effective it should have been essential that a more pro-active, sceptical, less cosy and more forthright approach be taken. Forewarning the potential malefactor that you have a suspicion and then asking him voluntarily to provide evidence to convict himself strains credulity too far. If this is the investigatory model to be adopted in future cases, no breaches of the competition provisions will ever be substantiated.

8.4.3 Reflections on the telecommunications and broadcasting competition regimes

The structural and investigatory weaknesses identified in this and the previous section demonstrate substantial problems in the current legislative and administrative structures set up to regulate competition in the broadcasting and telecommunication industries in Hong Kong. Legislative amendment to align the regimes in these complementary markets is urgently required to rationalise the current illogical differences between the two. The fact that the government has legislated three times in three years in these sectors and still cannot even manage to produce a coherent set of principles and procedures to govern these markets is lamentable.

The government maintains, without giving reasons, that the regulatory incongruities observed are due to policy decisions and substantive differences between the telecommunications and broadcasting markets. However, it is submitted that the contradictions inherent in these two sets of regulations, concerning two closely related sectors but subject to the illogical and irrational sectoral approach, are all too easy to see, if not to understand. The government's muddled approach to these issues again shows the need for a clear and comprehensive competition policy in these two industries backed up by a general competition statute but the government is apparently blind to the logic of such arguments. The key question is why does the government adopt this illogical and irrational approach.

8.5 Conclusion

The bankruptcy and confusion of government policy in the competition field has been amply demonstrated in these three regulated industries. No clear set of principles, no legislative uniformity in treatment, indeed none at all in relation to electricity, illuminates the government's thinking or, more accurately, the lack of it. This demonstrates that the objective of light-touch, non-interventionist government committed to free-market principles but without a mechanism to protect the competitive process is a chimera. The failure to adopt a congruent legislative framework simply emphasises the seriousness of the policy failure.

One might argue that as far as electricity is concerned, at least the government has kept the lights on in Hong Kong and it has not suffered the chaos of power blackouts that have afflicted California's deregulated market. But this is disingenuous; California's problems stem from a botched legislative framework, not from a failure of markets to supply power. Hong Kong has paid a very high price for keeping the lights on and will continue to do so until at least 2008. There is no competition in the electricity market and unlikely to be any in the near future. Competition policy simply does not apply in this market; there are two private monopolies that have effectively guaranteed rates of return, whatever the vicissitudes of the economy as a whole.

As regards the telecommunications and the broadcasting markets, on a practical level the government's policy of liberalisation has been a success. There is much more choice at lower cost than before the structural changes began in earnest a decade ago. But is this success due to enlightened, pro-active government policy or simply a function of the twin engines of reform in the communications market globally, coupled with rapid technological advances and a more liberal international trade in services, especially after the successful creation of the WTO. Apportioning the laurels is problematic but it would be impossible to lay the success of the liberalisation at the door of the government's sectoral competition policy. Firstly, the overlap and artificial separation of the regulatory regimes is a function of the political requirement for separate sets of rules and administrative responsibilities to bolster the policy of sectoral regulation. This has even been confirmed to the author by the civil servants concerned.[92] Secondly, as can be appreciated from the analysis proffered above, the technical faults with the existing statutory schemes are serious and obvious.

In telecommunications and broadcasting, the lack of congruity between two sets of recently updated rules in markets that have many similarities, is perplexing to say the least. The coverage of the statutes is artificially limited – in terms of jurisdiction, merger and acquisition applications and appeal procedures. There appear to be two possible explanations. Either the policy decisions were not well thought out and the legislative draftsmen simply prepared the provisions as instructed by the policy bureaux, who did not co-ordinate their legislative schemes; or, the official philosophy of sectoral regulation required that no regard is taken of other legislative provisions to preserve the philosophical coherence of the segmented sectoral policy. A third reason might be purely political, namely, the industry lobbies in each case had different concerns that the government heeded in drafting the legislation.

---

[92] Meeting 29 August 2002 and in e-mail confirmations.

Extensive correspondence and a subsequent meeting with the government officials confirmed that indeed the true explanation was a mixture of rigid application of the sector-specific approach and administrative procedures in promulgating draft legislation designed to ensure that the end result was distinct, no matter how inconvenient or irrational. This discovery was a surprising insight into HKSAR government policy making.

Finally, therefore, what assessment can be made of the government's policy of sectoral regulation? A disinterested observer might opine that in electricity it has been a relative failure with great waste of scarce economic resources. In telecommunications and broadcasting it has been a relative success, not because of the extant regulations but in spite of them; allowing more entrants into the market has had a corrective effect in removing many monopoly rents. But active competition policy appears to have had relatively little effect to date, though recent cases seem to show that this may be changing.

However, the absence of a general competition law is a glaring weakness, as has been amply demonstrated by the various telecommunications cases analysed above. The sector-specific policy is riddled with incongruities, inconsistencies, and lacunae rendering it, at best, sub-optimal and, at worst, fatally flawed.

Taiwan – the Third China

9.1 Introduction

The Republic of China on Taiwan is the final part of Greater China that requires examination as to the type and nature of competition regulation. As we shall see, Taiwan has a well-developed and comprehensive competition law system that has been in place for over twelve years. Therefore, it is possible not only to chart the genesis of competition law but also to assess both the political and economic context within which the law has operated and, crucially, whether a conclusion can be drawn that the law has been effectively implemented. Further, the examination of Taiwan's experience may provide some clues as to the essential prerequisites that are needed for successful competition law adoption, should a judicious analysis of the facts lead us to the conclusion that Taiwanese adoption has been a success. Contrast of the Taiwanese situation with that pertaining in Mainland China and Hong Kong may also reveal some essential features of politico-economic structures that enable the postulation of a satisfactory explanation of the competition policy situation extant there. Analysis of the Taiwanese experience may also help in the creation of a predictive model as to whether competition policy and legal enforcement will be effective in any given jurisdiction that proposes to adopt a competition regime; this theme will be further elaborated in the next chapter.

9.2 History and politics

The history of Greater China (Mainland, Hong Kong, Macau and Taiwan) is inextricably intertwined, as is the political impulse, particularly on the part of the Beijing government, to reunite the fractured polity of China. Indeed, Taiwan is regarded by China as a renegade province.

Taiwan was partially colonised by the Dutch East India Company (VOC) in 1624. The Spanish also established out-posts on the island from 1626 but were expelled by the Dutch in 1642. The Dutch authorities encouraged ethnic Chinese immigration to the island in the 1630s to provide labour to grow sugar cane. Taiwan became an important entrepôt-trading centre and came to represent 26 per cent of the VOC's profits by 1649. However, harsh treatment of the inhabitants by the Dutch caused a revolt in 1652, resulting in a bloody repression of the insurrectionists. The overthrow of the Ming dynasty in China caused much political instability and Ming loyalists contrived to resist the Manchu usurpers for many years. In 1662, the Dutch were forced to abandon Taiwan by a Ming loyalist who used Taiwan as a base for anti-Manchu operations until 1683, when a Chinese imperial force finally ended the resistance. Thus, Taiwan became part of the Chinese empire in the late seventeenth century. In the late nineteenth century, Taiwan was ceded to Japan following the Sino-Japanese war of 1894–5. The island was re-occupied by the nationalist Chinese government in 1945 as a result of Japan's defeat in the Second World War. In 1949, as a result of losing the civil war in China, the nationalist Kuo Ming Tang (KMT) government decamped to Taiwan.[1]

The return of Chinese administration after fifty years of Japanese colonisation was not an unalloyed success. Taiwanese natives regarded the Nationalist army as little better than another occupying force. Between 1945 and early 1947, the Nationalist troops sent to re-occupy Taiwan, caused huge discontent as a result of ill discipline, brutality, corruption and outright theft. Economic mismanagement by incompetent government officials also inflamed animosity. Local resentment exploded in February 1947. A trivial incident quickly escalated into widespread rioting. The KMT authorities responded with a reign of terror during which many thousands of civilians were killed. These inauspicious events fostered lingering resentment by the native Taiwanese against the huge influx of Mainland KMT supporters who fled, with the ROC government, to Taiwan as a result of the end of the civil war on the Mainland and the Nationalist defeat in 1949.

Recognised, promoted and sponsored as the legitimate government of the whole of China, principally by the United States, Taiwan endured forty years of statist, authoritarian KMT government with little political freedom. The island was governed by a set of emergency decrees that suspended the operation of parts of the ROC constitution. Slowly however, the politics of dictatorship was superseded by the politics of democracy.

---

[1] A short official history of Taiwan can be found at www.ftc.gov.tw/taiwan-website/5-gp/yearbook/chpt03.htm#2.

The rump of the ROC on Taiwan was subject to the nominal authority of the 1946 ROC Constitution but in reality Taiwan was run by the KMT as a one-party state. Similarly to the position on the Mainland, the KMT party hierarchy were also the principal officers of state. The KMT was essentially an alien political force on Taiwan, given that until the late 1970s almost all positions of importance were occupied by Mainland migrants or their descendants, rather than by indigenous Taiwanese natives. Integration of the Taiwanese into the government and party apparatus was a sensitive issue given the disastrous beginning of KMT rule after the Second World War but gradually the native population began to occupy influential party and government positions. The KMT remained the only legal political party until the formation of the Democratic Progress Party (DPP) in 1986, which primarily provided an alternative political vehicle for disgruntled Taiwanese natives, who had come to consider Taiwan and the Mainland as separate entities.

The organisation of the state followed recognisably Western notions of a separation of powers and provided for a government structure consisting of an Executive President, whose lack of formal powers was easily supplemented by his *de facto* control of both the KMT party machine and the armed forces. Secondly, the Executive Yuan, headed by a Premier, who oversaw government administration but was not a member of the legislature and neither were his Cabinet colleagues. The Legislative Yuan held primary law-making powers, whilst the Judicial Yuan embodied a formally recognised judicial branch of government with powers over the conduct of all civil and criminal cases.

In addition to these familiar organisations of government, the ROC constitution also provided for an Examination Yuan that administered admission to the civil service and the employment terms of public servants. Finally, a Control Yuan was constituted to act as a watchdog over the other organs of government. This system had been originally devised by Sun Yat-sen in the 1920s.

As a result of emergency legislation, premised on the imminent threat of invasion and the continuing 'Communist Rebellion' on the Mainland, election to government offices was suspended indefinitely until it was possible to hold elections throughout Mainland China. Taiwanese natives concluded that this mechanism was a convenient pretext to forestall the expression of discontent with KMT rule on Taiwan and also to ensure continued Mainlander dominance of the political system.

Upon his death, Generalissimo Chiang Kai-shek was succeeded in 1975 as President by Yen Chia-kon who was replaced by Chiang's son,

Chiang Ching-kuo, in 1978. Ching-kuo's political pedigree stretched back to KMT rule on the Mainland and he had been an instrumental figure in the belated attempt to reduce corruption levels in late 1940s Shanghai. He had also promoted the integration of Taiwanese natives into the KMT. This background partly explains the decision to introduce radical political reform in Taiwan taken at a KMT Central Committee meeting in early 1986, as urged by Chiang Ching-kuo. However, it was not until October of that year that an announcement was made that martial law was to be repealed, the Legislative Yuan reformed and that new political parties would be legalised. The reasons for this bold decision were varied. Firstly, in 1984, a dissident journalist was murdered in California by a Triad hit-squad, which had been commissioned to conduct the assassination by Taiwan's military intelligence organisation. This incident caused huge damage to Taiwan's reputation in America and led to suggestions that America should cancel future sales of military equipment to Taiwan, which would have had potentially disastrous consequences for Taiwanese security.

Secondly, in 1985, a financial scandal erupted involving a savings and loan organisation owned by a senior KMT official, who was subsequently charged with fraud. The collapse of the Tenth Credit Co-operative led to a run on other financial institutions, threatening a full-scale banking crisis. These series of events were linked to pervasive corruption in the KMT and the government, so causing a collapse in public confidence in both the probity and competence of government.

Both these incidents – an out-of-control intelligence organisation and endemic corruption – were all too reminiscent of the political environment in the post-war Chinese Mainland. There, KMT abuses, coupled with military defeat, desertion and hyper-inflation ultimately created the conditions that led to a collapse in morale and the overthrow of the KMT government.

Chiang Ching-kuo presumably came to the view that the great economic success of Taiwan since 1945 was insufficient to maintain long-term political stability and that a widening of the political support base was essential to ensure the survival of the ROC on Taiwan. Having inherited his father's mantle, Chiang Ching-kuo was able to impose the political liberalisation, notwithstanding reservations by the KMT leadership and the military. He began moves towards democratisation in 1987 by lifting the state of martial law, which had pertained since 1949. Amendment of various repressive laws, the repeal of the Temporary Provisions of 1948 which had suspended the constitution and the ending of the 'Period of National Mobilisation for the Suppression of the Communist Rebellion' in May

1990, all moved Taiwan away from the authoritarian stance of the KMT. On Chiang's death in 1988, Lee Teng-hui assumed the Presidency of the ROC. A power struggle subsequently divided the KMT into conservative and liberal factions, but the liberals were able to hold the ring. Lee Teng-hui permitted the consolidation of press freedom, opposition political parties and civil society.

The new President also inaugurated a constitutional convention with broad-based participation, which resolved that the fundamentally divisive issues of reunification with the Mainland and outright Taiwanese independence would not be discussed, for fear of provoking the PRC into a military reaction. The Convention decided to repeal the Temporary Provisions that had suspended parts of the ROC Constitution. Retention of the structure of the 1946 ROC Constitution and the extension of democratic elections to local political posts were also endorsed. As a result of a judicial interpretation of the Constitution, all legislative members were required to resign and new elections were called.

The democratic movement had coalesced around middle-class professionals. Elections for mayoral offices, then the full elections for the legislature were held in 1991 and 1992, with a presidential election in 1996.[2] In 2000, the leader of the opposition DPP, Chen Shui-bian, became the first head of state to obtain office through a peaceful transition of political power in 4,000 years of Chinese history. As a result of the 2000 election, the Taiwanese political system came of age; it marked the 'consolidation' of the country's democracy, defined by most scholars as a transfer of political power to an opposition party.[3] The DPP, the main opposition party to the KMT, was the principal beneficiary of the liberalisation policies of the mid-1980s. The success of its leader in the 2000 and 2004 elections has had serious repercussions in respect of relations with the Mainland. The PRC authorities view the DPP as fundamentally opposed to reunification. The level of overt hostility towards Taiwan's political settlement has markedly increased during the years of the DPP ascendancy.

The extraordinary events of the 2004 Presidential election, with an apparent assassination attempt on the lives of both the President and Vice President on the eve of the poll by a mysterious assailant, continue to cause serious consequences. The KMT alleged that the whole event

---

[2] For a detailed account of the process of democratisation see Tien Hung Mao and Chu Yun-han, 'Building democracy in Taiwan', *The China Quarterly*, Issue 148, 1141–70 (1996); Keith Maguire, *The rise of modern Taiwan*, Aldershot: Ashgate (1998).

[3] J. F. Copper, 'Taiwan: democracy's gone awry?' *Journal of Contemporary China* (2003), 12 (34), pp. 145–62 at p. 145.

was staged so as to create a wave of sympathy for the incumbent DPP President, in order to skew a very tight election result in his favour. The apparent assassination attempt also triggered an immediate mobilisation of all army units, so preventing many KMT-supporting military personnel from voting in the election that was held the following day. Again, the KMT has alleged that this was all part of a political strategy to ensure that the DPP retained the highest offices of state.

The election result, a win by the DPP candidates by the narrowest possible margin, inflamed political passions in Taiwan with suspicions of a Machiavellian plot to retain power at any price and created scenes of grave public disorder. Additionally, allegations of electoral fraud have also been made by the KMT against the successful DPP candidates. Despite a court-supervised recount of the votes, Chen Shui-bian has retained the Presidency. The elections were followed by weeks of angry protests from KMT supporters and this whole series of events has clouded belief in the legitimacy of the DPP's second electoral success. Recently parliamentary enquiries into the whole affair have been announced but whether the truth of this matter will ever be discovered is currently impossible to say. Various legal challenges have been made to the electoral result and final determination of them may take until 2006.[4]

A central element of Chen Shui-bian's 2004 manifesto was a radical reform of Taiwan's political machinery including a constitutional review. This has caused consternation in the PRC. Mainland officials have increased both the volume and frequency of bellicose political rhetoric. Some have even stated openly that any political changes that appear to move Taiwan towards a declaration of separate statehood would be sufficient to trigger an immediate military response.

Thus, it seems that whilst Taiwan's political institutions are democratically constituted, there are clear weaknesses in the maturity of the political system and the populist pronouncements of the DPP tread a very fine line between continued peace and maintenance of the *modus vivendi* with the Mainland and a disastrous military conflagration.

9.3 The nature of Taiwan's democracy and institutions of government

In order to determine the nature of Taiwan's political system, several factors need to be considered. Taiwan does have representative government,

---

[4] Several challenges to the electoral results have been made and are subject to the appeal process. See http://news.bbc.co.uk/1/hi/world/asia-pacific/3981259.stm.

chosen by open elections with universal suffrage with voters having a plurality of candidates representing different political parties. An independent assessment of political structures and the functioning of civil society can be found in the Transparency International's Global Corruption Report 2004.[5] It notes peaceful democratic political evolution and the growth of civil society. Similar views are also echoed in the 2002 Index of Economic Freedom.[6] However, it must be added that Taiwan's democracy is not perfect. Political institutions are immature and serious corruption remains a significant problem. The Chen government has sought to take more effective measures to deal with it. The Global Corruption Report's Corruption Perception Index 2004 ranks Taiwan at thirtieth position out of 133 jurisdictions surveyed, with no. 1 being the least corrupt. By comparison, Hong Kong was ranked fourteenth and China sixty-sixth. As Rowan Callick noted in the Global Corruption Report 2001 at pp. 12–13: 'Vote buying persists in Taiwan but Chen's victory demonstrated that both the practise and the effect [of corrupt political practices] have waned. However, the problem of 'Black-Gold' politics remains a serious challenge.'[7]

Further, some observers contend that the Taiwanese public has become disillusioned with democracy as the election of the first Chen government coincided with a significant economic recession caused by the collapse of the hi-tech bubble in 2000. The computer hardware industry in Taiwan was severely affected and the global economic slowdown exacerbated Taiwan's economic malaise. As a direct result of this recession, the Taipei stock market fell by about 50 per cent from the high-water mark of 2000. Copper argues that the first Chen government mishandled the economy through a mixture of incompetence and inexperience, the constitutional-political system is faulty and the election of the Chen government has lead to a dangerous form of 'majority tyranny and ethnic discrimination'.[8] The original inhabitants of Taiwan are the principal supporters of Chen's DPP, who had previously chafed under successive KMT governments that favoured KMT supporters from the Mainland who had decamped to the island in 1949. Copper further argues that Chen's original election as President polarised Taiwan society, heightened ethnic tensions and caused a haemorrhage of capital out of Taiwan and into China, where manufacturers can take advantage of lower land and

[5] Transparency International Global Corruption Report 2004. See http://www.globalcorruption.org.
[6] http://www.heritage.org.   [7] See http://www.globalcorruption.org/index.shtml.
[8] Copper, Taiwan: democracy's gone awry, pp. 145–62.

labour costs, so causing a 'hollowing-out' of the economic base and feeding public discontent with the political system. This view is supported by a Beijing-based political scientist Wei Pan, who suggests that: 'Today's Taiwan seems in deep social strife and that is out of a very primitive kind of partisan politics – partisan politics of sub-ethnic groups, which has made nearly all politicians notorious.'[9] However, this analysis is not universally accepted. Friedman argues that support for both the DPP and KMT is not determined exclusively on ethnic lines,[10] with considerable ethnic-majority support for the KMT and that the democratic transition has allowed the peaceful political evolution of the island. Thus, it appears that the perception of the success of democracy on Taiwan is clearly divided, but it is also clear that the institution exists in a functional form.

Taiwan also has sound, constitutionally mandated, state institutions with a functional separation of powers. The Constitution of the ROC provides for the establishment of separate government organs and it appears that they do function independently as legislative, executive and judicial branches, with the addition of the Control Yuan, an overall supervisory organ that monitors the performance of all other branches of government. The institutional structures appear to be both rational and legally legitimate.

9.4 The judicial system and the rule of law

Taiwan appears to have a reasonably reliable judicial system but judicial partiality, incompetence and corruption are present, a legacy of forty years of KMT patronage. Measures to improve the calibre of the judiciary are in place but more needs to be done. In 1997, the *Taiwan Human Rights Report*[11] highlighted cases of judicial corruption and political interference in individual cases which its authors suggested led to a widespread lack of public confidence in the judicial system. The Chen government has instituted a high-level reform of judicial training and has passed several measures aimed at improving the quality of the judicial system and ensuring high standards of adjudication and ethics. The President of the Judicial Yuan (the Chief Justice) has stated that

---

[9] Wei Pan, 'Toward a consultative rule of law regime in China', *Journal of Contemporary China* (2003), 12 (34), pp. 3–43 at p. 32.

[10] Edward Friedman, 'A comparative politics of democratization in China', *Journal of Contemporary China* (2003), 12 (34), pp. 103–23.

[11] http://www.tahr.org.tw/data/report97/eng97/index.html.

his objectives since his appointment in 1999 have been: 'the protection of human rights, the improvement of judicial efficiency, accessibility, and transparency, and, finally the promotion of fairness and judicial integrity'.[12]

He acknowledges failings in the integrity of some judges and gave as an example the involvement of a judge in a prostitution business who was dismissed and subjected to criminal prosecution. As regards judicial ethics, some seventy-four cases have been investigated by internal self-disciplinary committees, with sixty-three persons subject to sanction since 2000. However, despite the ongoing reforms, problems persist especially in relation to the competence of some judicial personnel and severe problems in bringing to justice politicians accused of corrupt practices. A scandal involving vote buying in a Kaoshung City Council election took over ten years to come to court. The Judicial Yuan has accused sixteen judges of incompetence in relation to delaying trials in twenty-nine cases without justification. Further, in another political corruption case which began in 1989, a DPP legislator was finally imprisoned in 2003 for six years. All these examples demonstrate the range of outstanding problems. However, the determination of the DPP government to reform the system is seen as bearing fruit and the seriousness of the Chen administration in improving the justice system does not appear to be in doubt, since, despite a very thin parliamentary majority, the government did nothing to prevent one of its own parliamentary deputies being convicted and sentenced.[13]

As regards legal professionals, lawyers' qualifications are generally up to internationally accepted standards and a four- or five-year university-level legal education is required. There is an independent legal profession. The qualification system follows civilian practice with law graduates choosing either to take the civil service examination, the judicial – prosecutorial examination or the lawyers' practising examination. Judges follow the civilian method of promotion through the courts' hierarchy but at the apex of the system the fifteen Grand Justices are selected by the Taiwanese President and may be judges, prosecutors, practising lawyers or academics.[14]

Thus, it is suggested that, whilst Taiwan's judicial and legal system is not spotless, it does have enough of the necessary hallmarks to characterise it as effective in ensuring that there is an operable rule of law.

---

[12] Wang Yueh-sheng, President of the Judicial Yuan, http://www.judicial.gov.tw.
[13] Editorial Comment: 'Taiwan's human right improving', *Taipei Times*, 4 February 2003.
[14] http://www.loc.gov/law/glin/taiwan/html.

9.5 Competence of executive government

The performance of the current democratically elected government is not without its critics. Inexperience, factionalism, economic recession and the perils of navigating the uncharted waters of a fully democratic system, make it difficult to arrive at a definitive conclusion as to the competence of the present administration. Clearly, promoting communal interests, populism and continuing corruption problems are factors which could potentially tarnish or prevent the competent exercise of government power. But these are pressures that many elected regimes have to face, to some extent or other; they are part of the fabric of pluralistic politics. In any event, the elected politicians have the unelected civil service to bolster any deficiency in administrative skill. Specific consideration will be given later to the enforcement of competition law, as well as to the structure and competence of the Taiwan Fair Trade Commission.

9.6 Civil society in Taiwan

The 1987 liberalisations in Taiwan set the stage for the growth of civil society. A critical mass of middle-class citizens had developed by that time, which exerted political pressure through the pro-democracy movement. Taiwan now exhibits all the signs of having a thriving civil society – as of 2002 there were ninety-nine political parties registered with the Ministry of the Interior of which thirty-four were national, though only three were very significant.[15] In addition to political parties, non-governmental organisations of all types flourish, the media is free and there is actual freedom of association, respectable universities and considerable academic capacity to support the formation of competition policy and to provide academic courses to train lawyers and officials. For example, there are at least ten full professors of competition law teaching at various universities and three research institutes that have a specialisation in competition law.[16] Therefore, it can be reasonably suggested that Taiwan does indeed have a vibrant civil society that can monitor government action effectively, promote consumer interests and bolster the creation of a pro-competition ethos in society at large.

However, a darker side of Taiwan society also exists. Organised criminal gangs, the Triad societies, often with close connections to the old KMT

[15] http://www.moi.gov.tw Ministry of the Interior, Department of Statistics.
[16] http://www.ftc.gov.tw APEC Competition Law Data Base – Chinese Teipei.

elite, continue to be a problem. Government appears to have made a continued, high-profile effort to reduce the threat posed by organised crime, but the results of such campaigns must inevitably take a considerable time to come to fruition.

Thus, despite reservations, Taiwan does seem to satisfy the necessary elements of a functioning democracy – representative government, independent state institutions that exhibit a separation of powers, the rule of law, competent exercise of executive power and a lively civil society.

9.7 Economic development and structure

Taiwan is an island of some 22 million people, three times the population of Hong Kong, with a GDP per capita of US$12,916 in 2000.[17] The economy is now 32 per cent industrial, mainly hi-tech computer hardware, third only after United States and Japan, 66 per cent services and 2 per cent agriculture. Taiwan exports in 1999 were US$121 billion, giving a trade surplus of US$10.9 billion. Economic links with Mainland China have seen Taiwanese entrepreneurs invest over US$17 billion in Mainland production facilities since 1987, so as to take advantage of the lower-cost environment. Direct trade links, including shipping and aviation, with China are still impossible, but with WTO accession, political movement on this issue is expected. This will have a detrimental impact on Hong Kong as it has acted as the transport intersection between the two entities.

As for economic policy, during the authoritarian phase of government, the KMT transformed Taiwan from an agricultural economy to an industrial one. GDP per capita rose from US$196 in 1952 to US$3,993 in 1986 and in overall terms grew from US$1.674 billion to US$77.296 billion over the same period.[18] By the mid-1960s, Taiwan had become a predominantly industrial products exporter and the contribution of private enterprises gradually overtook the previous predominance of state-owned firms. For example, in 1952 state enterprises contributed 57 per cent of industrial production but in 1980 less than 20 per cent. However, many strategic enterprises were monopolised by the state – petroleum, electricity, gas, water, steel, railways, shipbuilding, posts and telecommunications, tobacco, alcoholic spirits and banking.

---

[17] The Republic of China Year Book http://www.gio.gov.tw/taiwan-website/5-gp/yearbook.
[18] I. Marsh, J. Blondel and T. Inoguchi (eds.), *Democracy, governance and economic performance: East and South Asia,* Tokyo: United Nations University Press, chapter 5, 'Taiwan' by Michael Hsiao and Cheng Hsiao-shih at p. 111.

Moreover, the KMT had significant influence over and ownership of many strategic business sectors in Taiwan. The party owned or controlled over fifty enterprises via two very influential investment houses and so had the ability to intervene directly in a number of economic sectors. The private sector was divided essentially into two groups – the 100 large-scale business conglomerates composed of some 700 or 800 component firms accounting for 34 per cent of GNP in 1988 but employing only 4.6 per cent of the workforce and which were concentrated in the high technology sector and in domestic businesses, and a large number of small and medium-sized enterprises (SMEs); in 1961 there were 178,916 of them and in 1986 there were around 750,000. They had several distinguishing characteristics. They were predominantly in the commercial sector, concentrating on export markets, most had less than fifty employees, they utilised private capital, were family operated and were less supported and protected by government than the large-scale businesses.[19]

The KMT had learnt from its politico-economic mistakes on the Mainland that had been an important factor in its loss of support of the majority of the Mainland population after the defeat of the Japanese. Failure to reform land ownership and to control inflation, especially consumer prices, were key factors in the KMT's loss of legitimacy. Thus, in Taiwan land reform, direct intervention to control commodity prices and a sound monetary policy were key objectives pursued with vigour in the 1950s.

Whilst the KMT ran Taiwan as an authoritarian party state, the political economy adopted was a mixed-economy variant ideologically labelled 'The Principle of Social Welfare', which envisaged public control over certain key sectors of the economy but allowed ample room for the development of the private market economy. In some ways it mirrored the German Ordoliberal ideology (see chapter 2), but with an emphasis on primary economic development and a greater role for the state in certain strategic industries and also a stronger co-ordinating role, whereby competition was not necessarily seen as beneficial. Hsiao and Cheng have demarcated Taiwan's economic development into four phases:[20] (1) the import-substitution phase (1949–59), during which the embryonic industrial sector developed to out-grow both agriculture and textiles. (2) The export-orientated industrialisation phase (1960s) which was stimulated by a policy of devaluation, liberalising the foreign trade regime, allowing foreign direct investment to promote export processing in

---

[19] The factual information in this paragraph is a précis of chapter 5, 'Taiwan', pp. 110–115, ibid.
[20] Ibid. at pp. 117–121.

special zones and eliminating certain import restrictions. In some ways this policy was mirrored by the PRC some twenty years later. The 1960s also saw the expansion of the two-tier economy – large firms dominated the domestic economy and the SMEs concentrated on export. (3) A further import-substitution phase occurred in the 1970s as a result of the economic shocks of the oil crisis and the diplomatic isolation caused by the de-recognition of the KMT as the government of China. High inflation and world recession forced consolidation but by the end of the decade the large firms and state businesses had recovered and consolidated into various conglomerates; the SME sector had also weathered the storm in good shape. (4) The last phase identified by the authors was the liberalisation and globalisation of the economy in the 1980s. A free-market philosophy began to pervade policy making in the 1980s. In 1985, the KMT government accepted the Committee for Economic Reform proposals and took an important economic policy decision to liberalise the domestic economy, privatise many state firms and to reduce protectionist tariffs and non-tariff barriers to trade. Capital flows were liberalised and foreign banks allowed to be established from 1989.[21] The decision to abandon import-substitution policies and to reduce protectionist trade measures hurt state and KMT-owned enterprises most of whom operated mainly in government-licensed sectors of the economy. Import penetration and the removal of regulatory protection allowed an increase in both foreign and domestic competition in many previously restricted sectors. However, the rising power of privatised and deregulated businesses increased the demands for a competition law to set out the ground rules for the new market-orientated economy.[22] The results of the reform policy were impressive, with Taiwan becoming the world's third largest supplier of computer hardware by 1995. The party-state had been instrumental in guiding Taiwan's economic development but liberalisation of the economy went hand in hand with political change.[23] As part of the economic liberalisation plan, a comprehensive competition statute was proposed. This radical change in policy resulted from a realisation that cartels and monopolies were undermining Taiwan's competitive edge. Previously, a Price

---

[21] For a detailed description of Taiwan's economic transformation since 1980 see Marsh et al., *Democracy, governance and economic performance.*

[22] For a detailed description and analysis of Taiwan's policy of deregulation and trade liberalisation, see Chen Tain Jy, 'Democratisation and trade liberalisation', chapter 9, *Taiwan's economic success since 1980,* ed. Chao Cheng Mai and Chien-Sheng Shih, Cheltenham: Edward Elgar (2001).

[23] See Cheng Tun Jen, 'The Economic Significance of Taiwan's Democratisation', chapter 4 in Mai and Shih, *Taiwan's economic success since 1980.*

Supervision Council directly attempted to regulate supply and demand by co-ordinating suppliers' production levels by administrative fiat.[24]

9.8 Adopting competition policy and law

By the 1990s, as a result of the change in the political climate, monopolies and cartels (many sponsored by the KMT as sources of economic and political patronage) were seen to be less economically effective and could potentially hold back the next stage of economic development and liberalisation. The move towards liberalisation was also thought to be essential in preparing local firms for the rigours of competition to be faced after Taiwan's accession to GATT and the WTO.[25]

The history of the adoption of a competition law flowed from the political decision in 1985 to liberalise the economy. However, the implementation of that liberalisation policy has been criticised by Professor Lawrence Liu, an eminent Taiwanese academic observer, as being 'gradual and haphazard' and he suggests that the prevarication by Premier Yu and President Chiang Ching-quo in 1985 about introducing a 'big bang' reform resulted in wasting an opportunity to open the economy and reform the economic structure in the mid-1980s. Professor Liu suggests that such a policy choice would have allowed the early enactment of a general competition law.[26] Nevertheless, the decision to liberalise the economy and to abandon import substitution policies did lead to the eventual enactment of the Taiwanese Fair Trade Law 1992 (FTL).

The process of adoption began in 1986, when the government forwarded a draft of the FTL to the Legislative Yuan for enactment. The draft had been prepared by a committee of academic experts under the aegis of the Ministry of Economic Affairs (MOEA). The government's case for a new law was based on two arguments. Firstly, the liberalising economic environment had unleashed unrestrained market forces in some sectors of the economy, which had created, or at least had the potential to create, monopolies, oligopolies and cartels, which were seen to be detrimental to the public welfare. Secondly, other unfair trade practices, such

---

[24] Information on the pre-1992 position was provided to the author by Liu Chien-hsuen of the Taiwan Fair Trade Commission during an interview on 15 September 2002.

[25] Lawrence S. Liu, *In search of free and fair trade – the experience of the Republic of China on Taiwan as an Asian model of implementing competition law and policy,* paper delivered at the Conference on Competition Regulation within the APEC Region: Commonality and Divergence, Georgetown University Law Centre, Washington, D.C., 1–3 May 1995.

[26] Lawrence S. Liu, *Fostering competition law and policy: a façade of Taiwan's political economy,* Washington Global Studies Law Review, vol. 1, 77–160 (2002).

as counterfeiting, abuse of trademarks, false and misleading advertising and pyramid-selling frauds were also serious imperfections in the market. The government had also come under increasing international pressure, particularly from America, to deal with these practices. Thus, the government's proposed bill dealt with both pure competition concerns as well as with unfair trade practices.[27]

In the Legislative Yuan, the opposition DPP welcomed the proposed legislation but for reasons other than those propounded by the KMT government. The DPP saw the draft law as a potentially useful tool to break up the symbiotic relationships of the KMT with many powerful industries, either as a result of indirect influence or because of outright control by the KMT party.

However, despite the welcome accorded to the draft legislation by both main political parties, the bill still took over six years to achieve enactment. Essentially, three main issues dominated debate and held up progress. Firstly, there was the fundamental question of whether a comprehensive competition law was needed, given the state of economic development in Taiwan. Secondly, a vigorous merger and acquisition policy was controversial as some thought it might delay or prevent economically necessary and beneficial consolidation in various fragmented industries. Thirdly, a political issue arose as to whether or not a powerful economic regulator should be politically independent of a state ministry; how would such an important bureaucracy be politically accountable?

During the passage of the legislation, these matters were debated on several occasions. Taiwan might be considered a small economy, so giving rise to special concerns, such as an appropriate merger policy and the inevitable conflict between the maintenance of competition with the demands of efficiency promoted by economies of scale.[28] These concerns were raised by several parties during the protracted legislative process. Arguments that the bulk of the domestic economy consisted of SMEs meant that consolidation, which could be adversely affected by an intrusive regulatory scheme, might be delayed or prevented. The government's response was that the purpose of the law was 'to protect competition, not competitors',[29] so emphasising a policy of economic efficiency. Thus, mergers and consolidations that promoted efficiency would not be prohibited, where this did not lead to market structures that would result in

---

[27] The Legislation Record of the Fair Trade Law, Legislative Yuan, Republic of China, page 1 (1992).
[28] See Mical Gal, *Competition policy in small market economies.*
[29] The Legislation Record of the Fair Trade Law.

uncontestable markets because of the erection of unassailable barriers to entry.

Also on the merger issue, there were technical concerns that the originally proposed thresholds and scrutiny procedures were too heavy handed and would inhibit economically desirable consolidations of SMEs. It was also said that the original merger proposals were at odds with the government's own policy, which encouraged the merger of family-owned enterprises, so as to promote economies of scale that would allow the merged businesses to complete with large domestic and foreign entities. Multi-nationals had been granted much wider access to Taiwan's domestic markets and so consolidation of domestic industry was seen to be essential in order to meet the foreign challenge.

Potential administrative inefficiency and delay by the new regulator were also seen as a drag on business responsiveness that would inevitably follow from *ex ante* regulation rather than an *ex post* system of notification. After protracted debate, the government agreed to a moratorium on enforcement of the merger provisions for one year from the date of enactment and that time limits for scrutiny of qualifying mergers would be reduced to two months from the date of completed notification.

The final political issue of importance in the debate on competition law was that of the institutional architecture and the need for, or desirability of, the *de facto* and *de jure* independence of the enforcement body. Under the government's original proposals, the new Fair Trade Commission (FTC) was to be an organ of the MOEA, the ministry which had sponsored the drafting and promoted the bill through both the Executive and Legislative Yuans. However, during the passage of the bill, both the impartiality and competence of the MOEA to police the new law were questioned. Consequently, it was decided to make the new Fair Trade Commission answerable to the Executive Yuan (effectively the Taiwanese Cabinet) and not to the MOEA. Further, the Chair of the Commission would hold Cabinet rank, so as to be able to act as a more effective advocate of competition policy at the heart of government. This Cabinet position for the Commission chair was welcomed in the sense that it evidenced a seriousness of purpose to change the business environment in Taiwan irrevocably and so to make it more competitive. However, it was also argued that the Cabinet position of the Chairman made him a component part of the highest level of government, that might also lead to potential conflicts of interest when industrial policy and competition policy came into conflict. On balance, the positive impact of a dedicated competition advocate mandated to promote competition in all fields of government endeavour probably outweighed the possible conflicts of interest. This was especially so in a society, such as Taiwan, where ingrained business practices were more likely to conflict with the tenets of market competition and so a strong advocate was an essential element in ensuring successful adoption. Further, many of the concepts in competition law would also have been alien to the general population and so having a high-profile advocate has obvious advantages in newly adopting jurisdictions such as Taiwan.

Thus, after a protracted gestation, the FTL was finally passed on 4 February 1992, having been preceded by the promulgation of the Organic Statute of the Fair Trade Commission on 13 January 1992, which made detailed provisions for the administration of the new FTC and its operations. The Organic Statute stipulated that each Commissioner would hold office for a fixed term of three years, with the possibility of re-appointment for a second term. The membership of the Commission was to be politically balanced, and the appointees had to have requisite experience in law, economics, finance, tax, accountancy or management. Specifically, Commissioners were enjoined to act independently and not as representatives of factional interests.

In the view of Professor Lawrence Liu, the structure and most of the substantive provisions of FTL can be traced to twin developments. Firstly, pressure from trading partners, particularly America, to improve domestic unfair competition rules on counterfeiting and passing-off. Secondly, the predominant legal–academic culture in Taiwan has been heavily influenced by German jurisprudence and training. Consequently, many Taiwanese legal academics admired the German competition law system for its intellectual elegance and Ordoliberal pedigree. The German system was thought to be a desirable object for transplantation to Taiwan, especially as much of the Taiwanese legal system originated in the adoption of a German inspired codal system by the ROC in the 1920s.

Further, Professor Liu suggests that there was considerable disagreement about the form and content of the competition provisions due to lawyers favouring a German model, whilst most academic economists were more familiar with the terminology and case law of the American anti-trust system.[30] Despite this divergence of preferences, the FTL is recognisably European in orientation, rather than American, though there are some specific provisions that reflect American, Japanese and Korean jurisprudence.

---

[30] Liu, *Fostering Competition Law and Policy.*

9.9 Substantive provisions of the Fair Trade Law

The FTL has two distinct functions. Firstly, to set out the rules for promoting competition in the Taiwanese market. Secondly, the law also seeks to prevent unfair trade practices, generally involving some type of deception. The present analysis is concerned only with the market-competition provisions. In this regard, the law contains stipulations to control restrictive practices and agreements, the abuse of dominance and to regulate overly concentrative mergers.

The FTL has been amended on three occasions since initial enactment in 1992. The 1999 amendment substantially increased penalty provisions, the 2000 amendment adjusted administrative practices and the 2002 amendment changed the merger notification system by raising threshold trigger points and also improved procedural transparency. For convenience, this analysis will consider the existing version of the law (2002) making reference to amendments as appropriate.

The FTL is divided into several chapters, beginning with a set of General Principles in chapter 1. The stated objectives of the law are to:

- maintain the trading order;
- protect consumers' interests;
- ensure fair competition;
- promote economic stability and prosperity.[31]

It is immediately apparent that some of these laudable objectives are potentially incompatible with a competitive economic system. For example, maintaining 'trading order' and 'promoting economic stability' might appear to be exactly the opposite of a market-based system where many enterprises seek supremacy through a Darwinian struggle for survival. The market paradigm would seem to require at least a certain element of uncertainty and instability for the market process to operate.

The suggestion has been made that these policy goals create confusion on the part of the Commission as to its core rationale.[32] Some FTC decisions seem to use mercantilist logic,[33] or protect employee welfare,[34] or social customs[35] or attempt to maintain employment opportunities. These differing rationales constitute the justification, in the early decisions

---

[31] Article 1, Fair Trade Law 2002 www.ftl.gov.tu/2000010/2999010//376.htm.
[32] Liu, *Fostering competition law and policy*, pp. 89–91.
[33] FTC Approval No. 81, Gazette of Fair Trade Commission, September 1992.
[34] FTC Interpretation No. 011, Gazette of Fair Trade Commission September 1992.
[35] Ibid.

made under the FTL to approve or reject regulatory intervention without
any apparent coherence, though on the whole the decisions to do appear
to support market forces as opposed to non-market solutions.

The FTL applies only to 'enterprises' which are defined as 'companies,
partnerships, sole traders, trade associations or any other entity engaged
in the same market with one or more enterprise offering more favourable
prices, quantities, quality or services'.[36] The position of entities exempt
from the operation of the law will be considered later.

Monopolistic enterprises are then defined as those that face no competition or have a dominant position in a market. Two or more enterprises
that do not engage in price competition may be deemed to constitute a
joint monopolistic enterprise for the purposes of the law. The relevant
market is defined somewhat crudely in merely geographic terms and in
respect of 'particular' goods or services.[37] This definition appears to ignore the temporal element of markets and does not deal with issues of
substitutability. However, this faulty definition provides the basis for the
later prohibitions of abusive conduct.

No enterprise shall be classified as a monopolistic enterprise, unless certain thresholds are met. A single enterprise with a market share
of more than 50 per cent may be monopolistic. Two firms that enjoy
66 per cent of a market may be a duopoly. Three firms having 75 per cent
of a market may constitute an oligopoly. However, enterprises which are
caught by the thresholds also must have individually at least 10 per cent of
the relevant market or turnover of at least NT$1 billion (US$29 million).

Notwithstanding these tests, an enterprise may also be classified as
monopolistic in the following circumstances: 'If the establishment of
the enterprise or any of the goods or services supplied by the enterprise to relevant markets is subject to legal or technological restraints
or there exist other circumstances under which supply and demand
on the relevant market are affected and the ability of others to compete is thereby impaired.' Under the original version of the law, such
monopolistic enterprises were to be designated, after investigation by
the Commission, and placed on a public register. This process follows
Korean practice. However, by 1999 this procedure was seen as wasteful
of Commission resources and of little effect in determination of individual investigations of abuse, as any data used in the registration process
was likely to be stale at the time of commission of a potential competition offence. Thus, the listing duty on the Commission was removed

[36] Article 2 Fair Trade Law (2002).   [37] Ibid. Article 5.

in the 1999 amendment to the law, so saving both time and scarce resources.

Originally, some forty enterprises had been listed as 'monopolistic enterprises', so giving a distorted picture that the whole economy was dominated by such businesses. Whilst it is true that many important sectors of the economy were subject to the dominance of former state or KMT-preferred entities, the reality of Taiwan's economy was of numerous small and medium-sized enterprises. Also, the opening of the external trading environment meant that many of the incumbents were, by the mid-1990s, under discernable competitive pressure.

The removal of the listing provision made good administrative and policy sense. Further, it should not be forgotten that Taiwan might be expected to have a somewhat concentrated domestic economy, given its relatively small size and the requirements of economies of scale in certain capital-intensive industries.

Mergers are defined as:

- the complete take over of one enterprise by another; or
- where one enterprise owns or acquires more than 33 per cent of the shares or assets of another enterprise; or
- where an enterprise leases or receives assignment of the whole or most of the goodwill or assets of another enterprise; or
- when an enterprise forms a joint venture to operate its business or entrusts the operation of its business to another enterprise; or
- where one enterprise directly or indirectly controls the operations of another enterprise or the appointment or removal of the staff of that other enterprise.[38]

Thus all the manifestations of ownership and control, both indirect and direct, are contemplated in the FTL. The consequences of this definition are discussed below.

Concerted action is defined as such 'conduct between competing enterprises, by way of formal agreement or informal understanding, to jointly determine the price of goods or services or to limit competition between them by reference to quantities, technology, products, facilities or trading territories'.[39] These acts are prohibited. However, the prohibition only relates to horizontal agreements between enterprises at the same stage of production or marketing and which would adversely affect the market for the relevant goods or services. The definition also confirms that no legally

[38] Ibid. Article 6.   [39] Ibid. Article 7.

binding agreement is necessary to come within the ambit of the definition, merely that a meeting of minds 'which would in effect lead to joint action' is required, so apparently utilising an objective test of concerted action.

Chapter 2 of the FTL explains the substantive prohibitions. Any monopolistic enterprise, as defined, shall not:

- directly or indirectly prevent any other enterprise from competing by unfair means;
- improperly set, maintain or change the price for goods or the remuneration of services;
- require a trading counterpart to give preferential treatment without justification; or
- otherwise abuse its market power.[40]

Whilst the language of the statute may be open to criticism, the essential features required to control abuse of market power appear to be present; the implementation and enforcement of these provisions will be considered later.

The law then provides for an *ex ante* system of merger notification. Mergers that fall within the perimeters of Article 11 of the law must be pre-notified for consideration before they are concluded. The relevant criteria are:

- the merged enterprise has more than 33 per cent of a relevant market;
- one of the merging enterprises has 25 per cent of the relevant market; or
- turnover of one of the merging enterprises exceeds currently for non-financial enterprises NT$10 billion (US$90 million approximately) and for financial enterprises NT$20 billion (US$180 million approximately). These thresholds have been raised substantially since 1992.

The nature of the original merger provisions was found to be far too wide, in that both parent/subsidiary share alterations and many franchising agreements met the statutory tests. As a result, in the period from 1992 to 2004, over 6,125 merger filings were made, a remarkable number for a small island economy. The over-broad definitions of qualifying mergers were amended in 2002 and the FTC statistics show that whilst between 1999 and 2001 there were over 1,000 merger notifications, in 2000 there were only 132 and in 2003 only 50 cases.[41]

---

[40] Ibid. Article 10.
[41] http://www.ftc.gov.tw/200000/029991231191.htm.

This drastic reduction in merger notifications simply reflects the amendment made to the law in 2002,[42] not a collapse in economic activity, though Taiwan did experience a sharp economic contraction due to the collapse of the internet bubble and the subsequent decline in computer and telecommunications hardware sales worldwide.

Administratively, the FTC has thirty days from the filing of a complete set of data to reach a decision. In default of a positive prohibition, the notified transaction may proceed unhindered. However, the FTC has the power to extend the examination period by an additional thirty days. This 'negative clearance' procedure was adopted in 2002 to replace the need for a positive permission from the FTC in relation to qualifying mergers. Thus, both substantive grounds for merger control and the scrutiny process have been substantially improved as a result of the 2002 amendments.

The test applied by the FTC in merger cases is whether the qualifying merger produces 'overall economic benefits that outweigh the reduction in competition'. Thus, the law does not adopt a pure economic test of a substantial lessening of competition and the FTC has taken many (possibly extraneous) factors into account in deciding merger cases. Political factors, such as 'fairness' and a concern for an over-concentration of economic power in few hands, may be a trait in some of the decisions but in the event these considerations have only had a marginal effect on merger activity. In the period from 1992 to 2004, of the 6,125 notifications made to the FTC, only four were refused permission to proceed. Thus, whilst the substantive provisions were originally far too wide and the test adopted might be thought to be too 'political', the net effect of the merger-control system has been minimal in preventing the consolidation of the Taiwanese economy. The FTL's 'bark' was clearly worse than its 'bite' but a great deal of business time and professional costs may have been wasted pre-2002 on redundant and unnecessary compliance with an ill-considered legislative provision. This provides an object lesson in the need for caution when drafting notification procedures in competition cases, either for exemption from restrictive trade practices provisions or in relation to mergers that have little economic consequence. Not only may a newly established competition authority be overwhelmed by a deluge of applications for exemption or approval and thus waste or divert scarce administrative resources but the true function of a competition law – discovering and punishing pernicious cartels and abuses of market power – may be sidelined, so bringing the whole system into disrepute.

---

[42] See Article 11.1.

Turning now to permissible restrictions of competition, the absolute prohibition on concerted action by enterprises is ameliorated by Article 14 of the FTL, which provides that in certain instances, such conduct may be permitted if it consists of one of the enumerated activities, and is beneficial to the economy as a whole, as well as being approved by the FTC.

The types of act that can be condoned include:

• unifying specifications or standards, so reducing the cost of goods or
• improving efficiency or quality;
• research and development joint ventures;
• specialisation agreements;
• export cartels;
• import cartels of foreign goods;
• crisis cartels; and
• agreements between small and medium-sized enterprises that improve efficiency or strengthen their competitiveness.

The FTC has three months after receipt of notification by participating enterprises to reach a decision on the notified agreement, which may be permitted subject to conditions, and may not extend for more than three years. However, enterprises can seek a three-year extension for the FTC-sanctioned restrictive agreement.[43] Permission may be revoked if its scope is exceeded or economic conditions change.[44] All such exemptions must be published in the public register and in the Government Gazette, so as to provide a transparency check on exemptions granted by the FTC.

These provisions are largely replicated from former EC jurisprudence but the allowance of import/export, specialisation and crisis cartels should be viewed with scepticism and may be the result of special pleading by self-interested businesses and so may reduce the overall economic benefit of the primary prohibition contained in the FTL. Also, the notification process is imitative of the former EC system, which of course, has now been reformed to remove these provisions.[45] Such notification processes might be justified when the whole competition law system was newly established but the diversion of resources needed to scrutinise such notified agreements clearly hampers the proper investigation of cartels and abuses of dominance. The desire for legal certainty in the business community when a new competition law is adopted is understandable but,

---

[43] Ibid. Article 15.   [44] Article 16.
[45] See the Modernisation Regulation, 1/2003, OJ [2003] L 1/1, [2003] 4 CMLR 551. For a full explanation of this provision see, Whish, *Competition law*, chapter 7.

as the system matures, consideration for shifting the compliance burden to enterprises and their professional advisors from the shoulders of the competition authority, should be seriously considered.

As regards vertical restraints, the law categorises these as acts of unfair competition, which includes consumer protection measures against trade fraud. This categorisation reflects the influence of Japanese jurisprudence. Consequently, chapter 3 of the FTL prohibits resale price maintenance.[46] Enterprises will lessen or impede competition by:

- causing another enterprise to boycott a third party with the intent to injure that party;
- imposing unjust discriminatory trading conditions;
- using coercion or improper inducements or other improper means to require another enterprise to trade with it;
- forcing another enterprise not to compete on price or to enter a merger;
- coercing a rival to divulge trade secrets or other business information; or
- imposing restrictions on enterprise business activities by contract (these might include tying, exclusive dealing or exclusive territories).

Other provisions in chapter 3 relate to passing-off and trademark infringement,[47] misleading advertisements,[48] trade libel,[49] regulation of multi-level selling schemes[50] and finally a catch-all provision: Article 24 bans enterprises from engaging in any 'deceptive or obviously unfair conduct that is liable to affect the trading order'. This provision was apparently taken from Section 5 of the United States Federal Trade Commission Act (1914).[51] The Article appears to apply in both competition and unfair trade practice cases. Arguably, the width of the provision could make the specific provisions on abuse of dominance, cartels, re-sale price maintenance and even passing-off, redundant, such is the statutory language. The FTC has utilised this provision in over 770 cases since 1992, which is second only to the 920 misleading advertising infringement cases in the same period.[52] The statistics do not break down how many of these cases were quasi-competition matters and how many were unfair trade practice complaints. However, the catch-all nature of the provision has the potential for substantial application in situations where it might be difficult for definitional, or evidential reasons, to utilise the specific competition provisions in the FTL. This may obviously raise concerns about

---

[46] Article 18 FTL.   [47] Ibid. Article 20.   [48] Ibid. Article 21.
[49] Ibid. Article 22.   [50] Ibid. Article 23.   [51] 15 USC §§ 41–51.
[52] http://www.ftc.gov.tw/200010129991231800.htm at P 3.

the interface between overlapping provisions as well as the consistency of application and resulting legal uncertainty. An assessment of the use of this provision by the FTC will be given later.

9.10 The Fair Trade Commission

Chapter 4 of the FTL entrusts enforcement of the Law to a Fair Trade Commission,[53] which is responsible for the formation of policy and law-reform measures on fair trade issues, as well as the investigation and adjudication of fair trade cases. No specific mandate is given for competition advocacy, though as we shall see, the FTC has devoted considerable resources to this activity. The FTC is given general investigatory powers and required to adhere to the principles of natural justice.[55] The organisational structure of the FTC is contained in the Organic Statute of the FTC. This law provides that the FTC be composed of seven Commissioners and a Chairman and Vice Chairman. Political neutrality is required, as is professional expertise. Most of the Commissioners over the first decade of the existence of the FTC had doctorates in law, economics or business management as well as experience in industry, government, academia or the professions. The issue of political independence has already been raised, given that the FTC is not fully independent of government, being a creature of the Executive Yuan and the Chairman being a member of the Taiwanese Cabinet. An assessment of the FTC's performance will be given below. The model for this administrative enforcement of the competition regime clearly follows the EC pattern.

9.11 Private rights of action

Chapter 5 of the FTL provides for private rights of action against infringers allowing both injunction and damages to be claimed in respect of both competition provisions and unfair trade practice breaches.[55] The FTL borrows the concept of treble damages from the United States anti-trust system. A court is empowered to grant more than the actual damage suffered, provided that the violation of the law was intentional, though these additional damages should not exceed three times the amount of actual damage.[56] Any claim for damages under the FTL must be commenced within two years of the claimant's date of knowledge, with an absolute time bar of ten years from the date of the infringing conduct.

[53] Article 25 FTL.   [54] Ibid. Article 31.
[55] Ibid. Articles 30 and 31.   [56] Ibid. Article 32.

9.12 Penalties under the Fair Trade Law

The FTL provides that obstruction of an FTC investigation or the destruction of evidence can cause the imposition of an administrative penalty of not less than NT$20,000 (US$600) but no more than NT$250,000 (US$7,400) This penalty can be imposed again in case of continuing refusal to co-operate.[57]

In relation to abuses of dominance or the operation of non-exempt restrictive agreement, the FTL provides that the FTC may issue a cease-and-desist order, including positive injunctions to rectify conduct or take corrective action as necessary.[58] Refusal to obey such an order could result in the imposition of a fine of up to NT$100 million (US$3 million) or three years' imprisonment or both.[59] Additionally, even where no cease-and-desist order has been made or discharged, the FTC can levy an administrative penalty for breach of not less than NT$50,000 (US$1,500) nor more than NT$25 million (US$750,000).[60] Repeat offences may attract higher fines between NT$100,000 (US$3,000) and NT$50 million (US$1.5 million).

As regards breach of the merger provisions, failure to file or seek permission to merge in qualifying cases can result in an administrative order to divest all or part of the acquired enterprise. Should an enterprise proceed with a merger in contravention of an order not to do so by the FTC, orders for divestiture can be supplemented by an administrative penalty of not less than NT$100,000 (US$3,000) nor more than NT$50 million (US$1.5 million).[61]

The penalty regime appears relatively modest in that even where breaches of the law are discovered, the primary remedy is injunctive relief rather than punishment. In these circumstances, one must call into question whether or not these penalty provisions are sufficiently punitive to achieve the purposes of the FTL. However, the cease-and-desist powers plus administrative penalties of the FTC coupled with the potential for treble damages actions by aggrieved parties might, in combination, ameliorate the relatively modest levels of administrative penalties.

The penalty provisions were amended in 1999. Previously abuses of monopolistic power and concerted practices were subject to criminal sanctions. However, as a result of substantial criticism from industry that these penalties were too harsh, the government amended the FTL to delete these penal provisions. This decriminalisation, especially in

---

[57] Ibid. Article 41.   [58] Ibid.   [59] Ibid. Article 35.
[60] Ibid. Article 41.   [61] Ibid. Article 40.

relation to cartels, is directly at odds with developments in recent years of reinvigorated criminal prosecutions of cartels in America[62] and recent criminalisation of such conduct in the UK.[63] Given the international trend towards enhanced cartel enforcement, the Taiwanese amendment, in this respect, seems retrograde.

9.13 Fair Trade Commission: strategy and policy implementation 1992–2004

The FTC came into existence on 27 January 1992. Prior to this date the MOEA Price Surveillance Task Force, which had previously been responsible for the control of prices in the economy, established a preliminary working group to determine who would staff the Commission once it came into existence. Clearly, it was open to question whether staff steeped in the traditions of bureaucratic price-fixing would be able to make the cultural and intellectual leap to the promotion of competition.[64] However, the Commissioners of the FTC appear to be more than adequately qualified with experience in the legal and economics fields. There are nine full-time Commissioners, with the Chairman ranked at the apex of the government administrative hierarchy. They are all direct presidential appointees and appear to have adequate status, resources and independence. The staff of the FTC consists of 218 civil servants, 25 per cent of whom are qualified lawyers, 18 per cent are economists, the balance of 57 per cent being administrators. Over 35 per cent have Master's degree qualifications and a further 55 per cent have at least a Bachelor's degree.[65]

In addition to ensuring the re-training of the existing staff of the former Price Surveillance Taskforce, other members of the bureaucracy, including the judiciary, also needed to be made aware of the nature and substance of the FTL. Competition advocacy to the general population was also a priority of the new FTC. In the period from 1992 to 1995, the FTC conducted 735 seminars for the business community and general public

---

[62] Examples of recent US prosecutorial activism in this field include the Vitamins, Graphite Electrodes, Lysine, Citric Acid and Sotheby's cases. For a discussion of their importance, see Whish, *Competition law*, pp. 545–6.

[63] See s.188 Enterprise Act 2002.

[64] Similar but much more severe problems have been observed in relation to the creation of a competition agency to enforce a new competition regime in Thailand. See Mark Williams, *Competition law in Thailand: seeds of success or fated to fail?* World Competition 27(3) 459–94 (2004).

[65] *Statistical yearbook of the Taiwan Fair Trade Commission* (2001), Taiwan: Taipei, p. 128.

to explain the nature and substance of the FTL. The FTC established a specialised unit to disseminate information about the FTL and to handle enquiries and complaints from businesses or private individuals. During the twelve years of the existence of the FTC, almost 17,000 complaints have been received.[66] Unfortunately, this figure is not broken down in respect of competition and unfair business practice cases, though it would appear that misleading advertising and passing-off type cases formed the bulk of this total. Thus, it would seem that FTC efforts at public education have been relatively successful, at least insofar as generating a substantial number of complaints is concerned. As regards industry, the original penalty provisions of the FTL imposed criminal sanctions in respect of cartelisation and abuse of dominance. The Commission actively sought to educate industry as to the content of these new provisions. In fact, so successful was the Commission in alerting business leaders to the perils that they might run, that the business lobby was able to persuade government, in 1999, to amend the law to decriminalise both abuse of dominance and cartelisation. Perhaps the Commission was too successful in this aspect of its work!

In order to promote transparency, all administrative decisions of the FTC were to be published in the FTC Gazette and media briefings were given on major decisions, so as to inform the public of the deliberations of the Commissioners. Again to encourage transparency, guidelines in relation to various aspects of the competition regime were promulgated and published, so that industry and professional advisers were made aware of the necessary interpretative detail of the legal prohibitions and the procedures by which the FTC would investigate, assess and adjudicate cases.[67]

The FTC was also anxious to ensure that its procedures and policy outlook were communicated to other departments of government that had sectoral responsibilities in agriculture, health, energy, telecommunications and financial services, ensuring that demarcation disputes did not arise, or when they did, they were minimised. This was a crucial part of the relatively smooth introduction of the FTL.

---

[66] FTC Statistics.
[67] The FTC has published Guidelines on the following subjects: Extraterritorial Mergers; Trade Associations; Impeding Fair Competition; the Application of Articles 20, 21 and 24; Technology Licensing; the Holding of Public Hearings; the Imposition of Additional Fees in the Retail Industry; procedures in relation to Case Handling; the Approval of Concerted Practices, Cable TV Amalgamations and Enterprise Mergers. See http://www.ftc.gov.tw/indexEnglish.html.

The Commission also considered it important to attempt to achieve a consensus on purely legal matters in relation to the new law, to which end an annual consultation exercise was conducted whereby senior judges were invited to a conference where the legal aspects of the competition regime could be aired and discussed in order to attempt to reach consensus in relation to achieving a better understanding of the principles underlying the FTL.

However, not all aspects of the initiation of the FTC have been universally praised. Professor Liu has suggested that the FTC 'failed to achieve sufficient independence and professionalism during its first decade'.[68] He argues that whilst Commissioners were on the whole well qualified to perform their tasks, the institutional architecture of Taiwan's constitution prevented the establishment of a properly independent body and, as a result of the Chairman being a member of the Cabinet, political pressure was applied to take enforcement action in relation to certain products such as imported foreign cosmetics, as a result of complaints about inflationary pressure and unfair import prices, rather than matters of purely competition concern. Professor Liu also suggests that the influence of the FTC Chairman for the first six years of the Commission's operation was decisive. The first Chairman apparently had a substantial input into the selection of individual Commissioners and, as a result of the bureaucratic culture in Taiwan, the personality of the Chairman was an important factor in the success or failure of the system. Professor Liu suggests that the first Chairman, a professor of marketing with a well-developed political sense, concentrated on raising public awareness of the new law rather than heavy-handed enforcement. Liu comments that this may well have been the best strategy for introducing a radical new law such as the FTL but the downside of this was that, by raising public awareness of competition matters, the efficiency of the FTC was compromised due to the generation of an avalanche of complaints. Further, as was noted above, the ill-drafted merger-control regime and requests for exemption of restrictive agreements also created a huge case-load of fillings, most of which proved to be innocuous, though highly distractive for the FTC, whose attention was taken off much more important and egregious competition failures. These defects, which caused the excessive number of complaints and unimportant merger and restrictive agreement notifications, were clearly unfortunate. More foresight and better strategic thinking at the inception of the FTL would have allowed the FTC to focus its

---

[68] Liu, *Fostering competition law and policy.*

enforcement policy on those matters that were most significant in competition terms.

In addition to its domestic work, the FTC has been active in making bilateral contacts with other national enforcement agencies and even signing co-operation agreements with some.[69] The FTC has participated extensively in OECD competition fora (after a long wait caused by political considerations regarding its observer status that might have provoked a negative reaction from the PRC). As part of APEC, the FTC has housed the Asia Pacific Regional Operations Centre and also hosts a competition policy database for that organisation.[70] These attempts at international recognition and integration on the part of the FTC may well not only be motivated by a desire to ensure best practice in its own operations but also to raise Taiwan's diplomatic profile, given the very limited international space that Taiwan is granted by the hostile attitude of the PRC authorities to any Taiwanese involvement in international governmental organisations.[71] Notwithstanding the attitude of the PRC authorities, the FTC has also signed bilateral co-operation agreements with the competition authorities of Australia, New Zealand and France.

9.14 The Fair Trade Law and public sector enterprises

As will be recalled, the FTL applies only to 'enterprises' as defined by Article 2. These include companies, sole traders, partnerships, trade associations and other persons or organisations engaged in transactions for the sales of goods or the provision of services. As the FTL does not specifically exempt wholly publicly owned entities from its reach, the issue of whether or not the FTL applies to government agencies and public-sector organisations is important. Clearly, public-sector organisations that engage in trade in goods or services do appear to fall within the definition but government ministries or other public bodies exercising public law functions could argue that they are not 'enterprises' within the meaning of Article 2.

The FTC has been faced with various situations where a clear-cut line between the exercise of official functions and engagement in market

---

[69] Co-operation agreements have been signed with New Zealand, Australia and France http://www.ftc.gov.tw/indexEngklishg,html.

[70] See http://www.ftc.gov.tw/indexEnglish.html.

[71] An instance of this intransigent attitude by the PRC was the veto exercised against Taiwanese membership of the World Health Organisation at the height of the SARS outbreak in 2003.

activity has been difficult to discern. Two cases involving the provincial layer of government in Taiwan illustrate this point. A government owned printing unit was declared not to be an enterprise within the meaning of the FTL and a decision by the provincial government to require all official documents and publications to be printed by the government press was not subject to the FTL.[72] However, in another case involving the provincial government, the Taiwan bookstore, an emanation of the government, was given responsibility to prepare new textbooks for primary schools. The FTC decided that a monopoly granted by the government to the Taiwan bookstore was within the sphere of government conduct and so the FTL did not apply. But the Commission went on to decide that the supply of other textbooks was not within the ambit of government prerogatives and the FTL could apply to such supply in these circumstances.[73] As regards state-owned trading enterprises, the original FTL contained an exemption for all public-sector enterprises for the first four years of the operation of the FTL.

The original Article 46 of the FTL also provided that the FTL 'shall not apply to any activity carried out by any enterprise in accordance with other laws'. This provision provided, essentially, for industries regulated by other statutes not to fall within the purview of the FTL. Gradually, over the twelve years of the operation of the FTL it has become appreciated that a reduction in the number and scope of anomalous exemptions and a better alignment of other regulatory regimes with the objectives of the FTL, is essential. In 1999, Article 46 was amended so that where other statutes govern the conduct of businesses, they can only be invoked where they do not conflict with the statutory objectives of the FTL.

Whilst there have clearly been tensions between the FTC and other regulatory bodies in Taiwan, the general perception is that many industries have been substantially deregulated during the existence of the FTL and that the FTC has been the principal motivating force behind this liberalisation of overly regulated sectors.

Thus, having surveyed the economic landscape in Taiwan prior to 1992 and that pertaining twelve years later, one is struck by the fact that both the external trading regime and the internal economy are considerably more competitive than had been the case previously. This change cannot be entirely credited to the FTC and the enforcement of the new FTL. Clearly, the removal of specific regulatory barriers, both in respect of external trade

---

[72] FTC, Interpretation No. 034, 1 Gazette of the FTC, September 1992, p. 31.
[73] FTC, Interpretation No. 041, 1 Gazette of the FTC, December 1992, p. 53.

and in relation to domestic industries, has played a very important role in liberalising the economy. The entry of multi-national enterprises into the Taiwan market has had a salutary effect on previously protected domestic incumbents. However, notwithstanding the achievements of liberal economic policies, one should not underestimate the impact and effect, both psychological and real, of the competition advocacy undertaken by the FTC and the enforcement of the new law. Raising public consciousness, through the effective use of the media and other methods of familiarising the public and industry with the precepts of competition, has no doubt contributed to a change in attitudes towards competition and assisted in achieving government liberalisation goals.

9.15 Enforcement capacity of the FTC

As we have seen, during the first six years of the FTL's existence investigation and enforcement was to some extent secondary to the promotion of the aims and objectives of the legislation to both the general public and industry. Added to this, the penalty regime under the original statute was limited, in that offenders were not liable to punishment in the first instance of being found in breach of the law and merely had to cease the infringing conduct. The available criminal sanctions were hardly ever used in competition cases. Consequently, many in industry took the view that since any discovered breach would not attract penalty, old methods of doing business were acceptable unless and until they were discovered. On being censured by the FTC, a business decision would have to be taken whether to continue the practice and run the risk of a financial penalty and/or possible criminal prosecution, or else to come into compliance with the FTL.

This unsatisfactory situation was remedied in 1999 with an amendment to the penalty provisions, which substantially increased administrative penalties. Whilst this structural defect in the initial phase of the implementation of the law was serious, the FTC did undertake specific information campaigns to industry in relation to particular breaches of the FTL that were widespread in particular sectors of the economy. This process of seeking out specific, widespread anti-competitive practices and then publicising them to the industry and the public as a whole had a generally salutary effect.

Another pressure on the newly constituted FTC was that of resources. The first Chairman was keen to publicise the provisions of the FTL, which generated a considerable volume of complaints, which unfortunately the

FTC did not have sufficient resources, or perhaps expertise, at that stage, to deal with or to select the most egregious cases for full-scale investigation and adjudication.

From the outset, the FTC appreciated that substantial resources in relation to staff training, recruitment of appropriate professionals and retention of experienced staff was a vital matter to ensure that institutional capability was increased, so as effectively to enforce the new FTL. Whilst many of the Commissioners themselves had received postgraduate education in the USA, Germany, France and Japan in law and/or economics, many of the junior staff were not as well qualified. The FTC also sought to develop bilateral links with established enforcement authorities as well as participating in international fora on experience-sharing and capacity-building hosted by, amongst others, the OECD.

The Commission also established enforcement guidelines to ensure transparency and to provide for procedural safeguards for the interests of the subjects of investigations.[74] Thus, the evidence in relation to the institutional organisation of the FTC, its procedures and personnel capacity appears to indicate that Taiwan has successfully undertaken the creation of a competent, though by no means perfect, competition enforcement authority.

Next we need to consider a sample of actual decisions to evaluate enforcement of the main prohibitions of the FTL, namely cases involving abuse of market power, restrictive agreements and mergers and acquisitions.

9.16 Investigations and adjudication

The purpose of this section is to describe and analyse a selection of cases decided under the various provisions of the FTL. It is not intended to be exhaustive but merely illustrative of the development of decisional practice under the Taiwanese legislation. After the cases have been considered, this section will conclude with an assessment of the investigational and decisional practice of the FTC and consider whether or not the new law has been effectively implemented during the first decade of its existence.

In any jurisdiction adopting a new competition law, with no previous experience of such legislation, it is to be expected that the enforcement learning curve will be a steep one and that almost inevitably errors will be made. In assessing the effectiveness of the law, it is suggested that one

---

[74] See the FTC website for full details at http://www.ftc.gov.tw/indexEnglish.html.

should ask several questions. Firstly, whether the decisions on selection of cases for investigation may have been arrived at on the basis of cogent evidence. Secondly, whether the investigation of complaints has been thorough and impartial. Thirdly, whether the alleged wrongdoer has had an opportunity to meet the charges made and fourthly, whether the adjudication process has been transparent and the decision arrived at based on a rational assessment of the facts. If a breach of the law has been found, it is necessary to consider whether or not the remedy imposed in terms of injunctive relief or financial penalty was appropriate to the offence and was able to rectify the offending conduct or provide sufficient deterrence or to improve the structural conditions that gave rise to the anti-competitive effect. Again, it should be emphasised that in a new system, such as Taiwan's, perfection cannot be expected. However, an important element in deciding the effectiveness of both the law and the enforcement authority is, whether or not lessons have been learned from decisional experience and amendments to the statute or other substantive rules and procedures have been made to improve the original system. This element of reflection by the competition authority and the sponsoring government department must be an important factor in arriving at a judgement as to whether the system has been reasonably effective in the initial stage but, also, as to whether it has been improved as a result of a rational assessment of that decisional experience.

This section will now consider a selection of cases decided by the FTC in relation to abuse of dominance, cartels, restrictive agreements and mergers.

9.16.1 Abuse of dominance

An interesting example of the process of monopoly liberalisation and enforcement action is the case of the LPG market in Taiwan. LPG is a very important energy source in Taiwan. The product was first introduced and produced in Taiwan in 1958. By 1971, LPG usage had reached 176,200 tonnes and by 2001 consumption had increased to 1.6 million tonnes. By that same year, around 3.5 million households on the island used LPG as their primary fuel; this amounts to over 50 per cent of the total.

The monopoly supplier of LPG in Taiwan was previously the Chinese Petroleum Corporation (CPC) until the market was liberalised in 1999. In 1978, the government instructed CPC to grant the Veterans Affairs Commission (VAC) an exclusive dealership in relation to bottled LPG, which was used as a domestic cooking fuel. Measures were adopted to restrict new entrants to the LPG bottling and transportation markets. No new retail licences for LPG dealerships were issued, existing retailers were prohibited from changing their business location or from selling in the territory of another dealer. Both quotas and retail price maintenance were also enforced.

After establishment of the FTL numerous complaints were received concerning monopolistic abuses within the LPG market. The FTC investigated these complaints, completed a report and submitted it to CPC's sponsoring government department, the MOEA and also to the VAC.

The report concluded that CPC held the monopoly in the supply of LPG and that the relevant department of the VAC held the distribution monopoly. The exclusive dealing arrangement between CPC and the VAC contravened the FTL. The CPC should not renew its exclusive dealership arrangement after the expiry of the present agreement as from February 1993. Further, CPC should, within a reasonable time, propose a fair and transparent scheme for opening up the distribution market for LPG.

In September 1993, CPC did indeed draft and promulgate a set of transparent regulations dealing with qualification and approval of participants in the bottled-LPG market in respect of retail dealerships, bottling and transport. By the end of 1994, four wholesale dealerships had been approved as had the opening of LPG bottling, transport and retailing markets.

In relation to this downstream market, the FTC had no direct regulatory oversight, as the state-owned monopoly, CPC was directly regulated by the MOEA. However, the passage of the FTL and the investigation by the FTC of the then existing state monopoly prompted substantial deregulation in the bottled-LPG market so considerably improving consumer choice and reducing retail prices.

This was not the only liberalisation measure in the hydrocarbons market. In 1996, the government decided to allow the establishment of private oil refineries, a sector which had also previously been monopolised by CPC. This measure created multiple sources of supply of wholesale LPG into the market. In January 1999, businesses who had merely acted as traders, rather than refiners, were also allowed to enter the market, so further diversifying the sources of supply of LPG. By 2001, there were four wholesale suppliers of LPG and wholesale distributors had increased to ten. Further downstream, there were almost 100 bottling and transport companies and just over 3,000 retailers. Again, whilst the FTL acted as a catalyst to this structural change in the LPG market, it was not the policy tool used to deregulate this industry. The adoption of market policies, as opposed to monopoly by government, which formed the core philosophy of the FTL, clearly reinforced each other and together had a major impact in this structural reorientation.

However, this outwardly more competitive market did have problems. A newly established retailer of bottled LPG filed a complaint with the FTC in August 2000 alleging that no bottling company would supply this retailer with bottled LPG. Consequently, the new retailer had sought to obtain supply from other retailers in wholesale quantities. Those retailers who had sold to the new market player were put under pressure by various bottling companies not to continue to supply the new entrant. The complaint triggered a comprehensive investigation of the whole LPG industry. As a result FTC concluded that thirty LPG bottling and transport companies in the north of Taiwan formed two regional cartels in relation to the bottling and retail markets.[75] The details of the cartel investigation and sanctions will be discussed below.

There are several other examples where the passing of the FTL has allowed the FTC to intervene formally in monopolised markets authorised under other legislation which was supervised by other government departments. In relation to the financial securities market, the Taiwan stock exchange, the telecommunications market, the potable water supply industry and the sugar market, the FTC has had notable successes in using its powers under the FTL to raise competition-related concerns with sponsoring ministries and regulatory authorities, so that competition policies have then been adopted in these sectors by government. This, of course, was primarily because the original 1992 version of the FTL excluded regulated monopolies from the effects of the provisions in the FTL. Further, the FTL did not contain powers to order structural remedies in relation to monopolised sectors and therefore, as regards structural impediments to competition, the ability of the FTC to intervene effectively was compromised. But, as a result of most structural monopoly situations being under the control of the state, the implementation of liberalisation policies through other regulatory changes has substantially restructured these markets. When added to a much liberalised foreign-trade policy, structural impediments have been addressed relatively well in most sectors.

As regards actual enforcement of the abuse of dominance, there have been relatively few decisions. In 2001, three leading foreign firms, Phillips,

---

[75] Details of the liberalisation of the Taiwan LPG market can be found in 'How enforcement against private anti-competitive conduct has contributed to economic development' – contribution of Chinese Taipei, OECD Global Forum on Competition, 12 February 2004 – CCNM/GF/COMP/WD/(2004)26.

Sony and Taiyo Yunden, were investigated in relation to allegations of abuse of collective dominance in relation to CD-R products. The foreign companies owned 'blocking' patents and undertook joint licensing agreements in relation to technology essential to the manufacture of CD-R hardware. Local Taiwanese manufacturers had, at this stage, become leading manufacturers of these products worldwide and had some 70 per cent of the market. The result of the licensing regime was to impose relatively high costs on the Taiwanese hardware manufacturers on a fixed royalty per machine produced, which hurt Taiwanese companies as hardware prices fell globally as the market matured in these products. At the end of an eighteen-month investigation, the FTL ruled against the collective licensing agreements imposed by foreign intellectual property owners and levied a substantial administrative fine as well as ordering them to adopt a new licensing regime.

The FTC has been criticised in relation to its decision in this case, in that one of the main bases of the decision appears to be an idea that the price demanded by the intellectual property owners for the relevant licences was excessive. Not only is the interface between competition law and intellectual property rights an extremely contentious one but the FTC appears to have adopted a very narrow definition of the relevant market, excluding potentially close substitute storage media. Consequently, a finding of dominance in relation to this narrowly defined market was relatively easy. The decision has also been criticised on the basis that it clearly favoured domestic hardware manufacturers over the interests of foreign intellectual property owners, a suspicion being that the FTC may often have unduly favoured domestic business interests over those of foreign intellectual property owners.

In 2002, Microsoft's software licensing regime was investigated as part of potential abuse of its dominance in the software operating systems market. The Microsoft case has also raised suspicions that politics, rather than a fair application of competition principles, may lie at the root of the decision to investigate Microsoft's licensing activities in Taiwan. The investigation in Taiwan followed on from similar probes in the United States and in the EU. The FTC gave its reason for investigating Microsoft operating systems and the company's trading practices in Taiwan as being consumer concerns relating to the high price of legitimate copies of Microsoft products. The result of the FTC investigation was that on 27 February 2003 the FTC approved an administrative settlement of the complaints against Microsoft, in which the company agreed to reduce its prices on average by 26.7 per cent. Additionally, Microsoft Taiwan also agreed to modify its licence agreements in respect of Taiwanese consumers and certain retail price maintenance practices were amended or abandoned. The company also agreed to enter into negotiations with the government in connection with sharing source-code information that would ultimately advantage both software and hardware producers in Taiwan.

In surveying the first decade of implementation of the FTL concerning monopolisation, one is struck by the fact that the number of decisions in which enforcement penalties have been levied is small but that the structural changes in the overall economy in relation to formerly monopolised products and services, has been great. It appears that the FTC has used its position within the government structure as an advocate for pro-competition policies, both in respect of domestic regulation of individual industries and in relation to liberalisation of foreign trade. Thus, whilst traditional enforcement may appear to have had some significant problems, the net effect of the overall policy in relation to competition advocacy and in the creation or enhancement of competitive markets in formerly monopolised sectors, appears to have been substantial. The enactment of the FTL in 1992 has had a catalytic effect in expediting and facilitating the government's pro-competition and pro-market policy that was initially enunciated in the mid 1980s. It may well be that in the second decade of the FTL's existence the FTC will concentrate more on individual abuse of dominance cases. The overall judgement however in relation to this area of enforcement and implementation must be cautious, though broadly favourable.

9.16.2 Cartels and restrictive agreements

Cartels are expressly prohibited by Article 14 FTL, as noted above, though there are seven exceptions to this general prohibition, subject to a public-interest test and approval by the FTC. A pervasive problem in a relatively small economy such as Taiwan's, especially given long-established business practices of co-operation through trade associations, is the basic notion that co-operation between participants in the same trade or industry had become a social norm. Thus, it would seem appropriate that, given such a background, the FTC should first concentrate on explaining the disadvantages of cartels to the general public and then ensuring that the prohibitions contained within the FTL were fully understood by business associations and then by individual enterprises. It is noteworthy that trade associations are defined as enterprises in the FTL and it appears this was done specifically to ensure that such organisations were, without doubt, within specific ambit of the law.

This section will examine enforcement of the anti-cartel provisions and will highlight a number of examples of cartel behaviour that have been uncovered and punished. However, the FTC has appreciated that cartel enforcement is difficult in some situations primarily because of a lack of cogent proof of price fixing or market sharing conspiracies.[76] However, this does not mean that cartel enforcement has been neglected or that significant competitive improvements in relation to various markets have not been made during the first decade of the existence of the FTL.

An example of a cartel organised by a trade association was the Taiwan Flour Mills Association case. The Taiwan Noodle Producers Association complained that the Flour Mills Producers Association had organised a cartel. The FTC investigation discovered that in 1998 the Flour Mills Association had issued a joint purchasing policy for thirty-two flour producers, which was justified on the entirely understandable basis of 'co-existence and co-prosperity'. A cartel was organised on the basis of import wheat quotas allocated to each of the flour producers and regular meetings were held by the Association to police the agreement. The purpose of quota allocation was, of course, to limit production and thus, artificially maintain a higher than market price for the resulting flour. The FTC investigations concluded that the operation of the Flour Mills Association knowingly breached Article 14 of the FTL. The FTC issued a cease-and-desist order in relation to the cartel's practices and imposed a fine of NT$20 million (US$600,000).

Another market in which an extensive cartel was found to operate was in the LPG market. Following the deregulation of the production and supply of domestic LPG in cylinders (see the previous section), the more vigorous competition that resulted from the liberalisation of this market was, in some areas, subject to a suppression of competition by concerted action of the players in that newly liberalised market. From late 1999 to early 2000 the retail price of LPG supplied in cylinders increased markedly, well in excess of a rise in international oil prices. This steep increase in price resulted in numerous complaints to the FTC who launched an investigation. The FTC found that LPG cylinder distribution and supply

---

[76] Cse Tay-Chung and Ma Chang-hung, *An analysis of the decisions in collusive cases made under the Fair Trade Law*, Fair Trade Quarterly, Fair Trade Commission (Taiwan) April 2001, p. 37.

was essentially organised in three separate geographical areas. A three-tier pricing system was created by the bottling stations, organised by three separate trade associations in the relevant geographical areas. The FTC discovered that operators in two of the three geographical areas held regular meetings to restrict the number of downstream operators and to enforce the standard pricing policy. In order to enforce the price-fixing arrangement, retailers who refused to join the scheme were threatened with the refusal of supply by the bottling companies. Nineteen bottling companies in one area accounted for 97 per cent of the total volume of LPG sold in that area and the eight bottling stations in the Tainan area accounted for over 80 per cent of market volume there. The FTC found that the price-fixing agreements made between the respective operators and organised by the trade associations was in breach of Article 14 of the FTL. The investigation was extensive and complex given the number of participants. Administrative fines were imposed on the participants, which varied from NT$1 million to NT$15 million (US$450,000). The totals fines imposed amounted to NT$133 million (US$4 million). Other illustrative examples of action taken by the FTC include the uncovering of a cement cartel[77] and concerted action by a trade association in the optometry industry.[78]

In answer to a questionnaire issued by the OECD in 2001 the FTC produced a table of cartel cases[79] that it had investigated during the period 1 January 2000 to 6 October 2001. Twenty-five cases were listed and eighteen out of twenty-five cases resulted in administrative penalties being imposed that varied from NT$ 50,000 million to NT$ 133 million (US$1,500 million to US$4 million), depending on the nature and gravity of the offence in accordance with the enforcement guidelines issued by the FTC. It seems that given this level of enforcement activity the FTC has undertaken significant anti-cartel action. These cases illustrate that cartels clearly are matters of concern in relation to the Taiwanese domestic economy and that the FTC appears to be taking substantial action in relation to them.

However, Professor Lawrence Liu has criticised the FTC on the basis that the Commission has concentrated enforcement efforts on cartels organised by small business operators, rather than leading players in the

[77] Llan District Mixed Concrete case (1998), as described on the FTC website. See http://www.ftc.gov.tw.
[78] Chia Yi City Clock and Optometry Association case (2001), ibid.
[79] OECD Global Forum on Competition, *Contribution from Chinese Taipei*, 5 October 2001, CCNM/GF/COMP/WD(2001)16.

market.[80] He also considers that the approvals process under Article 14 is too bureaucratic and cumbersome, so leaving businesses in a state of uncertainty as to whether or not they will be liable under the law and also that, because of the former monopoly control rules, the FTC's resources had been misallocated in the initial years of the FTC's existence. The new merger and revised monopoly provisions will now allow greater concentration of resources on anti-cartel enforcement. He also criticises the explicit exemption of small businesses from the cartel provisions on the basis that there is no logical justification for such an exemption simply based on the small size of the enterprise, rather than the effect on competition in the relevant market.

An assessment of anti-cartel enforcement would appear to show that the FTC has made good progress in advocating the case for prohibiting cartel activity. Enforcement has been reasonably effective but whilst the system has not been perfect, it has been adequate and, given Taiwan's participation in OECD and other fora, it appears that greater emphasis will now be placed on the detection and punishment of cartels and that larger market operators will now be targeted. However, the removal of the criminal sanctions for cartel operations, as noted above, does appear to be a retrograde step, given international developments in this aspect of competition policy.

9.16.3 Vertical restraints

The FTL, as we have seen above, treats vertical restrictions as essentially part of the rules concerned with unfair trade practices, as opposed to their being pure competition concerns. Article 18 of the FTL prohibits retail price maintenance and Article 19.6 forbids an enterprise from 'limiting its trading counterparts business activity improperly by means of the requirements of business engagement', which are likely to lessen competition or impede fair competition. The FTC has interpreted Article 19.6 to include tying, exclusive dealing and any restrictions imposed on operators concerning consumers or geographical areas. As was mentioned above, both these provisions were thought to be primarily concerned with reducing inflationary pressures, especially in relation to commodities that were imported and subject to retail price maintenance and other onerous restrictions. The cost of imported luxury cosmetics was a populist issue that arose during the early years of implementation of the FTL.

---

[80] See Liu, *Fostering competition law and policy*.

There has also been concern with the activities of retailers as demonstrated by a programme initiated by the FTC in 1995 to deal with the relationship between retail chain stores and their suppliers and also issues concerned with the growth of franchised retailers.

Despite a 1995 programme to identify egregious practices, the FTC continued to receive a high volume of complaints in relation to marketing and distribution practices in Taiwan. In 2000, the FTC adopted additional guidelines in relation to fees demanded of suppliers by retailers with market power. These fees were in addition to the price of the goods supplied. Under the new guidelines fees charged, not related directly to the promotion of the goods in question or contributions to equipment, research and development or general promotional activities were declared to be improper.[81]

Another issue of concern in relation to retailing in Taiwan has been the explosive growth of franchised retailing. 7-Eleven Convenience Stores and China Petroleum Corporation (CPC) respectively operate large franchised chains of convenience stores and petrol stations. Taiwan has over 3,200 7-Eleven stores. Apparently in Taiwan, 7-Eleven franchises are organised differently to other jurisdictions. The Taiwan franchisor not only supplies goods to be sold in the shops as well as a business format but also agrees to share business risk and provide various online services. In the view of the FTC, the franchise is more akin to a joint venture between the franchisee and the franchisor. This method of franchise operations meant that they were caught by the FTL merger provisions until the 2001 amendments. Whilst acknowledging the benefits that franchised operations can bring, the FTC has remained alert to the possibility of collusion or exclusionary practices, although no enforcement proceedings have yet been brought in this regard.

Franchising of CPC retail filling stations also caused the FTC some concern, in that because of the previous vertically monopolised structure of the industry, the policy decision by government to liberalise oil product imports and refining in Taiwan, made the distribution of oil produce difficult due to a shortage of sites for new petrol stations, as all the existing stations were owned and operated by the former monopolist CPC.

The franchise agreements granted by CPC to divest itself of direct ownership of filling stations were viewed by the FTC with some suspicion

[81] See *Taiwan's competition law enforcement experience and cases relating to retailing businesses,* Lin Gin-lan Taiwan Fair Trade Commission ww2.jftc.go.jp/eacpf/o5/ APECTrainingProgramme 2003/LINGin.pdf.

as they might be a method by which CPC might seek to perpetuate its dominant status in the petroleum market. Shortages of suitable sites for new petrol stations, particularly in urban areas, exacerbated the problem. The FTC has taken a vigilant attitude towards CPC market practices, as any attempt to consolidate the monopolistic power of the CPC would undermine the policy to liberalise the retail petroleum market.

Lastly, as regards vertical restraints, the use of Article 24 of the FTL should also be mentioned. This provision provides that 'no enterprise shall otherwise have any deceptive or obviously unfair conduct that is able to affect the trading order [*sic*]'. This catch-all provision is additional to the previous prohibitions set out in the FTL and might be seen as primarily a consumer-protection measure. The provision has been used in a wide variety of cases and in particular in relation to vertical restraints. The Carrefour case of 2001 provides an example of its utilisation. The FTC received a complaint from Tang Chia Co., a supplier to Carrefour of tobacco and alcohol products. The complaint alleged that Carrefour exploited its position in the retail market to collect 'additional fees' from Tang Chia Co. The FTC found that Carrefour had indeed charged eleven 'additional fees' during the period 1999 to 2000. These appeared to be in contravention of Article 24. At the relevant time, Carrefour had 27.35 per cent of the turnover of hypermarkets in Taiwan. This was not of the whole of the retail market in groceries but limited to large-format stores. Even on that narrow market definition Carrefour was not dominant and could not have been dealt with under the monopolisation provisions of the FTL. However, instead of concluding that suppliers could merely have refused to supply Carrefour with products, on the terms offered, given that there were many other competitors in the general grocery retail market and also in the hypermarket sector, the FTC concluded that as Carrefour had 'a significant market position' and that as the supplier had continued to trade with Carrefour notwithstanding these disadvantageous terms, Carrefour had breached Article 24 by being able to rely on its advantageous market position to collect 'these additional fees'.

Whilst one might have some sympathy with the supplier in this case, the interpretation of Article 24 appears to be unduly wide and seems to show that protection of the supplier, rather than a concern with the process of competition, was actually at the heart of the FTC's decision. Presumably the central issue in deciding this case was one of 'obvious unfairness', which Article 24 prohibits. However, it does seem in this case the decision of the FTC is questionable on purely competition grounds.

Thus, in relation to vertical restraints, the FTC appears to have taken the view that whilst the FTL provisions are essentially consumer protection measures in the case of Article 24, a mechanism to enforce rules of 'fair play' in the commercial market place exists. This policy decision appears to reflect provisions in Japanese statutes and is also perhaps an undesirable widening of a concept found in US law. Thus, it is open to question whether the provision is being implemented appropriately.

9.16.4 Merger cases

As will be recalled from the earlier discussion, the pre-2002 merger provisions were too widely drawn and so captured a very large number of small-scale franchise agreements that were of little or no concern in competition terms. The huge number of notifications diverted attention away from matters of real competition importance and wasted valuable resources. As will also be remembered, one of the principle reasons for the delay in enactment of the FTL was in relation to the possibility that over-intrusive rules would inhibit the beneficial restructuring and consolidation of small and medium-sized businesses. However, over a decade of experience of merger control has shown these fears to have been unfounded as only four notified merger cases were actually refused permission to proceed and three of them related to the cable television market (CTV).

The Taiwanese CTV market had several idiosyncratic characteristics. Firstly, broadcasting channels were previously tightly controlled and largely owned by the KMT; only in the 1990s, as the political environment changed, was an even-handed regulation of the television industry adopted. The broadcasting law provided for a licensing and regulatory regime, dividing Taiwan into a number of franchise areas with a maximum of five operators licensed for each locality. The law required diversity of ownership of licensees in particular areas and restrictions on foreign ownership. This plurality of ownership resulted in keen competition for viewers and so, advertising revenues. Thus, some consolidation would have given substantial efficiency gains as a result of economies of scale. The three decisions by the FTC on merger applications in this highly fragmented and politically sensitive industry should not be seen as a reliable indication of FTC competence as regards merger review, because many potentially forbidden consolidations occurred in the CTV sector without triggering FTC action as a result of the legalistic and rigid threshold requirements of the FTL. Thus, it is very difficult to form a view as to the appropriateness of decisions in these cases given these complicating extraneous factors.

9.17 The process of policy formation and execution

If one considers Taiwan's performance in competition policy matters as against that of China and Hong Kong, one is struck by the fact that Taiwan has been able both to legislate and implement a full competition regime, despite the difficulties inherent in that process. It is submitted that the reason Taiwan has been able to achieve this is the existence of an effective democratic process which has encompassed the inclusion of a competition regime as part of economic and political liberalisation. This view is confirmed by officials at the FTC[82] and by independent observers.

Professor Lawrence Liu has written:

> It is not easy to embrace competition policy. But Taiwan's experience is one of voluntary adoption of rules that seek to preserve market forces... For post-war Taiwan seeking to modernise its economy and society... industrial policy had its heyday in Taiwan, trade liberalisation begun in the 1980s was not easy. But since the 1980s Taiwan has increasingly relied on competition policy to guide economic progress... market liberalisation paved the way for the enforcement of the FTL. The fact that Taiwan had undergone significant political reforms when the FTL was enacted helped to solidify the political support required to make competition policy enforceable [through] law.[83]

It is submitted that the core reason for the difference in competition adoption success between China/Hong Kong and Taiwan is the existence of this functioning, albeit imperfect, democracy in Taiwan.

9.18 Conclusion

Taiwan has adopted and operated a comprehensive competition law system for over twelve years. Legislating a suitable statute and proceeding to implement a new law of this type is an undertaking fraught with the possibility of failure.

Taiwan has achieved notable success in its progress towards operating a more efficient, flexible and responsive economy, to which end the competition law has been a not insignificant contributor. The commitment of

[82] Liu Chien-hsuen of the Fair Trade Commission.
[83] Liu, *In search of free and fair trade*, above.

politicians, the long-term public advocacy of competition policy and the effective implementation of the new law by the FTC have been impressive.

The results have not always been perfect but the system and those who operate it have shown themselves to be both reflective and responsive. The law has been amended to improve deficiencies and the bureaucracy has matured in its approach to enforcement.

The achievements of Taiwan's adoption should be seen as a useful case study for transitional and developing states that wish to succeed in creating and implementing a pro-competition policy and a legal regime to enforce it effectively.

10

Political economy: an explanation of competition policy in Greater China

10.1 Introduction

This book has considered the political and economic arguments in favour of a pro-competition policy enforced by statutory provisions. The influence of international organisations on potential adopter nations to rely on competitive markets with appropriate protections for the competitive mechanism has also been outlined, with particular reference to Greater China. The actual and contemplated competition law systems of China, Hong Kong and Taiwan have been described and analysed in the context of their own particular political, economic and legal settings. However, no comprehensive explanation of the existing state of affairs in the studied jurisdictions has yet been offered.

This chapter will provide that explanation by using grounded theory to create a hypothesis. The key to understanding both the current features of the competition systems in each jurisdiction and their likely future development, lies in their unique political and institutional environment.

This chapter will also sketch the relevant aspects of their respective political economy conditions; describe and analyse the arguments on the merits of whether authoritarian or democratic structures are best in optimising economic market-orientated growth and link this debate to the ability of a jurisdiction successfully to adopt and operate a pro-competition regime. The particular circumstances pertaining in Greater China will then be recalled from the narrative chapters, so allowing the creation of the explanatory hypothesis.

10.2 Political economy of Greater China

Competition policy and law have deep roots in the economic theory that informs the rationale for the political choice to adopt a market basis for economic management. However, it cannot safely be assumed that a laissez-faire policy will always promote economically efficient outcomes through innate competition in any given market and policy makers would be wise to bear in mind what the founder of modern economics had to say on the subject: 'People of the same trade seldom meet together but the conversation ends in a conspiracy against the public or in some diversion to raise prices' (Adam Smith, *The Wealth of Nations*, 1776).

Consequently, if one accepts on the one hand that economies do not benefit from government *dirigiste* micro-management but that, on the other hand, markets cannot be trusted to self-correct by reason of conspiring competitors or dominant abusers, then politicians may well seek to achieve optimal economic outcomes by imposing a set of rules upon the economic game. As Professor Manfred Neuman says in relation to Germany's adoption of a competition regime after the Second World War: '[The pre-existing proliferation of cartels in Germany] provides overwhelming evidence for competition policy to be indispensable for maintaining competition... Adopting a laissez-faire stance of competition policy bodes the danger for a free-market economy to be corrupted and its social legitimacy to be undermined.'[1] Thus, a serious commitment to optimal free-market operations necessarily involves some measure of government interference in market processes whether as a prescriptive regulator or as a light-touch umpire. It is submitted that the subject of competition is infused with economic and political concepts concerning wealth creation and the control of that process, including distribution of that wealth amongst the population. At bottom, the root question becomes, who should make economic decisions, and this is inherently a political question.

As we have seen in China, until relatively recently, all economic and political decisions were taken by the party-state. That monolithic economic structure has now broken down and may well collapse under the impact of market opening consequent upon WTO entry. The government has accepted that this new economic paradigm needs a new set of rules and is endeavouring to promulgate the new rulebook. Whether the rules will be appropriate or enforceable is a moot point.

In stark contrast, the Hong Kong government claims to be a quintessential example of limited government that allows a free market to allocate economic resources and denies the need for a comprehensive regulatory regime. However, we have seen that this is not entirely accurate, either in respect of ownership and control of a number of vital factors of

---

[1] Manfred Neuman, *Competition policy: history, theory and practice*, Cheltenham: Edward Elgar (2001), pp. 27–8.

production, nor in relation to the sector-specific approach adopted to regulate several parts of the economy. It is true to say, however, that in industries not subject to external competitive pressures, much of the domestic market is left to its own devices. Unsurprisingly, as Adam Smith predicted, significant collusion and monopoly has resulted, though the government wilfully refuses to accept this analysis even though it is derived from the best available evidence. The government emphatically rejects the need for a set of transparent and universal competition rules, implicitly rejecting the majority of academic and political opinion internationally. Presumably, the Hong Kong government would agree with the minority opinion, most trenchantly expressed by Dominick Armentano, who denies the need for anti-trust policies on the basis that they are contrary to natural law, the economic theory that underpins them is insufficiently objective and that perfect competition as the ultimate goal of competition policy is unrealistic and unattainable.[2] Armentano's views, which are even more critical than those of Bork,[3] are a useful counterpoint to the majority opinion but they have not been influential in causing an abandonment of competition regulation, in fact quite the opposite, as a large number of countries have rushed to legislate since the 1980s. Armentano's objections to competition policy have been subjected to telling criticism,[4] which has exposed them as being an unreliable basis on which to found a do-nothing laissez-faire policy, as is advocated by the Hong Kong authorities.

Yet, the official Hong Kong policy has not been accepted by everyone. As the former Governor of Hong Kong, Chris Patten, says:

> How economically literate or sensible were the pressures that came from the anti-democratic camp in Hong Kong? A number of the most prominent business spokesmen and lobbyists (though, to be fair, not by any means all) gave every appearance of wanting to audition for walk-on parts as those businessmen whom Adam Smith memorably described in *The Wealth of Nations* as seldom being able to meet together 'even for merriment and diversion' without getting involved in a conspiracy against competition, found monopolies extremely cosy, disliked open tendering (or open anything for that matter), and believed that any regulation of markets or of corporate governance was thinly disguised socialism.[5]

---

[2] Armentano, *Anti-trust*.   [3] Bork, *The Anti-trust paradox*.

[4] For a forthright and convincing critique of Armentano's views see, F. M. Scherer, *Anti-trust ideology or economics?* (3) Critical Review, vol. 5, no. 4. (1992), Center for Independent Thought. Also reproduced as a chapter in F. M. Scherer, *Competition policy: domestic and international*, Cheltenham: Edward Elgar (2000).

[5] Christopher Patten, *East and west*, London: Macmillan (1998), p. 195.

Whilst this paradoxical situation is, in itself, worthy of description and analysis, the author believes that an explanation should be sought to synthesise the observed phenomena. This inevitably leads to the question of how a theory can be created that encapsulates the observed phenomena in both China and Hong Kong that have been analysed here and then explain them satisfactorily. As was explained in chapter 1, grounded theory has been the methodology selected to attempt to rationalise the evidence uncovered. The facts discovered will become the constructs of a hypothesis that will then be measured against the available information to confirm its internal validity. Once the internal validity of the hypothesis has been confirmed it is necessary, in accordance with grounded theory, to show that the hypothesis also has external validity. In order to do so, contrast will be made with competition law developments in Taiwan. The selection of Taiwan as the control jurisdiction is deliberate. Taiwan has largely the same historical, political, legal, economic, cultural, linguistic and racial characteristics as China and Hong Kong but with the crucial difference that it has an effective competition law regime and also has a functioning democracy. It will be demonstrated that the proposed hypothesis is both internally and externally valid and, thus, may provide a workable test as to whether or not, in any given jurisdiction, competition law and policy will have the necessary environmental preconditions to achieve the domestically set objectives of a market-based economic policy. This will demonstrate that the theory created is generalisable. Thus, the linkages between monopolies in the economy and monopolies in politics identified by Woodrow Wilson (see section 1.1) will be explained in theoretical terms. Potential criticisms of the hypothesis will also be discussed below (10.7).

10.3 Economics and democracy

The literature on the relationship between a nation's political system and its economic success is very extensive. The crux of the debate is whether authoritarian regimes are better than democratic ones in delivering economic growth, since most states, whether democratic or not, now, at least theoretically, subscribe to market economy principles. Another heated debate also rages as to what, precisely, are the hallmarks of a democracy and whether partial democracies or quasi-authoritarian governments can also achieve significant, stable, long-term growth. Allied to this debate is the question of competence in government, whatever its political typology, and that the key to economic success lies in the efficiency and fairness of the system, rather than the peculiarities of individual political arrangements.

This complex, multi-faceted dispute is not just the preserve of arid academes, as the promotion of 'good governance' has become part of the political lexicon of the principal aid-donor countries and the international development organisations since the fall of the Soviet Union. The need for Western donors to ignore the poor economic and political performance of many client states that had sided with the West during the Cold War has evaporated. The 'good governance' issue and the form of political arrangements that best achieve competence in government are also central to the question of whether or not a competition regime will be effective. As will be shown later, the evidence presented in this study of China, Hong Kong and Taiwan suggests that political arrangements determine whether a jurisdiction can successfully adopt and enforce a competition regime.

The debate about the linkages between politics and economic achievement is riven with controversy over disputes about taxonomy, arguments about cause and effect and the relative importance of the sequencing of reforms, whether political, economic or legal. The significance of law as the definer of property rights, that allows efficient transfer of those rights and the ability to use them effectively as collateral for loans is also part of the ongoing debate of how best to promote prosperity. Capital formation via reliable collateral security also promotes the creation, expansion and efficient operation of markets which has also been highlighted in the literature and will be discussed below.

A useful over-view of aspects of this debate has been provided by Christopher Clague.[6] Firstly, he suggests that political scientists and economists address the inter-linkage of decisions about liberalisation differently, which reflects the internal paradigms of their respective disciplines. Political scientists look at individual national case histories and try to extract generalisations that explain changes in political fashion and waves of politico-economic reform. In contrast, economists looking at the same data attempt to create a stylised list of facts whereby the construction of a predictive model may be achieved, which assumes rationality, self-interest and foresight on the part of policy makers. These divergent approaches colour the explanations provided for the success or failure of reform.

---

[6] *The Political economy of liberalisation: analytical approaches from economics and political science*, ch. 5 in *The expansion of economics: toward a more inclusive social science*, ed. Shoshana Grossbard-Shechtman and Christopher Clague, New York: M. E. Sharpe (2002).

As regards which system of government best provides optimal results, in the 1960s and 1970s autocracies were generally thought to be best at delivering economic reform and growth in developing countries. Authoritarian regimes were thought best because they could withstand the clamour of special-interest groups, which democratic governments might have to placate to ensure electoral success. Thus, democratic governments would have a short time-horizon that would be inimical to the long-term stability needed for the promotion of economic success. Authoritarian regimes, provided they were not irredeemably corrupt or incompetent, were thought best placed to achieve market-based reforms; the cases of Taiwan, South Korea, Indonesia and Chile were often cited in support of this contention. However, by the 1980s the conventional wisdom was under attack when a number of studies, particularly related to South America, appeared to show that there was no necessary correlation between authoritarianism and economic success.[7] These surveys concluded that, in relation to economic success, the quality of the civil service was a key factor and that resistance to reform came from ruling power elites. A change of regime was the catalyst that promoted reform, as those with vested interests to protect were ousted from office and so lost the power to protect them; this was true whether the regime change was from democratic to authoritarian or vice versa.

Thus, on this view there was no clear evidence as to the universal superiority of authoritarian or democratic forms of government in relation to the promotion of long-term economic success or as to the effectiveness of governments reacting to periodic economic crises. This ambivalence as to the best form of government to deliver economic success has also become entwined in the related issue of whether a country needs a period of benevolent dictatorship, so as to develop constitutionalism, that is to say a reliable rule of law, separation of powers, and protection of the basic liberties of speech, assembly, religion and property ownership. Some have argued that a clear distinction should be drawn between a liberal democratic state and an illiberal democracy, where constitutionalism has been subverted by majoritarian rule, unconstrained by respect for individual rights. Fareed Zakaria, in his influential article 'The Rise

---

[7] K. L. Remmer, 'The politics of economic stabilisation: IMF standby programmes in Latin America 1954–84', *Comparative Politics*, 19(1996), pp. 1–24; 'Democracy and economic crisis: the Latin American experience', *World Politics*, 42(1990), pp. 315–35; 'The political economy of elections in Latin America 1980–91', *American Political Science Review*, 87(1993), pp. 393–407.

of Illiberal Democracy',[8] argued that an over-concentration on political liberty in choosing a government is dangerous, as newly democratising countries can fall prey to majoritarian oppression of minorities and disregard individual liberties.

Zakaria opined that the development of a constitutional liberalism that protects civil rights is much more difficult to cultivate than merely adopting an open electoral system. He suggested that constitutional liberalism could lead to democratic politics but that democratic elections, of themselves, do not bring constitutional liberalism. He also suggested that the attainment of constitutional liberalism is a key factor in optimising economic reform. He considered it safer and more successful for states to undergo a transition to full democracy via a process of benevolent authoritarianism, which inculcates the virtues of constitutionalism before permitting full political liberty.[9]

These views have been criticised as ignoring the fact that authoritarian regimes, even when allowing some personal liberties and protecting property rights, often resort to abuses of human rights. They rarely have a comprehensive and robust conception of the rule of law, as press freedom is tightly controlled and dissidents and protesters are victimised by oppressive state surveillance or detained without due process of law.[10] Clearly, if one narrows the definition of rule of law to exclude the protection of basic human rights against state abuse, the attraction of a philosopher-king type sovereign, as against majoritarian tyranny, is clear. But if a more inclusive definition of the breadth of the rule of law is adopted, the balance of advantage diminishes.

The relationship between a political system and economic success has also been analysed by Hernando de Soto. He has examined the relationship between fair and effective regulatory systems and economic growth

---

[8] Fareed Zakaria, 'The rise of illiberal democracy', *Foreign Affairs*, 76(6) (Nov./Dec. 1997), p. 22. Whether the phenomenon of illiberal democracy worldwide is increasing or reducing is controversial. Some suggest that the high-water mark of illiberal democracy has now past. See Adrian Karatncky, 'The decline of illiberal democracy', *Journal of Democracy*, 10(1), (Jan. 1999), pp. 112–25.

[9] Fareed Zakaria, *The future of freedom: illiberal democracy at home and abroad*, New York: Norton (2003).

[10] Larry Diamond, 'The illusion of illiberal democracy', *Journal of Democracy*, 14(4), (Oct. 2003), pp. 167–71. Other criticism of Zakaria's postulation concentrates on the view that the triumph of the liberal principle has created an almost unchallengeable right to universal suffrage, so rendering untenable the suggestion that a less than democratic but liberal government is preferable. Marc Plattner, 'From liberalism to liberal democracy', *Journal of Democracy*, 10(3) (July 1999), pp. 121–34.

and wealth creation. In his book, *The Mystery of Capital: Why Capitalism Triumphs in the West and Fails Everywhere Else*,[11] he argued that there is a direct correlation between simple and effective recognition of property rights and successful capitalism. Such a system would benefit the widest proportion of any given society, rather than just a small elite. This proposition has been supported by a recent empirical study of over 130 countries between 1995 and 1999, which suggested that in addition to securing property rights, other factors are also decisive in creating a prosperous society. Roll and Talbot[12] concluded that in addition to strong property rights, political rights (elections), civil liberties (human rights), press freedom and government spending are the most significant and positive influences. Excessive regulation, poor monetary policy, informal economic activity (black market) and foreign trade barriers are the most important negative factors. They also suggest that the statistical evidence they produce shows that democratic states, that are also constitutionally liberal, *cause* economic growth and prosperity to develop more rapidly than in countries subject to undemocratic regimes or illiberal democracies. Amartya Sen also suggested that political incentives (democracy) can be just as important to economic growth as a market economy; the two must proceed in tandem to promote an optimal outcome.[13]

A recent book, *The Democracy Advantage: How Democracies Promote Peace and Prosperity*,[14] supports this thesis and provides a statistical comparison of the relative economic progress of democracies against non-democratic states worldwide over the period 1960 to 2001. The conclusions reached from the quantitative data are somewhat surprising and show that on average rates of GDP per capita growth in democracies are higher and a range of development indicators – life expectancy, school enrolment, cereal crop yields, infant mortality – amongst others, are all better in democracies than in autocracies. The authors suggest that this superior performance is due to a range of factors that give democracies an advantage over authoritarian regimes. These include more accountability, greater equality of opportunity, higher levels of access to information and so transparency, better political stability and a greater ability to learn

[11] Hernando de Soto, *The mystery of capital: why capitalism triumphs in the west and fails everywhere else*, New York: Basic Books (2000).
[12] Richard Roll and John Talbot, 'Political freedom, economic liberty and prosperity', *Journal of Democracy*, 14(3) (July 2003), pp. 75–89.
[13] Amartya Sen, 'Democracy as a universal value', *Journal of Democracy*, 10(3) (July 1999), pp. 3–17.
[14] Morton H. Halperin, Joseph T. Siegle and Michael M. Weinstein, *The democracy advantage: how democracies promote prosperity and peace*, New York: Routledge (2005).

from mistakes and take effective corrective action more quickly. They do not say that authoritarian regimes cannot ever produce stellar economic results but rather that this is highly exceptional. They note the progress made by China in the last twenty-five years but suggest that the continued sustainability of high growth rates is uncertain, for the reasons analysed in the preceding chapters.

This evidence suggests that, contrary to popular assumption, authoritarian government is not necessarily better for economic growth and development. Thus, it seems that there is also evidence that democracy is causative of economic growth and development via markets.

Turning now to the specifics of competition regulation, what impact does this debate have on the creation of a hypothesis to explain the factual situation currently observed in China, Hong Kong and Taiwan? The literature appears to suggest that, in respect of use of markets as a tool of economic management, democracies have a better record than autocracies. Democracies may even be causative of superior economic outcomes. Democracies also appear to be at least as capable of promoting efficient institutional infrastructure as autocracies and may even surpass them. Thus, democracies appear to be better suited to optimise economic growth based on foundations of rule of law and efficient administration. These strands of economic rectitude coupled with rule of law, and efficient, impartial and uncorrupt government all seem necessary prerequisites for a system of competition regulation adoption and appropriate implementation; Kovacic and other competition law commentators confirm this (see chapter 2).

10.4 The hypothesis

The theory of knowledge explained in section 1.4.3 was used as the principal foundation for the recording, analysis and assimilation of the data in the substantive chapters on China, Hong Kong and Taiwan. The evidence concerning the state of competition in China and Hong Kong has been presented in the relevant chapters in this book. This has led the author to consider how they can be rationalised to form an overarching theory to test whether competition policy is achieving its stated goals in greater China or any other given jurisdiction. Further, it is necessary to consider what are the fundamental factors that underlie the success or failure of any given set of competition policies and laws.

In the first instance we have to define what is meant by the term 'competition'. As was discussed in chapter 2, the economic literature on this subject is very large. Classical economics considered an atomistic state of perfect competition to be the market structure that would produce optimal economic results but the constraints extant in the real world have meant that this vision is utopian. Perfect competition can only exist in the mind of the economic theorist, not in the world of real people and real businesses. The contemporary theories of contestable markets and workable competition provide more realistic policy goals that have been adopted pragmatically as the primary objective of most pro-competition governments. But it is inevitable that even the more limited objectives that these models imply will be subject to the exigencies of exemptions to the stated policy resulting from the political and social demands of voters and firms fearful of unrestricted competition in sensitive markets. However, although competition policies are hedged by these caveats, most governments in developed economies espouse pro-competition policies of one type or another backed by law. For the purposes of this book, it is postulated that without, at least, the tacit acceptance of economic competition by the general population, their political representatives and government officials, no competition policy will ever achieve its objectives; in other words a successful campaign of competition advocacy must have been undertaken to convince the political elite and the general population of the merits of an active pro-competition policy.

Assuming that this basis of political support applies, and a pro-competition policy is chosen, what measures are needed to ensure that the objectives of such a policy are achieved? The Hong Kong government believes that exhortation is all that is required, save in exceptional circumstances. However, most other jurisdictions disagree and have decided that law, properly drafted and enforced, is an essential tool to achieve competition policy goals.

Whether a competition policy 'works' in practice can be encapsulated by the word 'effective'. This adjective in the context of this discussion has, it is submitted, three elements:-

- A usable *legislative instrument*, namely, a coherent and consistent law, not subject to extraneous exceptions or ambiguities;
- Competent and impartial *administration* of the law, that is it needs to be efficiently implemented by government agencies staffed with suitable expert, uncorrupted, personnel; and
- *Enforcement*, that is the ability to coerce persons who break the law into compliance by administrative or judicial sanctions, this is essential to guarantee the integrity and utility of the competition system.

It is submitted that without these three elements, no competition regime can be 'effective'.

However, it is further submitted that more is needed to ensure that competition policy is effective. Clearly, the three factors mentioned above are a necessary but not a sufficient framework to ensure the integrity of a competition system. In the author's view, there is a fundamental condition to make competition policy effective. This necessary foundational element is that the territory in which the policy operates must have a 'functioning democracy'; this is the core reason why neither China nor Hong Kong can ensure that a pro-competition policy can be made effective through law. This bold assertion will be tested below.

In the hypothesis the term 'functioning democracy' has a special meaning. It does not mean a territory that merely conducts popular elections at regular intervals where the population has the right to vote. This is, of course, a necessary requirement of a democracy but it is not a sufficient determinant of the extant political structures that are fundamental to a successful competition policy. There are many nations that hold elections but nevertheless do not have effective competition policy, and that is because they do not have a functioning democracy as defined here. Functioning democracy, as used here, encompasses a set of values, procedures and conditions that is much wider than the mere holding of elections. The term does not mean an idealised, referenda-based, plebiscite system with voters taking direct decisions on every major political issue. This would be an unrealistic model of government in most jurisdictions.[15] 'Functioning democracy', is not an abstract theoretical construct but rather a system of government that includes all, or at least most, of the following elements:

- Representative government
  Mandated by universal suffrage where government's legitimacy and power derive from the consent of the governed as expressed in free and fair elections where the voters have a real choice of alternative political representatives.

- State institutions
  Established on a sound legal basis and exhibiting a division of powers between the legislative, executive and judicial branches with respect by each branch for the functions and powers granted to the other organs of state power.

- Rule of law
  Respect for the rule of law in terms of independent, fearless and un-corrupt judges and legal professionals, impartial decision-making and

---

[15] Though of course Switzerland does still operate a variant of this system.

respect for the judicial determinations of litigants' legal rights by the
population and other government agencies.

- Competent exercise of executive power
  Government policies should be executed by competent and skilful public officials who make decisions on the basis of the public good and
  do not protect or favour one section of society as a result of corrupt
  practices, whether financial or political.

- Civil society
  An active citizenry that has the ability to organise effective and vibrant
  non-governmental organisations that enjoy freedoms of speech and
  association, including consumer-advocacy organisations, single-issue
  pressure groups, trade unions, expert professional groups, academic
  commentators and, crucially, a free and independent media that has
  the ability to expose abuses of power and corrupt activities and can
  provide an active medium for public debate on policy issues.

'Functioning democracy', therefore, has all the characteristics of constitutional liberalism discussed above in section 10.3. Thus, we have now
identified two strands or constructs, namely, effectiveness and functioning democracy. This allows the conceptualisation of the core issues identified in this book. In considering all the facts discovered, two substantive questions have presented themselves to the author. Firstly, in what
circumstances can competition law be observed to function satisfactorily, in terms of achieving the domestically set policy objectives? This
clearly relates to the political context within which policy is made and
implemented and it is submitted that the existence or absence of a 'functioning democracy', as defined above, is the crucial determinant of the
success or failure of competition law in any given society. Secondly,
what factors determine the operational success of competition policy?
To achieve competition policy goals an 'effective' law, as defined above, is
needed.

The answer to these questions allows a linkage to be suggested and so
the postulation of the following hypothesis:

> Competition law can only be effective in a functioning democracy

The hypothesis, therefore, consists of three key elements or constructs
that have been identified and defined above: 'competition', 'effectiveness'
and 'functioning democracy'. Each of these constructs is derived from the
evidence examined in this book, competition being derived from economic theory, effectiveness being deconstructed into its component parts

as relevant here – the legislative instrument itself, administration and enforcement. Further, it is submitted that, the substratum that provides the only foundation upon which an effective competition policy can be erected is the concept of a 'functioning democracy'; illiberal or authoritarian regimes are not capable of effective implementation, as will be argued below (see section 10.7). The process undertaken to reach this proposition seems to accord with the grounded theory model of theory generation explained in section 1.4.5.

As regards 'competition' the studied jurisdictions now appear, at least formally, to accept the economic rationale of competition, though the extent to which all parts of Chinese society do so is open to question. These matters were examined in chapters 5 and 6. In Hong Kong, whilst competition is lauded in theory, the actions of government call into question the nature and level of its commitment to the concept, as was demonstrated in chapters 6, 7 and 8. Taiwan's contrasting experiences were examined in chapter 9.

In relation to 'effectiveness', China, as was shown in chapter 4, has major hurdles to overcome whereas Hong Kong could apply and enforce a competition law if only government policy towards adoption changed. Taiwan, on the evidence appears to have a reasonably well functioning competition system.

So far as the existence of 'functioning democracy' is concerned, China is very far from achieving this goal given the lack of universal suffrage, the absence of any political choice, corruption, hazy relationships between the CCP and the state, no separation of powers, no rule of law and a virtual absence of civil society, as defined.

Hong Kong's position is very different, as it fulfils most of the requirements of a 'functioning democracy', in that it already has good government, thriving civil society, the rule of law, low corruption rates and only needs to pass a political reform bill to adopt universal suffrage. But this may well be impossible given the obstacle of Beijing's consent to a systemic change and the need to override the internal veto power of the merchant oligarchy. This power matrix was explained and analysed in chapters 6 and 7.

Taiwan by contrast has made the transition from authoritarianism to democratic pluralism over the last two decades and appears to have all or at least almost all of the identified constituent elements of a functioning democracy, as defined.

Therefore the constructs that form the elements of the hypothesis are derived from the evidence exposed and analysed in this book.

10.5 Testing and validating the hypothesis

It is submitted that on the evidence provided in the analytical chapters, the conditions in both China and Hong Kong are not conducive to competition policy being made effective through law, within the meaning of the hypothesis. At root, this is because of the prevailing political conditions in both jurisdictions. But the reasons why competition policy is unlikely to be effective in either place are quite different.

In China, most of the conditions both in relation to effectiveness and functioning democracy are absent. In Hong Kong, by contrast, most of them are present. It is suggested that effective competition policy will not be achieved unless the underlying political conditions change. In accordance with grounded theory, the hypothesis generated from the research findings must be tested to prove its validity.

The evidence adduced in the work should provide the internal validity required by grounded theory as explained by Glasser and Strauss, in section 1.4.5. Yin, as will be recalled, suggested that to be confident of the validity of the generated theory multiple sources of evidence should be used and the veracity of the information should be checked with knowledgeable interlocutors (see section 1.4.6). Once the validity of the constructs is ascertained, the linkages between them can be used to form the hypothesis and the internal validity of the hypothesis can be measured against them. In order to cross-check whether the hypothesis is robust and if it can apply to situations beyond the studied jurisdictions, external validity also needs to be ascertained. This can be done by examining the effectiveness of competition law in a comparator jurisdiction, in this case Taiwan. This control analogue has been selected for the reasons mentioned above and will provide external confirmation that the hypothesis is, indeed, valid.

10.5.1 Internal validity – China

Essentially we need to ask several questions to determine whether China can adopt an effective competition policy. These relate to the same elements that constitute 'effectiveness' as defined and explained above.

Firstly, can China legislate a competition regime? As we have seen in section 5.7, China already has a draft competition law (the 1999, 2001 and 2004 drafts). These essentially include the norms usually associated with comprehensive competition regimes, namely control of anti-competitive agreements, abuse of dominant position and merger control. Additionally, the draft law contains a section relating to 'administrative monopoly'.

The proposals also provide a superficially attractive enforcement structure. Given the nature of the political system in China, should the CCP
hierarchy decide to legislate on this topic, the NPC would enact the statute
into law without difficulty. Thus, it appears that China can fulfil the first
element of 'effectiveness'.

Secondly, can China administer a competition law? The answer to this
must be no. China lacks sufficient competent personnel and its state institutions are notoriously susceptible to corruption of both the political
and/or financial type. Thus, on the evidence related in chapter 4, China
will not be able to administer a new competition law, within the definition offered in the hypothesis; support for this proposition can be found
in the way in which the existing provisions are not implemented by the
bureaucracies charged with this task.

Thirdly, can China enforce a competition law? Again the answer is
no. China does not have robust legal institutions and cannot ensure that
administrative or legal decisions are faithfully carried into effect because
of the structure of Chinese political society, local protectionism and a very
weak legal system in which corruption is rampant, as was demonstrated
in chapter 4.

Thus, it is suggested that China cannot implement an effective pro-
competition policy regime, even though one might be legislated. However,
these answers lead to the logical question of why this situation pertains
in China. In the author's submission, it is because China lacks the basic
condition for competition policy; China lacks a 'functioning democracy'.

If China had a functioning democracy, as defined, it would be able
to legislate, administer and enforce such rules but in the absence of this
political settlement any attempt at an effective competition policy regime
is doomed to failure. It is even possible that the additional powers granted
to the state apparently to promote competition could be used by corrupt
and partial officials to protect failing domestic industries from effective
competition provided by new entrants to the domestic Chinese market.
Those newcomers include efficient domestic private firms and foreign-
owned businesses, whether the goods are produced in China or imported,
and can now compete in the domestic market more effectively, as a result
of the loosening of trade controls following WTO accession. There is a
significant risk that given the current political, economic and financial
conditions in China competition policy could be perverted to perform
a protectionist, as opposed to a pro-competitive function. The danger
signals are already present – the recent merger regulations that only seek
to regulate foreign-connected transactions and the May 2004 government

report that claimed that sections of the economy were being monopolised by foreigners and that this was the principal reason for the need for the swift enactment of a new comprehensive competition statute.

10.5.2 Internal validity – Hong Kong

Adopting the same process for Hong Kong to test the internal validity of the hypothesis, we need to answer the same set of questions.

Firstly, can Hong Kong legislate a competition regime? As has been seen in chapter 8, Hong Kong is quite capable of drafting and legislating competition provisions, should the government see fit. The current sectoral approach, it is submitted, is a technical failure but notwithstanding that, it would be perfectly possible for Hong Kong to legislate a general competition law, should the government take the political decision to do so. But, as has been explained in chapters 6 and 7, this is highly unlikely to happen given the preponderant political weight of the commercial oligarchy. The decisive influence of this group means that the Hong Kong government is unwilling to change its policy stance for fear of the political consequences of such action. Thus, issues of competition policy are not being decided on the basis of the public good but rather on the basis of the policy that best suits the oligarchic vested interests that dominate Hong Kong's interlocking economic and political life. In these circumstances, the possibility of comprehensive legislation is remote. Again, one must ask the question, how can this situation be remedied? It is clear that the only way in which the political viewpoint of the government can be changed is the introduction of a 'functioning democracy' in Hong Kong. Crucially, this means in Hong Kong's case, the adoption of universal suffrage for LEGCO, and either a Westminster Cabinet system for the Executive Council and Chief Executive or a directly elected Presidential-type system. This could be achieved under the Basic Law in 2008 but the chances of universal suffrage being adopted within the next five years now appear unlikely given Beijing's ruling on the relevant Basic Law provisions in April 2004. Democratic parties are still attempting to force the pace of change but the powerful commercial oligarchs remain resolutely opposed to early adoption of universal suffrage. Thus, it can confidently be asserted that legislating an effective competition law in Hong Kong is most unlikely in present circumstances. Only if influential business interests could be persuaded to back competition legislation could the government be pressured into a policy reversal in present conditions. But given the extant vested interests, this would be a difficult or, indeed, an impossible task.

Secondly, can Hong Kong administer a competition law? Current evidence, on the basis of existing competition provisions in the telecommunications and broadcasting ordinances, suggests that, with some provisos, sufficient competent expertise exists within Hong Kong to administer any competition regime that might be legislated. Given Hong Kong's financial resources, should domestic expertise not be available, it could be purchased from abroad. The integrity of the civil service in matters of administration is undoubted and so, if a comprehensive law were to be introduced, it could be efficiently and fairly administered.

Thirdly, can Hong Kong enforce a competition law? Fortunately, Hong Kong has the benefit of the rule of law. Decisions of the courts and of the administration are, generally, faithfully implemented. There is constitutional liberalism in Hong Kong but not political liberalism in the form of universal suffrage. Public and private disputants accept decisions of government and the courts and abide by such rulings. Thus, again, if a competition law were enacted the necessary conditions exist for it to be enforceable.

As has been demonstrated in this section, an effective competition regime in Hong Kong is possible. The political conditions in Hong Kong are much more favourable than those that pertain in China. Such a law could be effectively administered and decisions made under it would be respected but given current political conditions, it is very unlikely that a comprehensive competition policy will be enacted into legislation due to the existence of the blocking power of the merchant oligarchs. An analogy might be made with the refusal of the House of Lords in England in 1909 to pass the tax-and-spend Peoples' Budget proposed by Lloyd George. King George V had to be persuaded to threaten to create a sufficient number of new peers sympathetic to the Liberal government's policy to force the Lords to abandon their opposition. The political situation in Hong Kong is not as favourable to change as the one that pertained in London in 1910 and there is no benign philosopher-king able to trump the extant vested interests. Therefore, it is submitted, that unless Hong Kong institutes constitutional reforms to commit to introducing a 'functioning democracy', comprehensive competition law will be most unlikely to reach the statute book, save for a Damascene conversion of the vested interest groups that hold effective political power to an active role for government in competition regulation.

Thus, it is submitted, for the reasons outlined in this section, as regards Hong Kong and the previous section as regards China, that the internal validity of the hypothesis is confirmed and it is provisionally valid. However, in order to be sure that the hypothesis is of general application one also needs to test its external validity by reference to a control analogue, in this case Taiwan. Further, the thrust of these arguments is also supported by knowledgeable interlocutors, as will be demonstrated below.

10.5.3 External validity – Taiwan

In order to show that the postulated hypothesis has external validity, as mandated by grounded theory, it is necessary to measure it against the experience of another jurisdiction. For the purposes of this book, it was both appropriate and convenient to select Taiwan for this purpose, given that it is a close analogue to China and Hong Kong. This choice avoids potential criticism based on historical, political, legal, economic, cultural or linguistic differences. However, since the liberalisation of the economy and the political system began in the 1980s, Taiwan has become increasingly divergent from the other parts of China.

Therefore, it is now necessary to consider the effectiveness of competition law and policy on Taiwan. This assessment is retrospective and based on the actual performance of a system that has been in place for twelve years, and so not a prospective exercise as to effectiveness, as was the case in respect of both the Mainland and Hong Kong, save for those provisions that actually exist and have been implemented.

Thus, the situation in respect of Taiwan is substantially different to that which pertains in China or Hong Kong.

Firstly, in contrast to the Mainland and Hong Kong, Taiwan has already legislated a comprehensive statute and revised it twice in light of operational experience. The Fair Trade Law (FTL) is an amalgam of elements of European, American and Asian regimes but appears to have been broadly suitable to the needs of the Taiwanese economy. The FTL formed a logical part of a package of economic liberalisation and deregulation measures first announced by the then authoritarian KMT government in the mid-1980s. This rolling programme of economic liberalisation has been implemented over the last two decades, subject to the exigencies of the economic cycle and the political situation at any given time. Thus, the legislative instrument required for the effectiveness of competition law exists and, given the analysis in chapter 9, appears to be appropriate to Taiwan's needs.

Secondly, the FTL in Taiwan appears to have been appropriately and fairly administered. A balanced assessment of the available evidence appears to be that the administration of the law has been both reasonably fair and efficient. The FTC has suitable expertise and resources to conduct its operations and over the first decade of its existence, selection, investigation and adjudication of cases appears to have been generally transparent and fair. Thus, on the evidence, whilst criticism of some policy issues and of some isolated individual cases has been made, the integrity of the administrative arrangements appears not to have been doubted.

Thirdly, the administration and adjudication of the FTL has been enforceable so as to give meaning to decisions of the FTC. The levying of fines and the adoption of injunctive relief does indeed appear to have been enforced. Private litigation, whilst theoretically possible, has been of little practical importance in the enforcement arrangements of the FTL. That is unsurprising given the nature of Chinese society and the very significant cost and uncertainty involved in individual litigation where there is little culture of aggressive private actions of this type. However, the Taiwanese record of public enforcement has indeed been impressive for a newly adopted regime.

Thus, a fair assessment of the evidence, as set out in chapter 9, in respect of Taiwan's performance in competition matters, shows that the adoption of competition law in Taiwan has been an effective instrument in assisting the restructuring of the Taiwanese domestic economy, so helping it to be more competitive and thus efficient.

Therefore, given that competition law is effective in Taiwan and ineffective in China and Hong Kong (both in relation to existing arrangements – save for the Hong Kong telecommunications regime – and as regards the immediate future), one is driven to consider why this is the case. The answer that presents itself is a political one. Taiwan's political arrangements are clearly very different from those on the Mainland and in Hong Kong. The key questions to ask are, do they accord with the hypothesis tendered in this book – namely do the political arrangements in Taiwan constitute a 'functioning democracy', as defined – and further is the existence of such a functioning democracy causative of the effectiveness of the competition system?

Based on the evidence set out in chapter 9, whilst Taiwan's democracy is immature and has been under considerable strain especially as a result of the events surrounding the 2004 Presidential election, the system does seem to fulfil the positive requirements of a functioning democracy; alignment is not perfect, but perfection in political systems is hardly to be expected. However, Taiwan does possess enough of the elements set out in the suggested hypothesis to pass the test of being a functioning democracy.

Further, it is possible to link the decision to liberalise the political system with the simultaneous process of economic liberalisation that was begun in the mid-1980s. The process was not perfectly synchronised but it seems abundantly clear that without the political impetus to adopt markets as the key economic regulator, the subsequent adoption of a competition law as a component of the reformatory process would not have been possible. The subsequent effectiveness of the law has been sustained by the underlying political support that the democratising society has supplied. Political liberalisation has loosened the grip of vested interests, enabling the creation and effective implementation of the new system. Thus, it is suggested that the key success factor in creating an effective competition law system in Taiwan has been the development of a functioning democracy. The future sustainability of the continued effectiveness of Taiwan's competition law system is inextricably linked to the maturing and consolidation of that functioning democracy within the island. This conclusion appears to accord with the academic literature discussed above (see section 10.3).

10.6 Interlocutors

A final piece of corroboration to lend support to the validation of the hypothesis are the views of knowledgeable interlocutors. The issues raised by Kovacic, described in chapter 2, concerning the hallmarks of successful adoption and implementation provide a framework or check-list to determine competition policy effectiveness (as defined above) in any given jurisdiction. His criteria have been referred to throughout this work when analysing the situation in both China and Hong Kong. His observations are equally apposite as regards Taiwan. But it is submitted that whilst his observations are most valuable they do not go to the root of the conundrum as to what factors underlie successful adoption of competition policy. This investigation of circumstances in Greater China has advanced his work by not only suggesting a theoretical explanation of the circumstances necessary for success but also by suggesting a predictive tool to assess the likelihood of competition policy success. This book's emphasis on the political and economic context within which competition policy adoption and enforcement operates represents a development and extension of Kovacic's observations. Support for the intimate linkage of a favourable political environment to successful adoption is also provided by Liu[16] in relation to Taiwan, and Patten in relation to Hong Kong.[17]

---

[16] See various articles quoted by Professor Liu in chapter 9.
[17] Patten, *East and west*, p. 195.

10.7   Criticisms of the hypothesis

Whilst the posited hypothesis appears to explain the observed phenomena pertaining to competition law in China, Hong Kong and Taiwan, several objections to this explanation can be envisaged. Firstly, it might be argued that the proposed explanation is too general and is not specifically related to competition law. Another branch of law might just as easily be substituted in place of competition law, which might well also only be effectively applied in a functional democracy; this argument may have some force. For example, human rights, may only be effectively enforced in a functioning democracy. But even if this is so, it is suggested that this does not detract from the validity of the hypothesis specifically in relation to competition law systems. As has been demonstrated, the success or failure of a competition system is intimately connected with the choice of economic model and the nature of the government machine that administers it. Competition law adoption, administration and enforcement is a uniquely difficult and complex task that juxtaposes questions of political and economic judgement that most other laws do not; it is for this reason that the hypothesis specifically links the ideas of competition law effectiveness with a functioning democracy.

Secondly, the concept of a functioning democracy might be criticised as being too vague and amorphous, to the extent that it is not amenable to precise definition or measurement. Arriving at a conclusion that country X has a functioning democracy but that country Z does not, is a matter of subjective judgement and so, has little or no value, as two dispassionate observers might reasonably disagree as to whether or not a country's system qualifies as a functioning democracy, within the meaning of the definition proffered above. Again, it is admitted that judgement, not empirical calculation, as to the qualitative nature of the system, is inherent in the notion of functioning democracy but that does mean that the concept has no value. To some extent an analogy may be made with the difficulty of describing an elephant. A comprehensive description of such an animal might be difficult and no doubt there would be a wide variety of opinion as to the essence of a pachyderm but almost everyone would be able to recognise whether or not the animal in front of them was or was not an elephant. Utilising a set of similar criteria and applying them to the factual situation in any given jurisdiction should allow for a reasonable (though not absolute) degree of certainty as to whether or not a country has a functioning democracy or not. Presumably it might be possible to create a set of precise criteria with some method of statistically treating each element and then giving weight to it, so that a numerical index could be created to assess quantitatively whether or not a functioning democracy exists. However, inevitably, any such index would be open to criticism as to the inclusion or exclusion of one or other factor and the relative weightings given to them in calculating the index. Thus, any attempt at quantification would be subject to just as much controversy as an honestly attempted and robust qualitative assessment. The superficial attraction that an index number might provide greater objectivity or certainty is, it is submitted, an illusion.

Thirdly, objection to causation might be advanced. It might be argued as to whether or not it was necessary for a functioning democracy to exist prior to the creation of an effective competition system or, might it not be possible for some other form of government such as an enlightened autocrat or an efficient authoritarian regime that is less than a fully functional democracy, to have the ability to create and operate an effective competition system?

Clearly, it is possible for a state that is less than a functioning democracy to create a competition policy and to pass a competition law, though in general authoritarian governments favour corporatism.[18] But the acid test is whether such a state is able to appropriately administer and enforce the law even-handedly. Therefore, we need to consider whether in theory a wise but authoritarian philosopher-king might be able to achieve this feat and also whether there are any examples of such a regime in practice.

For the purposes of dealing with this argument, let us consider a state that has most of the trappings of a political democracy but which is, in fact, not a functioning democracy, within the definition under discussion here. It is necessary in developing this argument to consider how such an illiberal democracy or authoritarian regime might treat competition law. The concept of the illiberal democracy was considered earlier.

When considering the theoretical possibility of such a regime adopting, administering and enforcing a competition system, it is suggested that whilst a less-than-functioning democracy will be able to legislate a competition law, administration and enforcement will be sub-optimal due to inherent weaknesses in the system of rule of law, even if the executive and administrative organs of the state are competent. This is because

---

[18] For example, as Neuman notes, Nazi Germany extended the reach of pre-existing cartels so that every German business was required to belong to one, see Neuman, *Competition policy*.

it is likely that an authoritarian state or an illiberal democracy will have close linkages or actual control of various economic sectors, so creating irreconcilable conflicts of interest between on the one hand promoting competition and on the other state or regime members' personal economic goals, which will trump pro-competition interests. Authoritarian regimes and illiberal democracies will rarely brook opposition to the government line on what the regime considers a vital national interest and so competition sentiments will inevitably yield to anti-competitive forces when the two collide.

Thus, a well-administered, uncorrupt authoritarian state might well protect property rights through a judicial system when private interests are at stake, but the impartial administration of a competition law system causes particularly acute problems of conflicts of interest, especially where the state is a substantial or even dominant stakeholder in the national economy. Authoritarian states, by their nature, hold great sway in the national economy either directly or indirectly so making impartiality difficult, if not impossible. Open-textured rules and inherent discretion in application are an intimate part of all competition law systems. Enforcement, by an administrative body, which would be an intrinsic part of the authoritarian state's machinery, must raise the substantial suspicion that when state economic interests conflict with the maintenance of a competitive market, the state interest would prevail. This would be so even if appeal were possible to a court, as the loyalty of judicial appointees to the status quo would probably mean that a pro-state bias would be apparent. The nature of authoritarianism is to ensure compliance with corporatist objectives, for the greater good of the nation, and individual interests, of necessity, will be subservient to perceived national economic imperatives. Thus, in authoritarian states the rule of law will be attenuated in such a way as to make it less than complete. Only in a functioning democracy can there be sufficient checks and balances to counter the overwhelming presence of the state, which allow the attainment of a comprehensive and complete rule of law, essential to the effectiveness of a competition system.

Finally, an argument might be advanced that the hypothesis is too absolutist. By insisting that effectiveness is either present or absent in any given system and that only in jurisdictions that fulfil all the criteria of a functioning democracy can this occur, the theory is unrealistic in that no extant system can be absolutely effective, for if it were, presumably, it would become redundant, as it would have achieved its purpose by attaining a state of workable competition in the economy. This point is flawed, as competition is a dynamic, not a static, concept that constantly shifts through time as economic structures change and adapt to new circumstances, buffeted by developments in politics or technology. Further, effectiveness, as defined, is a qualitative concept and a rational, balanced assessment of all the elements of effectiveness must be made to ascertain whether any particular system is effective in combating anti-competitive practices and economic structures. A sub-optimal outcome may be achieved in any competition regime and this means that it is less than effective. Effective does not mean a perfect outcome, merely an optimal one. The evidence suggests that only in a functional democracy will effectiveness be achieved.

Consequently, it is suggested that a functioning democracy is a necessary condition for effective competition law and that authoritarian or illiberal democracies are unlikely to have effective competition law systems.

10.8 Conclusion

This chapter has sought to discuss and analyse the various issues of political economy relevant to the creation of a viable market economy and has related them to the specific conditions found in China, Hong Kong and Taiwan. This has allowed the creation of an explanatory hypothesis, that has been tested in accordance with grounded theory principles and found to be robust, even after critical analysis of potential weaknesses and the theory. The explanation offered of the present state of competition law and the probable future direction of this subject in Greater China hopefully commends itself to the reader.

11

Competition policy and law in Greater China: where next?

11.1 Introduction

This book has sought to examine and explain the prevailing competition regimes in Greater China. A theoretical explanation of the existing states of affairs in China, Hong Kong and Taiwan that is robust has been offered in the last chapter. The final matter to be addressed is what is likely to happen, in the near-term future, in competition matters in each of the three jurisdictions. Clearly, this author does not pretend to be able to foretell the future of competition regulation in Greater China but it is possible to extrapolate from the present position, based on the most recent intelligence, in each jurisdiction to offer a reasonable prognosis of the most likely developments.

However, on the assumption that the author's hypothesis is a valid explanation of the existing situation in Greater China, it would seem apparent that without the adoption of a functioning democracy, effective competition regulation is impossible. Whilst that is indeed the author's contention, some measures may be able to be taken to attempt to ameliorate the situation, though in the final analysis fundamental political change is the only viable route to achieve an effective competition policy in both China and Hong Kong. The exception to this radical prescription is clearly Taiwan, where less drastic measures are necessary to ensure that an existing working system of competition regulation continues to develop and improve through experience, reflection and adaptation.

11.2 China

In China, the obstacles to achieving a better competitive regime based on law are formidable. But, certain suggestions can be made that could alleviate some of the most pressing problems. Firstly, China might adopt simple, clear, limited, competition rules. In the first instance, a ban on cartels should be made. This might be absolute or subject to a rule-of-reason approach, in the EC sense. Abuse of dominance provisions would also be needed, given the structure of the Chinese economy. This would also necessitate a merger-control rule, otherwise competitors would simply combine to achieve monopolistic status. The rules could be implemented in stages to provide experience for officers handling competition cases. Prior to implementation of such rules, a significant period of high-quality education and training of all relevant civil servants staffing the new competition authority would be needed. Clearly, this would vary depending on function but without the enforcers having a clear understanding of the function and purpose of a competition law, the enterprise is doomed. This preparatory stage might take several years, as China simply does not have anything like enough qualified personnel at present. This process, if carried out appropriately, might involve hundreds of officials and would be very expensive. Foreign assistance would undoubtedly be needed, either by sending officials to universities in countries that have developed competition jurisprudence similar in structure and content to the new Chinese legislation or by importing qualified educators into China to conduct dedicated courses *in situ*. The language of instruction might well be a barrier to effective learning as in general, most Chinese students concentrate on English as their only foreign language. But this would not be the end of the process, as whilst university courses might well provide a valuable grounding in principles of foreign law and the decisions of foreign tribunals, Chinese officials would also need substantial practical training in all aspects of the enforcement of a competition statute. Investigation techniques, application of principles to actual case scenarios, analytical skills and the reasoning of decisions as to liability and penalty calculation would also be needed to be taught. This type of training is not available at university institutes and only private-practice law firms or government agencies have the necessary resources and/or experience. But in practice it is most unlikely that leading competition agencies, in primarily English speaking countries, will have the time, resources or motivation to offer more than token assistance. Private-practice law firms would have even less incentive to divulge their know-how, even if they were to be paid at very high corporate rates. Therefore, the practical obstacles for the training of Chinese officials to an appropriate standard to deal with the immensely complex fact-finding and analytical tasks that competition law demands are very great indeed.

Moreover, not only lawyers would need to be trained but also economists, forensic accountants and judicial personnel – both judges who might hear appeals and private lawyers who would have to advise enterprises. Additionally, a substantial number of academic teachers would also be needed. Extensive use of postgraduate courses at foreign universities would appear to be the only way to address this issue, though new methods of course delivery, such as through the preparation of dedicated Chinese-language materials or delivery of courses via the internet with intensive short-term traditional class contact to supplement delivery, might prove viable academically and financially. In total these measures represent an immense task and would involve a very substantial allocation of public resources and private funds too. In reality, with all the demands on the public purse, it is unlikely that even if training places were available through foreign universities or foreign agencies or law firms, the funds would be available to pay for them.

An alternative might be to deploy local training resources and this might have some success, but it is unlikely that the huge demand could be met by internal supply, especially as regards practical application of the law to individual situations, as to date there is no experience within the government machine or in universities of undertaking the sophisticated market analysis needed in relation to competition enquiries or the investigation of multi-national enterprises.

Another significant problem is the unreliability of domestic statistical and accounting information upon which to base enforcement decisions. China does not have a culture of open market information that has any substantial degree of reliability; it is likely that even information obtained, for example, from the tax authorities would be significantly inaccurate. Therefore, even to get to the stage of having a credibly staffed enforcement agency would be a huge task, never mind the actual operation of a sophisticated system.

From the experience of other transitional countries as examined in chapter 2, other issues beside training and education are fundamentally important too. In addition to adequate resources to run a competition agency, the architecture and position of the authority within the government machine would be crucial. In China, the place of that agency in the bureaucratic hierarchy would be critical in determining its credibility to enforce its decisions, especially as against other government agencies. At present, bureaucratic in-fighting has stalled progress towards legislation but if that log-jam is broken and a suitable niche found for the agency in the hierarchy, the problems of effectiveness are still far from overcome. A national authority with the highest administrative status and no affiliation to local government is essential to give the enforcement body political 'clout' and the kudos to attract high-calibre staff. The budget would have been generous to allow the employment of well-qualified staff to administer the law, so as to remove a basic reason for corruption. Unfortunately, the possibility of even a nominally independent competition agency in China is now remote and it is likely that the body will become a mere appendage of an existing bureaucracy. This prospect is depressing, as it probably condemns the enforcement of competition law to a subservient role to the other political priorities of the parent department. However, this potential marginalisation of competition enforcement might not be a wholly bad thing especially if it allows unconstrained economic forces more freedom to continue to erode the predominance of the state-owned sector and so assist in the creation of a functioning market; this is especially true if heavy-handed or discriminatory enforcement tactics were adopted by the new agency. Weak enforcement might, paradoxically, be better for the economy than zealous but partial application of the new rules.

All the relevant literature also places great emphasis on the need to undertake a comprehensive programme of competition advocacy to extol the virtue of market competition to officials, business operators and the consuming public; exactly how this could be achieved effectively in China is difficult to envisage. State control of all media outlets and a long history of expansive political propaganda campaigns certainly provide the necessary channels of communication to all sectors of society. However, propaganda exercises tend to be short term and aimed at a particular social or political problem that is limited in scope, such as violent crime or aspects of corruption; interest often wanes after the expiry of the campaign's limited duration with little long-term effect on the identified problem. Explanation of the complex theories of competition and putting them into a domestic Chinese context, so as to make them comprehensible to the population, is a formidable task. Incomprehension and scepticism are the likely responses of government officials and the barons of the state-owned enterprises, especially if enforcing pro-competition rules means loss of domestic-sector jobs or greater market opening that favours foreign firms. The general population will have the greatest difficulty in comprehending a pro-competition system and should they do so, and later their expectations are dashed by an inability to enforce legal decisions, their enthusiasm might be quickly undermined. Any actual increase in unemployment caused by increased competition might create severe public discontent.

Notwithstanding the creation of a corps of qualified professionals, a suitable agency and an effective advocacy campaign, the closely intertwined nexus of party, state and publicly owned enterprises will in-evitably cause significant problems of conflict of interest, even allowing for a good-faith desire to implement competitive reforms. This will be the case at both the policy level and also in respect of individual decisions, both within the competition agency and on appeal to the courts. This in-herent difficulty will be compounded by the ubiquity of corrupt practices. Consequently, the systemic problems identified here do indeed present substantial obstacles to the creation of an operational competition regime and it is difficult to envisage how all of them can be addressed in the near term, even though all the signs indicate that China will enact a new law soon and create a body to enforce it.

The anticipated new statute would not only deal with the traditional anti-trust-type competition problems of commercial enterprises; the hy-dra of administrative monopoly would also be tackled, again. Effective rules on administrative monopoly, though sorely needed, would be most difficult to enforce given China's political arrangements and should either be left until last to implement or else the existing administrative disci-plinary structures should be used as an alternative, though the utility of these procedures is doubtful.

Turning now to enforcement of decisions of the envisaged competition agency, since obtaining satisfaction of a money judgement or administra-tive penalty in China is so problematic, penal provisions aimed at a strict liability regime of imprisonment for culpable senior managers or respon-sible officers would seem to be the only practical way to secure compliance with competition enforcement directions, however draconian this might, at first, appear; after all an increasing number of countries now criminalise cartelisation.

But however sincere the advocates of a pro-competition system in China are, there is a real danger that such a new competition law might actually worsen competition conditions after WTO market-opening rules come into effect. They may be used selectively to disadvantage incoming foreign firms and protect domestic national champions, principally state enter-prises. Perversely, without the legal powers to control competition or com-petitors, the competitive forces unleashed by tariff and quota reductions might be a more effective pro-competitive force than ineptly or menda-ciously applied competition rules. In the worst-case scenario, competition law in China might be used to prevent, not encourage competition. Thus, it is submitted that given the reality of the political and legal conditions in China a competition regime might actually do more harm than good.

These suggestions are offered with a great deal of trepidation, given the expressed concerns about the possible misapplication of competition powers. Consequently, it might be best simply to allow the market forces, unleashed by WTO membership, free reign, so as to facilitate the import of goods and services and thereby to act as a proxy competition regime. This policy might allow the creation of markets in previously monopolised sectors. This might also promote the growth of the domestic private sector. Such a solution would also keep government intervention in the nascent market to an absolute minimum. At some later stage, once economic restructuring had proceeded and politico-legal conditions improved, consideration might then be given to competition regulation. At that time, the new competition regime would have more chance of an efficacious outcome. As to when an appropriate stage for implementation has been reached, only the passage of time will tell.

11.3 Hong Kong

Improving competitive conditions in Hong Kong is both, in a way, a simpler and yet at the same time a more difficult problem to address. Without a competition law to administer and enforce, suggestions for palliation are futile, given that one cannot recommend a removal of external government barriers to trade, such as tariffs and quotas, as there are so few of them. Reducing state intervention in enterprises would be limited to disengagement from health and educational services or the provision of potable water. There are no state enterprises to privatise (save government interests in the two railway companies) and the current laissez-faire policy could not be more business friendly. Reform of the land system and the change of use of real estate would certainly improve this vital sector of the economy. In the absence of a general competition law, the 'voluntary' system of exhortation to private business not to engage in anti-competitive practices is all that can be accomplished. The government will continue to protest its faith in unrestrained market forces and business will continue to pay lip service to the mantra of non-intervention. At the same time, however, enterprises will act rationally to maximise profits, blithely monopolising and cartelising the economy to the satisfaction of their shareholders and the chagrin of consumers.

The existing sector-specific rules in telecommunications and broadcasting clearly, as a minimum, need to be aligned but their effectiveness, even as regards their own domains, is dubious given the interconnected nature of Hong Kong conglomerates and the outcome of the Banyan Gardens case, which strictly limits the power of the regulator to the supervision of actual telecommunications licensees only.

In the face of implacable government intransigence, future progress in reforming competition regulation is unclear, despite the glaring defects in the competitive process in Hong Kong.

Those who are not convinced by the government's arguments for maintenance of the status quo will have to be mobilised to exert maximum political pressure to convince the administration that the existing arrangements are both illogical and ineffective in enhancing Hong Kong's future economic prosperity. The government's blind faith in the economic prescriptions of past British colonial administrations must be challenged, just as Hong Kong's once pre-eminent position as the only gateway to China is now also challenged.

Change of policy and enactment of a comprehensive law to ensure that all sectors of industry are subject to congruent rules is a clear and urgent necessity. Once enacted, the administration and enforcement of the law should not prove an insurmountable hurdle, given Hong Kong's strong infrastructure of rule of law, low corruption levels, substantial financial and human capital and a record of competent implementation of policy in many sectors.

To soften the hard heart of the Hong Kong authorities on this matter will be no easy matter, given the powerful vested interests that will fight tooth and nail to prevent such a change. They will deny that a problem exists, assert the primacy of economic non-intervention, hark back to the historical success of that policy, assert that there is no consensus internationally over the type and content of a competition regime, and wave the shroud of increased bureaucracy and an open-ended additional burden of public expenditure. At the end of the day, only a change in the structure of government and the head of the administration will allow such a significant policy reversal, in the absence of a WTO-mandated obligation which seems a very distant prospect at present.

In the meantime, the Consumer Council should continue its work of investigation and persuasion by publishing findings on competition complaints, notwithstanding the severe constraints under which it operates. Academics should highlight the inconsistencies and illogicalities of the government's policies. Non-governmental organisations should take up the cudgels. Civic Exchange, a fairly recently established public policy body, did so in 2002.[1] This organisation was founded by Christine Loh[2] and has conducted a project to investigate competition policy in Hong Kong. A principal objective of this intervention was to convince

---

[1] http://www.civic-exchange.org.
[2] Ms Loh is a prominent former member of LEGCO who did not seek re-election in 2000.

key business players that the current arrangements simply do not work. If business leaders can be persuaded that self-interest dictates that Hong Kong's increasingly uncompetitive economy needs a new set of rules for the economic game, then change in government policy may be possible.

Secondly, competition policy may be moving up the political agenda. The Frontier Party and the Democratic Party both advocate competition law adoption. Ronny Tong SC, a former Chairman of the Hong Kong Bar Association and elected as a member of LEGCO in September 2004, recently launched a new campaign to increase public pressure on the government to legislate a comprehensive competition statute.

Both of these initiatives may ultimately promote new legislation, though without a change in the composition of LEGCO and a new Chief Executive, progress will be neither quick nor easy, especially given the Beijing authorities' decision in April 2004 to rule out universal suffrage for the 2006 and 2007 elections. The recent change in leadership and the announcement of a review of COMPAG may herald a change of heart but the road to the enactment of a comprehensive competition statute in Hong Kong has been both long and tortuous thus far and, at present, the destination is not yet in sight.

11.4 Taiwan

The first decade of competition law enforcement in Taiwan has been essentially a story of successful implementation. This text has identified a number of defects in the substantive rules, their application and in the shifting emphasis that the competition authority has given to advocacy and later to specific enforcement of substantive rules. The success of Taiwanese adoption has also been shown in the resources and professionalism of the civil servants devoted to the task; the independence of the investigation, adjudication and enforcement procedures; the reflective attitude of the authority in seeking to improve the system by legislative and administrative means and their openness to embrace co-operation with established competition authorities worldwide, so as to absorb appropriate institutional wisdom.

Improvements in the Taiwanese system might include a more comprehensive review of the professional development of officials to ensure that they have the necessary skills needed for their tasks. Advocacy campaigns and educational activities should be maintained. Continued engagement with overseas competition authorities, including participation in OECD fora and in International Competition Network activities, can only strengthen Taiwan's competition regulation and enforcement regime.

Consequently, both the Mainland and Hong Kong should carefully study the experiences of Taiwan in adopting competition policy and law; both may have important lessons to learn from the Taiwanese experience, notwithstanding their differing economic and governmental circumstances.

11.5 Conclusion

This work has sought to describe and analyse the present arrangements for competition regulation in Greater China. Each of the examined jurisdictions have their unique characteristics but all of them face economic challenges brought about by liberalising international trade and commerce. To survive and prosper, economies must strive to be as competitive as possible or else they may lose the competitive race. Evidence exists that unless an economy is internally competitive, it will not remain internationally competitive for long.[3]

Adopting a tailored competition policy and law regime is no simple matter; ensuring that it is effectively and appropriately implemented is even more complex. The conclusion of this author is that to achieve optimal results in competition regulation, the underlying political arrangements of any given jurisdiction are crucial. The evidence presented here as regards Greater China suggests that in the absence of a functioning democracy this task is exceptionally difficult, if not impossible. This book does not seek to suggest that countries must become functioning democracies; that is a choice for the local inhabitants. But, on the basis of the evidence revealed here in relation to Greater China, without a functioning democracy any adopted competition law system will operate at best at a sub-optimal level and, at worst, as a protectionist engine.

Competition law developments in Greater China are not only of significance to domestic business operators; more liberal trade rules inevitably mean that China's international economic importance will only grow. Creating and maintaining fair rules for competition in Greater China is, therefore, not a purely domestic concern. The next decade in Greater China should prove just as interesting as the last and issues of economic competition are bound to become more prominent.

---

[3] Michael E. Porter, *The competitive advantage of nations*, New York: Free Press (1990).

BIBLIOGRAPHY

Amato, Giuliano, *Anti-trust and the bounds of power – the dilemma of liberal democracy in the history of the market*, Oxford: Hart Publishing (1997).

Armentano, Dominick T., *Antitrust policy: the case for repeal*, Washington, D.C.: Cato Institute (1986).

Bailey, David, *Contestability and the design of regulatory and anti-trust policy*, 71 AM Ec Rev. 178–83 (1981).

Becker, Jasper, *Hungry ghosts*, New York: Owl Books (1996).

The Chinese, London: John Murray (2000).

Bing Song, *Competition policy in a transitional economy: the case of China*, 31 Stanford Journal of International Law (1995).

Black, Bernard, Kraakman, Reiner and Tarassova, Anna, *Russian privatisation and corporate governance: what went wrong?* 52 Stan. L. Rev. 1731 (2000).

Blackstone, William, *Commentaries on the laws of England*, University of Chicago Press (1979).

Bork, Robert H., *The anti-trust paradox: a policy at war with itself*, New York: Basic Books (1978).

Brahm, Laurence J., *China's century: the awakening of the next economic powerhouse*, New York: Wiley (2002).

Brathwaite, John and Drahos, Peter, *Global business regulation*, Cambridge University Press (2000).

Broadcasting Authority, *Annual Report 2000–2001*, Hong Kong (2002).

Brown, A. W., Ickes, B. and Ryterman, R., 'The myth of monopoly: a new view of industrial structure in Russia', World Bank Research Working Paper, No. 1331 (1993).

Brzezinski, Carolyn, 'Competition and antitrust law in Central Europe: Poland, the Czech Republic, Slovakia and Hungary', Michigan Journal of International Law (Summer 1994).

Cadot, Olivier, Grether, Jean-Marie and de Melo, Jaime, 'Trade and competition: where do we stand?' *Journal of World Trade* 34 (2000), p. 1.

Calabresi, Guido, *Some thoughts on risk distribution and the Law of Torts*, 70 Yale Law Journal 499 (1961).

Capacity building for effective competition policy in developing and transitional economies, 16 April 2003, OECD Joint Global Forum on Trade and Competition (2003).

Capelik, V. E. 'Should monopoly be regulated in Russia?' *6 Communist Countries & Economic Transformation* 19 (1994) 22–4.

Cartel Report, Paris: OECD (2002).

Challenges/obstacles faced by competition authorities in achieving greater economic development through the promotion of competition, Contribution by Russian Federation, OECD Global Competition Forum, Paris (2004).

Chang, Gordon G. *The coming collapse of China*, New York: Random House (2000).

Chen, Albert, *Competition law and Hong Kong*, 23(3) HKLJ (1993).

Chen Jian-fu, 'Implementation of law as a politico-legal battle in China', *China Perspectives*, 43 (2002), pp. 26–39.

Cheng Leonard K. and Wu Chang qi, *Competition policy and the regulation of business*, City University of Hong Kong Press (1998).

China statistical year book, International Centre for Advancement of Science and Technology, Hong Kong (2000).

Choukroune, Leila, '*Rule of law through internationalisation: the objective of the reforms*', China Perspectives, 40 (2002), pp. 7–21.

Clark, John, 'Toward a concept of workable competition', AM Ec Rev. 30 (1940), pp. 241–56.

Clarke, Donald C., 'The Execution of Civil Judgements in China', *The China Quarterly*, 141 (1995), pp. 65–79.

Coase, Ronald, *The problem of social cost*, 3 J. Law and Econ. 1 (1960).

Competition law and policy in Russia, OECD Peer Review, Paris (2004).

Competition policy for Hong Kong, Trade and Industry Bureau, Hong Kong, November 1997.

Conrath, C. and Freeman, B., *A response to the effectiveness of proposed antitrust programmes for developing countries*, 19 NCILCR 233 (1994).

Cooter, Robert, 'Market modernization of the law; economic development through decentralised law', in *Economic dimensions in international law, comparative and empirical perspectives*, ed. Bhandari J. S. and Sykes, A. O., London: Sage (1997).

Copper, John F. 'Taiwan: democracy's gone awry?', *Journal of Contemporary China* 12 (34) (2003), pp. 145–62.

Corbin, Juliet and Strauss, Anselm, *Basics of qualitative research: techniques and procedures for developing grounded theory*, London: Sage (1998).

Dabbah, M., *Measuring the success of a system of competition law: a preliminary view*, 21(8) ECLR, 369–76 (2000).

'Definition of the relevant market for the purposes of community competition law', *European Commission OJ* C372 (1997).

De Leon, Ignacio, *The role of competition policy in the promotion of competitiveness and development in Latin America*, 23(4) Journal of World Competition Law 115 (1992).

An alternative approach to policies for the promotion of competition in developing countries, 6 SWJLTA 85 (1999).

'Should we promote antitrust in international trade?' 28 *J World Comp.* (1997), p. 35.

'Should we promote antitrust in international trade?' 28 *J World Comp.* 35 (1997).

De Soto, Hernando, *The mystery of capital: why capitalism triumphs in the west and fails everywhere else*, New York: Basic Books (2000).

Diamond, Larry, 'The rule of law as transition to democracy in China', *Journal of Contemporary China* 12 (35) (2003), 319–31.

'The illusion of illiberal democracy', *Journal of Democracy*, 14 (4) (2003), pp. 167–71.

Dodwell, D., *Competition policy and competitiveness*, The Hong Kong Service Economy, vol. 7 (February 1999).

Eisenhardt, K. M., 'Building theories from case study research', *Academy of Management Review*, 14 (4) (1989).

Emerging private enterprises: prospects for the new century, International Finance Corporation, Washington, D.C. (2000).

Eueken, W., Bohm, F. and Grossmann-Doerth, H., 'The Ordo Manifesto of 1936', in Peacock, Alan and Willgerodt, Hans (eds.), *German neo-liberals and the social market economy: origins and evolution*, New York: St Martin's Press (1989).

Friedman, Edward, 'A comparative politics of democratisation in China', *Journal of Contemporary China*, 12 (34) (2003), pp. 103–23.

Frischtak, C., Hadjimichael, B. and Zachau, U., *Competition policies for industrialising countries*, Policy and Research Series, No. 7, World Bank, Washington, D.C. (1989).

Gal, Mical, *Competition policy for small market economies*, Cambridge, Mass.: Harvard University Press (2003).

Garcia-Rodriguez, Sergio, *Mexico's new institutional framework for anti-trust enforcement*, 44 De Paul Law Review 1149 (1995).

Gellhorn, Ernest and Kovacic, William E., *Antitrust law and economics*, 4th edn, New York: West Publishing, New York (1994).

Glasser, Barney, *Basics of grounded theory analysis*, Mill Valley, Calif.: Sociology Press (1992).

Glasser, Barney and Strauss, Anselm, *The discovery of grounded theory: strategies for qualitative research*, New York: Aldine Pub. Co. (1967).

Global Corruption Report, Transparency International (2001).

Global Corruption Report 2004, Transparency International (2004).

Godek, Paul E., 'One U.S. export Eastern Europe does not need', *Regulation*, 20 (Winter 1992), p. 21.

Graham, Edward and Richardson, David, *Competition policies for a global economy*, Washington, D.C.: Institute for International Economics (1997).

Grossbard-Shechtman, Soshana and Clague, Christopher (eds.), *The expansion of economics: toward a more inclusive social science*, New York: M. E. Sharpe (2002).

Guba, Egon, *The paradigm dialogue*, London: Sage Publications (1990).

Halperin, Morton H., Siegle, Joseph T. and Weinstein, Michael M., *The democracy advantage: how democracies promote prosperity and peace*. New York: Routledge (2005).

Hayek, Fredrick, *The fortunes of liberalism: essays on Austrian economics and the ideal of freedom*, including *The rediscovery of freedom: personal recollections*, ed. Peter G. Klein, University of Chicago Press (1992).

Hao Yufon, 'From rule of man to rule of law: an unintended consequence of corruption in China in the 1990s', *Journal of Contemporary China* 8 (22) (1999), pp. 405–23.

Ho, Peter, 'Who owns China's land? Policies, property rights and deliberate institutional ambiguity', *The China Quarterly*, 66 (2001), pp. 394–421.

Hoekman, Bernard, Competition Policy, Developing Countries and the WTO, Policy Research Paper no. 2211, World Bank, Washington (1999).

Hoekman, Bernard and Djankov, Simeon, 'Competition law in post-central-planning Bulgaria', *The Antitrust Bulletin* (Spring 2000).

Holmes, Oliver Wendell, *The common law*, Boston: Little, Brown & Co. (1881).

The path of the law, 10 Harvard Law Rev. 457 (1897).

Hong, Yu-hung and Lam, Alven H. S., Opportunities and risks of capturing land values under Hong Kong's leasehold system, Lincoln Institute of Land Policy Working Paper, Cambridge, Mass. (1998).

Hong Kong Consumer Council, *Achieving competition in the liberalised telecommunications market*, Hong Kong (March 1966).

Are Hong Kong depositors fairly treated? Hong Kong (February 1994).

Report on the supermarket industry in Hong Kong, Hong Kong (November 1994).

Assessing competition in the water heating and cooking fuel market, Hong Kong (1995).

Ensuring competition in the dynamic television broadcasting market, Hong Kong (January 1996).

How competitive is the private residential property market?, Hong Kong (July 1996).

Energizing the energy market, Hong Kong (January 2000).

Hong Kong's telecommunications policy, Hong Kong Government, Economic Services Branch (January 1994).

Hong Kong 2001, Information Services Department of the Hong Kong SAR Government, Hong Kong (2002).

Hough, Jerry, *The logic of economic reform in Russia,* Washington, D.C.: Brookings Institution Press (2001).

Hu Ruying, *Competition and monopoly: micro-economic analysis of socialism,* Shanghai: Shanghai Shanlian Publishing House (1998).

Hu Weiwei, *Anti-monopoly law is a necessity in China,* 3 Jurisprudence (1995).

Huang Xin and Zhou Jun, *An approach to the legislative control of Administrative Monopoly and monopoly practices,* 3 China Jurists' Journal, National University of Politics and Law, Beijing (2001).

Impact and effectiveness of the single market. European Commission Report, SMN no. 6 (1996).

Jackson, John H., *The world trading system: law and policy of international economic relations,* Cambridge, Mass.: The MIT Press (1997).

The World Trade Organization, constitution and jurisprudence, London: The Royal Institute of International Affairs (1998).

The jurisprudence of GATT and the WTO, insights on treaty law and economic relations, Cambridge University Press (2000).

Jones, Clifford, 'Toward global competition policy? The expanding dialogue on multilateralism', *J World Comp* 23 (2000), p. 95.

Jorde, Thomas and Teece, David (eds.), *Antitrust, innovation and competitiveness,* Oxford University Press (1992).

Jung, Youngin, 'Modelling a WTO dispute mechanism in international antitrust agreement: an impossible dream?' *Journal of World Trade* 34 (2000), p. 89.

Karatncky, Adrian, 'The decline of illiberal democracy', *Journal of Democracy,* 10(1), (Jan. 1999), pp. 112–25.

Keay, John, *The honourable company: A history of the English East India Company,* London: Harper Collins Publishers (1993).

Kennedy, K. C., *Competition law and the World Trade Organisation: the limits of multilateralism,* London: Sweet and Maxwell (2001).

Kong QingJiang, 'Enforcement of WTO agreements in China: illusion or reality?', *Journal of World Trade* 35(6) (2001).

Kovacic, William, *Designing and implementing competition and consumer protection reforms in transitional economies: perspectives from Mongolia, Nepal, Ukraine and Zimbabwe,* 44 De Paul Law Review 1197 (1995).

Getting started: creating new competition policy institutions in transitional economies, 23 Brooklyn Journal of International Law 403 (1997).

Merger enforcement in transition: antitrust controls on acquisitions in emerging economies, University of Cincinnati Law Review (1998).

Kuhn, Thomas, *The structure of scientific revolutions,* University of Chicago Press (1962).

Laffont, Jean-Jacques, Competition Information and Development, Annual World Bank Conference on Development Economics, Washington, D.C. (1998).

Laird, Sam, *Transition economics, business and the WTO,* 22(1) Journal of World Competition Law 171, 184–5 (1999).

Lam Pun Lee, *Competition in energy*, The Hong Kong Economic Policy Series, City University of Hong Kong Press (1997).

Lardy, Nicholas, *China's unfinished economic revolution*, Washington D.C.: Brookings Institution Press (1998).

Lawrence, Lee, *Taiwan's antitrust statutes: proposals for a regulatory regime and comparison of U.S. and Taiwanese, antitrust law*, 6 Indiana International and Comparative Law Review, 583 (1996).

Lenaerts, Tom and Vandamme, Walter, *Procedural rights of private parties in community administrative proceedings*, 34 CML Rev. 531 (1997).

Liu Dashing, *The new field of anti-monopoly legislation in our country*, 82 Chinese Legal Science (1997).

Liu, Lawrence S., *Fostering competition law and policy: a façade of Taiwan's political economy*, 1 Washington Global Studies Law Review, 77–160 (2002).

Loasby, Brian, *Equilibrium and evolution: an exploration of connecting principles in economics*, Manchester University Press (1991).

Machiavelli, Nicolo, *The prince*, ed. Quentin Skinner and Russell Price, Cambridge University Press (1988).

Maguire, Keith, *The rise of modern Taiwan*, Aldershot: Ashgate (1998).

Malaguti, Maria, C., 'Restrictive business practices in international trade and the role of the WTO', *Journal of World Trade* 32 (1998), p. 117.

Marsh, Ian, Blondel, Jean and Inoguchi, Takashi (eds.), *Democracy, governance and economic performance: East and South East Asia*, Tokyo: United Nations University Press (1999).

Markesinis, Basil, *The German law of torts*, 3rd edn., Oxford: Clarendon Press (1994).

Moses, Naim, 'The launching of radical policy changes, the Venezuelan experience: 1989–1991', in *Venezuela: democracy and political and economic change*, ed. J. S. Tulchin, Oxford University Press (1992).

Monti, Mario, *The scope of collective dominance under Article 82 EC*, 38 CML Rev. 131 (2001).

Muchlinski, Peter, *Multinational enterprises and the law*, Oxford: Blackwell (1999).

Mueller, Milton, *International telecommunications in Hong Kong: a case for liberalisation*, Chinese University of Hong Kong (1992).

Nature and impact of hard core cartels, OECD, Paris (20 February 2002).

Neuman, Manfred, *Competition policy: history, theory and practice*, Cheltenham: Edward Elgar (2001).

North, Douglass C. *Institutions, institutional change, and economic performance*, Cambridge University Press (1990).

Understanding the process of economic change. Princeton University Press (2005).

Objectives of competition law and policy and the optimal design of a competition agency, 5 (1) OECD Journal of Competition Law and Policy (2003).

Office of the Telecommunications Authority, Consultation paper on the regulation of mergers and acquisitions, Hong Kong (April 2001).

Oksenberg, Michael, 'China's political system: challenges for the twenty-first-century', *The 45 China Journal* 21 (2001), p. 35.

Overholt, William, *China: the next economic superpower*, London: Weidenfeld and Nicolson (1993).

Pan Wei, 'Toward a consultative rule of law regime in China', *Journal of Contemporary China*, 12(34) (2003), pp. 3–43.

Parker, D., *The Competition Act 1998: change and continuity in U.K. competition policy*, 283 Journal of Business Law (July Issue 2000).

Patten, Christoper, *East and west*, London: Macmillan (1998).

Peerenboom, R., 'A government of laws: democracy, rule of law and administrative law reform in the PRC, *Journal of Contemporary China*, 12 (34) (2003), pp. 54–67.

Pei Minxin, 'China governance crisis', *Foreign Affairs* (Sept/Oct 2002).

Peritz, Rudolf, *Competition policy in America 1888–1992*, Oxford University Press (1996).

Pipes, Richard, 'Flight from freedom: what Russians think and want', *Foreign Affairs* (May/June 2004).

Plattner, Marc F., 'From liberalism to liberal democracy', *Journal of Democracy*, 10 (3) (July 1999), pp. 121–34.

Pollock, Fredrick, *The genius of the common law*, New York: Columbia University Press (1912).

Porter, Michael E., *The competitive advantage of nations*, New York: Free Press (1990).

Posner, Richard and Esterbrook, Frank, *Antitrust cases: economic notes and other materials*, 2nd edn, University of Chicago Press (1981).

Posner, Richard A., *Antitrust law: an economic approach*, University of Chicago Press (1976).

   Law and legal theory in the UK and USA, Oxford: Clarendon Press (1996).

   Economic Analysis of Law, New York: Little, Brown & Co. (1973) and 5th edn, New York: Aspen Law and Business (1998).

   Anti-trust, University of Chicago Press, 2nd edn. (2001).

Postema, Gerald, *Bentham and the common law tradition*, Clarendon Law Series, Oxford University Press (1986).

Potter, Pitman B., 'The Chinese legal system: continuing commitment to the primacy of state power', *China Quarterly*, 159 (1999), p. 674.

Press release on the government's opinion on the private member's Fair Competition Bill, Democratic Party Legislative Council Secretariat, Hong Kong, 23 November 2000.

Putter Man, Louis, 'The role of ownership and property rights in China's economic transition', *The China Quarterly*, 144 (1995).

Remmer, K., 'Democracy and economic crisis: the Latin American experience', *World Politics*, 42 (1990), pp. 315–35.

   'The political economy of elections in Latin America 1980–91', (87) *American Political Science Review*, pp. 393–407 (1993).

'The politics of economic stabilisation: IMF standby programmes in Latin America' 1954–84, *Comparative Politics*, 19 (1996), pp. 1–24.

Report of advocacy working group, International Competition Network (2002).

Report of 2000 Legislative *Council elections*, Hong Kong Electoral Commission, Hong Kong (2001).

Response to the Consumer Council report on competition, Hong Kong Special Administrative Region Government (1997).

Review of BSkyB's position in the wholesale pay-TV market, London: Office of Fair Trading, London (December 1996).

Review of legal education and training, Law Society of Hong Kong, Hong Kong (August 2001).

Review of technical assistance, advisory and training programmes on competition law and policy, United Nations Conference on Trade and Development, Geneva (23 April 2002).

Richardson, G. B., *Information and investment*, Oxford University Press (1960).

Rodriguez, A. E. and Williams, M. D., *The effectiveness of proposed anti-trust programmes for developing countries*, 19, NCILCR 209 (1994).

Roll, Richard and Talbot, John, 'Political freedom, economic liberty and prosperity', *Journal of Democracy*, 14(3) (July 2003), pp. 75–89.

Qi Duojun, *Research problems in Chinese anti-monopoly legislation*, Wuhan University Law Review (1998).

Sally, Razeen, *Classical liberalism and international economic order*, London: Routledge (1998).

Scherer, F. M., *Anti-trust ideology or economics?* (3) *Critical Review*, 5(4) Center for Independent Thought (1992).

 Competition policy: domestic and international, Cheltenham: Edward Elgar (2000).

Sen, A. 'Democracy as a universal value', *Journal of Democracy*, 10(3) (July 1999), pp. 3–17.

Shi JiChun, *Definition and regulation of Administrative Monopoly in China*, Frontiers of Jurisprudence (3), Law Publishing House, Beijing, 1999.

Shi Jishun, 'Anti-monopoly law analysis', *Intertrade*, Beijing, 4 (1998).

Shleifer, A. and Triesman, D., 'A normal country', *Foreign Affairs* (March/April 2004).

Shipp, Steven, *Macau, China: A political history of the Portuguese colony's transition to Chinese rule*, Jefferson, N.C.: McFarland & Co., Inc. (1997).

Slay, Ben and Capelik, Vladimir, 'Natural monopoly regulation and competition policy in Russia', *The Anti-Trust Bulletin* (Spring 1998).

Short, Philip, *Mao: a life*, London: *Hodder & Stoughton* (1999).

Singh, A. and Dhumale, R., Competition policy, development and developing countries, South Centre, Geneva, Working Paper no. 7 (November 1999).

Smith, Adam, *An inquiry into the nature and causes of the wealth of nations*, ed. Edwin, Cannan, London: Methuen (1950).

Spence, Jonathan D., *The search for modern China*, New York: Norton and Company, Inc. (1999).

Staley, Samuel, *Planning rules and urban economic performance: the case of Hong Kong*, The Hong Kong Centre for Economic Research, University of Hong Kong (1994).

Stark, Chuck, *Antitrust in the international business environment*, 27(3) NY J. Int'l Law and Pol. (1995).

*The Statesman year book, 138*th edn, New York: Palgrave (2002).

*Statistical year book, 45*th issue, New York: United Nations (2001).

Statistical yearbook of Fair Trade Commission 2001, Fair Trade Commission Executive Yuan, Taipei (2002).

Steiner, Josephine and Woods, Lorna, *Textbook on EC law, 8*th edn., Oxford University Press (2003).

Steinfeld, Edward, *Forging reform in China: the fate of state owned industry*, Cambridge University Press (1998).

'Strengthening enterprise governance' in *China in the world economy: the domestic challenges*, Paris: OECD (2002).

Supachai, Panitchpakdi and Clifford, Mark, *China and the WTO: changing China, changing world trade*, Singapore: Wiley (2002).

Supply of beer, Monopolies and Mergers Commission, London, Cmd 651 (1989).

Tan, Alexander C., 'Taiwan's economy at T + 1 and counting: challenges, dilemmas and opportunities', *Journal of Contemporary China*, 12 (34) (2003), pp. 163–71.

Tesch, Renata, *Qualitative research: analysis types and software tools*, London: Falmer (1990).

Theorelli, Hans, *The federal anti-trust policy – organisation of an American tradition*, Baltimore: The Johns Hopkins Press (1955).

Tien Hung Mao and Chu Yun-han, 'Building democracy in Taiwan', *The China Quarterly*, 148 (1996), pp. 1141–70.

Todino, Mario, 'International competition network: the state of play after Naples', *World Competition*, 26(2) (2002), pp. 283–302.

Trebilcock, M. and Iacobucci, E., 'Designing competition institution', *World Competition* 25(3) (2002), pp. 361–94.

Trefler, D., *Trade liberalisation and the theory of endogenous protection: an econometric study of U.S. import policy*, 101 J. Pol. Econ. 101 (1993), p. 138.

Triesman, D., 'Russia renewed?', *Foreign Affairs* (November/December 2002).

United Nations, Set of multilaterally agreed equitable principles and rules for the control of restrictive business practices, United Nations Conference on Trade and Development, Res. 35/63 (1980).

Wang Baoshu, 'Comments upon anti-trust law application to Administrative Monopoly', *Journal of the Graduate School of the Chinese Academy of Social Sciences*, 5 (1998).

Wang Chundi, *Monopoly through merger*, 3 Jurists' Review, Beijing (1998).

Wang Cunxue, *Price cartels and their regulation in China's market economy*, 2 Modern Law Science Review, Beijing (1998).

Wang Xianlin, 'An approach to the establishment of an anti-monopoly law enforcement authority and its, Functions', *China Administrative Supervision Journal* (August 2000).

Wang Xiaoye, 'Anti-monopoly law under the conditions of the socialist market economy', *Journal of Chinese Social Sciences*, 1, Beijing (1996).

Wang Xiaoye, *Anti-monopoly law should regulate the activities of public companies in the* market, 5 Chinese Academy of Social Sciences Journal of Law, Beijing (1997).

Wang Xiaoye, *Investigation on legislation to control mergers in China*, Beijing: People's Publishing House (1997).

Wang Xiaoye, 'Regulation of Administrative Monopoly', *Intertrade*, 4, Beijing (1998).

Wang Xiaoye, *Studies in competition law*, Beijing: China Legal System Press (1999).

Wang Xiaoye, Necessity of and conditions for an anti-monopoly law in China (working paper in English), Institute of European Studies, Chinese Academy of Social Sciences, Beijing (2001).

Wei Pan, 'Toward a consultative rule of law regime in China', *Journal of Contemporary China*', 12 (34) (2003) pp. 3–43.

Wei Zhao, 'China's WTO accession; commitments and prospects', *Journal of World Trade* 33(2) (1999).

Welsh, Frank, *A history of Hong Kong*, London: Harper Collins (1997).

Whish, Richard, *Competition Law*, London: Butterworth, 5th edn (2002).

Willem Van Der Geest, 'Bringing China into the Concert of nations; an analysis of its accession to the WTO', *Journal of World Trade* 33(3) (1999).

Williams, M., *Implications of the EU Competition Law for China's competition legislation*, 97(6) Wuhan University Law Review (1999).

Analysis and suggestions on the outline anti-monopoly law of the PRC, Contemporary Legal Studies, 1 Fudan University Press, Shanghai (2001).

An introduction to general principles and formation of contracts in the New Chinese Contract Law, 17 Journal of Contract Law 13 (2001).

Competition Law Developments in China, Journal of Business Law (May 2001).

Consumer Law in China, 18(2) UCLA Pacific Basin Law Journal (Spring 2001).

'Competition law in Thailand: seeds of success or fated to fail?' *J World Comp*, 27(3) (2004), pp. 459–04.

Williams, M. and Kong Yuk-choi, Shen Yan, 'Bonanza or Mirage? Textiles and China's accession to the WTO', *Journal of World Trade* 36(3) (2002).

World Bank, *China: internal market development and regulation*, Washington, D.C. (1984).

Wu Hongwei, *A discussion on China's Administrative Monopoly and avoidance*, 6 Jurist's Journal, Beijing (2001).

Wu Weiping and Yusuf Shahid, Shanghai rising in globalizing world, The World Bank Development Research Group, Washington, D.C. (June 2001).

Wu Wenlong, 'An economic constitution; a discussion of some ideas and problems in legislating a Chinese anti-monopoly law', *Intertrade*, 4, Beijing (1998).

Xu Shiqing, *Talks on American anti-monopoly law*, 1 Political Science and Law, Shanghai Academy of Social Science (1994).

Yang Yongzheng, 'China's WTO accession; the economics and politics', *Journal of World Trade*, 34(4) (2000).

Yin, R., *Applications of case study research*, London: Sage (1993).

Zach, Roger (Ed.), *Toward WTO Competition Rules*, The Hague: Kluwer Law International (1999).

Zakaria, Fareed, 'The rise of illiberal democracy', *Foreign Affairs* (Nov/Dec 1997). *The future of freedom: illiberal democracy at home and abroad*, New York: Norton (2003).

Zhang Deling, 'Monopoly and anti-monopoly legislation in China's contemporary situation', *Economic Studies*, 6 (1996).

Zhang Ruping, *Analysis of abuse of market power*, 3 Jurists' Review (1998).

Zhang Shufang, *Analysis of Administrative Monopoly and legal measures that can be taken to counter it*, 4 Chinese Academy of Social Sciences Journal of Law, Beijing (1999). *Causes and analysis of Administrative Monopoly and legal measures against it*, 4 Chinese Academy of Social Sciences Journal of Law (1999).

Zhao Sui-sheng, 'Political liberation without democratisation: Pan Wei's proposal for political reform', *Journal of Contemporary China*, 12 (35)(2003), pp. 333–55.

INDEX

abuse of dominance
  draft Anti-Monopoly Law, China,
    179–80, 207
  FTL case law, Taiwan, 399–403
  recommendations and future
    directions for China, 437
  telecommunications in Hong Kong,
    320–4, 334–6, 345
  television broadcasting in Hong
    Kong, 356–7
academic community
  democracy hypothesis, support for,
    431
  in China
    nature of and support for
      competition law, 149–51
    survey of domestic academic
      literature on competition policy,
      153–65
  in Hong Kong
    nature of and support for
      competition law, 236
    reaction to Consumer Council final
      report and government response,
      281–5
    survey of positions on competition
      policy, 254–7
acquis comunataire requirements of
  EU, 58
Administrative Monopoly (AM),
  China
  Anti-Unfair Competition Law
    (1993) outlawing, 166
  Chinese academic literature on,
    158–60, 161, 163
  Draft Anti-Monopoly Law on,
    183–4, 194–5, 197

government intervention and,
  215–16
local protectionism and, 138–44
SOEs and, 110–11
advocating competition, 62–4, 84,
  151–2
Agreement on Trade-Related
  Intellectual Property Rights
  (TRIPS), 86
AM *see* Administrative Monopoly
Anti-Monopoly Law *see* Draft
  Anti-Monopoly Law, China
Anti-Rightist Movement, 101, 132
Anti-Unfair Competition Law (1993),
  China, 166–70
APEC (Asia-Pacific Economic
  Co-operation), 63, 89–90, 395
appeals process in Hong Kong
  telecommunications, 333–4,
    341–4
  television broadcasting, 359–60
Armentano, Dominick T., 37, 414
Armstrong, Sir Robin, 278
ASEAN (Association of South-East
  Asian Nations), 64
Asia-Pacific Economic Co-operation
  (APEC), 63, 89–90, 395
Asian financial crisis of 1997–8, 80, 89,
  116, 244
assessment of competition regimes *see*
  evaluation of competition
  regimes
Association of South-East Asian
  Nations (ASEAN), 64
Australia, 116, 161, 174, 304, 327
authoritarian regimes and success with
  market-based reforms, 417

456